Seabrook boards the Mauretania, 1931.

WILLIAM BUEHLER SEABROOK
WRITER, EXPLORER,
ALCOHOLIC,
SADIST,
CANNIBAL...

...AND ALL THE REST
OF THE STORY...

# the Abominable Mr. Seabrook

## JOE OLLMANN

# DRAWN & QUARTERLY

www.drawnandquarterly.com

FIRST EDITION: JANUARY 2017
PRINTED IN CHINA
10 9 8 7 6 5 4 3 2 1

LIBRARY AND ARCHIVES CANADA CATALOGUING
IN PUBLICATION
OLLMANN, JOE, 1966-, AUTHOR, ILLUSTRATOR
    THE ABOMINABLE MR. SEABROOK / JOE OLLMANN
ISBN 978-1-77046-267-0 (PAPERBACK)
    1. SEABROOK, WILLIAM, 1884-1945 - COMIC BOOKS, STRIPS, ETC.
2. JOURNALISTS — UNITED STATES — BIOGRAPHY - COMIC BOOKS,
STRIPS, ETC. 3. GRAPHIC NOVELS. I. TITLE.
PN4874.S42046 2017  070.92  C2016-904132-8

PUBLISHED IN THE USA BY DRAWN & QUARTERLY, A CLIENT
PUBLISHER OF FARRAR, STRAUS AND GIROUX. ORDERS:
888-330-8477
PUBLISHED IN CANADA BY DRAWN & QUARTERLY, A CLIENT
PUBLISHER OF RAINCOAST BOOKS. ORDERS: 800-663-5714
PUBLISHED IN THE UNITED KINGDOM BY DRAWN & QUARTERLY,
A CLIENT PUBLISHER OF PUBLISHERS GROUP UK. ORDERS:
info@pguk.co.uk

DRAWN & QUARTERLY ACKNOWLEDGES THE SUPPORT OF THE
GOVERNMENT OF CANADA AND THE CANADA COUNCIL FOR
THE ARTS FOR OUR PUBLISHING PROGRAM.

JOE OLLMANN WOULD LIKE TO THANK THE CANADA COUNCIL
FOR THE ARTS FOR THEIR SUPPORT IN THE MAKING OF THIS
BOOK AND THE ONTARIO ARTS COUNCIL'S WRITERS' WORKS
IN PROGRESS PROGRAM FOR THEIR SUPPORT IN ITS
COMPLETION. MY SINCERE THANKS.

Canada Council    Conseil des Arts    Canadä
for the Arts      du Canada

ONTARIO ARTS COUNCIL
CONSEIL DES ARTS DE L'ONTARIO
an Ontario government agency
un organisme du gouvernement de l'Ontario

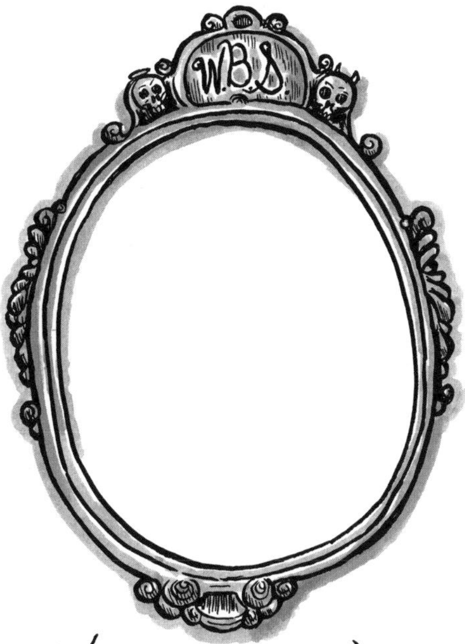
W.B.S.

(DRAW SEABROOK HERE.)

# TO WILLIAM SEABROOK

*I hope I've done justice to this thing, despite my limited abilities...*

"PEOPLE ARE NOT DISTURBED BY THINGS, BUT BY THE VIEW THEY TAKE OF THEM."

"THERE IS NOTHING GOOD OR EVIL SAVE IN THE WILL."

"WHEN YOU ARE OFFENDED AT ANY MAN'S FAULT, TURN TO YOURSELF AND STUDY YOUR OWN FAILINGS. THEN YOU WILL FORGET YOUR ANGER."

-EPICTETUS (ONE OF SEABROOK'S FAVOURITE WRITERS)

# Me and Mr. Seabrook

**WHEN** I CHECK THE DATES ON MY FIRST ROUGH NOTES ON WILLIAM SEABROOK, I SEE THEY DATE FROM TEN YEARS AGO. **TEN YEARS!** I'VE BEEN "RESEARCHING" THIS BOOK, OFF-AND-ON, FOR A DECADE! WHY WOULD ANYONE SPEND SO MUCH TIME WITH A "CANNIBAL, SADIST, ALCOHOLIC, SUICIDE?" WELL, SEABROOK IS AN INTERESTING GUY WHO LIVED AN INTERESTING LIFE — AS I HOPE YOU WILL SEE...

I'VE ALWAYS MAINTAINED THAT I FIND SEABROOK INTERESTING NOT *BECAUSE* OF HIS ABERRATIONS, BUT BECAUSE HE CHOSE TO TALK ABOUT THEM. THAT HONESTY IS WHAT APPEALS TO ME. SEABROOK'S ACTUAL INTERESTS ARE OF LITTLE INTEREST TO ME ACTUALLY. CANNIBAL ENTHUSIASTS, SAVE YOUR LETTERS, I'M NOT THE CANNIBAL GUY TO CORRESPOND WITH, BUT THANKS! (THOUGH, AS A VEGETARIAN OF TWENTY-EIGHT YEARS, I DON'T FIND EATING AN ALREADY DEAD HUMAN ANY WORSE THAN EATING A COW, DOG OR HORSE, REALLY.)

SEABROOK'S FASCINATION WITH BONDAGE INTERESTS ME MOSTLY BECAUSE HE WAS WILLING AND ABLE TO WRITE ABOUT IT IN BOOKS BY MAINSTREAM PUBLISHERS IN THE 30s AND 40s, WHEN PEOPLE KEPT THEIR DARK SIDES CONCEALED. SEABROOK SHARED THE MOTTO OF TERENCE, "I AM A MAN, AND HOLD THAT NOTHING HUMAN IS ALIEN TO ME." I LIKE THAT OPENNESS. THAT SAID, BONDAGE IS NO MORE AN

INTEREST OF MINE THAN EATING MEAT, BUT I'M SURE SOMEONE ELSE WILL WANT TO HEAR ALL OF YOUR BONDAGE STORIES.

THE ALCOHOLISM IS SOMETHING I RELATE TO MORE CLOSELY THAN ANYTHING ELSE ABOUT SEABROOK. AT THIS WRITING, I'M ENTERING MY THIRD YEAR OFF OF BOOZE. LIKE SEABROOK, I'M A GUY WHO LIKED TO DRINK TOO MUCH.

UNLIKE HIM, I WAS ABLE TO "PULL MYSELF OFF THE BOTTLE." IN HIS BOOK *ASYLUM*, WHEN HE BELIEVES HIMSELF CURED OF ALCOHOLISM AND THINKS HE CAN TAKE A DRINK AGAIN CASUALLY, I'M DEEPLY SADDENED EVERY TIME I THINK OF THIS MISCALCULATION AND HOW IT WOULD RUIN HIS LIFE.

I ALSO RELATE TO BEING A RELIGIOUS KID WHO LOST HIS FAITH AND SPENT A LOT OF TIME SEEKING ANY SUPERNATURAL EVENT TO STAND IN FOR GOD. I WENT IN TO DARK, EMPTY BARNS ALONE AT NIGHT AND DARED THE UNIVERSE TO MAKE ME BELIEVE IN ~~SOMETHING~~. I THINK THAT SAME FEELING WAS A LOT OF SEABROOK'S MOTIVATION FOR A LIFETIME SPENT SEEKING THE STRANGE AND SUPERNATURAL.

SEABROOK WAS A GOOD WRITER WHO WAS DEEPLY INSECURE AND EMBARRASSED OF BEING A GUTTER PRESS "YELLOW JOURNALIST." HIS WORK ALWAYS TRANSCENDED THE MATERIAL IT COVERED — IT SEEMS TO ME — THOUGH IT WAS NEVER ENOUGH FOR SEABROOK, WHO ASPIRED TO MAKE SOMETHING GREAT, SOMETHING BEAUTIFUL. HE WANTED TO BE A GREAT ARTIST, FELT HE WASN'T, AND THE FAILURE MADE HIM DRINK. WHO BETTER THAN A CARTOONIST — BOTH A FAILED WRITER **AND** ARTIST — TO DOCUMENT THIS KIND OF INSECURITY?

ANYWAY, AFTER SPENDING A DECADE RESEARCHING HIS LIFE — SPENDING THOUSANDS ON OUT-OF-PRINT BOOKS AND MAGAZINES, TRAVELLING TO OREGON AND NORTH CAROLINA, CHASING SEABROOK EPHEMERA — I WAS KIND OF OBLIGATED TO MAKE THIS BOOK. I REMEMBER MY FIRST ENCOUNTER WITH HIM: "DEAD MEN WORKING IN THE CANE FIELDS," IN A ZOMBIE COLLECTION EDITED BY THE GREAT ANTHOLOGIST PETER HAINING. THE STORY WAS WELL-WRITTEN AND ORIGINAL, BUT IT WAS HAINING'S SHORT BIO OF SEABROOK THAT SO INTRIGUED ME AND STARTED ME ON THE SEARCH THAT EVENTUALLY BECAME THIS BOOK.

I REALIZED THAT NO ONE KNEW ABOUT SEABROOK'S WORK — ALL HIS BOOKS WERE OUT OF PRINT AT THE TIME — OR HIS LIFE, AND EVERYONE I GAVE THE BRIEF, ELEVATOR-PITCH VERSION OF THAT LIFE TO WAS FASCINATED BY IT.

I KNEW AT THE BEGINNING THAT I WANTED TO DO A LINEAR BIOGRAPHY AND TO PUT AS LITTLE OF MY OWN EDITORIAL BIAS ONTO IT AS POSSIBLE, WHATEVER THE RESULT. SOMETIMES A LIFE DOESN'T FOLLOW A NEAT NARRATIVE ARC OR FULFILL THE REQUIREMENTS OF A BIOGRAPHER'S THESIS.

I'VE TRIED TO REMAIN TRUE TO THE FACTS, THOUGH ANY BIOGRAPHY THAT ADDS DIALOGUE — AS THIS ONE DOES, THOUGH I'VE TRIED TO USE DIRECT QUOTES AS MUCH AS POSSIBLE — HAS TO BE CALLED SPECULATIVE NON-FICTION. BUT METICULOUSLY RESEARCHED SPECULATIVE NON-FICTION!!

SOMETIMES I SMOOTHED OUT COMPLICATED EVENTS FOR CLARITY'S SAKE, OR COMBINED LESSER CHARACTERS AND PUT WORDS IN PEOPLE'S MOUTHS. THIS BOOK IS, AT TIMES, LESS SWORN AFFIDAVIT TRUTH THAN IT IS WERNER HERZOG'S POETIC TRUTH. STICKLERS, RELAX, IT'S PRETTY ACCURATE! SEABROOK EXPERTS, YOU SHOULD WRITE YOUR OWN VERSION, THIS ONE WILL NEVER SATISFY YOU.

THE BIGGEST THING I REALIZED IS THE HEAVY RESPONSIBILITY OF BIOGRAPHY. FICTION IS SO MUCH EASIER: MAKING YOUR PUPPETS DO YOUR BIDDING WITH NO CONCERN FOR FACTS. I REALLY DIDN'T WANT TO MAKE A MESS OF WILLIE'S LIFE, MESSY AS IT WAS. I'VE TRIED TO BE RESPECTFUL, WHILE BEING OPEN AND HONEST, AS HE WOULD HAVE APPRECIATED, I THINK. I GUESS THAT'S IT. I HOPE YOU ENJOY THIS. I HOPE IT DOES JUSTICE TO THE MAN'S LIFE. I HOPE IT INTRODUCES MORE PEOPLE TO SEABROOK'S WORK. AFTER TEN YEARS WITH SEABROOK, I LIKE HIM A LOT LESS IN SOME WAYS AND A BIT MORE IN OTHERS. YOU KNOW, LIKE ANYONE.

— JOE OLLMANN, MAY, 2016

A NOTE ON ACCENTS — I TRIED TO BE SPARING IN THE USE OF PEOPLE SPEAKING WITH ACCENTS OR IN BROKEN ENGLISH. (AND TRACY RIGHTLY SUGGESTED EDITING EVEN MORE.) REMAINING USES OF PEOPLE SPEAKING ACCENTED ENGLISH IS MOSTLY TO INDICATE SOMEONE NOT USING THEIR FIRST LANGUAGE IN ORDER TO ACCOMMODATE SEABROOK OR SOME OTHER WESTERN TRAVELLER. I HAD SEABROOK SPEAKING MANGLED FRENCH AT ONE POINT TO ATTEMPT TO REVERSE THE USUAL STEREOTYPE. ANYWAY, I HOPE IT WILL BE CLEAR MY INTENT WAS NOT TO DENIGRATE OR OFFEND. THERE ARE A LOT OF COMPLEX, SENSITIVE ISSUES OF RACE, CULTURE, SEX AND RELIGION IN THIS BOOK. I'VE TRIED TO TELL THE STORY HONESTLY, WHILE TRYING TO REMAIN COGNIZANT OF ALL THE PEOPLE WHO WILL READ IT. IF I FAILED, I APOLOGISE.

PROLOGUE

WHISKEY

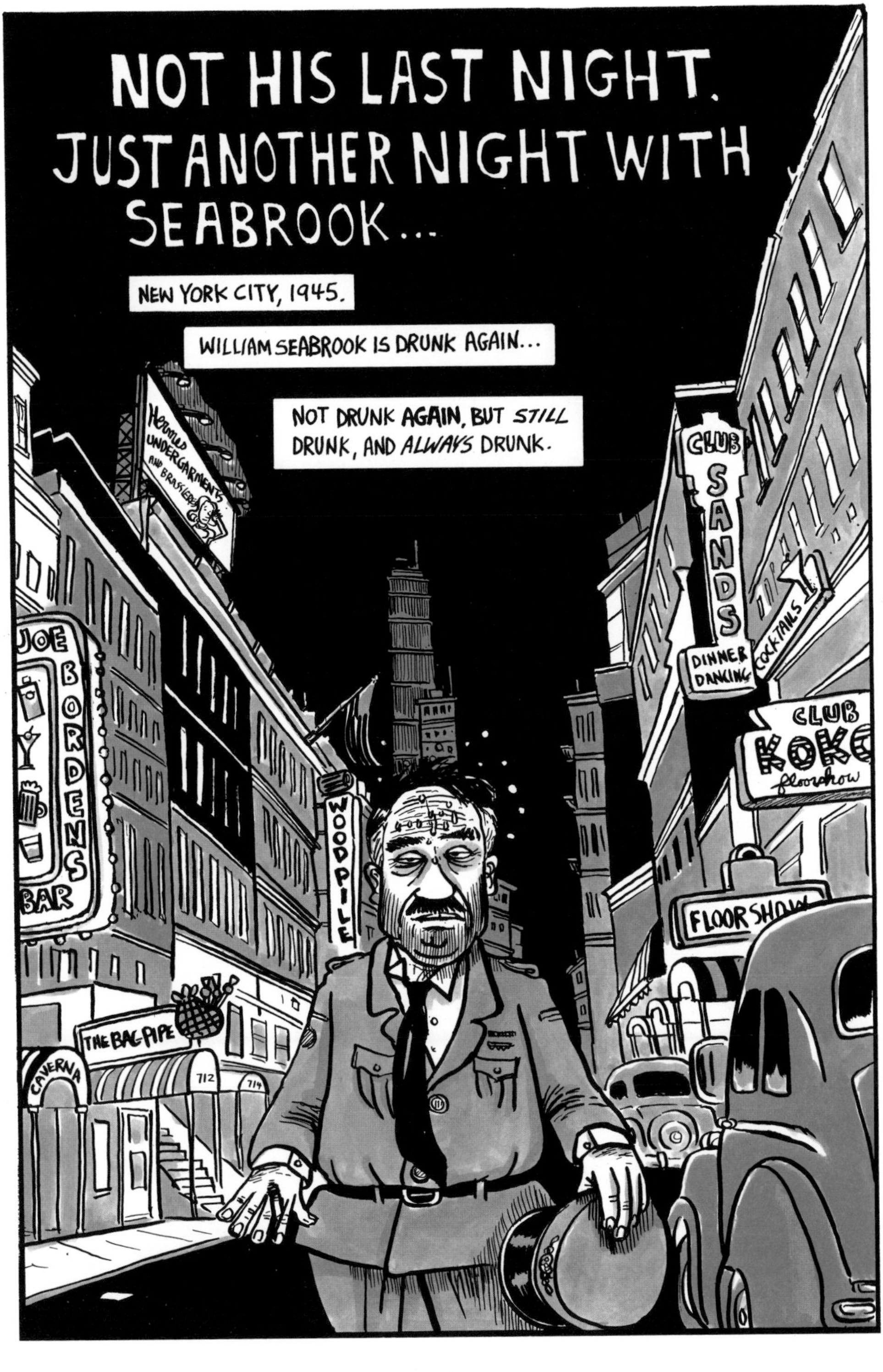
NOT HIS LAST NIGHT.
JUST ANOTHER NIGHT WITH SEABROOK...
NEW YORK CITY, 1945.
WILLIAM SEABROOK IS DRUNK AGAIN...
NOT DRUNK AGAIN, BUT STILL DRUNK, AND ALWAYS DRUNK.
UNDERGARMENTS AND BRASSIERES
JOE BORDENS BAR
WOODPILE
CLUB SANDS DINNER DANCING
COCKTAILS
CLUB
floorshow
THE BAG PIPE
CAVERNA
712
714

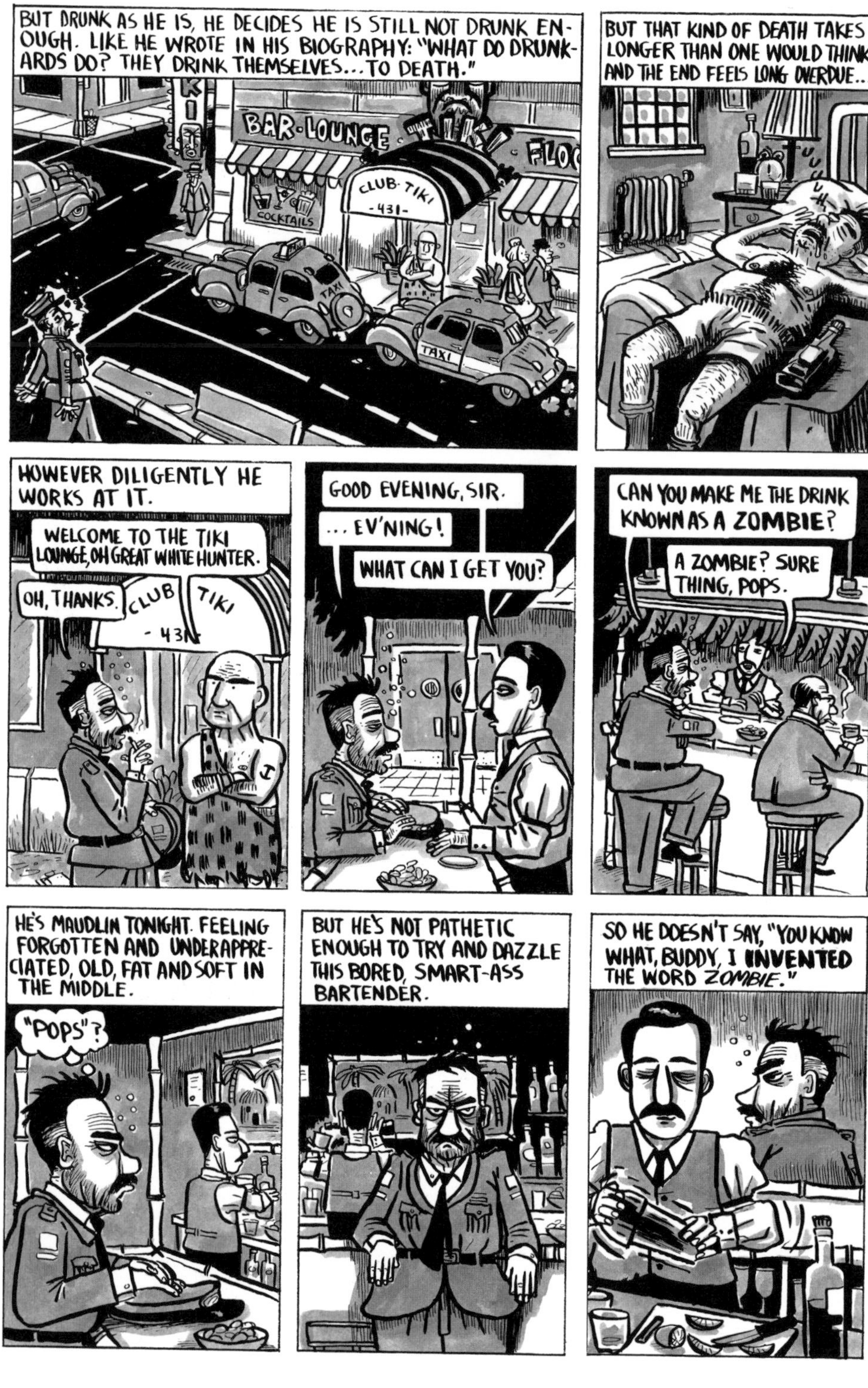
BUT DRUNK AS HE IS, HE DECIDES HE IS STILL NOT DRUNK ENOUGH. LIKE HE WROTE IN HIS BIOGRAPHY: "WHAT DO DRUNKARDS DO? THEY DRINK THEMSELVES... TO DEATH."
BAR·LOUNGE
CLUB·TIKI -431-
COCKTAILS
TAXI
TAXI
BUT THAT KIND OF DEATH TAKES LONGER THAN ONE WOULD THINK, AND THE END FEELS LONG OVERDUE...
HOWEVER DILIGENTLY HE WORKS AT IT.
WELCOME TO THE TIKI LOUNGE, OH GREAT WHITE HUNTER.
OH, THANKS.
CLUB TIKI - 431
GOOD EVENING, SIR.
... EV'NING!
WHAT CAN I GET YOU?
CAN YOU MAKE ME THE DRINK KNOWN AS A ZOMBIE?
A ZOMBIE? SURE THING, POPS.
HE'S MAUDLIN TONIGHT. FEELING FORGOTTEN AND UNDERAPPRECIATED, OLD, FAT AND SOFT IN THE MIDDLE.
"POPS"?
BUT HE'S NOT PATHETIC ENOUGH TO TRY AND DAZZLE THIS BORED, SMART-ASS BARTENDER.
SO HE DOESN'T SAY, "YOU KNOW WHAT, BUDDY, I INVENTED THE WORD ZOMBIE."

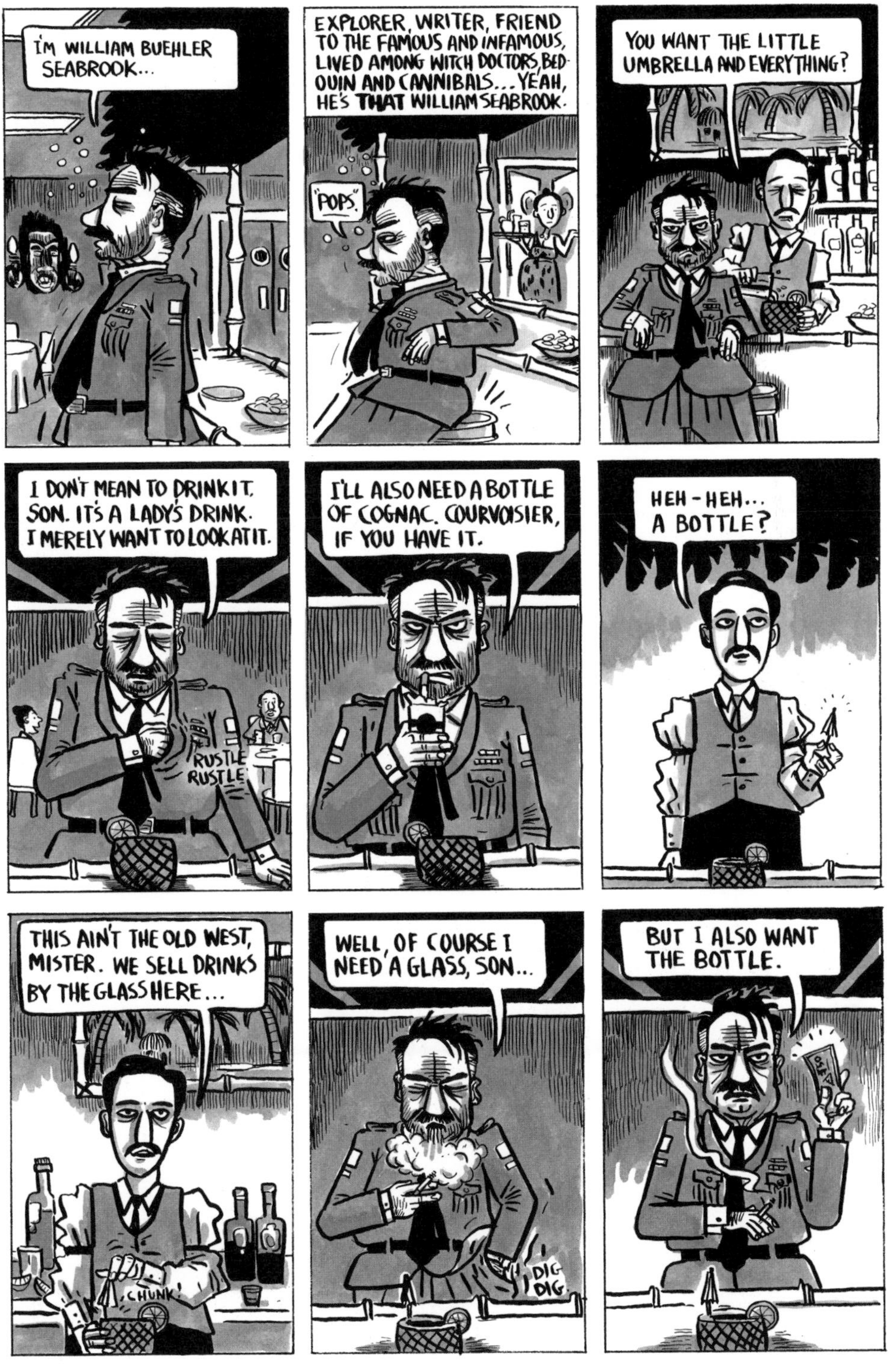
I'M WILLIAM BUEHLER SEABROOK...
EXPLORER, WRITER, FRIEND TO THE FAMOUS AND INFAMOUS, LIVED AMONG WITCH DOCTORS, BEDOUIN AND CANNIBALS... YEAH, HE'S **THAT** WILLIAM SEABROOK.
"POPS."
YOU WANT THE LITTLE UMBRELLA AND EVERYTHING?
I DON'T MEAN TO DRINK IT, SON. IT'S A LADY'S DRINK. I MERELY WANT TO LOOK AT IT.
RUSTLE RUSTLE
I'LL ALSO NEED A BOTTLE OF COGNAC. COURVOISIER, IF YOU HAVE IT.
HEH-HEH... A BOTTLE?
THIS AIN'T THE OLD WEST, MISTER. WE SELL DRINKS BY THE GLASS HERE...
CHUNK!
WELL, OF COURSE I NEED A GLASS, SON...
DIG DIG
BUT I ALSO WANT THE BOTTLE.

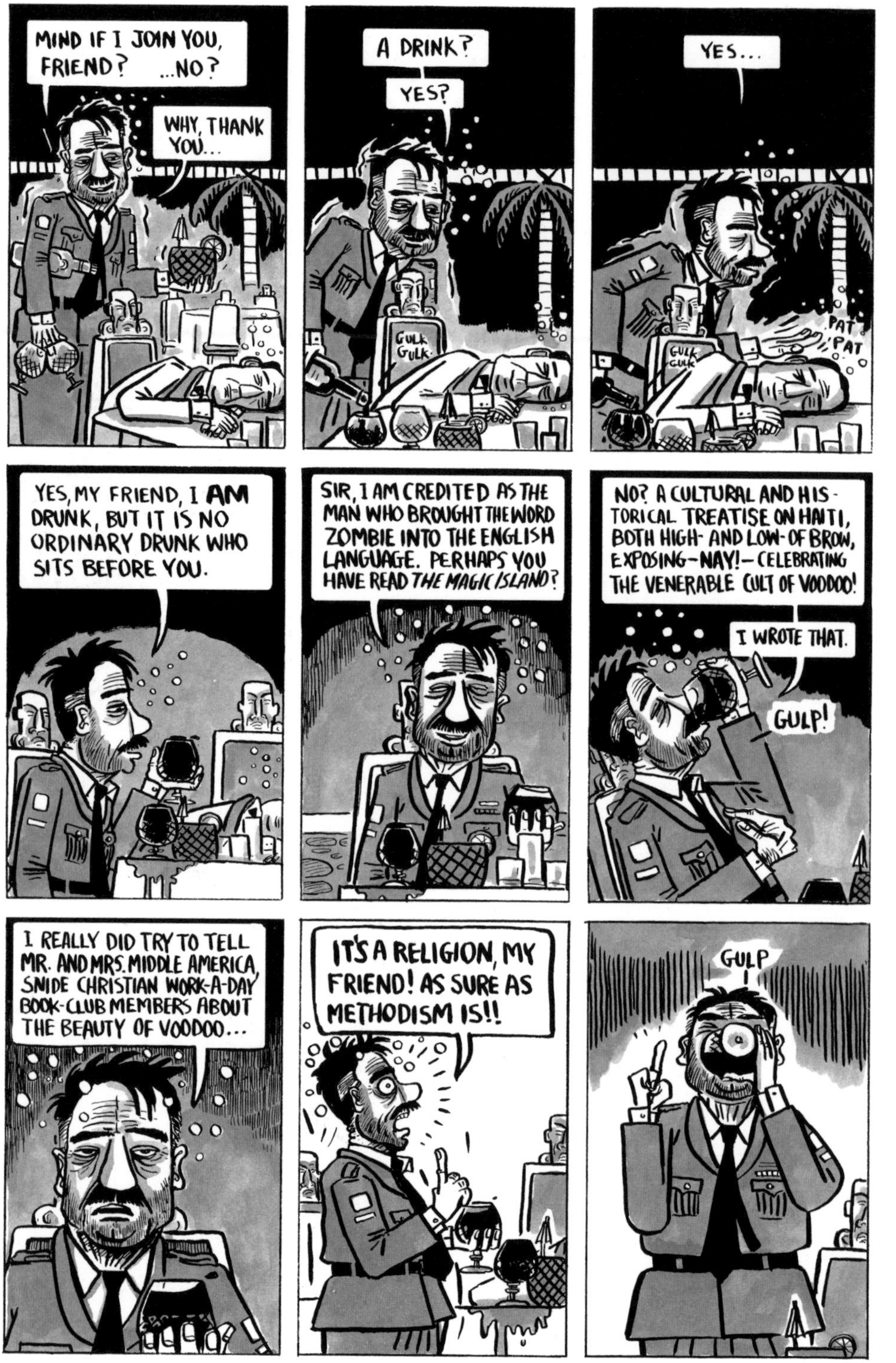
MIND IF I JOIN YOU, FRIEND? ...NO?
WHY, THANK YOU...
A DRINK?
YES?
GULK GULK
YES...
GULK GULK
PAT PAT
YES, MY FRIEND, I AM DRUNK, BUT IT IS NO ORDINARY DRUNK WHO SITS BEFORE YOU.
SIR, I AM CREDITED AS THE MAN WHO BROUGHT THE WORD ZOMBIE INTO THE ENGLISH LANGUAGE. PERHAPS YOU HAVE READ *THE MAGIC ISLAND*?
NO? A CULTURAL AND HISTORICAL TREATISE ON HAITI, BOTH HIGH- AND LOW-OF BROW, EXPOSING—NAY!—CELEBRATING THE VENERABLE CULT OF VOODOO!
I WROTE THAT.
GULP!
I REALLY DID TRY TO TELL MR. AND MRS. MIDDLE AMERICA, SNIDE CHRISTIAN WORK-A-DAY BOOK-CLUB MEMBERS ABOUT THE BEAUTY OF VOODOO...
IT'S A RELIGION, MY FRIEND! AS SURE AS METHODISM IS!!
GULP

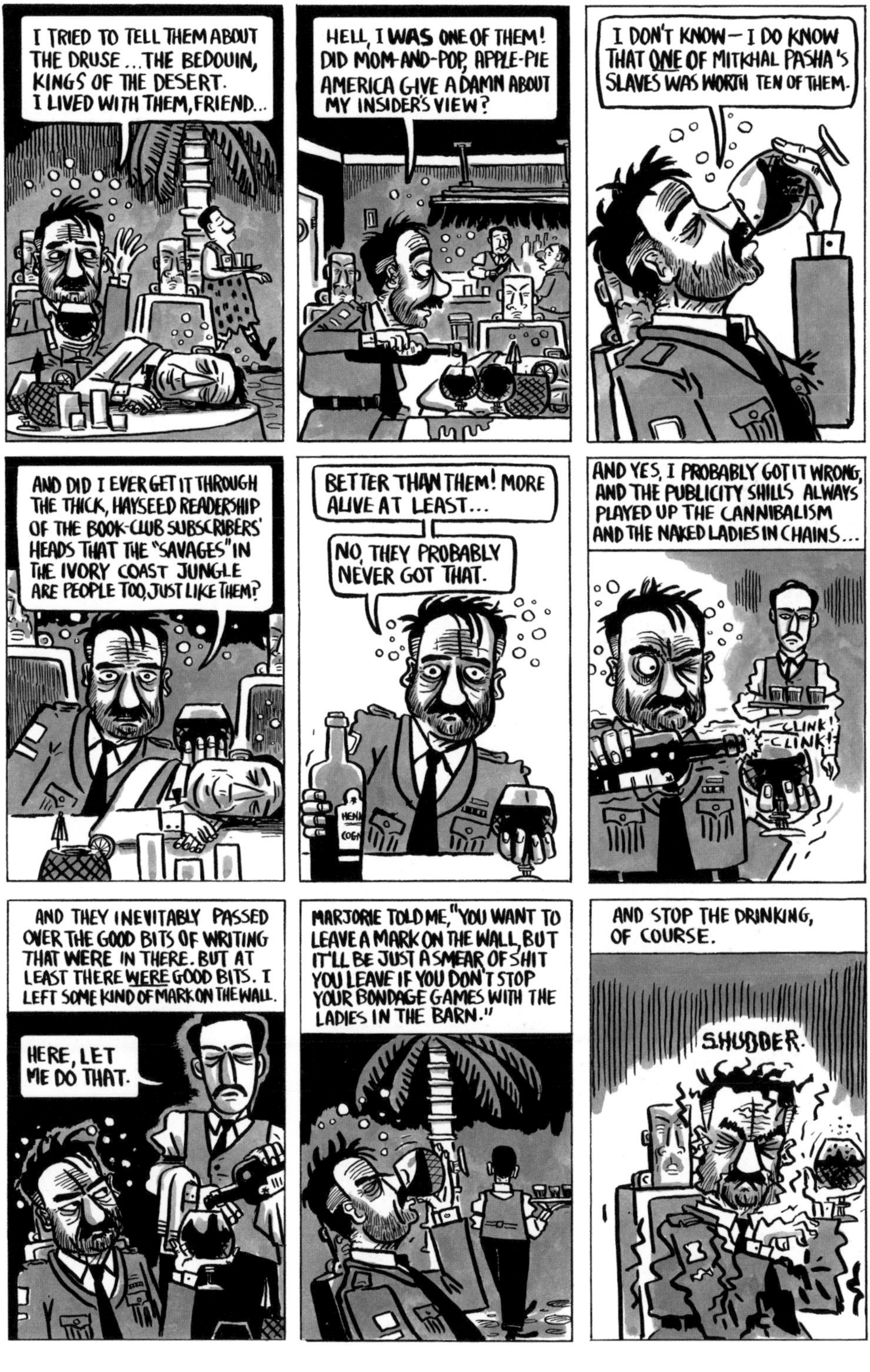
I TRIED TO TELL THEM ABOUT THE DRUSE ...THE BEDOUIN, KINGS OF THE DESERT. I LIVED WITH THEM, FRIEND...
HELL, I WAS ONE OF THEM! DID MOM-AND-POP, APPLE-PIE AMERICA GIVE A DAMN ABOUT MY INSIDER'S VIEW?
I DON'T KNOW— I DO KNOW THAT ONE OF MITKHAL PASHA'S SLAVES WAS WORTH TEN OF THEM.
AND DID I EVER GET IT THROUGH THE THICK, HAYSEED READERSHIP OF THE BOOK-CLUB SUBSCRIBERS' HEADS THAT THE "SAVAGES" IN THE IVORY COAST JUNGLE ARE PEOPLE TOO, JUST LIKE THEM?
BETTER THAN THEM! MORE ALIVE AT LEAST...
NO, THEY PROBABLY NEVER GOT THAT.
AND YES, I PROBABLY GOT IT WRONG, AND THE PUBLICITY SHILLS ALWAYS PLAYED UP THE CANNIBALISM AND THE NAKED LADIES IN CHAINS...
CLINK! CLINK!
AND THEY INEVITABLY PASSED OVER THE GOOD BITS OF WRITING THAT WERE IN THERE. BUT AT LEAST THERE WERE GOOD BITS. I LEFT SOME KIND OF MARK ON THE WALL.
HERE, LET ME DO THAT.
MARJORIE TOLD ME, "YOU WANT TO LEAVE A MARK ON THE WALL, BUT IT'LL BE JUST A SMEAR OF SHIT YOU LEAVE IF YOU DON'T STOP YOUR BONDAGE GAMES WITH THE LADIES IN THE BARN."
AND STOP THE DRINKING, OF COURSE.
SHUDDER.

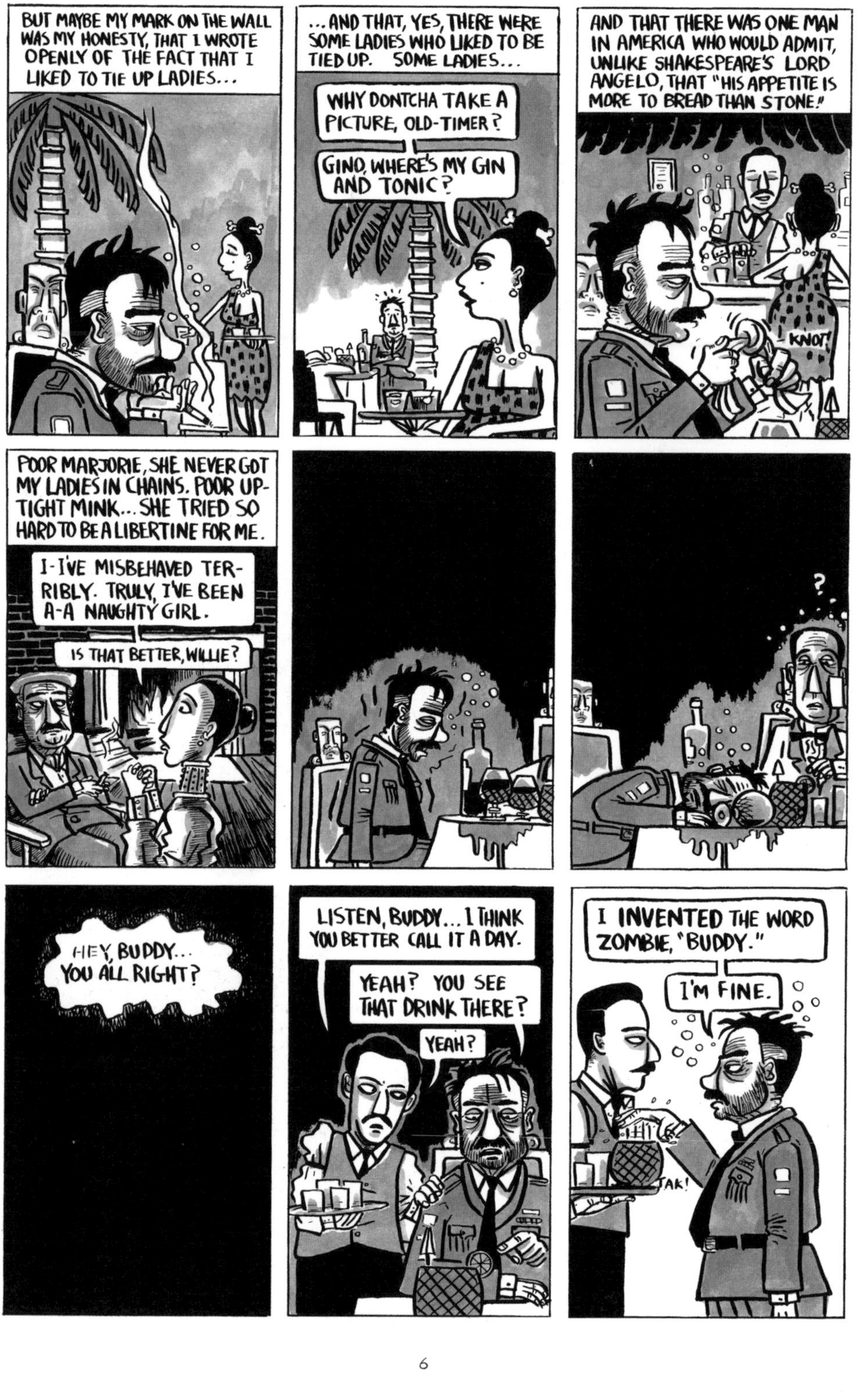

BUT MAYBE MY MARK ON THE WALL WAS MY HONESTY, THAT I WROTE OPENLY OF THE FACT THAT I LIKED TO TIE UP LADIES...
...AND THAT, YES, THERE WERE SOME LADIES WHO LIKED TO BE TIED UP. SOME LADIES...
WHY DONTCHA TAKE A PICTURE, OLD-TIMER?
GINO, WHERE'S MY GIN AND TONIC?
AND THAT THERE WAS ONE MAN IN AMERICA WHO WOULD ADMIT, UNLIKE SHAKESPEARE'S LORD ANGELO, THAT "HIS APPETITE IS MORE TO BREAD THAN STONE."
KNOT
POOR MARJORIE, SHE NEVER GOT MY LADIES IN CHAINS. POOR UP-TIGHT MINK... SHE TRIED SO HARD TO BE A LIBERTINE FOR ME.
I-I'VE MISBEHAVED TERRIBLY. TRULY, I'VE BEEN A-A NAUGHTY GIRL.
IS THAT BETTER, WILLIE?
?
HEY, BUDDY... YOU ALL RIGHT?
LISTEN, BUDDY... I THINK YOU BETTER CALL IT A DAY.
YEAH? YOU SEE THAT DRINK THERE?
YEAH?
I INVENTED THE WORD ZOMBIE, "BUDDY."
I'M FINE.
TAK!

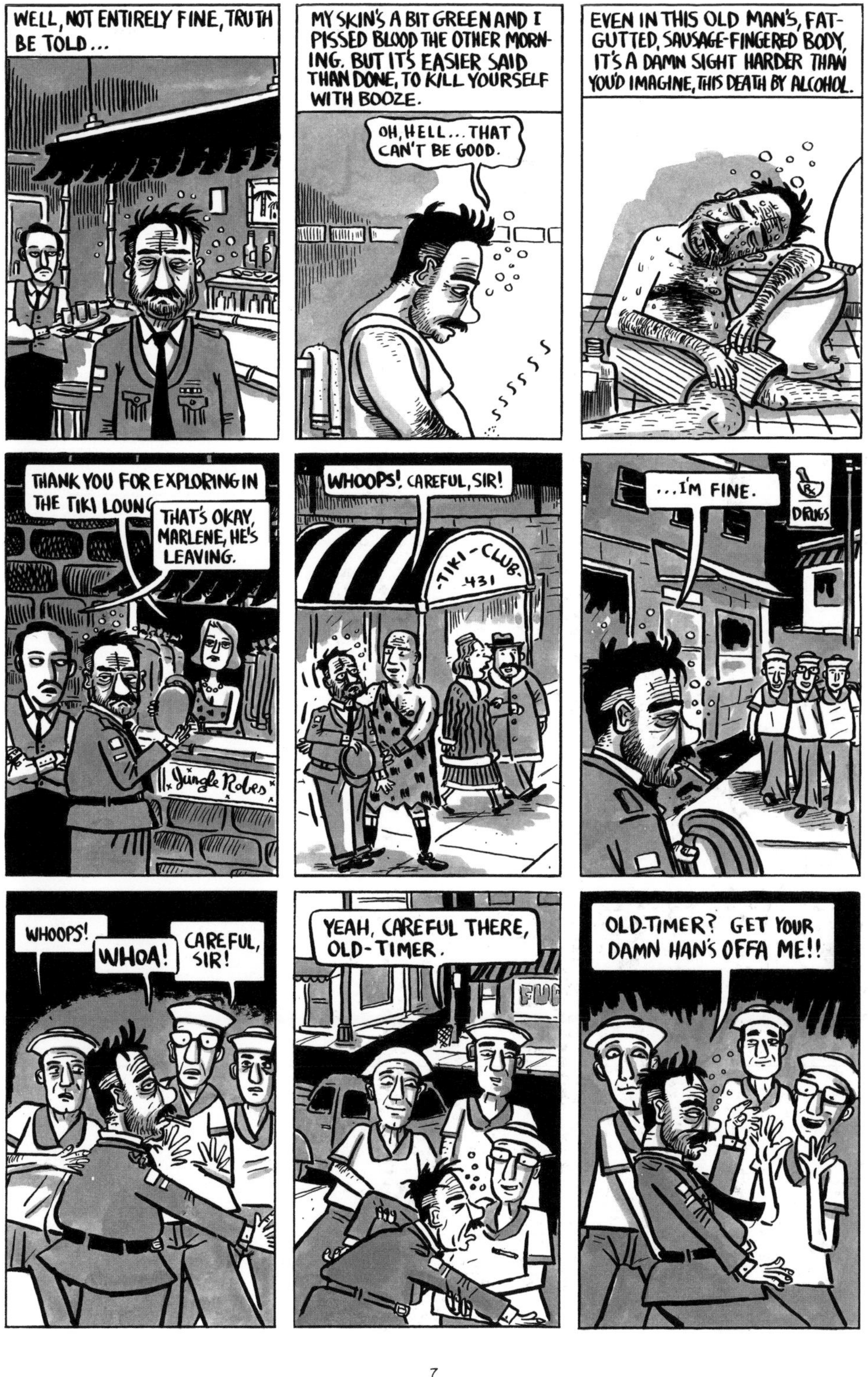
WELL, NOT ENTIRELY FINE, TRUTH BE TOLD...
MY SKIN'S A BIT GREEN AND I PISSED BLOOD THE OTHER MORNING. BUT IT'S EASIER SAID THAN DONE, TO KILL YOURSELF WITH BOOZE.
OH, HELL... THAT CAN'T BE GOOD.
EVEN IN THIS OLD MAN'S, FAT-GUTTED, SAUSAGE-FINGERED BODY, IT'S A DAMN SIGHT HARDER THAN YOU'D IMAGINE, THIS DEATH BY ALCOHOL.
THANK YOU FOR EXPLORING IN THE TIKI LOUNG
THAT'S OKAY, MARLENE, HE'S LEAVING.
Jungle Robes
WHOOPS! CAREFUL, SIR!
TIKI-CLUB 431
...I'M FINE.
DRUGS
WHOOPS!
WHOA!
CAREFUL, SIR!
YEAH, CAREFUL THERE, OLD-TIMER.
OLD-TIMER? GET YOUR DAMN HAN'S OFFA ME!!

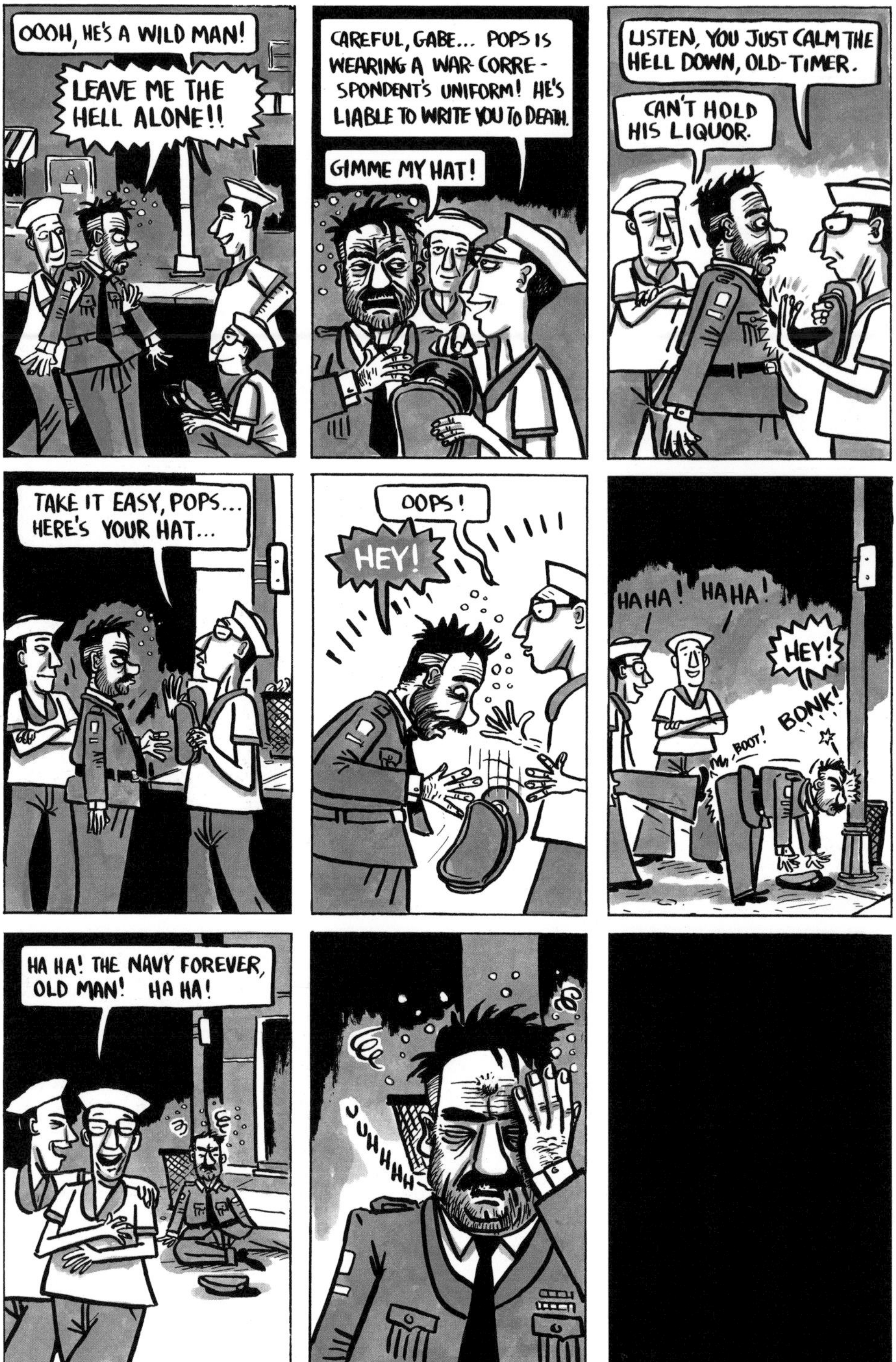
OOOH, HE'S A WILD MAN!
LEAVE ME THE HELL ALONE!!
CAREFUL, GABE... POPS IS WEARING A WAR-CORRESPONDENT'S UNIFORM! HE'S LIABLE TO WRITE YOU TO DEATH.
GIMME MY HAT!
LISTEN, YOU JUST CALM THE HELL DOWN, OLD-TIMER.
CAN'T HOLD HIS LIQUOR.
TAKE IT EASY, POPS... HERE'S YOUR HAT...
OOPS!
HEY!
HAHA! HAHA!
HEY!
BOOT!
BONK!
HA HA! THE NAVY FOREVER, OLD MAN! HA HA!
UUHHHH-

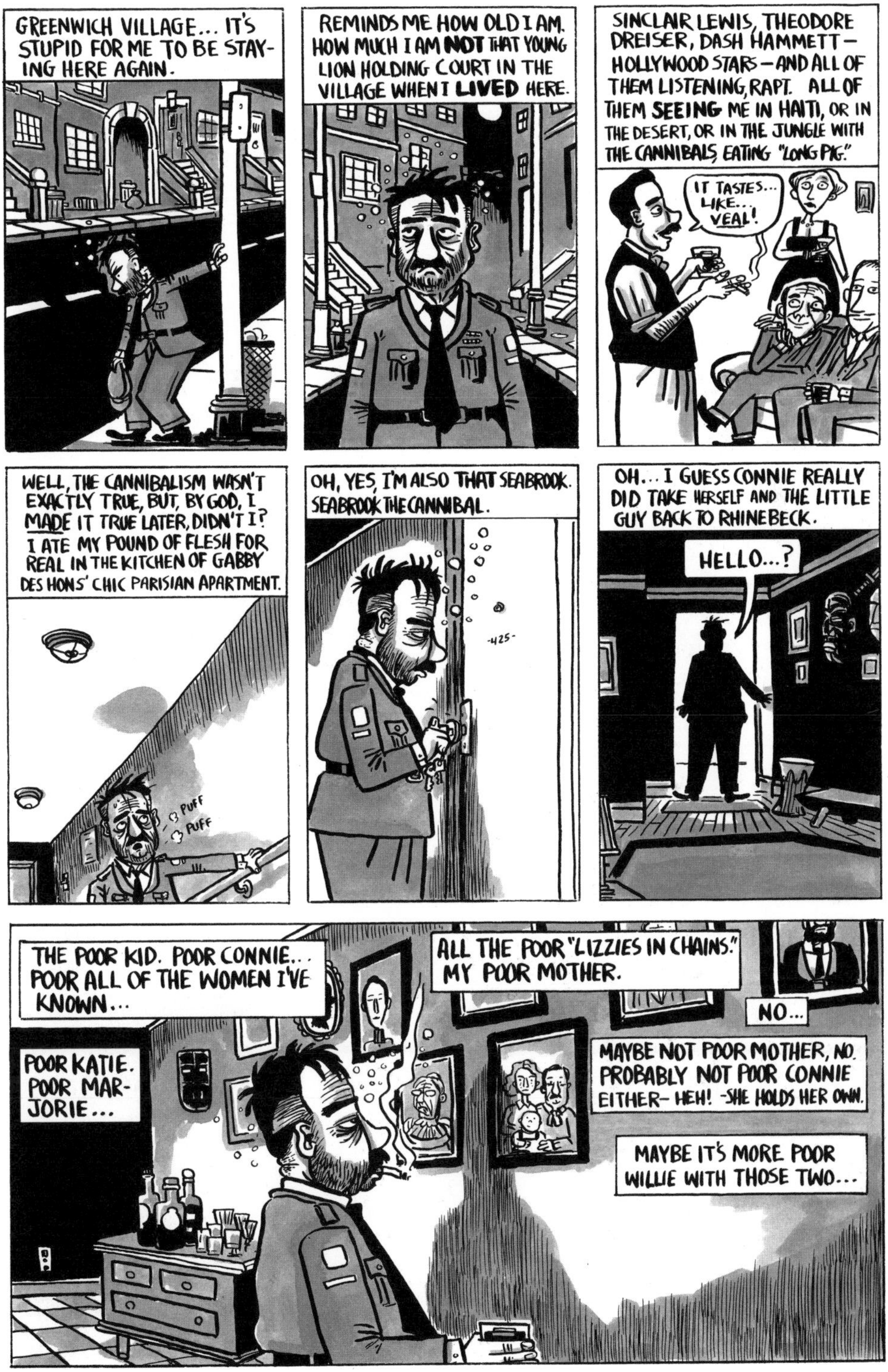
GREENWICH VILLAGE... IT'S STUPID FOR ME TO BE STAYING HERE AGAIN.
REMINDS ME HOW OLD I AM. HOW MUCH I AM NOT THAT YOUNG LION HOLDING COURT IN THE VILLAGE WHEN I LIVED HERE.
SINCLAIR LEWIS, THEODORE DREISER, DASH HAMMETT— HOLLYWOOD STARS—AND ALL OF THEM LISTENING, RAPT. ALL OF THEM SEEING ME IN HAITI, OR IN THE DESERT, OR IN THE JUNGLE WITH THE CANNIBALS, EATING "LONG PIG."
IT TASTES... LIKE... VEAL!
WELL, THE CANNIBALISM WASN'T EXACTLY TRUE, BUT, BY GOD, I MADE IT TRUE LATER, DIDN'T I? I ATE MY POUND OF FLESH FOR REAL IN THE KITCHEN OF GABBY DES HONS' CHIC PARISIAN APARTMENT.
PUFF
PUFF
OH, YES, I'M ALSO THAT SEABROOK. SEABROOK THE CANNIBAL.
-425-
OH... I GUESS CONNIE REALLY DID TAKE HERSELF AND THE LITTLE GUY BACK TO RHINEBECK.
HELLO...?
THE POOR KID. POOR CONNIE... POOR ALL OF THE WOMEN I'VE KNOWN...
ALL THE POOR "LIZZIES IN CHAINS." MY POOR MOTHER.
NO...
POOR KATIE. POOR MARJORIE...
MAYBE NOT POOR MOTHER, NO. PROBABLY NOT POOR CONNIE EITHER— HEH! -SHE HOLDS HER OWN.
MAYBE IT'S MORE POOR WILLIE WITH THOSE TWO...

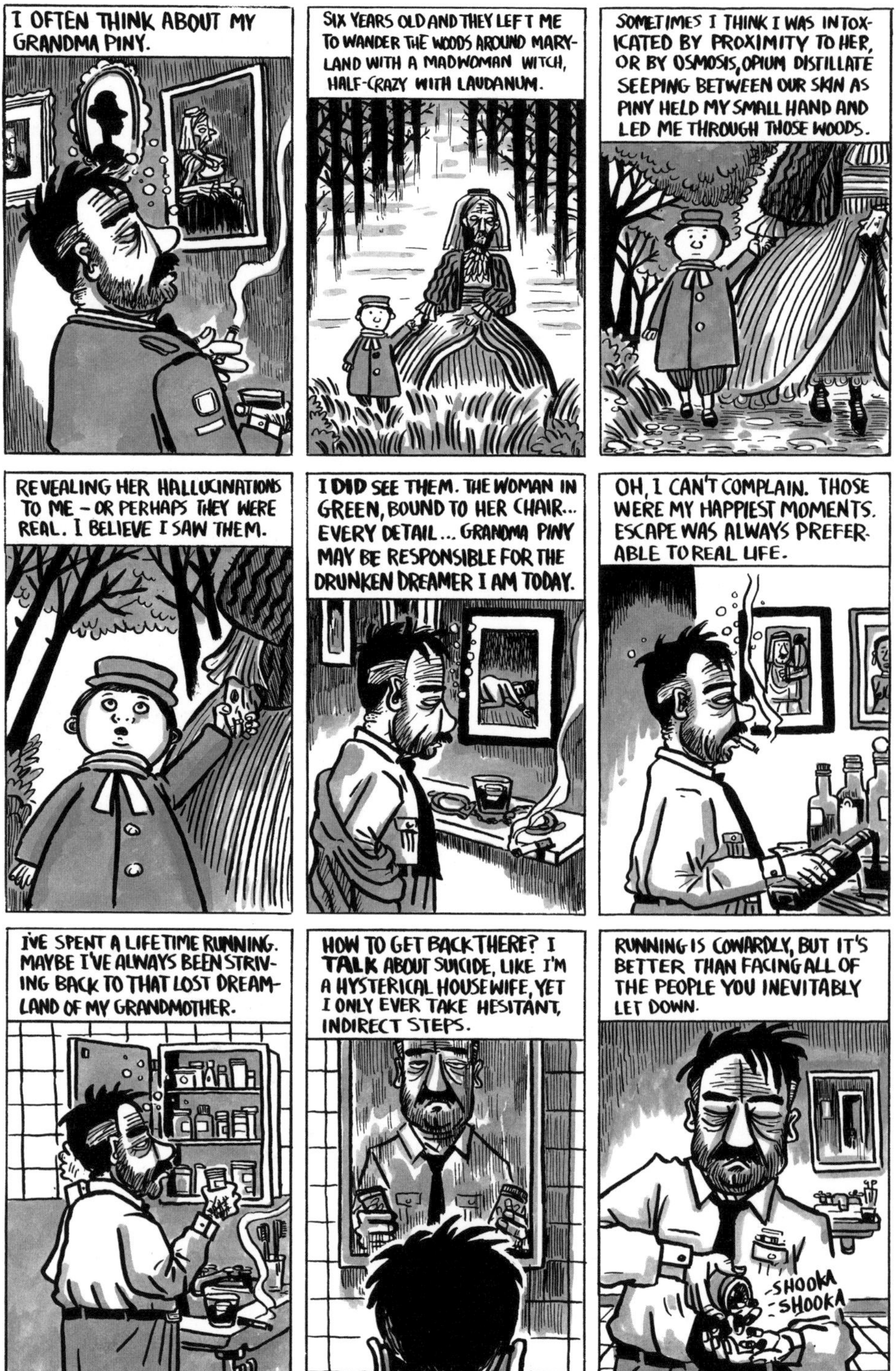
I OFTEN THINK ABOUT MY GRANDMA PINY.
SIX YEARS OLD AND THEY LEFT ME TO WANDER THE WOODS AROUND MARYLAND WITH A MADWOMAN WITCH, HALF-CRAZY WITH LAUDANUM.
SOMETIMES I THINK I WAS INTOXICATED BY PROXIMITY TO HER, OR BY OSMOSIS, OPIUM DISTILLATE SEEPING BETWEEN OUR SKIN AS PINY HELD MY SMALL HAND AND LED ME THROUGH THOSE WOODS.
REVEALING HER HALLUCINATIONS TO ME – OR PERHAPS THEY WERE REAL. I BELIEVE I SAW THEM.
I DID SEE THEM. THE WOMAN IN GREEN, BOUND TO HER CHAIR... EVERY DETAIL... GRANDMA PINY MAY BE RESPONSIBLE FOR THE DRUNKEN DREAMER I AM TODAY.
OH, I CAN'T COMPLAIN. THOSE WERE MY HAPPIEST MOMENTS. ESCAPE WAS ALWAYS PREFERABLE TO REAL LIFE.
I'VE SPENT A LIFETIME RUNNING. MAYBE I'VE ALWAYS BEEN STRIVING BACK TO THAT LOST DREAMLAND OF MY GRANDMOTHER.
HOW TO GET BACK THERE? I TALK ABOUT SUICIDE, LIKE I'M A HYSTERICAL HOUSEWIFE, YET I ONLY EVER TAKE HESITANT, INDIRECT STEPS.
RUNNING IS COWARDLY, BUT IT'S BETTER THAN FACING ALL OF THE PEOPLE YOU INEVITABLY LET DOWN.
SHOOKA
SHOOKA

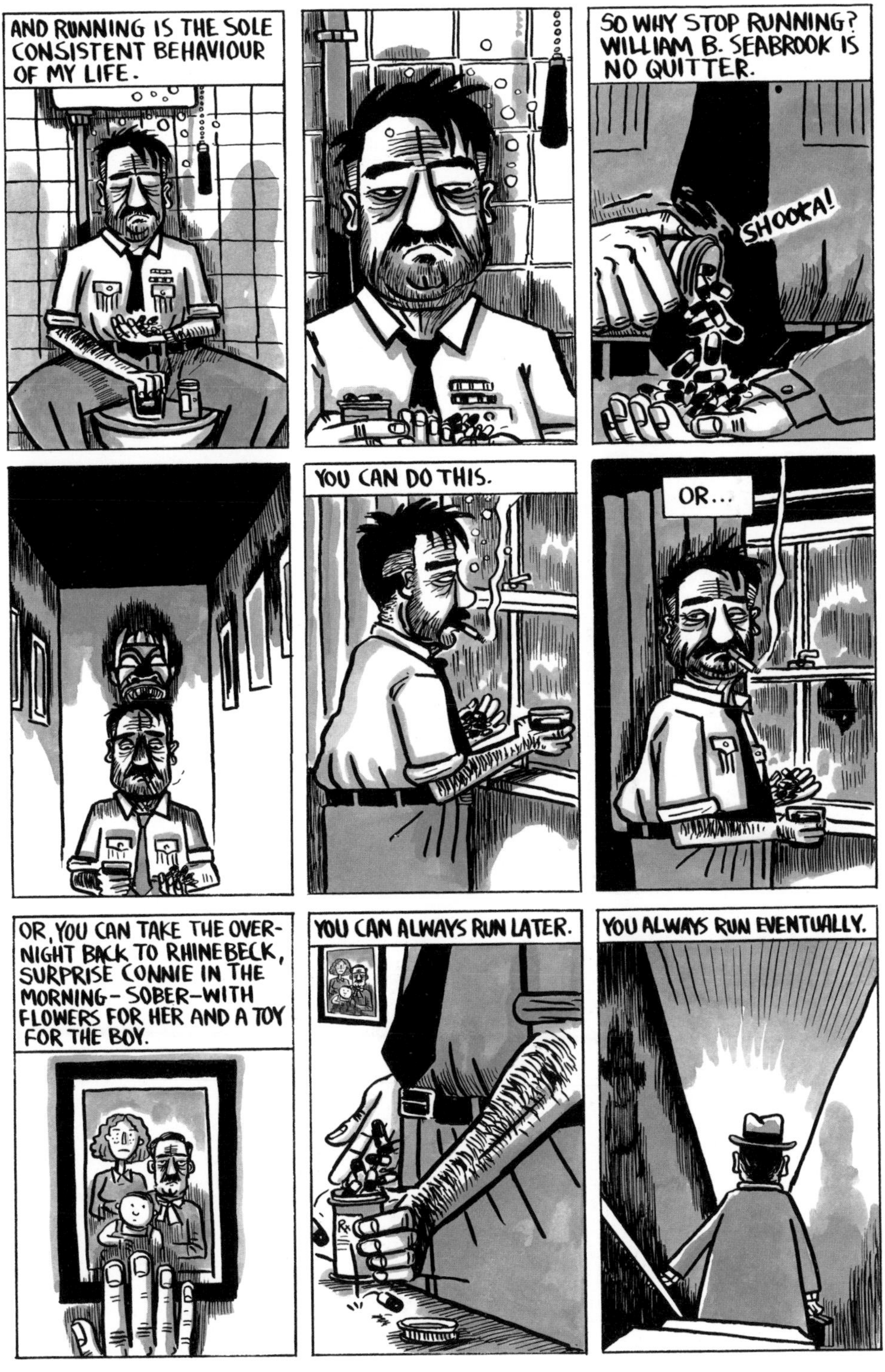
AND RUNNING IS THE SOLE CONSISTENT BEHAVIOUR OF MY LIFE.
SO WHY STOP RUNNING? WILLIAM B. SEABROOK IS NO QUITTER.
SHOOKA!
YOU CAN DO THIS.
OR...
OR, YOU CAN TAKE THE OVER-NIGHT BACK TO RHINEBECK, SURPRISE CONNIE IN THE MORNING–SOBER–WITH FLOWERS FOR HER AND A TOY FOR THE BOY.
YOU CAN ALWAYS RUN LATER.
Rx
YOU ALWAYS RUN EVENTUALLY.

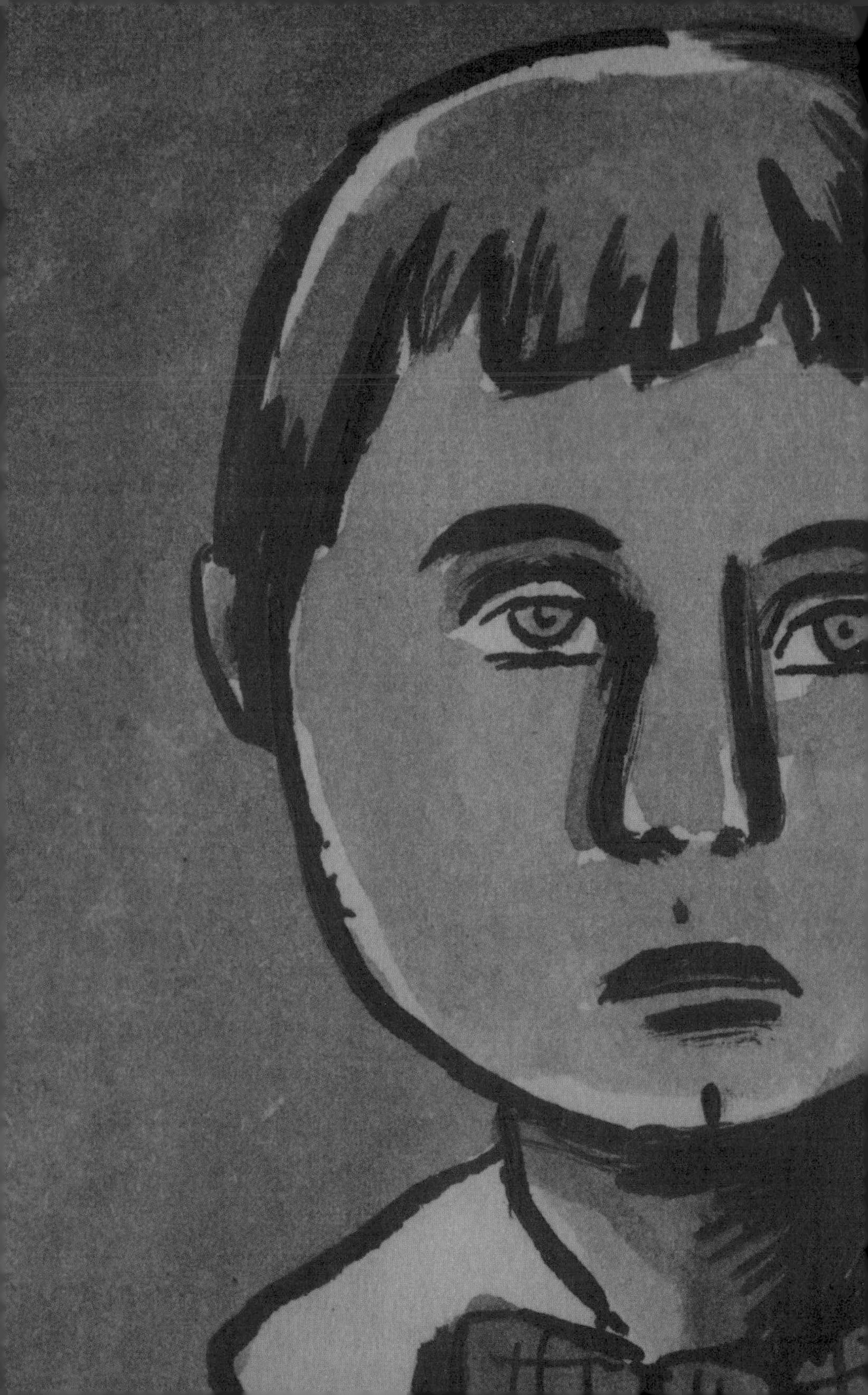

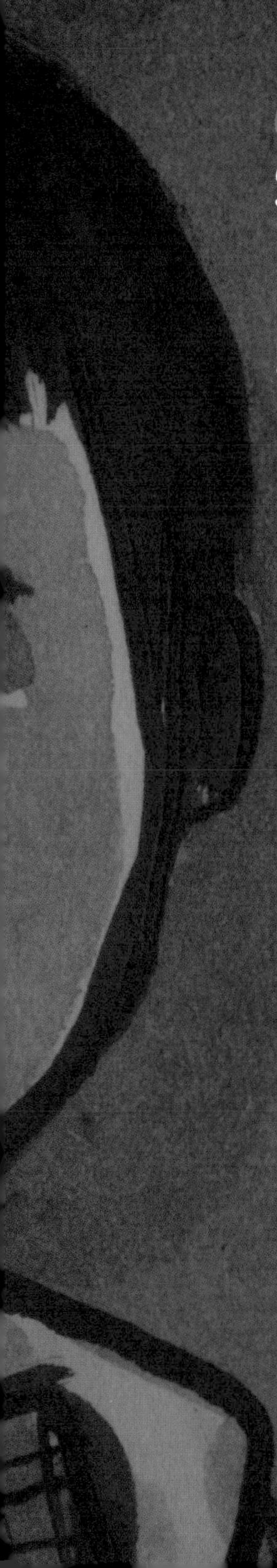

# CHAPTER ONE
# SUPREME WANTS: FROM SOUTHERN METHODIST TO SADOMASOCHIST

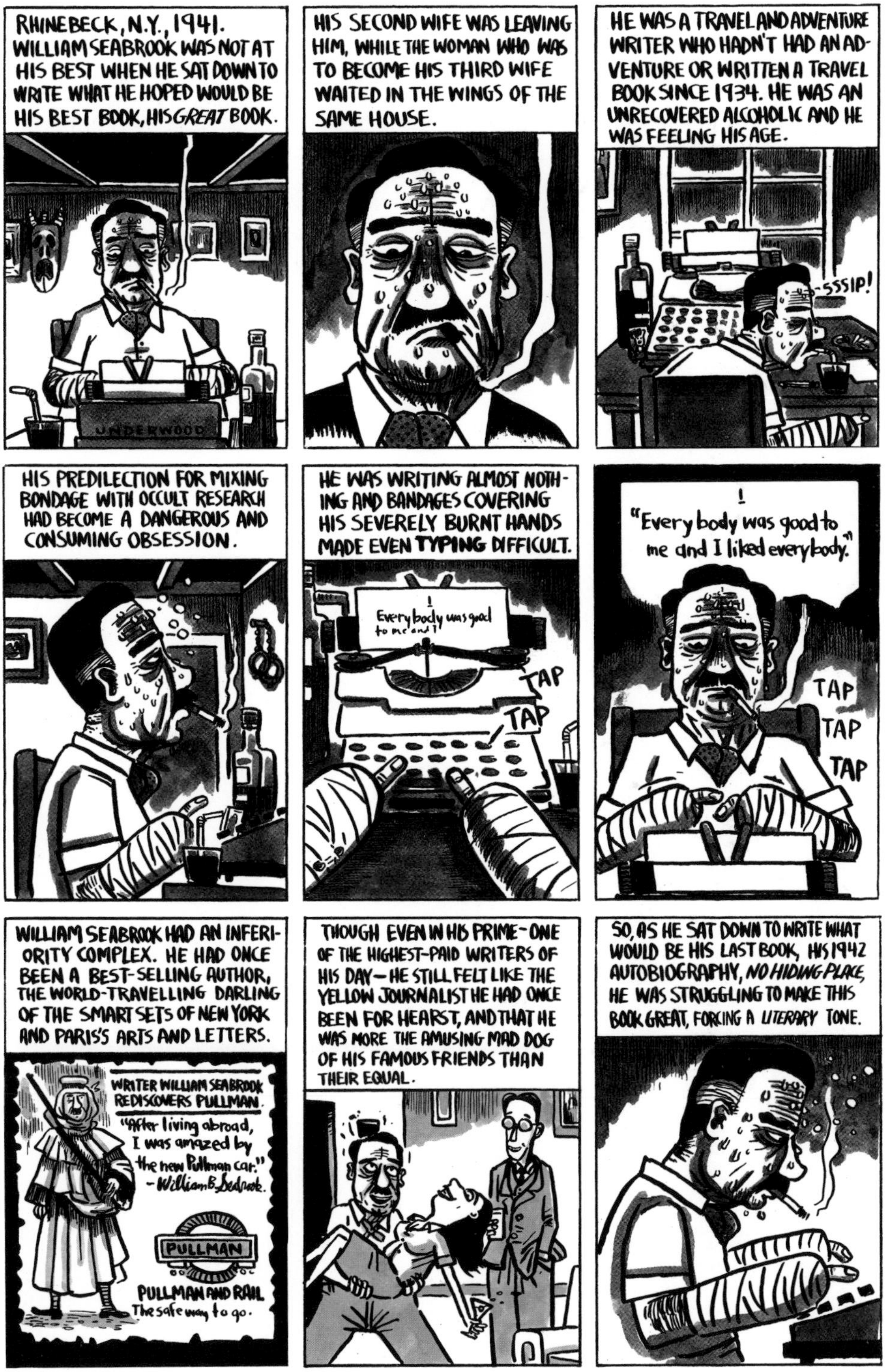
RHINEBECK, N.Y., 1941. WILLIAM SEABROOK WAS NOT AT HIS BEST WHEN HE SAT DOWN TO WRITE WHAT HE HOPED WOULD BE HIS BEST BOOK, HIS *GREAT* BOOK.
UNDERWOOD
HIS SECOND WIFE WAS LEAVING HIM, WHILE THE WOMAN WHO WAS TO BECOME HIS THIRD WIFE WAITED IN THE WINGS OF THE SAME HOUSE.
HE WAS A TRAVEL AND ADVENTURE WRITER WHO HADN'T HAD AN ADVENTURE OR WRITTEN A TRAVEL BOOK SINCE 1934. HE WAS AN UNRECOVERED ALCOHOLIC AND HE WAS FEELING HIS AGE.
SSSIP!
HIS PREDILECTION FOR MIXING BONDAGE WITH OCCULT RESEARCH HAD BECOME A DANGEROUS AND CONSUMING OBSESSION.
HE WAS WRITING ALMOST NOTHING AND BANDAGES COVERING HIS SEVERELY BURNT HANDS MADE EVEN **TYPING** DIFFICULT.
! Everybody was good to me and I
TAP
TAP
! "Every body was good to me and I liked everybody."
TAP
TAP
TAP
WILLIAM SEABROOK HAD AN INFERIORITY COMPLEX. HE HAD ONCE BEEN A BEST-SELLING AUTHOR, THE WORLD-TRAVELLING DARLING OF THE SMART SETS OF NEW YORK AND PARIS'S ARTS AND LETTERS.
WRITER WILLIAM SEABROOK REDISCOVERS PULLMAN.
"After living abroad, I was amazed by the new Pullman car." - William B. Seabrook.
PULLMAN
PULLMAN AND RAIL
The safe way to go.
THOUGH EVEN IN HIS PRIME—ONE OF THE HIGHEST-PAID WRITERS OF HIS DAY—HE STILL FELT LIKE THE YELLOW JOURNALIST HE HAD ONCE BEEN FOR HEARST, AND THAT HE WAS MORE THE AMUSING MAD DOG OF HIS FAMOUS FRIENDS THAN THEIR EQUAL.
SO, AS HE SAT DOWN TO WRITE WHAT WOULD BE HIS LAST BOOK, HIS 1942 AUTOBIOGRAPHY, *NO HIDING PLACE*, HE WAS STRUGGLING TO MAKE THIS BOOK GREAT, FORCING A *LITERARY* TONE.

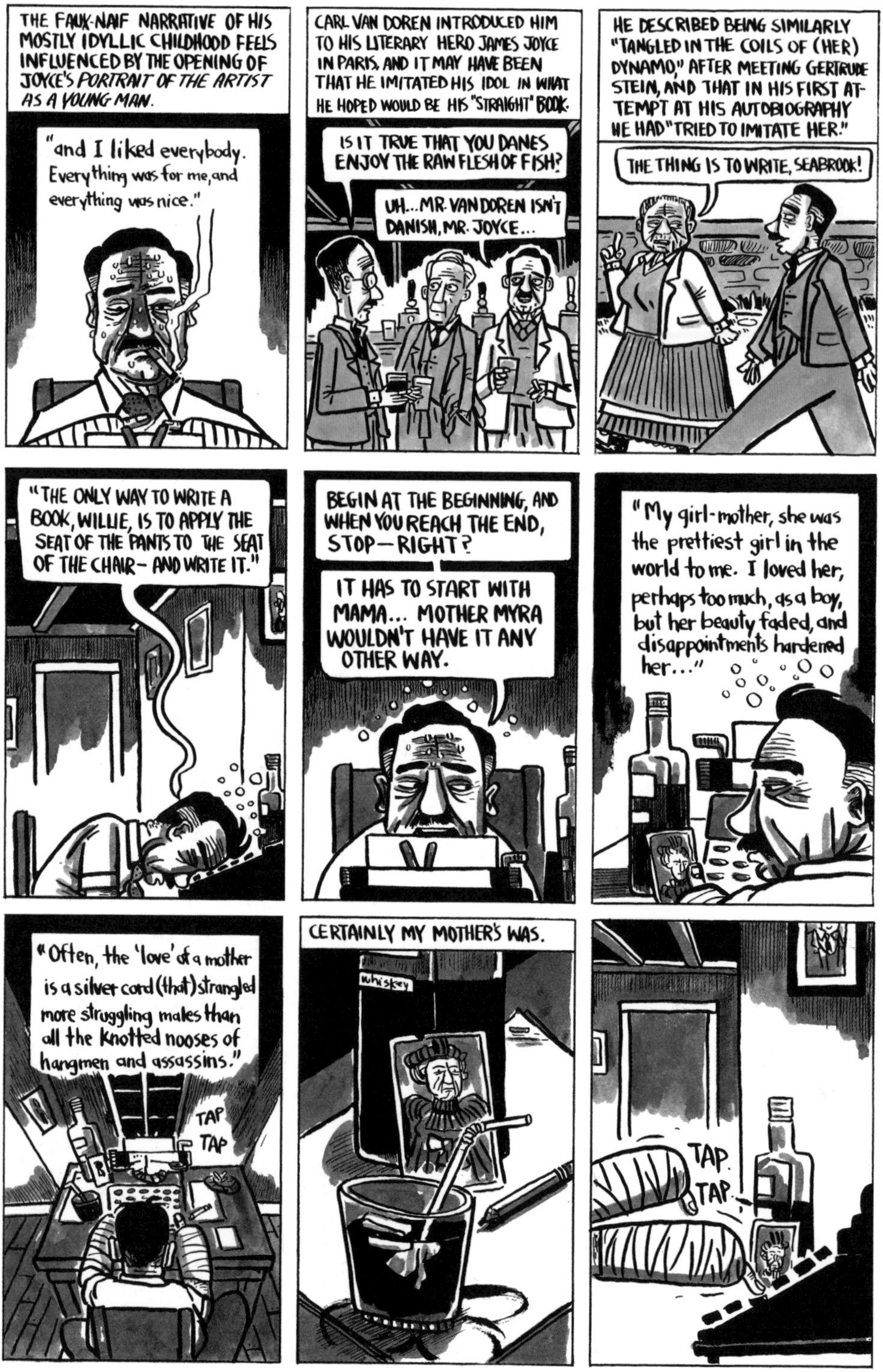
THE FAUX-NAIF NARRATIVE OF HIS MOSTLY IDYLLIC CHILDHOOD FEELS INFLUENCED BY THE OPENING OF JOYCE'S *PORTRAIT OF THE ARTIST AS A YOUNG MAN*.
"and I liked everybody. Everything was for me, and everything was nice."
CARL VAN DOREN INTRODUCED HIM TO HIS LITERARY HERO JAMES JOYCE IN PARIS, AND IT MAY HAVE BEEN THAT HE IMITATED HIS IDOL IN WHAT HE HOPED WOULD BE HIS "STRAIGHT" BOOK.
IS IT TRUE THAT YOU DANES ENJOY THE RAW FLESH OF FISH?
UH... MR. VAN DOREN ISN'T DANISH, MR. JOYCE...
HE DESCRIBED BEING SIMILARLY "TANGLED IN THE COILS OF (HER) DYNAMO," AFTER MEETING GERTRUDE STEIN, AND THAT IN HIS FIRST ATTEMPT AT HIS AUTOBIOGRAPHY HE HAD "TRIED TO IMITATE HER."
THE THING IS TO WRITE, SEABROOK!
"THE ONLY WAY TO WRITE A BOOK, WILLIE, IS TO APPLY THE SEAT OF THE PANTS TO THE SEAT OF THE CHAIR– AND WRITE IT."
BEGIN AT THE BEGINNING, AND WHEN YOU REACH THE END, STOP– RIGHT?
IT HAS TO START WITH MAMA... MOTHER MYRA WOULDN'T HAVE IT ANY OTHER WAY.
"My girl-mother, she was the prettiest girl in the world to me. I loved her, perhaps too much, as a boy, but her beauty faded, and disappointments hardened her..."
"Often, the 'love' of a mother is a silver cord (that) strangled more struggling males than all the knotted nooses of hangmen and assassins."
TAP TAP
CERTAINLY MY MOTHER'S WAS.
whiskey
TAP. TAP.

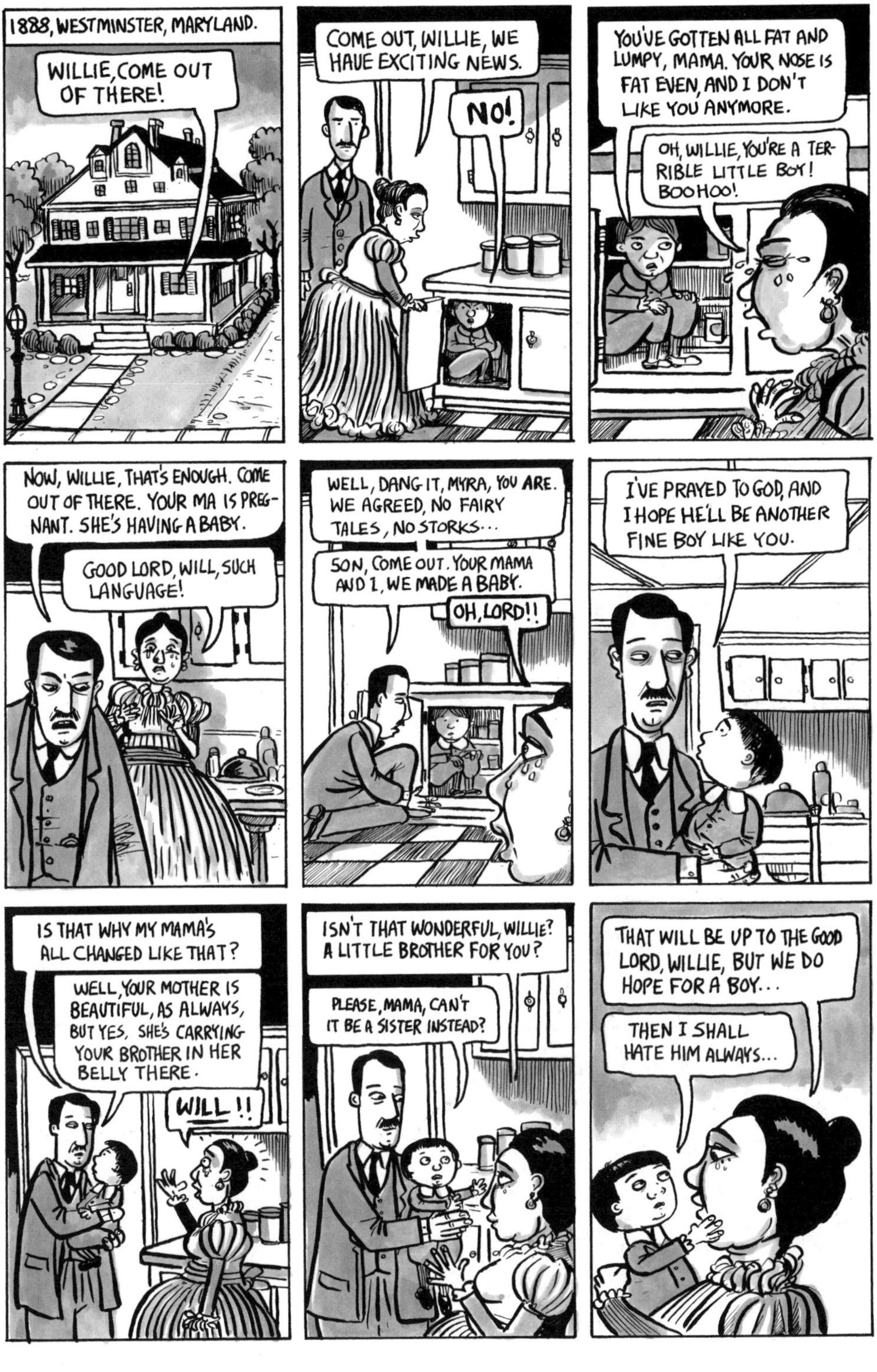
1888, WESTMINSTER, MARYLAND.
WILLIE, COME OUT OF THERE!
COME OUT, WILLIE, WE HAVE EXCITING NEWS.
NO!
YOU'VE GOTTEN ALL FAT AND LUMPY, MAMA. YOUR NOSE IS FAT EVEN, AND I DON'T LIKE YOU ANYMORE.
OH, WILLIE, YOU'RE A TERRIBLE LITTLE BOY! BOOHOO!
NOW, WILLIE, THAT'S ENOUGH. COME OUT OF THERE. YOUR MA IS PREGNANT. SHE'S HAVING A BABY.
GOOD LORD, WILL, SUCH LANGUAGE!
WELL, DANG IT, MYRA, YOU ARE. WE AGREED, NO FAIRY TALES, NO STORKS...
SON, COME OUT. YOUR MAMA AND I, WE MADE A BABY.
OH, LORD!!
I'VE PRAYED TO GOD, AND I HOPE HE'LL BE ANOTHER FINE BOY LIKE YOU.
IS THAT WHY MY MAMA'S ALL CHANGED LIKE THAT?
WELL, YOUR MOTHER IS BEAUTIFUL, AS ALWAYS, BUT YES, SHE'S CARRYING YOUR BROTHER IN HER BELLY THERE.
WILL!!
ISN'T THAT WONDERFUL, WILLIE? A LITTLE BROTHER FOR YOU?
PLEASE, MAMA, CAN'T IT BE A SISTER INSTEAD?
THAT WILL BE UP TO THE GOOD LORD, WILLIE, BUT WE DO HOPE FOR A BOY...
THEN I SHALL HATE HIM ALWAYS...

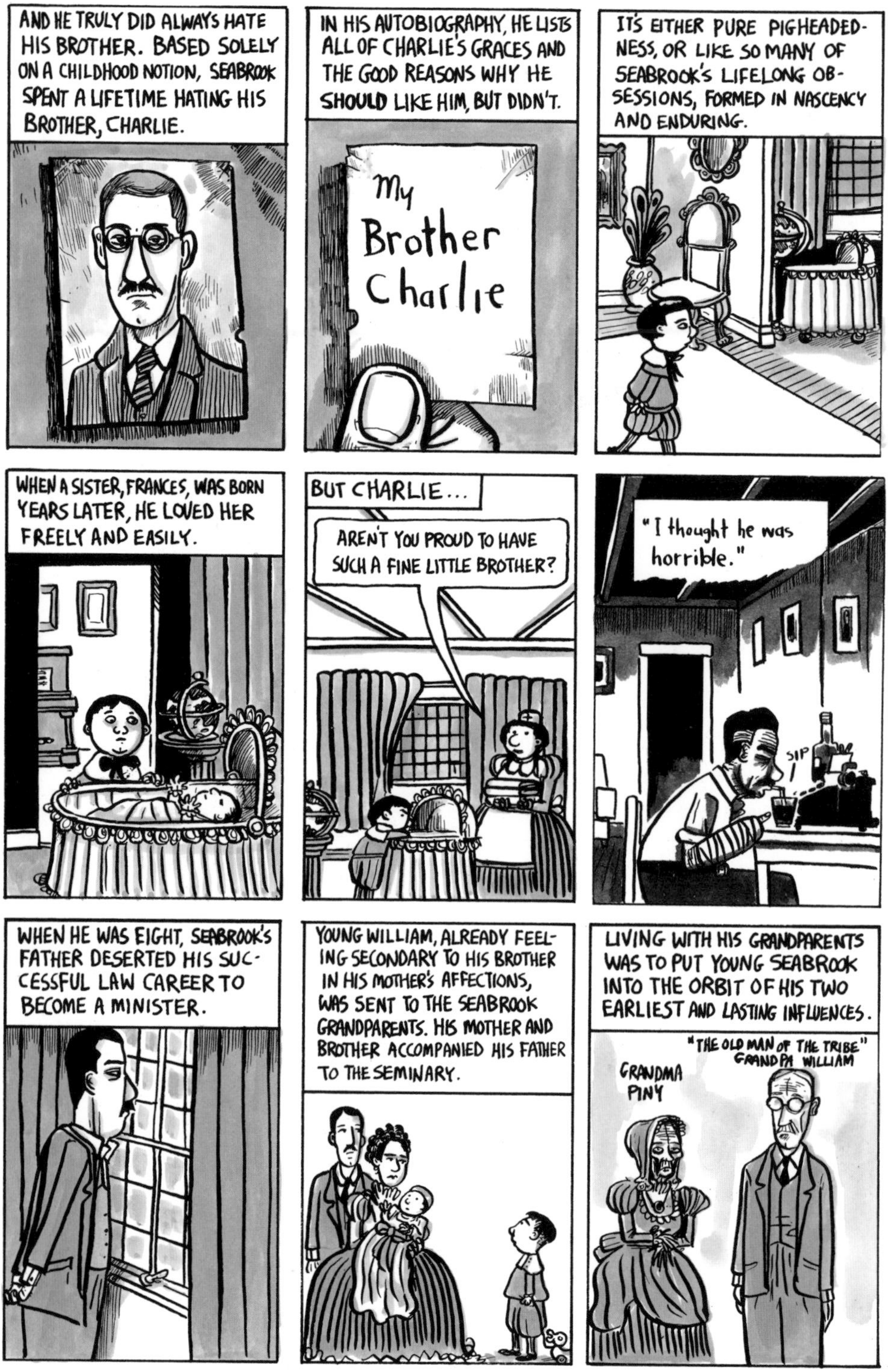
AND HE TRULY DID ALWAYS HATE HIS BROTHER. BASED SOLELY ON A CHILDHOOD NOTION, SEABROOK SPENT A LIFETIME HATING HIS BROTHER, CHARLIE.
IN HIS AUTOBIOGRAPHY, HE LISTS ALL OF CHARLIE'S GRACES AND THE GOOD REASONS WHY HE SHOULD LIKE HIM, BUT DIDN'T.
My Brother Charlie
IT'S EITHER PURE PIGHEADEDNESS, OR LIKE SO MANY OF SEABROOK'S LIFELONG OBSESSIONS, FORMED IN NASCENCY AND ENDURING.
WHEN A SISTER, FRANCES, WAS BORN YEARS LATER, HE LOVED HER FREELY AND EASILY.
BUT CHARLIE...
AREN'T YOU PROUD TO HAVE SUCH A FINE LITTLE BROTHER?
"I thought he was horrible."
SIP
WHEN HE WAS EIGHT, SEABROOK'S FATHER DESERTED HIS SUCCESSFUL LAW CAREER TO BECOME A MINISTER.
YOUNG WILLIAM, ALREADY FEELING SECONDARY TO HIS BROTHER IN HIS MOTHER'S AFFECTIONS, WAS SENT TO THE SEABROOK GRANDPARENTS. HIS MOTHER AND BROTHER ACCOMPANIED HIS FATHER TO THE SEMINARY.
LIVING WITH HIS GRANDPARENTS WAS TO PUT YOUNG SEABROOK INTO THE ORBIT OF HIS TWO EARLIEST AND LASTING INFLUENCES.
GRANDMA PINY
"THE OLD MAN OF THE TRIBE" GRANDPA WILLIAM

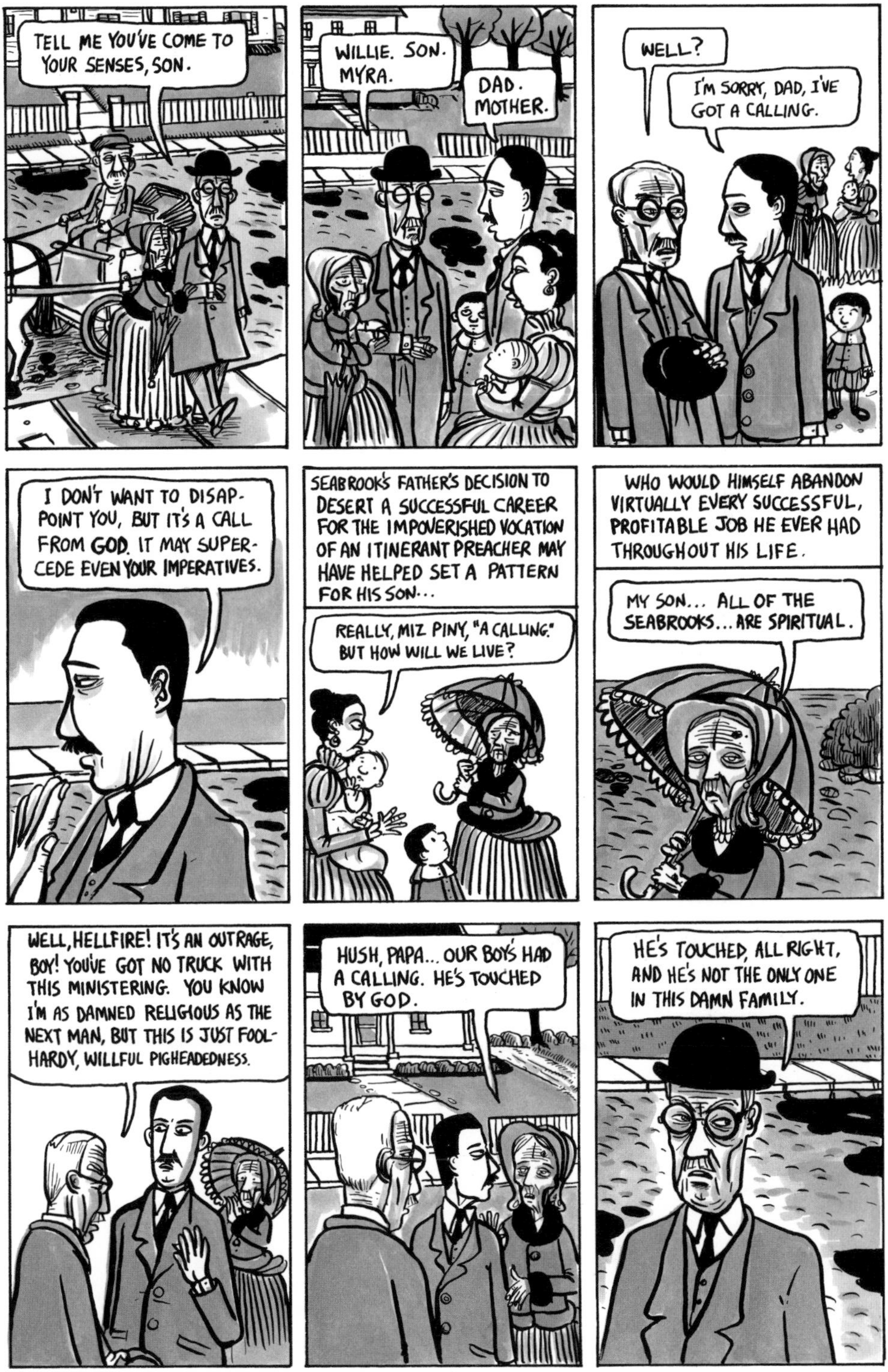
TELL ME YOU'VE COME TO YOUR SENSES, SON.
WILLIE. SON. MYRA.
DAD. MOTHER.
WELL?
I'M SORRY, DAD, I'VE GOT A CALLING.
I DON'T WANT TO DISAPPOINT YOU, BUT IT'S A CALL FROM GOD. IT MAY SUPERCEDE EVEN YOUR IMPERATIVES.
SEABROOK'S FATHER'S DECISION TO DESERT A SUCCESSFUL CAREER FOR THE IMPOVERISHED VOCATION OF AN ITINERANT PREACHER MAY HAVE HELPED SET A PATTERN FOR HIS SON...
REALLY, MIZ PINY, "A CALLING." BUT HOW WILL WE LIVE?
WHO WOULD HIMSELF ABANDON VIRTUALLY EVERY SUCCESSFUL, PROFITABLE JOB HE EVER HAD THROUGHOUT HIS LIFE.
MY SON... ALL OF THE SEABROOKS... ARE SPIRITUAL.
WELL, HELLFIRE! IT'S AN OUTRAGE, BOY! YOU'VE GOT NO TRUCK WITH THIS MINISTERING. YOU KNOW I'M AS DAMNED RELIGIOUS AS THE NEXT MAN, BUT THIS IS JUST FOOLHARDY, WILLFUL PIGHEADEDNESS.
HUSH, PAPA... OUR BOY'S HAD A CALLING. HE'S TOUCHED BY GOD.
HE'S TOUCHED, ALL RIGHT, AND HE'S NOT THE ONLY ONE IN THIS DAMN FAMILY.

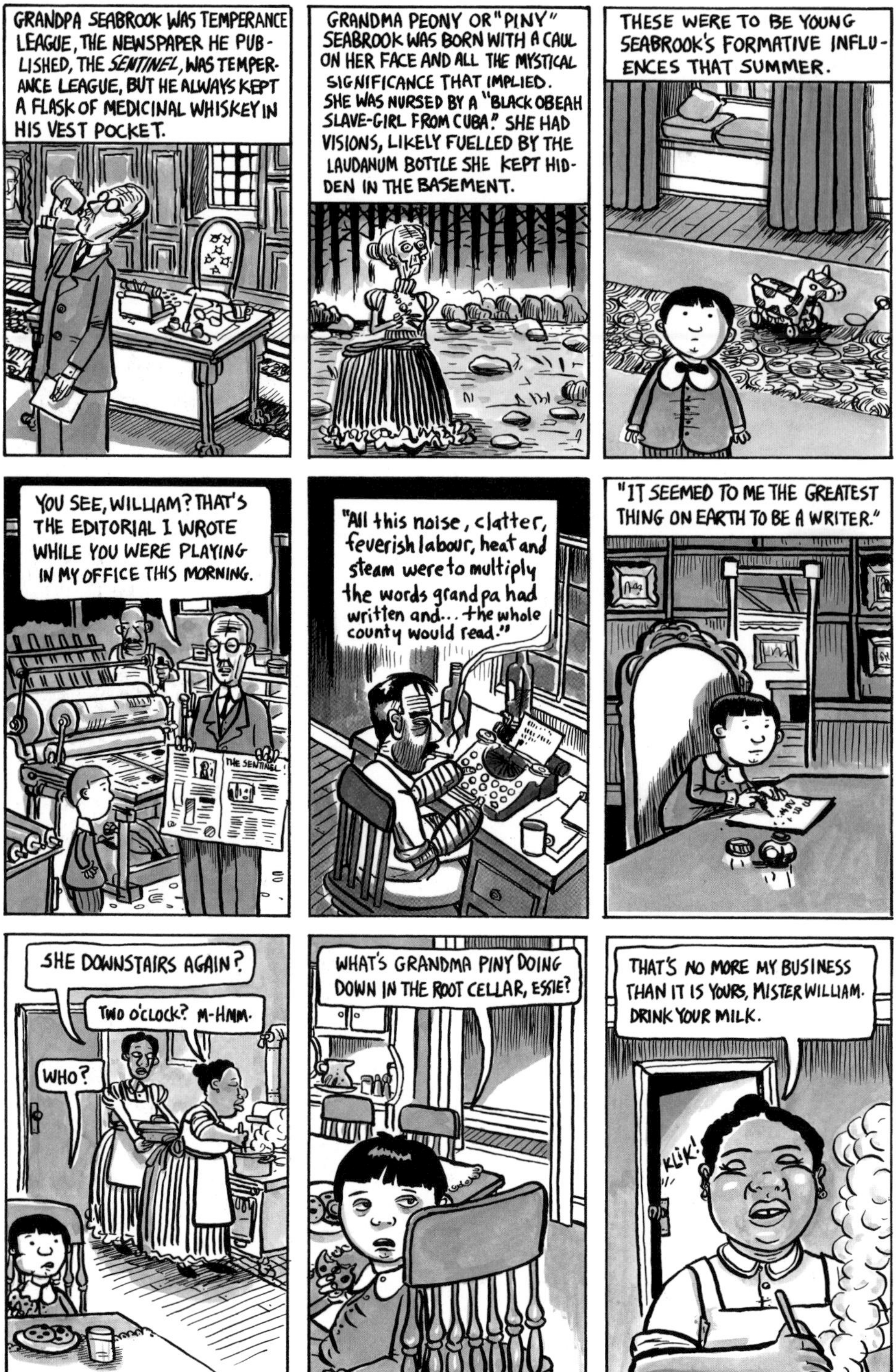

GRANDPA SEABROOK WAS TEMPERANCE LEAGUE, THE NEWSPAPER HE PUBLISHED, THE *SENTINEL*, WAS TEMPERANCE LEAGUE, BUT HE ALWAYS KEPT A FLASK OF MEDICINAL WHISKEY IN HIS VEST POCKET.
GRANDMA PEONY OR "PINY" SEABROOK WAS BORN WITH A CAUL ON HER FACE AND ALL THE MYSTICAL SIGNIFICANCE THAT IMPLIED. SHE WAS NURSED BY A "BLACK OBEAH SLAVE-GIRL FROM CUBA." SHE HAD VISIONS, LIKELY FUELLED BY THE LAUDANUM BOTTLE SHE KEPT HIDDEN IN THE BASEMENT.
THESE WERE TO BE YOUNG SEABROOK'S FORMATIVE INFLUENCES THAT SUMMER.
YOU SEE, WILLIAM? THAT'S THE EDITORIAL I WROTE WHILE YOU WERE PLAYING IN MY OFFICE THIS MORNING.
THE SENTINEL
"All this noise, clatter, feverish labour, heat and steam were to multiply the words grandpa had written and... the whole county would read."
"IT SEEMED TO ME THE GREATEST THING ON EARTH TO BE A WRITER."
SHE DOWNSTAIRS AGAIN?
TWO O'CLOCK? M-HMM.
WHO?
WHAT'S GRANDMA PINY DOING DOWN IN THE ROOT CELLAR, ESSIE?
THAT'S NO MORE MY BUSINESS THAN IT IS YOURS, MISTER WILLIAM. DRINK YOUR MILK.
KLIK!

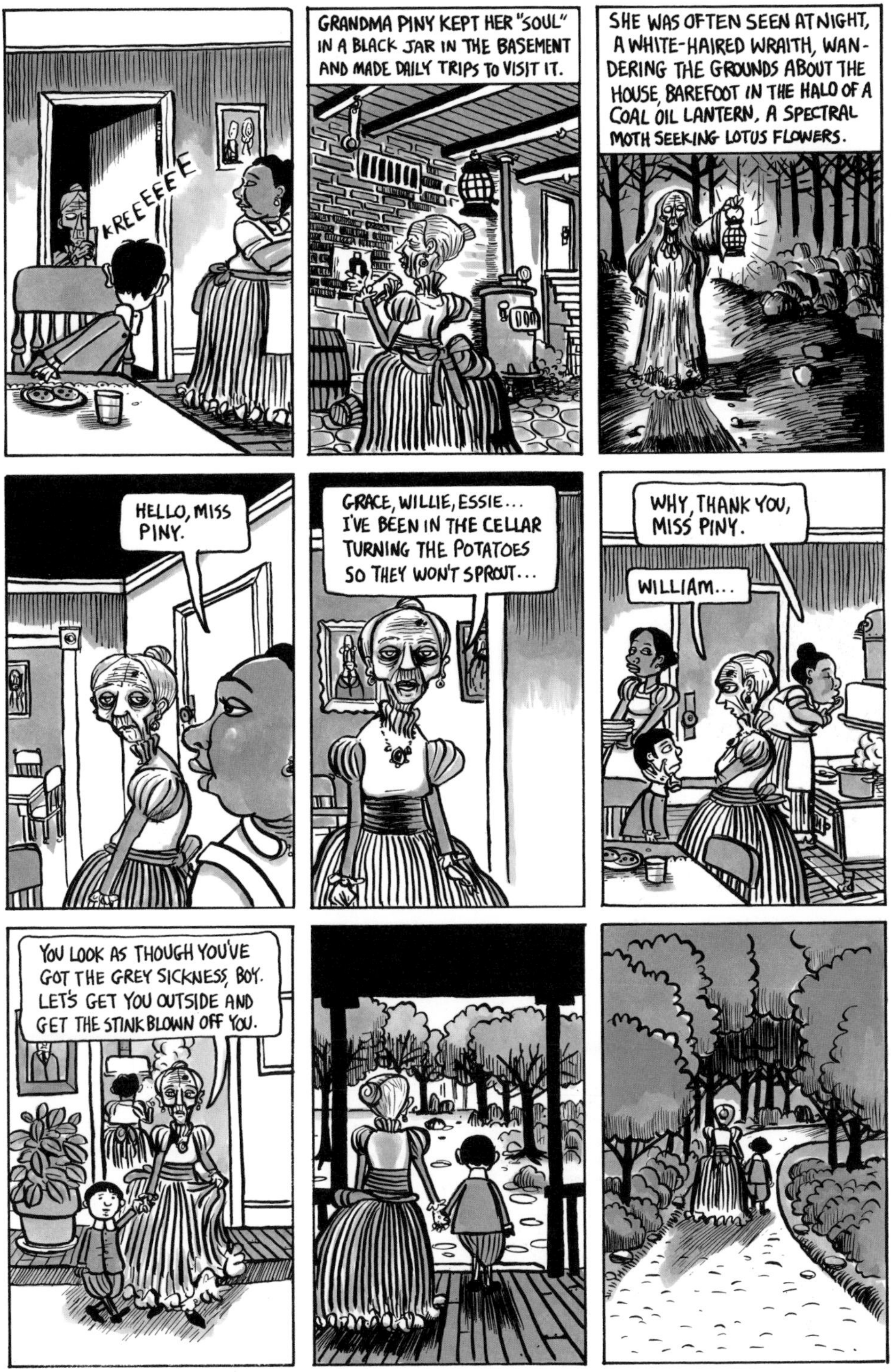
KREEEEEEE
GRANDMA PINY KEPT HER "SOUL" IN A BLACK JAR IN THE BASEMENT AND MADE DAILY TRIPS TO VISIT IT.
SHE WAS OFTEN SEEN AT NIGHT, A WHITE-HAIRED WRAITH, WANDERING THE GROUNDS ABOUT THE HOUSE, BAREFOOT IN THE HALO OF A COAL OIL LANTERN, A SPECTRAL MOTH SEEKING LOTUS FLOWERS.
HELLO, MISS PINY.
GRACE, WILLIE, ESSIE... I'VE BEEN IN THE CELLAR TURNING THE POTATOES SO THEY WON'T SPROUT...
WHY, THANK YOU, MISS PINY.
WILLIAM...
YOU LOOK AS THOUGH YOU'VE GOT THE GREY SICKNESS, BOY. LET'S GET YOU OUTSIDE AND GET THE STINK BLOWN OFF YOU.

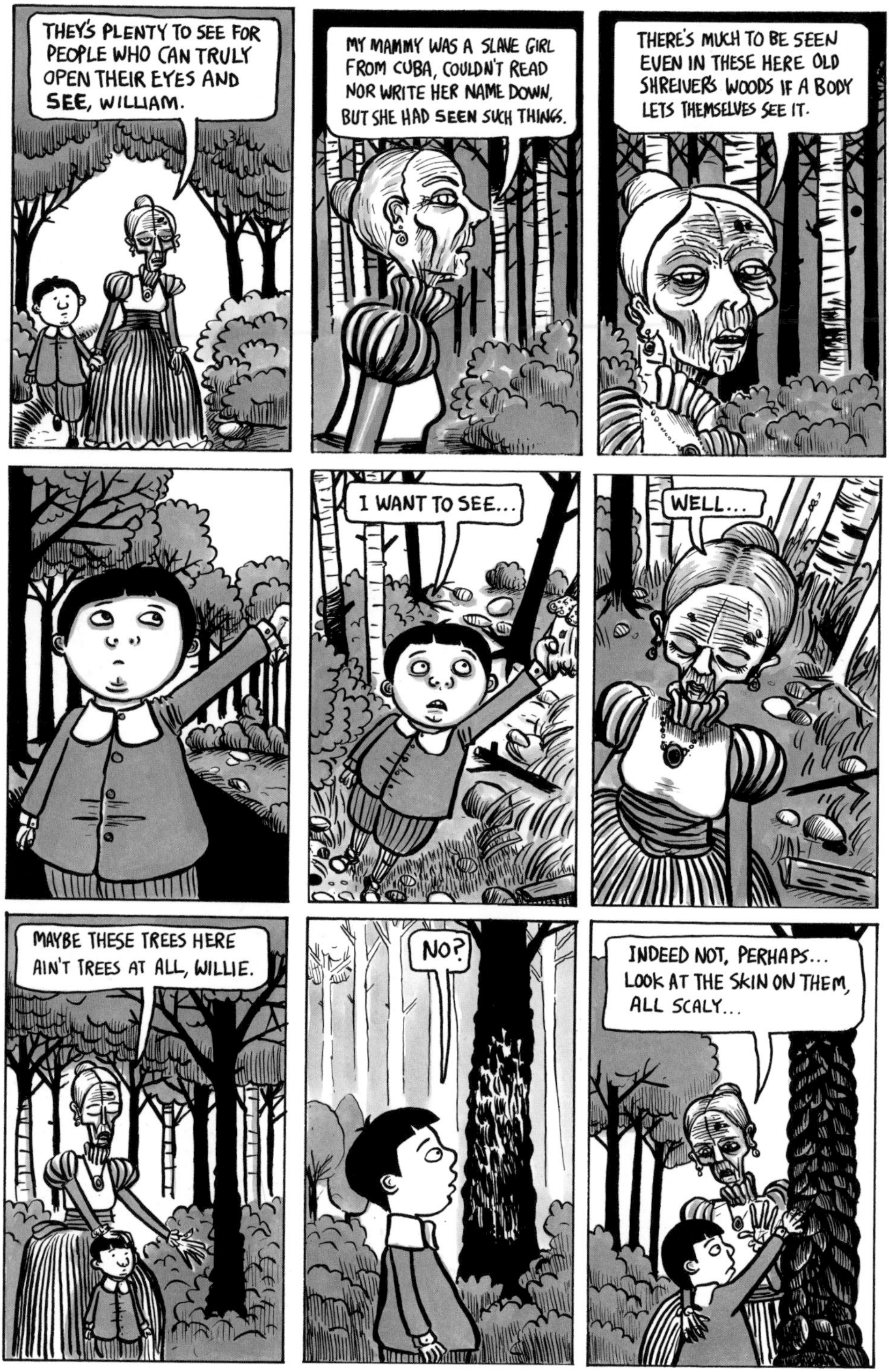
THEY'S PLENTY TO SEE FOR PEOPLE WHO CAN TRULY OPEN THEIR EYES AND **SEE**, WILLIAM.
MY MAMMY WAS A SLAVE GIRL FROM CUBA, COULDN'T READ NOR WRITE HER NAME DOWN, BUT SHE HAD SEEN SUCH THINGS.
THERE'S MUCH TO BE SEEN EVEN IN THESE HERE OLD SHREIVER'S WOODS IF A BODY LETS THEMSELVES SEE IT.
I WANT TO SEE...
WELL...
MAYBE THESE TREES HERE AIN'T TREES AT ALL, WILLIE.
NO?
INDEED NOT, PERHAPS... LOOK AT THE SKIN ON THEM, ALL SCALY...

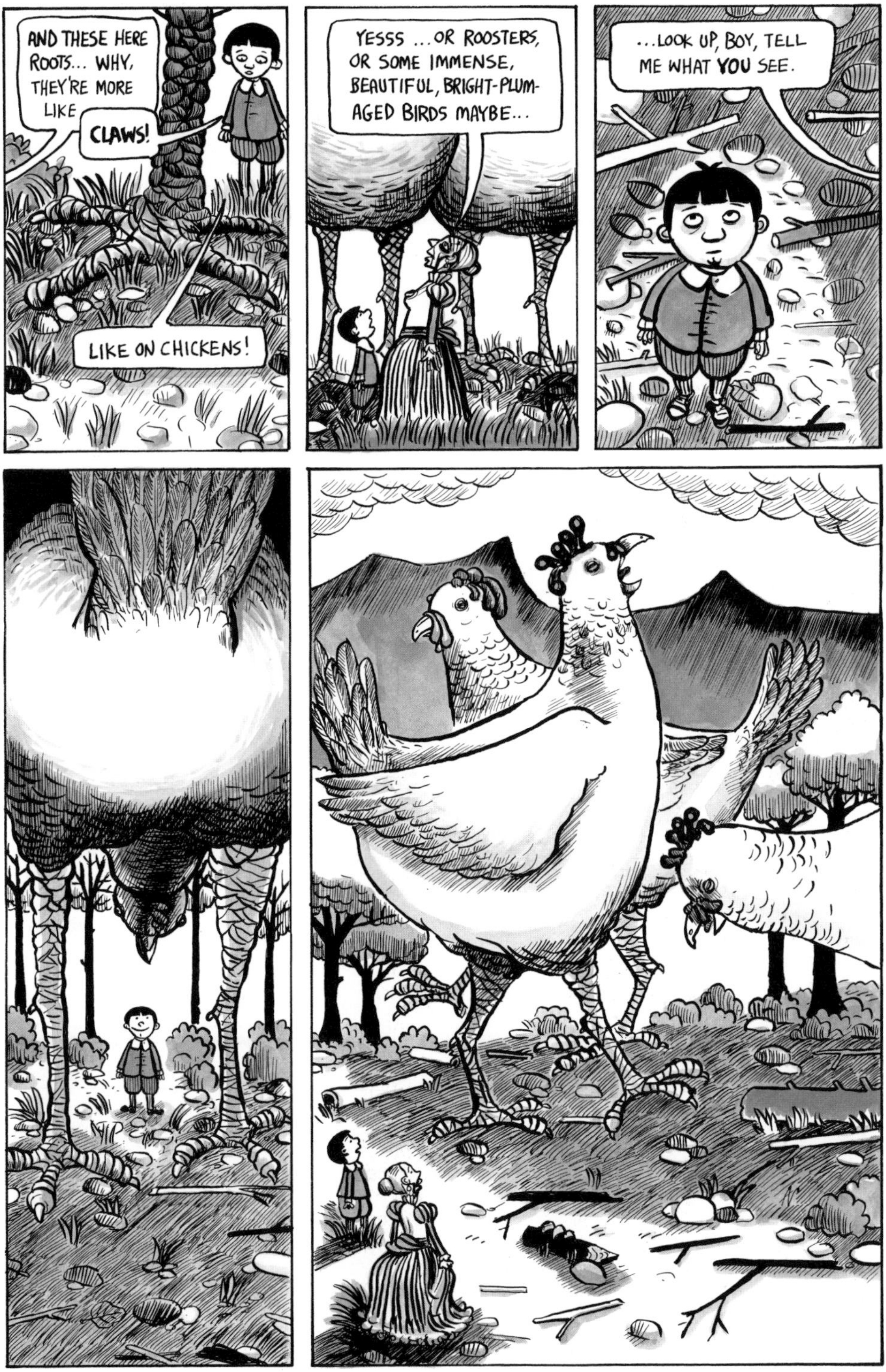
AND THESE HERE ROOTS... WHY, THEY'RE MORE LIKE
CLAWS!
LIKE ON CHICKENS!
YESSS ...OR ROOSTERS, OR SOME IMMENSE, BEAUTIFUL, BRIGHT-PLUMAGED BIRDS MAYBE...
...LOOK UP, BOY, TELL ME WHAT YOU SEE.

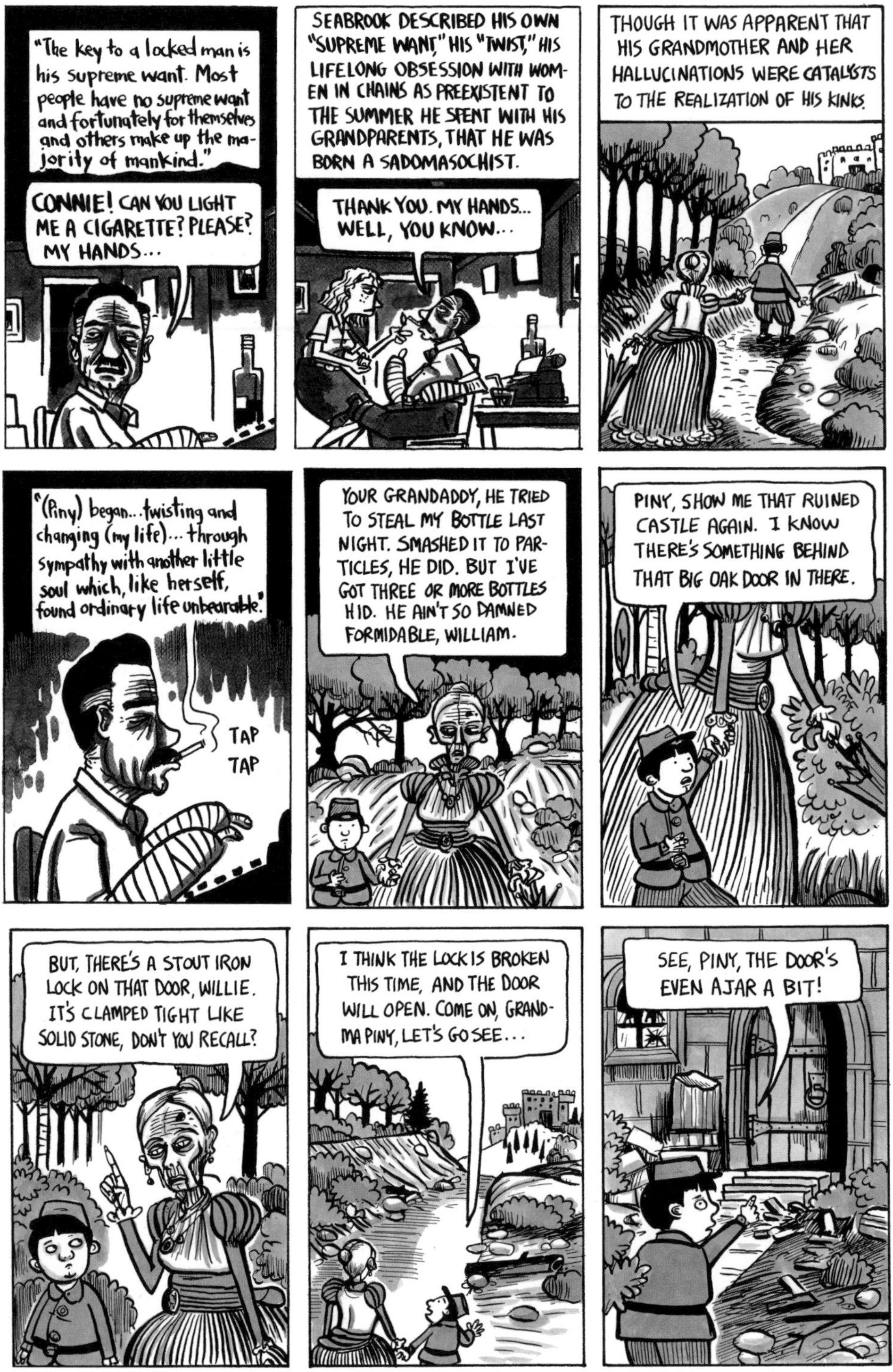
"The key to a locked man is his supreme want. Most people have no supreme want and fortunately for themselves and others make up the majority of mankind."
CONNIE! CAN YOU LIGHT ME A CIGARETTE? PLEASE? MY HANDS...
SEABROOK DESCRIBED HIS OWN "SUPREME WANT," HIS "TWIST," HIS LIFELONG OBSESSION WITH WOMEN IN CHAINS AS PREEXISTENT TO THE SUMMER HE SPENT WITH HIS GRANDPARENTS, THAT HE WAS BORN A SADOMASOCHIST.
THANK YOU. MY HANDS... WELL, YOU KNOW...
THOUGH IT WAS APPARENT THAT HIS GRANDMOTHER AND HER HALLUCINATIONS WERE CATALYSTS TO THE REALIZATION OF HIS KINKS.
"(Piny) began... twisting and changing (my life)... through sympathy with another little soul which, like herself, found ordinary life unbearable."
TAP TAP
YOUR GRANDADDY, HE TRIED TO STEAL MY BOTTLE LAST NIGHT. SMASHED IT TO PARTICLES, HE DID. BUT I'VE GOT THREE OR MORE BOTTLES HID. HE AIN'T SO DAMNED FORMIDABLE, WILLIAM.
PINY, SHOW ME THAT RUINED CASTLE AGAIN. I KNOW THERE'S SOMETHING BEHIND THAT BIG OAK DOOR IN THERE.
BUT, THERE'S A STOUT IRON LOCK ON THAT DOOR, WILLIE. IT'S CLAMPED TIGHT LIKE SOLID STONE, DON'T YOU RECALL?
I THINK THE LOCK IS BROKEN THIS TIME, AND THE DOOR WILL OPEN. COME ON, GRANDMA PINY, LET'S GO SEE...
SEE, PINY, THE DOOR'S EVEN AJAR A BIT!

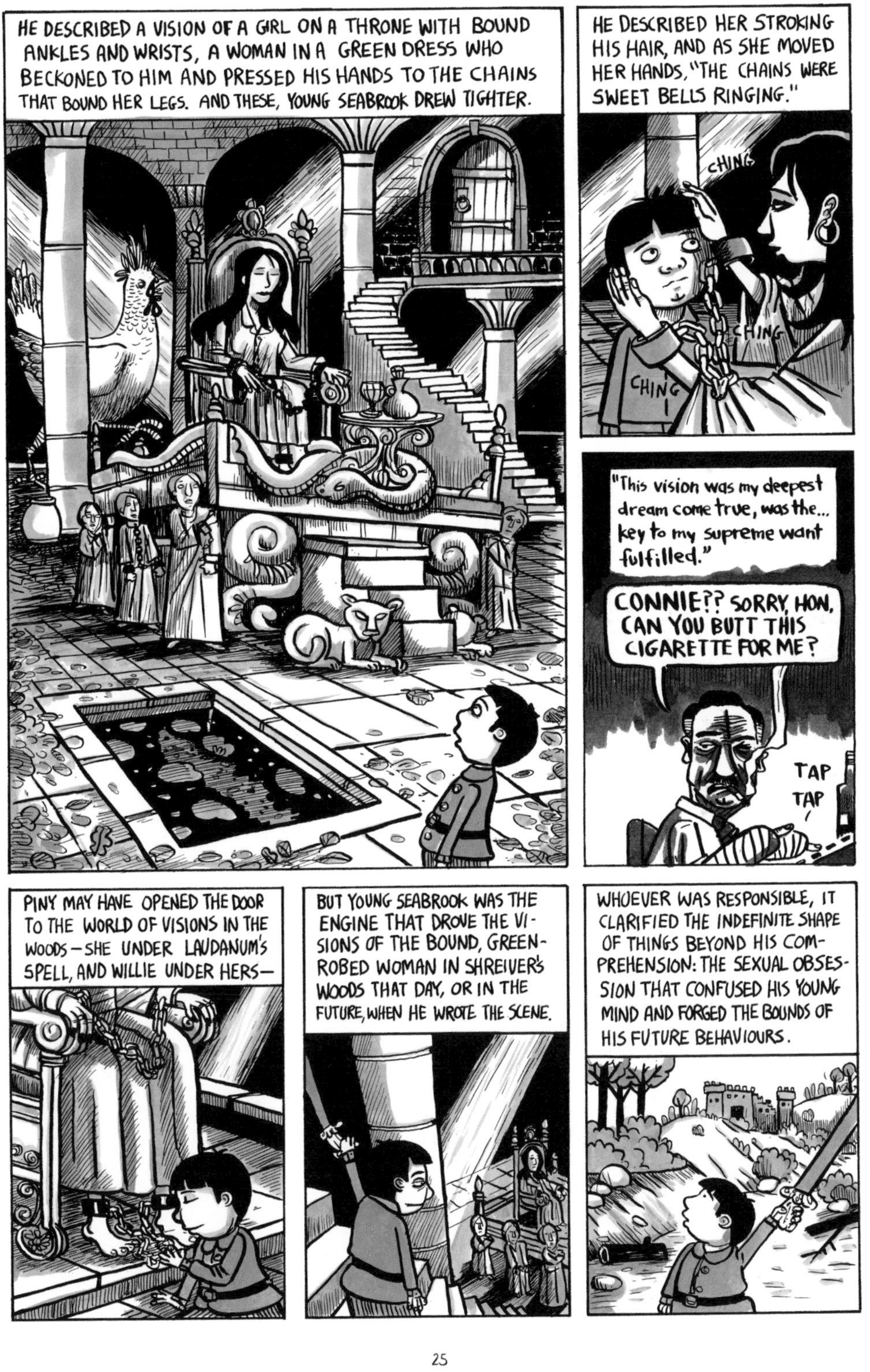
HE DESCRIBED A VISION OF A GIRL ON A THRONE WITH BOUND ANKLES AND WRISTS, A WOMAN IN A GREEN DRESS WHO BECKONED TO HIM AND PRESSED HIS HANDS TO THE CHAINS THAT BOUND HER LEGS. AND THESE, YOUNG SEABROOK DREW TIGHTER.
HE DESCRIBED HER STROKING HIS HAIR, AND AS SHE MOVED HER HANDS, "THE CHAINS WERE SWEET BELLS RINGING."
CHING
CHING
CHING
"This vision was my deepest dream come true, was the... key to my supreme want fulfilled."
CONNIE?? SORRY, HON, CAN YOU BUTT THIS CIGARETTE FOR ME?
TAP
TAP
PINY MAY HAVE OPENED THE DOOR TO THE WORLD OF VISIONS IN THE WOODS—SHE UNDER LAUDANUM'S SPELL, AND WILLIE UNDER HERS—
BUT YOUNG SEABROOK WAS THE ENGINE THAT DROVE THE VISIONS OF THE BOUND, GREEN-ROBED WOMAN IN SHREIVER'S WOODS THAT DAY, OR IN THE FUTURE, WHEN HE WROTE THE SCENE.
WHOEVER WAS RESPONSIBLE, IT CLARIFIED THE INDEFINITE SHAPE OF THINGS BEYOND HIS COMPREHENSION: THE SEXUAL OBSESSION THAT CONFUSED HIS YOUNG MIND AND FORGED THE BOUNDS OF HIS FUTURE BEHAVIOURS.

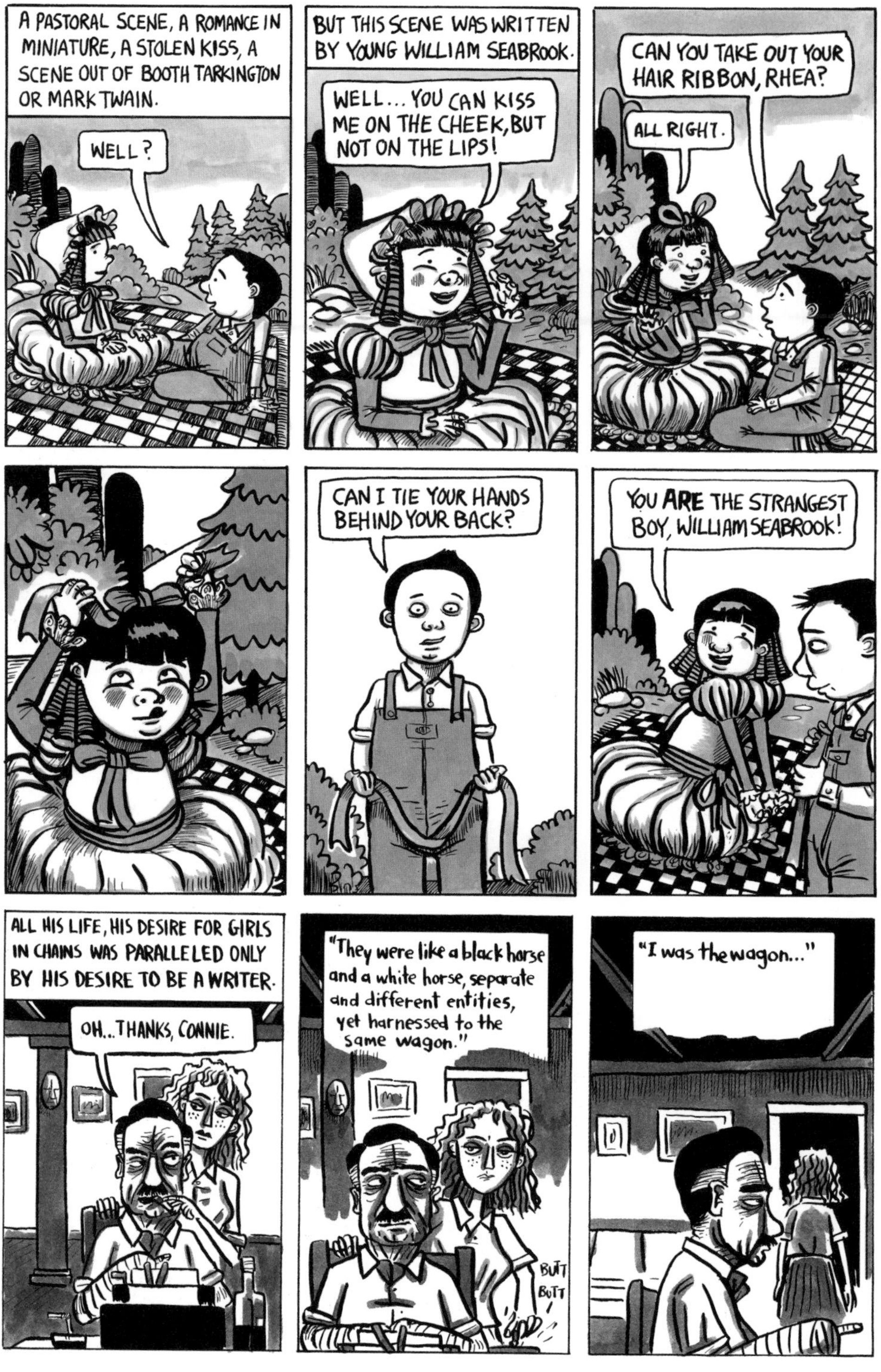
A PASTORAL SCENE, A ROMANCE IN MINIATURE, A STOLEN KISS, A SCENE OUT OF BOOTH TARKINGTON OR MARK TWAIN.
WELL?
BUT THIS SCENE WAS WRITTEN BY YOUNG WILLIAM SEABROOK.
WELL... YOU CAN KISS ME ON THE CHEEK, BUT NOT ON THE LIPS!
CAN YOU TAKE OUT YOUR HAIR RIBBON, RHEA?
ALL RIGHT.
CAN I TIE YOUR HANDS BEHIND YOUR BACK?
YOU **ARE** THE STRANGEST BOY, WILLIAM SEABROOK!
ALL HIS LIFE, HIS DESIRE FOR GIRLS IN CHAINS WAS PARALLELED ONLY BY HIS DESIRE TO BE A WRITER.
OH... THANKS, CONNIE.
"They were like a black horse and a white horse, separate and different entities, yet harnessed to the same wagon."
BUTT BUTT
"I was the wagon..."

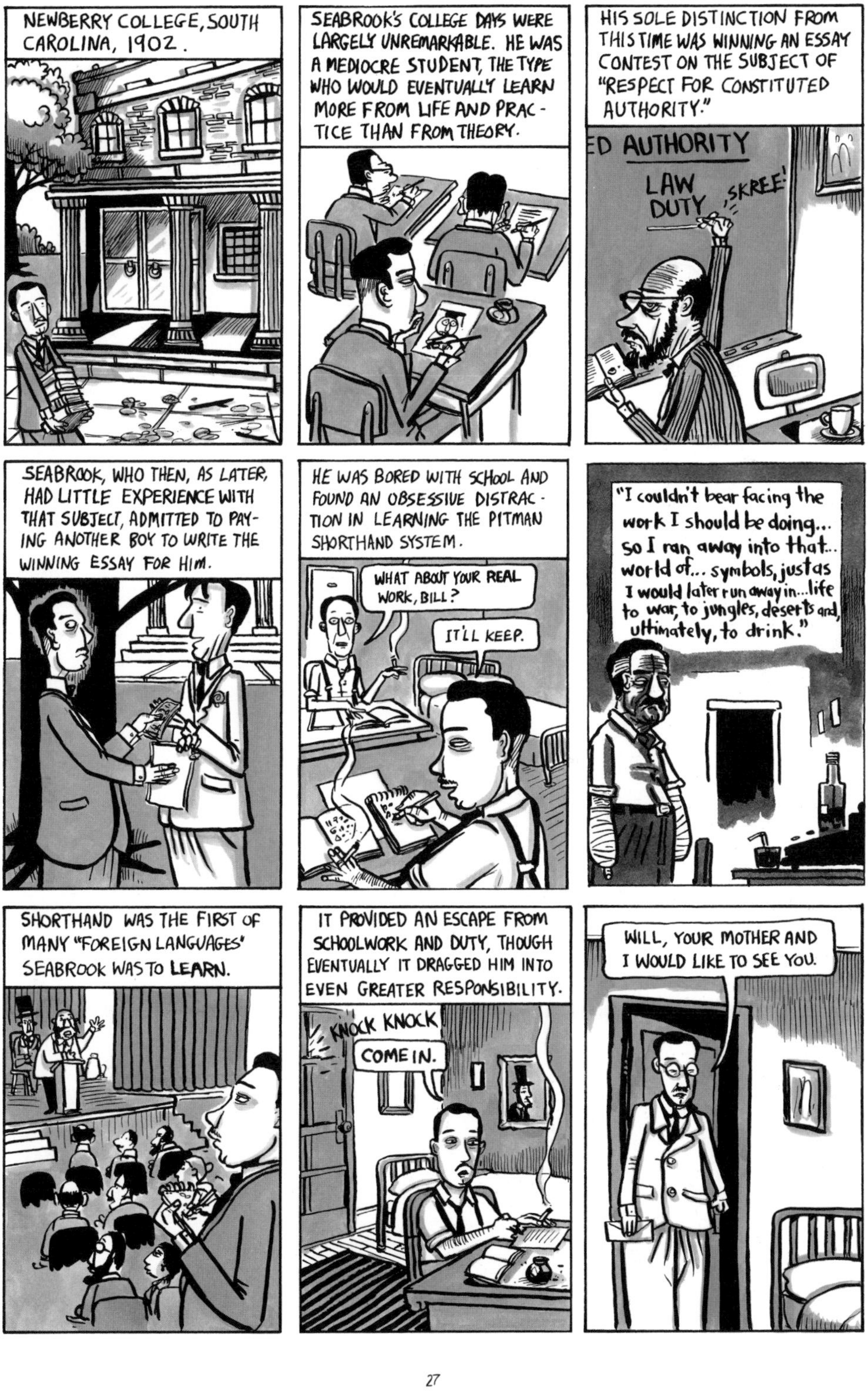
NEWBERRY COLLEGE, SOUTH CAROLINA, 1902.
SEABROOK'S COLLEGE DAYS WERE LARGELY UNREMARKABLE. HE WAS A MEDIOCRE STUDENT, THE TYPE WHO WOULD EVENTUALLY LEARN MORE FROM LIFE AND PRACTICE THAN FROM THEORY.
HIS SOLE DISTINCTION FROM THIS TIME WAS WINNING AN ESSAY CONTEST ON THE SUBJECT OF "RESPECT FOR CONSTITUTED AUTHORITY."
ED AUTHORITY
LAW
DUTY
SKREE!
SEABROOK, WHO THEN, AS LATER, HAD LITTLE EXPERIENCE WITH THAT SUBJECT, ADMITTED TO PAYING ANOTHER BOY TO WRITE THE WINNING ESSAY FOR HIM.
HE WAS BORED WITH SCHOOL AND FOUND AN OBSESSIVE DISTRACTION IN LEARNING THE PITMAN SHORTHAND SYSTEM.
WHAT ABOUT YOUR REAL WORK, BILL?
IT'LL KEEP.
"I couldn't bear facing the work I should be doing... so I ran away into that... world of... symbols, just as I would later run away in... life to war, to jungles, deserts and, ultimately, to drink."
SHORTHAND WAS THE FIRST OF MANY "FOREIGN LANGUAGES" SEABROOK WAS TO LEARN.
IT PROVIDED AN ESCAPE FROM SCHOOLWORK AND DUTY, THOUGH EVENTUALLY IT DRAGGED HIM INTO EVEN GREATER RESPONSIBILITY.
KNOCK KNOCK
COME IN.
WILL, YOUR MOTHER AND I WOULD LIKE TO SEE YOU.

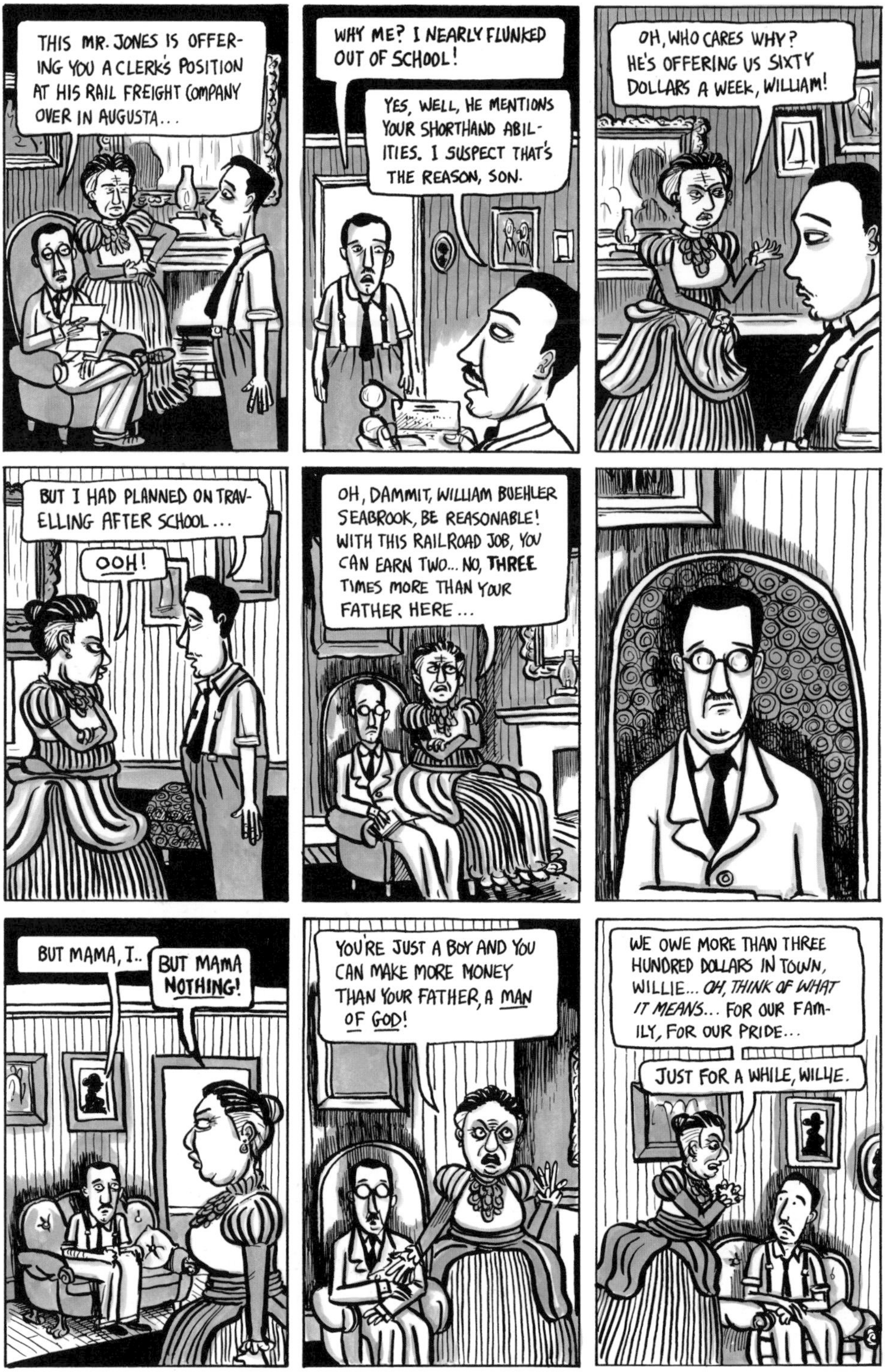
THIS MR. JONES IS OFFERING YOU A CLERK'S POSITION AT HIS RAIL FREIGHT COMPANY OVER IN AUGUSTA...
WHY ME? I NEARLY FLUNKED OUT OF SCHOOL!
YES, WELL, HE MENTIONS YOUR SHORTHAND ABILITIES. I SUSPECT THAT'S THE REASON, SON.
OH, WHO CARES WHY? HE'S OFFERING US SIXTY DOLLARS A WEEK, WILLIAM!
BUT I HAD PLANNED ON TRAVELLING AFTER SCHOOL...
OOH!
OH, DAMMIT, WILLIAM BUEHLER SEABROOK, BE REASONABLE! WITH THIS RAILROAD JOB, YOU CAN EARN TWO... NO, THREE TIMES MORE THAN YOUR FATHER HERE...
BUT MAMA, I..
BUT MAMA NOTHING!
YOU'RE JUST A BOY AND YOU CAN MAKE MORE MONEY THAN YOUR FATHER, A MAN OF GOD!
WE OWE MORE THAN THREE HUNDRED DOLLARS IN TOWN, WILLIE... OH, THINK OF WHAT IT MEANS... FOR OUR FAMILY, FOR OUR PRIDE...
JUST FOR A WHILE, WILLIE.

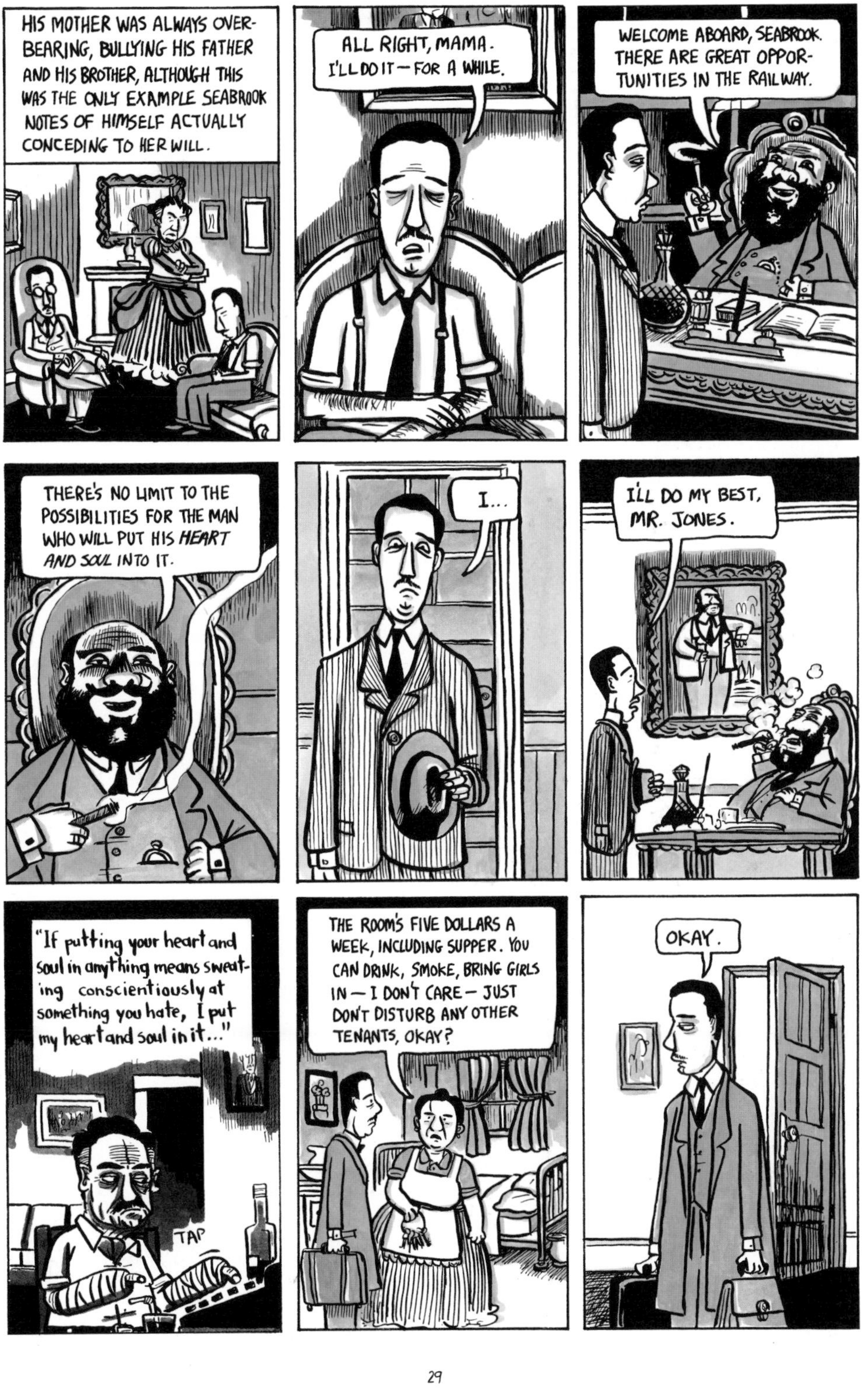
HIS MOTHER WAS ALWAYS OVER-BEARING, BULLYING HIS FATHER AND HIS BROTHER, ALTHOUGH THIS WAS THE ONLY EXAMPLE SEABROOK NOTES OF HIMSELF ACTUALLY CONCEDING TO HER WILL.
ALL RIGHT, MAMA. I'LL DO IT — FOR A WHILE.
WELCOME ABOARD, SEABROOK. THERE ARE GREAT OPPORTUNITIES IN THE RAILWAY.
THERE'S NO LIMIT TO THE POSSIBILITIES FOR THE MAN WHO WILL PUT HIS *HEART AND SOUL* INTO IT.
I...
I'LL DO MY BEST, MR. JONES.
"If putting your heart and soul in anything means sweating conscientiously at something you hate, I put my heart and soul in it..."
TAP
THE ROOM'S FIVE DOLLARS A WEEK, INCLUDING SUPPER. YOU CAN DRINK, SMOKE, BRING GIRLS IN — I DON'T CARE — JUST DON'T DISTURB ANY OTHER TENANTS, OKAY?
OKAY.

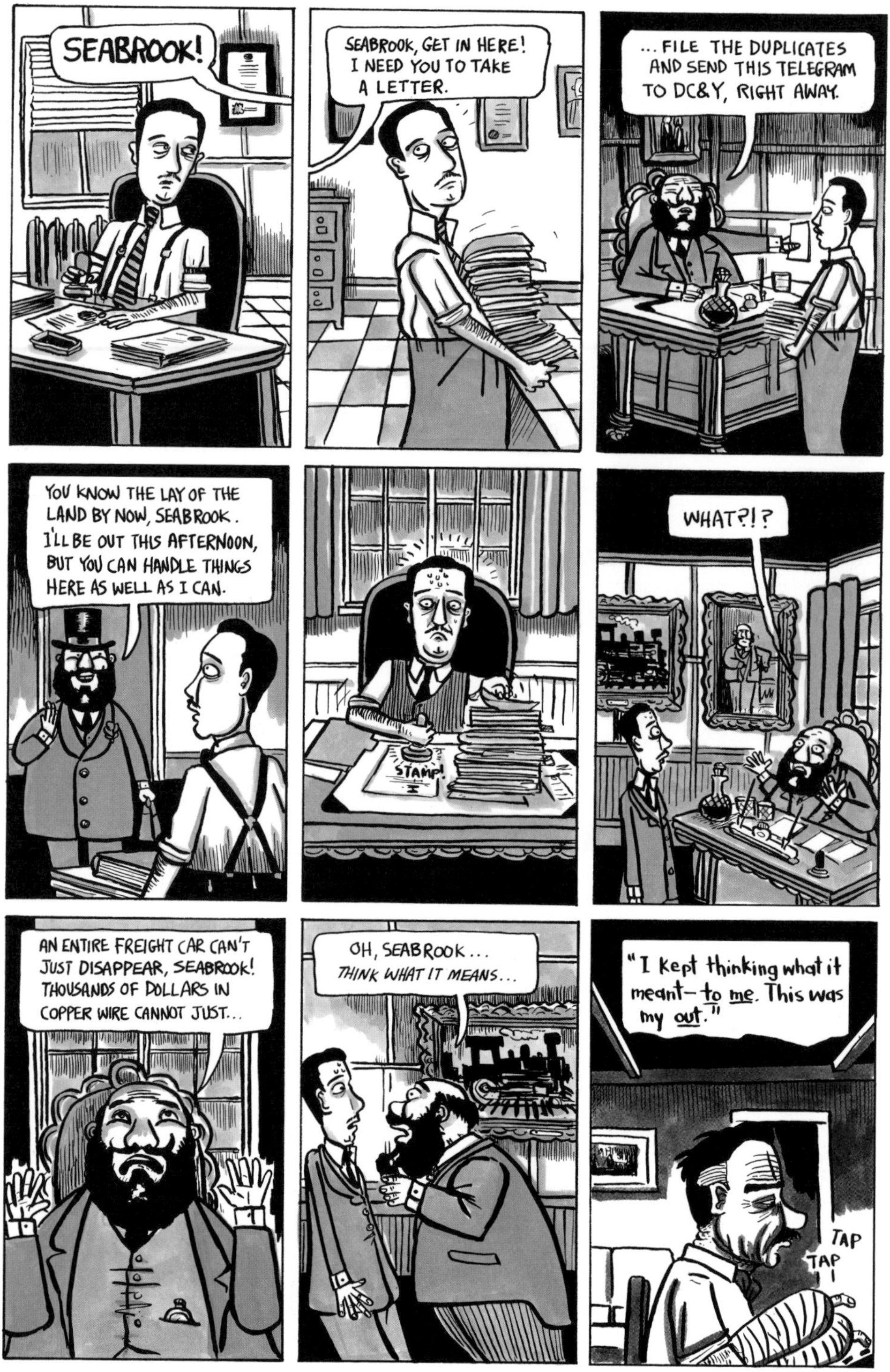
SEABROOK!
SEABROOK, GET IN HERE! I NEED YOU TO TAKE A LETTER.
... FILE THE DUPLICATES AND SEND THIS TELEGRAM TO DC&Y, RIGHT AWAY.
YOU KNOW THE LAY OF THE LAND BY NOW, SEABROOK. I'LL BE OUT THIS AFTERNOON, BUT YOU CAN HANDLE THINGS HERE AS WELL AS I CAN.
STAMP!
WHAT?!?
AN ENTIRE FREIGHT CAR CAN'T JUST DISAPPEAR, SEABROOK! THOUSANDS OF DOLLARS IN COPPER WIRE CANNOT JUST...
OH, SEABROOK... THINK WHAT IT MEANS...
"I kept thinking what it meant— to me. This was my out."
TAP
TAP

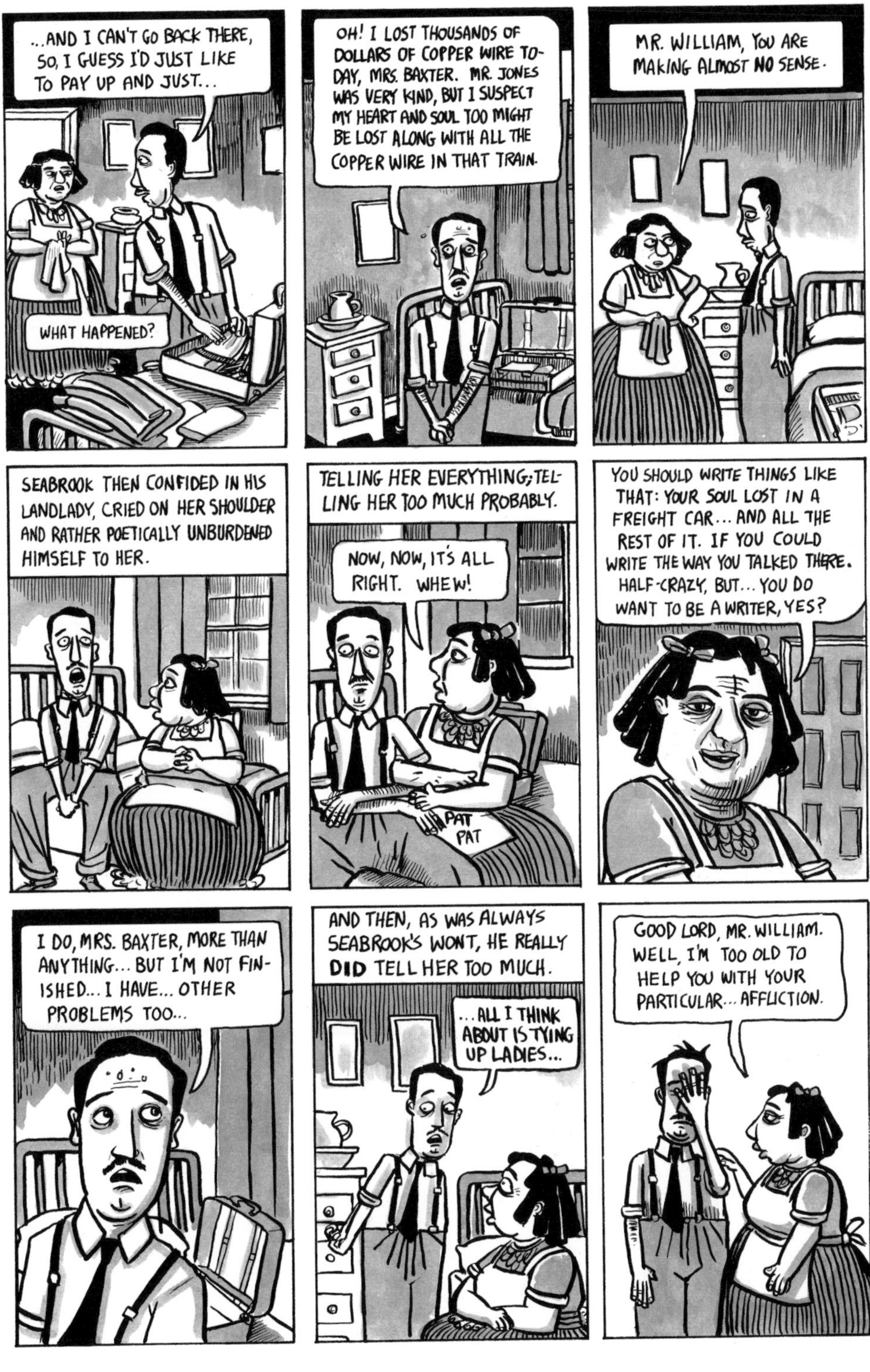
...AND I CAN'T GO BACK THERE, SO, I GUESS I'D JUST LIKE TO PAY UP AND JUST...
WHAT HAPPENED?
OH! I LOST THOUSANDS OF DOLLARS OF COPPER WIRE TO-DAY, MRS. BAXTER. MR. JONES WAS VERY KIND, BUT I SUSPECT MY HEART AND SOUL TOO MIGHT BE LOST ALONG WITH ALL THE COPPER WIRE IN THAT TRAIN.
MR. WILLIAM, YOU ARE MAKING ALMOST NO SENSE.
SEABROOK THEN CONFIDED IN HIS LANDLADY, CRIED ON HER SHOULDER AND RATHER POETICALLY UNBURDENED HIMSELF TO HER.
TELLING HER EVERYTHING; TELLING HER TOO MUCH PROBABLY.
NOW, NOW, IT'S ALL RIGHT. WHEW!
PAT
PAT
YOU SHOULD WRITE THINGS LIKE THAT: YOUR SOUL LOST IN A FREIGHT CAR... AND ALL THE REST OF IT. IF YOU COULD WRITE THE WAY YOU TALKED THERE. HALF-CRAZY, BUT... YOU DO WANT TO BE A WRITER, YES?
I DO, MRS. BAXTER, MORE THAN ANYTHING... BUT I'M NOT FINISHED... I HAVE... OTHER PROBLEMS TOO...
AND THEN, AS WAS ALWAYS SEABROOK'S WONT, HE REALLY DID TELL HER TOO MUCH.
...ALL I THINK ABOUT IS TYING UP LADIES...
GOOD LORD, MR. WILLIAM. WELL, I'M TOO OLD TO HELP YOU WITH YOUR PARTICULAR... AFFLICTION.

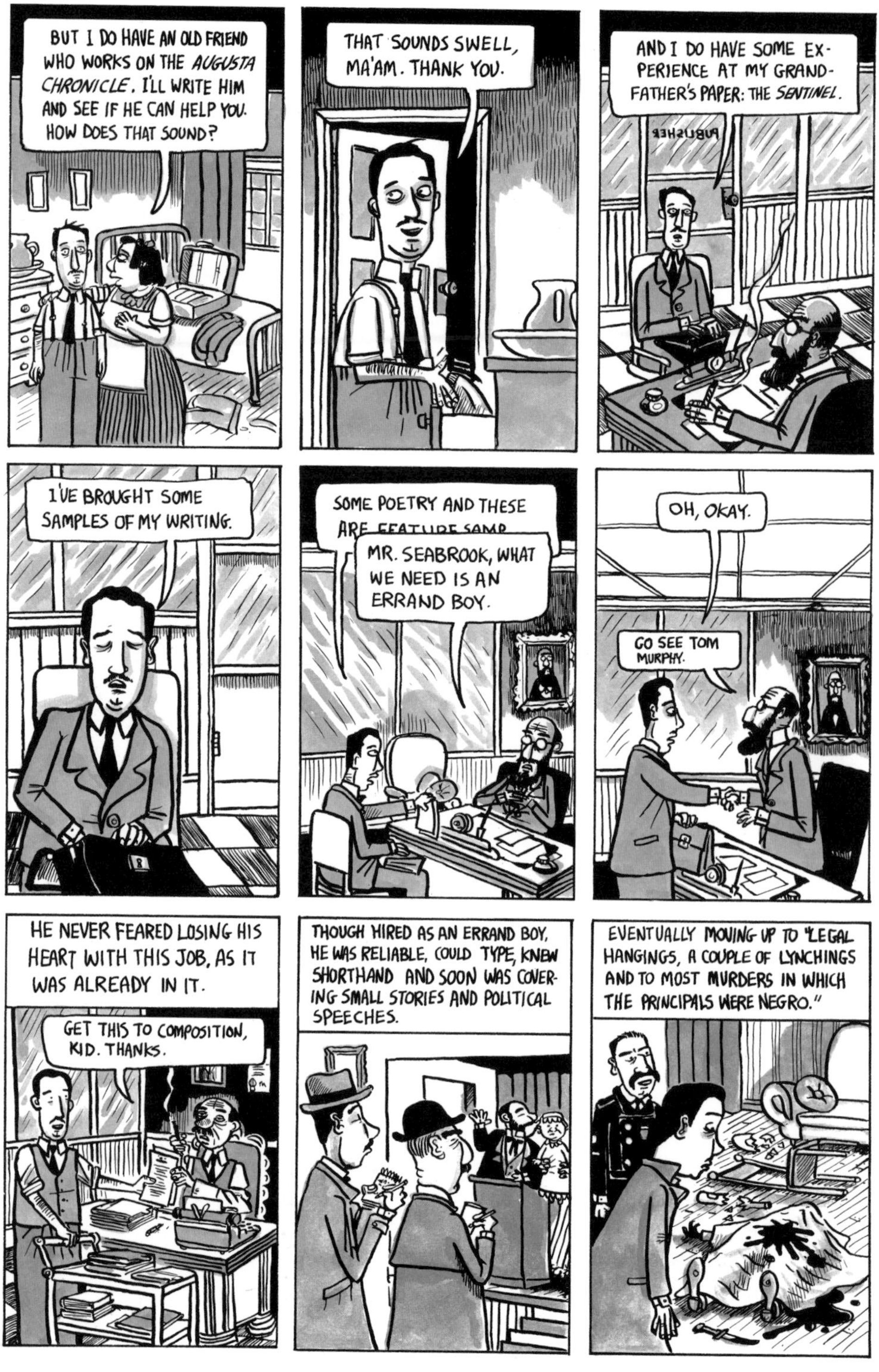
BUT I DO HAVE AN OLD FRIEND WHO WORKS ON THE AUGUSTA CHRONICLE. I'LL WRITE HIM AND SEE IF HE CAN HELP YOU. HOW DOES THAT SOUND?
THAT SOUNDS SWELL, MA'AM. THANK YOU.
AND I DO HAVE SOME EXPERIENCE AT MY GRANDFATHER'S PAPER: THE SENTINEL.
I'VE BROUGHT SOME SAMPLES OF MY WRITING.
SOME POETRY AND THESE
MR. SEABROOK, WHAT WE NEED IS AN ERRAND BOY.
OH, OKAY.
GO SEE TOM MURPHY.
HE NEVER FEARED LOSING HIS HEART WITH THIS JOB, AS IT WAS ALREADY IN IT.
GET THIS TO COMPOSITION, KID. THANKS.
THOUGH HIRED AS AN ERRAND BOY, HE WAS RELIABLE, COULD TYPE, KNEW SHORTHAND AND SOON WAS COVERING SMALL STORIES AND POLITICAL SPEECHES.
EVENTUALLY MOVING UP TO "LEGAL HANGINGS, A COUPLE OF LYNCHINGS AND TO MOST MURDERS IN WHICH THE PRINCIPALS WERE NEGRO."

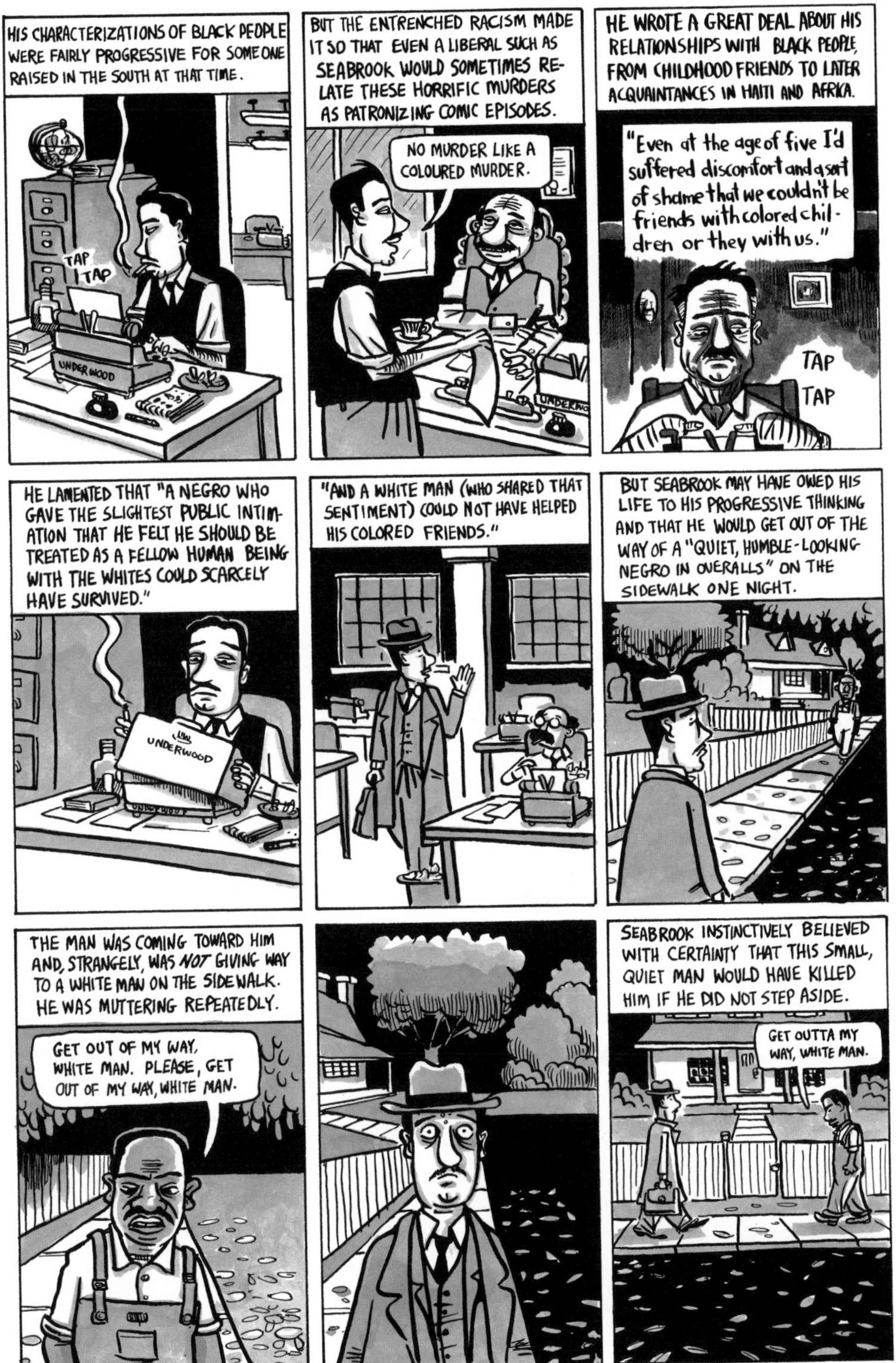
HIS CHARACTERIZATIONS OF BLACK PEOPLE WERE FAIRLY PROGRESSIVE FOR SOMEONE RAISED IN THE SOUTH AT THAT TIME.
TAP TAP
UNDERWOOD
BUT THE ENTRENCHED RACISM MADE IT SO THAT EVEN A LIBERAL SUCH AS SEABROOK WOULD SOMETIMES RELATE THESE HORRIFIC MURDERS AS PATRONIZING COMIC EPISODES.
NO MURDER LIKE A COLOURED MURDER.
HE WROTE A GREAT DEAL ABOUT HIS RELATIONSHIPS WITH BLACK PEOPLE, FROM CHILDHOOD FRIENDS TO LATER ACQUAINTANCES IN HAITI AND AFRICA.
"Even at the age of five I'd suffered discomfort and a sort of shame that we couldn't be friends with colored children or they with us."
TAP
TAP
HE LAMENTED THAT "A NEGRO WHO GAVE THE SLIGHTEST PUBLIC INTIMATION THAT HE FELT HE SHOULD BE TREATED AS A FELLOW HUMAN BEING WITH THE WHITES COULD SCARCELY HAVE SURVIVED."
UNDERWOOD
"AND A WHITE MAN (WHO SHARED THAT SENTIMENT) COULD NOT HAVE HELPED HIS COLORED FRIENDS."
BUT SEABROOK MAY HAVE OWED HIS LIFE TO HIS PROGRESSIVE THINKING AND THAT HE WOULD GET OUT OF THE WAY OF A "QUIET, HUMBLE-LOOKING NEGRO IN OVERALLS" ON THE SIDEWALK ONE NIGHT.
THE MAN WAS COMING TOWARD HIM AND, STRANGELY, WAS NOT GIVING WAY TO A WHITE MAN ON THE SIDEWALK. HE WAS MUTTERING REPEATEDLY.
GET OUT OF MY WAY, WHITE MAN. PLEASE, GET OUT OF MY WAY, WHITE MAN.
SEABROOK INSTINCTIVELY BELIEVED WITH CERTAINTY THAT THIS SMALL, QUIET MAN WOULD HAVE KILLED HIM IF HE DID NOT STEP ASIDE.
GET OUTTA MY WAY, WHITE MAN.

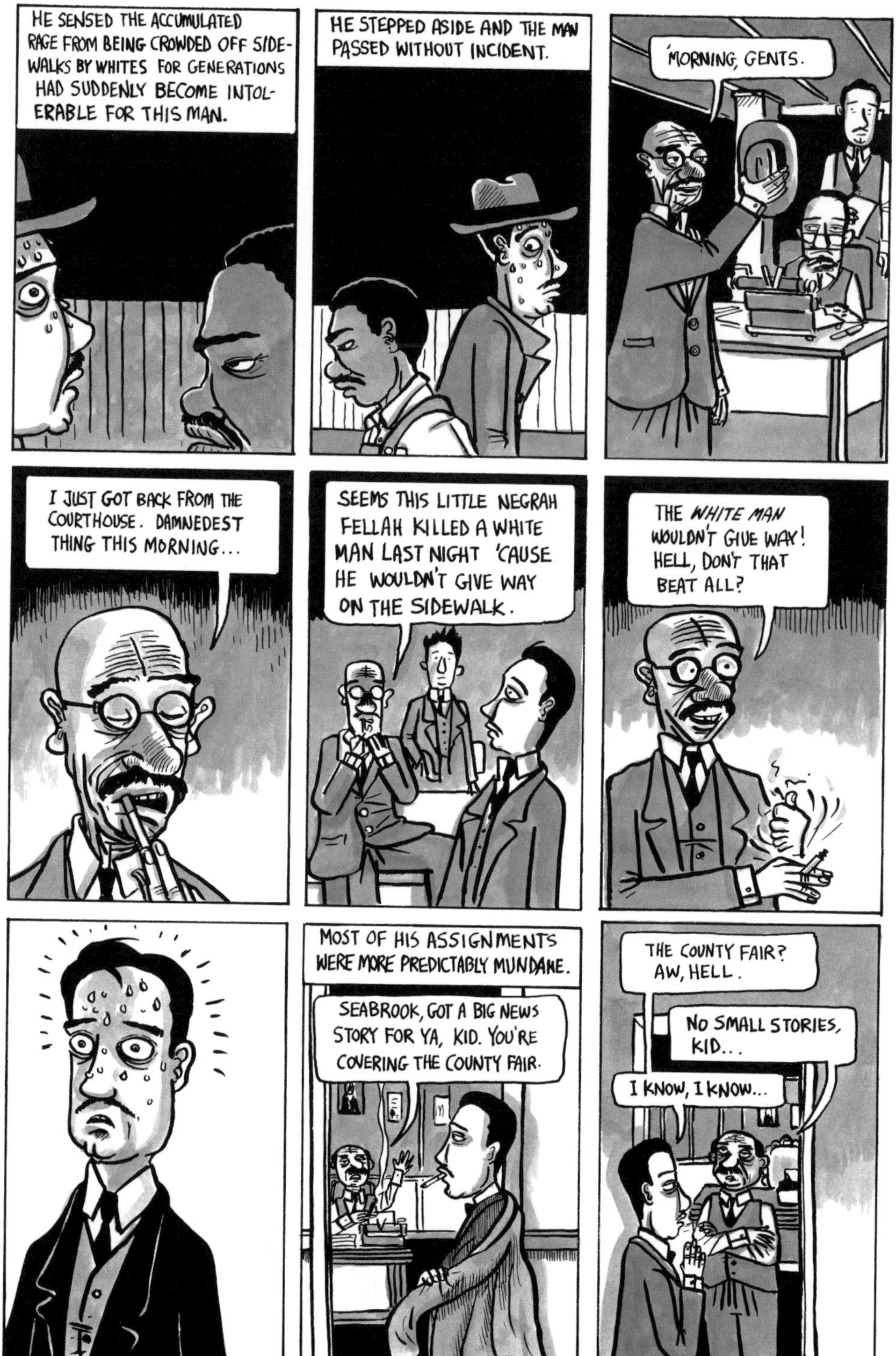
HE SENSED THE ACCUMULATED RAGE FROM BEING CROWDED OFF SIDE-WALKS BY WHITES FOR GENERATIONS HAD SUDDENLY BECOME INTOL-ERABLE FOR THIS MAN.
HE STEPPED ASIDE AND THE MAN PASSED WITHOUT INCIDENT.
'MORNING, GENTS.
I JUST GOT BACK FROM THE COURTHOUSE. DAMNEDEST THING THIS MORNING...
SEEMS THIS LITTLE NEGRAH FELLAH KILLED A WHITE MAN LAST NIGHT 'CAUSE HE WOULDN'T GIVE WAY ON THE SIDEWALK.
THE *WHITE MAN* WOULDN'T GIVE WAY! HELL, DON'T THAT BEAT ALL?
MOST OF HIS ASSIGNMENTS WERE MORE PREDICTABLY MUNDANE.
SEABROOK, GOT A BIG NEWS STORY FOR YA, KID. YOU'RE COVERING THE COUNTY FAIR.
THE COUNTY FAIR? AW, HELL.
NO SMALL STORIES, KID...
I KNOW, I KNOW...

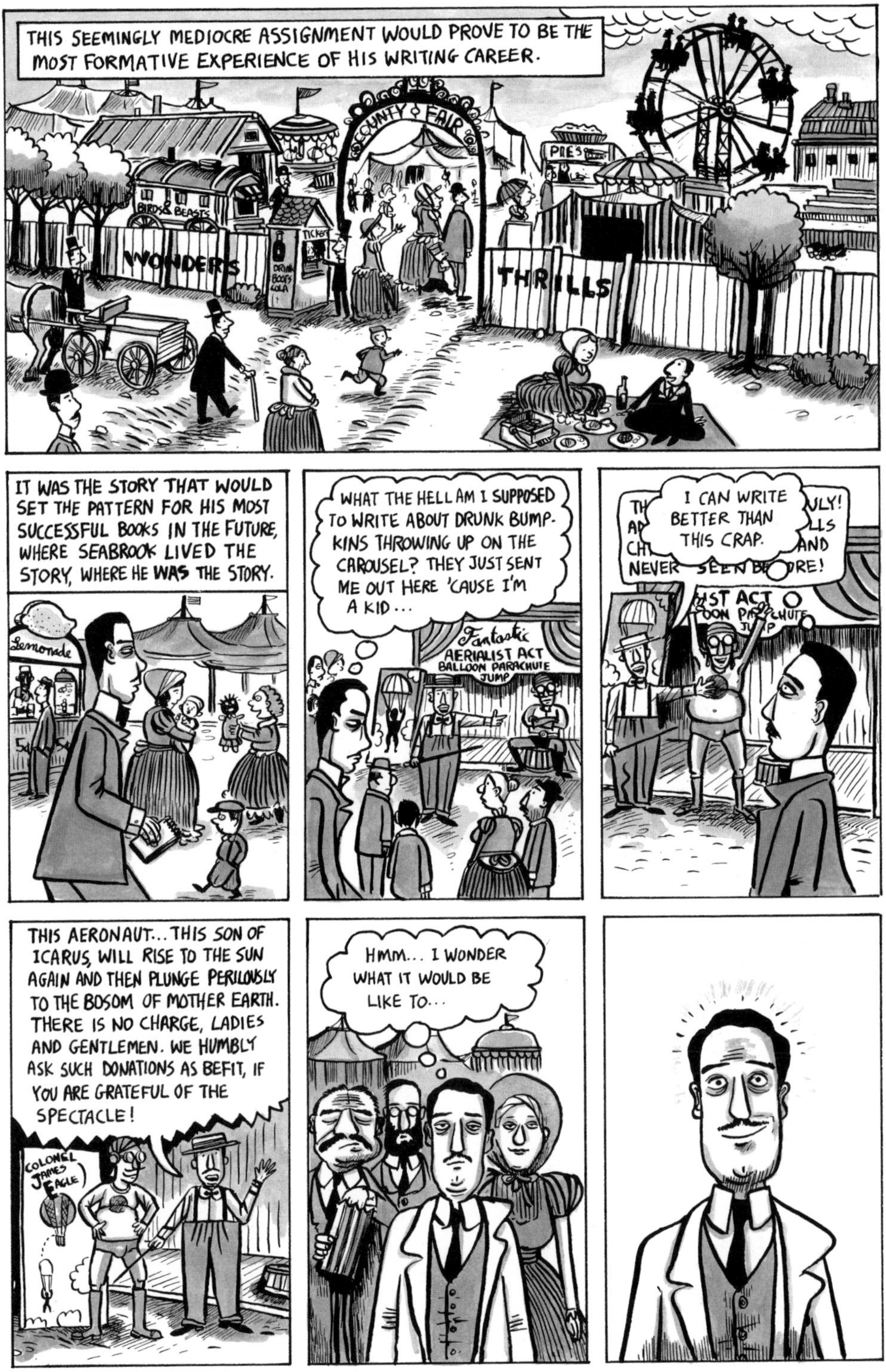
THIS SEEMINGLY MEDIOCRE ASSIGNMENT WOULD PROVE TO BE THE MOST FORMATIVE EXPERIENCE OF HIS WRITING CAREER.
COUNTY FAIR
PIES
BIRDS & BEASTS
WONDERS
THRILLS
IT WAS THE STORY THAT WOULD SET THE PATTERN FOR HIS MOST SUCCESSFUL BOOKS IN THE FUTURE, WHERE SEABROOK LIVED THE STORY, WHERE HE WAS THE STORY.
Lemonade
WHAT THE HELL AM I SUPPOSED TO WRITE ABOUT DRUNK BUMPKINS THROWING UP ON THE CAROUSEL? THEY JUST SENT ME OUT HERE 'CAUSE I'M A KID...
Fantastic AERIALIST ACT BALLOON PARACHUTE JUMP
I CAN WRITE BETTER THAN THIS CRAP.
THIS AERONAUT... THIS SON OF ICARUS, WILL RISE TO THE SUN AGAIN AND THEN PLUNGE PERILOUSLY TO THE BOSOM OF MOTHER EARTH. THERE IS NO CHARGE, LADIES AND GENTLEMEN. WE HUMBLY ASK SUCH DONATIONS AS BEFIT, IF YOU ARE GRATEFUL OF THE SPECTACLE!
COLONEL JAMES EAGLE
HMM... I WONDER WHAT IT WOULD BE LIKE TO...

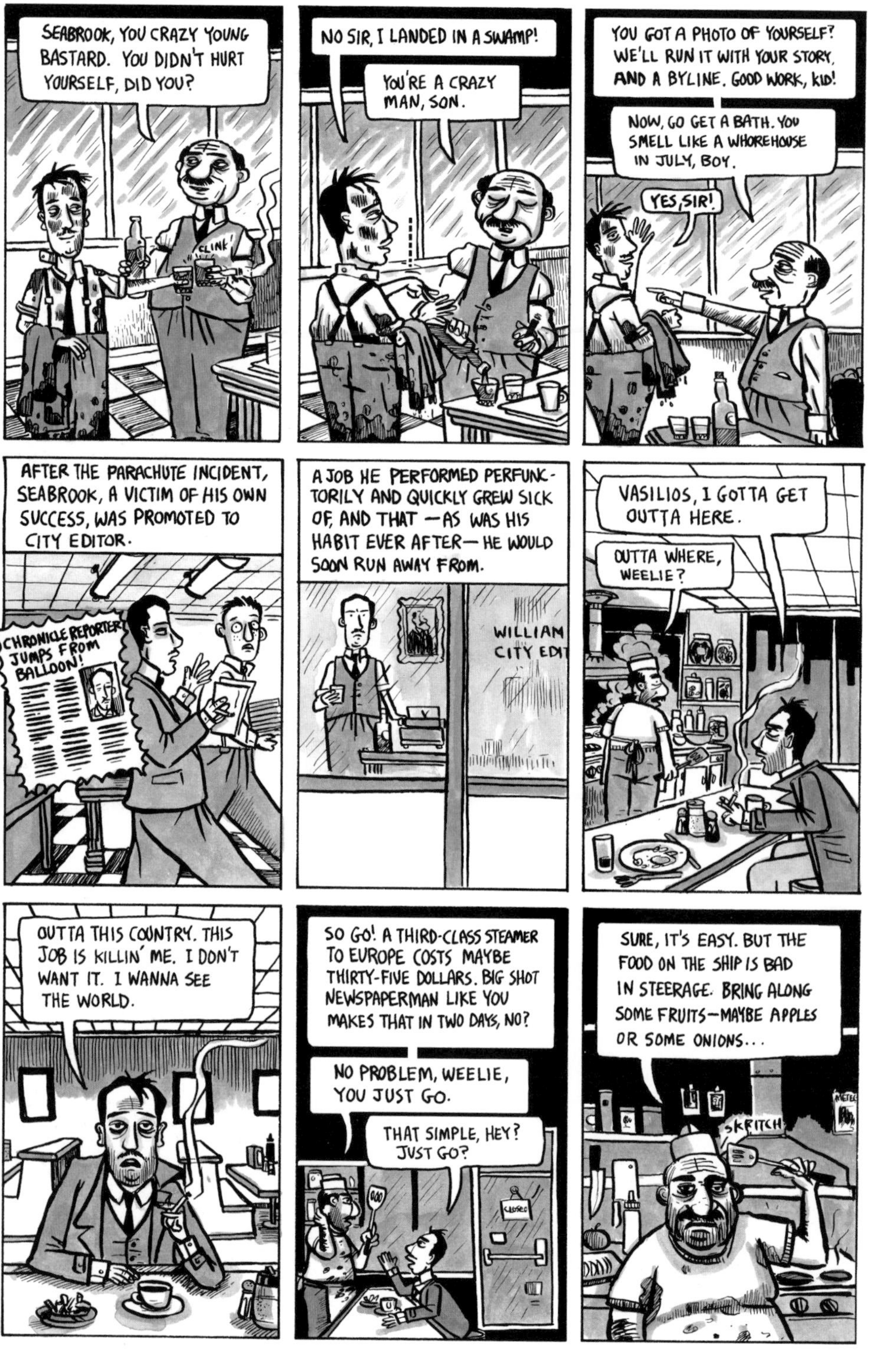

SEABROOK, YOU CRAZY YOUNG BASTARD. YOU DIDN'T HURT YOURSELF, DID YOU?
CLINK
NO SIR, I LANDED IN A SWAMP!
YOU'RE A CRAZY MAN, SON.
YOU GOT A PHOTO OF YOURSELF? WE'LL RUN IT WITH YOUR STORY, AND A BYLINE. GOOD WORK, KID!
NOW, GO GET A BATH. YOU SMELL LIKE A WHOREHOUSE IN JULY, BOY.
YES, SIR!
AFTER THE PARACHUTE INCIDENT, SEABROOK, A VICTIM OF HIS OWN SUCCESS, WAS PROMOTED TO CITY EDITOR.
CHRONICLE REPORTER JUMPS FROM BALLOON!
A JOB HE PERFORMED PERFUNCTORILY AND QUICKLY GREW SICK OF, AND THAT —AS WAS HIS HABIT EVER AFTER— HE WOULD SOON RUN AWAY FROM.
WILLIAM
CITY EDIT
VASILIOS, I GOTTA GET OUTTA HERE.
OUTTA WHERE, WEELIE?
OUTTA THIS COUNTRY. THIS JOB IS KILLIN' ME. I DON'T WANT IT. I WANNA SEE THE WORLD.
SO GO! A THIRD-CLASS STEAMER TO EUROPE COSTS MAYBE THIRTY-FIVE DOLLARS. BIG SHOT NEWSPAPERMAN LIKE YOU MAKES THAT IN TWO DAYS, NO?
NO PROBLEM, WEELIE, YOU JUST GO.
THAT SIMPLE, HEY? JUST GO?
CLOSED
SURE, IT'S EASY. BUT THE FOOD ON THE SHIP IS BAD IN STEERAGE. BRING ALONG SOME FRUITS—MAYBE APPLES OR SOME ONIONS...
SKRITCH

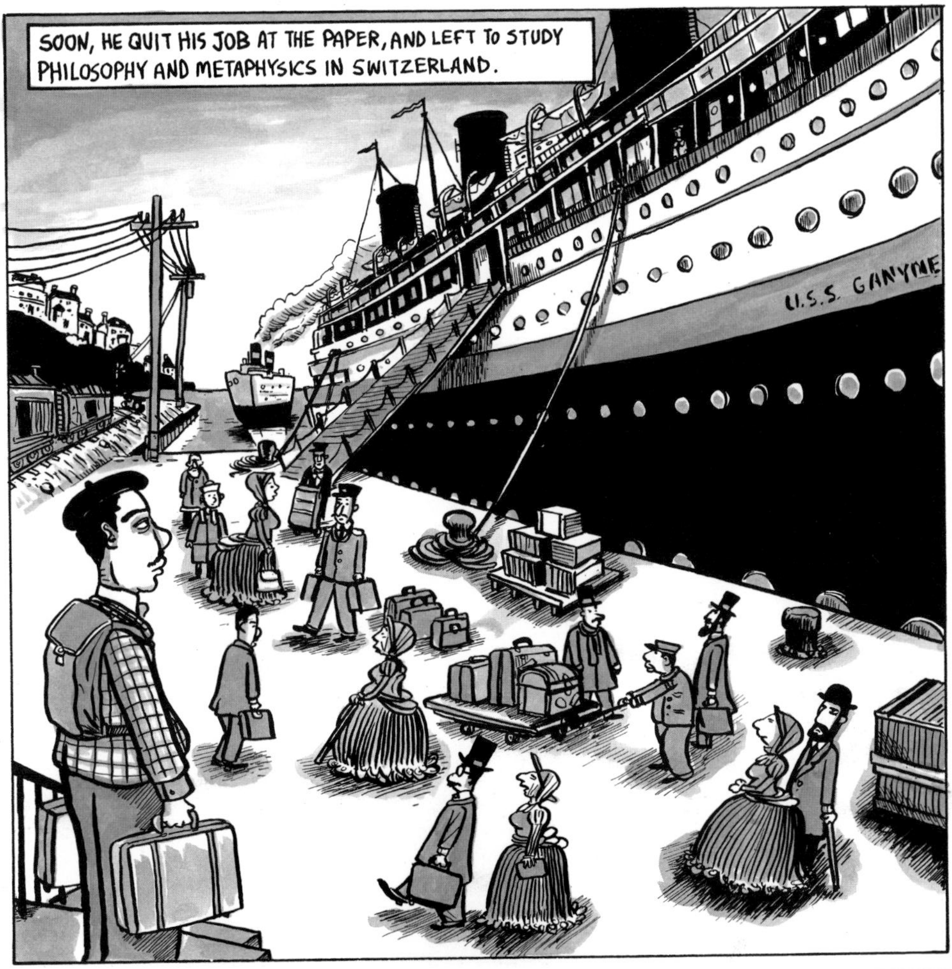
SOON, HE QUIT HIS JOB AT THE PAPER, AND LEFT TO STUDY PHILOSOPHY AND METAPHYSICS IN SWITZERLAND.
U.S.S. GANYME

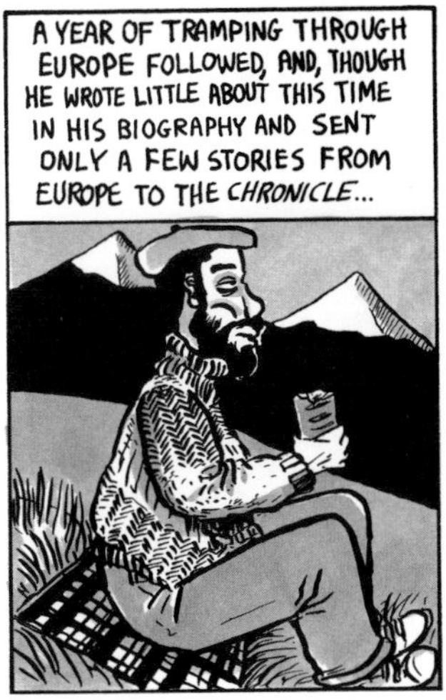
A YEAR OF TRAMPING THROUGH EUROPE FOLLOWED, AND, THOUGH HE WROTE LITTLE ABOUT THIS TIME IN HIS BIOGRAPHY AND SENT ONLY A FEW STORIES FROM EUROPE TO THE *CHRONICLE*...

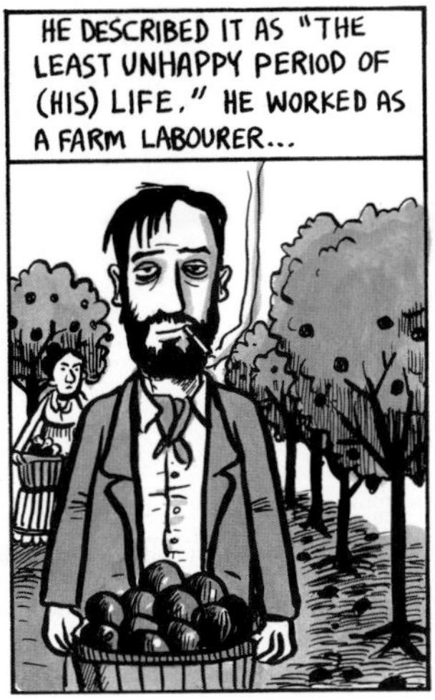
HE DESCRIBED IT AS "THE LEAST UNHAPPY PERIOD OF (HIS) LIFE." HE WORKED AS A FARM LABOURER...

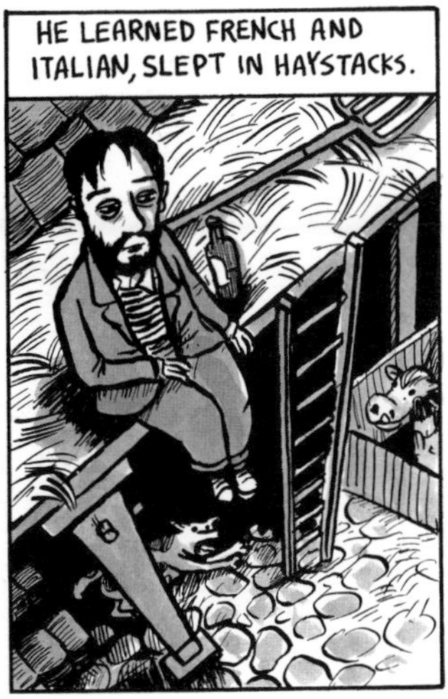
HE LEARNED FRENCH AND ITALIAN, SLEPT IN HAYSTACKS.

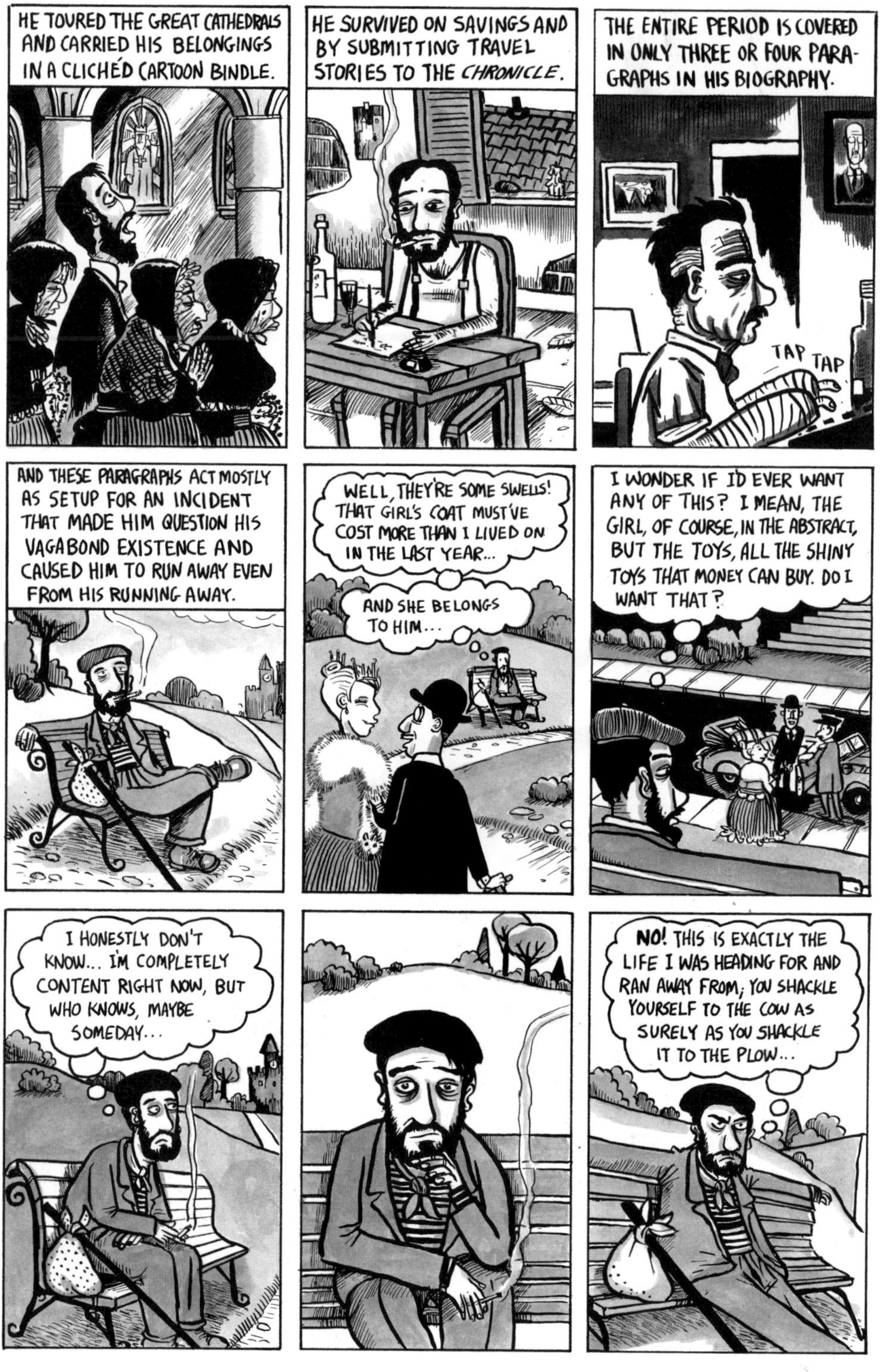
HE TOURED THE GREAT CATHEDRALS AND CARRIED HIS BELONGINGS IN A CLICHÉD CARTOON BINDLE.
HE SURVIVED ON SAVINGS AND BY SUBMITTING TRAVEL STORIES TO THE *CHRONICLE*.
THE ENTIRE PERIOD IS COVERED IN ONLY THREE OR FOUR PARAGRAPHS IN HIS BIOGRAPHY.
TAP TAP
AND THESE PARAGRAPHS ACT MOSTLY AS SETUP FOR AN INCIDENT THAT MADE HIM QUESTION HIS VAGABOND EXISTENCE AND CAUSED HIM TO RUN AWAY EVEN FROM HIS RUNNING AWAY.
WELL, THEY'RE SOME SWELLS! THAT GIRL'S COAT MUST'VE COST MORE THAN I LIVED ON IN THE LAST YEAR...
AND SHE BELONGS TO HIM...
I WONDER IF I'D EVER WANT ANY OF THIS? I MEAN, THE GIRL, OF COURSE, IN THE ABSTRACT, BUT THE TOYS, ALL THE SHINY TOYS THAT MONEY CAN BUY. DO I WANT THAT?
I HONESTLY DON'T KNOW... I'M COMPLETELY CONTENT RIGHT NOW, BUT WHO KNOWS, MAYBE SOMEDAY...
NO! THIS IS EXACTLY THE LIFE I WAS HEADING FOR AND RAN AWAY FROM; YOU SHACKLE YOURSELF TO THE COW AS SURELY AS YOU SHACKLE IT TO THE PLOW...

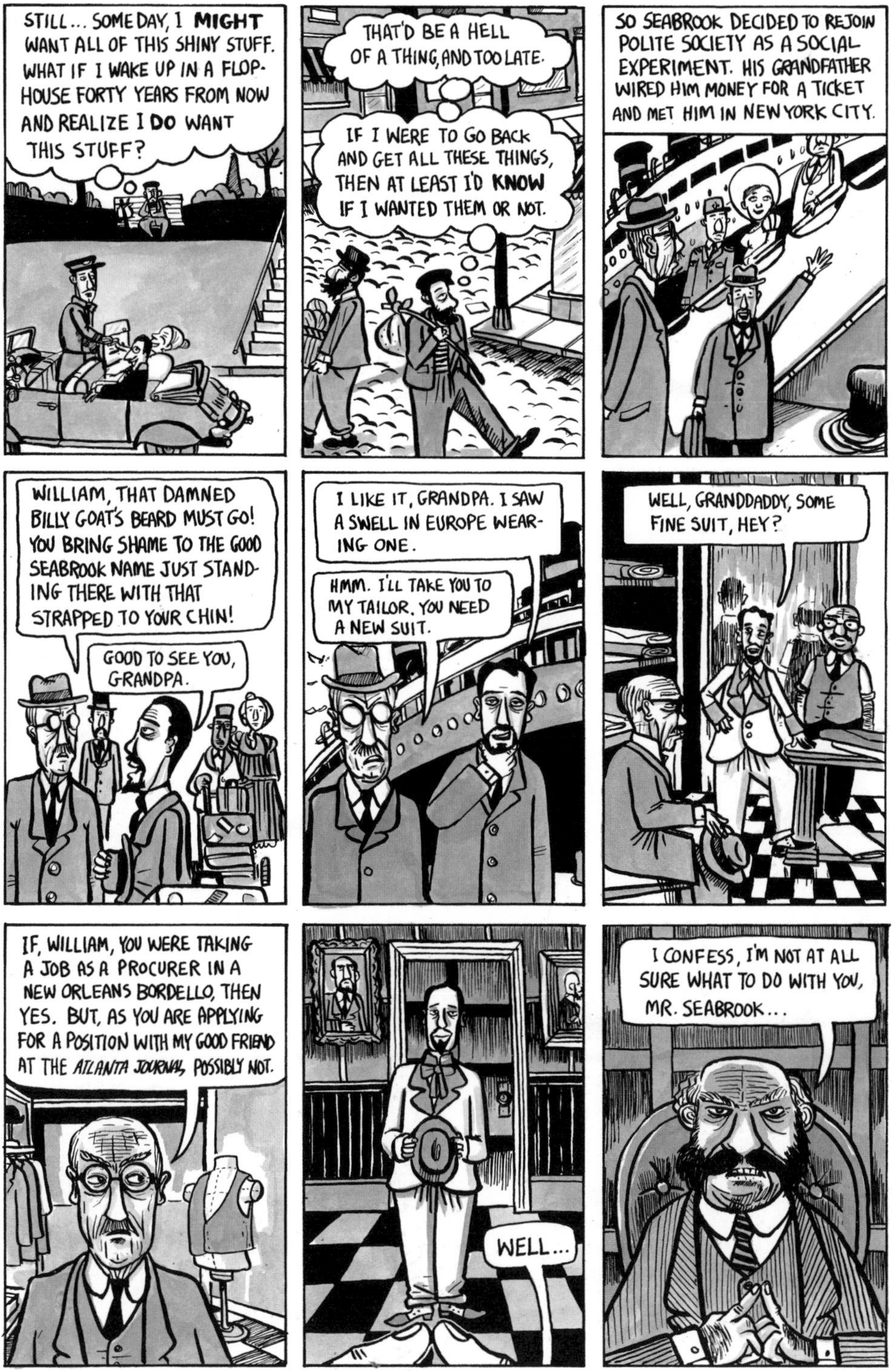
STILL... SOMEDAY, I MIGHT WANT ALL OF THIS SHINY STUFF. WHAT IF I WAKE UP IN A FLOP-HOUSE FORTY YEARS FROM NOW AND REALIZE I DO WANT THIS STUFF?
THAT'D BE A HELL OF A THING, AND TOO LATE.
IF I WERE TO GO BACK AND GET ALL THESE THINGS, THEN AT LEAST I'D KNOW IF I WANTED THEM OR NOT.
SO SEABROOK DECIDED TO REJOIN POLITE SOCIETY AS A SOCIAL EXPERIMENT. HIS GRANDFATHER WIRED HIM MONEY FOR A TICKET AND MET HIM IN NEW YORK CITY.
WILLIAM, THAT DAMNED BILLY GOAT'S BEARD MUST GO! YOU BRING SHAME TO THE GOOD SEABROOK NAME JUST STANDING THERE WITH THAT STRAPPED TO YOUR CHIN!
GOOD TO SEE YOU, GRANDPA.
I LIKE IT, GRANDPA. I SAW A SWELL IN EUROPE WEARING ONE.
HMM. I'LL TAKE YOU TO MY TAILOR. YOU NEED A NEW SUIT.
WELL, GRANDDADDY, SOME FINE SUIT, HEY?
IF, WILLIAM, YOU WERE TAKING A JOB AS A PROCURER IN A NEW ORLEANS BORDELLO, THEN YES. BUT, AS YOU ARE APPLYING FOR A POSITION WITH MY GOOD FRIEND AT THE ATLANTA JOURNAL, POSSIBLY NOT.
WELL...
I CONFESS, I'M NOT AT ALL SURE WHAT TO DO WITH YOU, MR. SEABROOK...

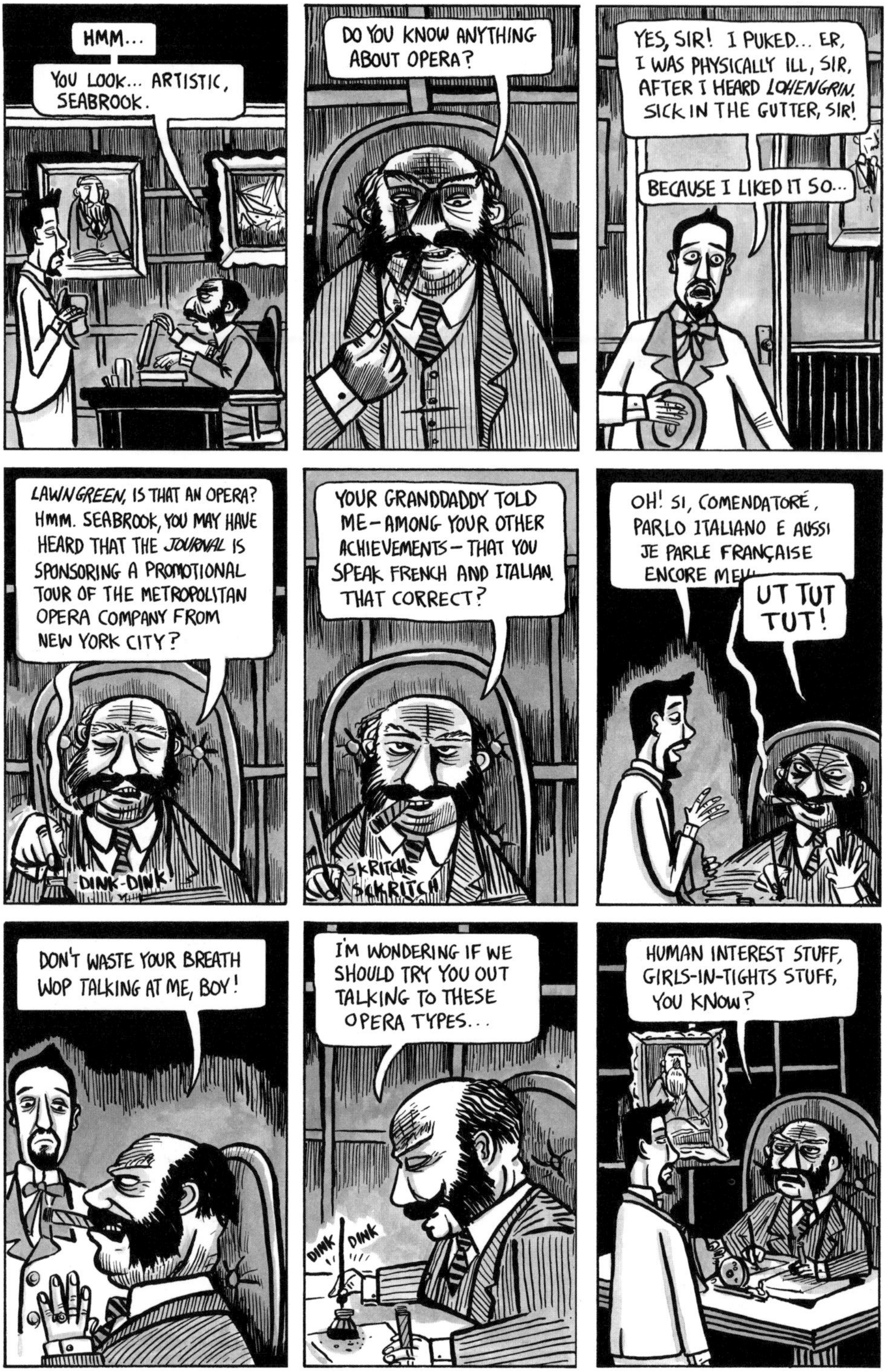
HMM...
YOU LOOK... ARTISTIC, SEABROOK.
DO YOU KNOW ANYTHING ABOUT OPERA?
YES, SIR! I PUKED... ER, I WAS PHYSICALLY ILL, SIR, AFTER I HEARD LOHENGRIN. SICK IN THE GUTTER, SIR!
BECAUSE I LIKED IT SO...
LAWNGREEN, IS THAT AN OPERA? HMM. SEABROOK, YOU MAY HAVE HEARD THAT THE JOURNAL IS SPONSORING A PROMOTIONAL TOUR OF THE METROPOLITAN OPERA COMPANY FROM NEW YORK CITY?
DINK-DINK
YOUR GRANDDADDY TOLD ME—AMONG YOUR OTHER ACHIEVEMENTS—THAT YOU SPEAK FRENCH AND ITALIAN. THAT CORRECT?
SKRITCH SKRITCH
OH! SI, COMENDATORÉ, PARLO ITALIANO E AUSSI JE PARLE FRANÇAISE ENCORE ME
UT TUT TUT!
DON'T WASTE YOUR BREATH WOP TALKING AT ME, BOY!
I'M WONDERING IF WE SHOULD TRY YOU OUT TALKING TO THESE OPERA TYPES...
DINK DINK
HUMAN INTEREST STUFF, GIRLS-IN-TIGHTS STUFF, YOU KNOW?

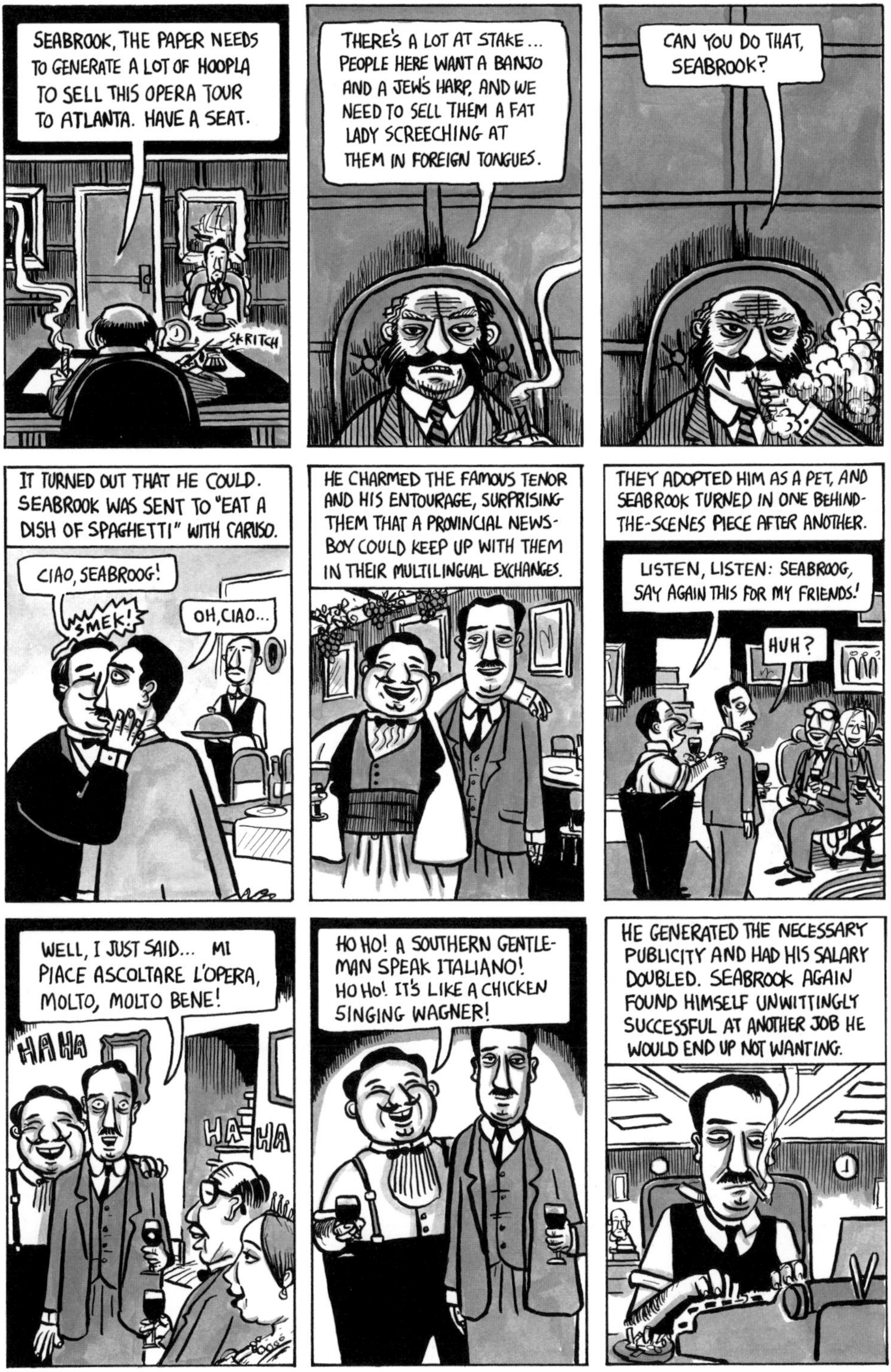
SEABROOK, THE PAPER NEEDS TO GENERATE A LOT OF HOOPLA TO SELL THIS OPERA TOUR TO ATLANTA. HAVE A SEAT.
SKRITCH
THERE'S A LOT AT STAKE... PEOPLE HERE WANT A BANJO AND A JEW'S HARP, AND WE NEED TO SELL THEM A FAT LADY SCREECHING AT THEM IN FOREIGN TONGUES.
CAN YOU DO THAT, SEABROOK?
IT TURNED OUT THAT HE COULD. SEABROOK WAS SENT TO "EAT A DISH OF SPAGHETTI" WITH CARUSO.
CIAO, SEABROOG!
SMEK!
OH, CIAO...
HE CHARMED THE FAMOUS TENOR AND HIS ENTOURAGE, SURPRISING THEM THAT A PROVINCIAL NEWS-BOY COULD KEEP UP WITH THEM IN THEIR MULTILINGUAL EXCHANGES.
THEY ADOPTED HIM AS A PET, AND SEABROOK TURNED IN ONE BEHIND-THE-SCENES PIECE AFTER ANOTHER.
LISTEN, LISTEN: SEABROOG, SAY AGAIN THIS FOR MY FRIENDS!
HUH?
WELL, I JUST SAID... MI PIACE ASCOLTARE L'OPERA, MOLTO, MOLTO BENE!
HA HA
HA HA
HO HO! A SOUTHERN GENTLE-MAN SPEAK ITALIANO! HO HO! IT'S LIKE A CHICKEN SINGING WAGNER!
HE GENERATED THE NECESSARY PUBLICITY AND HAD HIS SALARY DOUBLED. SEABROOK AGAIN FOUND HIMSELF UNWITTINGLY SUCCESSFUL AT ANOTHER JOB HE WOULD END UP NOT WANTING.

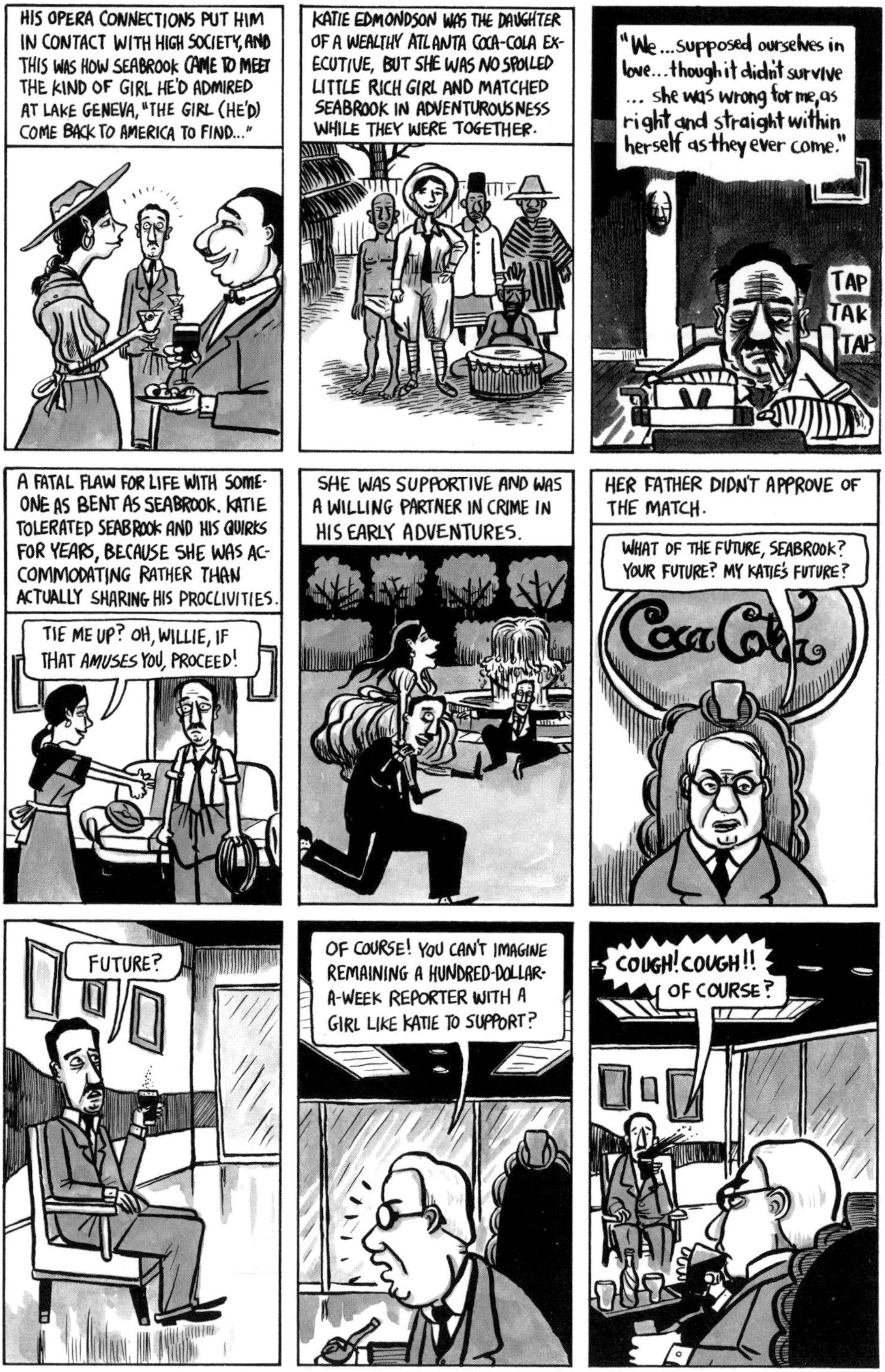
HIS OPERA CONNECTIONS PUT HIM IN CONTACT WITH HIGH SOCIETY, AND THIS WAS HOW SEABROOK CAME TO MEET THE KIND OF GIRL HE'D ADMIRED AT LAKE GENEVA, "THE GIRL (HE'D) COME BACK TO AMERICA TO FIND..."
KATIE EDMONDSON WAS THE DAUGHTER OF A WEALTHY ATLANTA COCA-COLA EXECUTIVE, BUT SHE WAS NO SPOILED LITTLE RICH GIRL AND MATCHED SEABROOK IN ADVENTUROUSNESS WHILE THEY WERE TOGETHER.
"We...supposed ourselves in love...though it didn't survive ... she was wrong for me, as right and straight within herself as they ever come."
TAP
TAK
TAP
A FATAL FLAW FOR LIFE WITH SOMEONE AS BENT AS SEABROOK. KATIE TOLERATED SEABROOK AND HIS QUIRKS FOR YEARS, BECAUSE SHE WAS ACCOMMODATING RATHER THAN ACTUALLY SHARING HIS PROCLIVITIES.
TIE ME UP? OH, WILLIE, IF THAT AMUSES YOU, PROCEED!
SHE WAS SUPPORTIVE AND WAS A WILLING PARTNER IN CRIME IN HIS EARLY ADVENTURES.
HER FATHER DIDN'T APPROVE OF THE MATCH.
WHAT OF THE FUTURE, SEABROOK? YOUR FUTURE? MY KATIE'S FUTURE?
Coca-Cola
FUTURE?
OF COURSE! YOU CAN'T IMAGINE REMAINING A HUNDRED-DOLLAR-A-WEEK REPORTER WITH A GIRL LIKE KATIE TO SUPPORT?
COUGH! COUGH!!
OF COURSE?

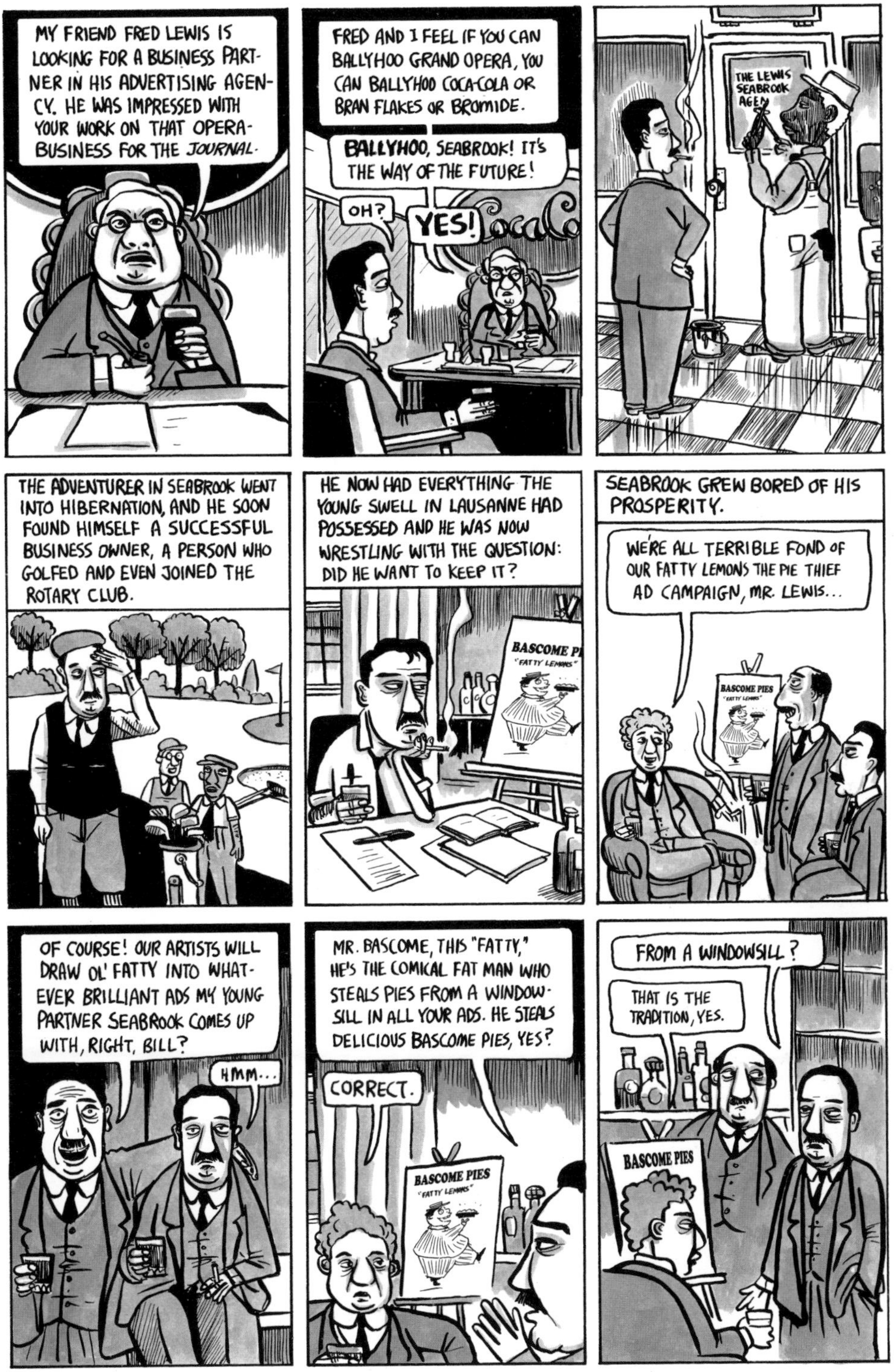
MY FRIEND FRED LEWIS IS LOOKING FOR A BUSINESS PARTNER IN HIS ADVERTISING AGENCY. HE WAS IMPRESSED WITH YOUR WORK ON THAT OPERA-BUSINESS FOR THE JOURNAL.
FRED AND I FEEL IF YOU CAN BALLYHOO GRAND OPERA, YOU CAN BALLYHOO COCA-COLA OR BRAN FLAKES OR BROMIDE.
BALLYHOO, SEABROOK! IT'S THE WAY OF THE FUTURE!
OH?
YES!
THE LEWIS SEABROOK AGEN
THE ADVENTURER IN SEABROOK WENT INTO HIBERNATION, AND HE SOON FOUND HIMSELF A SUCCESSFUL BUSINESS OWNER, A PERSON WHO GOLFED AND EVEN JOINED THE ROTARY CLUB.
HE NOW HAD EVERYTHING THE YOUNG SWELL IN LAUSANNE HAD POSSESSED AND HE WAS NOW WRESTLING WITH THE QUESTION: DID HE WANT TO KEEP IT?
BASCOME PI
"FATTY LEMONS"
SEABROOK GREW BORED OF HIS PROSPERITY.
WE'RE ALL TERRIBLE FOND OF OUR FATTY LEMONS THE PIE THIEF AD CAMPAIGN, MR. LEWIS...
BASCOME PIES
"FATTY LEMONS"
OF COURSE! OUR ARTISTS WILL DRAW OL' FATTY INTO WHATEVER BRILLIANT ADS MY YOUNG PARTNER SEABROOK COMES UP WITH, RIGHT, BILL?
HMM...
MR. BASCOME, THIS "FATTY," HE'S THE COMICAL FAT MAN WHO STEALS PIES FROM A WINDOWSILL IN ALL YOUR ADS. HE STEALS DELICIOUS BASCOME PIES, YES?
CORRECT.
BASCOME PIES
"FATTY LEMONS"
FROM A WINDOWSILL?
THAT IS THE TRADITION, YES.
BASCOME PIES

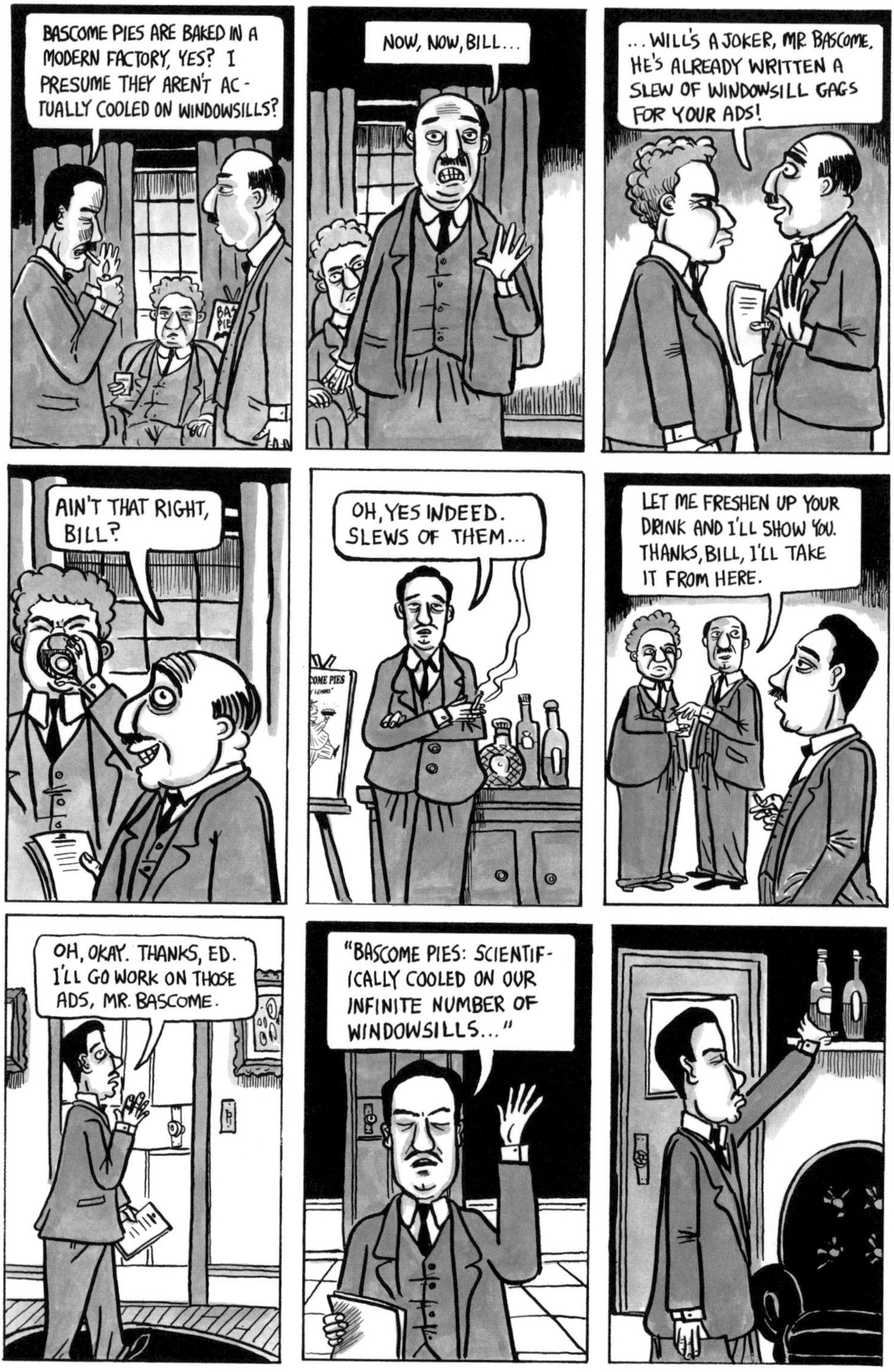
BASCOME PIES ARE BAKED IN A MODERN FACTORY, YES? I PRESUME THEY AREN'T ACTUALLY COOLED ON WINDOWSILLS?
NOW, NOW, BILL...
...WILL'S A JOKER, MR. BASCOME. HE'S ALREADY WRITTEN A SLEW OF WINDOWSILL GAGS FOR YOUR ADS!
AIN'T THAT RIGHT, BILL?
OH, YES INDEED. SLEWS OF THEM...
LET ME FRESHEN UP YOUR DRINK AND I'LL SHOW YOU. THANKS, BILL, I'LL TAKE IT FROM HERE.
OH, OKAY. THANKS, ED. I'LL GO WORK ON THOSE ADS, MR. BASCOME.
"BASCOME PIES: SCIENTIFICALLY COOLED ON OUR INFINITE NUMBER OF WINDOWSILLS..."

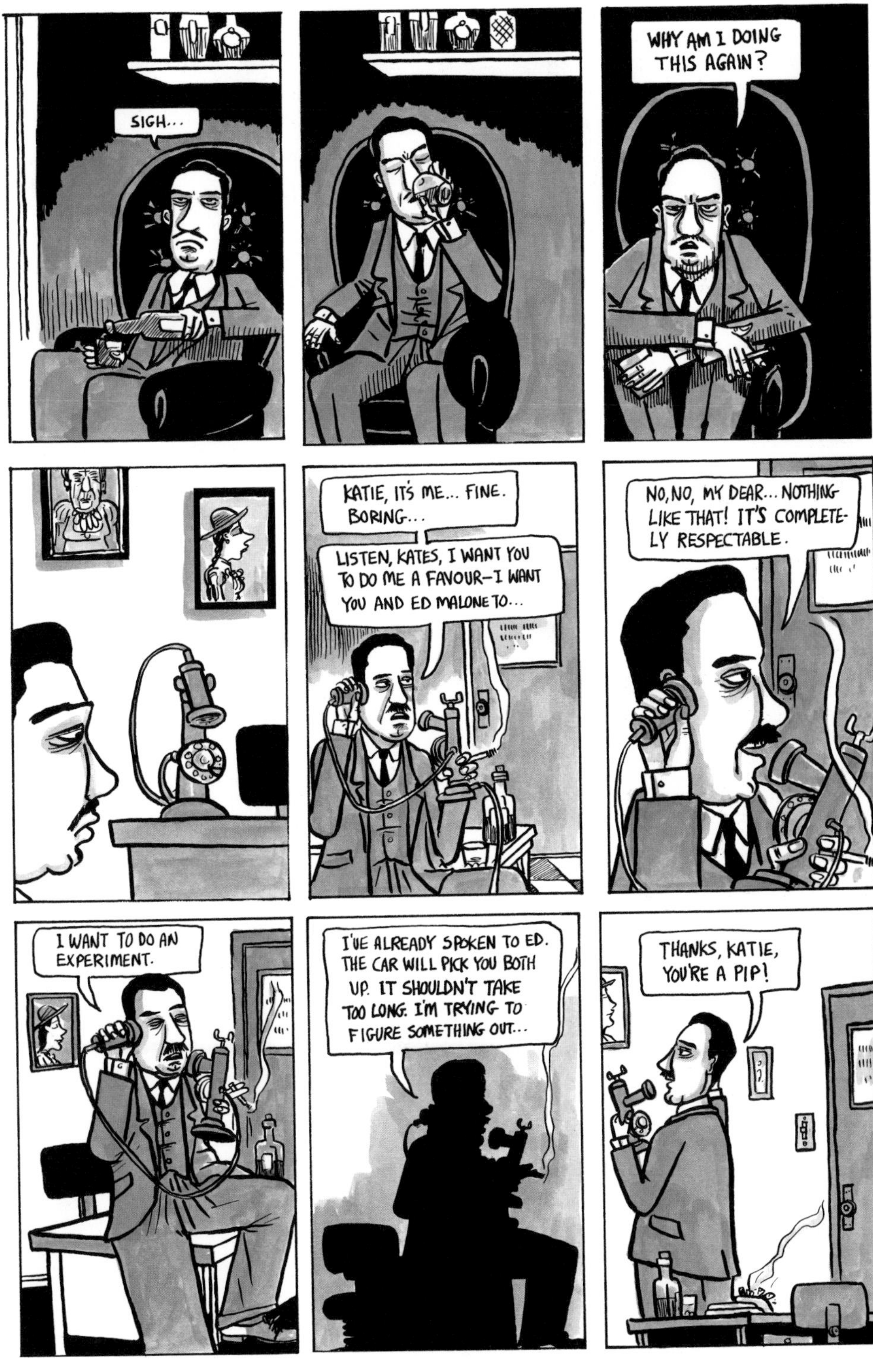
SIGH...
WHY AM I DOING THIS AGAIN?
KATIE, IT'S ME... FINE. BORING...
LISTEN, KATES, I WANT YOU TO DO ME A FAVOUR–I WANT YOU AND ED MALONE TO...
NO, NO, MY DEAR... NOTHING LIKE THAT! IT'S COMPLETELY RESPECTABLE.
I WANT TO DO AN EXPERIMENT.
I'VE ALREADY SPOKEN TO ED. THE CAR WILL PICK YOU BOTH UP. IT SHOULDN'T TAKE TOO LONG. I'M TRYING TO FIGURE SOMETHING OUT...
THANKS, KATIE, YOU'RE A PIP!

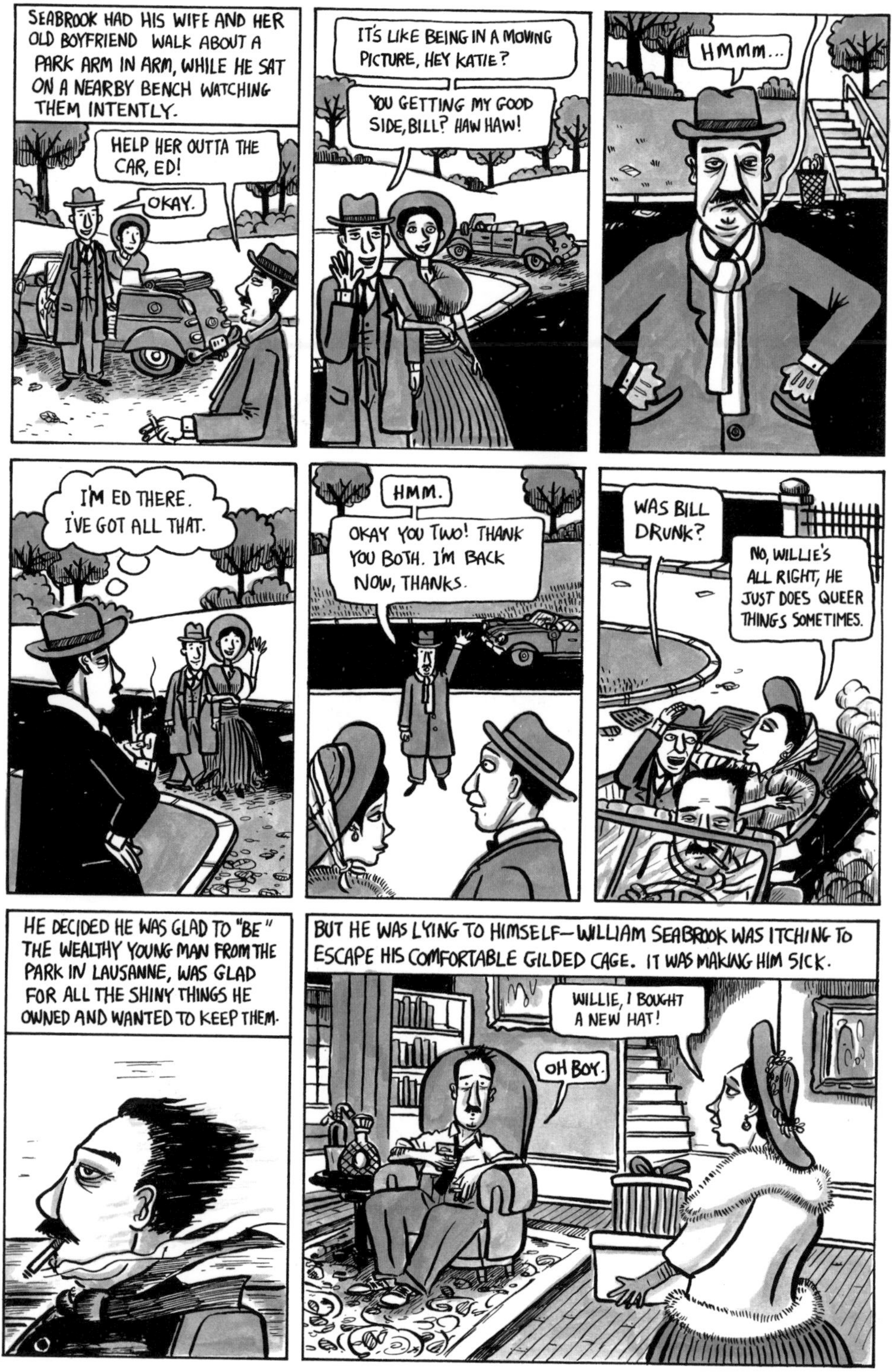
SEABROOK HAD HIS WIFE AND HER OLD BOYFRIEND WALK ABOUT A PARK ARM IN ARM, WHILE HE SAT ON A NEARBY BENCH WATCHING THEM INTENTLY.
HELP HER OUTTA THE CAR, ED!
OKAY.
IT'S LIKE BEING IN A MOVING PICTURE, HEY KATIE?
YOU GETTING MY GOOD SIDE, BILL? HAW HAW!
HMMM...
I'M ED THERE. I'VE GOT ALL THAT.
HMM.
OKAY YOU TWO! THANK YOU BOTH. I'M BACK NOW, THANKS.
WAS BILL DRUNK?
NO, WILLIE'S ALL RIGHT, HE JUST DOES QUEER THINGS SOMETIMES.
HE DECIDED HE WAS GLAD TO "BE" THE WEALTHY YOUNG MAN FROM THE PARK IN LAUSANNE, WAS GLAD FOR ALL THE SHINY THINGS HE OWNED AND WANTED TO KEEP THEM.
BUT HE WAS LYING TO HIMSELF— WILLIAM SEABROOK WAS ITCHING TO ESCAPE HIS COMFORTABLE GILDED CAGE. IT WAS MAKING HIM SICK.
WILLIE, I BOUGHT A NEW HAT!
OH BOY.

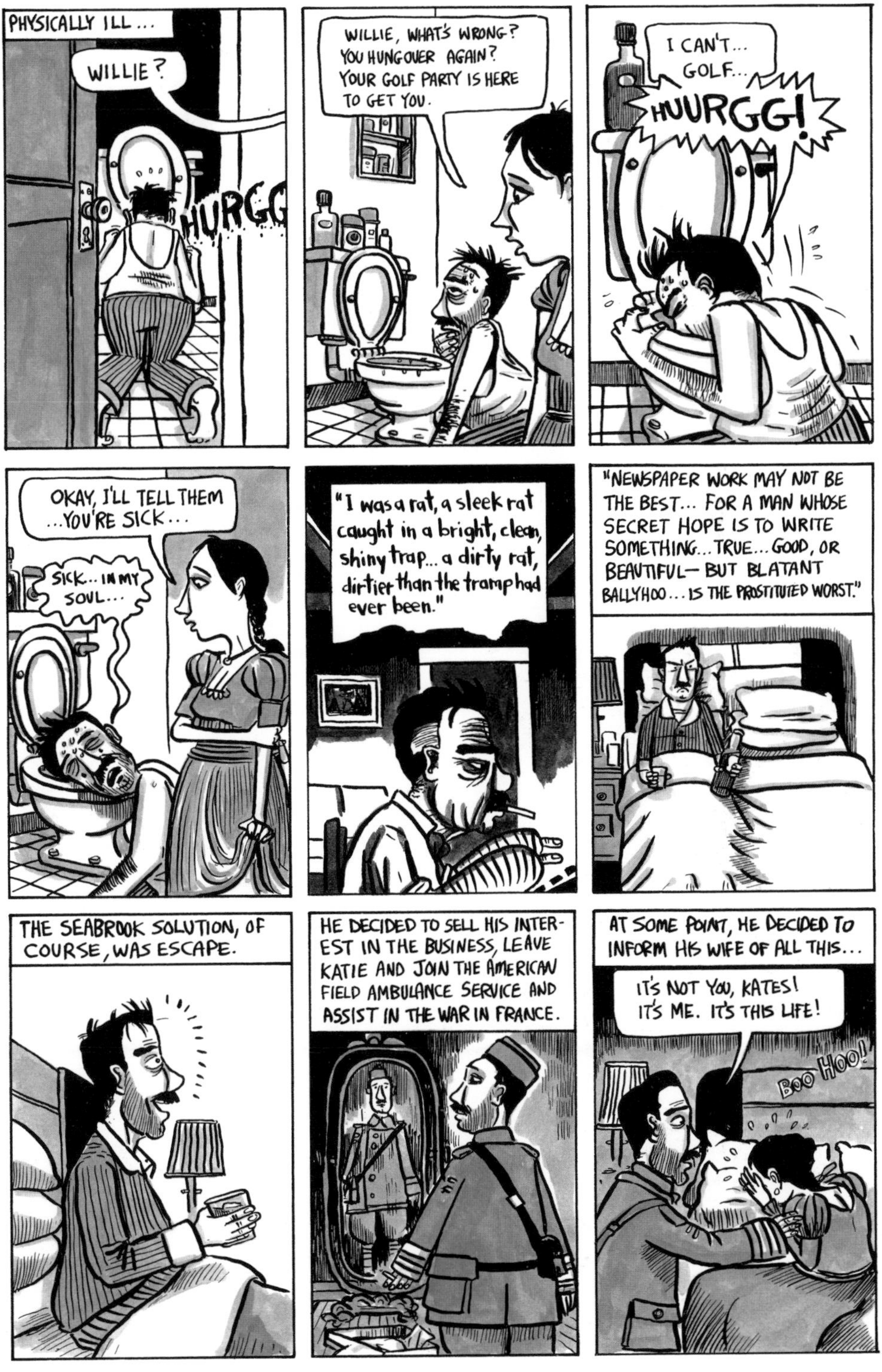
PHYSICALLY ILL...
WILLIE?
HURGG
WILLIE, WHAT'S WRONG? YOU HUNGOVER AGAIN? YOUR GOLF PARTY IS HERE TO GET YOU.
I CAN'T... GOLF...
HUURGG!
OKAY, I'LL TELL THEM ...YOU'RE SICK...
SICK... IN MY SOUL...
"I was a rat, a sleek rat caught in a bright, clean, shiny trap... a dirty rat, dirtier than the tramp had ever been."
"NEWSPAPER WORK MAY NOT BE THE BEST... FOR A MAN WHOSE SECRET HOPE IS TO WRITE SOMETHING... TRUE... GOOD, OR BEAUTIFUL— BUT BLATANT BALLYHOO... IS THE PROSTITUTED WORST."
THE SEABROOK SOLUTION, OF COURSE, WAS ESCAPE.
HE DECIDED TO SELL HIS INTEREST IN THE BUSINESS, LEAVE KATIE AND JOIN THE AMERICAN FIELD AMBULANCE SERVICE AND ASSIST IN THE WAR IN FRANCE.
AT SOME POINT, HE DECIDED TO INFORM HIS WIFE OF ALL THIS...
IT'S NOT YOU, KATES! IT'S ME. IT'S THIS LIFE!
BOO HOO!

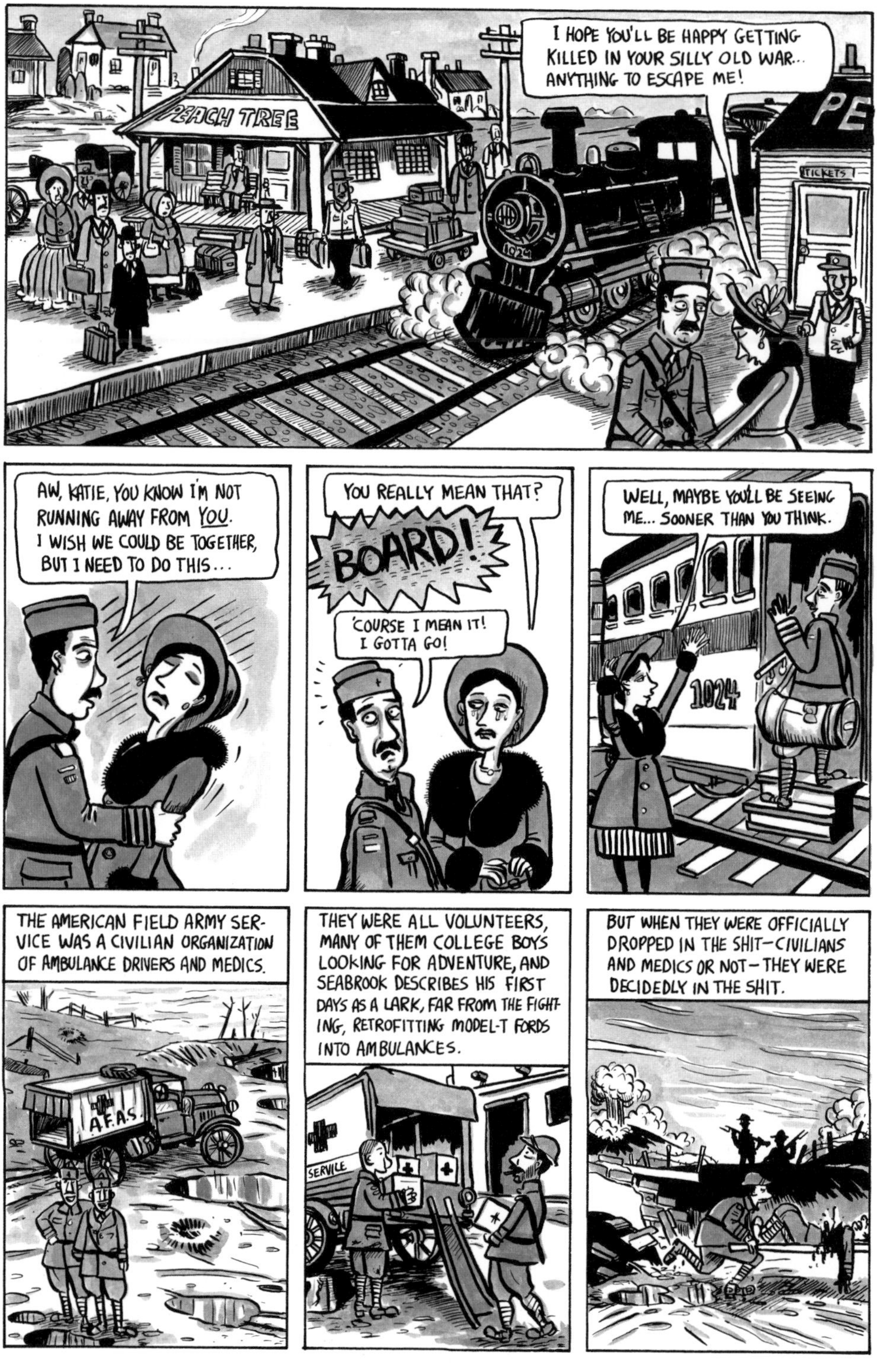
PEACH TREE
I HOPE YOU'LL BE HAPPY GETTING KILLED IN YOUR SILLY OLD WAR... ANYTHING TO ESCAPE ME!
PE
TICKETS
1024
AW, KATIE, YOU KNOW I'M NOT RUNNING AWAY FROM YOU. I WISH WE COULD BE TOGETHER, BUT I NEED TO DO THIS...
YOU REALLY MEAN THAT?
BOARD!
'COURSE I MEAN IT! I GOTTA GO!
WELL, MAYBE YOU'LL BE SEEING ME... SOONER THAN YOU THINK.
1024
THE AMERICAN FIELD ARMY SERVICE WAS A CIVILIAN ORGANIZATION OF AMBULANCE DRIVERS AND MEDICS.
A.F.A.S.
THEY WERE ALL VOLUNTEERS, MANY OF THEM COLLEGE BOYS LOOKING FOR ADVENTURE, AND SEABROOK DESCRIBES HIS FIRST DAYS AS A LARK, FAR FROM THE FIGHTING, RETROFITTING MODEL-T FORDS INTO AMBULANCES.
SERVICE
BUT WHEN THEY WERE OFFICIALLY DROPPED IN THE SHIT—CIVILIANS AND MEDICS OR NOT—THEY WERE DECIDEDLY IN THE SHIT.

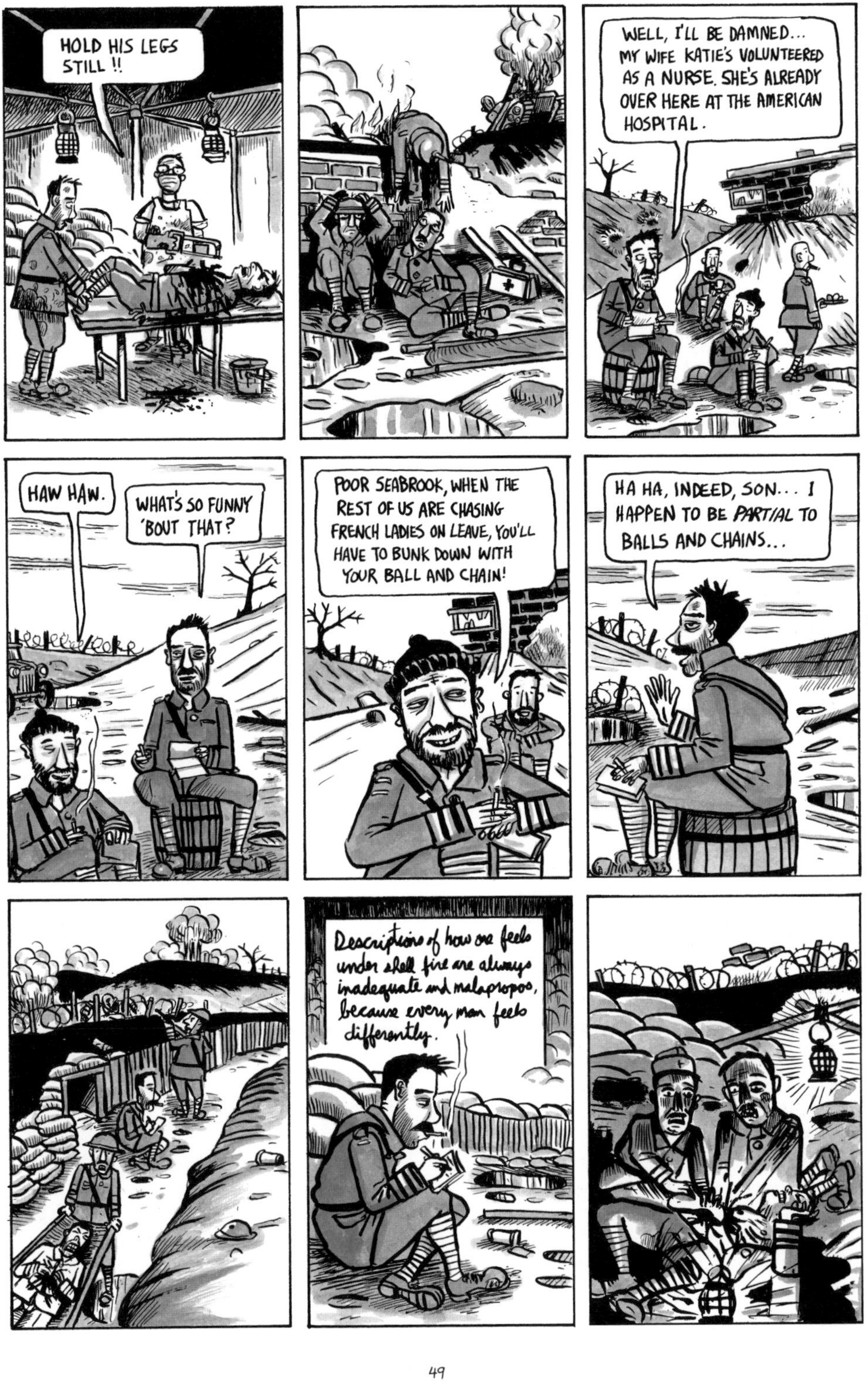
HOLD HIS LEGS STILL !!
WELL, I'LL BE DAMNED... MY WIFE KATIE'S VOLUNTEERED AS A NURSE. SHE'S ALREADY OVER HERE AT THE AMERICAN HOSPITAL.
HAW HAW.
WHAT'S SO FUNNY 'BOUT THAT?
POOR SEABROOK, WHEN THE REST OF US ARE CHASING FRENCH LADIES ON LEAVE, YOU'LL HAVE TO BUNK DOWN WITH YOUR BALL AND CHAIN!
HA HA, INDEED, SON... I HAPPEN TO BE PARTIAL TO BALLS AND CHAINS...
Descriptions of how one feels under shell fire are always inadequate and malapropos, because every man feels differently.

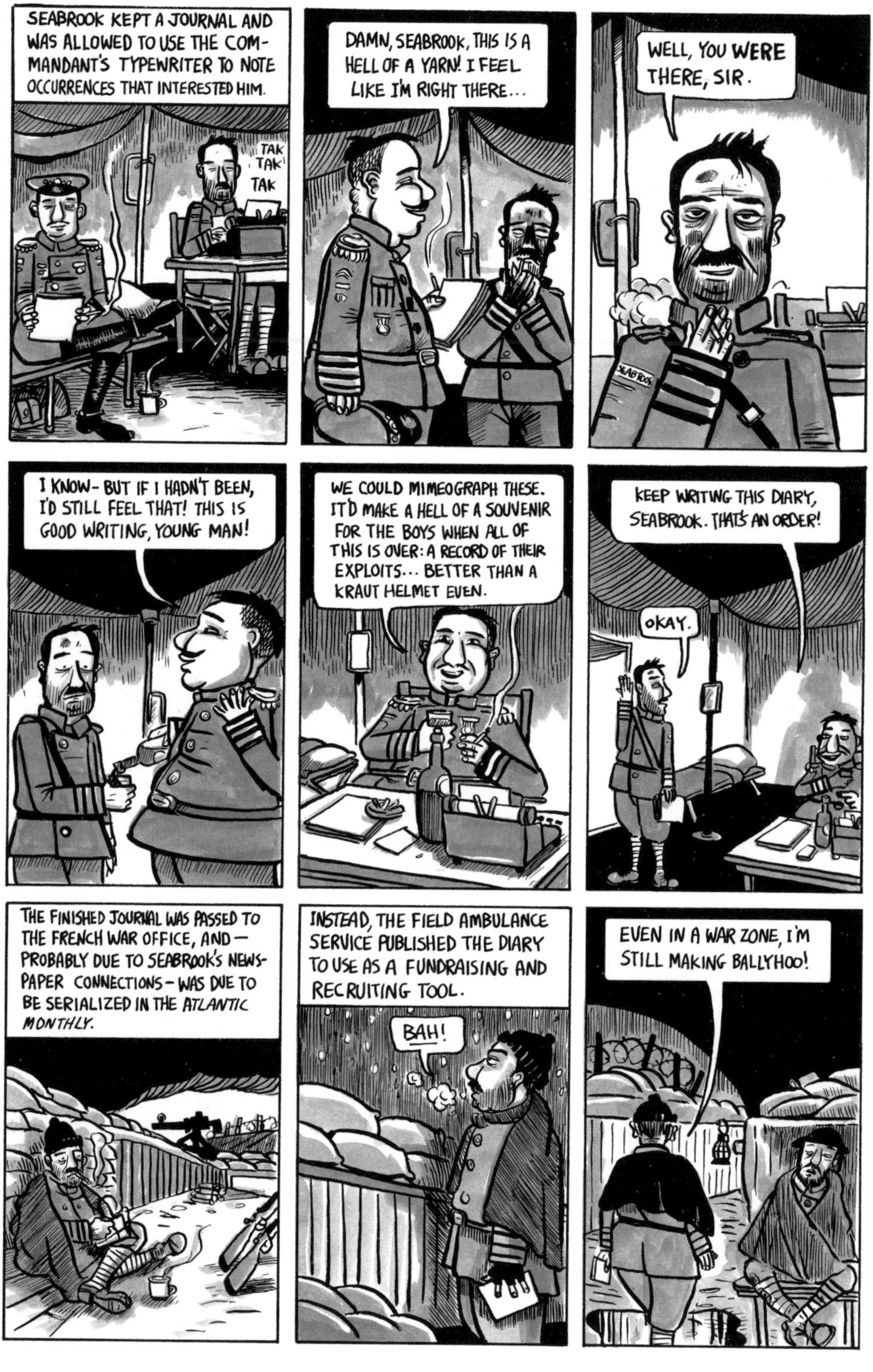
SEABROOK KEPT A JOURNAL AND WAS ALLOWED TO USE THE COMMANDANT'S TYPEWRITER TO NOTE OCCURRENCES THAT INTERESTED HIM.
TAK TAK TAK
DAMN, SEABROOK, THIS IS A HELL OF A YARN! I FEEL LIKE I'M RIGHT THERE...
WELL, YOU WERE THERE, SIR.
SEABROOK
I KNOW- BUT IF I HADN'T BEEN, I'D STILL FEEL THAT! THIS IS GOOD WRITING, YOUNG MAN!
WE COULD MIMEOGRAPH THESE. IT'D MAKE A HELL OF A SOUVENIR FOR THE BOYS WHEN ALL OF THIS IS OVER: A RECORD OF THEIR EXPLOITS... BETTER THAN A KRAUT HELMET EVEN.
KEEP WRITING THIS DIARY, SEABROOK. THAT'S AN ORDER!
OKAY.
THE FINISHED JOURNAL WAS PASSED TO THE FRENCH WAR OFFICE, AND—PROBABLY DUE TO SEABROOK'S NEWSPAPER CONNECTIONS—WAS DUE TO BE SERIALIZED IN THE ATLANTIC MONTHLY.
INSTEAD, THE FIELD AMBULANCE SERVICE PUBLISHED THE DIARY TO USE AS A FUNDRAISING AND RECRUITING TOOL.
BAH!
EVEN IN A WAR ZONE, I'M STILL MAKING BALLYHOO!

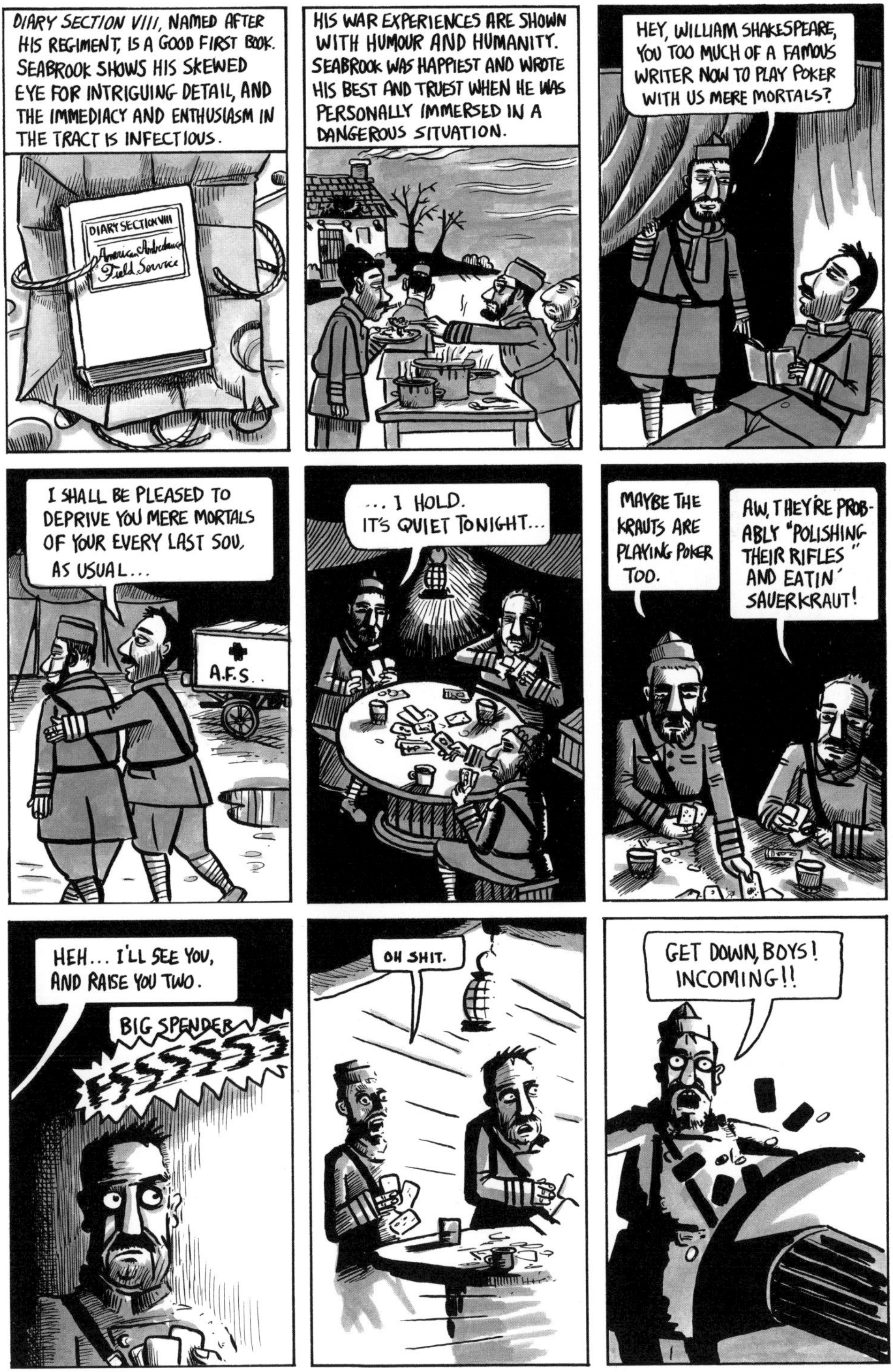
DIARY SECTION VIII, NAMED AFTER HIS REGIMENT, IS A GOOD FIRST BOOK. SEABROOK SHOWS HIS SKEWED EYE FOR INTRIGUING DETAIL, AND THE IMMEDIACY AND ENTHUSIASM IN THE TRACT IS INFECTIOUS.
DIARY SECTION VIII
American Ambulance Field Service
HIS WAR EXPERIENCES ARE SHOWN WITH HUMOUR AND HUMANITY. SEABROOK WAS HAPPIEST AND WROTE HIS BEST AND TRUEST WHEN HE WAS PERSONALLY IMMERSED IN A DANGEROUS SITUATION.
HEY, WILLIAM SHAKESPEARE, YOU TOO MUCH OF A FAMOUS WRITER NOW TO PLAY POKER WITH US MERE MORTALS?
I SHALL BE PLEASED TO DEPRIVE YOU MERE MORTALS OF YOUR EVERY LAST SOU, AS USUAL...
A.F.S.
... I HOLD. IT'S QUIET TONIGHT...
MAYBE THE KRAUTS ARE PLAYING POKER TOO.
AW, THEY'RE PROBABLY "POLISHING THEIR RIFLES" AND EATIN' SAUERKRAUT!
HEH... I'LL SEE YOU, AND RAISE YOU TWO.
BIG SPENDER
FSSSSSSS
OH SHIT.
GET DOWN, BOYS! INCOMING!!

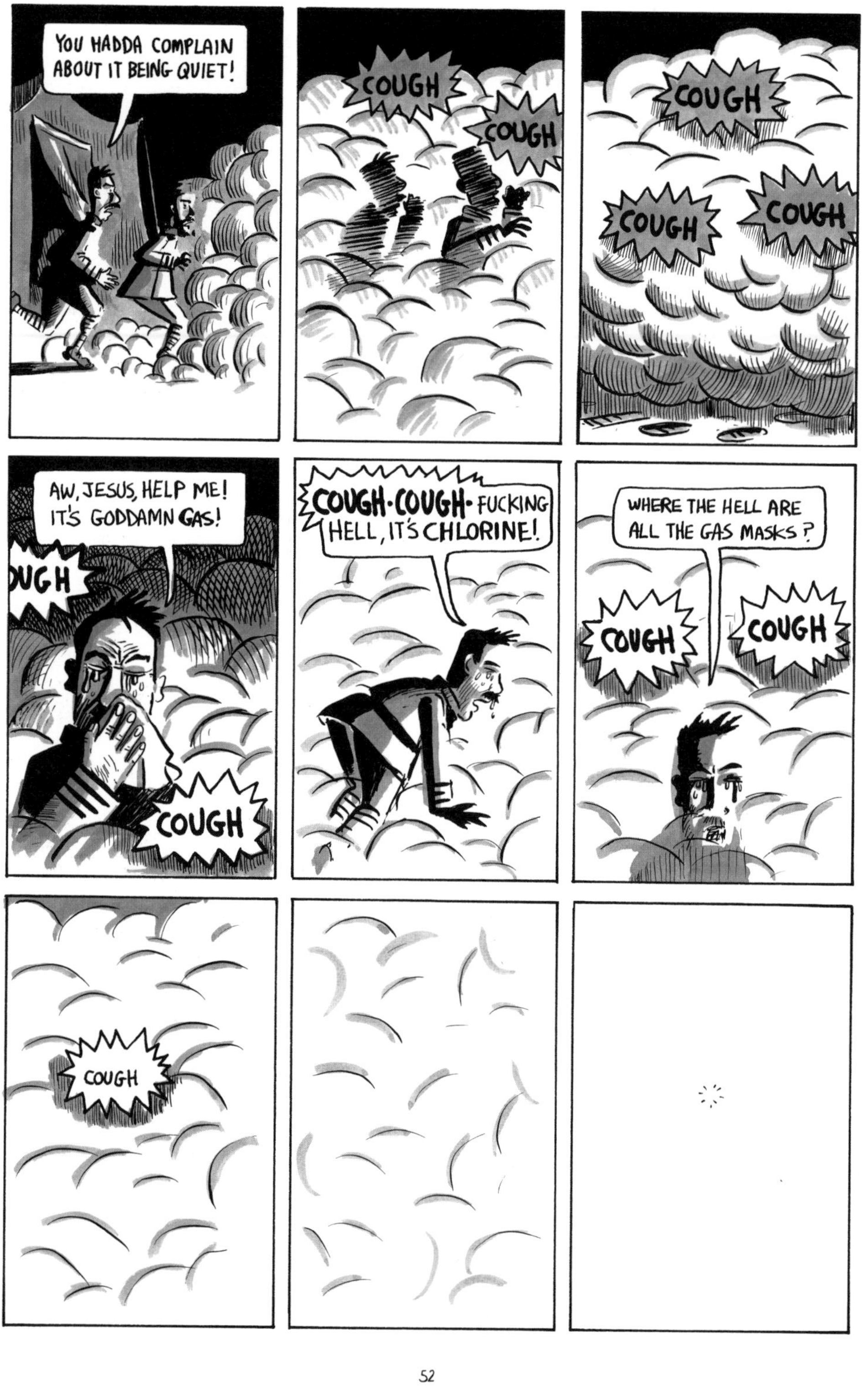
YOU HADDA COMPLAIN ABOUT IT BEING QUIET!
COUGH
COUGH
COUGH
COUGH
COUGH
AW, JESUS, HELP ME! IT'S GODDAMN GAS!
COUGH
COUGH·COUGH· FUCKING HELL, IT'S CHLORINE!
WHERE THE HELL ARE ALL THE GAS MASKS?
COUGH
COUGH
COUGH

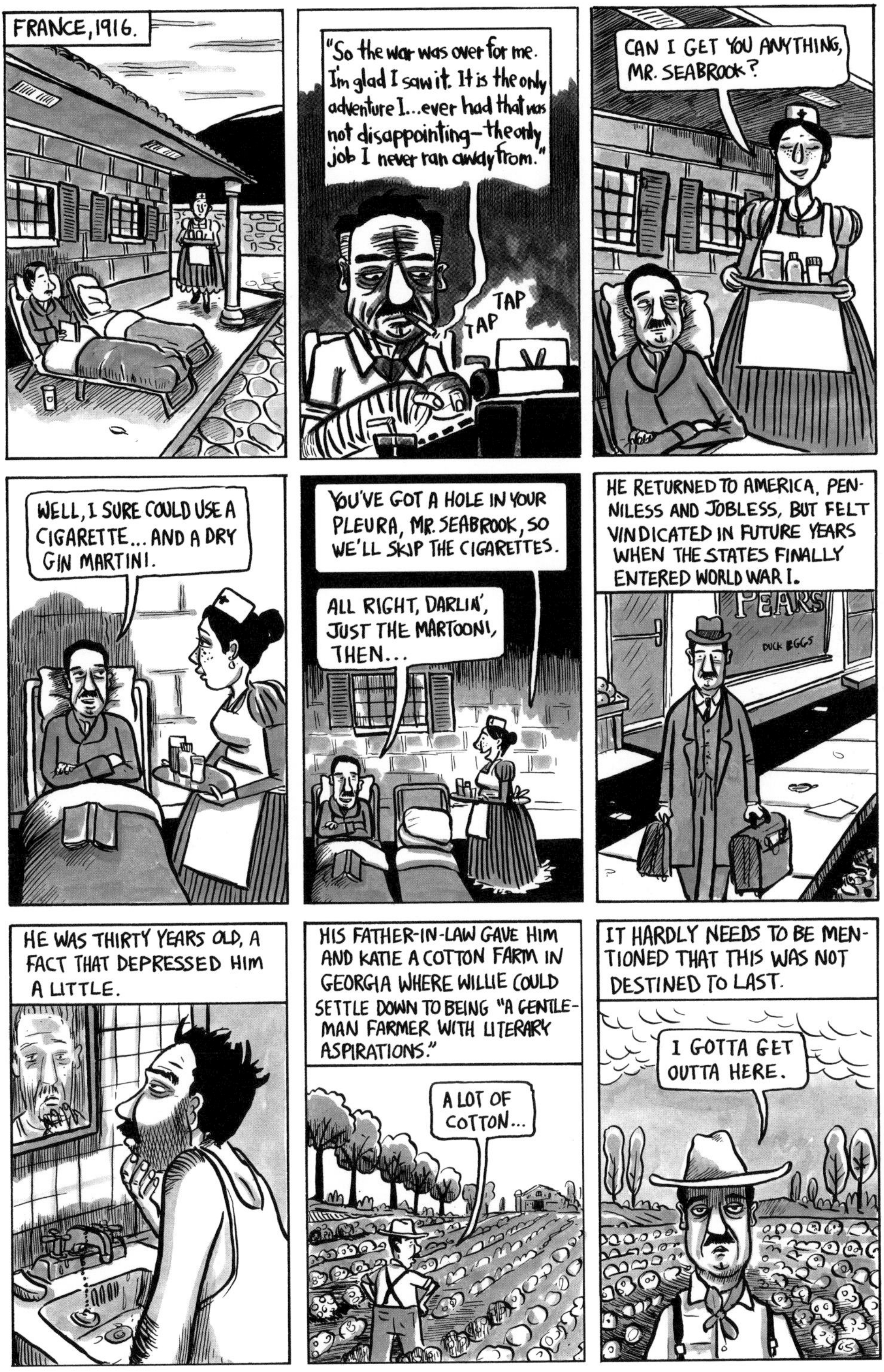
FRANCE, 1916.
"So the war was over for me. I'm glad I saw it. It is the only adventure I...ever had that was not disappointing—the only job I never ran away from."
TAP TAP
CAN I GET YOU ANYTHING, MR. SEABROOK?
WELL, I SURE COULD USE A CIGARETTE... AND A DRY GIN MARTINI.
YOU'VE GOT A HOLE IN YOUR PLEURA, MR. SEABROOK, SO WE'LL SKIP THE CIGARETTES.
ALL RIGHT, DARLIN', JUST THE MARTOONI, THEN...
HE RETURNED TO AMERICA, PENNILESS AND JOBLESS, BUT FELT VINDICATED IN FUTURE YEARS WHEN THE STATES FINALLY ENTERED WORLD WAR I.
PEARS
DUCK EGGS
HE WAS THIRTY YEARS OLD, A FACT THAT DEPRESSED HIM A LITTLE.
HIS FATHER-IN-LAW GAVE HIM AND KATIE A COTTON FARM IN GEORGIA WHERE WILLIE COULD SETTLE DOWN TO BEING "A GENTLEMAN FARMER WITH LITERARY ASPIRATIONS."
A LOT OF COTTON...
IT HARDLY NEEDS TO BE MENTIONED THAT THIS WAS NOT DESTINED TO LAST.
I GOTTA GET OUTTA HERE.

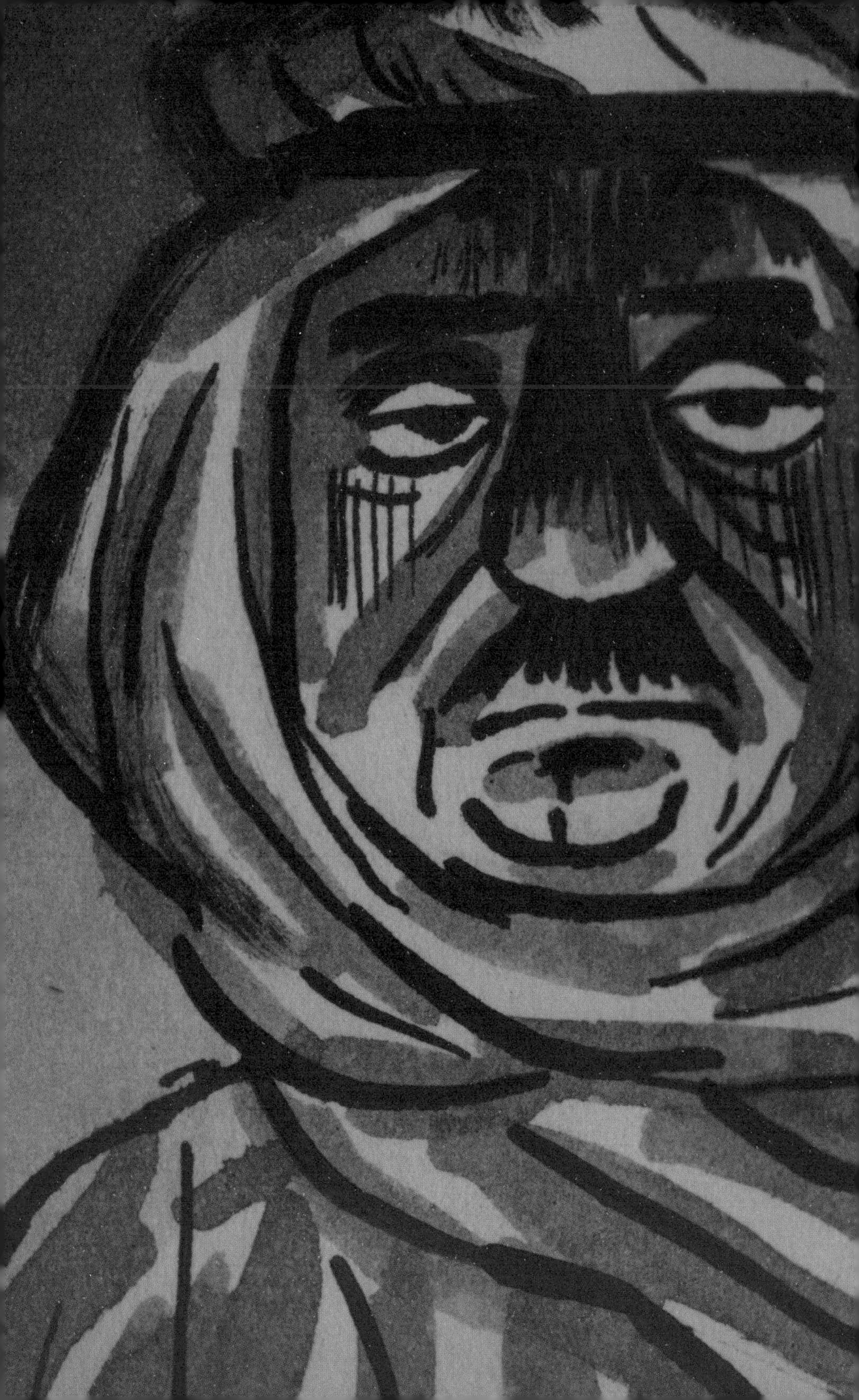

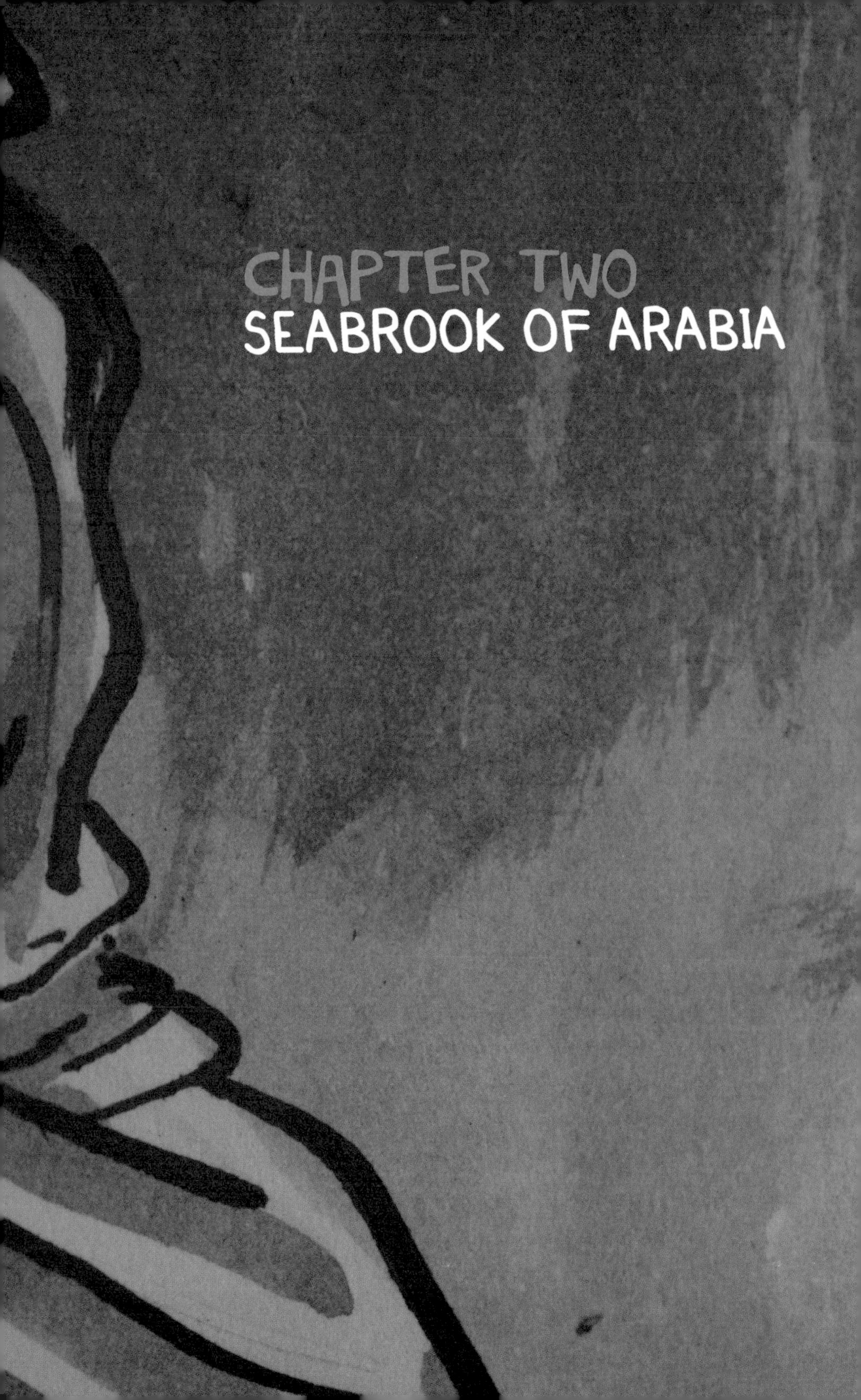

# CHAPTER TWO
# SEABROOK OF ARABIA

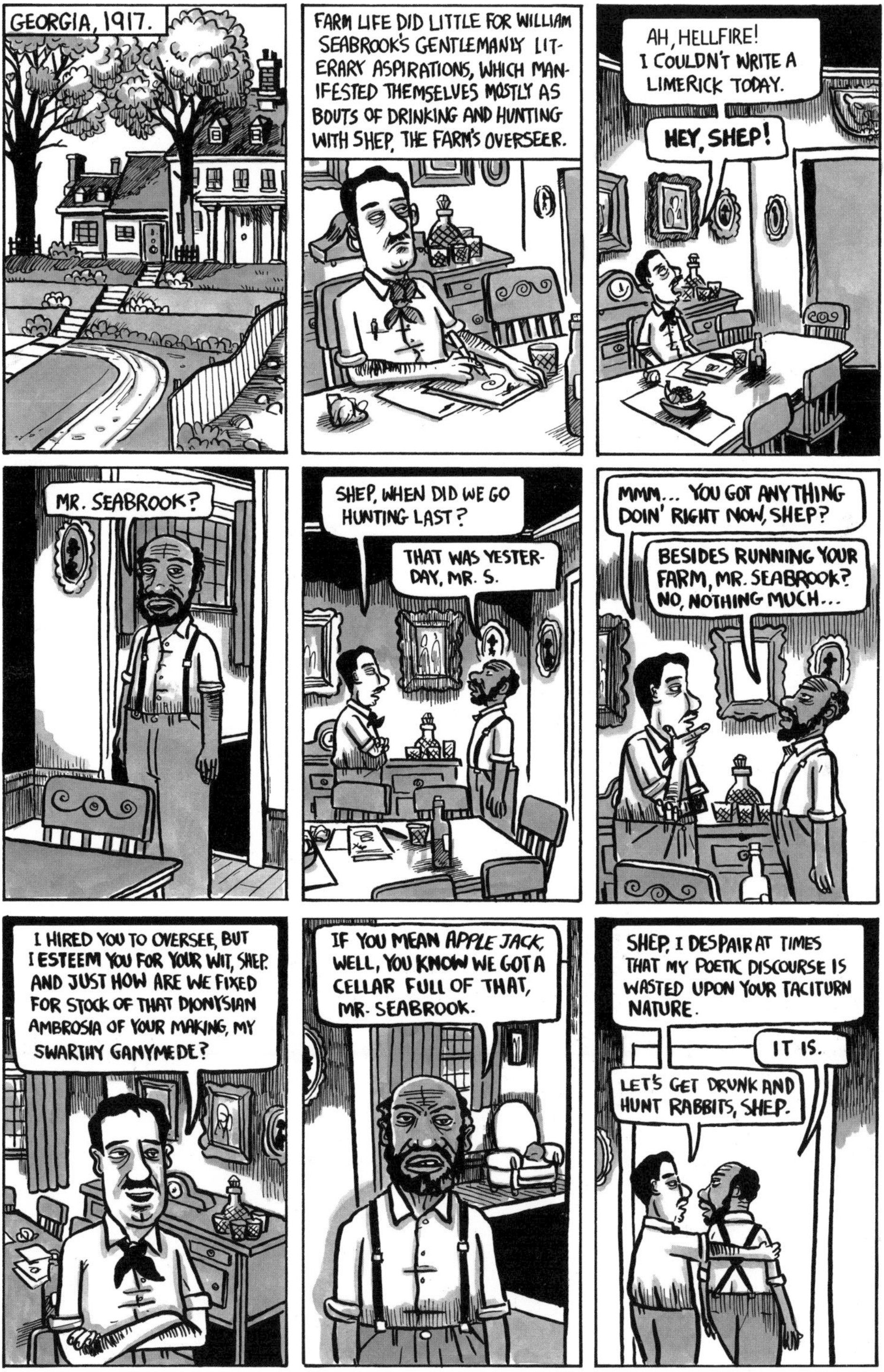
GEORGIA, 1917.
FARM LIFE DID LITTLE FOR WILLIAM SEABROOK'S GENTLEMANLY LITERARY ASPIRATIONS, WHICH MANIFESTED THEMSELVES MOSTLY AS BOUTS OF DRINKING AND HUNTING WITH SHEP, THE FARM'S OVERSEER.
AH, HELLFIRE! I COULDN'T WRITE A LIMERICK TODAY.
HEY, SHEP!
MR. SEABROOK?
SHEP, WHEN DID WE GO HUNTING LAST?
THAT WAS YESTERDAY, MR. S.
MMM... YOU GOT ANYTHING DOIN' RIGHT NOW, SHEP?
BESIDES RUNNING YOUR FARM, MR. SEABROOK? NO, NOTHING MUCH...
I HIRED YOU TO OVERSEE, BUT I ESTEEM YOU FOR YOUR WIT, SHEP. AND JUST HOW ARE WE FIXED FOR STOCK OF THAT DIONYSIAN AMBROSIA OF YOUR MAKING, MY SWARTHY GANYMEDE?
IF YOU MEAN APPLE JACK, WELL, YOU KNOW WE GOT A CELLAR FULL OF THAT, MR. SEABROOK.
SHEP, I DESPAIR AT TIMES THAT MY POETIC DISCOURSE IS WASTED UPON YOUR TACITURN NATURE.
IT IS.
LET'S GET DRUNK AND HUNT RABBITS, SHEP.

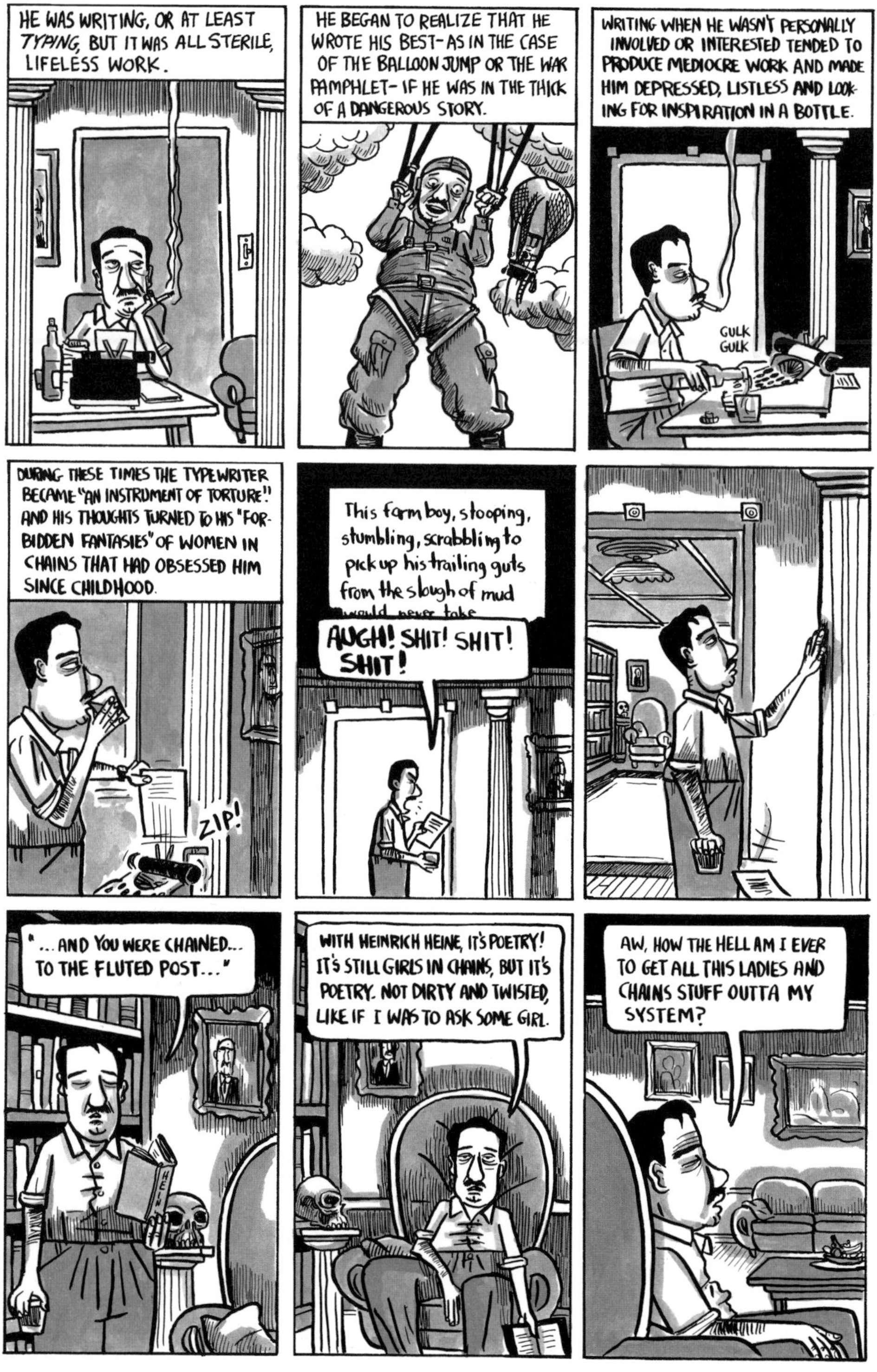
HE WAS WRITING, OR AT LEAST TYPING, BUT IT WAS ALL STERILE, LIFELESS WORK.
HE BEGAN TO REALIZE THAT HE WROTE HIS BEST– AS IN THE CASE OF THE BALLOON JUMP OR THE WAR PAMPHLET– IF HE WAS IN THE THICK OF A DANGEROUS STORY.
WRITING WHEN HE WASN'T PERSONALLY INVOLVED OR INTERESTED TENDED TO PRODUCE MEDIOCRE WORK AND MADE HIM DEPRESSED, LISTLESS AND LOOKING FOR INSPIRATION IN A BOTTLE.
GULK GULK
DURING THESE TIMES THE TYPEWRITER BECAME "AN INSTRUMENT OF TORTURE." AND HIS THOUGHTS TURNED TO HIS "FORBIDDEN FANTASIES" OF WOMEN IN CHAINS THAT HAD OBSESSED HIM SINCE CHILDHOOD.
ZIP!
This farm boy, stooping, stumbling, scrabbling to pick up his trailing guts from the slough of mud
AUGH! SHIT! SHIT! SHIT!
"...AND YOU WERE CHAINED... TO THE FLUTED POST..."
WITH HEINRICH HEINE, IT'S POETRY! IT'S STILL GIRLS IN CHAINS, BUT IT'S POETRY. NOT DIRTY AND TWISTED, LIKE IF I WAS TO ASK SOME GIRL.
AW, HOW THE HELL AM I EVER TO GET ALL THIS LADIES AND CHAINS STUFF OUTTA MY SYSTEM?

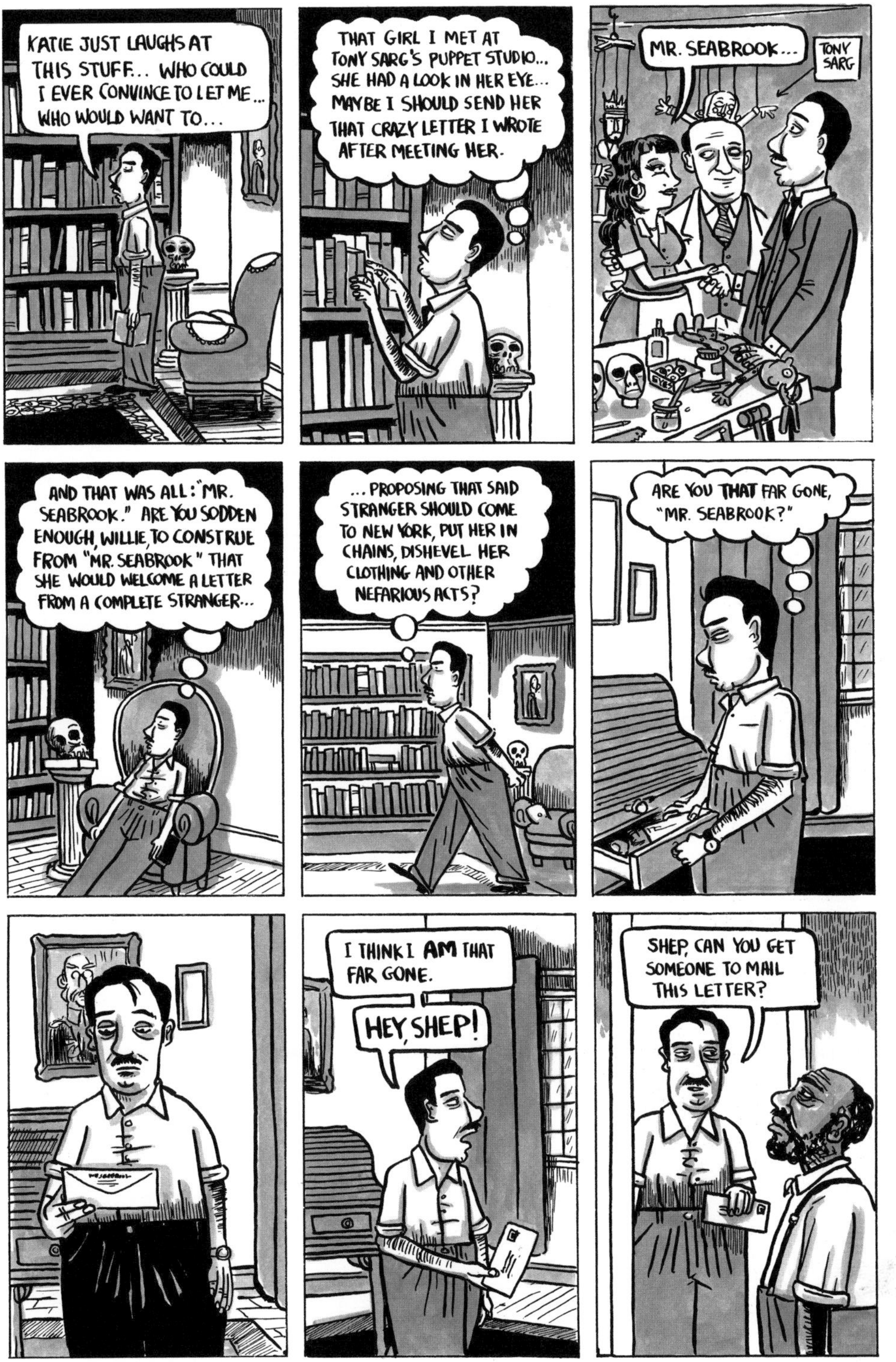
KATIE JUST LAUGHS AT THIS STUFF... WHO COULD I EVER CONVINCE TO LET ME... WHO WOULD WANT TO...
THAT GIRL I MET AT TONY SARG'S PUPPET STUDIO... SHE HAD A LOOK IN HER EYE... MAYBE I SHOULD SEND HER THAT CRAZY LETTER I WROTE AFTER MEETING HER.
MR. SEABROOK...
TONY SARG
AND THAT WAS ALL: "MR. SEABROOK." ARE YOU SODDEN ENOUGH, WILLIE, TO CONSTRUE FROM "MR. SEABROOK" THAT SHE WOULD WELCOME A LETTER FROM A COMPLETE STRANGER...
...PROPOSING THAT SAID STRANGER SHOULD COME TO NEW YORK, PUT HER IN CHAINS, DISHEVEL HER CLOTHING AND OTHER NEFARIOUS ACTS?
ARE YOU THAT FAR GONE, "MR. SEABROOK?"
I THINK I AM THAT FAR GONE.
HEY, SHEP!
SHEP, CAN YOU GET SOMEONE TO MAIL THIS LETTER?

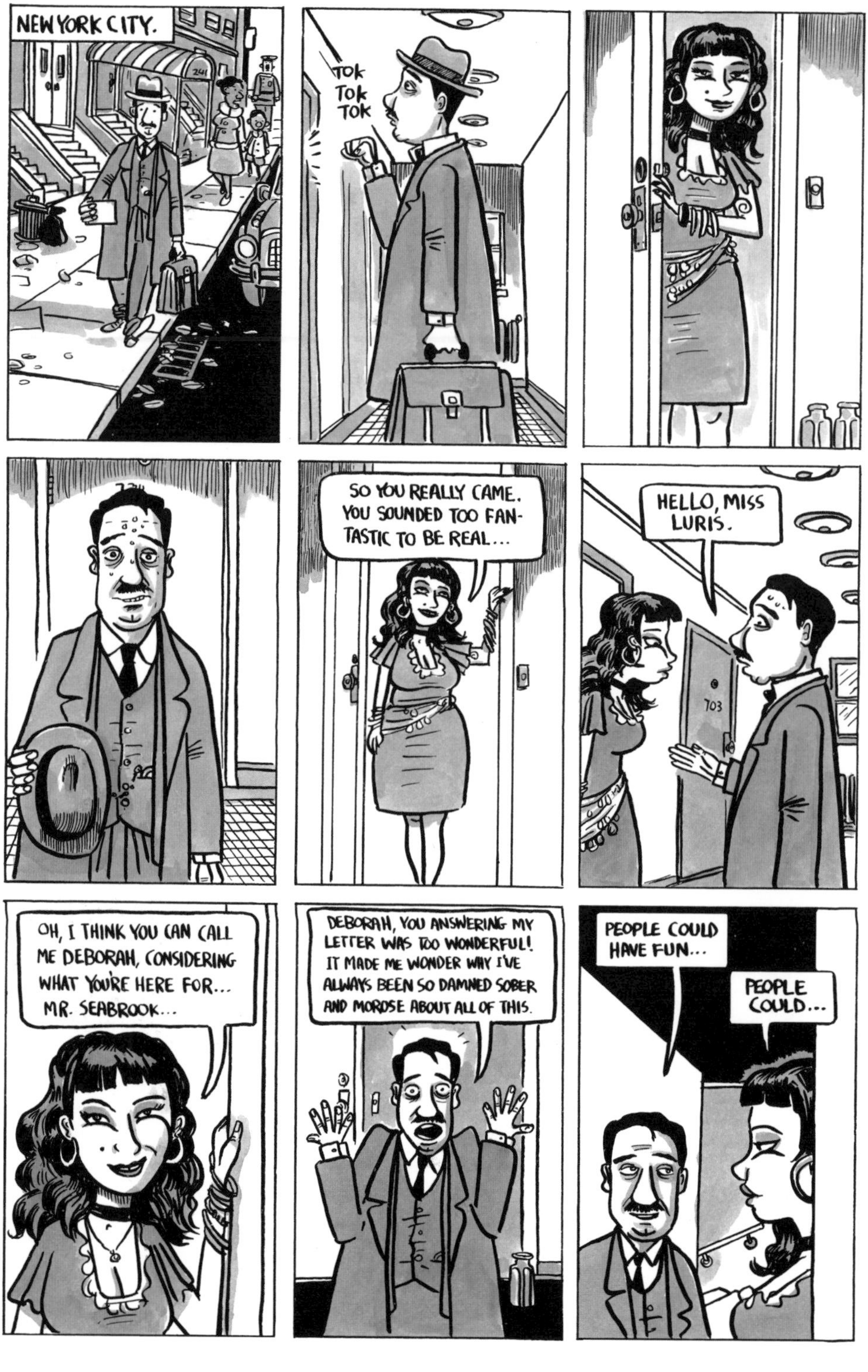
NEW YORK CITY.
TOK TOK TOK
SO YOU REALLY CAME. YOU SOUNDED TOO FANTASTIC TO BE REAL...
HELLO, MISS LURIS.
OH, I THINK YOU CAN CALL ME DEBORAH, CONSIDERING WHAT YOU'RE HERE FOR... MR. SEABROOK...
DEBORAH, YOU ANSWERING MY LETTER WAS TOO WONDERFUL! IT MADE ME WONDER WHY I'VE ALWAYS BEEN SO DAMNED SOBER AND MOROSE ABOUT ALL OF THIS.
PEOPLE COULD HAVE FUN...
PEOPLE COULD...

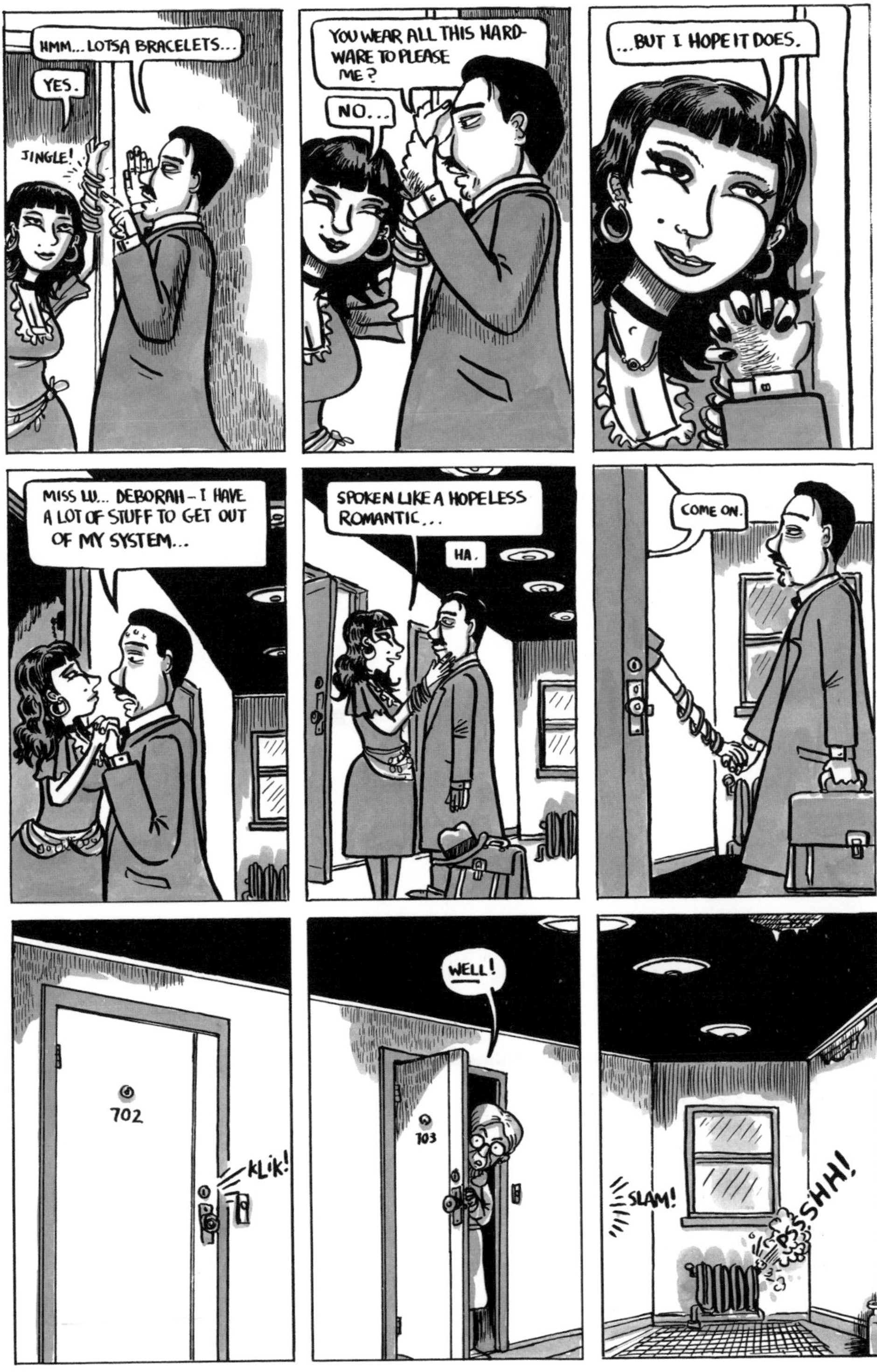
HMM... LOTSA BRACELETS...
YES.
JINGLE!
YOU WEAR ALL THIS HARD-WARE TO PLEASE ME?
NO...
...BUT I HOPE IT DOES.
MISS LU... DEBORAH - I HAVE A LOT OF STUFF TO GET OUT OF MY SYSTEM...
SPOKEN LIKE A HOPELESS ROMANTIC...
HA.
COME ON.
702
KLIK!
WELL!
703
SLAM!
PSSHH!

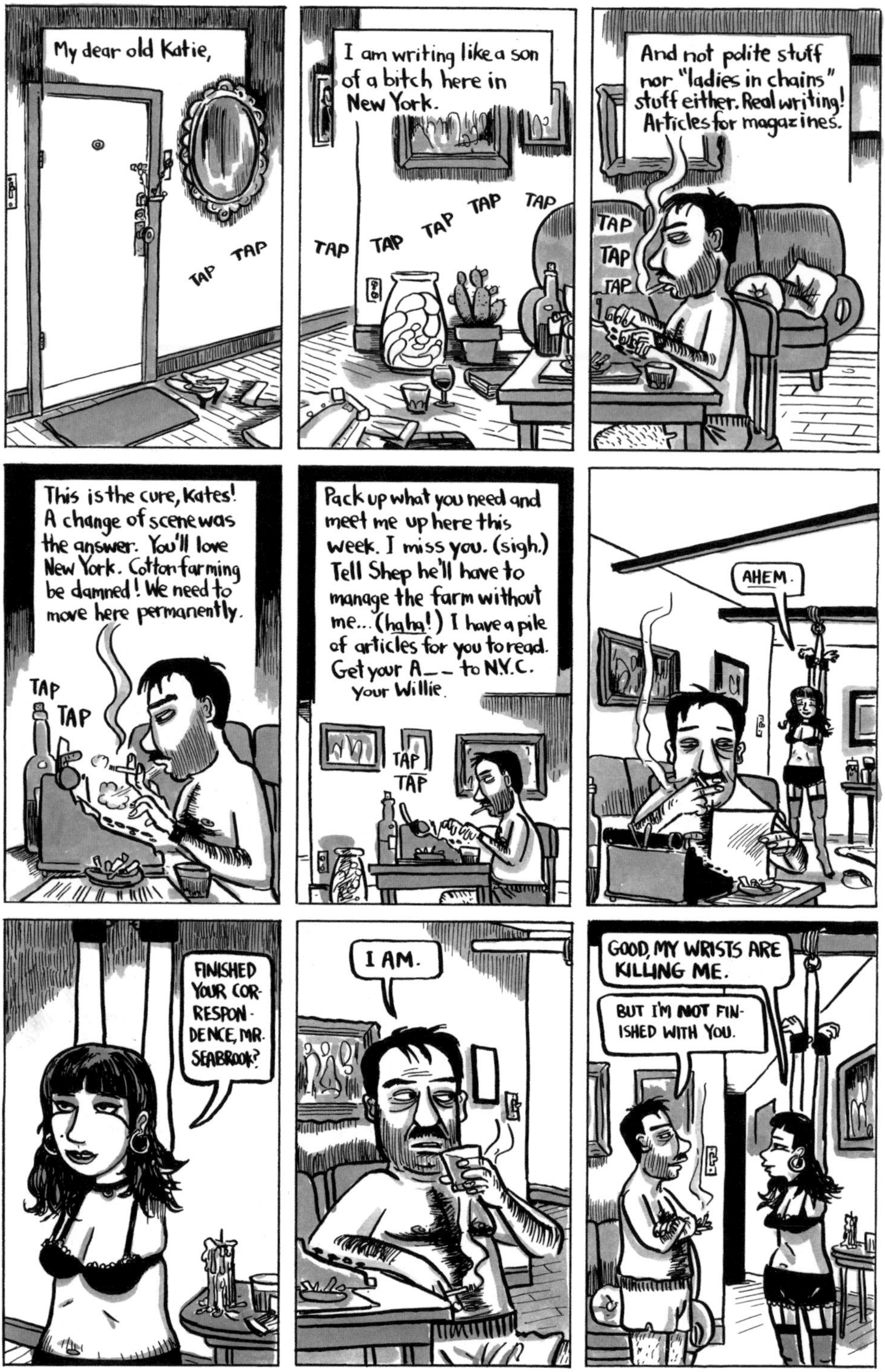
My dear old Katie,
TAP TAP
I am writing like a son of a bitch here in New York.
TAP TAP TAP TAP TAP
And not polite stuff nor "ladies in chains" stuff either. Real writing! Articles for magazines.
TAP TAP TAP
This is the cure, Kates! A change of scene was the answer. You'll love New York. Cotton-farming be damned! We need to move here permanently.
TAP TAP
Pack up what you need and meet me up here this week. I miss you. (sigh.) Tell Shep he'll have to manage the farm without me... (haha!) I have a pile of articles for you to read. Get your A__ to N.Y.C. Your Willie.
TAP TAP
AHEM.
FINISHED YOUR COR-RESPON-DENCE, MR. SEABROOK?
I AM.
GOOD, MY WRISTS ARE KILLING ME.
BUT I'M NOT FIN-ISHED WITH YOU.

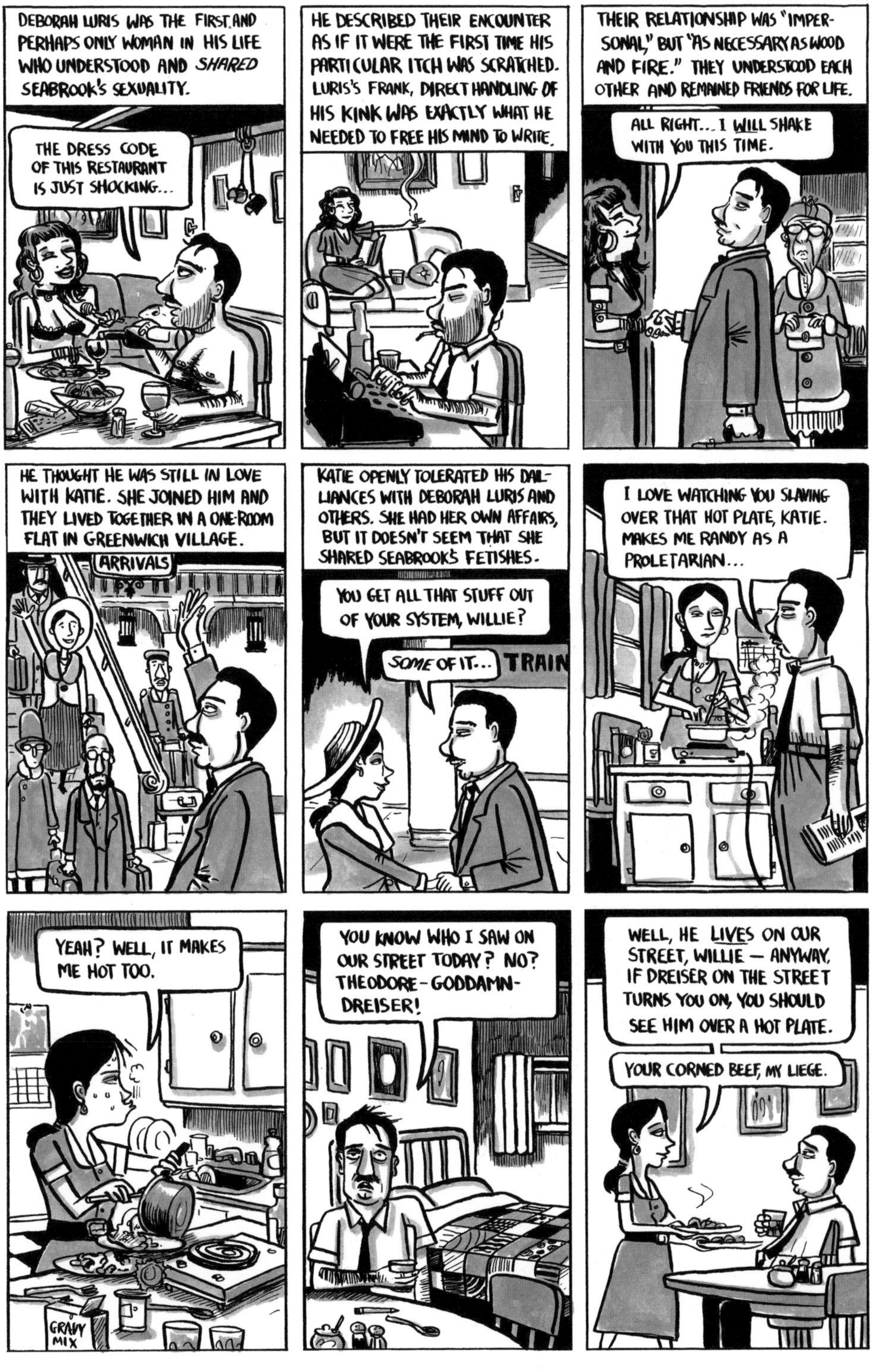
DEBORAH LURIS WAS THE FIRST AND PERHAPS ONLY WOMAN IN HIS LIFE WHO UNDERSTOOD AND *SHARED* SEABROOK'S SEXUALITY.
THE DRESS CODE OF THIS RESTAURANT IS JUST SHOCKING...
HE DESCRIBED THEIR ENCOUNTER AS IF IT WERE THE FIRST TIME HIS PARTICULAR ITCH WAS SCRATCHED. LURIS'S FRANK, DIRECT HANDLING OF HIS KINK WAS EXACTLY WHAT HE NEEDED TO FREE HIS MIND TO WRITE.
THEIR RELATIONSHIP WAS "IMPERSONAL," BUT "AS NECESSARY AS WOOD AND FIRE." THEY UNDERSTOOD EACH OTHER AND REMAINED FRIENDS FOR LIFE.
ALL RIGHT... I WILL SHAKE WITH YOU THIS TIME.
HE THOUGHT HE WAS STILL IN LOVE WITH KATIE. SHE JOINED HIM AND THEY LIVED TOGETHER IN A ONE-ROOM FLAT IN GREENWICH VILLAGE.
ARRIVALS
KATIE OPENLY TOLERATED HIS DALLIANCES WITH DEBORAH LURIS AND OTHERS. SHE HAD HER OWN AFFAIRS, BUT IT DOESN'T SEEM THAT SHE SHARED SEABROOK'S FETISHES.
YOU GET ALL THAT STUFF OUT OF YOUR SYSTEM, WILLIE?
*SOME* OF IT...
TRAIN
I LOVE WATCHING YOU SLAVING OVER THAT HOT PLATE, KATIE. MAKES ME RANDY AS A PROLETARIAN...
YEAH? WELL, IT MAKES ME HOT TOO.
GRAVY MIX
YOU KNOW WHO I SAW ON OUR STREET TODAY? NO? THEODORE-GODDAMN-DREISER!
WELL, HE LIVES ON OUR STREET, WILLIE — ANYWAY, IF DREISER ON THE STREET TURNS YOU ON, YOU SHOULD SEE HIM OVER A HOT PLATE.
YOUR CORNED BEEF, MY LIEGE.

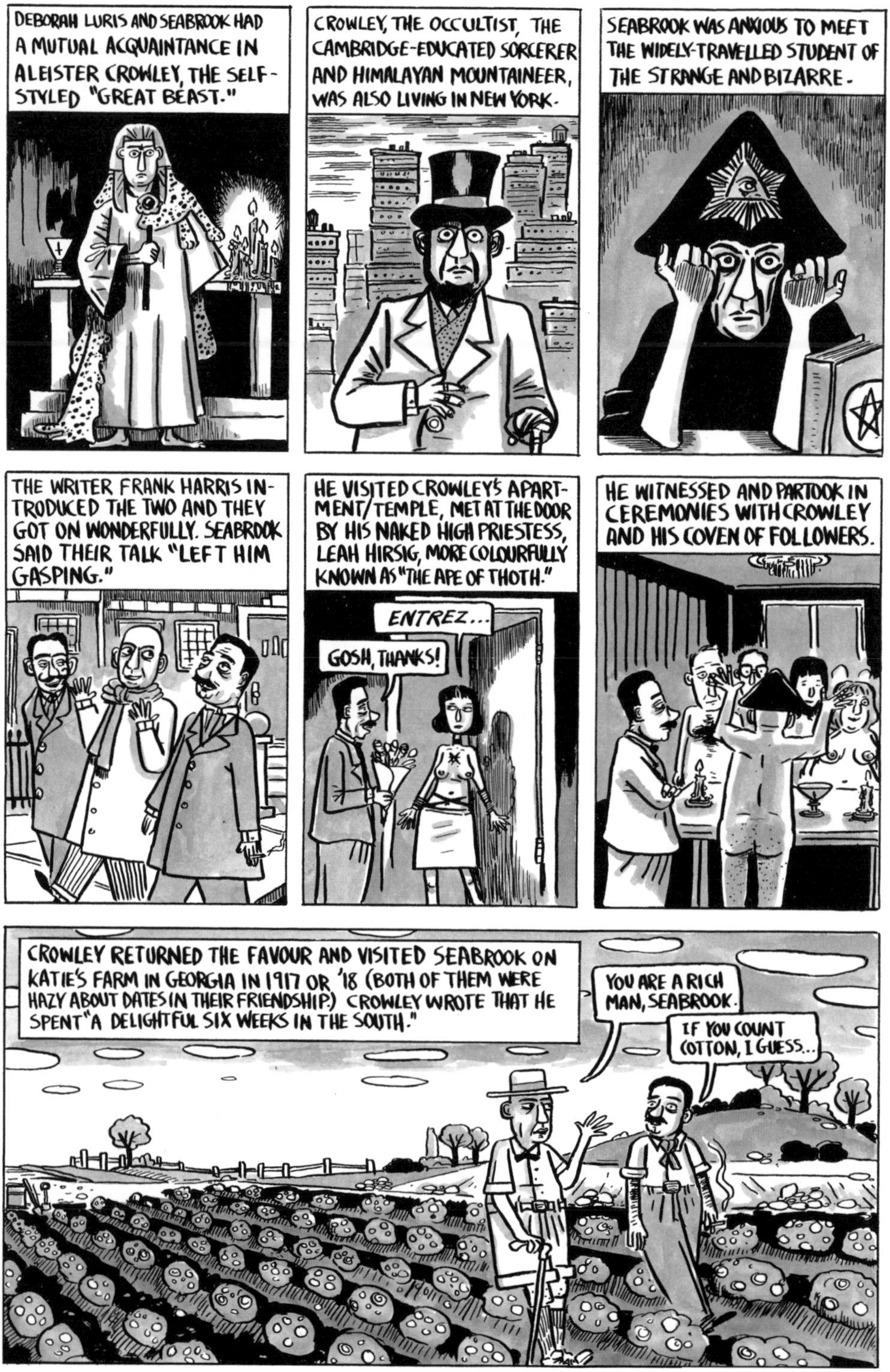
DEBORAH LURIS AND SEABROOK HAD A MUTUAL ACQUAINTANCE IN ALEISTER CROWLEY, THE SELF-STYLED "GREAT BEAST."
CROWLEY, THE OCCULTIST, THE CAMBRIDGE-EDUCATED SORCERER AND HIMALAYAN MOUNTAINEER, WAS ALSO LIVING IN NEW YORK.
SEABROOK WAS ANXIOUS TO MEET THE WIDELY-TRAVELLED STUDENT OF THE STRANGE AND BIZARRE.
THE WRITER FRANK HARRIS INTRODUCED THE TWO AND THEY GOT ON WONDERFULLY. SEABROOK SAID THEIR TALK "LEFT HIM GASPING."
HE VISITED CROWLEY'S APARTMENT/TEMPLE, MET AT THE DOOR BY HIS NAKED HIGH PRIESTESS, LEAH HIRSIG, MORE COLOURFULLY KNOWN AS "THE APE OF THOTH."
ENTREZ...
GOSH, THANKS!
HE WITNESSED AND PARTOOK IN CEREMONIES WITH CROWLEY AND HIS COVEN OF FOLLOWERS.
CROWLEY RETURNED THE FAVOUR AND VISITED SEABROOK ON KATIE'S FARM IN GEORGIA IN 1917 OR '18 (BOTH OF THEM WERE HAZY ABOUT DATES IN THEIR FRIENDSHIP.) CROWLEY WROTE THAT HE SPENT "A DELIGHTFUL SIX WEEKS IN THE SOUTH."
YOU ARE A RICH MAN, SEABROOK.
IF YOU COUNT COTTON, I GUESS...

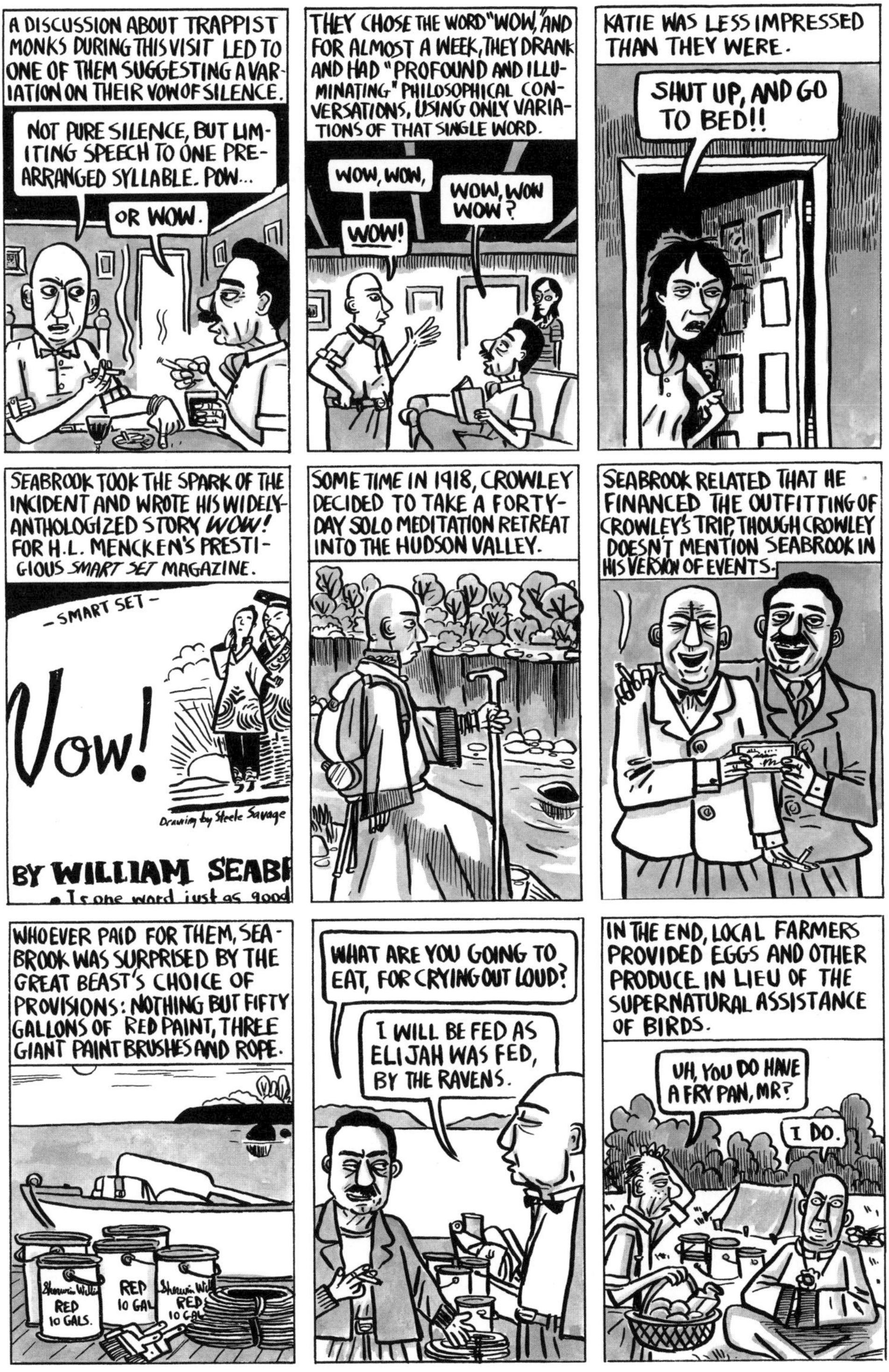
A DISCUSSION ABOUT TRAPPIST MONKS DURING THIS VISIT LED TO ONE OF THEM SUGGESTING A VARIATION ON THEIR VOW OF SILENCE.
NOT PURE SILENCE, BUT LIMITING SPEECH TO ONE PRE-ARRANGED SYLLABLE. POW...
OR WOW.
THEY CHOSE THE WORD "WOW," AND FOR ALMOST A WEEK, THEY DRANK AND HAD "PROFOUND AND ILLUMINATING" PHILOSOPHICAL CONVERSATIONS, USING ONLY VARIATIONS OF THAT SINGLE WORD.
WOW, WOW,
WOW!
WOW, WOW WOW?
KATIE WAS LESS IMPRESSED THAN THEY WERE.
SHUT UP, AND GO TO BED!!
SEABROOK TOOK THE SPARK OF THE INCIDENT AND WROTE HIS WIDELY-ANTHOLOGIZED STORY WOW! FOR H.L. MENCKEN'S PRESTIGIOUS SMART SET MAGAZINE.
– SMART SET –
Wow!
Drawing by Steele Savage
BY WILLIAM SEAB
Is one word just as good
SOME TIME IN 1918, CROWLEY DECIDED TO TAKE A FORTY-DAY SOLO MEDITATION RETREAT INTO THE HUDSON VALLEY.
SEABROOK RELATED THAT HE FINANCED THE OUTFITTING OF CROWLEY'S TRIP, THOUGH CROWLEY DOESN'T MENTION SEABROOK IN HIS VERSION OF EVENTS.
WHOEVER PAID FOR THEM, SEABROOK WAS SURPRISED BY THE GREAT BEAST'S CHOICE OF PROVISIONS: NOTHING BUT FIFTY GALLONS OF RED PAINT, THREE GIANT PAINT BRUSHES AND ROPE.
RED 10 GALS.
RED 10 GAL
RED 10 GAL
WHAT ARE YOU GOING TO EAT, FOR CRYING OUT LOUD?
I WILL BE FED AS ELIJAH WAS FED, BY THE RAVENS.
IN THE END, LOCAL FARMERS PROVIDED EGGS AND OTHER PRODUCE IN LIEU OF THE SUPERNATURAL ASSISTANCE OF BIRDS.
UH, YOU DO HAVE A FRY PAN, MR?
I DO.

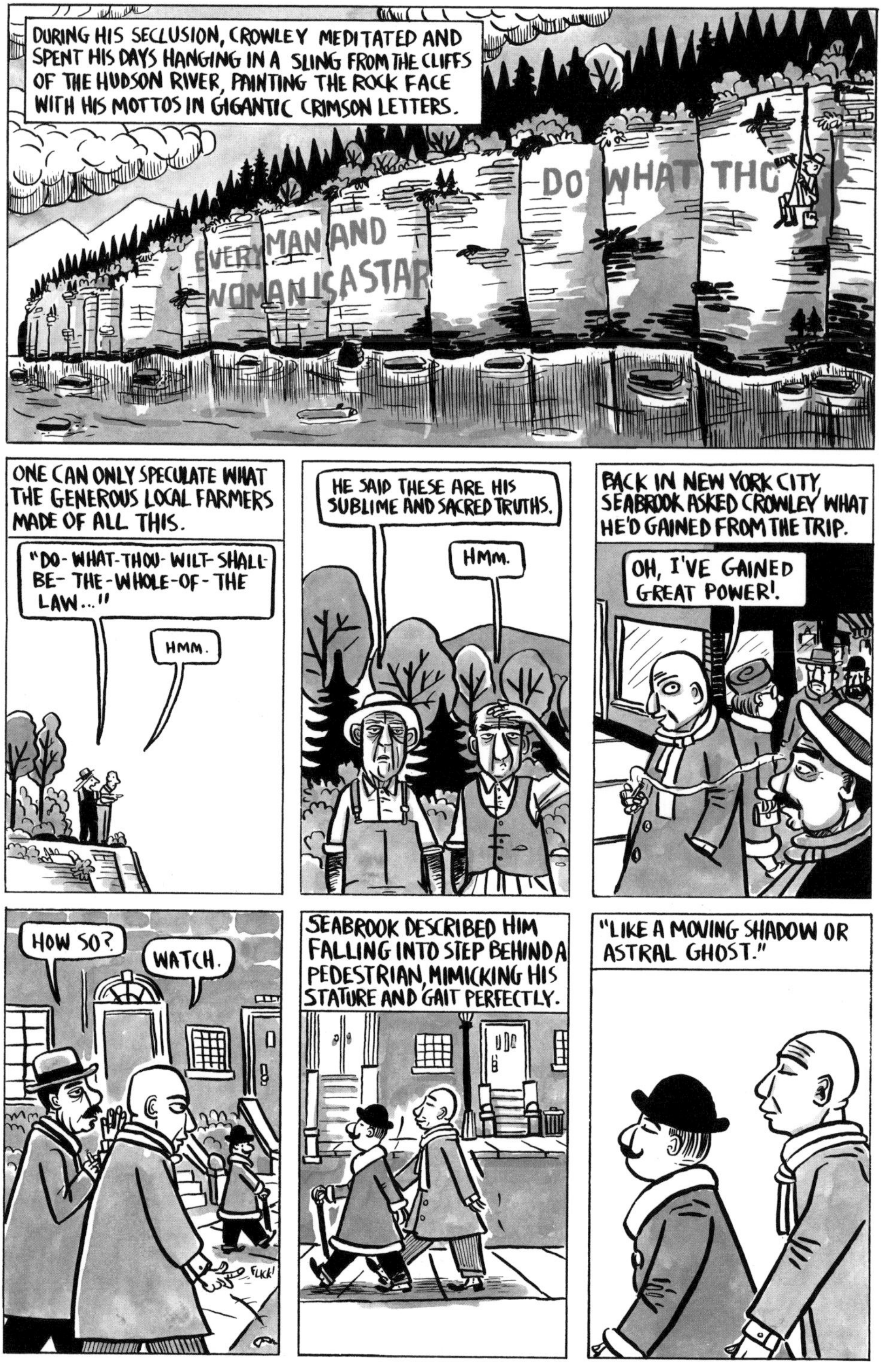
DURING HIS SECLUSION, CROWLEY MEDITATED AND SPENT HIS DAYS HANGING IN A SLING FROM THE CLIFFS OF THE HUDSON RIVER, PAINTING THE ROCK FACE WITH HIS MOTTOS IN GIGANTIC CRIMSON LETTERS.
EVERY MAN AND WOMAN IS A STAR
DO WHAT THO
ONE CAN ONLY SPECULATE WHAT THE GENEROUS LOCAL FARMERS MADE OF ALL THIS.
"DO-WHAT-THOU-WILT-SHALL-BE-THE-WHOLE-OF-THE LAW..."
HMM.
HE SAID THESE ARE HIS SUBLIME AND SACRED TRUTHS.
HMM.
BACK IN NEW YORK CITY, SEABROOK ASKED CROWLEY WHAT HE'D GAINED FROM THE TRIP.
OH, I'VE GAINED GREAT POWER!
HOW SO?
WATCH.
FLICK!
SEABROOK DESCRIBED HIM FALLING INTO STEP BEHIND A PEDESTRIAN, MIMICKING HIS STATURE AND GAIT PERFECTLY.
"LIKE A MOVING SHADOW OR ASTRAL GHOST."

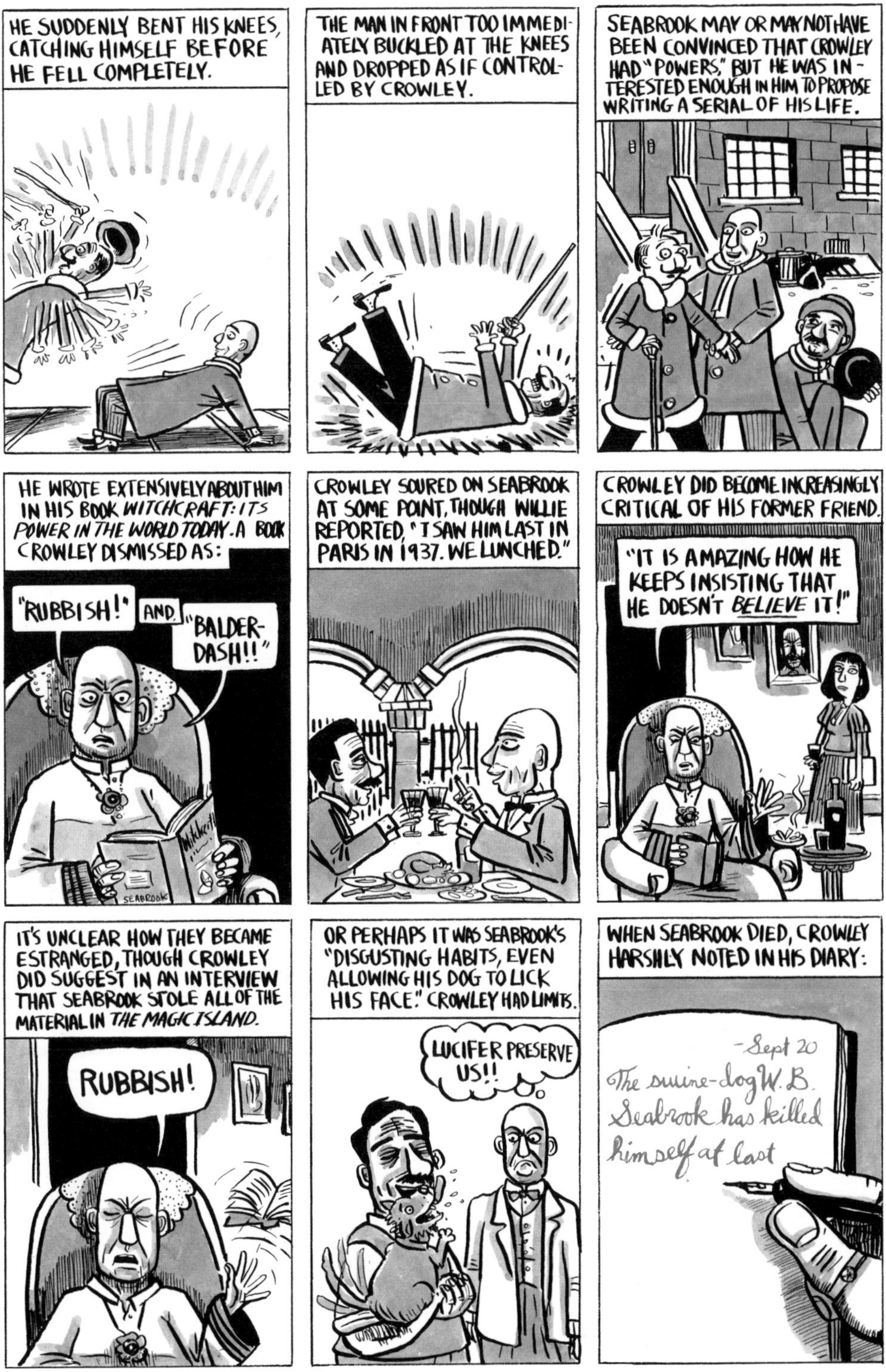
HE SUDDENLY BENT HIS KNEES, CATCHING HIMSELF BEFORE HE FELL COMPLETELY.
THE MAN IN FRONT TOO IMMEDIATELY BUCKLED AT THE KNEES AND DROPPED AS IF CONTROLLED BY CROWLEY.
SEABROOK MAY OR MAY NOT HAVE BEEN CONVINCED THAT CROWLEY HAD "POWERS," BUT HE WAS INTERESTED ENOUGH IN HIM TO PROPOSE WRITING A SERIAL OF HIS LIFE.
HE WROTE EXTENSIVELY ABOUT HIM IN HIS BOOK *WITCHCRAFT: ITS POWER IN THE WORLD TODAY*. A BOOK CROWLEY DISMISSED AS:
"RUBBISH!"
AND
"BALDERDASH!!"
SEABROOK
CROWLEY SOURED ON SEABROOK AT SOME POINT, THOUGH WILLIE REPORTED, "I SAW HIM LAST IN PARIS IN 1937. WE LUNCHED."
CROWLEY DID BECOME INCREASINGLY CRITICAL OF HIS FORMER FRIEND.
"IT IS AMAZING HOW HE KEEPS INSISTING THAT HE DOESN'T BELIEVE IT!"
IT'S UNCLEAR HOW THEY BECAME ESTRANGED, THOUGH CROWLEY DID SUGGEST IN AN INTERVIEW THAT SEABROOK STOLE ALL OF THE MATERIAL IN *THE MAGIC ISLAND*.
RUBBISH!
OR PERHAPS IT WAS SEABROOK'S "DISGUSTING HABITS, EVEN ALLOWING HIS DOG TO LICK HIS FACE." CROWLEY HAD LIMITS.
LUCIFER PRESERVE US!!
WHEN SEABROOK DIED, CROWLEY HARSHLY NOTED IN HIS DIARY:
-Sept 20
The swine-dog W. B. Seabrook has killed himself at last

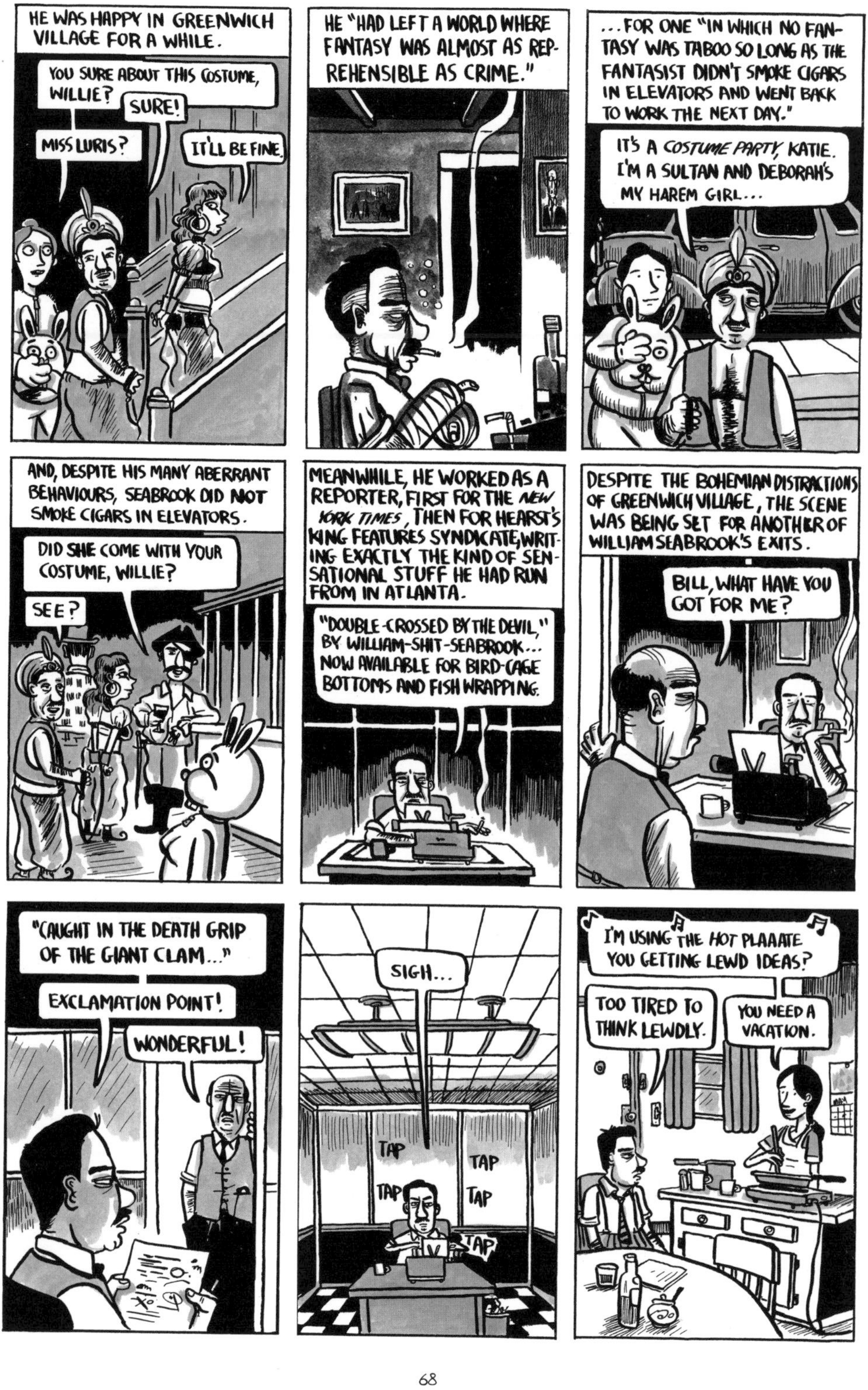
HE WAS HAPPY IN GREENWICH VILLAGE FOR A WHILE.
YOU SURE ABOUT THIS COSTUME, WILLIE?
SURE!
MISS LURIS?
IT'LL BE FINE.
HE "HAD LEFT A WORLD WHERE FANTASY WAS ALMOST AS REPREHENSIBLE AS CRIME."
...FOR ONE "IN WHICH NO FANTASY WAS TABOO SO LONG AS THE FANTASIST DIDN'T SMOKE CIGARS IN ELEVATORS AND WENT BACK TO WORK THE NEXT DAY."
IT'S A COSTUME PARTY, KATIE. I'M A SULTAN AND DEBORAH'S MY HAREM GIRL...
AND, DESPITE HIS MANY ABERRANT BEHAVIOURS, SEABROOK DID NOT SMOKE CIGARS IN ELEVATORS.
DID SHE COME WITH YOUR COSTUME, WILLIE?
SEE?
MEANWHILE, HE WORKED AS A REPORTER, FIRST FOR THE NEW YORK TIMES, THEN FOR HEARST'S KING FEATURES SYNDICATE, WRITING EXACTLY THE KIND OF SENSATIONAL STUFF HE HAD RUN FROM IN ATLANTA.
"DOUBLE-CROSSED BY THE DEVIL," BY WILLIAM-SHIT-SEABROOK... NOW AVAILABLE FOR BIRD-CAGE BOTTOMS AND FISH WRAPPING.
DESPITE THE BOHEMIAN DISTRACTIONS OF GREENWICH VILLAGE, THE SCENE WAS BEING SET FOR ANOTHER OF WILLIAM SEABROOK'S EXITS.
BILL, WHAT HAVE YOU GOT FOR ME?
"CAUGHT IN THE DEATH GRIP OF THE GIANT CLAM..."
EXCLAMATION POINT!
WONDERFUL!
SIGH...
TAP
TAP
TAP
TAP
TAP
I'M USING THE HOT PLAAATE YOU GETTING LEWD IDEAS?
TOO TIRED TO THINK LEWDLY.
YOU NEED A VACATION.

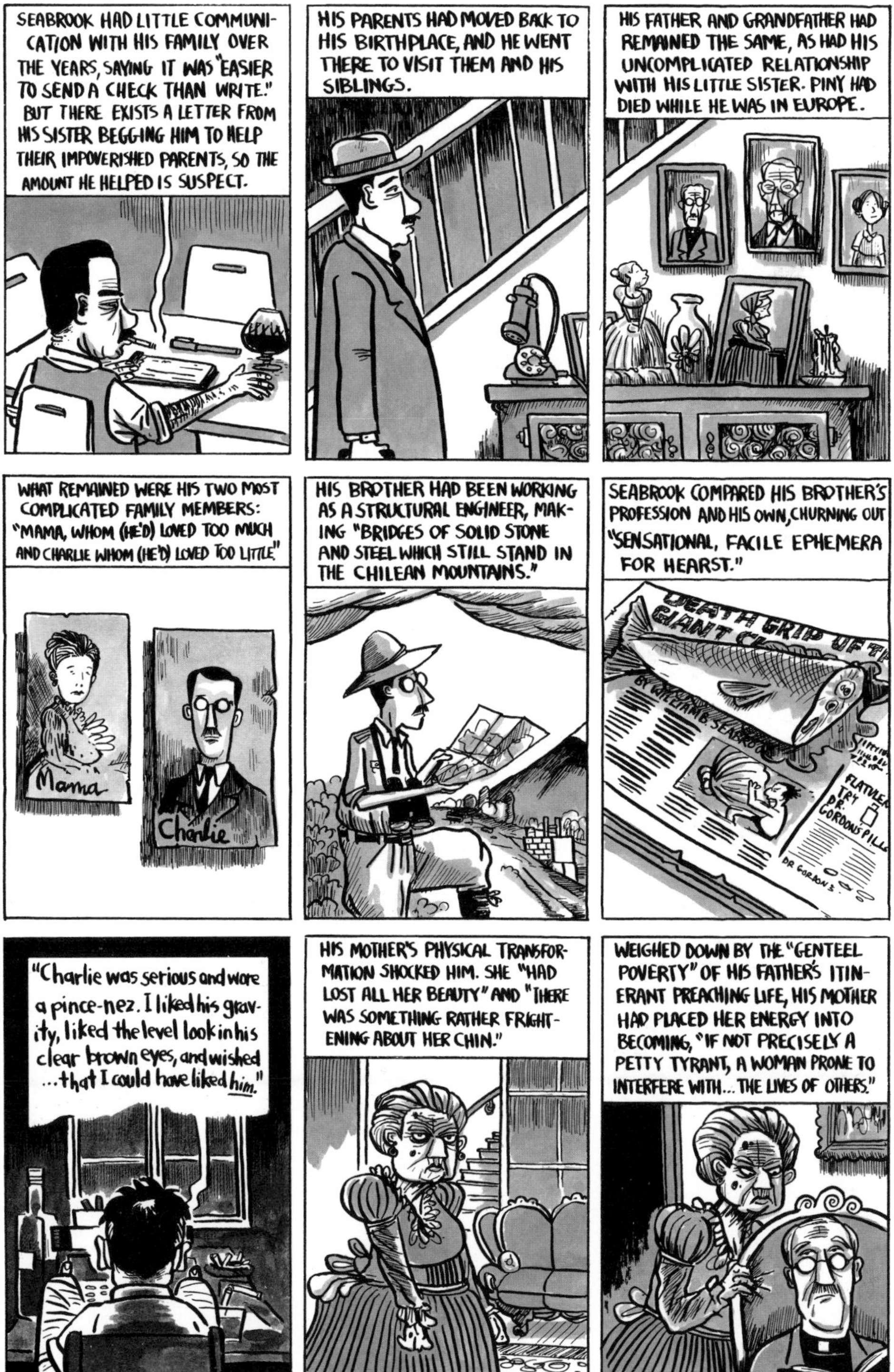
SEABROOK HAD LITTLE COMMUNICATION WITH HIS FAMILY OVER THE YEARS, SAYING IT WAS "EASIER TO SEND A CHECK THAN WRITE." BUT THERE EXISTS A LETTER FROM HIS SISTER BEGGING HIM TO HELP THEIR IMPOVERISHED PARENTS, SO THE AMOUNT HE HELPED IS SUSPECT.
HIS PARENTS HAD MOVED BACK TO HIS BIRTHPLACE, AND HE WENT THERE TO VISIT THEM AND HIS SIBLINGS.
HIS FATHER AND GRANDFATHER HAD REMAINED THE SAME, AS HAD HIS UNCOMPLICATED RELATIONSHIP WITH HIS LITTLE SISTER. PINY HAD DIED WHILE HE WAS IN EUROPE.
WHAT REMAINED WERE HIS TWO MOST COMPLICATED FAMILY MEMBERS: "MAMA, WHOM (HE'D) LOVED TOO MUCH AND CHARLIE WHOM (HE'D) LOVED TOO LITTLE."
Mama
Charlie
HIS BROTHER HAD BEEN WORKING AS A STRUCTURAL ENGINEER, MAKING "BRIDGES OF SOLID STONE AND STEEL WHICH STILL STAND IN THE CHILEAN MOUNTAINS."
SEABROOK COMPARED HIS BROTHER'S PROFESSION AND HIS OWN, CHURNING OUT "SENSATIONAL, FACILE EPHEMERA FOR HEARST."
DEATH GRIP OF THE GIANT
BY WILLIAM B. SEABROOK
TRY DR. GORDON'S PILLS
"Charlie was serious and wore a pince-nez. I liked his gravity, liked the level look in his clear brown eyes, and wished ...that I could have liked him."
HIS MOTHER'S PHYSICAL TRANSFORMATION SHOCKED HIM. SHE "HAD LOST ALL HER BEAUTY" AND "THERE WAS SOMETHING RATHER FRIGHTENING ABOUT HER CHIN."
WEIGHED DOWN BY THE "GENTEEL POVERTY" OF HIS FATHER'S ITINERANT PREACHING LIFE, HIS MOTHER HAD PLACED HER ENERGY INTO BECOMING, "IF NOT PRECISELY A PETTY TYRANT, A WOMAN PRONE TO INTERFERE WITH... THE LIVES OF OTHERS."

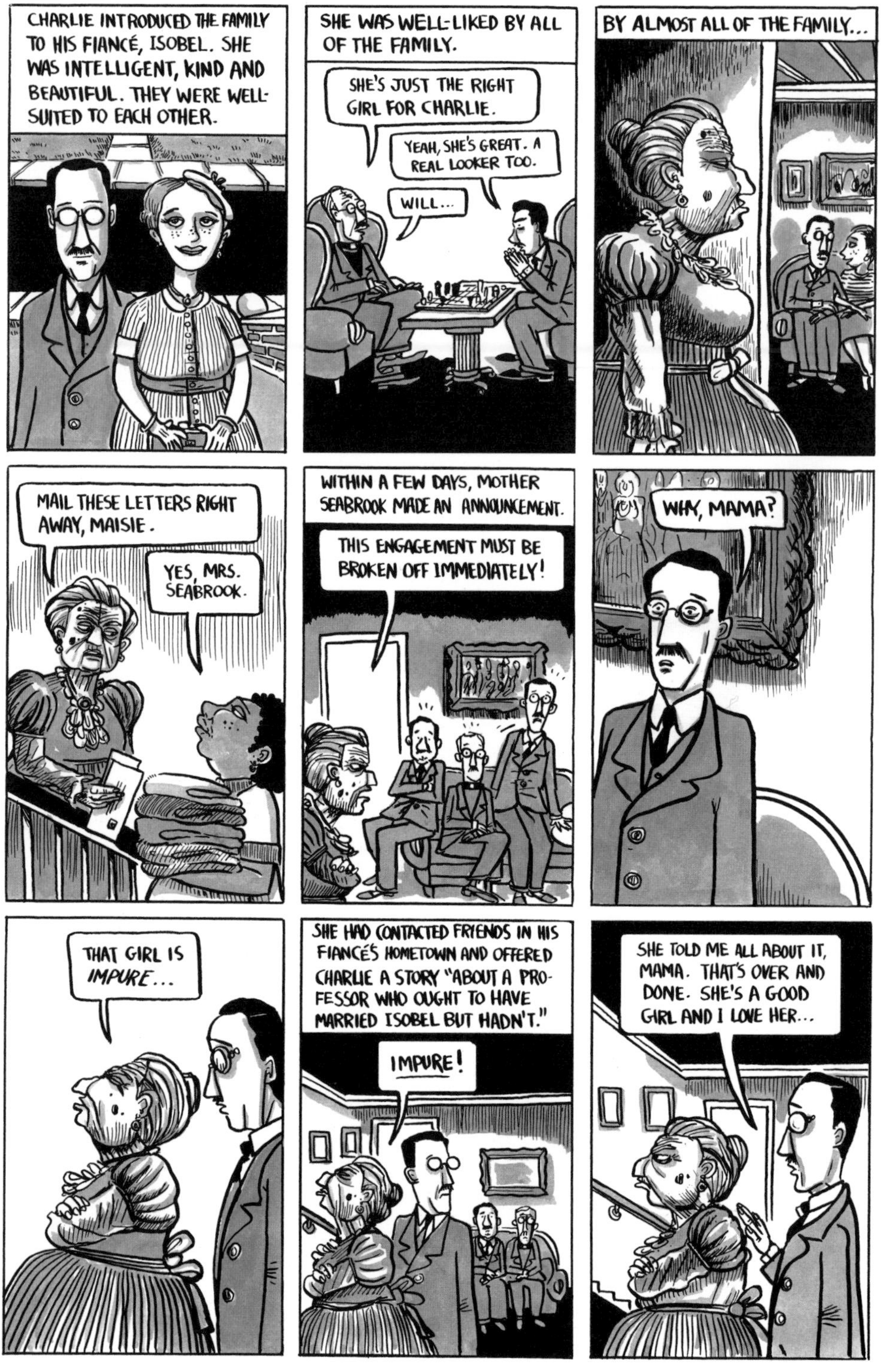
CHARLIE INTRODUCED THE FAMILY TO HIS FIANCÉ, ISOBEL. SHE WAS INTELLIGENT, KIND AND BEAUTIFUL. THEY WERE WELL-SUITED TO EACH OTHER.
SHE WAS WELL-LIKED BY ALL OF THE FAMILY.
SHE'S JUST THE RIGHT GIRL FOR CHARLIE.
YEAH, SHE'S GREAT. A REAL LOOKER TOO.
WILL...
BY ALMOST ALL OF THE FAMILY...
MAIL THESE LETTERS RIGHT AWAY, MAISIE.
YES, MRS. SEABROOK.
WITHIN A FEW DAYS, MOTHER SEABROOK MADE AN ANNOUNCEMENT.
THIS ENGAGEMENT MUST BE BROKEN OFF IMMEDIATELY!
WHY, MAMA?
THAT GIRL IS *IMPURE*...
SHE HAD CONTACTED FRIENDS IN HIS FIANCÉ'S HOMETOWN AND OFFERED CHARLIE A STORY "ABOUT A PROFESSOR WHO OUGHT TO HAVE MARRIED ISOBEL BUT HADN'T."
IMPURE!
SHE TOLD ME ALL ABOUT IT, MAMA. THAT'S OVER AND DONE. SHE'S A GOOD GIRL AND I LOVE HER...

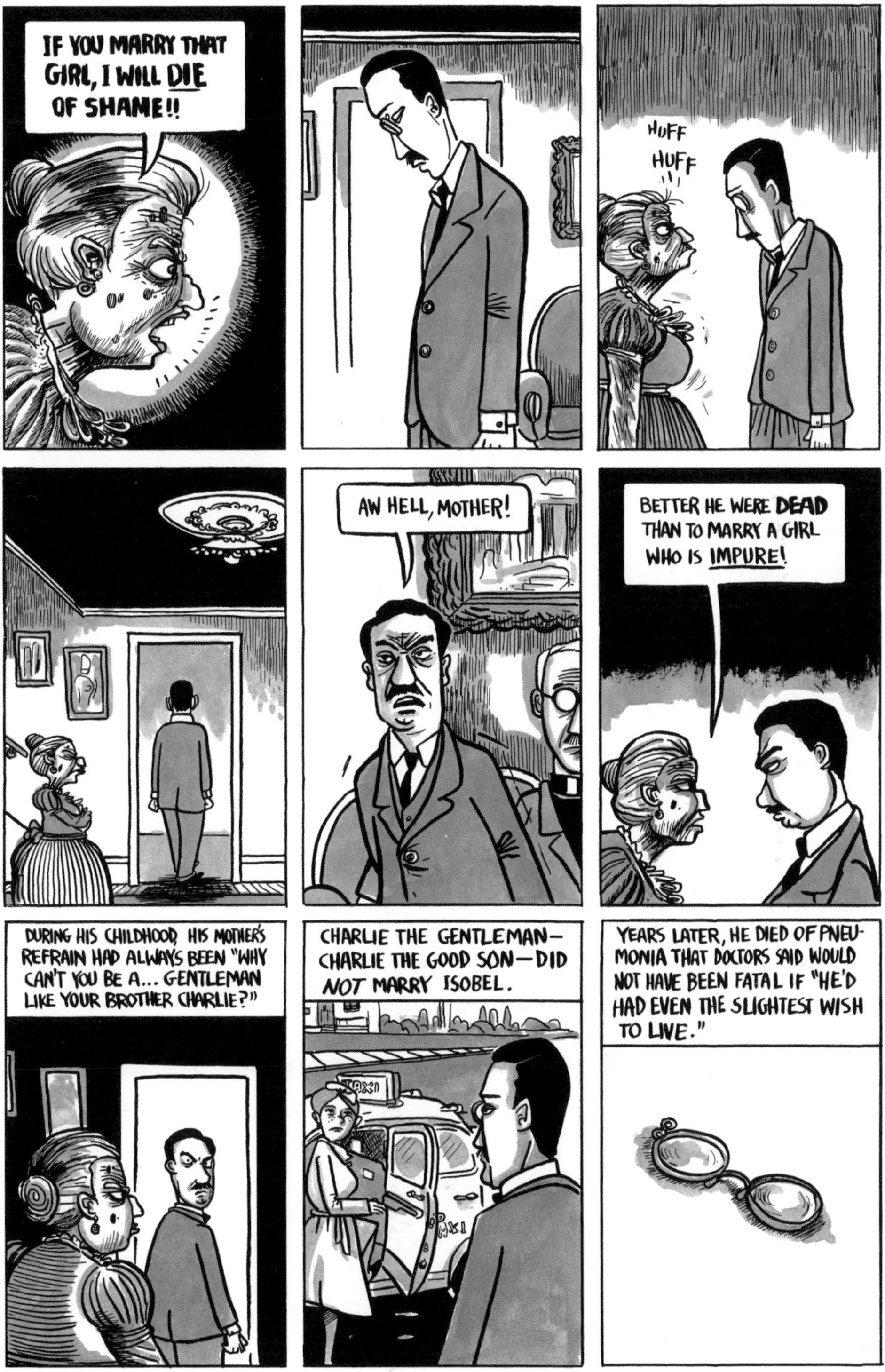
IF YOU MARRY THAT GIRL, I WILL DIE OF SHAME!!
HUFF
HUFF
AW HELL, MOTHER!
BETTER HE WERE DEAD THAN TO MARRY A GIRL WHO IS IMPURE!
DURING HIS CHILDHOOD, HIS MOTHER'S REFRAIN HAD ALWAYS BEEN "WHY CAN'T YOU BE A... GENTLEMAN LIKE YOUR BROTHER CHARLIE?"
CHARLIE THE GENTLEMAN— CHARLIE THE GOOD SON—DID NOT MARRY ISOBEL.
YEARS LATER, HE DIED OF PNEUMONIA THAT DOCTORS SAID WOULD NOT HAVE BEEN FATAL IF "HE'D HAD EVEN THE SLIGHTEST WISH TO LIVE."

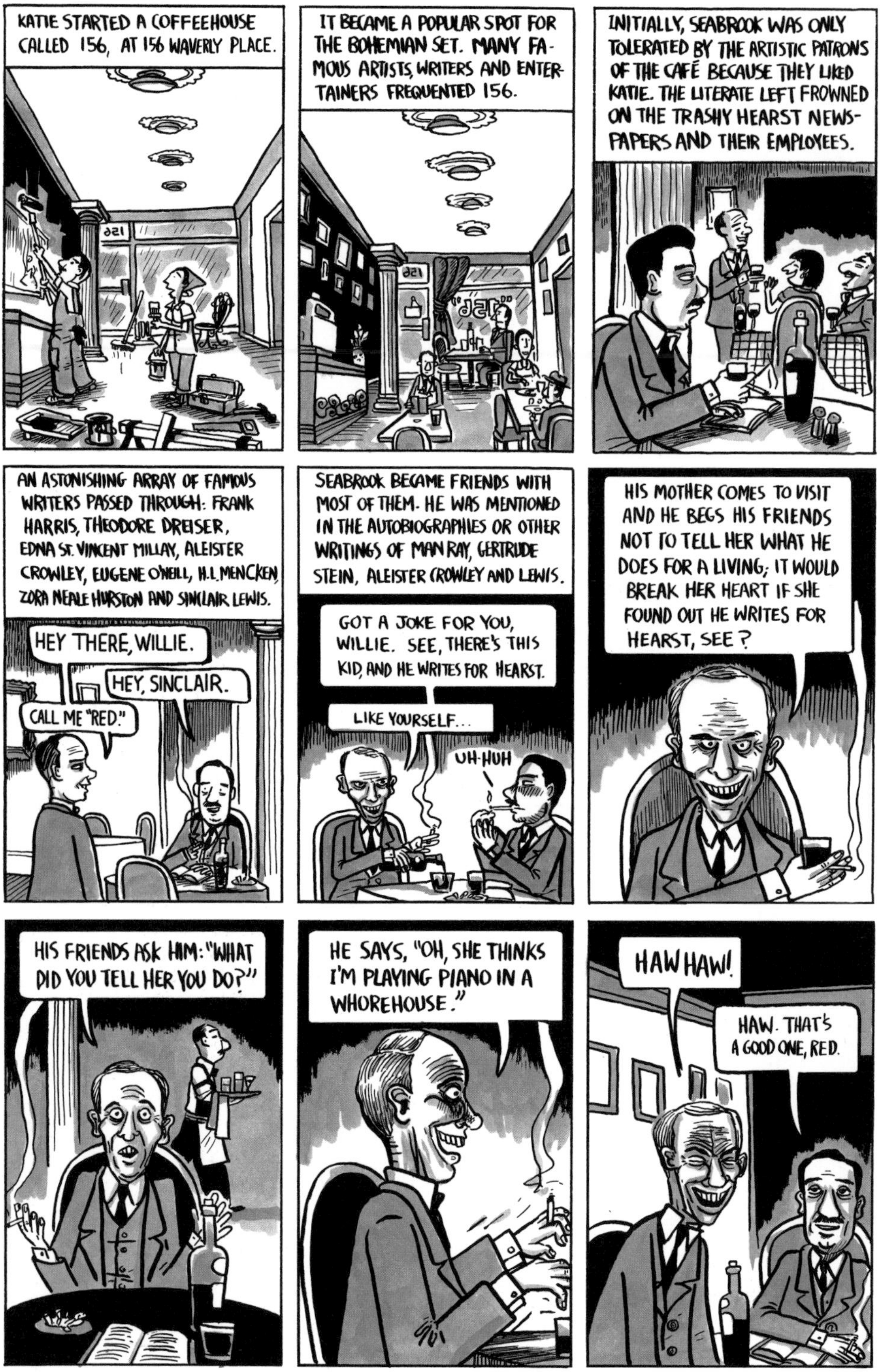
KATIE STARTED A COFFEEHOUSE CALLED 156, AT 156 WAVERLY PLACE.
IT BECAME A POPULAR SPOT FOR THE BOHEMIAN SET. MANY FAMOUS ARTISTS, WRITERS AND ENTERTAINERS FREQUENTED 156.
INITIALLY, SEABROOK WAS ONLY TOLERATED BY THE ARTISTIC PATRONS OF THE CAFÉ BECAUSE THEY LIKED KATIE. THE LITERATE LEFT FROWNED ON THE TRASHY HEARST NEWSPAPERS AND THEIR EMPLOYEES.
AN ASTONISHING ARRAY OF FAMOUS WRITERS PASSED THROUGH: FRANK HARRIS, THEODORE DREISER, EDNA ST. VINCENT MILLAY, ALEISTER CROWLEY, EUGENE O'NEILL, H.L. MENCKEN, ZORA NEALE HURSTON AND SINCLAIR LEWIS.
HEY THERE, WILLIE.
HEY, SINCLAIR.
CALL ME "RED."
SEABROOK BECAME FRIENDS WITH MOST OF THEM. HE WAS MENTIONED IN THE AUTOBIOGRAPHIES OR OTHER WRITINGS OF MAN RAY, GERTRUDE STEIN, ALEISTER CROWLEY AND LEWIS.
GOT A JOKE FOR YOU, WILLIE. SEE, THERE'S THIS KID, AND HE WRITES FOR HEARST.
LIKE YOURSELF...
UH-HUH
HIS MOTHER COMES TO VISIT AND HE BEGS HIS FRIENDS NOT TO TELL HER WHAT HE DOES FOR A LIVING; IT WOULD BREAK HER HEART IF SHE FOUND OUT HE WRITES FOR HEARST, SEE?
HIS FRIENDS ASK HIM: "WHAT DID YOU TELL HER YOU DO?"
HE SAYS, "OH, SHE THINKS I'M PLAYING PIANO IN A WHOREHOUSE."
HAW HAW!
HAW. THAT'S A GOOD ONE, RED.

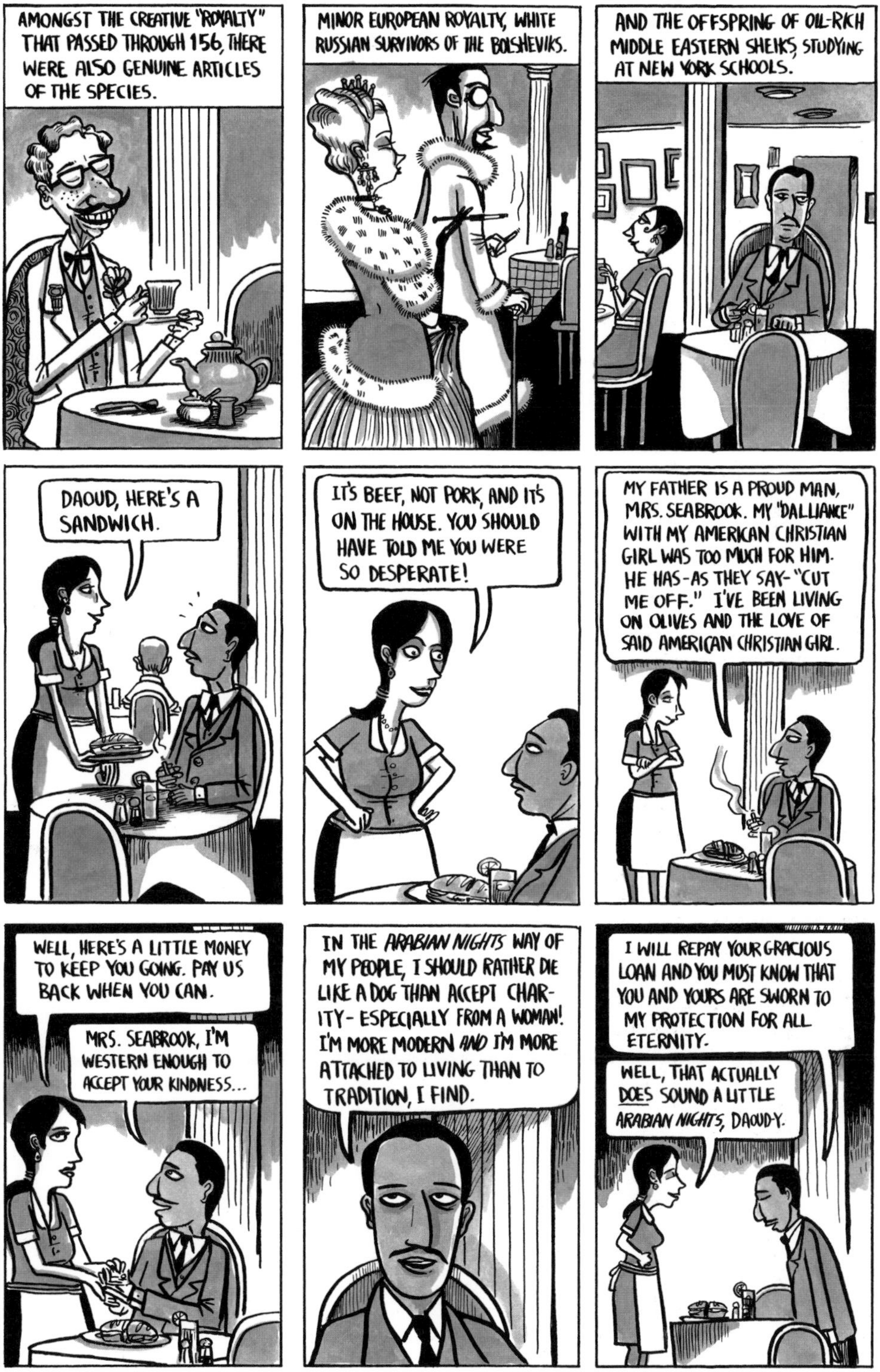
AMONGST THE CREATIVE "ROYALTY" THAT PASSED THROUGH 156, THERE WERE ALSO GENUINE ARTICLES OF THE SPECIES.
MINOR EUROPEAN ROYALTY, WHITE RUSSIAN SURVIVORS OF THE BOLSHEVIKS.
AND THE OFFSPRING OF OIL-RICH MIDDLE EASTERN SHEIKS, STUDYING AT NEW YORK SCHOOLS.
DAOUD, HERE'S A SANDWICH.
IT'S BEEF, NOT PORK, AND IT'S ON THE HOUSE. YOU SHOULD HAVE TOLD ME YOU WERE SO DESPERATE!
MY FATHER IS A PROUD MAN, MRS. SEABROOK. MY "DALLIANCE" WITH MY AMERICAN CHRISTIAN GIRL WAS TOO MUCH FOR HIM. HE HAS-AS THEY SAY-"CUT ME OFF." I'VE BEEN LIVING ON OLIVES AND THE LOVE OF SAID AMERICAN CHRISTIAN GIRL.
WELL, HERE'S A LITTLE MONEY TO KEEP YOU GOING. PAY US BACK WHEN YOU CAN.
MRS. SEABROOK, I'M WESTERN ENOUGH TO ACCEPT YOUR KINDNESS...
IN THE ARABIAN NIGHTS WAY OF MY PEOPLE, I SHOULD RATHER DIE LIKE A DOG THAN ACCEPT CHARITY- ESPECIALLY FROM A WOMAN! I'M MORE MODERN AND I'M MORE ATTACHED TO LIVING THAN TO TRADITION, I FIND.
I WILL REPAY YOUR GRACIOUS LOAN AND YOU MUST KNOW THAT YOU AND YOURS ARE SWORN TO MY PROTECTION FOR ALL ETERNITY.
WELL, THAT ACTUALLY DOES SOUND A LITTLE ARABIAN NIGHTS, DAOUD-Y.

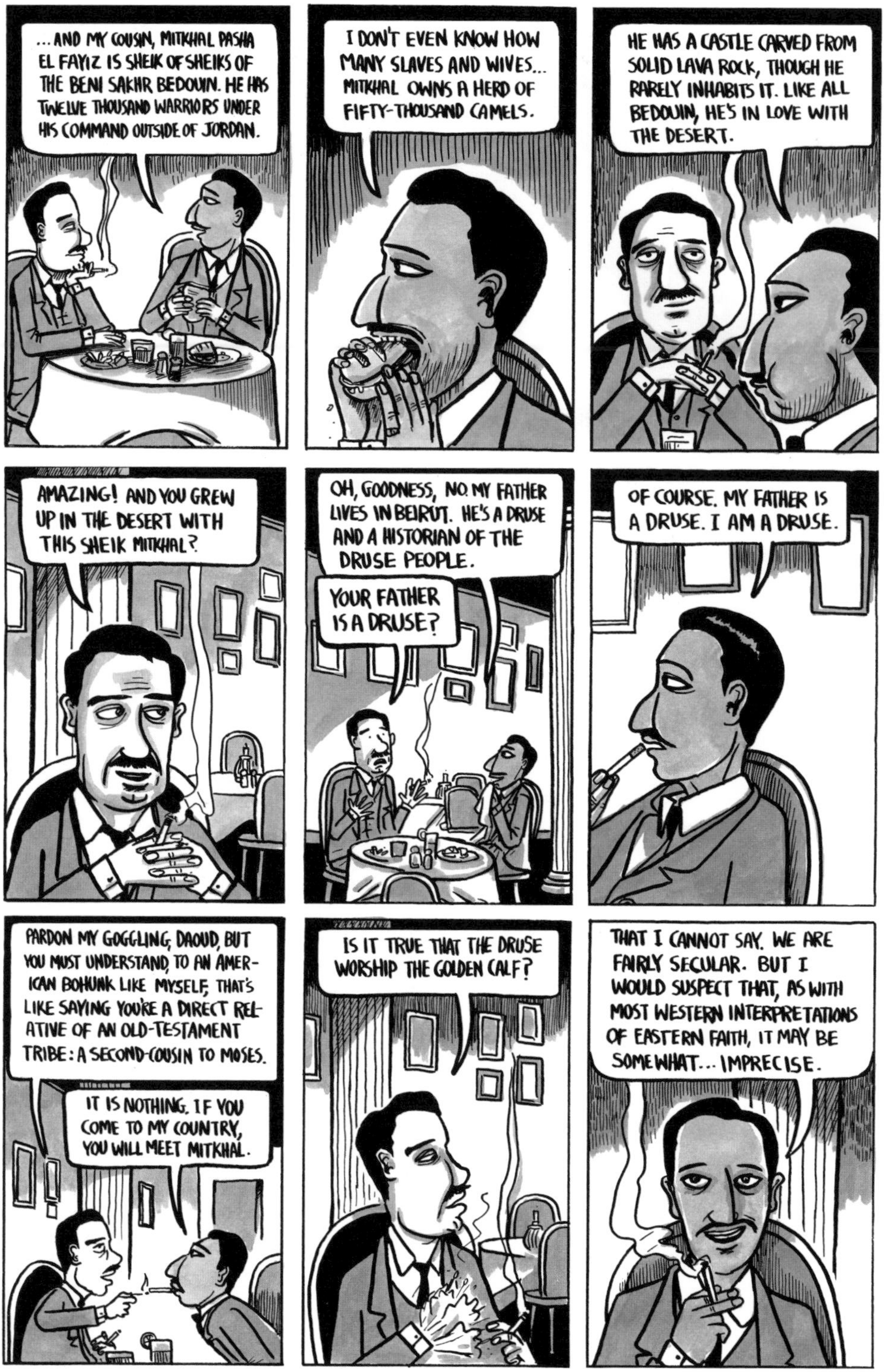
...AND MY COUSIN, MITKHAL PASHA EL FAYIZ IS SHEIK OF SHEIKS OF THE BENI SAKHR BEDOUIN. HE HAS TWELVE THOUSAND WARRIORS UNDER HIS COMMAND OUTSIDE OF JORDAN.
I DON'T EVEN KNOW HOW MANY SLAVES AND WIVES... MITKHAL OWNS A HERD OF FIFTY-THOUSAND CAMELS.
HE HAS A CASTLE CARVED FROM SOLID LAVA ROCK, THOUGH HE RARELY INHABITS IT. LIKE ALL BEDOUIN, HE'S IN LOVE WITH THE DESERT.
AMAZING! AND YOU GREW UP IN THE DESERT WITH THIS SHEIK MITKHAL?
OH, GOODNESS, NO. MY FATHER LIVES IN BEIRUT. HE'S A DRUSE AND A HISTORIAN OF THE DRUSE PEOPLE.
YOUR FATHER IS A DRUSE?
OF COURSE. MY FATHER IS A DRUSE. I AM A DRUSE.
PARDON MY GOGGLING, DAOUD, BUT YOU MUST UNDERSTAND, TO AN AMERICAN BOHUNK LIKE MYSELF, THAT'S LIKE SAYING YOU'RE A DIRECT RELATIVE OF AN OLD-TESTAMENT TRIBE: A SECOND-COUSIN TO MOSES.
IT IS NOTHING. IF YOU COME TO MY COUNTRY, YOU WILL MEET MITKHAL.
IS IT TRUE THAT THE DRUSE WORSHIP THE GOLDEN CALF?
THAT I CANNOT SAY. WE ARE FAIRLY SECULAR. BUT I WOULD SUSPECT THAT, AS WITH MOST WESTERN INTERPRETATIONS OF EASTERN FAITH, IT MAY BE SOMEWHAT... IMPRECISE.

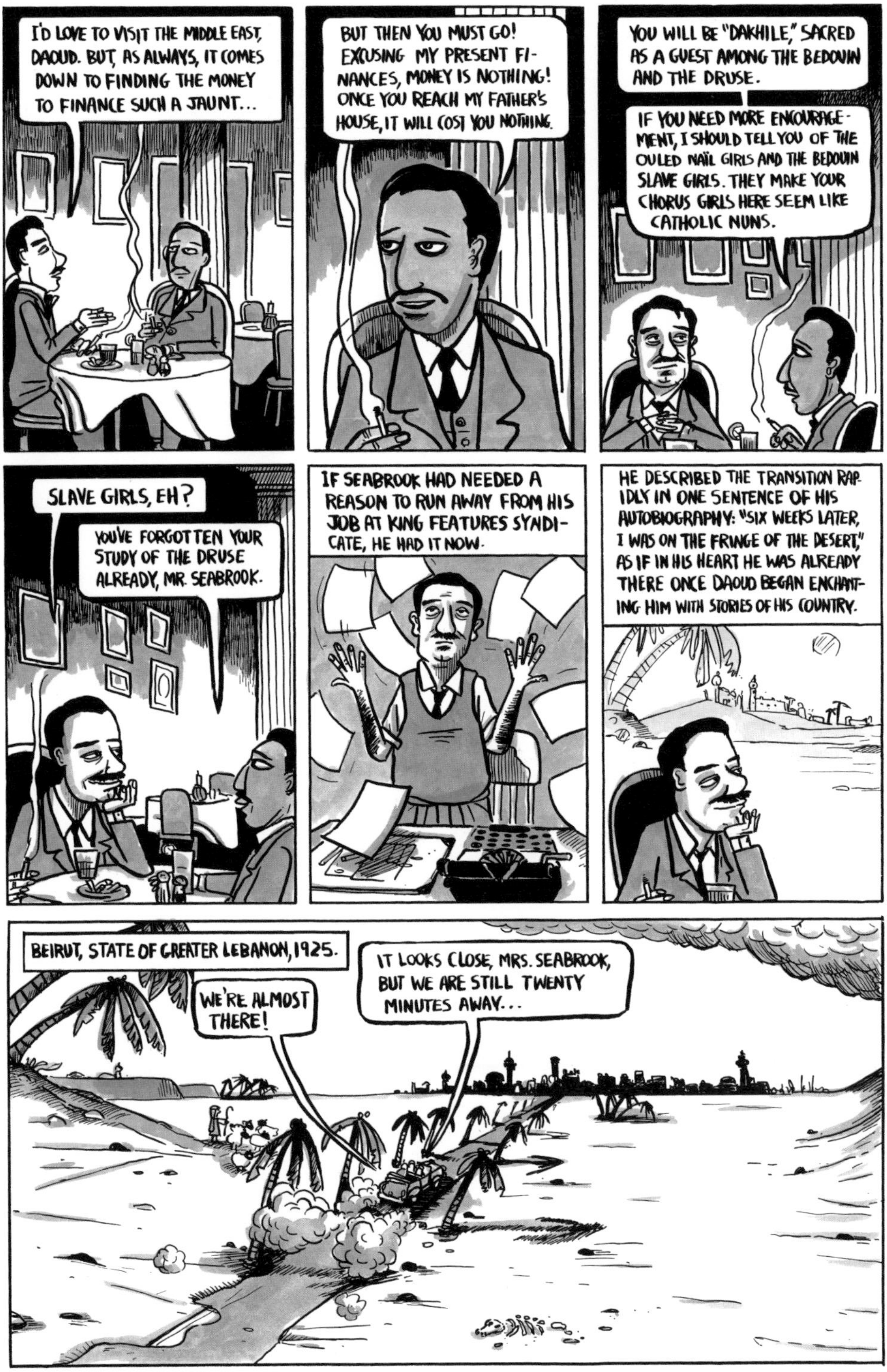
I'D LOVE TO VISIT THE MIDDLE EAST, DAOUD. BUT, AS ALWAYS, IT COMES DOWN TO FINDING THE MONEY TO FINANCE SUCH A JAUNT...
BUT THEN YOU MUST GO! EXCUSING MY PRESENT FINANCES, MONEY IS NOTHING! ONCE YOU REACH MY FATHER'S HOUSE, IT WILL COST YOU NOTHING.
YOU WILL BE "DAKHILE," SACRED AS A GUEST AMONG THE BEDOUIN AND THE DRUSE.
IF YOU NEED MORE ENCOURAGEMENT, I SHOULD TELL YOU OF THE OULED NAÏL GIRLS AND THE BEDOUIN SLAVE GIRLS. THEY MAKE YOUR CHORUS GIRLS HERE SEEM LIKE CATHOLIC NUNS.
SLAVE GIRLS, EH?
YOU'VE FORGOTTEN YOUR STUDY OF THE DRUSE ALREADY, MR. SEABROOK.
IF SEABROOK HAD NEEDED A REASON TO RUN AWAY FROM HIS JOB AT KING FEATURES SYNDICATE, HE HAD IT NOW.
HE DESCRIBED THE TRANSITION RAPIDLY IN ONE SENTENCE OF HIS AUTOBIOGRAPHY: "SIX WEEKS LATER, I WAS ON THE FRINGE OF THE DESERT," AS IF IN HIS HEART HE WAS ALREADY THERE ONCE DAOUD BEGAN ENCHANTING HIM WITH STORIES OF HIS COUNTRY.
BEIRUT, STATE OF GREATER LEBANON, 1925.
WE'RE ALMOST THERE!
IT LOOKS CLOSE, MRS. SEABROOK, BUT WE ARE STILL TWENTY MINUTES AWAY...

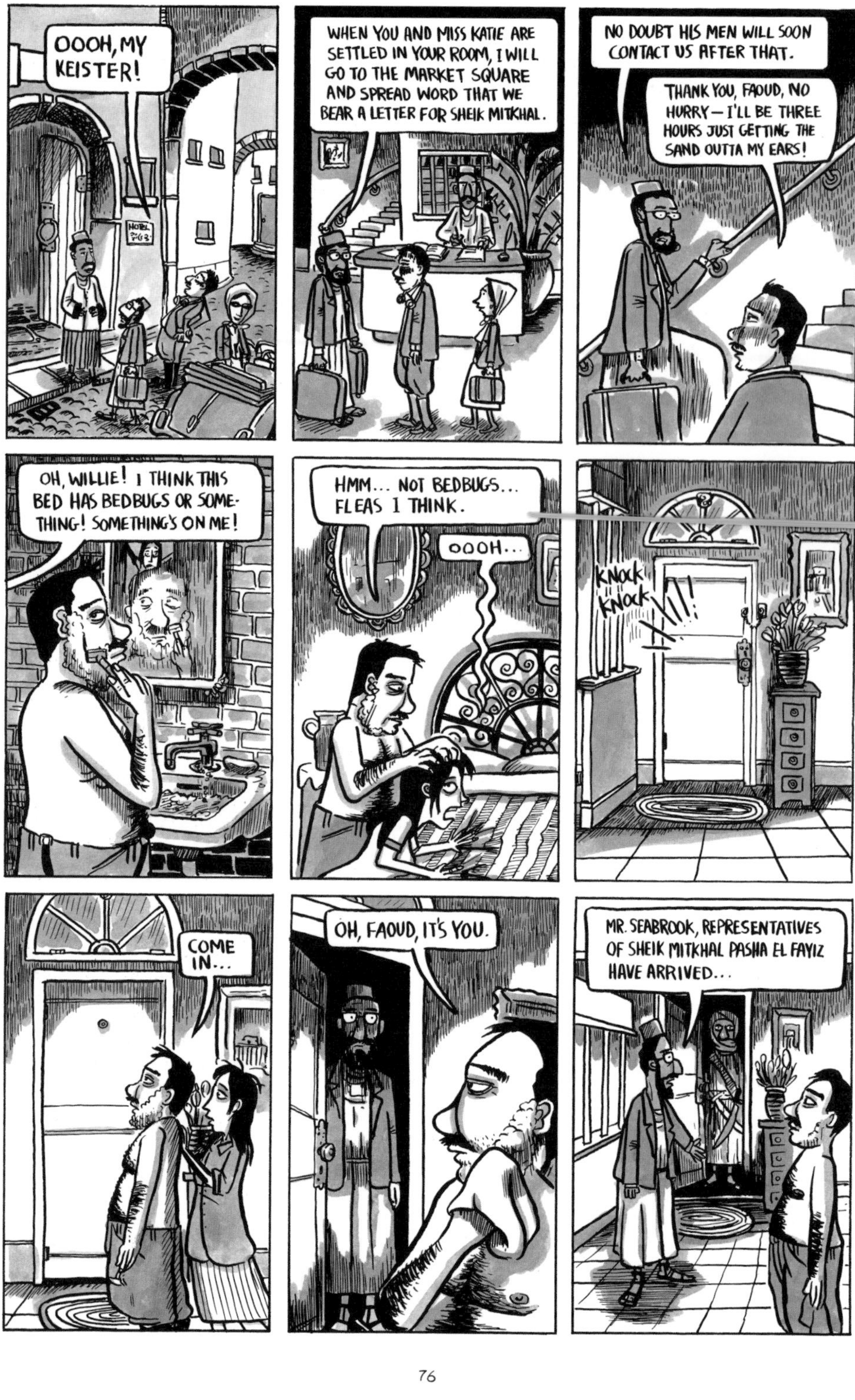
OOOH, MY KEISTER!
HOTEL
WHEN YOU AND MISS KATIE ARE SETTLED IN YOUR ROOM, I WILL GO TO THE MARKET SQUARE AND SPREAD WORD THAT WE BEAR A LETTER FOR SHEIK MITKHAL.
NO DOUBT HIS MEN WILL SOON CONTACT US AFTER THAT.
THANK YOU, FAOUD, NO HURRY — I'LL BE THREE HOURS JUST GETTING THE SAND OUTTA MY EARS!
OH, WILLIE! I THINK THIS BED HAS BEDBUGS OR SOMETHING! SOMETHING'S ON ME!
HMM... NOT BEDBUGS... FLEAS I THINK.
OOOH...
KNOCK KNOCK
COME IN...
OH, FAOUD, IT'S YOU.
MR. SEABROOK, REPRESENTATIVES OF SHEIK MITKHAL PASHA EL FAYIZ HAVE ARRIVED...

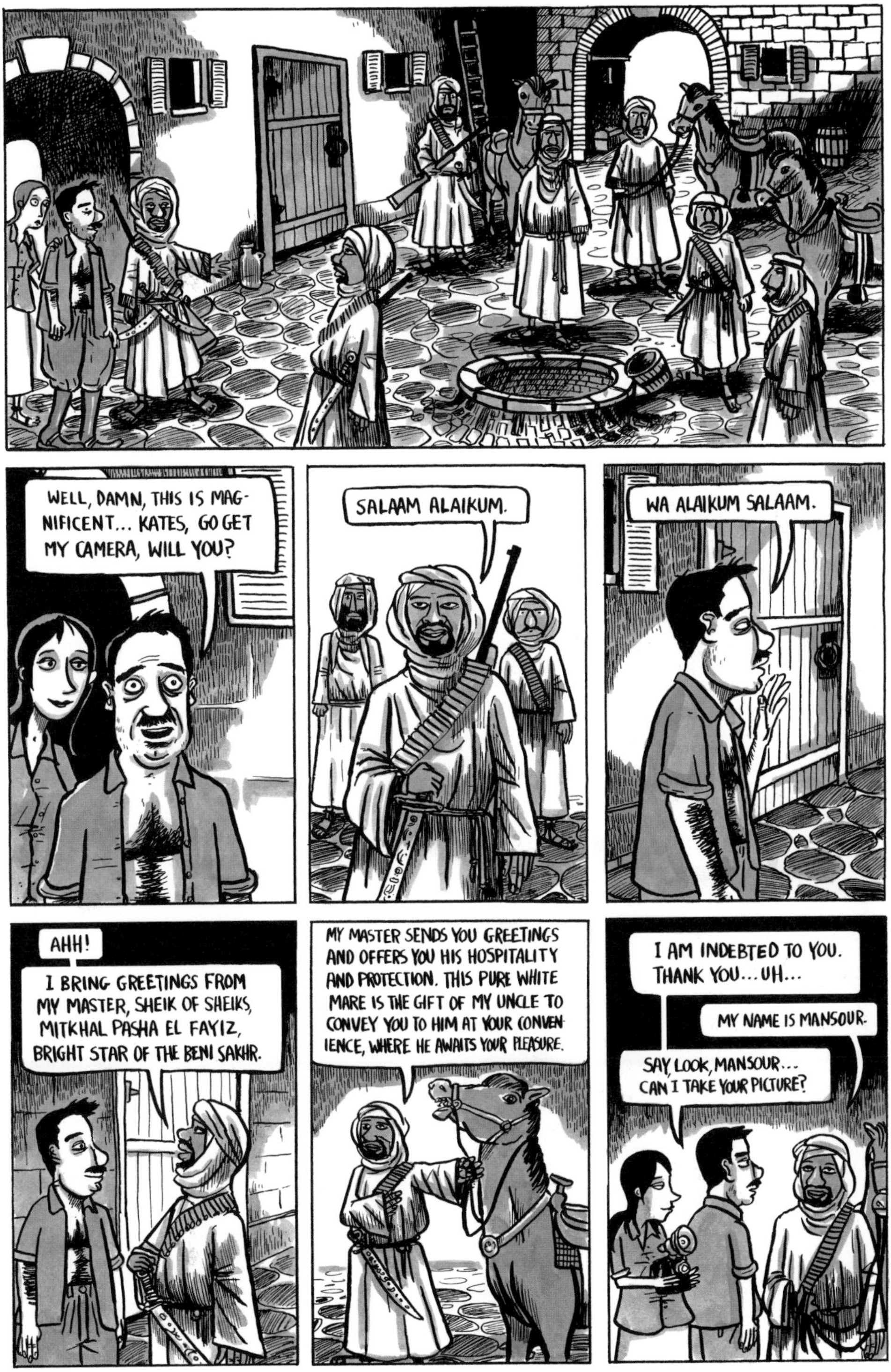
WELL, DAMN, THIS IS MAGNIFICENT... KATES, GO GET MY CAMERA, WILL YOU?
SALAAM ALAIKUM.
WA ALAIKUM SALAAM.
AHH!
I BRING GREETINGS FROM MY MASTER, SHEIK OF SHEIKS, MITKHAL PASHA EL FAYIZ, BRIGHT STAR OF THE BENI SAKHR.
MY MASTER SENDS YOU GREETINGS AND OFFERS YOU HIS HOSPITALITY AND PROTECTION. THIS PURE WHITE MARE IS THE GIFT OF MY UNCLE TO CONVEY YOU TO HIM AT YOUR CONVENIENCE, WHERE HE AWAITS YOUR PLEASURE.
I AM INDEBTED TO YOU. THANK YOU... UH...
MY NAME IS MANSOUR.
SAY, LOOK, MANSOUR... CAN I TAKE YOUR PICTURE?

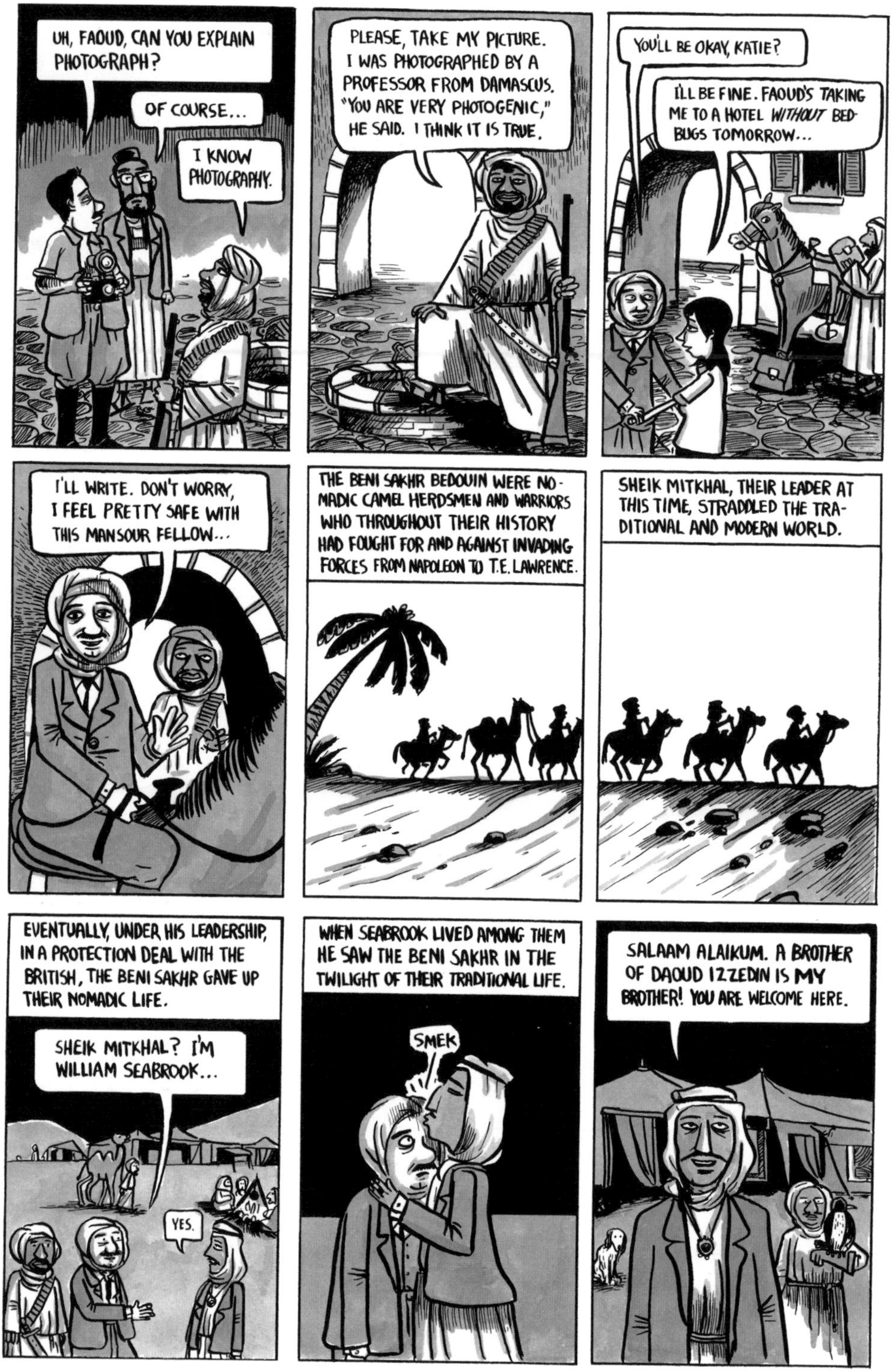
UH, FAOUD, CAN YOU EXPLAIN PHOTOGRAPH?
OF COURSE...
I KNOW PHOTOGRAPHY.
PLEASE, TAKE MY PICTURE. I WAS PHOTOGRAPHED BY A PROFESSOR FROM DAMASCUS. "YOU ARE VERY PHOTOGENIC," HE SAID. I THINK IT IS TRUE.
YOU'LL BE OKAY, KATIE?
I'LL BE FINE. FAOUD'S TAKING ME TO A HOTEL WITHOUT BED-BUGS TOMORROW...
I'LL WRITE. DON'T WORRY, I FEEL PRETTY SAFE WITH THIS MANSOUR FELLOW...
THE BENI SAKHR BEDOUIN WERE NOMADIC CAMEL HERDSMEN AND WARRIORS WHO THROUGHOUT THEIR HISTORY HAD FOUGHT FOR AND AGAINST INVADING FORCES FROM NAPOLEON TO T.E. LAWRENCE.
SHEIK MITKHAL, THEIR LEADER AT THIS TIME, STRADDLED THE TRADITIONAL AND MODERN WORLD.
EVENTUALLY, UNDER HIS LEADERSHIP, IN A PROTECTION DEAL WITH THE BRITISH, THE BENI SAKHR GAVE UP THEIR NOMADIC LIFE.
SHEIK MITKHAL? I'M WILLIAM SEABROOK...
YES.
WHEN SEABROOK LIVED AMONG THEM HE SAW THE BENI SAKHR IN THE TWILIGHT OF THEIR TRADITIONAL LIFE.
SMEK
SALAAM ALAIKUM. A BROTHER OF DAOUD IZZEDIN IS MY BROTHER! YOU ARE WELCOME HERE.

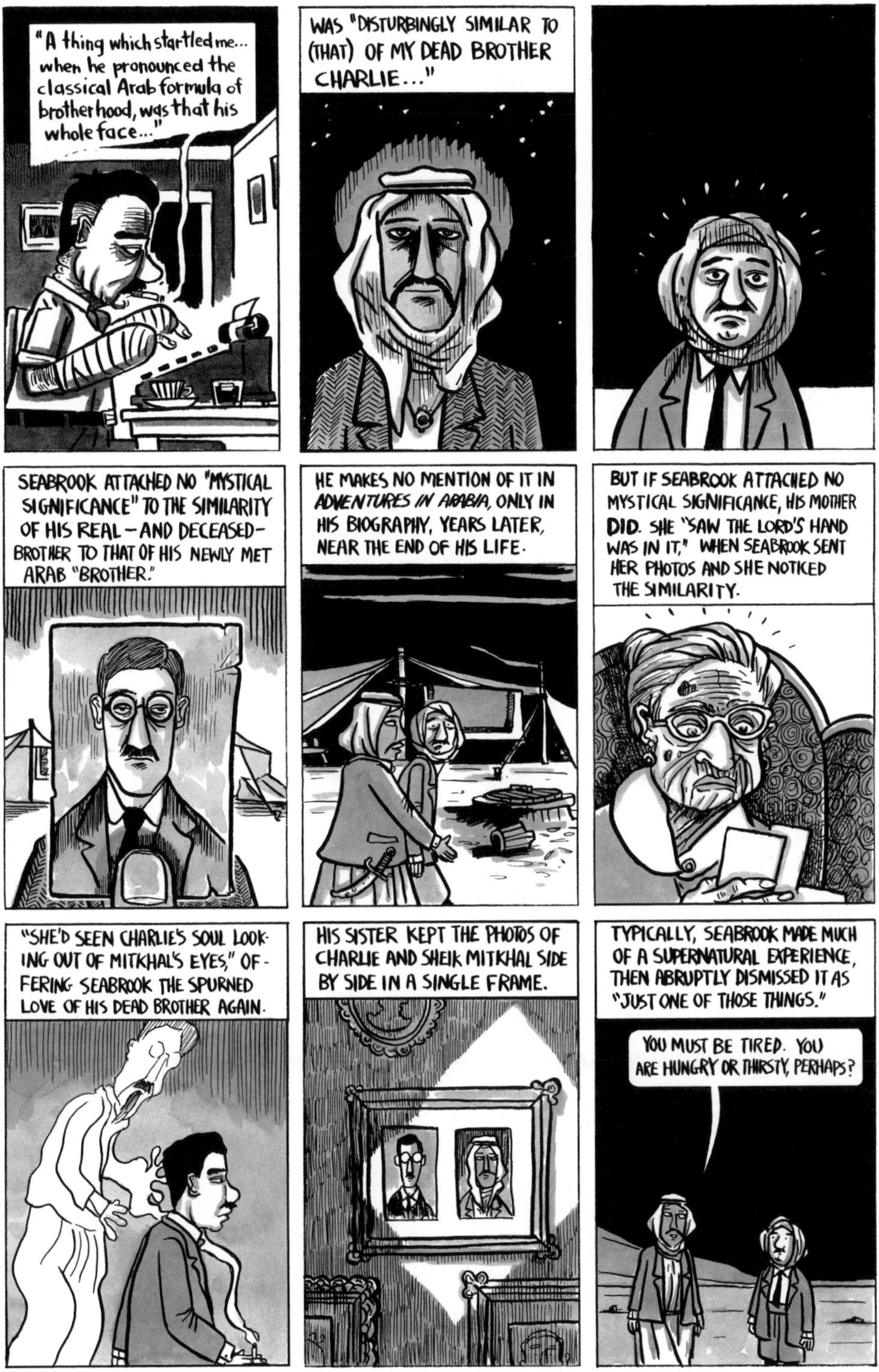
"A thing which startled me... when he pronounced the classical Arab formula of brotherhood, was that his whole face..."
WAS "DISTURBINGLY SIMILAR TO (THAT) OF MY DEAD BROTHER CHARLIE..."
SEABROOK ATTACHED NO "MYSTICAL SIGNIFICANCE" TO THE SIMILARITY OF HIS REAL – AND DECEASED – BROTHER TO THAT OF HIS NEWLY MET ARAB "BROTHER."
HE MAKES NO MENTION OF IT IN *ADVENTURES IN ARABIA*, ONLY IN HIS BIOGRAPHY, YEARS LATER, NEAR THE END OF HIS LIFE.
BUT IF SEABROOK ATTACHED NO MYSTICAL SIGNIFICANCE, HIS MOTHER **DID**. SHE "SAW THE LORD'S HAND WAS IN IT," WHEN SEABROOK SENT HER PHOTOS AND SHE NOTICED THE SIMILARITY.
"SHE'D SEEN CHARLIE'S SOUL LOOKING OUT OF MITKHAL'S EYES," OFFERING SEABROOK THE SPURNED LOVE OF HIS DEAD BROTHER AGAIN.
HIS SISTER KEPT THE PHOTOS OF CHARLIE AND SHEIK MITKHAL SIDE BY SIDE IN A SINGLE FRAME.
TYPICALLY, SEABROOK MADE MUCH OF A SUPERNATURAL EXPERIENCE, THEN ABRUPTLY DISMISSED IT AS "JUST ONE OF THOSE THINGS."
YOU MUST BE TIRED. YOU ARE HUNGRY OR THIRSTY, PERHAPS?

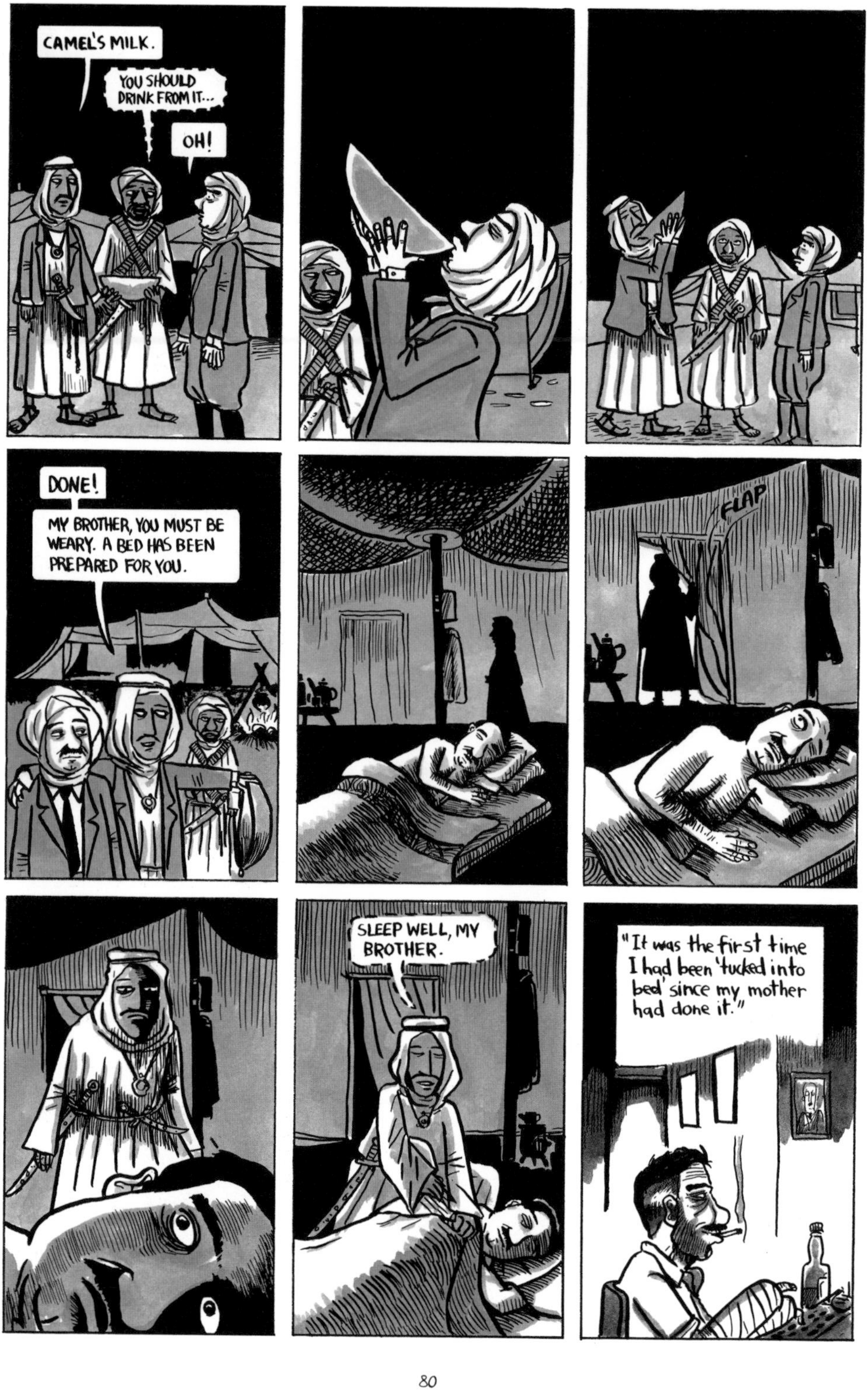
CAMEL'S MILK.
YOU SHOULD DRINK FROM IT...
OH!
DONE!
MY BROTHER, YOU MUST BE WEARY. A BED HAS BEEN PREPARED FOR YOU.
FLAP
SLEEP WELL, MY BROTHER.
"It was the first time I had been 'tucked into bed' since my mother had done it."

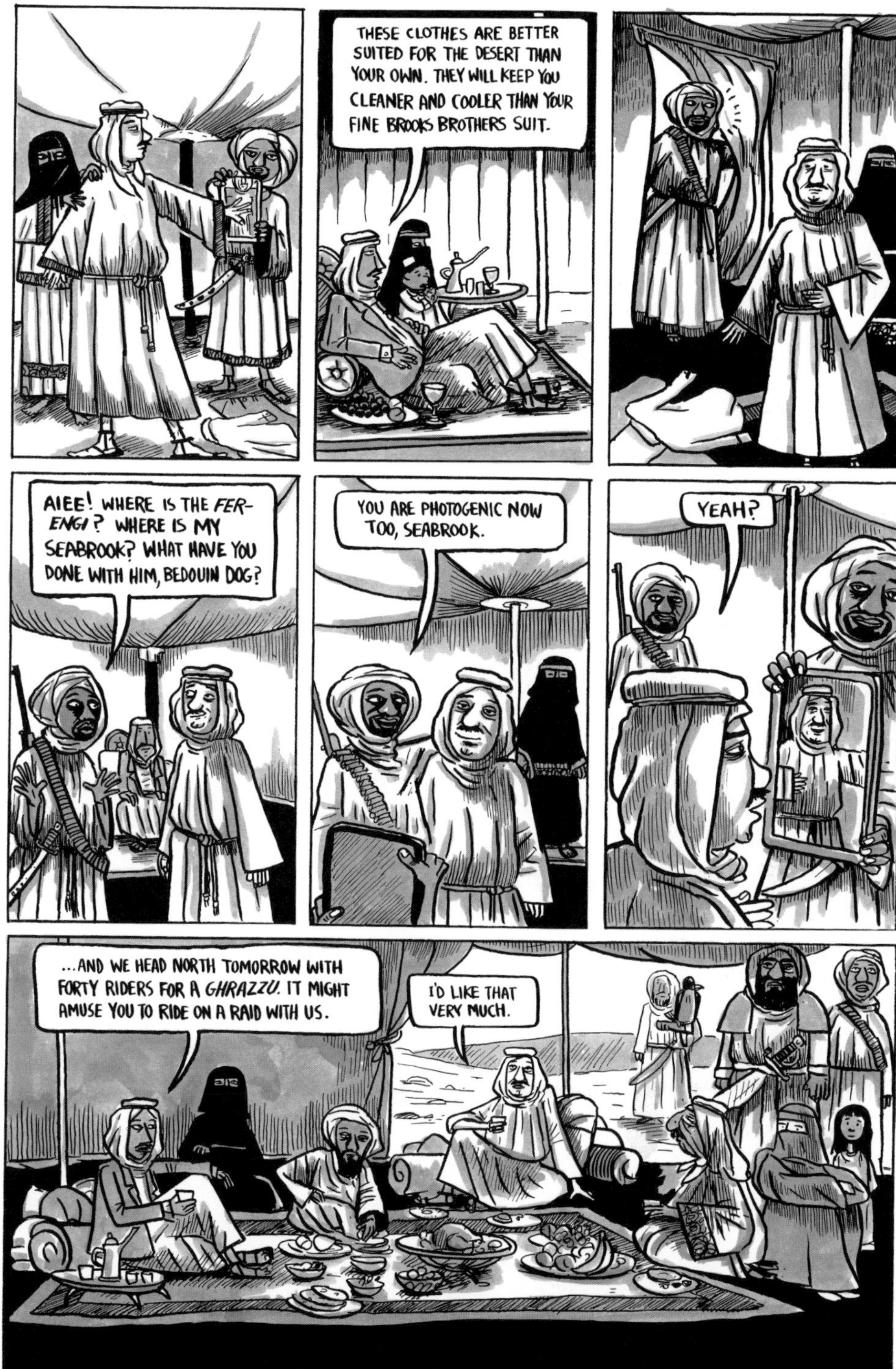
THESE CLOTHES ARE BETTER SUITED FOR THE DESERT THAN YOUR OWN. THEY WILL KEEP YOU CLEANER AND COOLER THAN YOUR FINE BROOKS BROTHERS SUIT.
AIEE! WHERE IS THE *FERENGI*? WHERE IS MY SEABROOK? WHAT HAVE YOU DONE WITH HIM, BEDOUIN DOG?
YOU ARE PHOTOGENIC NOW TOO, SEABROOK.
YEAH?
...AND WE HEAD NORTH TOMORROW WITH FORTY RIDERS FOR A *GHRAZZU*. IT MIGHT AMUSE YOU TO RIDE ON A RAID WITH US.
I'D LIKE THAT VERY MUCH.

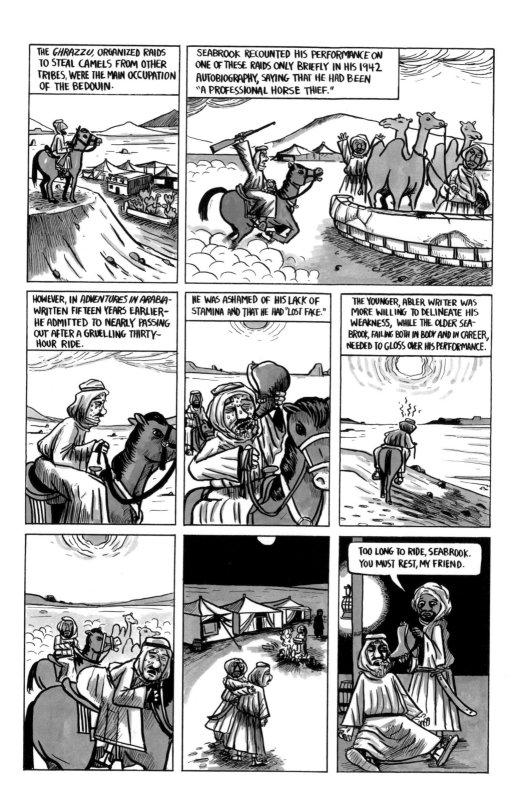

THE *GHRAZZU*, ORGANIZED RAIDS TO STEAL CAMELS FROM OTHER TRIBES, WERE THE MAIN OCCUPATION OF THE BEDOUIN.

SEABROOK RECOUNTED HIS PERFORMANCE ON ONE OF THESE RAIDS ONLY BRIEFLY IN HIS 1942 AUTOBIOGRAPHY, SAYING THAT HE HAD BEEN "A PROFESSIONAL HORSE THIEF."

HOWEVER, IN *ADVENTURES IN ARABIA*—WRITTEN FIFTEEN YEARS EARLIER—HE ADMITTED TO NEARLY PASSING OUT AFTER A GRUELLING THIRTY-HOUR RIDE.

HE WAS ASHAMED OF HIS LACK OF STAMINA AND THAT HE HAD "LOST FACE."

THE YOUNGER, ABLER WRITER WAS MORE WILLING TO DELINEATE HIS WEAKNESS, WHILE THE OLDER SEABROOK, FAILING BOTH IN BODY AND IN CAREER, NEEDED TO GLOSS OVER HIS PERFORMANCE.

TOO LONG TO RIDE, SEABROOK. YOU MUST REST, MY FRIEND.

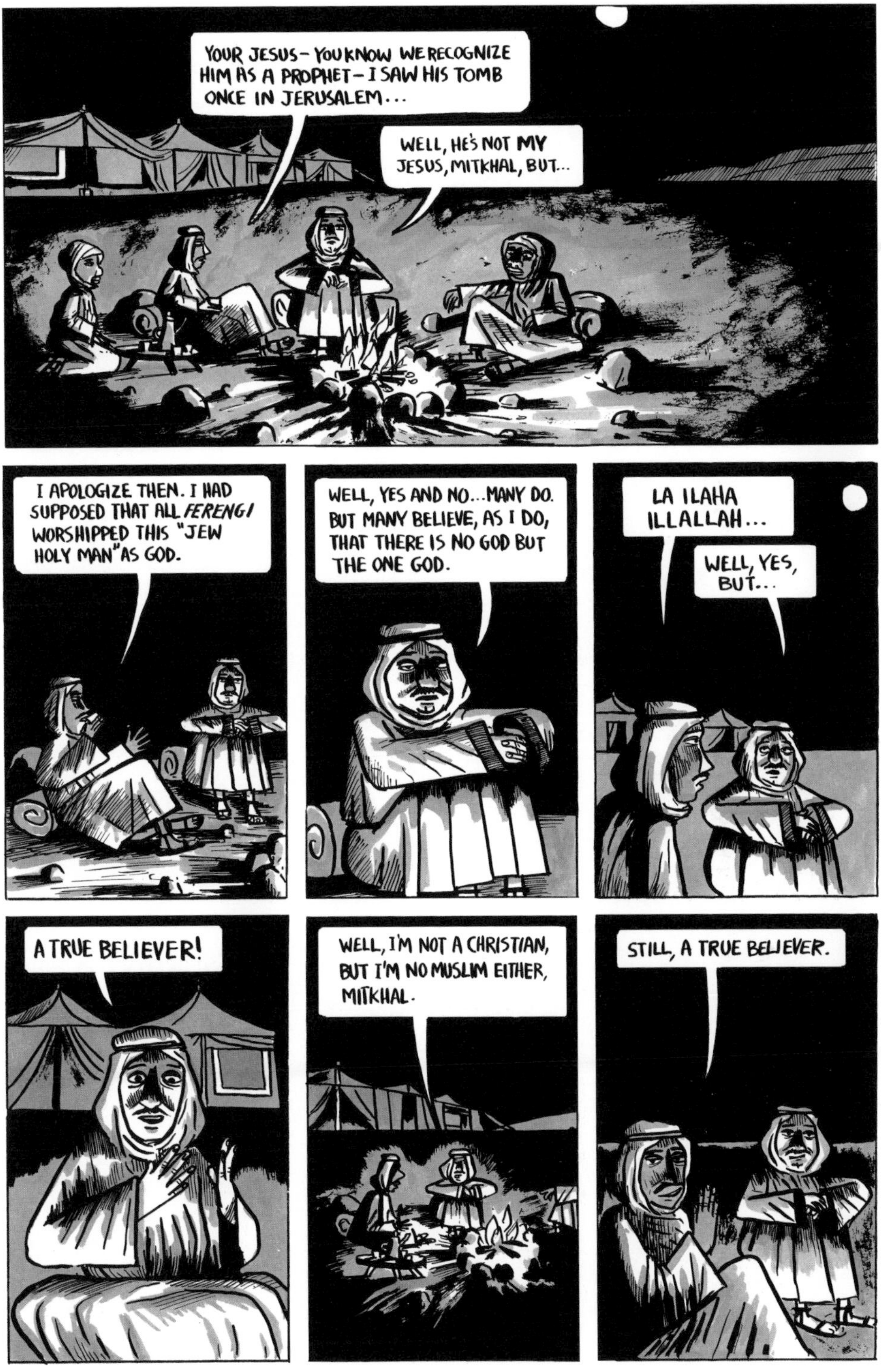
YOUR JESUS– YOU KNOW WE RECOGNIZE HIM AS A PROPHET– I SAW HIS TOMB ONCE IN JERUSALEM...
WELL, HE'S NOT MY JESUS, MITKHAL, BUT...
I APOLOGIZE THEN. I HAD SUPPOSED THAT ALL *FERENGI* WORSHIPPED THIS "JEW HOLY MAN" AS GOD.
WELL, YES AND NO... MANY DO. BUT MANY BELIEVE, AS I DO, THAT THERE IS NO GOD BUT THE ONE GOD.
LA ILAHA ILLALLAH...
WELL, YES, BUT...
A TRUE BELIEVER!
WELL, I'M NOT A CHRISTIAN, BUT I'M NO MUSLIM EITHER, MITKHAL.
STILL, A TRUE BELIEVER.

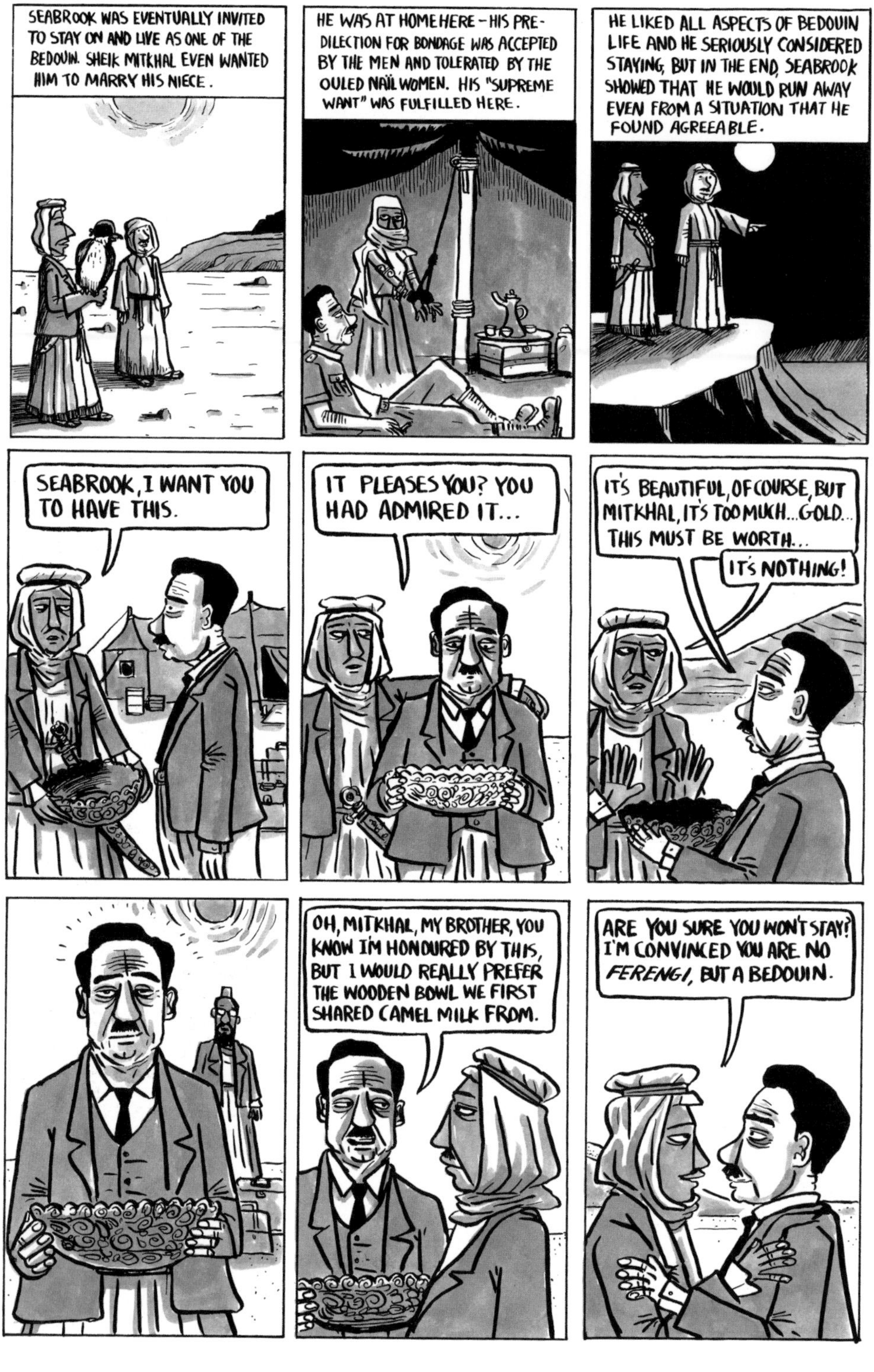
SEABROOK WAS EVENTUALLY INVITED TO STAY ON AND LIVE AS ONE OF THE BEDOUIN. SHEIK MITKHAL EVEN WANTED HIM TO MARRY HIS NIECE.
HE WAS AT HOME HERE - HIS PREDILECTION FOR BONDAGE WAS ACCEPTED BY THE MEN AND TOLERATED BY THE OULED NAÏL WOMEN. HIS "SUPREME WANT" WAS FULFILLED HERE.
HE LIKED ALL ASPECTS OF BEDOUIN LIFE AND HE SERIOUSLY CONSIDERED STAYING, BUT IN THE END, SEABROOK SHOWED THAT HE WOULD RUN AWAY EVEN FROM A SITUATION THAT HE FOUND AGREEABLE.
SEABROOK, I WANT YOU TO HAVE THIS.
IT PLEASES YOU? YOU HAD ADMIRED IT...
IT'S BEAUTIFUL, OF COURSE, BUT MITKHAL, IT'S TOO MUCH... GOLD... THIS MUST BE WORTH...
IT'S NOTHING!
OH, MITKHAL, MY BROTHER, YOU KNOW I'M HONOURED BY THIS, BUT I WOULD REALLY PREFER THE WOODEN BOWL WE FIRST SHARED CAMEL MILK FROM.
ARE YOU SURE YOU WON'T STAY? I'M CONVINCED YOU ARE NO *FERENGI*, BUT A BEDOUIN.

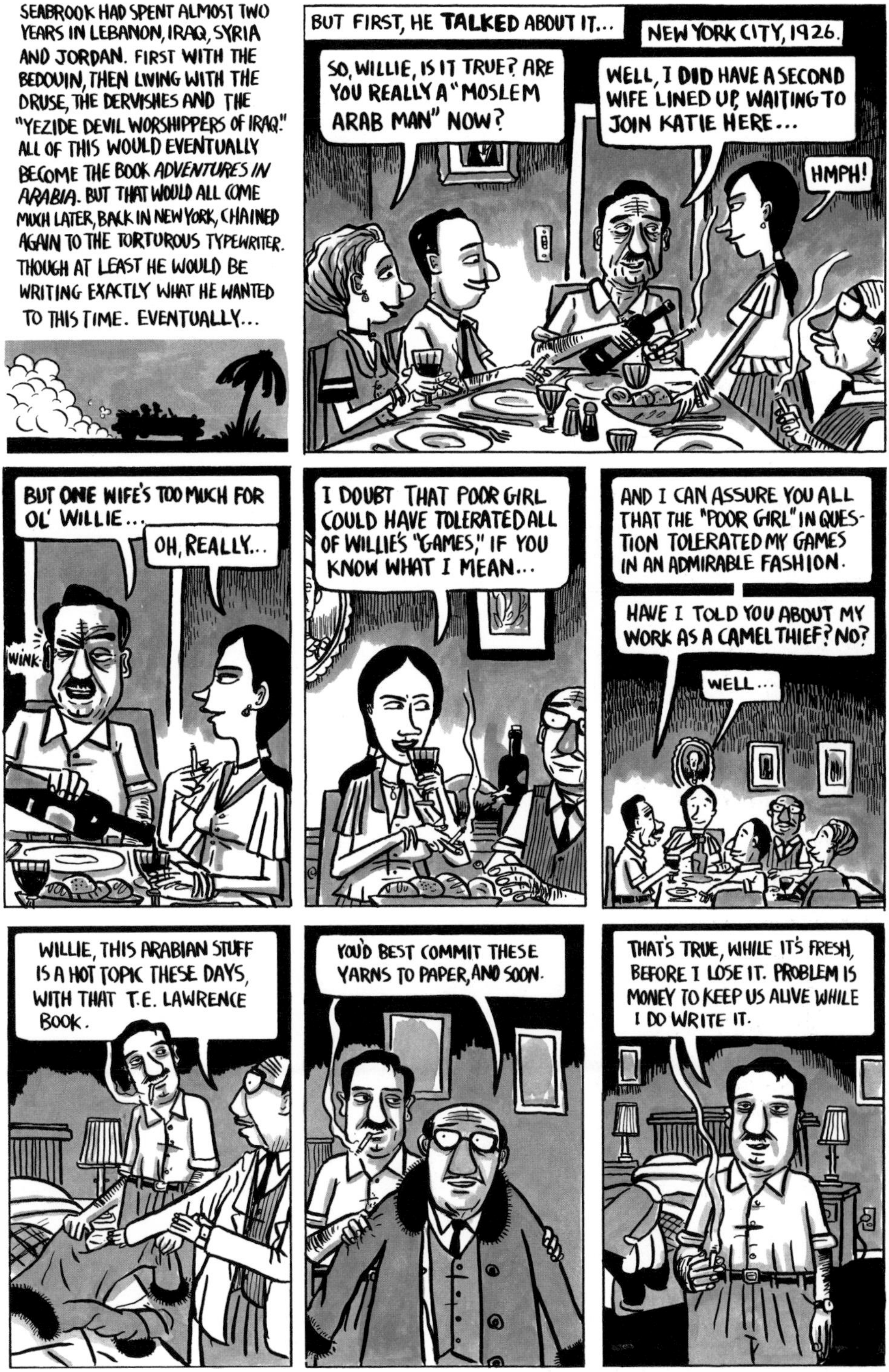
SEABROOK HAD SPENT ALMOST TWO YEARS IN LEBANON, IRAQ, SYRIA AND JORDAN. FIRST WITH THE BEDOUIN, THEN LIVING WITH THE DRUSE, THE DERVISHES AND THE "YEZIDE DEVIL WORSHIPPERS OF IRAQ." ALL OF THIS WOULD EVENTUALLY BECOME THE BOOK *ADVENTURES IN ARABIA*. BUT THAT WOULD ALL COME MUCH LATER, BACK IN NEW YORK, CHAINED AGAIN TO THE TORTUROUS TYPEWRITER. THOUGH AT LEAST HE WOULD BE WRITING EXACTLY WHAT HE WANTED TO THIS TIME. EVENTUALLY...
BUT FIRST, HE **TALKED** ABOUT IT...
NEW YORK CITY, 1926.
SO, WILLIE, IS IT TRUE? ARE YOU REALLY A "MOSLEM ARAB MAN" NOW?
WELL, I **DID** HAVE A SECOND WIFE LINED UP, WAITING TO JOIN KATIE HERE...
HMPH!
BUT **ONE** WIFE'S TOO MUCH FOR OL' WILLIE...
WINK
OH, REALLY...
I DOUBT THAT POOR GIRL COULD HAVE TOLERATED ALL OF WILLIE'S "GAMES," IF YOU KNOW WHAT I MEAN...
AND I CAN ASSURE YOU ALL THAT THE "POOR GIRL" IN QUESTION TOLERATED MY GAMES IN AN ADMIRABLE FASHION.
HAVE I TOLD YOU ABOUT MY WORK AS A CAMEL THIEF? NO?
WELL...
WILLIE, THIS ARABIAN STUFF IS A HOT TOPIC THESE DAYS, WITH THAT T.E. LAWRENCE BOOK.
YOU'D BEST COMMIT THESE YARNS TO PAPER, AND SOON.
THAT'S TRUE, WHILE IT'S FRESH, BEFORE I LOSE IT. PROBLEM IS MONEY TO KEEP US ALIVE WHILE I DO WRITE IT.

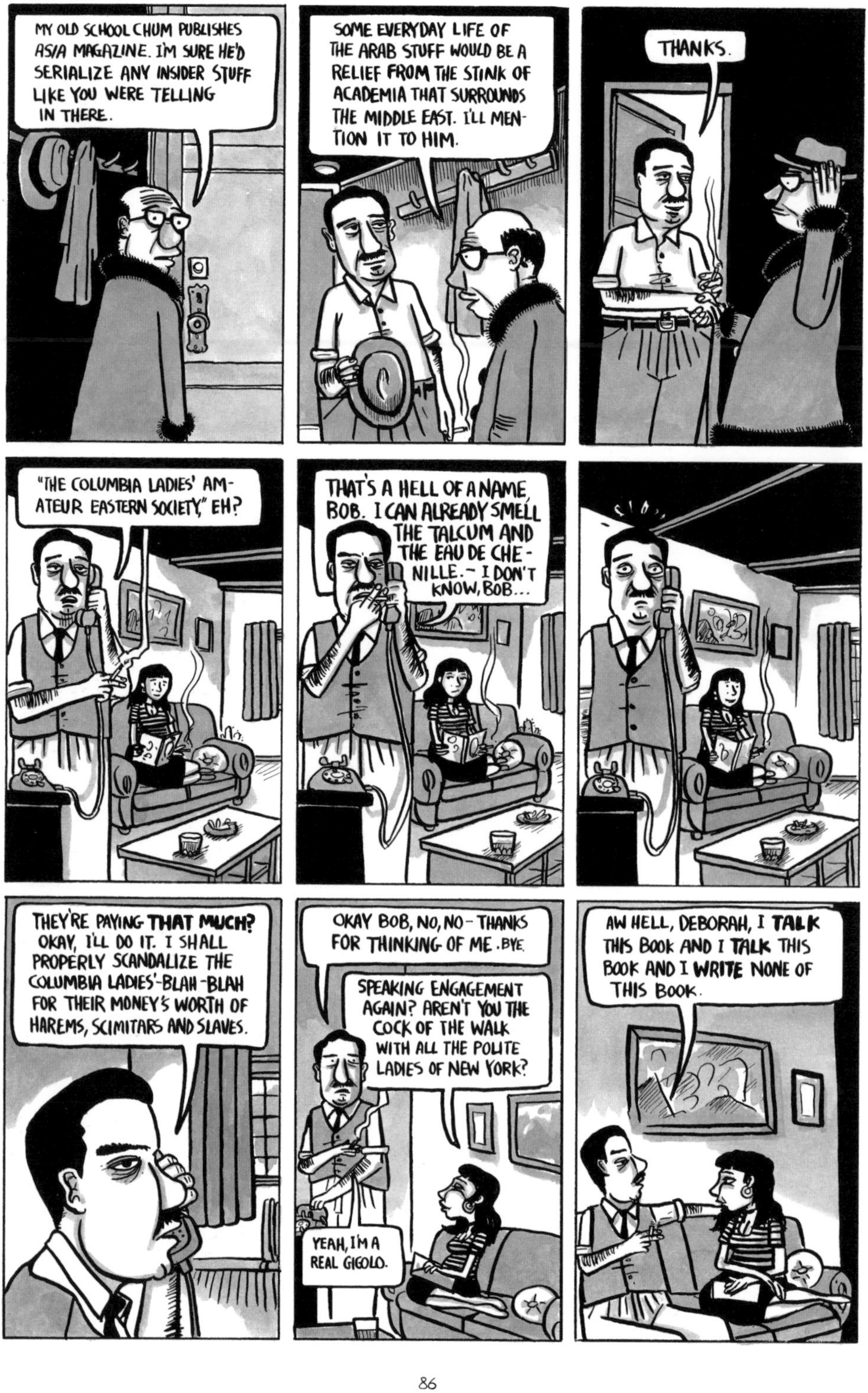
MY OLD SCHOOL CHUM PUBLISHES ASIA MAGAZINE. I'M SURE HE'D SERIALIZE ANY INSIDER STUFF LIKE YOU WERE TELLING IN THERE.
SOME EVERYDAY LIFE OF THE ARAB STUFF WOULD BE A RELIEF FROM THE STINK OF ACADEMIA THAT SURROUNDS THE MIDDLE EAST. I'LL MENTION IT TO HIM.
THANKS.
"THE COLUMBIA LADIES' AMATEUR EASTERN SOCIETY," EH?
THAT'S A HELL OF A NAME, BOB. I CAN ALREADY SMELL THE TALCUM AND THE EAU DE CHENILLE.— I DON'T KNOW, BOB...
THEY'RE PAYING THAT MUCH? OKAY, I'LL DO IT. I SHALL PROPERLY SCANDALIZE THE COLUMBIA LADIES'-BLAH-BLAH FOR THEIR MONEY'S WORTH OF HAREMS, SCIMITARS AND SLAVES.
OKAY BOB, NO, NO- THANKS FOR THINKING OF ME. BYE.
SPEAKING ENGAGEMENT AGAIN? AREN'T YOU THE COCK OF THE WALK WITH ALL THE POLITE LADIES OF NEW YORK?
YEAH, I'M A REAL GIGOLO.
AW HELL, DEBORAH, I TALK THIS BOOK AND I TALK THIS BOOK AND I WRITE NONE OF THIS BOOK.

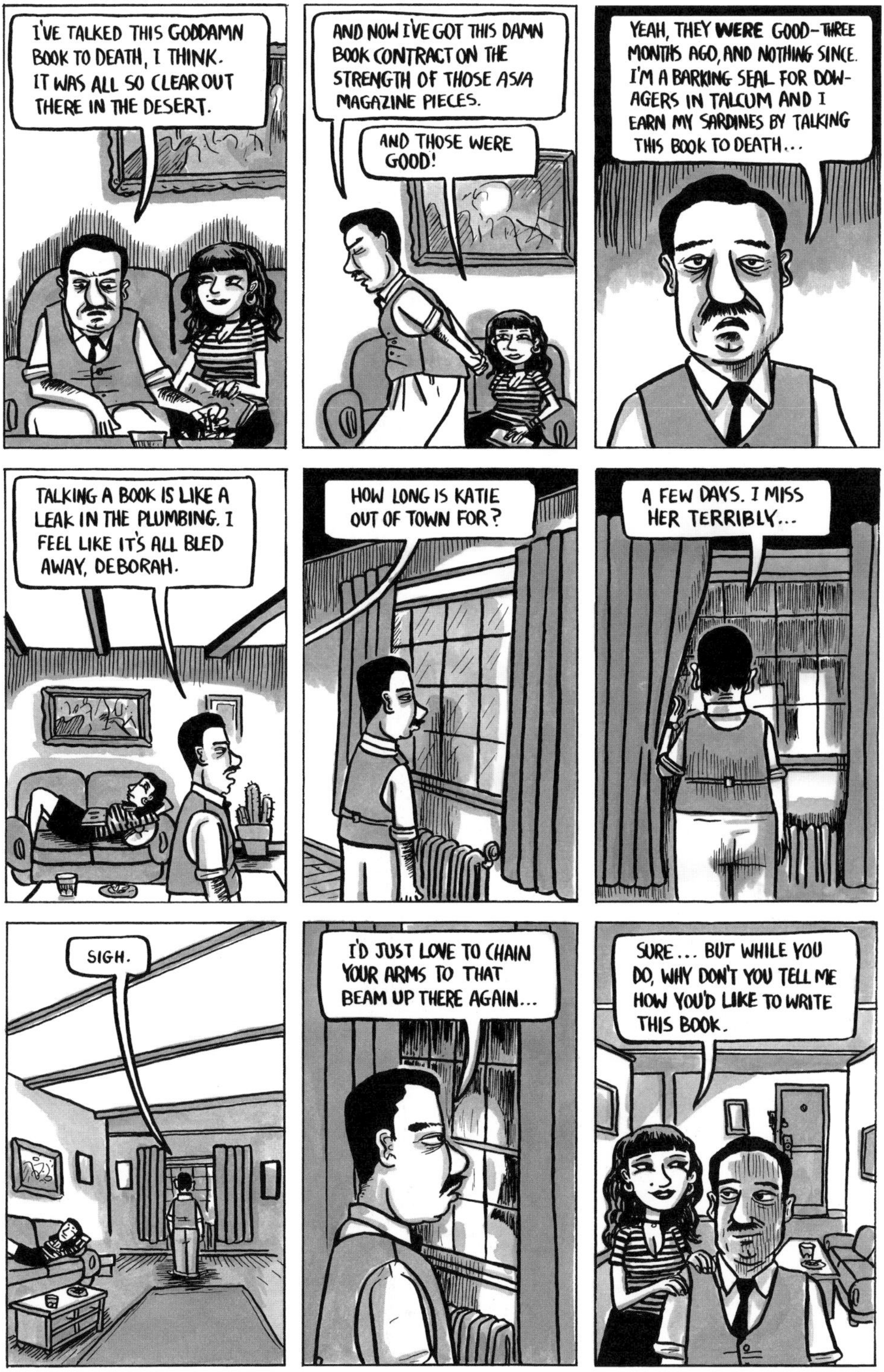
I'VE TALKED THIS GODDAMN BOOK TO DEATH, I THINK. IT WAS ALL SO CLEAR OUT THERE IN THE DESERT.
AND NOW I'VE GOT THIS DAMN BOOK CONTRACT ON THE STRENGTH OF THOSE ASIA MAGAZINE PIECES.
AND THOSE WERE GOOD!
YEAH, THEY WERE GOOD—THREE MONTHS AGO, AND NOTHING SINCE. I'M A BARKING SEAL FOR DOWAGERS IN TALCUM AND I EARN MY SARDINES BY TALKING THIS BOOK TO DEATH...
TALKING A BOOK IS LIKE A LEAK IN THE PLUMBING. I FEEL LIKE IT'S ALL BLED AWAY, DEBORAH.
HOW LONG IS KATIE OUT OF TOWN FOR?
A FEW DAYS. I MISS HER TERRIBLY...
SIGH.
I'D JUST LOVE TO CHAIN YOUR ARMS TO THAT BEAM UP THERE AGAIN...
SURE... BUT WHILE YOU DO, WHY DON'T YOU TELL ME HOW YOU'D LIKE TO WRITE THIS BOOK.

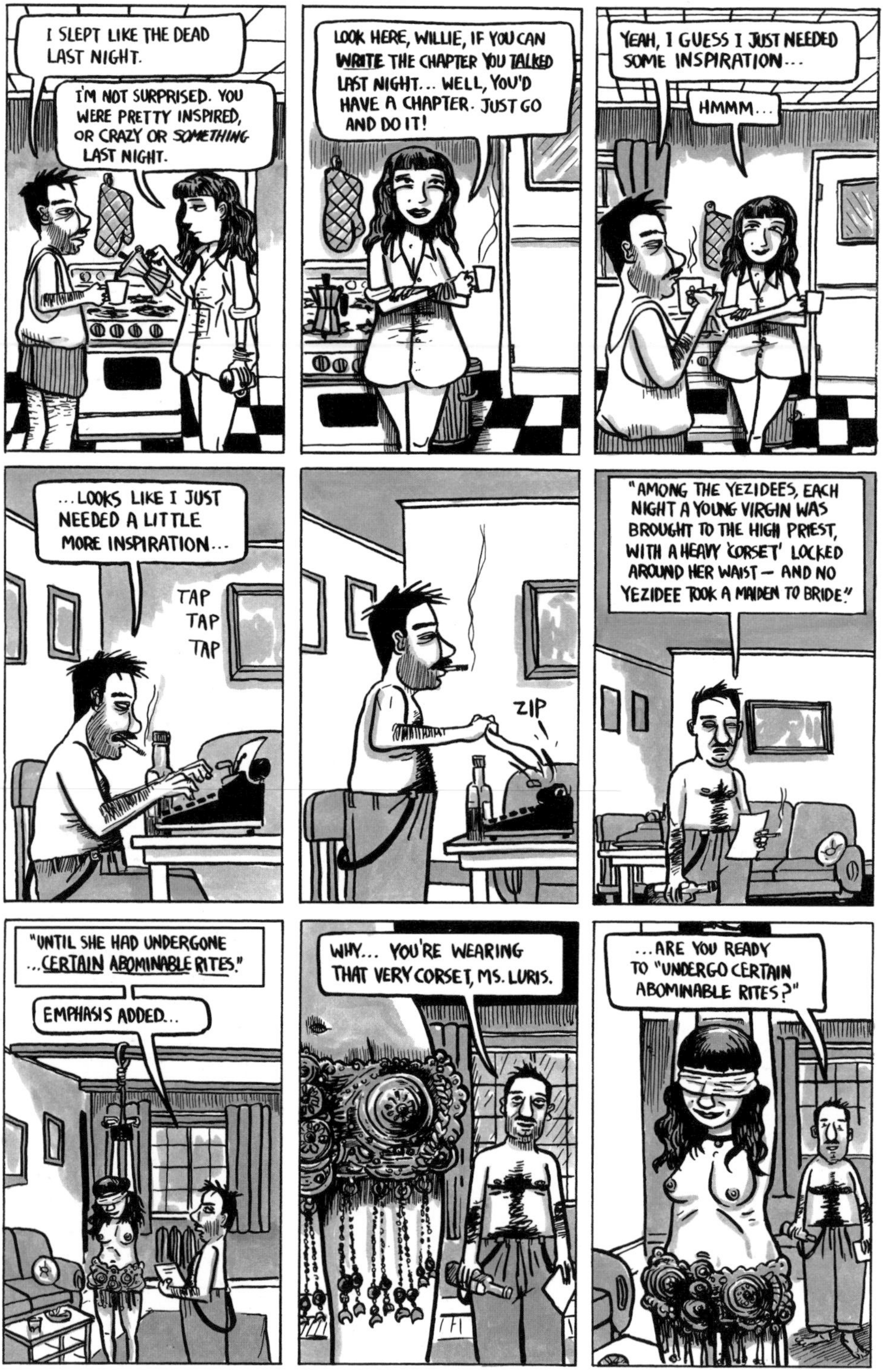
I SLEPT LIKE THE DEAD LAST NIGHT.
I'M NOT SURPRISED. YOU WERE PRETTY INSPIRED, OR CRAZY OR SOMETHING LAST NIGHT.
LOOK HERE, WILLIE, IF YOU CAN WRITE THE CHAPTER YOU TALKED LAST NIGHT... WELL, YOU'D HAVE A CHAPTER. JUST GO AND DO IT!
YEAH, I GUESS I JUST NEEDED SOME INSPIRATION...
HMMM...
...LOOKS LIKE I JUST NEEDED A LITTLE MORE INSPIRATION...
TAP TAP TAP
ZIP
"AMONG THE YEZIDEES, EACH NIGHT A YOUNG VIRGIN WAS BROUGHT TO THE HIGH PRIEST, WITH A HEAVY 'CORSET' LOCKED AROUND HER WAIST — AND NO YEZIDEE TOOK A MAIDEN TO BRIDE."
"UNTIL SHE HAD UNDERGONE ...CERTAIN ABOMINABLE RITES."
EMPHASIS ADDED...
WHY... YOU'RE WEARING THAT VERY CORSET, MS. LURIS.
...ARE YOU READY TO "UNDERGO CERTAIN ABOMINABLE RITES?"

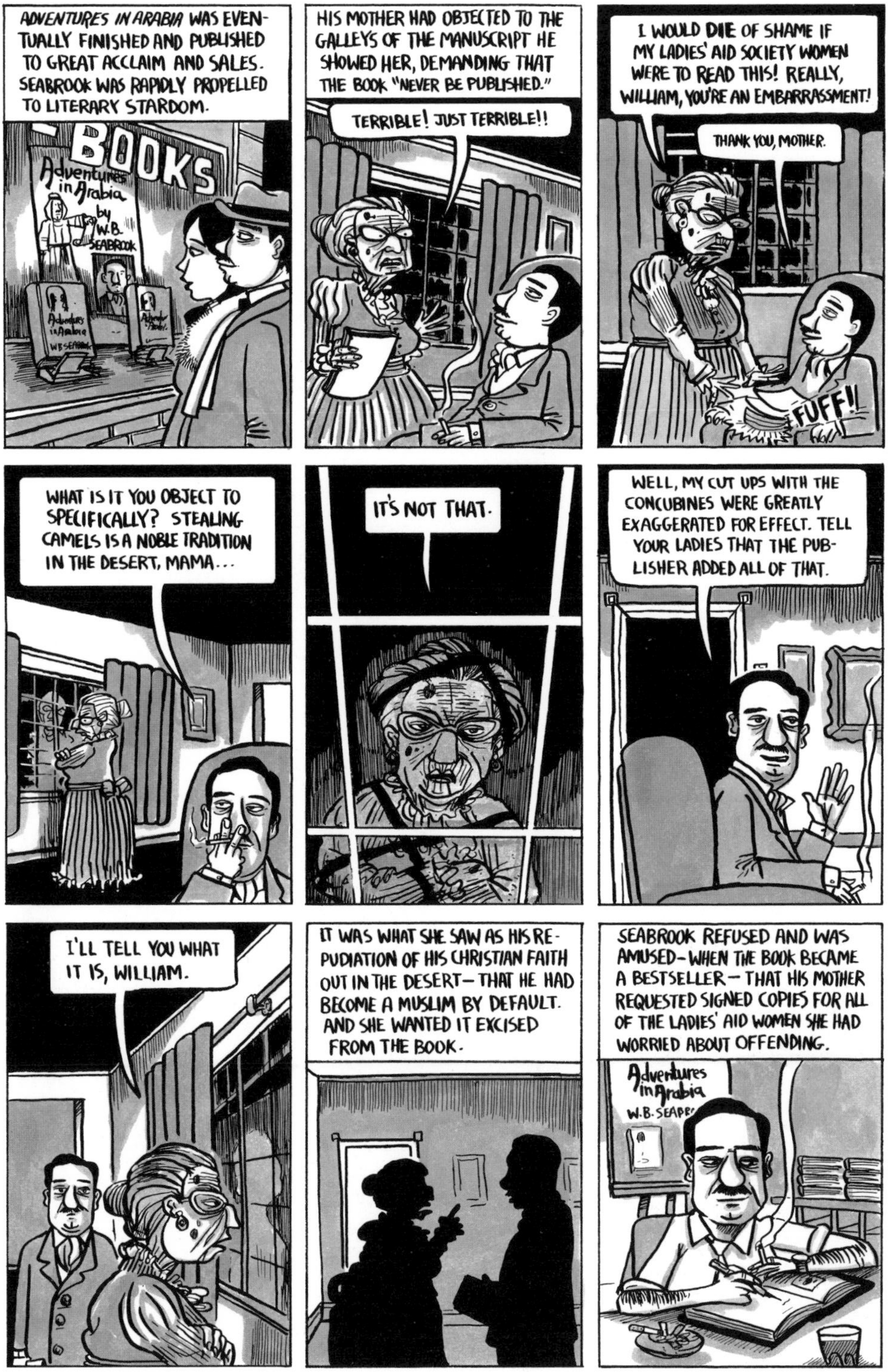
ADVENTURES IN ARABIA WAS EVENTUALLY FINISHED AND PUBLISHED TO GREAT ACCLAIM AND SALES. SEABROOK WAS RAPIDLY PROPELLED TO LITERARY STARDOM.
BOOKS
Adventures in Arabia by W.B. SEABROOK
HIS MOTHER HAD OBJECTED TO THE GALLEYS OF THE MANUSCRIPT HE SHOWED HER, DEMANDING THAT THE BOOK "NEVER BE PUBLISHED."
TERRIBLE! JUST TERRIBLE!!
I WOULD DIE OF SHAME IF MY LADIES' AID SOCIETY WOMEN WERE TO READ THIS! REALLY, WILLIAM, YOU'RE AN EMBARRASSMENT!
THANK YOU, MOTHER.
FUFF!
WHAT IS IT YOU OBJECT TO SPECIFICALLY? STEALING CAMELS IS A NOBLE TRADITION IN THE DESERT, MAMA...
IT'S NOT THAT.
WELL, MY CUT UPS WITH THE CONCUBINES WERE GREATLY EXAGGERATED FOR EFFECT. TELL YOUR LADIES THAT THE PUBLISHER ADDED ALL OF THAT.
I'LL TELL YOU WHAT IT IS, WILLIAM.
IT WAS WHAT SHE SAW AS HIS REPUDIATION OF HIS CHRISTIAN FAITH OUT IN THE DESERT— THAT HE HAD BECOME A MUSLIM BY DEFAULT. AND SHE WANTED IT EXCISED FROM THE BOOK.
SEABROOK REFUSED AND WAS AMUSED— WHEN THE BOOK BECAME A BESTSELLER— THAT HIS MOTHER REQUESTED SIGNED COPIES FOR ALL OF THE LADIES' AID WOMEN SHE HAD WORRIED ABOUT OFFENDING.
Adventures in Arabia W.B. SEAB

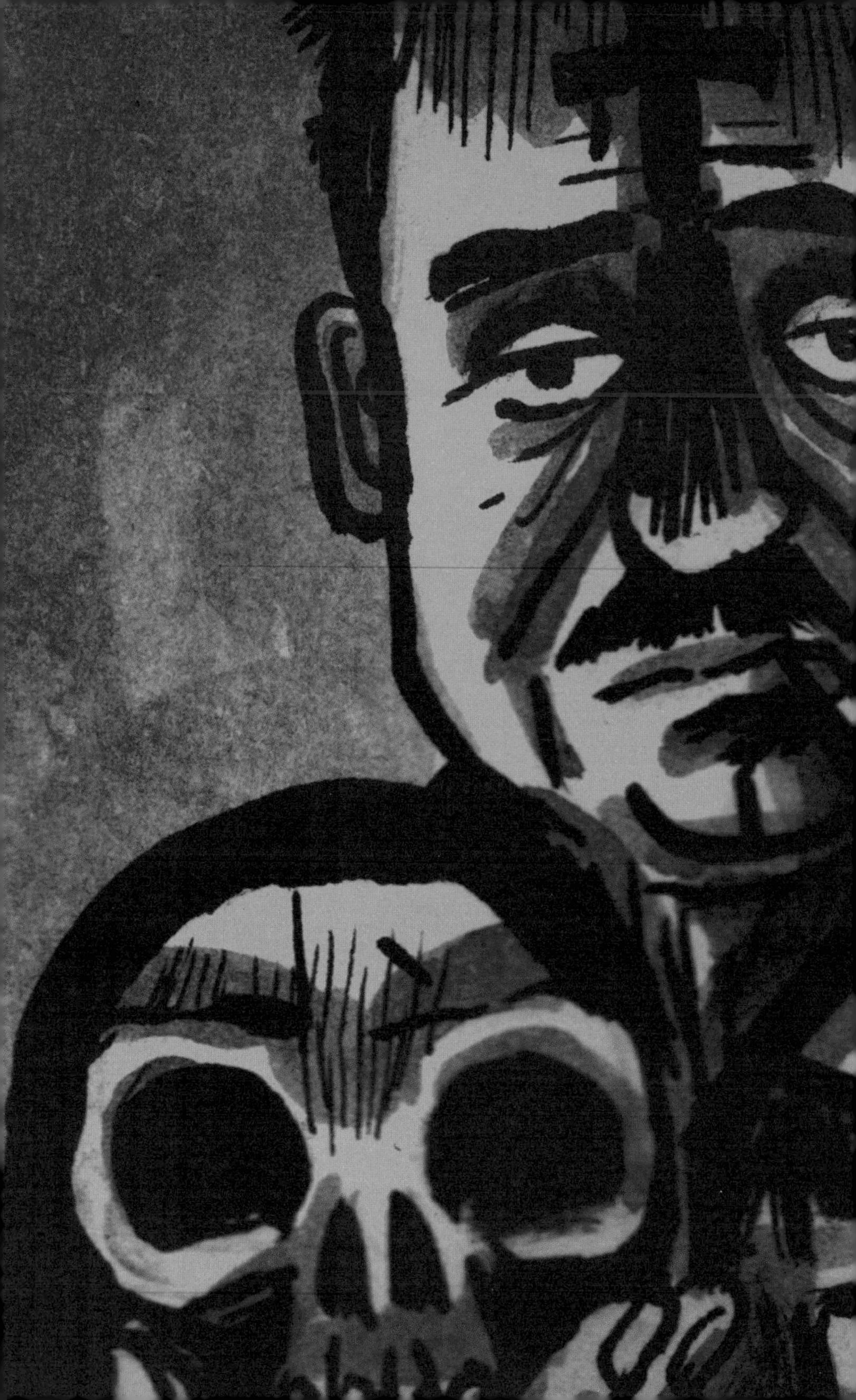

# CHAPTER THREE

## "INVENTING" THE ZOMBIE, LIKE THEY "DISCOVERED" AMERICA

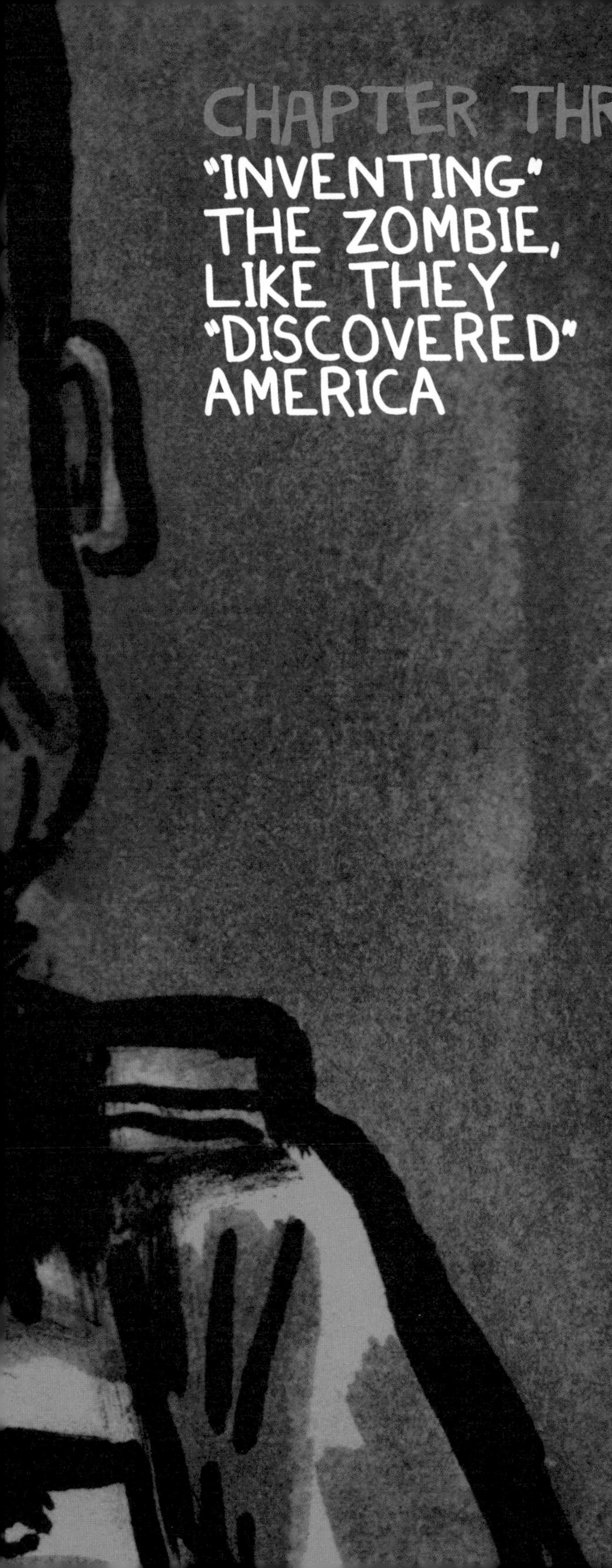

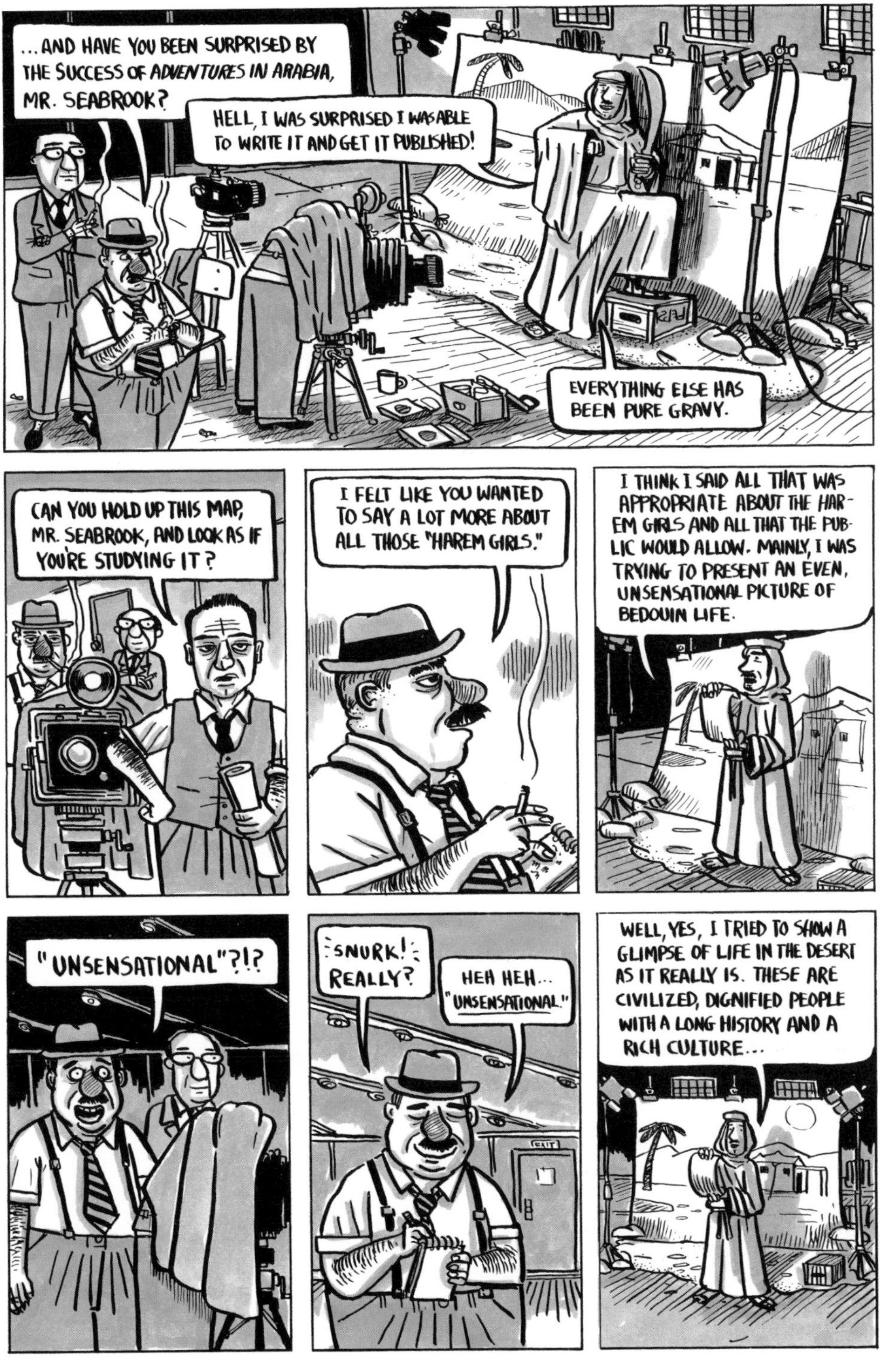
...AND HAVE YOU BEEN SURPRISED BY THE SUCCESS OF ADVENTURES IN ARABIA, MR. SEABROOK?
HELL, I WAS SURPRISED I WAS ABLE TO WRITE IT AND GET IT PUBLISHED!
EVERYTHING ELSE HAS BEEN PURE GRAVY.
CAN YOU HOLD UP THIS MAP, MR. SEABROOK, AND LOOK AS IF YOU'RE STUDYING IT?
I FELT LIKE YOU WANTED TO SAY A LOT MORE ABOUT ALL THOSE "HAREM GIRLS."
I THINK I SAID ALL THAT WAS APPROPRIATE ABOUT THE HAREM GIRLS AND ALL THAT THE PUBLIC WOULD ALLOW. MAINLY, I WAS TRYING TO PRESENT AN EVEN, UNSENSATIONAL PICTURE OF BEDOUIN LIFE.
"UNSENSATIONAL"?!?
SNURK! REALLY?
HEH HEH... "UNSENSATIONAL."
WELL, YES, I TRIED TO SHOW A GLIMPSE OF LIFE IN THE DESERT AS IT REALLY IS. THESE ARE CIVILIZED, DIGNIFIED PEOPLE WITH A LONG HISTORY AND A RICH CULTURE...

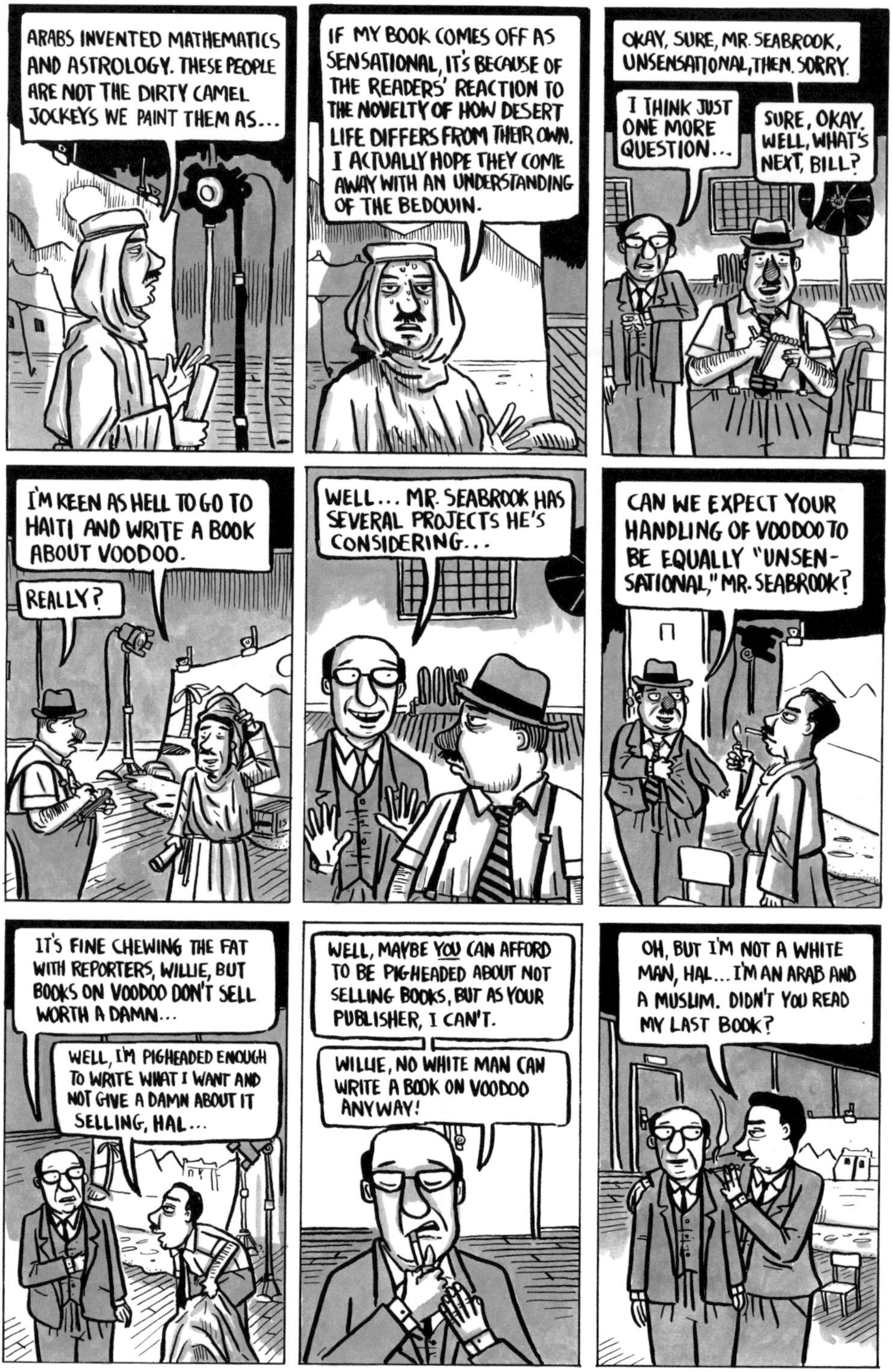
ARABS INVENTED MATHEMATICS AND ASTROLOGY. THESE PEOPLE ARE NOT THE DIRTY CAMEL JOCKEYS WE PAINT THEM AS...
IF MY BOOK COMES OFF AS SENSATIONAL, IT'S BECAUSE OF THE READERS' REACTION TO THE NOVELTY OF HOW DESERT LIFE DIFFERS FROM THEIR OWN. I ACTUALLY HOPE THEY COME AWAY WITH AN UNDERSTANDING OF THE BEDOUIN.
OKAY, SURE, MR. SEABROOK, UNSENSATIONAL, THEN. SORRY.
I THINK JUST ONE MORE QUESTION...
SURE, OKAY. WELL, WHAT'S NEXT, BILL?
I'M KEEN AS HELL TO GO TO HAITI AND WRITE A BOOK ABOUT VOODOO.
REALLY?
WELL... MR. SEABROOK HAS SEVERAL PROJECTS HE'S CONSIDERING...
CAN WE EXPECT YOUR HANDLING OF VOODOO TO BE EQUALLY "UNSENSATIONAL," MR. SEABROOK?
IT'S FINE CHEWING THE FAT WITH REPORTERS, WILLIE, BUT BOOKS ON VOODOO DON'T SELL WORTH A DAMN...
WELL, I'M PIGHEADED ENOUGH TO WRITE WHAT I WANT AND NOT GIVE A DAMN ABOUT IT SELLING, HAL...
WELL, MAYBE YOU CAN AFFORD TO BE PIGHEADED ABOUT NOT SELLING BOOKS, BUT AS YOUR PUBLISHER, I CAN'T.
WILLIE, NO WHITE MAN CAN WRITE A BOOK ON VOODOO ANYWAY!
OH, BUT I'M NOT A WHITE MAN, HAL... I'M AN ARAB AND A MUSLIM. DIDN'T YOU READ MY LAST BOOK?

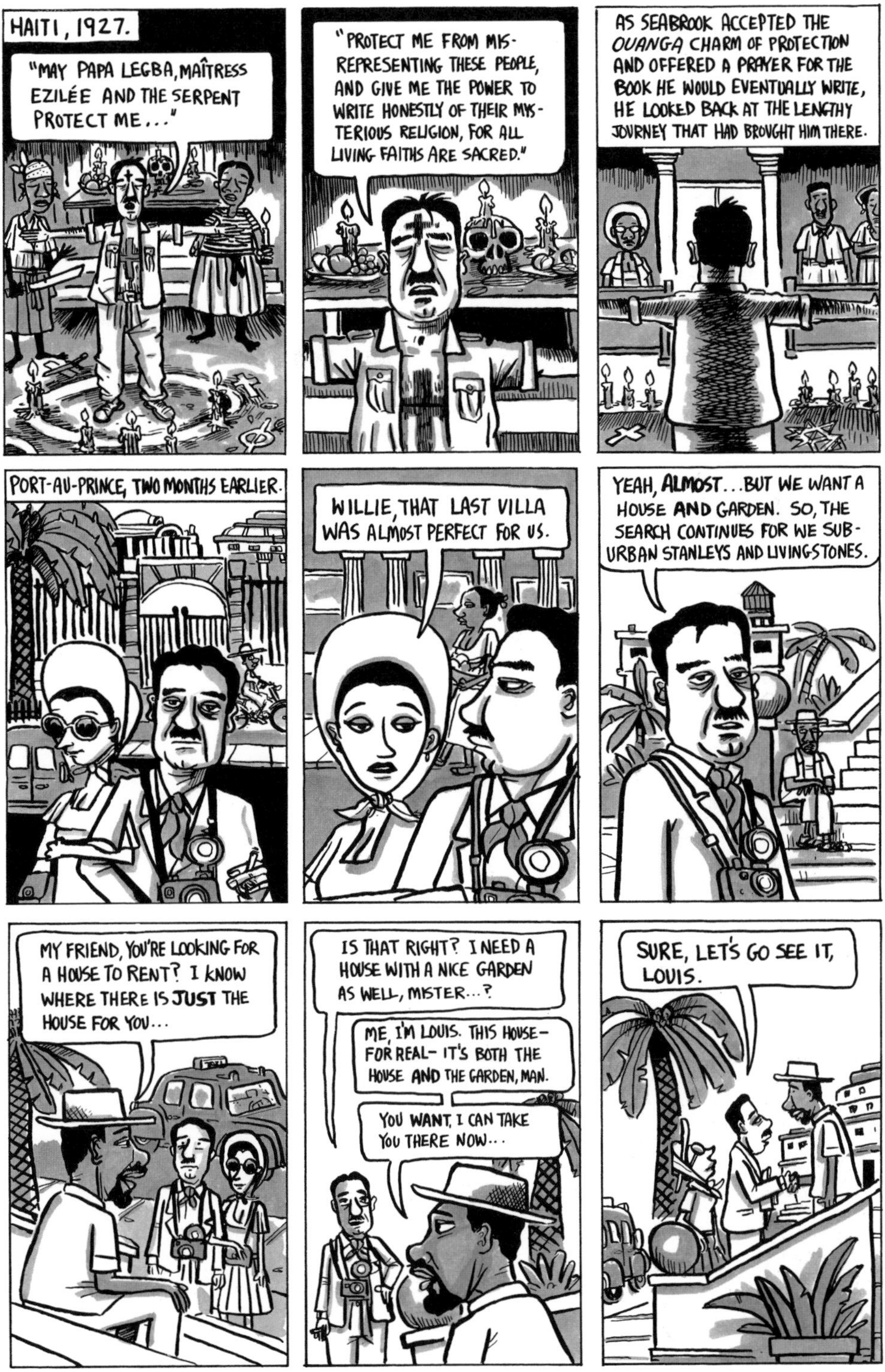
HAITI, 1927.
"MAY PAPA LEGBA, MAÎTRESS EZILÉE AND THE SERPENT PROTECT ME..."
"PROTECT ME FROM MIS-REPRESENTING THESE PEOPLE, AND GIVE ME THE POWER TO WRITE HONESTLY OF THEIR MYS-TERIOUS RELIGION, FOR ALL LIVING FAITHS ARE SACRED."
AS SEABROOK ACCEPTED THE OUANGA CHARM OF PROTECTION AND OFFERED A PRAYER FOR THE BOOK HE WOULD EVENTUALLY WRITE, HE LOOKED BACK AT THE LENGTHY JOURNEY THAT HAD BROUGHT HIM THERE.
PORT-AU-PRINCE, TWO MONTHS EARLIER.
WILLIE, THAT LAST VILLA WAS ALMOST PERFECT FOR US.
YEAH, ALMOST...BUT WE WANT A HOUSE AND GARDEN. SO, THE SEARCH CONTINUES FOR WE SUB-URBAN STANLEYS AND LIVINGSTONES.
MY FRIEND, YOU'RE LOOKING FOR A HOUSE TO RENT? I KNOW WHERE THERE IS JUST THE HOUSE FOR YOU...
IS THAT RIGHT? I NEED A HOUSE WITH A NICE GARDEN AS WELL, MISTER...?
ME, I'M LOUIS. THIS HOUSE- FOR REAL- IT'S BOTH THE HOUSE AND THE GARDEN, MAN.
YOU WANT, I CAN TAKE YOU THERE NOW...
SURE, LET'S GO SEE IT, LOUIS.

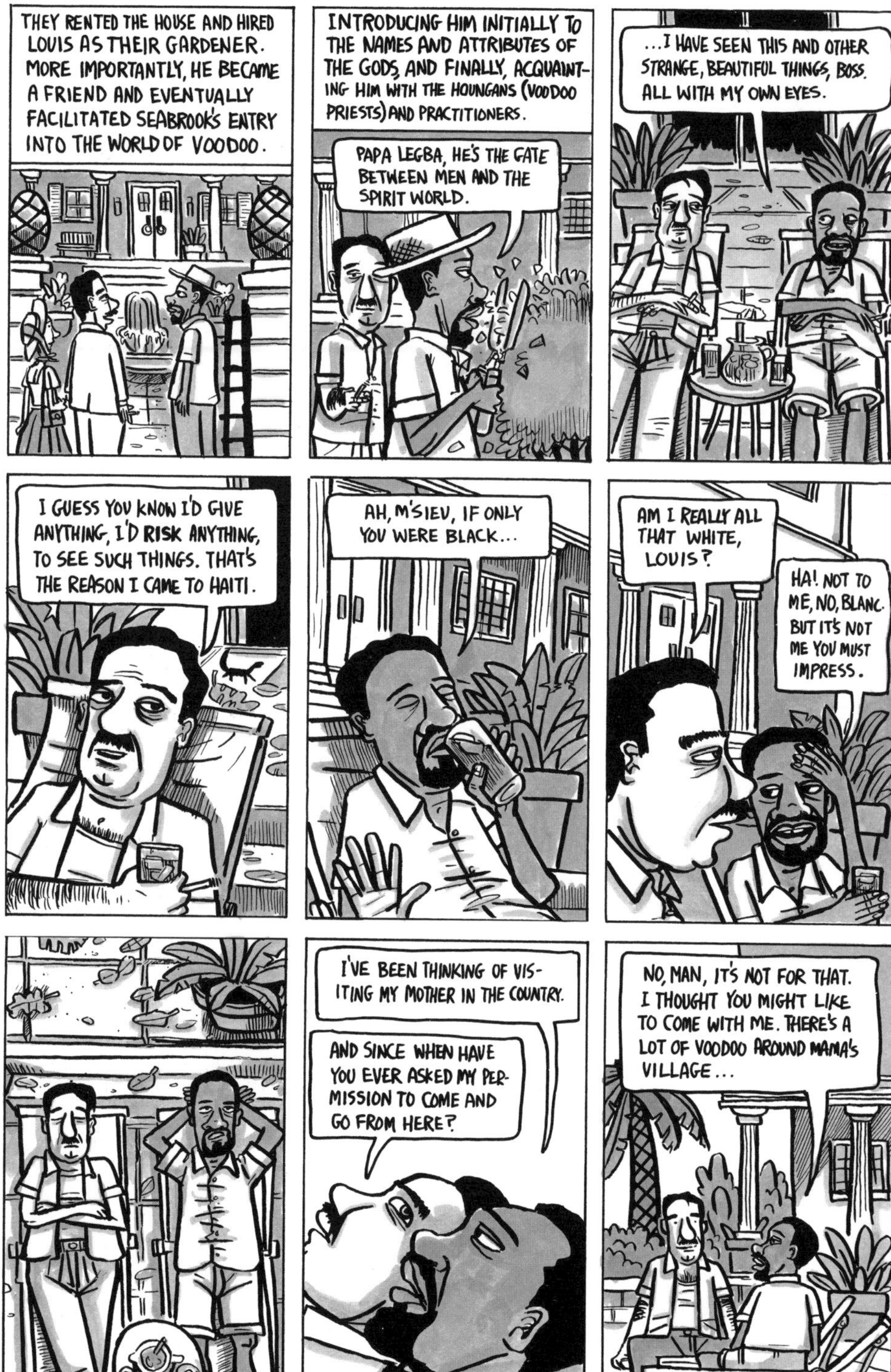
THEY RENTED THE HOUSE AND HIRED LOUIS AS THEIR GARDENER. MORE IMPORTANTLY, HE BECAME A FRIEND AND EVENTUALLY FACILITATED SEABROOK'S ENTRY INTO THE WORLD OF VOODOO.
INTRODUCING HIM INITIALLY TO THE NAMES AND ATTRIBUTES OF THE GODS, AND FINALLY, ACQUAINTING HIM WITH THE HOUNGANS (VOODOO PRIESTS) AND PRACTITIONERS.
PAPA LEGBA, HE'S THE GATE BETWEEN MEN AND THE SPIRIT WORLD.
...I HAVE SEEN THIS AND OTHER STRANGE, BEAUTIFUL THINGS, BOSS. ALL WITH MY OWN EYES.
I GUESS YOU KNOW I'D GIVE ANYTHING, I'D RISK ANYTHING, TO SEE SUCH THINGS. THAT'S THE REASON I CAME TO HAITI.
AH, M'SIEU, IF ONLY YOU WERE BLACK...
AM I REALLY ALL THAT WHITE, LOUIS?
HA! NOT TO ME, NO, BLANC. BUT IT'S NOT ME YOU MUST IMPRESS.
I'VE BEEN THINKING OF VISITING MY MOTHER IN THE COUNTRY.
AND SINCE WHEN HAVE YOU EVER ASKED MY PERMISSION TO COME AND GO FROM HERE?
NO, MAN, IT'S NOT FOR THAT. I THOUGHT YOU MIGHT LIKE TO COME WITH ME. THERE'S A LOT OF VOODOO AROUND MAMA'S VILLAGE...

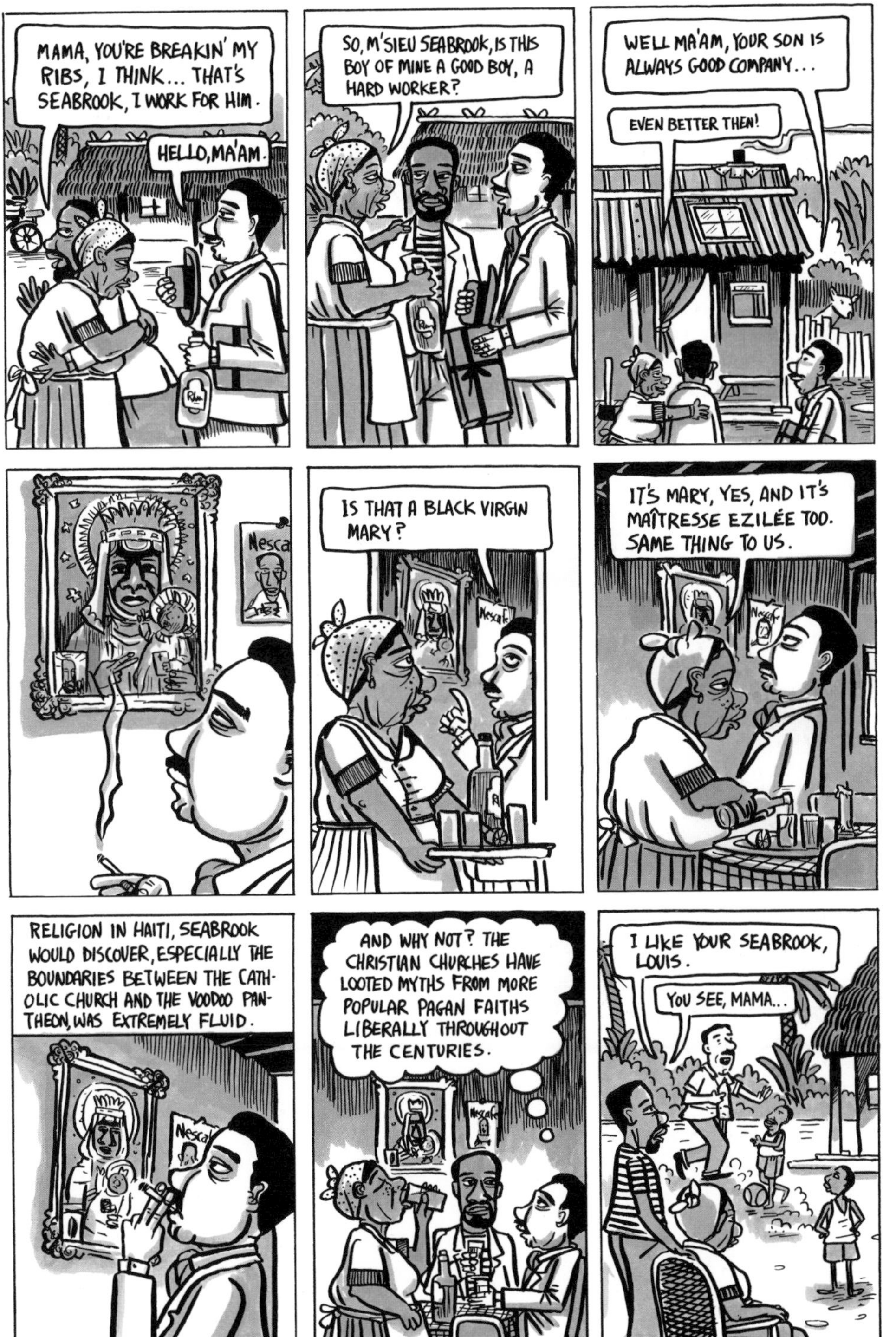
MAMA, YOU'RE BREAKIN' MY RIBS, I THINK... THAT'S SEABROOK, I WORK FOR HIM.
HELLO, MA'AM.
SO, M'SIEU SEABROOK, IS THIS BOY OF MINE A GOOD BOY, A HARD WORKER?
WELL MA'AM, YOUR SON IS ALWAYS GOOD COMPANY...
EVEN BETTER THEN!
Nesca
IS THAT A BLACK VIRGIN MARY?
Nescafé
IT'S MARY, YES, AND IT'S MAÎTRESSE EZILÉE TOO. SAME THING TO US.
RELIGION IN HAITI, SEABROOK WOULD DISCOVER, ESPECIALLY THE BOUNDARIES BETWEEN THE CATHOLIC CHURCH AND THE VOODOO PANTHEON, WAS EXTREMELY FLUID.
Nesca
AND WHY NOT? THE CHRISTIAN CHURCHES HAVE LOOTED MYTHS FROM MORE POPULAR PAGAN FAITHS LIBERALLY THROUGHOUT THE CENTURIES.
Nescafé
I LIKE YOUR SEABROOK, LOUIS.
YOU SEE, MAMA...

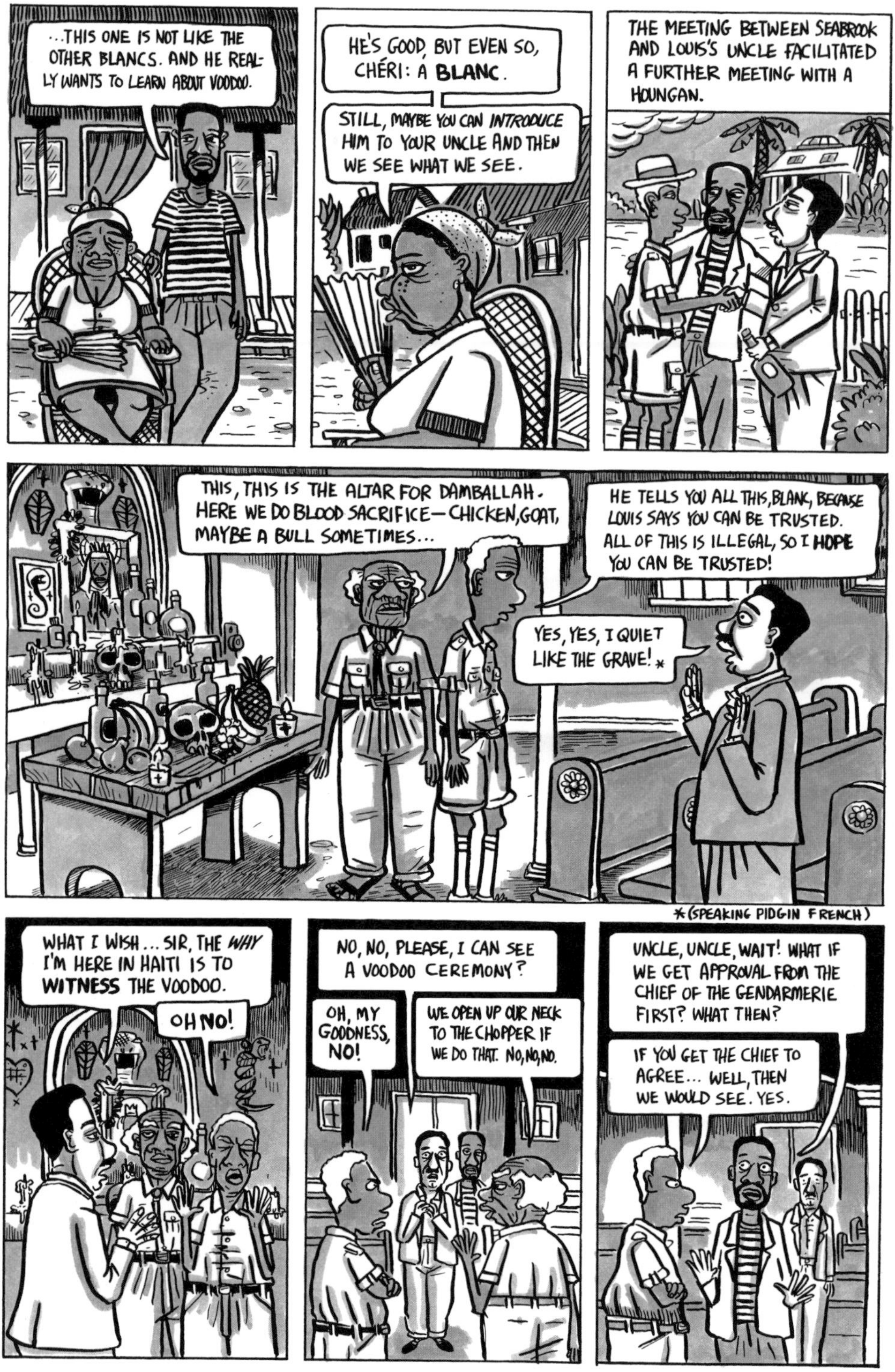
...THIS ONE IS NOT LIKE THE OTHER BLANCS. AND HE REALLY WANTS TO LEARN ABOUT VOODOO.
HE'S GOOD, BUT EVEN SO, CHÉRI: A BLANC.
STILL, MAYBE YOU CAN INTRODUCE HIM TO YOUR UNCLE AND THEN WE SEE WHAT WE SEE.
THE MEETING BETWEEN SEABROOK AND LOUIS'S UNCLE FACILITATED A FURTHER MEETING WITH A HOUNGAN.
THIS, THIS IS THE ALTAR FOR DAMBALLAH. HERE WE DO BLOOD SACRIFICE—CHICKEN, GOAT, MAYBE A BULL SOMETIMES...
HE TELLS YOU ALL THIS, BLANK, BECAUSE LOUIS SAYS YOU CAN BE TRUSTED. ALL OF THIS IS ILLEGAL, SO I HOPE YOU CAN BE TRUSTED!
YES, YES, I QUIET LIKE THE GRAVE! *
*(SPEAKING PIDGIN FRENCH)
WHAT I WISH... SIR, THE WHY I'M HERE IN HAITI IS TO WITNESS THE VOODOO.
OH NO!
NO, NO, PLEASE, I CAN SEE A VOODOO CEREMONY?
OH, MY GOODNESS, NO!
WE OPEN UP OUR NECK TO THE CHOPPER IF WE DO THAT. NO, NO, NO.
UNCLE, UNCLE, WAIT! WHAT IF WE GET APPROVAL FROM THE CHIEF OF THE GENDARMERIE FIRST? WHAT THEN?
IF YOU GET THE CHIEF TO AGREE... WELL, THEN WE WOULD SEE. YES.

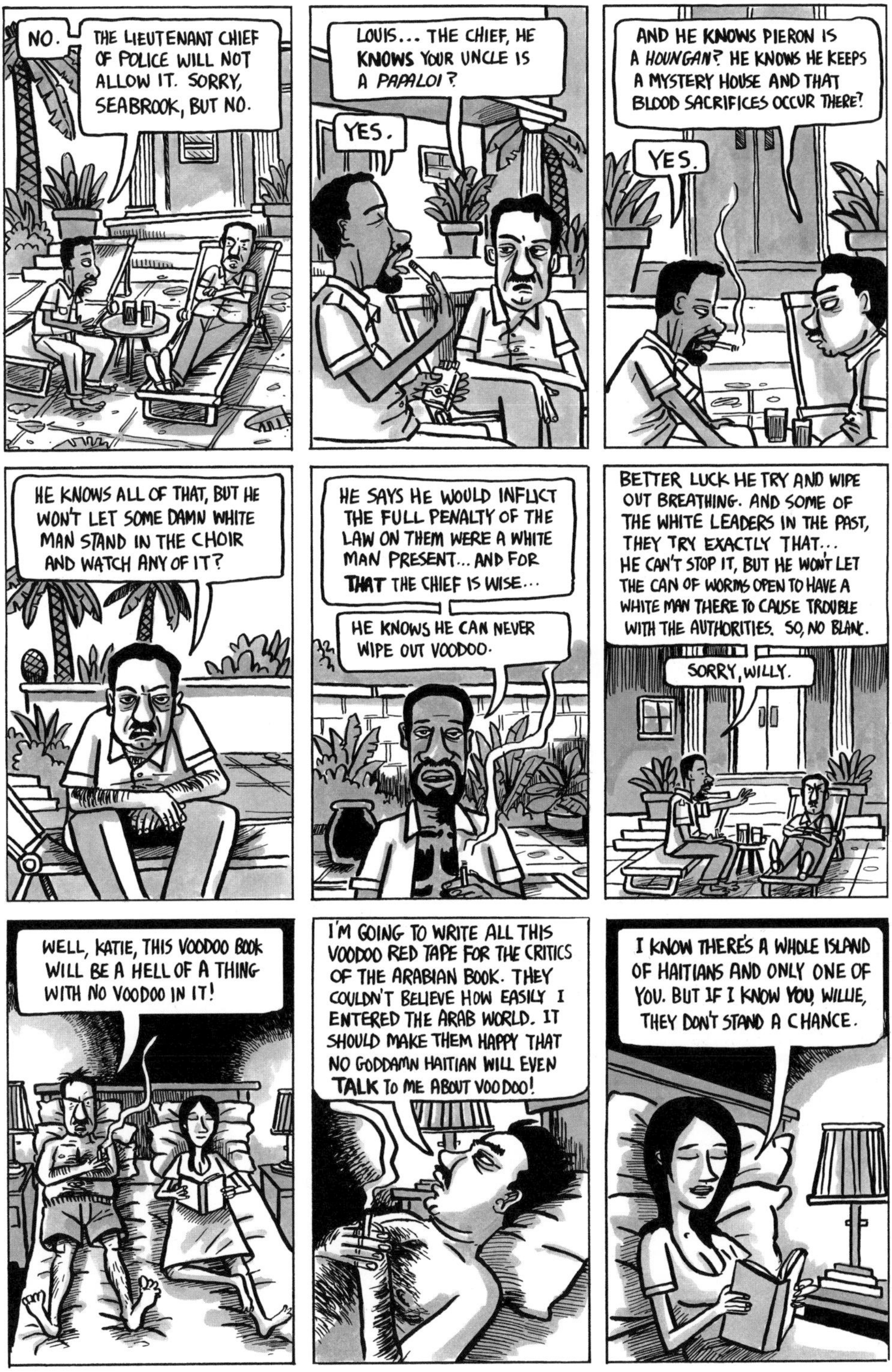
NO.
THE LIEUTENANT CHIEF OF POLICE WILL NOT ALLOW IT. SORRY, SEABROOK, BUT NO.
LOUIS... THE CHIEF, HE KNOWS YOUR UNCLE IS A PAPALOI?
YES.
AND HE KNOWS PIERON IS A HOUNGAN? HE KNOWS HE KEEPS A MYSTERY HOUSE AND THAT BLOOD SACRIFICES OCCUR THERE?
YES.
HE KNOWS ALL OF THAT, BUT HE WON'T LET SOME DAMN WHITE MAN STAND IN THE CHOIR AND WATCH ANY OF IT?
HE SAYS HE WOULD INFLICT THE FULL PENALTY OF THE LAW ON THEM WERE A WHITE MAN PRESENT... AND FOR THAT THE CHIEF IS WISE...
HE KNOWS HE CAN NEVER WIPE OUT VOODOO.
BETTER LUCK HE TRY AND WIPE OUT BREATHING. AND SOME OF THE WHITE LEADERS IN THE PAST, THEY TRY EXACTLY THAT... HE CAN'T STOP IT, BUT HE WON'T LET THE CAN OF WORMS OPEN TO HAVE A WHITE MAN THERE TO CAUSE TROUBLE WITH THE AUTHORITIES. SO, NO BLANC.
SORRY, WILLY.
WELL, KATIE, THIS VOODOO BOOK WILL BE A HELL OF A THING WITH NO VOODOO IN IT!
I'M GOING TO WRITE ALL THIS VOODOO RED TAPE FOR THE CRITICS OF THE ARABIAN BOOK. THEY COULDN'T BELIEVE HOW EASILY I ENTERED THE ARAB WORLD. IT SHOULD MAKE THEM HAPPY THAT NO GODDAMN HAITIAN WILL EVEN TALK TO ME ABOUT VOODOO!
I KNOW THERE'S A WHOLE ISLAND OF HAITIANS AND ONLY ONE OF YOU. BUT IF I KNOW YOU, WILLIE, THEY DON'T STAND A CHANCE.

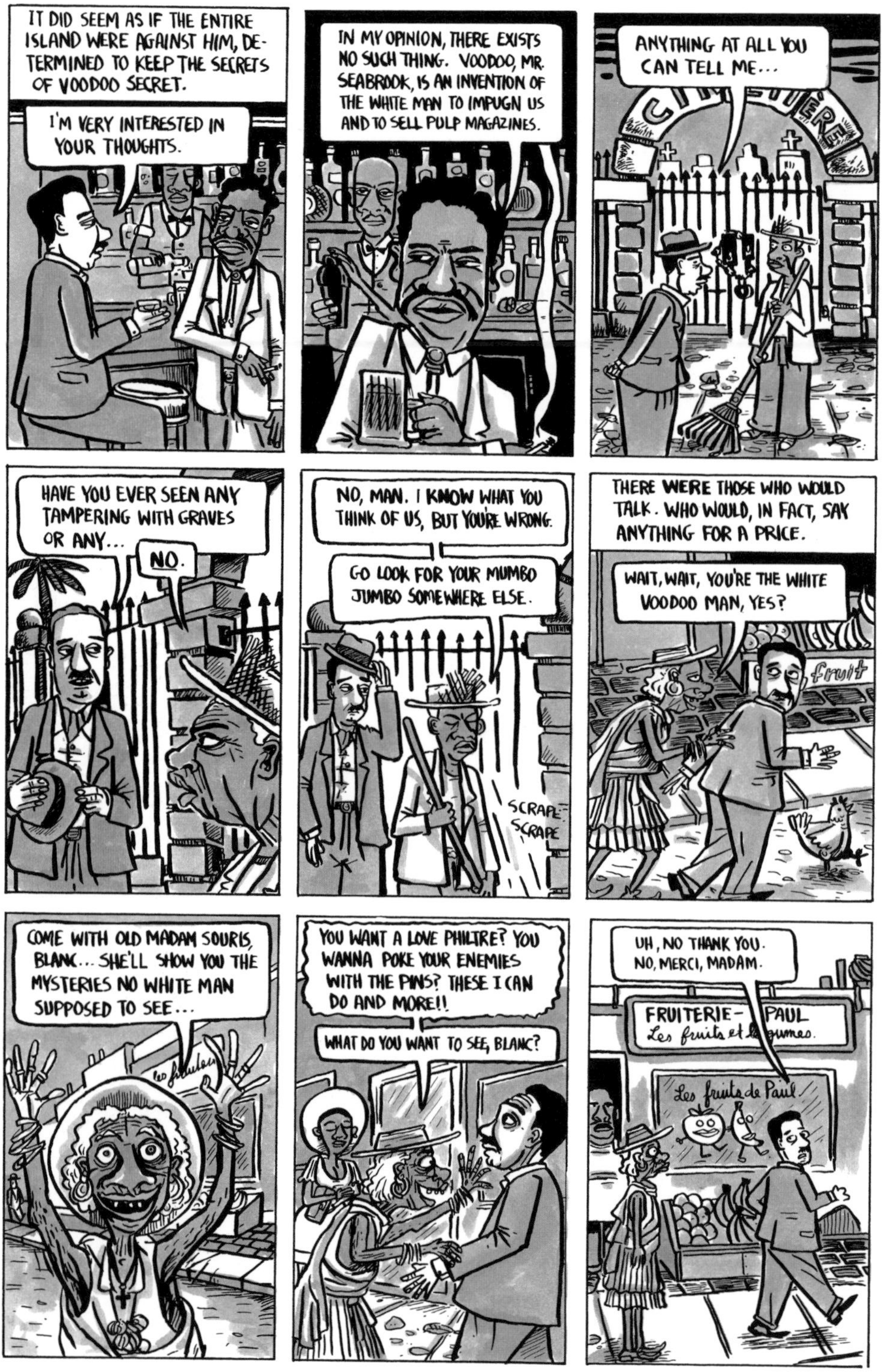
IT DID SEEM AS IF THE ENTIRE ISLAND WERE AGAINST HIM, DETERMINED TO KEEP THE SECRETS OF VOODOO SECRET.
I'M VERY INTERESTED IN YOUR THOUGHTS.
IN MY OPINION, THERE EXISTS NO SUCH THING. VOODOO, MR. SEABROOK, IS AN INVENTION OF THE WHITE MAN TO IMPUGN US AND TO SELL PULP MAGAZINES.
ANYTHING AT ALL YOU CAN TELL ME...
HAVE YOU EVER SEEN ANY TAMPERING WITH GRAVES OR ANY...
NO.
NO, MAN. I KNOW WHAT YOU THINK OF US, BUT YOU'RE WRONG.
GO LOOK FOR YOUR MUMBO JUMBO SOMEWHERE ELSE.
SCRAPE SCRAPE
THERE WERE THOSE WHO WOULD TALK. WHO WOULD, IN FACT, SAY ANYTHING FOR A PRICE.
WAIT, WAIT, YOU'RE THE WHITE VOODOO MAN, YES?
fruit
COME WITH OLD MADAM SOURIS, BLANC... SHE'LL SHOW YOU THE MYSTERIES NO WHITE MAN SUPPOSED TO SEE...
YOU WANT A LOVE PHILTRE? YOU WANNA POKE YOUR ENEMIES WITH THE PINS? THESE I CAN DO AND MORE!!
WHAT DO YOU WANT TO SEE, BLANC?
UH, NO THANK YOU. NO, MERCI, MADAM.
FRUITERIE- PAUL
Les fruits et
Les fruits de Paul

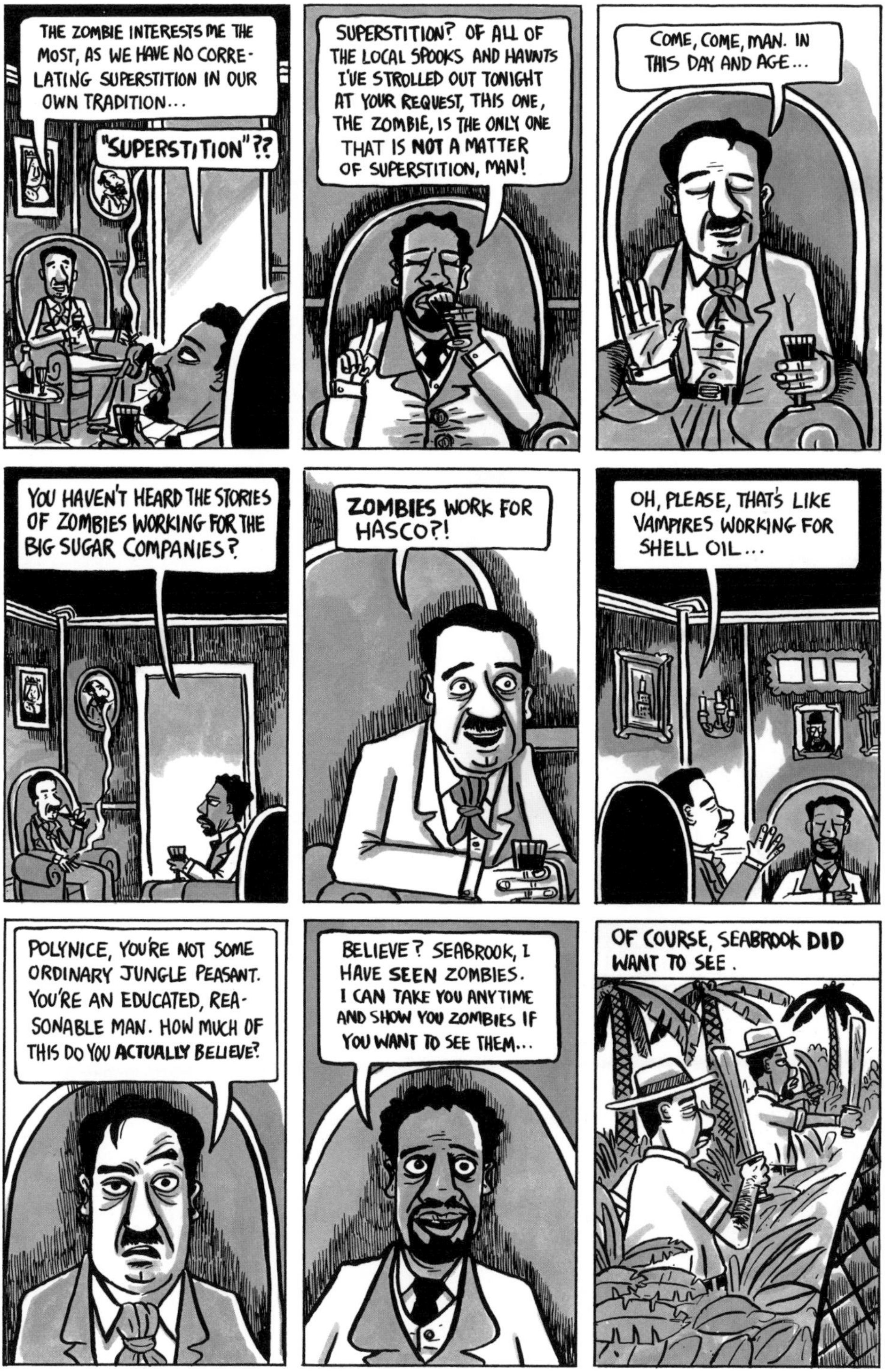
THE ZOMBIE INTERESTS ME THE MOST, AS WE HAVE NO CORRE-LATING SUPERSTITION IN OUR OWN TRADITION...
"SUPERSTITION"??
SUPERSTITION? OF ALL OF THE LOCAL SPOOKS AND HAUNTS I'VE STROLLED OUT TONIGHT AT YOUR REQUEST, THIS ONE, THE ZOMBIE, IS THE ONLY ONE THAT IS NOT A MATTER OF SUPERSTITION, MAN!
COME, COME, MAN. IN THIS DAY AND AGE...
YOU HAVEN'T HEARD THE STORIES OF ZOMBIES WORKING FOR THE BIG SUGAR COMPANIES?
ZOMBIES WORK FOR HASCO?!
OH, PLEASE, THAT'S LIKE VAMPIRES WORKING FOR SHELL OIL...
POLYNICE, YOU'RE NOT SOME ORDINARY JUNGLE PEASANT. YOU'RE AN EDUCATED, REA-SONABLE MAN. HOW MUCH OF THIS DO YOU ACTUALLY BELIEVE?
BELIEVE? SEABROOK, I HAVE SEEN ZOMBIES. I CAN TAKE YOU ANYTIME AND SHOW YOU ZOMBIES IF YOU WANT TO SEE THEM...
OF COURSE, SEABROOK DID WANT TO SEE.

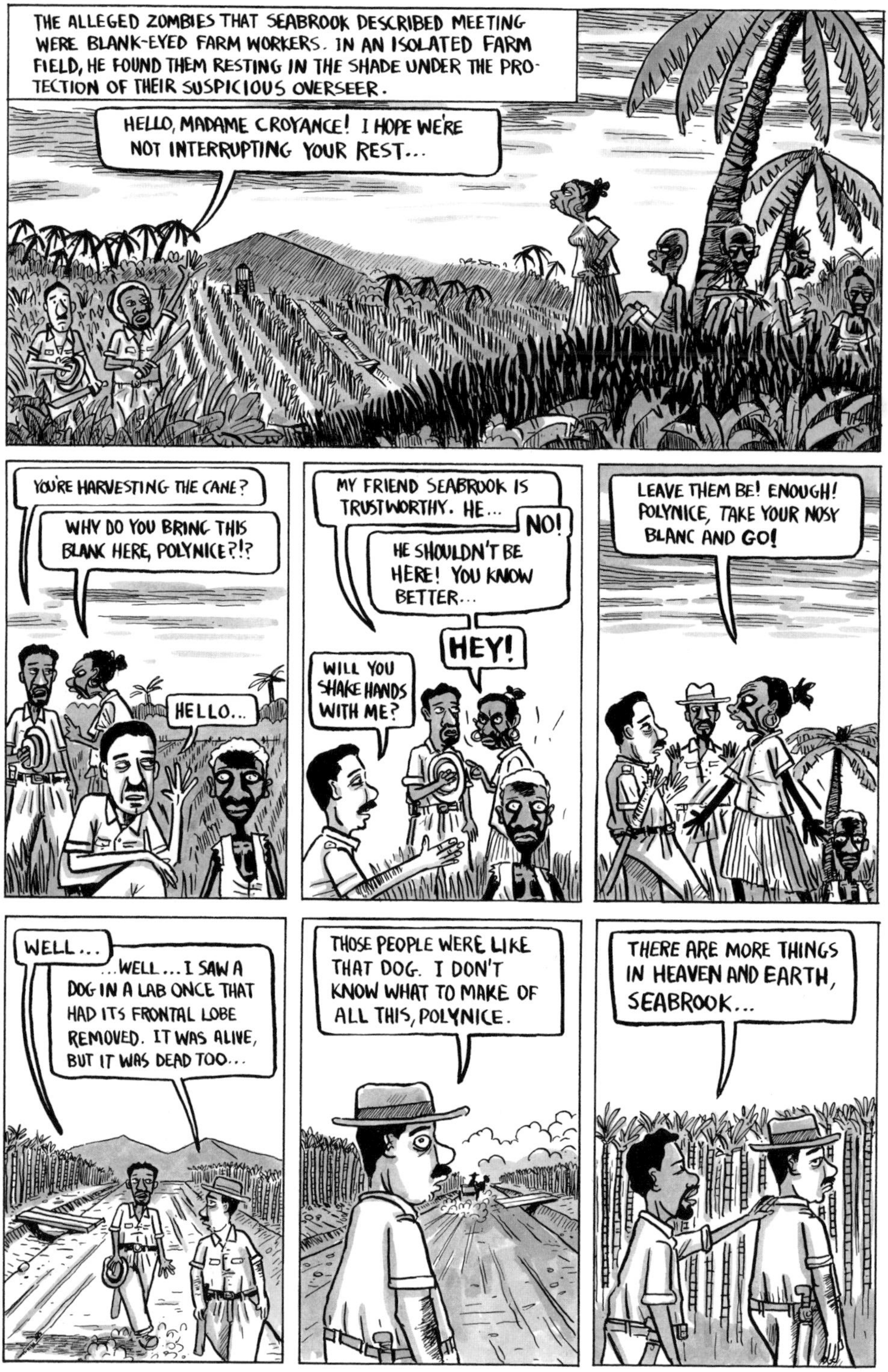

THE ALLEGED ZOMBIES THAT SEABROOK DESCRIBED MEETING WERE BLANK-EYED FARM WORKERS. IN AN ISOLATED FARM FIELD, HE FOUND THEM RESTING IN THE SHADE UNDER THE PROTECTION OF THEIR SUSPICIOUS OVERSEER.
HELLO, MADAME CROYANCE! I HOPE WE'RE NOT INTERRUPTING YOUR REST...
YOU'RE HARVESTING THE CANE?
WHY DO YOU BRING THIS BLANK HERE, POLYNICE?!?
HELLO...
MY FRIEND SEABROOK IS TRUSTWORTHY. HE...
NO!
HE SHOULDN'T BE HERE! YOU KNOW BETTER...
HEY!
WILL YOU SHAKE HANDS WITH ME?
LEAVE THEM BE! ENOUGH! POLYNICE, TAKE YOUR NOSY BLANC AND GO!
WELL...
...WELL... I SAW A DOG IN A LAB ONCE THAT HAD ITS FRONTAL LOBE REMOVED. IT WAS ALIVE, BUT IT WAS DEAD TOO...
THOSE PEOPLE WERE LIKE THAT DOG. I DON'T KNOW WHAT TO MAKE OF ALL THIS, POLYNICE.
THERE ARE MORE THINGS IN HEAVEN AND EARTH, SEABROOK...

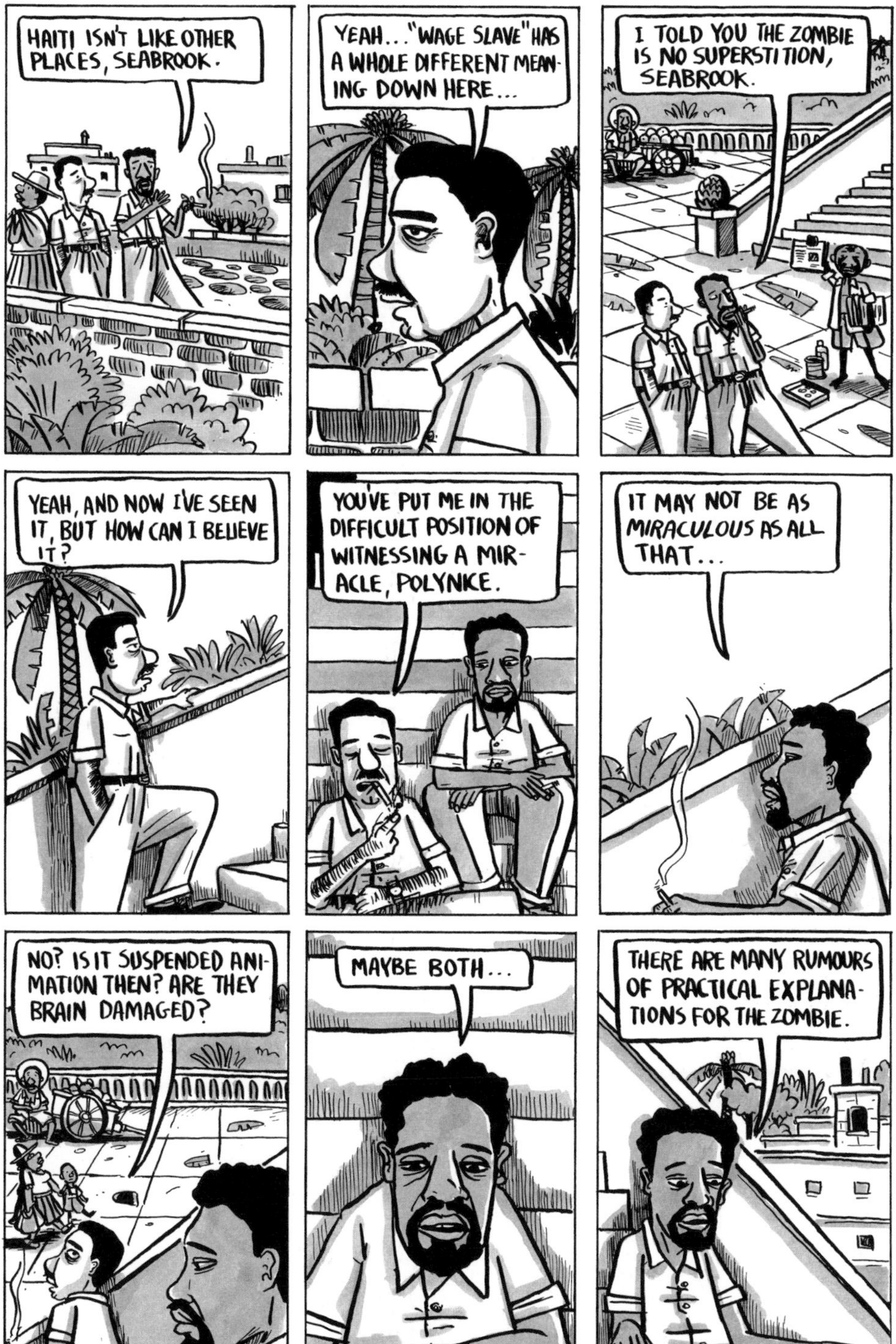
HAITI ISN'T LIKE OTHER PLACES, SEABROOK.
YEAH... "WAGE SLAVE" HAS A WHOLE DIFFERENT MEANING DOWN HERE...
I TOLD YOU THE ZOMBIE IS NO SUPERSTITION, SEABROOK.
YEAH, AND NOW I'VE SEEN IT, BUT HOW CAN I BELIEVE IT?
YOU'VE PUT ME IN THE DIFFICULT POSITION OF WITNESSING A MIRACLE, POLYNICE.
IT MAY NOT BE AS *MIRACULOUS* AS ALL THAT...
NO? IS IT SUSPENDED ANIMATION THEN? ARE THEY BRAIN DAMAGED?
MAYBE BOTH...
THERE ARE MANY RUMOURS OF PRACTICAL EXPLANATIONS FOR THE ZOMBIE.

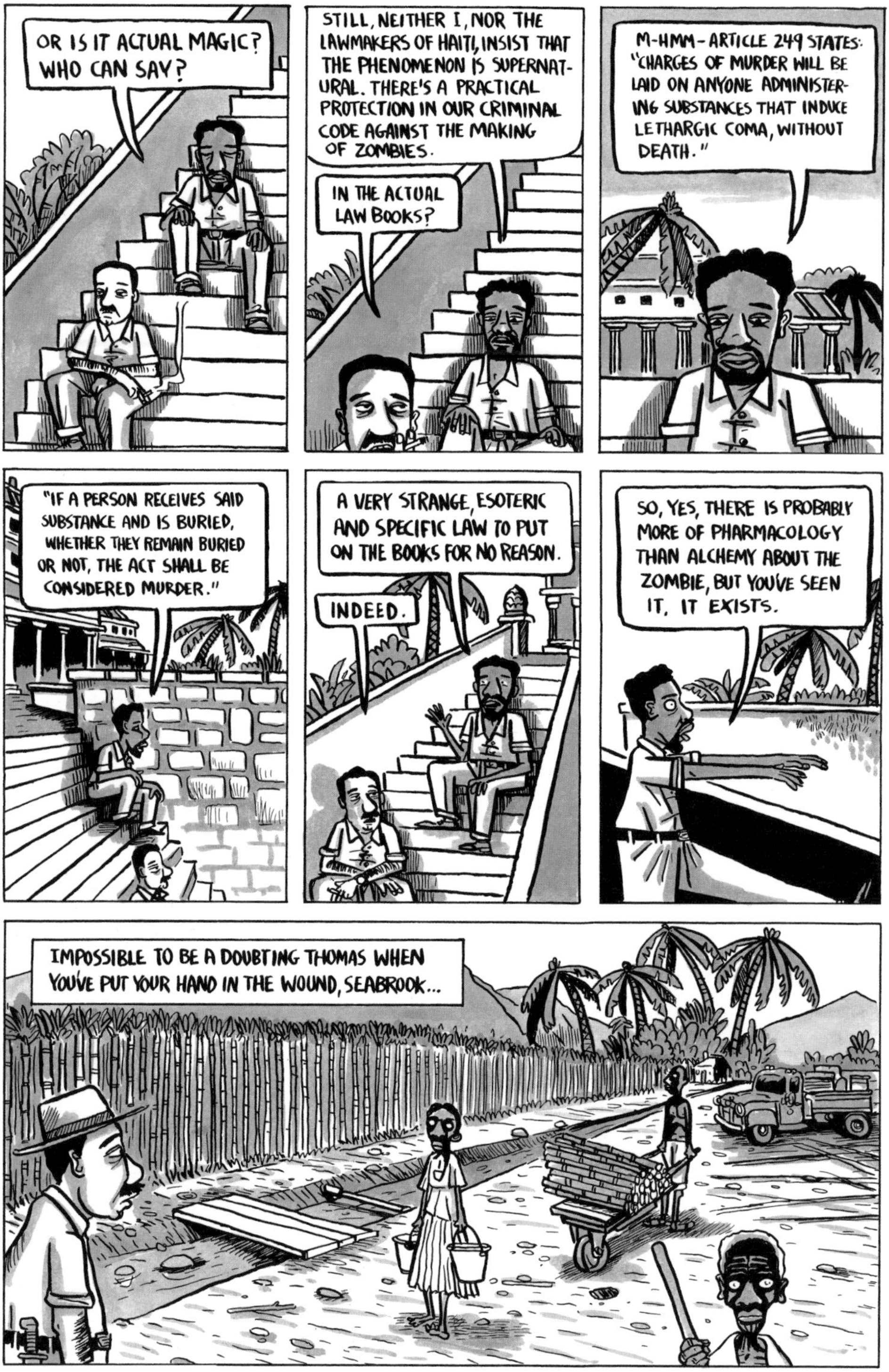
OR IS IT ACTUAL MAGIC? WHO CAN SAY?
STILL, NEITHER I, NOR THE LAWMAKERS OF HAITI, INSIST THAT THE PHENOMENON IS SUPERNATURAL. THERE'S A PRACTICAL PROTECTION IN OUR CRIMINAL CODE AGAINST THE MAKING OF ZOMBIES.
IN THE ACTUAL LAW BOOKS?
M-HMM - ARTICLE 249 STATES: "CHARGES OF MURDER WILL BE LAID ON ANYONE ADMINISTERING SUBSTANCES THAT INDUCE LETHARGIC COMA, WITHOUT DEATH."
"IF A PERSON RECEIVES SAID SUBSTANCE AND IS BURIED, WHETHER THEY REMAIN BURIED OR NOT, THE ACT SHALL BE CONSIDERED MURDER."
A VERY STRANGE, ESOTERIC AND SPECIFIC LAW TO PUT ON THE BOOKS FOR NO REASON.
INDEED.
SO, YES, THERE IS PROBABLY MORE OF PHARMACOLOGY THAN ALCHEMY ABOUT THE ZOMBIE, BUT YOU'VE SEEN IT, IT EXISTS.
IMPOSSIBLE TO BE A DOUBTING THOMAS WHEN YOU'VE PUT YOUR HAND IN THE WOUND, SEABROOK...

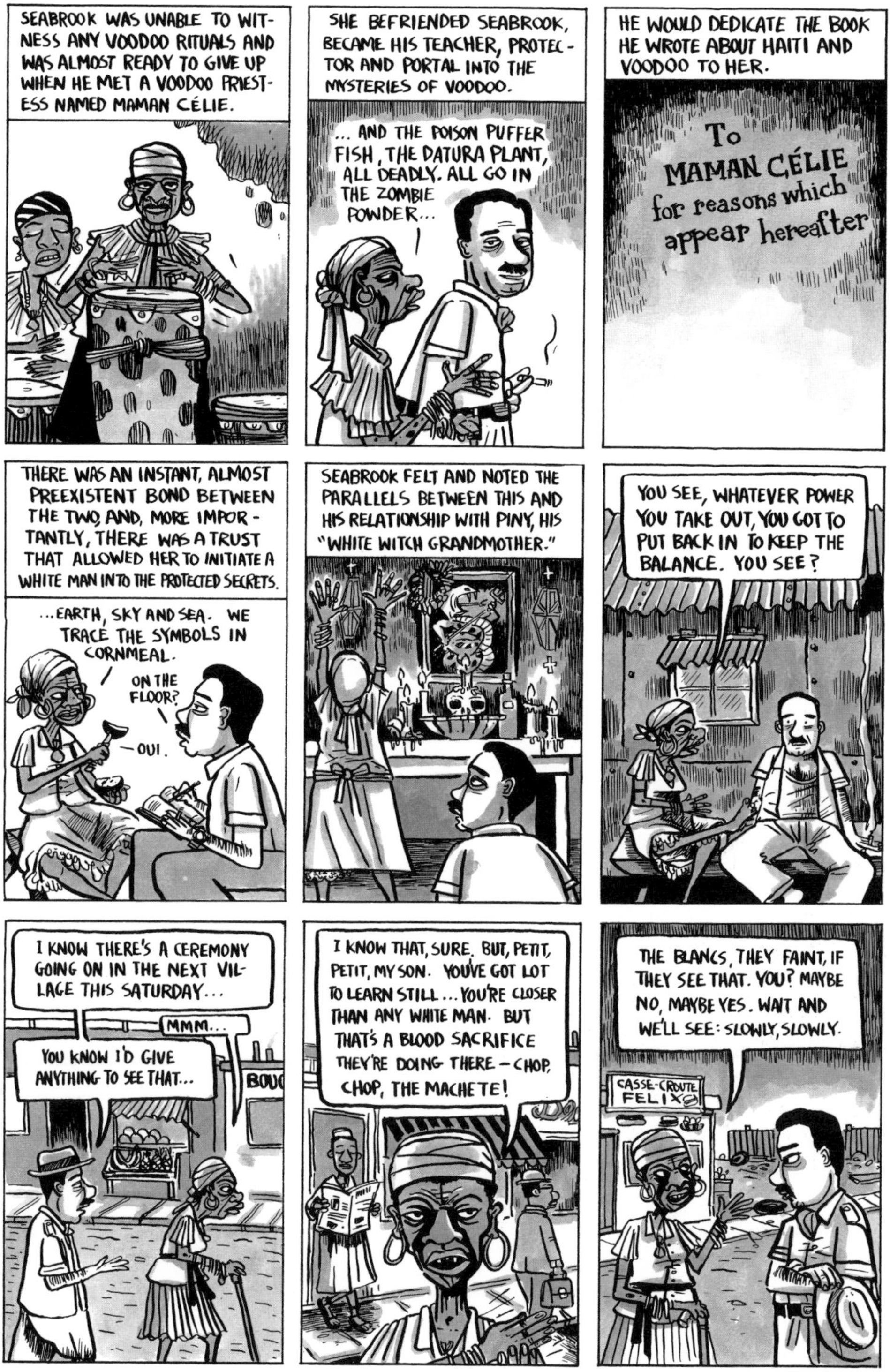
SEABROOK WAS UNABLE TO WITNESS ANY VOODOO RITUALS AND WAS ALMOST READY TO GIVE UP WHEN HE MET A VOODOO PRIESTESS NAMED MAMAN CÉLIE.
SHE BEFRIENDED SEABROOK, BECAME HIS TEACHER, PROTECTOR AND PORTAL INTO THE MYSTERIES OF VOODOO.
... AND THE POISON PUFFER FISH, THE DATURA PLANT, ALL DEADLY. ALL GO IN THE ZOMBIE POWDER...
HE WOULD DEDICATE THE BOOK HE WROTE ABOUT HAITI AND VOODOO TO HER.
To
MAMAN CÉLIE
for reasons which
appear hereafter
THERE WAS AN INSTANT, ALMOST PREEXISTENT BOND BETWEEN THE TWO, AND, MORE IMPORTANTLY, THERE WAS A TRUST THAT ALLOWED HER TO INITIATE A WHITE MAN INTO THE PROTECTED SECRETS.
...EARTH, SKY AND SEA. WE TRACE THE SYMBOLS IN CORNMEAL.
ON THE FLOOR?
OUI.
SEABROOK FELT AND NOTED THE PARALLELS BETWEEN THIS AND HIS RELATIONSHIP WITH PINY, HIS "WHITE WITCH GRANDMOTHER."
YOU SEE, WHATEVER POWER YOU TAKE OUT, YOU GOT TO PUT BACK IN TO KEEP THE BALANCE. YOU SEE?
I KNOW THERE'S A CEREMONY GOING ON IN THE NEXT VILLAGE THIS SATURDAY...
MMM...
YOU KNOW I'D GIVE ANYTHING TO SEE THAT...
BOU
I KNOW THAT, SURE. BUT, PETIT, PETIT, MY SON. YOU'VE GOT LOT TO LEARN STILL... YOU'RE CLOSER THAN ANY WHITE MAN. BUT THAT'S A BLOOD SACRIFICE THEY'RE DOING THERE — CHOP, CHOP, THE MACHETE!
THE BLANCS, THEY FAINT, IF THEY SEE THAT. YOU? MAYBE NO, MAYBE YES. WAIT AND WE'LL SEE: SLOWLY, SLOWLY.
CASSE-CROUTE
FELIX

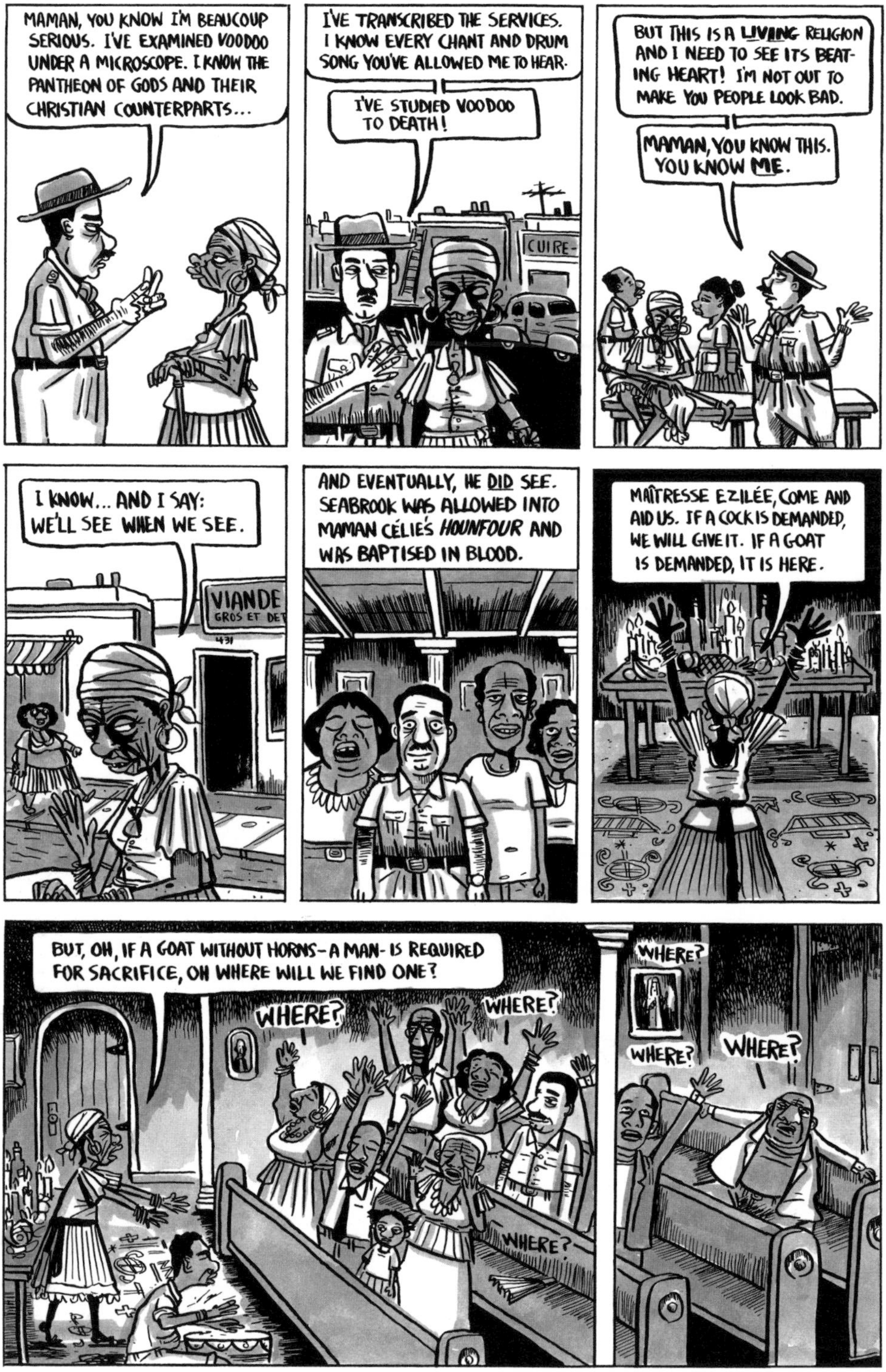
MAMAN, YOU KNOW I'M BEAUCOUP SERIOUS. I'VE EXAMINED VOODOO UNDER A MICROSCOPE. I KNOW THE PANTHEON OF GODS AND THEIR CHRISTIAN COUNTERPARTS...
I'VE TRANSCRIBED THE SERVICES. I KNOW EVERY CHANT AND DRUM SONG YOU'VE ALLOWED ME TO HEAR.
I'VE STUDIED VOODOO TO DEATH!
CUIRE-
BUT THIS IS A LIVING RELIGION AND I NEED TO SEE ITS BEATING HEART! I'M NOT OUT TO MAKE YOU PEOPLE LOOK BAD.
MAMAN, YOU KNOW THIS. YOU KNOW ME.
I KNOW... AND I SAY: WE'LL SEE WHEN WE SEE.
VIANDE
GROS ET DET
431
AND EVENTUALLY, HE DID SEE. SEABROOK WAS ALLOWED INTO MAMAN CÉLIE'S HOUNFOUR AND WAS BAPTISED IN BLOOD.
MAÎTRESSE EZILÉE, COME AND AID US. IF A COCK IS DEMANDED, WE WILL GIVE IT. IF A GOAT IS DEMANDED, IT IS HERE.
BUT, OH, IF A GOAT WITHOUT HORNS- A MAN- IS REQUIRED FOR SACRIFICE, OH WHERE WILL WE FIND ONE?
WHERE?
WHERE?
WHERE?
WHERE?
WHERE?
WHERE?

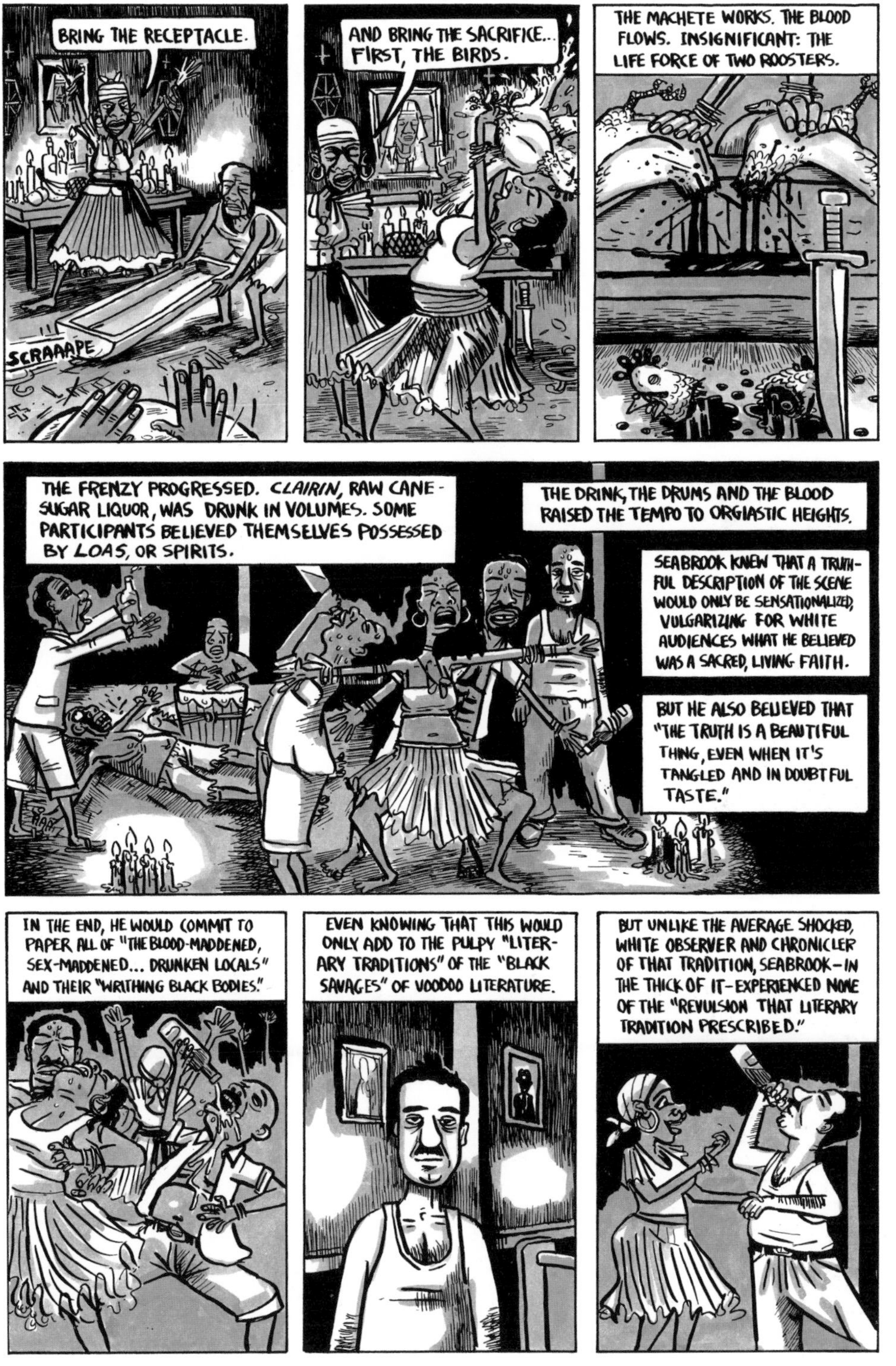
BRING THE RECEPTACLE.
SCRAAAPE
AND BRING THE SACRIFICE... FIRST, THE BIRDS.
THE MACHETE WORKS. THE BLOOD FLOWS. INSIGNIFICANT: THE LIFE FORCE OF TWO ROOSTERS.
THE FRENZY PROGRESSED. CLAIRIN, RAW CANE-SUGAR LIQUOR, WAS DRUNK IN VOLUMES. SOME PARTICIPANTS BELIEVED THEMSELVES POSSESSED BY LOAS, OR SPIRITS.
THE DRINK, THE DRUMS AND THE BLOOD RAISED THE TEMPO TO ORGIASTIC HEIGHTS.
SEABROOK KNEW THAT A TRUTHFUL DESCRIPTION OF THE SCENE WOULD ONLY BE SENSATIONALIZED, VULGARIZING FOR WHITE AUDIENCES WHAT HE BELIEVED WAS A SACRED, LIVING FAITH.
BUT HE ALSO BELIEVED THAT "THE TRUTH IS A BEAUTIFUL THING, EVEN WHEN IT'S TANGLED AND IN DOUBTFUL TASTE."
IN THE END, HE WOULD COMMIT TO PAPER ALL OF "THE BLOOD-MADDENED, SEX-MADDENED... DRUNKEN LOCALS" AND THEIR "WRITHING BLACK BODIES."
EVEN KNOWING THAT THIS WOULD ONLY ADD TO THE PULPY "LITERARY TRADITIONS" OF THE "BLACK SAVAGES" OF VOODOO LITERATURE.
BUT UNLIKE THE AVERAGE SHOCKED, WHITE OBSERVER AND CHRONICLER OF THAT TRADITION, SEABROOK—IN THE THICK OF IT—EXPERIENCED NONE OF THE "REVULSION THAT LITERARY TRADITION PRESCRIBED."

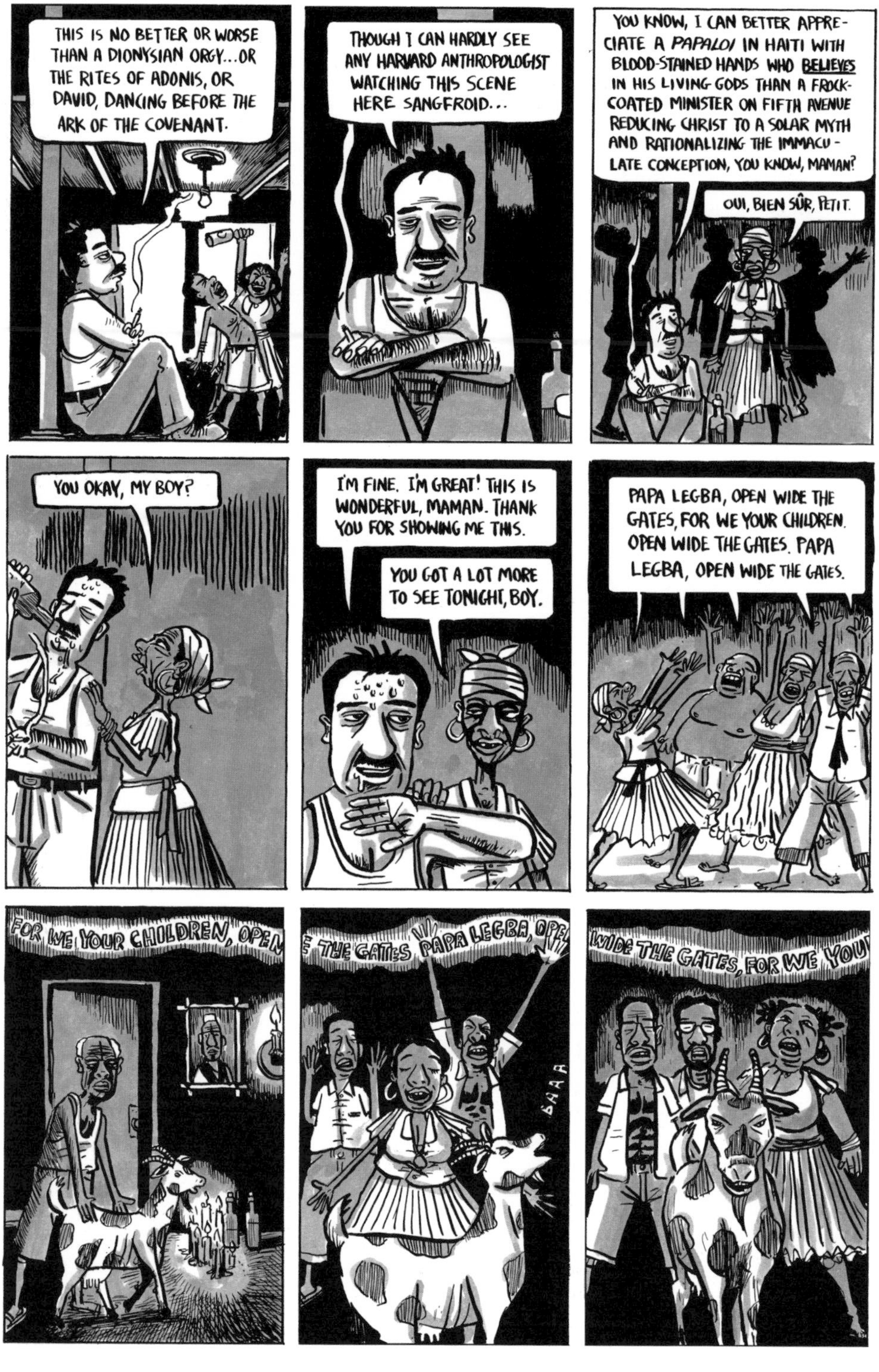
THIS IS NO BETTER OR WORSE THAN A DIONYSIAN ORGY...OR THE RITES OF ADONIS, OR DAVID, DANCING BEFORE THE ARK OF THE COVENANT.
THOUGH I CAN HARDLY SEE ANY HARVARD ANTHROPOLOGIST WATCHING THIS SCENE HERE SANGFROID...
YOU KNOW, I CAN BETTER APPRECIATE A PAPALOI IN HAITI WITH BLOOD-STAINED HANDS WHO BELIEVES IN HIS LIVING GODS THAN A FROCK-COATED MINISTER ON FIFTH AVENUE REDUCING CHRIST TO A SOLAR MYTH AND RATIONALIZING THE IMMACULATE CONCEPTION, YOU KNOW, MAMAN?
OUI, BIEN SÛR, PETIT.
YOU OKAY, MY BOY?
I'M FINE. I'M GREAT! THIS IS WONDERFUL, MAMAN. THANK YOU FOR SHOWING ME THIS.
YOU GOT A LOT MORE TO SEE TONIGHT, BOY.
PAPA LEGBA, OPEN WIDE THE GATES, FOR WE YOUR CHILDREN. OPEN WIDE THE GATES. PAPA LEGBA, OPEN WIDE THE GATES.
FOR WE YOUR CHILDREN, OPEN
E THE GATES PAPA LEGBA, OPE
BAAA
WIDE THE GATES, FOR WE YOU

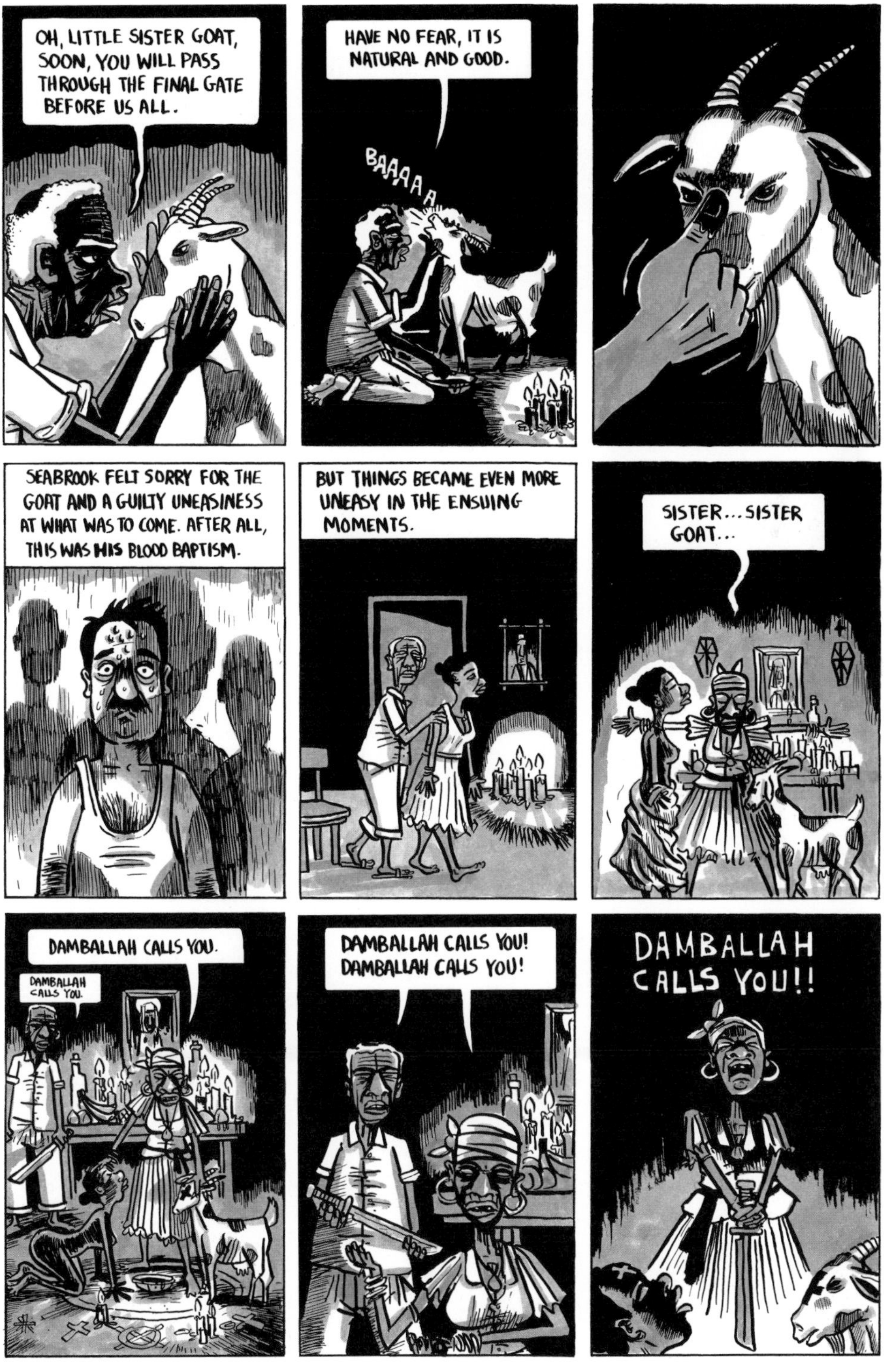
OH, LITTLE SISTER GOAT, SOON, YOU WILL PASS THROUGH THE FINAL GATE BEFORE US ALL.
HAVE NO FEAR, IT IS NATURAL AND GOOD.
BAAAAAA
SEABROOK FELT SORRY FOR THE GOAT AND A GUILTY UNEASINESS AT WHAT WAS TO COME. AFTER ALL, THIS WAS HIS BLOOD BAPTISM.
BUT THINGS BECAME EVEN MORE UNEASY IN THE ENSUING MOMENTS.
SISTER... SISTER GOAT...
DAMBALLAH CALLS YOU.
DAMBALLAH CALLS YOU.
DAMBALLAH CALLS YOU! DAMBALLAH CALLS YOU!
DAMBALLAH CALLS YOU!!

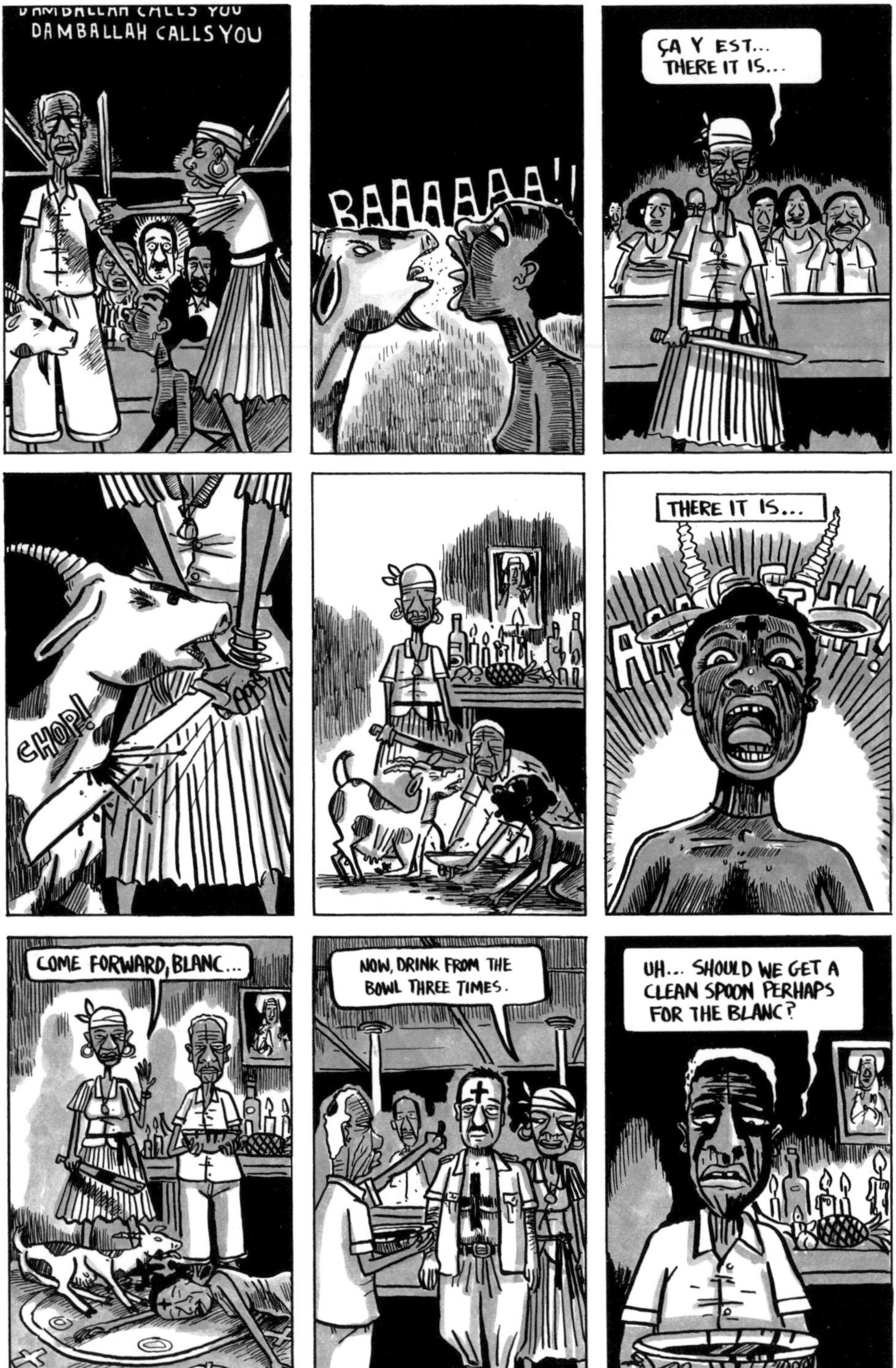
DAMBALLAH CALLS YOU
DAMBALLAH CALLS YOU
BAAAAAA!!
ÇA Y EST...
THERE IT IS...
CHOP!
THERE IT IS...
COME FORWARD, BLANC...
NOW, DRINK FROM THE BOWL THREE TIMES.
UH... SHOULD WE GET A CLEAN SPOON PERHAPS FOR THE BLANC?

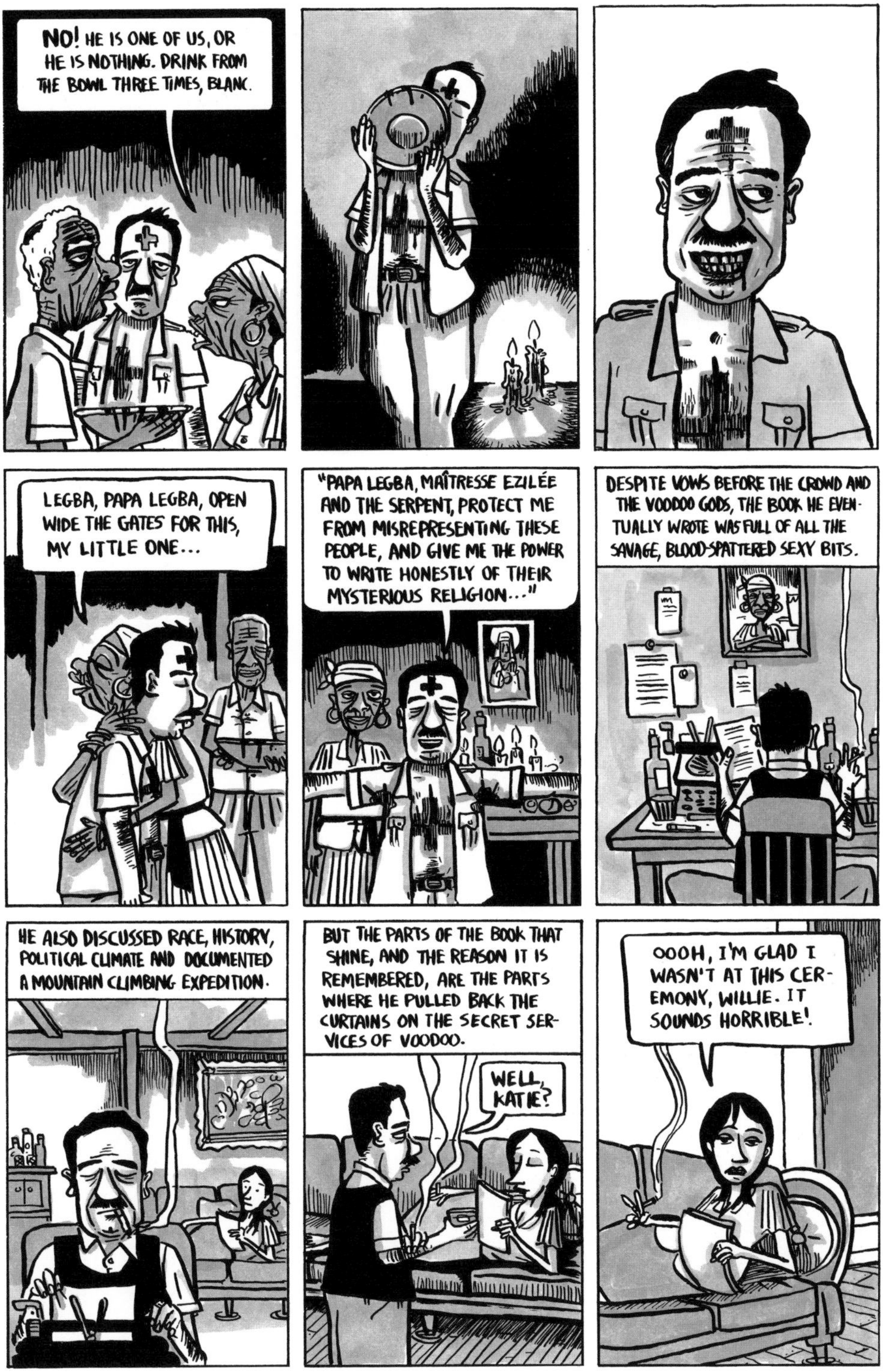
NO! HE IS ONE OF US, OR HE IS NOTHING. DRINK FROM THE BOWL THREE TIMES, BLANC.
LEGBA, PAPA LEGBA, OPEN WIDE THE GATES FOR THIS, MY LITTLE ONE...
"PAPA LEGBA, MAÎTRESSE EZILÉE AND THE SERPENT, PROTECT ME FROM MISREPRESENTING THESE PEOPLE, AND GIVE ME THE POWER TO WRITE HONESTLY OF THEIR MYSTERIOUS RELIGION..."
DESPITE VOWS BEFORE THE CROWD AND THE VOODOO GODS, THE BOOK HE EVENTUALLY WROTE WAS FULL OF ALL THE SAVAGE, BLOOD-SPATTERED SEXY BITS.
HE ALSO DISCUSSED RACE, HISTORY, POLITICAL CLIMATE AND DOCUMENTED A MOUNTAIN CLIMBING EXPEDITION.
BUT THE PARTS OF THE BOOK THAT SHINE, AND THE REASON IT IS REMEMBERED, ARE THE PARTS WHERE HE PULLED BACK THE CURTAINS ON THE SECRET SERVICES OF VOODOO.
WELL, KATIE?
OOOH, I'M GLAD I WASN'T AT THIS CEREMONY, WILLIE. IT SOUNDS HORRIBLE!

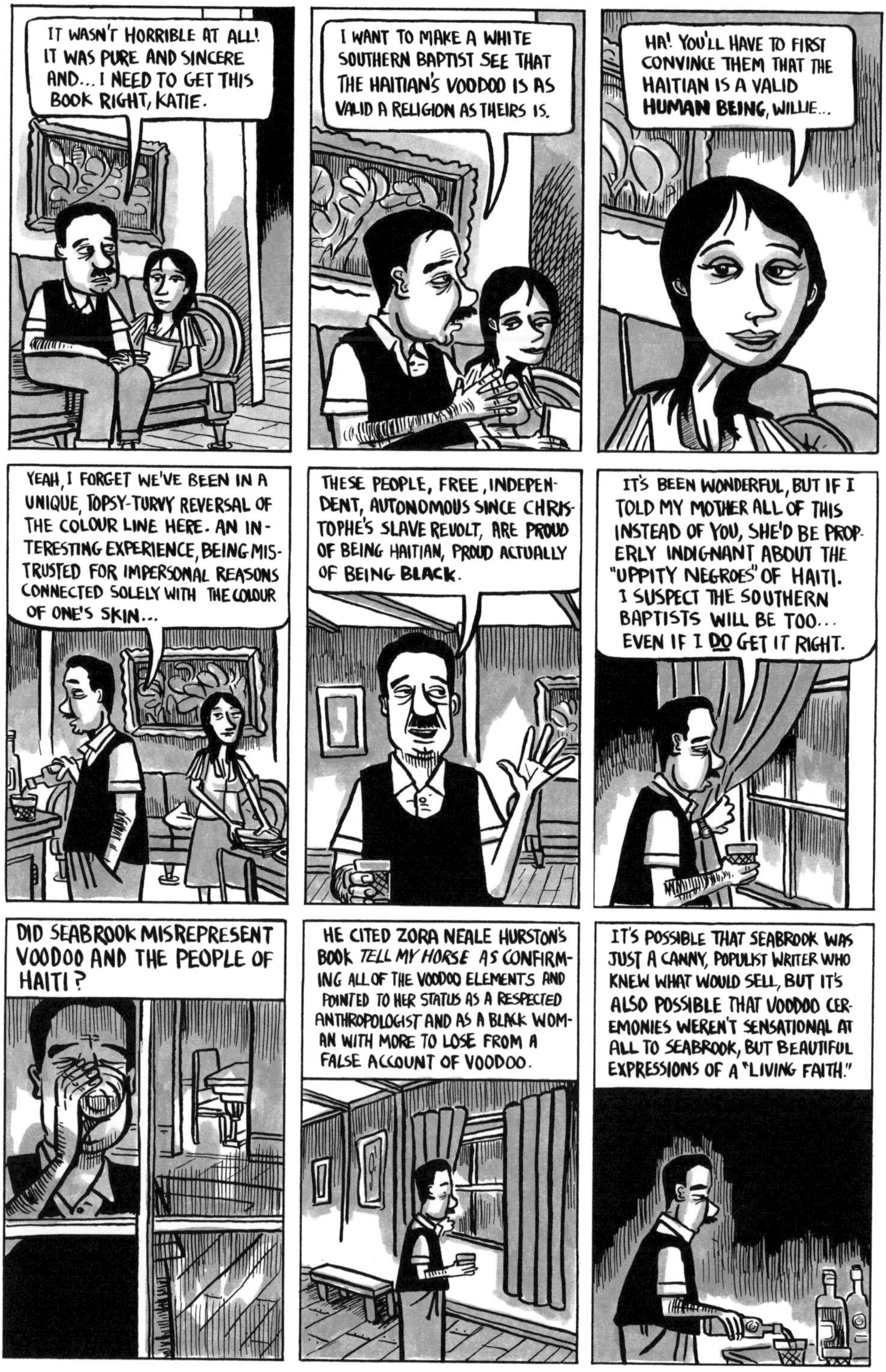
IT WASN'T HORRIBLE AT ALL! IT WAS PURE AND SINCERE AND... I NEED TO GET THIS BOOK RIGHT, KATIE.
I WANT TO MAKE A WHITE SOUTHERN BAPTIST SEE THAT THE HAITIAN'S VOODOO IS AS VALID A RELIGION AS THEIRS IS.
HA! YOU'LL HAVE TO FIRST CONVINCE THEM THAT THE HAITIAN IS A VALID **HUMAN BEING**, WILLIE...
YEAH, I FORGET WE'VE BEEN IN A UNIQUE, TOPSY-TURVY REVERSAL OF THE COLOUR LINE HERE. AN INTERESTING EXPERIENCE, BEING MISTRUSTED FOR IMPERSONAL REASONS CONNECTED SOLELY WITH THE COLOUR OF ONE'S SKIN...
THESE PEOPLE, FREE, INDEPENDENT, AUTONOMOUS SINCE CHRISTOPHE'S SLAVE REVOLT, ARE PROUD OF BEING HAITIAN, PROUD ACTUALLY OF BEING **BLACK**.
IT'S BEEN WONDERFUL, BUT IF I TOLD MY MOTHER ALL OF THIS INSTEAD OF YOU, SHE'D BE PROPERLY INDIGNANT ABOUT THE "UPPITY NEGROES" OF HAITI. I SUSPECT THE SOUTHERN BAPTISTS WILL BE TOO... EVEN IF I DO GET IT RIGHT.
DID SEABROOK MISREPRESENT VOODOO AND THE PEOPLE OF HAITI?
HE CITED ZORA NEALE HURSTON'S BOOK *TELL MY HORSE* AS CONFIRMING ALL OF THE VOODOO ELEMENTS AND POINTED TO HER STATUS AS A RESPECTED ANTHROPOLOGIST AND AS A BLACK WOMAN WITH MORE TO LOSE FROM A FALSE ACCOUNT OF VOODOO.
IT'S POSSIBLE THAT SEABROOK WAS JUST A CANNY, POPULIST WRITER WHO KNEW WHAT WOULD SELL, BUT IT'S ALSO POSSIBLE THAT VOODOO CEREMONIES WEREN'T SENSATIONAL AT ALL TO SEABROOK, BUT BEAUTIFUL EXPRESSIONS OF A "LIVING FAITH."

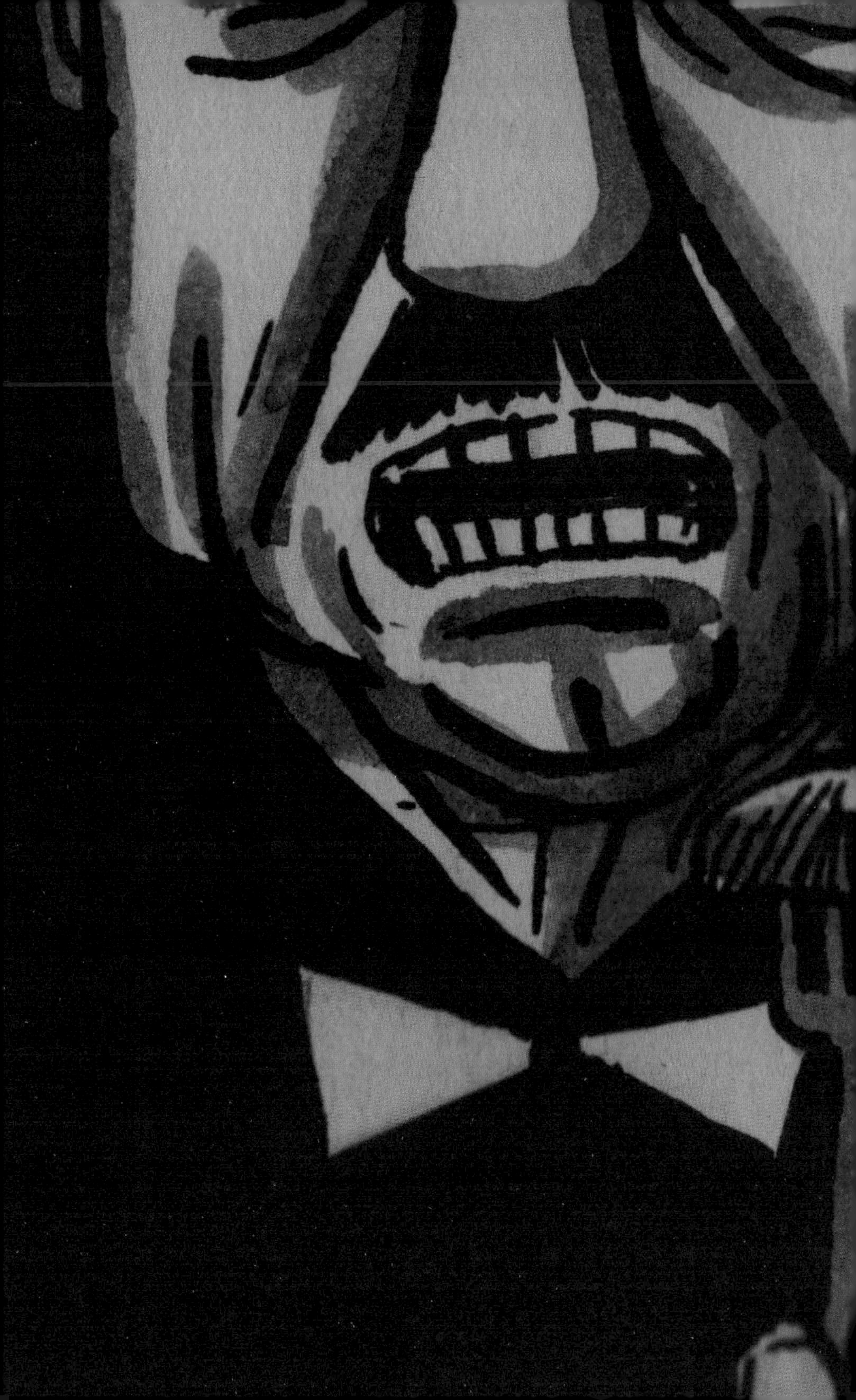

# CHAPTER FOUR
# THE URBAN CANNIBAL

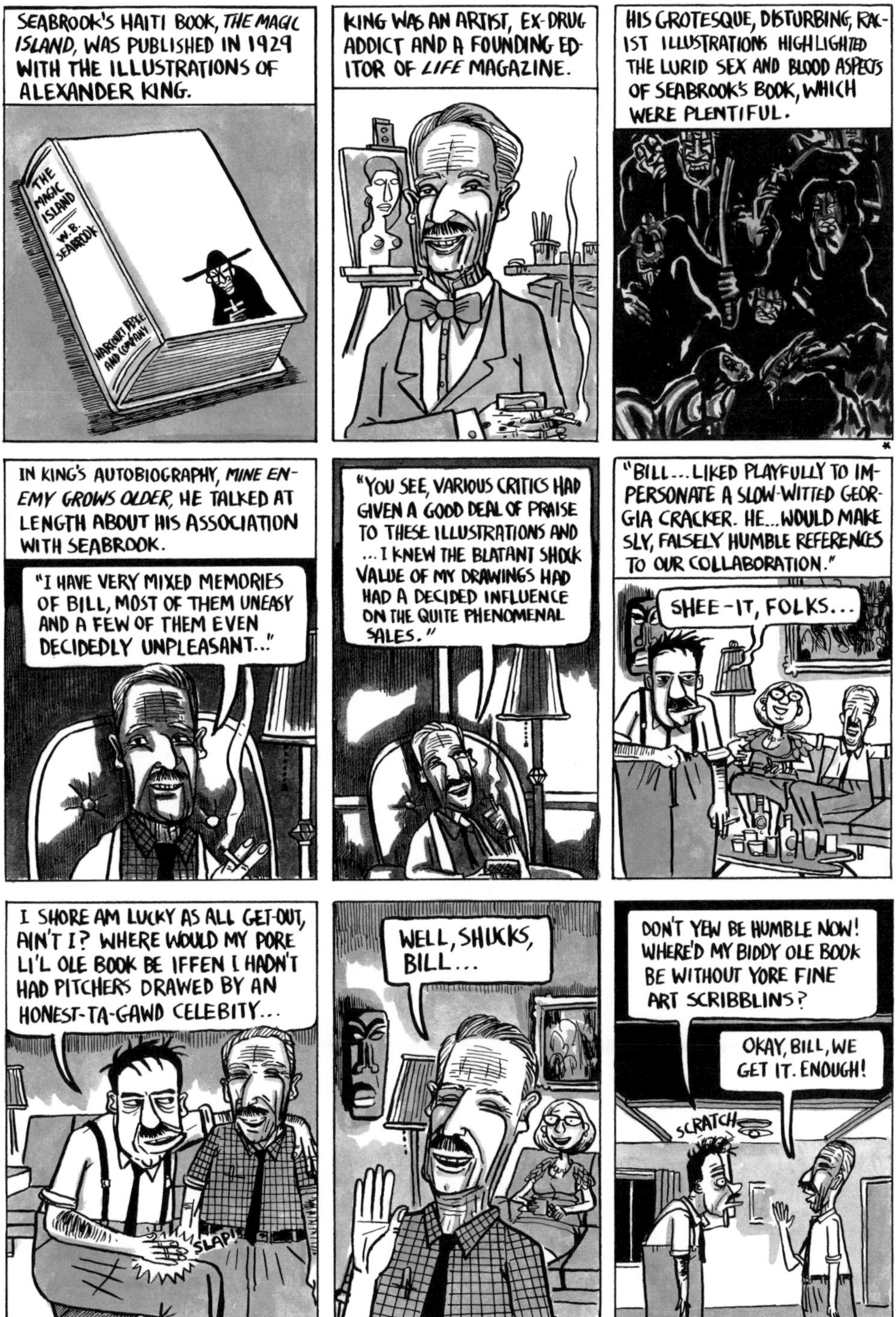
SEABROOK'S HAITI BOOK, *THE MAGIC ISLAND*, WAS PUBLISHED IN 1929 WITH THE ILLUSTRATIONS OF ALEXANDER KING.
THE MAGIC ISLAND
W.B. SEABROOK
HARCOURT BRACE AND COMPANY
KING WAS AN ARTIST, EX-DRUG ADDICT AND A FOUNDING EDITOR OF *LIFE* MAGAZINE.
HIS GROTESQUE, DISTURBING, RACIST ILLUSTRATIONS HIGHLIGHTED THE LURID SEX AND BLOOD ASPECTS OF SEABROOK'S BOOK, WHICH WERE PLENTIFUL.
*
IN KING'S AUTOBIOGRAPHY, *MINE ENEMY GROWS OLDER*, HE TALKED AT LENGTH ABOUT HIS ASSOCIATION WITH SEABROOK.
"I HAVE VERY MIXED MEMORIES OF BILL, MOST OF THEM UNEASY AND A FEW OF THEM EVEN DECIDEDLY UNPLEASANT..."
"YOU SEE, VARIOUS CRITICS HAD GIVEN A GOOD DEAL OF PRAISE TO THESE ILLUSTRATIONS AND ... I KNEW THE BLATANT SHOCK VALUE OF MY DRAWINGS HAD HAD A DECIDED INFLUENCE ON THE QUITE PHENOMENAL SALES."
"BILL... LIKED PLAYFULLY TO IMPERSONATE A SLOW-WITTED GEORGIA CRACKER. HE...WOULD MAKE SLY, FALSELY HUMBLE REFERENCES TO OUR COLLABORATION."
SHEE-IT, FOLKS...
I SHORE AM LUCKY AS ALL GET-OUT, AIN'T I? WHERE WOULD MY PORE LI'L OLE BOOK BE IFFEN I HADN'T HAD PITCHERS DRAWED BY AN HONEST-TA-GAWD CELEBITY...
SLAP!
WELL, SHUCKS, BILL...
DON'T YEW BE HUMBLE NOW! WHERE'D MY BIDDY OLE BOOK BE WITHOUT YORE FINE ART SCRIBBLINS?
OKAY, BILL, WE GET IT. ENOUGH!
SCRATCH

* (BASED ON AN ALEXANDER KING ILLUSTRATION FROM *THE MAGIC ISLAND*.)

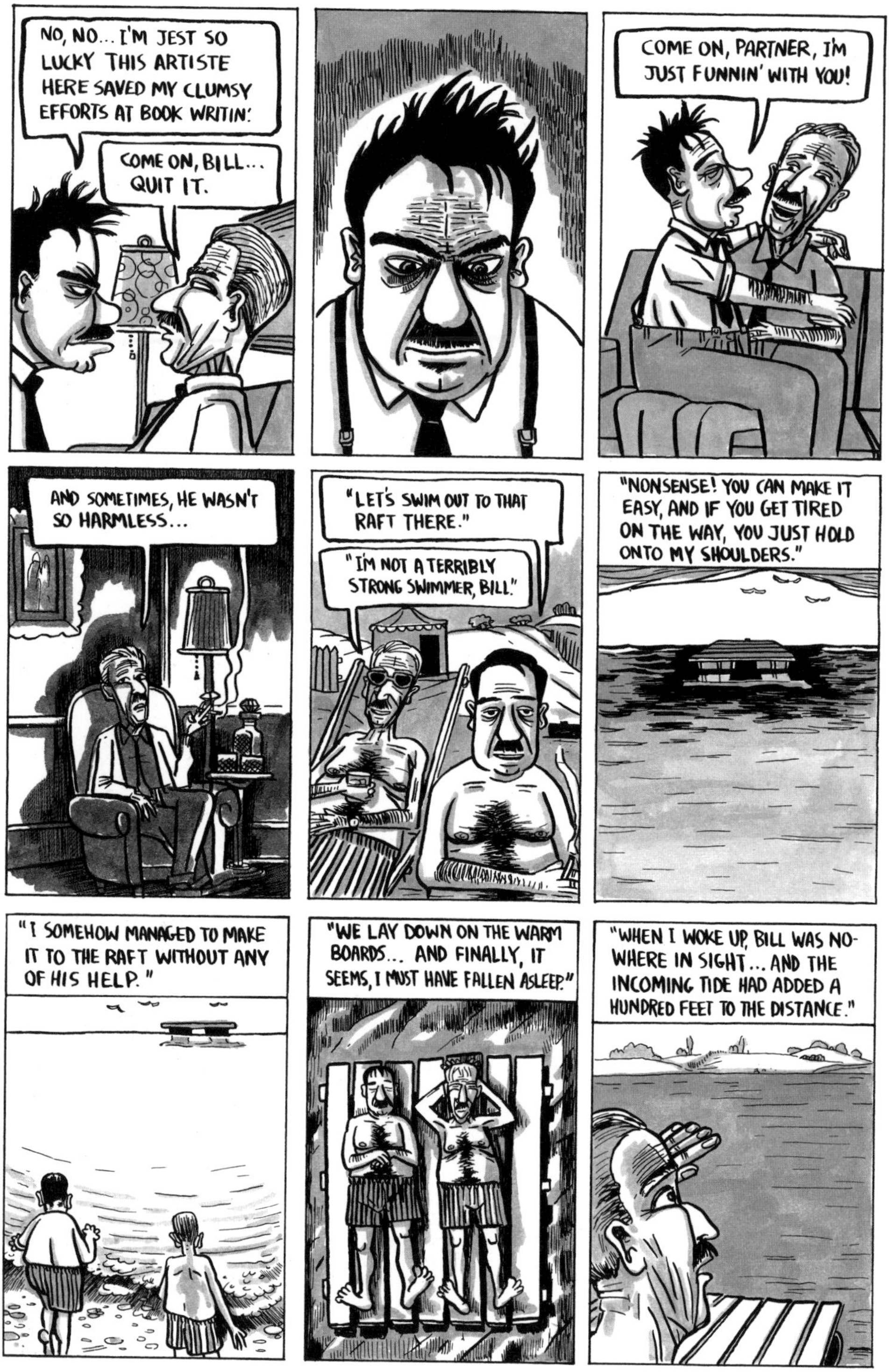
NO, NO... I'M JEST SO LUCKY THIS ARTISTE HERE SAVED MY CLUMSY EFFORTS AT BOOK WRITIN'.
COME ON, BILL... QUIT IT.
COME ON, PARTNER, I'M JUST FUNNIN' WITH YOU!
AND SOMETIMES, HE WASN'T SO HARMLESS...
"LET'S SWIM OUT TO THAT RAFT THERE."
"I'M NOT A TERRIBLY STRONG SWIMMER, BILL."
"NONSENSE! YOU CAN MAKE IT EASY, AND IF YOU GET TIRED ON THE WAY, YOU JUST HOLD ONTO MY SHOULDERS."
"I SOMEHOW MANAGED TO MAKE IT TO THE RAFT WITHOUT ANY OF HIS HELP."
"WE LAY DOWN ON THE WARM BOARDS... AND FINALLY, IT SEEMS, I MUST HAVE FALLEN ASLEEP."
"WHEN I WOKE UP, BILL WAS NOWHERE IN SIGHT... AND THE INCOMING TIDE HAD ADDED A HUNDRED FEET TO THE DISTANCE."

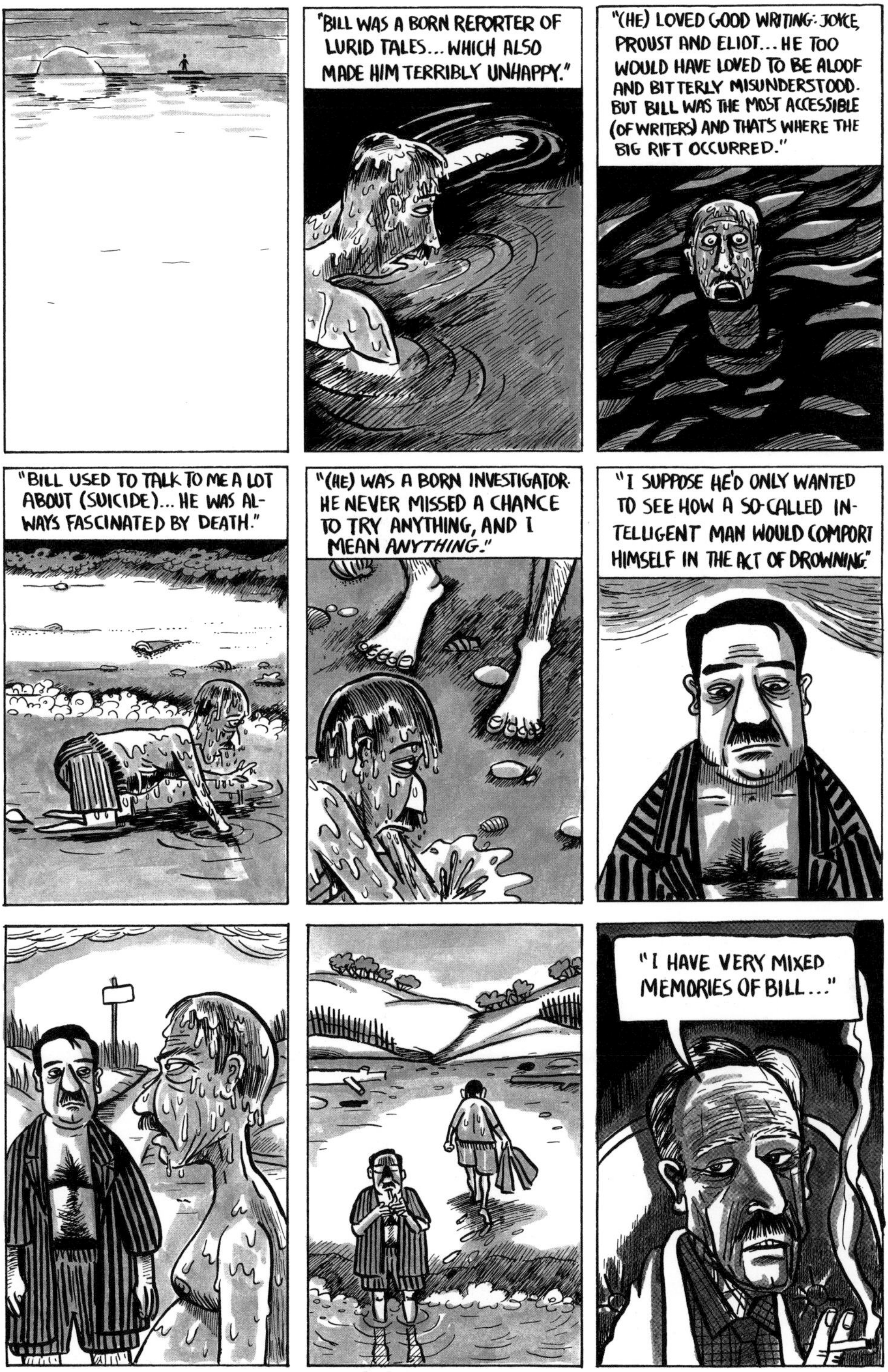
"BILL WAS A BORN REPORTER OF LURID TALES... WHICH ALSO MADE HIM TERRIBLY UNHAPPY."
"(HE) LOVED GOOD WRITING: JOYCE, PROUST AND ELIOT... HE TOO WOULD HAVE LOVED TO BE ALOOF AND BITTERLY MISUNDERSTOOD. BUT BILL WAS THE MOST ACCESSIBLE (OF WRITERS) AND THAT'S WHERE THE BIG RIFT OCCURRED."
"BILL USED TO TALK TO ME A LOT ABOUT (SUICIDE)... HE WAS ALWAYS FASCINATED BY DEATH."
"(HE) WAS A BORN INVESTIGATOR. HE NEVER MISSED A CHANCE TO TRY ANYTHING, AND I MEAN *ANYTHING*."
"I SUPPOSE HE'D ONLY WANTED TO SEE HOW A SO-CALLED INTELLIGENT MAN WOULD COMPORT HIMSELF IN THE ACT OF DROWNING."
"I HAVE VERY MIXED MEMORIES OF BILL..."

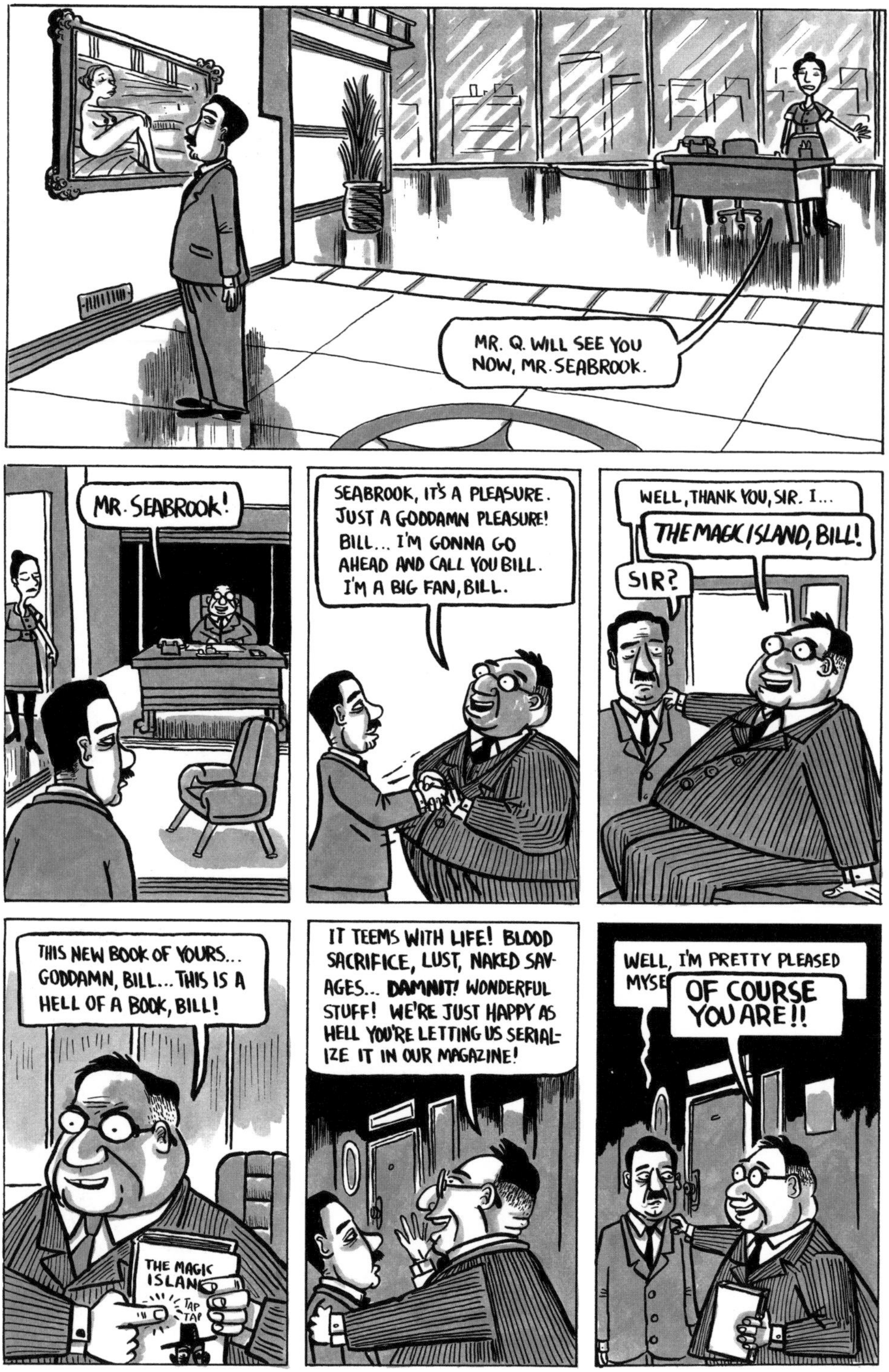
MR. Q. WILL SEE YOU NOW, MR. SEABROOK.
MR. SEABROOK!
SEABROOK, IT'S A PLEASURE. JUST A GODDAMN PLEASURE! BILL... I'M GONNA GO AHEAD AND CALL YOU BILL. I'M A BIG FAN, BILL.
WELL, THANK YOU, SIR. I...
THE MAGIC ISLAND, BILL!
SIR?
THIS NEW BOOK OF YOURS... GODDAMN, BILL... THIS IS A HELL OF A BOOK, BILL!
THE MAGIC ISLAN
TAP TAP
IT TEEMS WITH LIFE! BLOOD SACRIFICE, LUST, NAKED SAVAGES... DAMNIT! WONDERFUL STUFF! WE'RE JUST HAPPY AS HELL YOU'RE LETTING US SERIALIZE IT IN OUR MAGAZINE!
WELL, I'M PRETTY PLEASED MYSE
OF COURSE YOU ARE!!

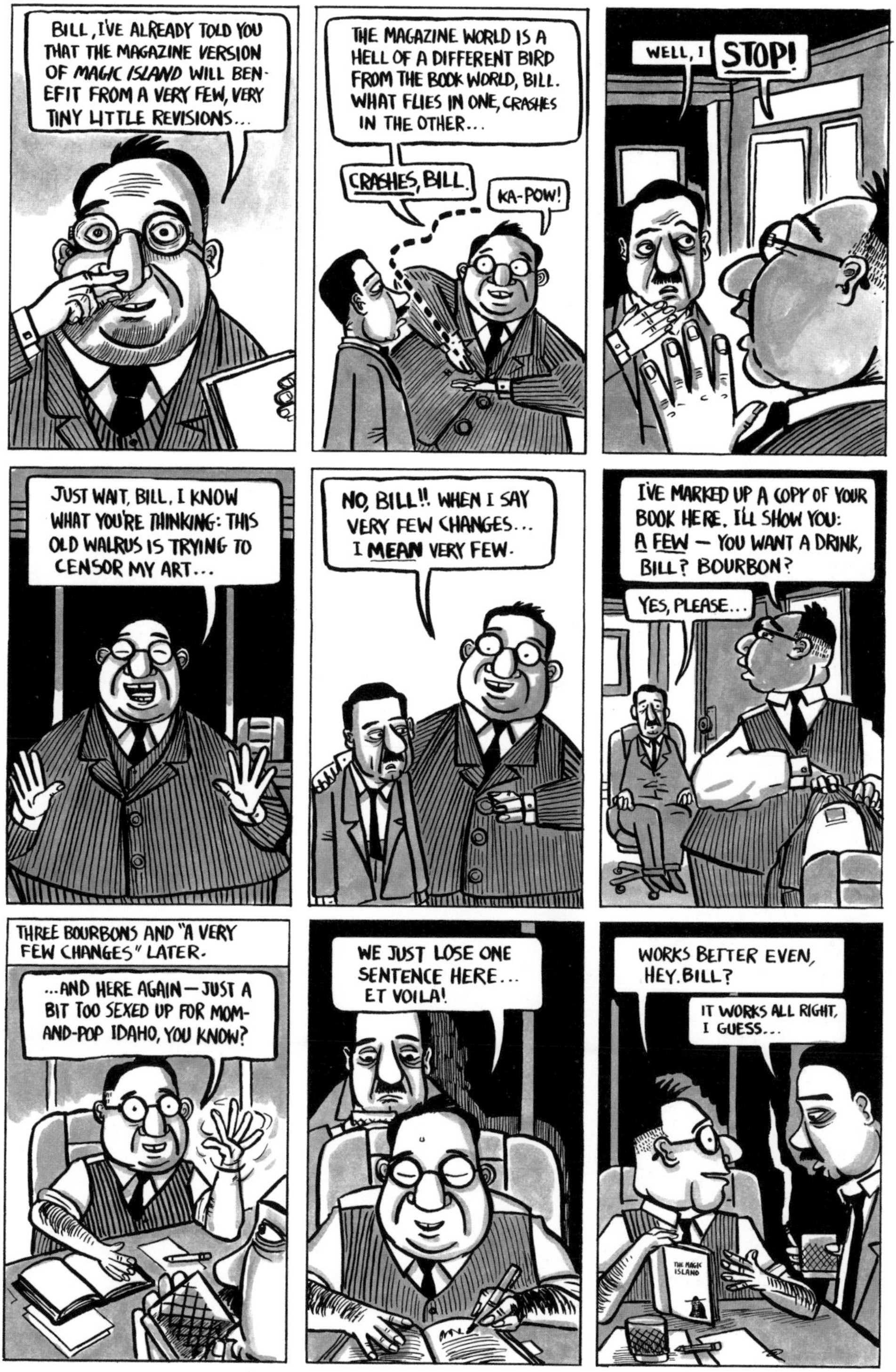
BILL, I'VE ALREADY TOLD YOU THAT THE MAGAZINE VERSION OF *MAGIC ISLAND* WILL BENEFIT FROM A VERY FEW, VERY TINY LITTLE REVISIONS...
THE MAGAZINE WORLD IS A HELL OF A DIFFERENT BIRD FROM THE BOOK WORLD, BILL. WHAT FLIES IN ONE, CRASHES IN THE OTHER...
CRASHES, BILL.
KA-POW!
WELL, I
STOP!
JUST WAIT, BILL, I KNOW WHAT YOU'RE THINKING: THIS OLD WALRUS IS TRYING TO CENSOR MY ART...
NO, BILL!! WHEN I SAY VERY FEW CHANGES... I MEAN VERY FEW.
I'VE MARKED UP A COPY OF YOUR BOOK HERE. I'LL SHOW YOU: A FEW — YOU WANT A DRINK, BILL? BOURBON?
YES, PLEASE...
THREE BOURBONS AND "A VERY FEW CHANGES" LATER.
...AND HERE AGAIN — JUST A BIT TOO SEXED UP FOR MOM-AND-POP IDAHO, YOU KNOW?
WE JUST LOSE ONE SENTENCE HERE... ET VOILA!
WORKS BETTER EVEN, HEY. BILL?
IT WORKS ALL RIGHT, I GUESS...
THE MAGIC ISLAND

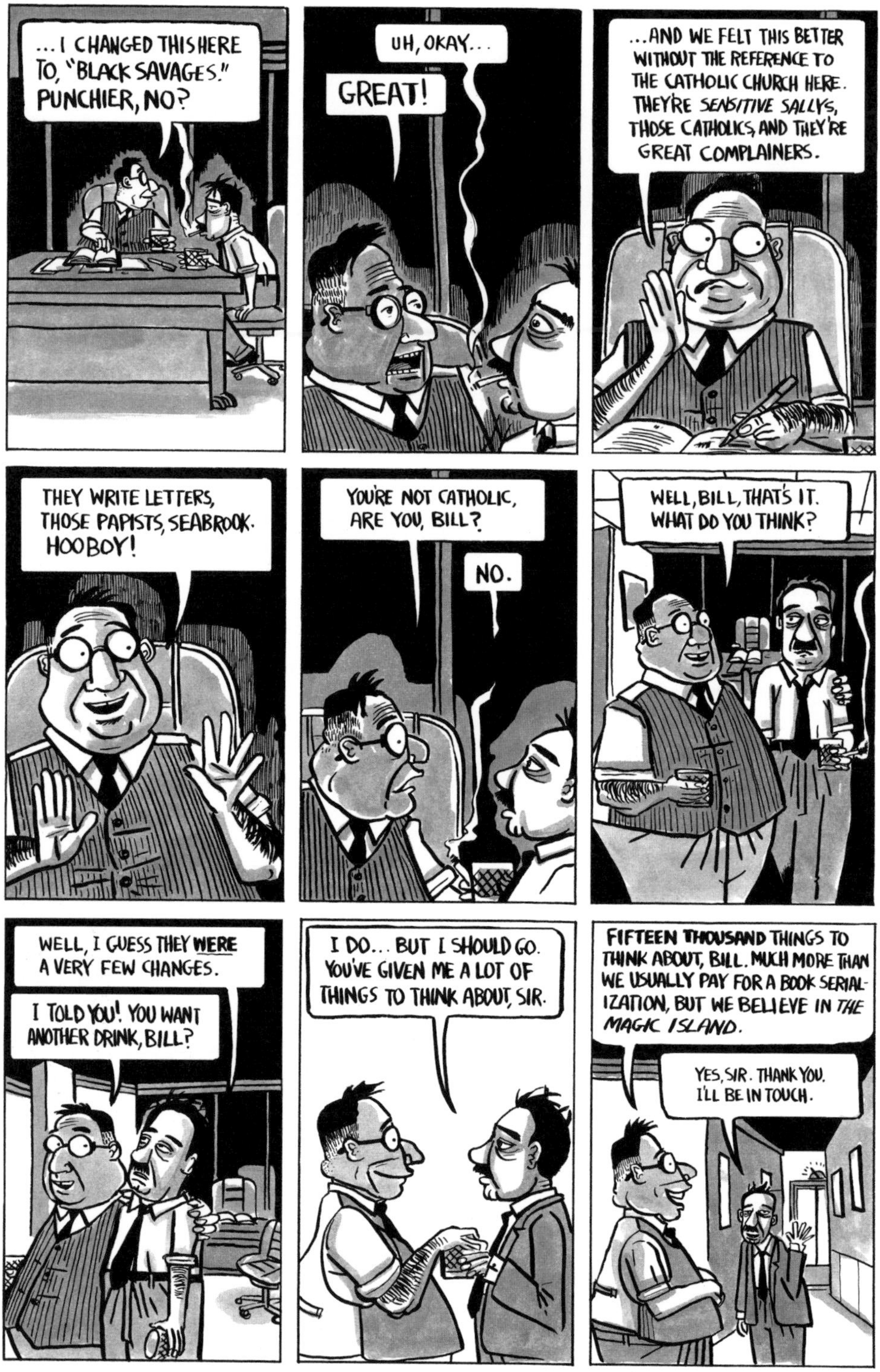
...I CHANGED THIS HERE TO, "BLACK SAVAGES." PUNCHIER, NO?
UH, OKAY...
GREAT!
...AND WE FELT THIS BETTER WITHOUT THE REFERENCE TO THE CATHOLIC CHURCH HERE. THEY'RE *SENSITIVE SALLYS*, THOSE CATHOLICS, AND THEY'RE GREAT COMPLAINERS.
THEY WRITE LETTERS, THOSE PAPISTS, SEABROOK. HOOBOY!
YOU'RE NOT CATHOLIC, ARE YOU, BILL?
NO.
WELL, BILL, THAT'S IT. WHAT DO YOU THINK?
WELL, I GUESS THEY WERE A VERY FEW CHANGES.
I TOLD YOU! YOU WANT ANOTHER DRINK, BILL?
I DO... BUT I SHOULD GO. YOU'VE GIVEN ME A LOT OF THINGS TO THINK ABOUT, SIR.
FIFTEEN THOUSAND THINGS TO THINK ABOUT, BILL. MUCH MORE THAN WE USUALLY PAY FOR A BOOK SERIALIZATION, BUT WE BELIEVE IN *THE MAGIC ISLAND*.
YES, SIR. THANK YOU. I'LL BE IN TOUCH.

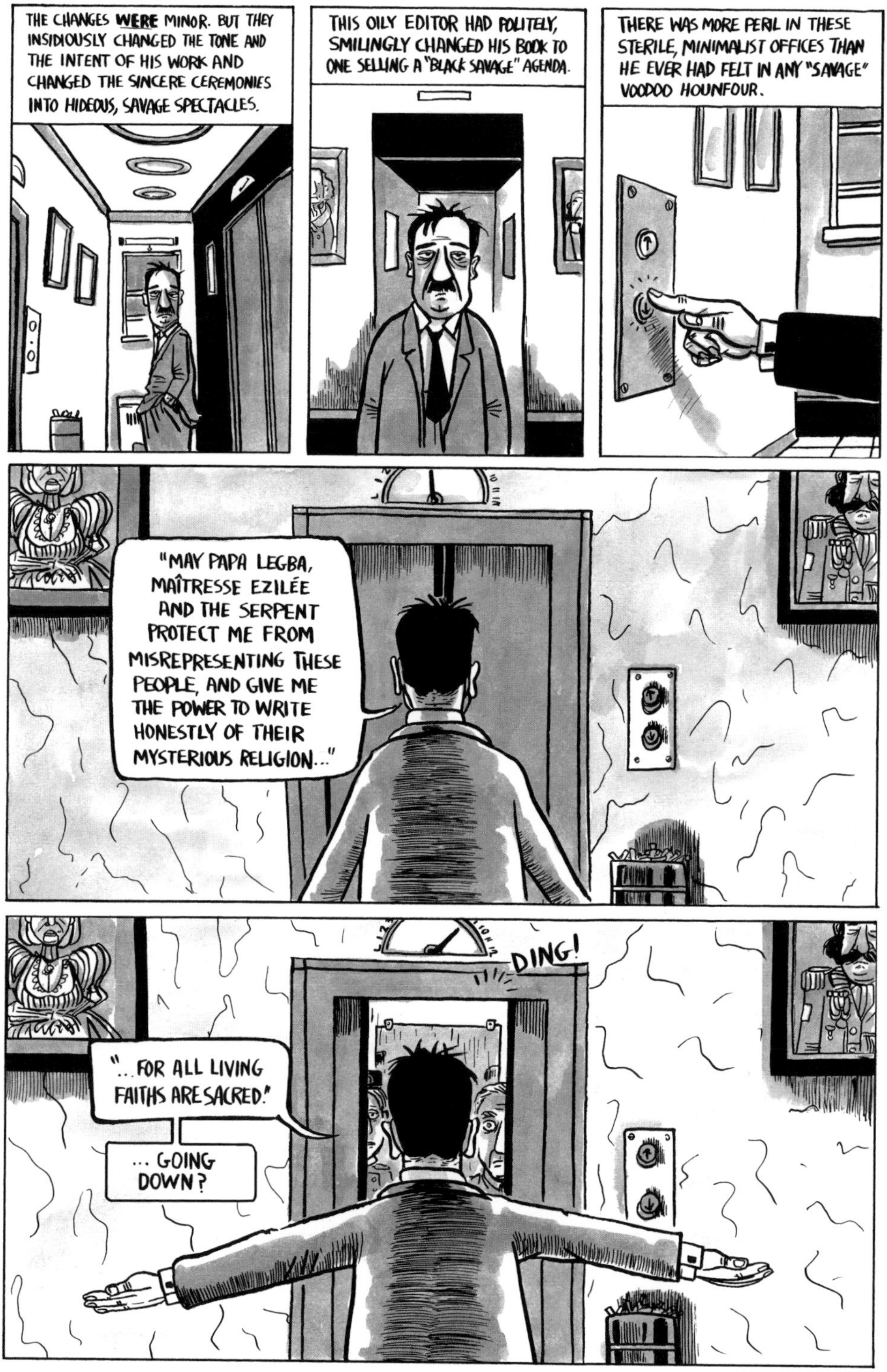
THE CHANGES WERE MINOR. BUT THEY INSIDIOUSLY CHANGED THE TONE AND THE INTENT OF HIS WORK AND CHANGED THE SINCERE CEREMONIES INTO HIDEOUS, SAVAGE SPECTACLES.
THIS OILY EDITOR HAD POLITELY, SMILINGLY CHANGED HIS BOOK TO ONE SELLING A "BLACK SAVAGE" AGENDA.
THERE WAS MORE PERIL IN THESE STERILE, MINIMALIST OFFICES THAN HE EVER HAD FELT IN ANY "SAVAGE" VOODOO HOUNFOUR.
"MAY PAPA LEGBA, MAÎTRESSE EZILÉE AND THE SERPENT PROTECT ME FROM MISREPRESENTING THESE PEOPLE, AND GIVE ME THE POWER TO WRITE HONESTLY OF THEIR MYSTERIOUS RELIGION..."
DING!
"...FOR ALL LIVING FAITHS ARE SACRED."
... GOING DOWN?

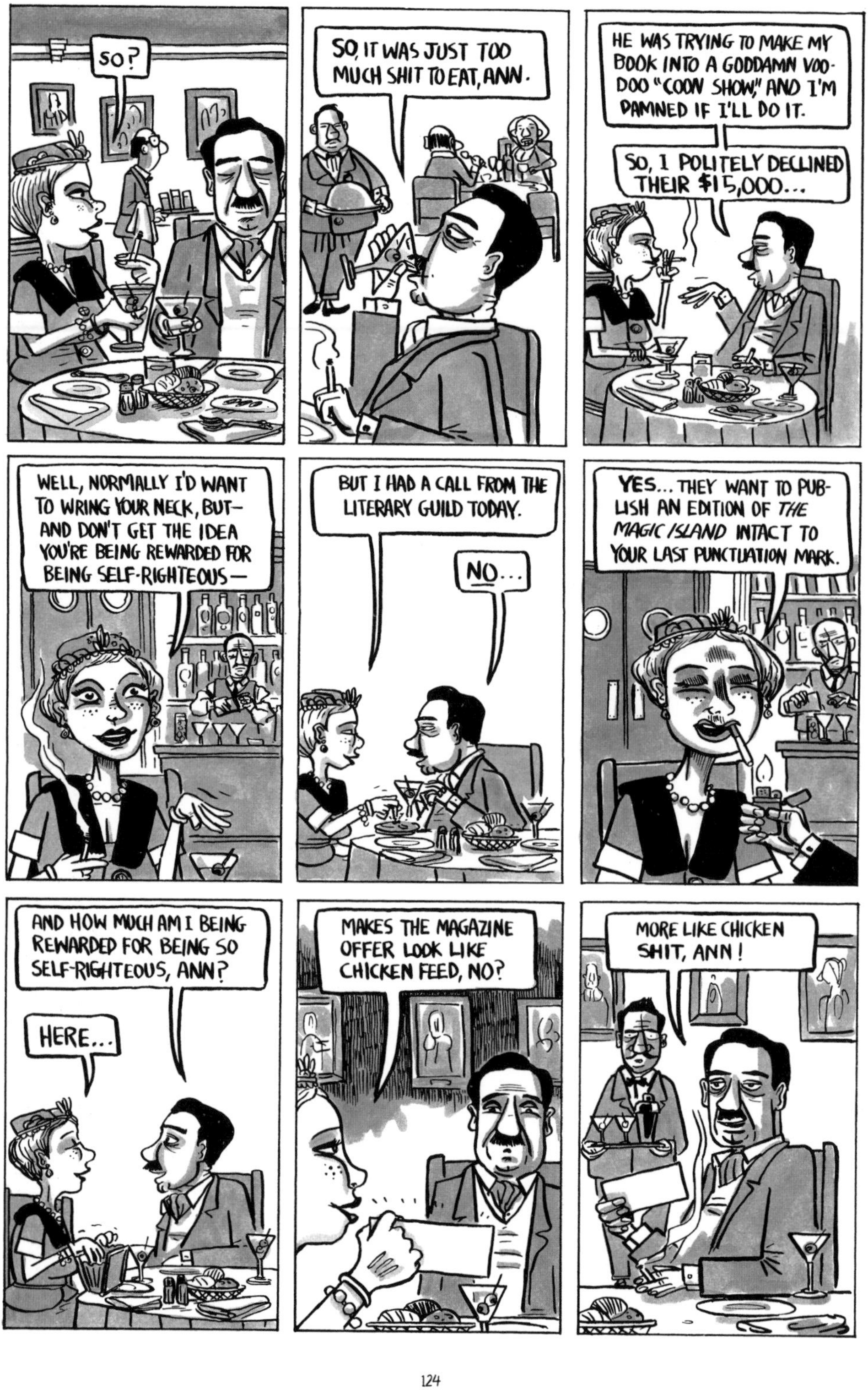
SO?
SO, IT WAS JUST TOO MUCH SHIT TO EAT, ANN.
HE WAS TRYING TO MAKE MY BOOK INTO A GODDAMN VOO-DOO "COON SHOW," AND I'M DAMNED IF I'LL DO IT.
SO, I POLITELY DECLINED THEIR $15,000...
WELL, NORMALLY I'D WANT TO WRING YOUR NECK, BUT— AND DON'T GET THE IDEA YOU'RE BEING REWARDED FOR BEING SELF-RIGHTEOUS—
BUT I HAD A CALL FROM THE LITERARY GUILD TODAY.
NO...
YES... THEY WANT TO PUB-LISH AN EDITION OF THE MAGIC ISLAND INTACT TO YOUR LAST PUNCTUATION MARK.
AND HOW MUCH AM I BEING REWARDED FOR BEING SO SELF-RIGHTEOUS, ANN?
HERE...
MAKES THE MAGAZINE OFFER LOOK LIKE CHICKEN FEED, NO?
MORE LIKE CHICKEN SHIT, ANN!

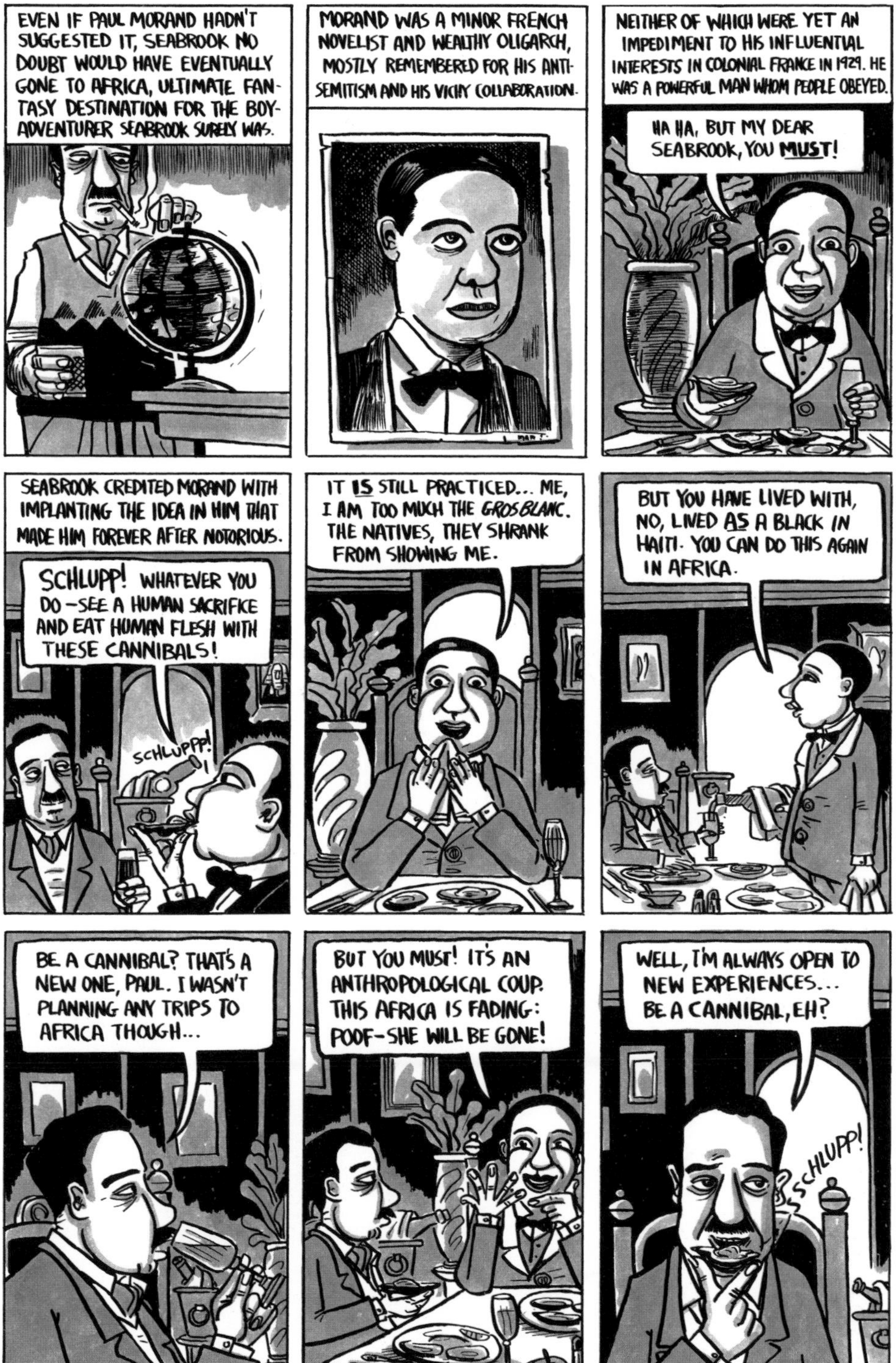
EVEN IF PAUL MORAND HADN'T SUGGESTED IT, SEABROOK NO DOUBT WOULD HAVE EVENTUALLY GONE TO AFRICA, ULTIMATE FANTASY DESTINATION FOR THE BOY-ADVENTURER SEABROOK SURELY WAS.
MORAND WAS A MINOR FRENCH NOVELIST AND WEALTHY OLIGARCH, MOSTLY REMEMBERED FOR HIS ANTI-SEMITISM AND HIS VICHY COLLABORATION.
NEITHER OF WHICH WERE YET AN IMPEDIMENT TO HIS INFLUENTIAL INTERESTS IN COLONIAL FRANCE IN 1929. HE WAS A POWERFUL MAN WHOM PEOPLE OBEYED.
HA HA, BUT MY DEAR SEABROOK, YOU MUST!
SEABROOK CREDITED MORAND WITH IMPLANTING THE IDEA IN HIM THAT MADE HIM FOREVER AFTER NOTORIOUS.
SCHLUPP! WHATEVER YOU DO—SEE A HUMAN SACRIFICE AND EAT HUMAN FLESH WITH THESE CANNIBALS!
SCHLUPPP!
IT IS STILL PRACTICED... ME, I AM TOO MUCH THE *GROS BLANC*. THE NATIVES, THEY SHRANK FROM SHOWING ME.
BUT YOU HAVE LIVED WITH, NO, LIVED AS A BLACK IN HAITI. YOU CAN DO THIS AGAIN IN AFRICA.
BE A CANNIBAL? THAT'S A NEW ONE, PAUL. I WASN'T PLANNING ANY TRIPS TO AFRICA THOUGH...
BUT YOU MUST! IT'S AN ANTHROPOLOGICAL COUP. THIS AFRICA IS FADING: POOF—SHE WILL BE GONE!
WELL, I'M ALWAYS OPEN TO NEW EXPERIENCES... BE A CANNIBAL, EH?
SCHLUPP!

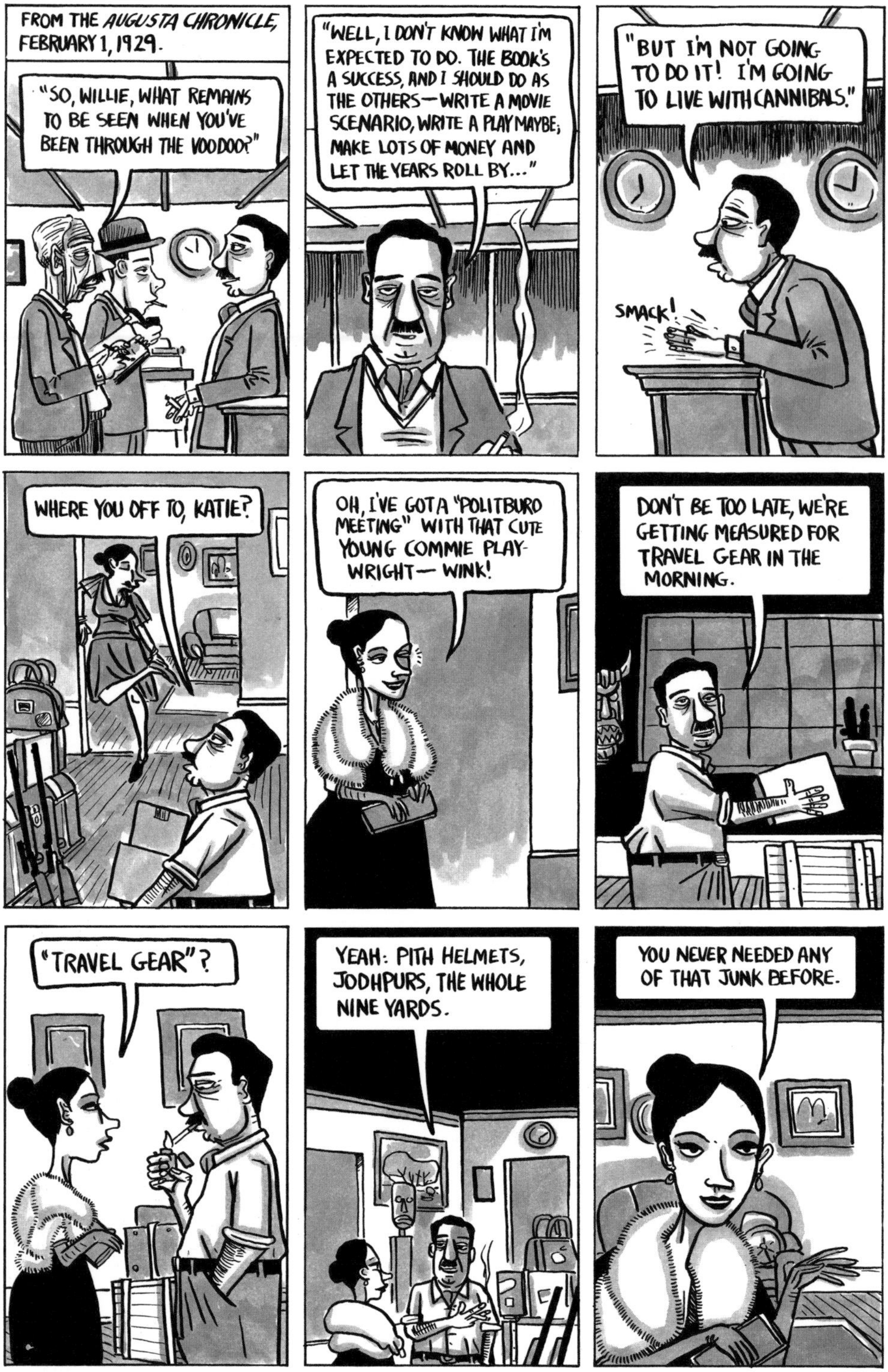
FROM THE AUGUSTA CHRONICLE, FEBRUARY 1, 1929.
"SO, WILLIE, WHAT REMAINS TO BE SEEN WHEN YOU'VE BEEN THROUGH THE VOODOO?"
"WELL, I DON'T KNOW WHAT I'M EXPECTED TO DO. THE BOOK'S A SUCCESS, AND I SHOULD DO AS THE OTHERS—WRITE A MOVIE SCENARIO, WRITE A PLAY MAYBE; MAKE LOTS OF MONEY AND LET THE YEARS ROLL BY..."
"BUT I'M NOT GOING TO DO IT! I'M GOING TO LIVE WITH CANNIBALS."
SMACK!
WHERE YOU OFF TO, KATIE?
OH, I'VE GOT A "POLITBURO MEETING" WITH THAT CUTE YOUNG COMMIE PLAYWRIGHT— WINK!
DON'T BE TOO LATE, WE'RE GETTING MEASURED FOR TRAVEL GEAR IN THE MORNING.
"TRAVEL GEAR"?
YEAH: PITH HELMETS, JODHPURS, THE WHOLE NINE YARDS.
YOU NEVER NEEDED ANY OF THAT JUNK BEFORE.

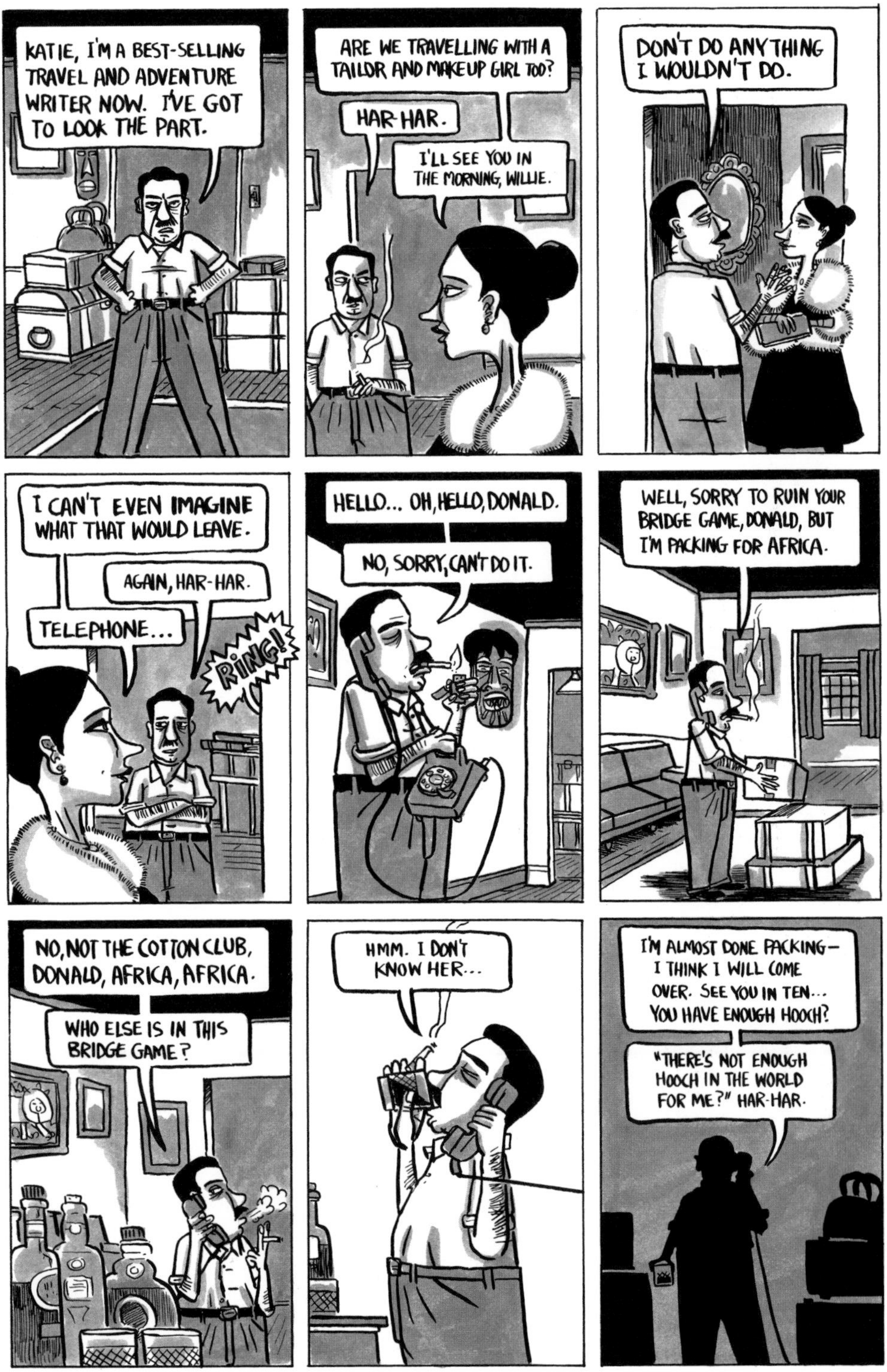
KATIE, I'M A BEST-SELLING TRAVEL AND ADVENTURE WRITER NOW. I'VE GOT TO LOOK THE PART.
ARE WE TRAVELLING WITH A TAILOR AND MAKEUP GIRL TOO?
HAR-HAR.
I'LL SEE YOU IN THE MORNING, WILLIE.
DON'T DO ANYTHING I WOULDN'T DO.
I CAN'T EVEN IMAGINE WHAT THAT WOULD LEAVE.
AGAIN, HAR-HAR.
TELEPHONE...
RING!
HELLO... OH, HELLO, DONALD.
NO, SORRY, CAN'T DO IT.
WELL, SORRY TO RUIN YOUR BRIDGE GAME, DONALD, BUT I'M PACKING FOR AFRICA.
NO, NOT THE COTTON CLUB, DONALD, AFRICA, AFRICA.
WHO ELSE IS IN THIS BRIDGE GAME?
HMM. I DON'T KNOW HER...
I'M ALMOST DONE PACKING— I THINK I WILL COME OVER. SEE YOU IN TEN... YOU HAVE ENOUGH HOOCH?
"THERE'S NOT ENOUGH HOOCH IN THE WORLD FOR ME?" HAR-HAR.

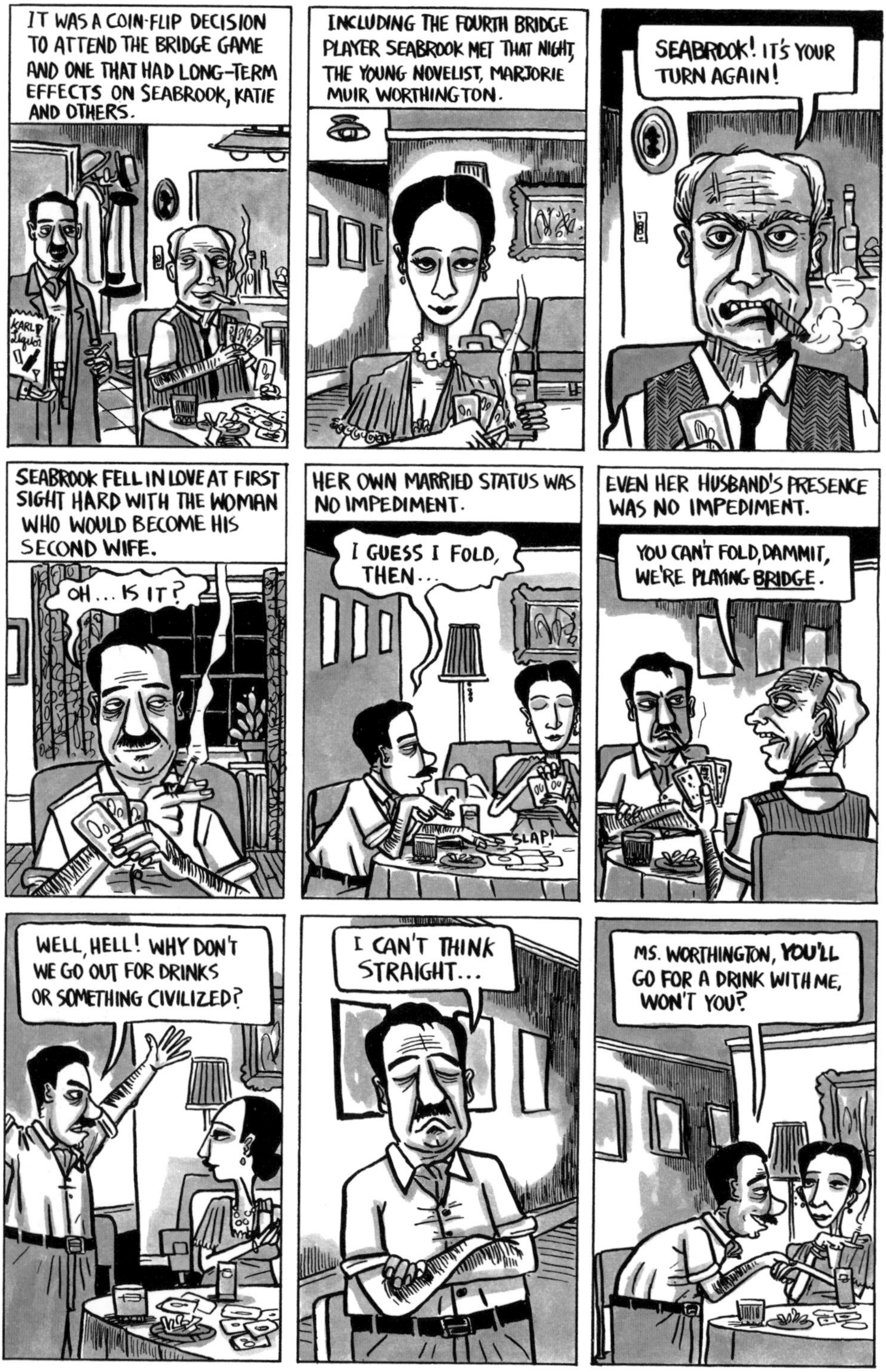
IT WAS A COIN-FLIP DECISION TO ATTEND THE BRIDGE GAME AND ONE THAT HAD LONG-TERM EFFECTS ON SEABROOK, KATIE AND OTHERS.
KARL'S Liquor
INCLUDING THE FOURTH BRIDGE PLAYER SEABROOK MET THAT NIGHT, THE YOUNG NOVELIST, MARJORIE MUIR WORTHINGTON.
SEABROOK! IT'S YOUR TURN AGAIN!
SEABROOK FELL IN LOVE AT FIRST SIGHT HARD WITH THE WOMAN WHO WOULD BECOME HIS SECOND WIFE.
OH... IS IT?
HER OWN MARRIED STATUS WAS NO IMPEDIMENT.
I GUESS I FOLD, THEN...
SLAP!
EVEN HER HUSBAND'S PRESENCE WAS NO IMPEDIMENT.
YOU CAN'T FOLD, DAMMIT, WE'RE PLAYING BRIDGE.
WELL, HELL! WHY DON'T WE GO OUT FOR DRINKS OR SOMETHING CIVILIZED?
I CAN'T THINK STRAIGHT...
MS. WORTHINGTON, YOU'LL GO FOR A DRINK WITH ME, WON'T YOU?

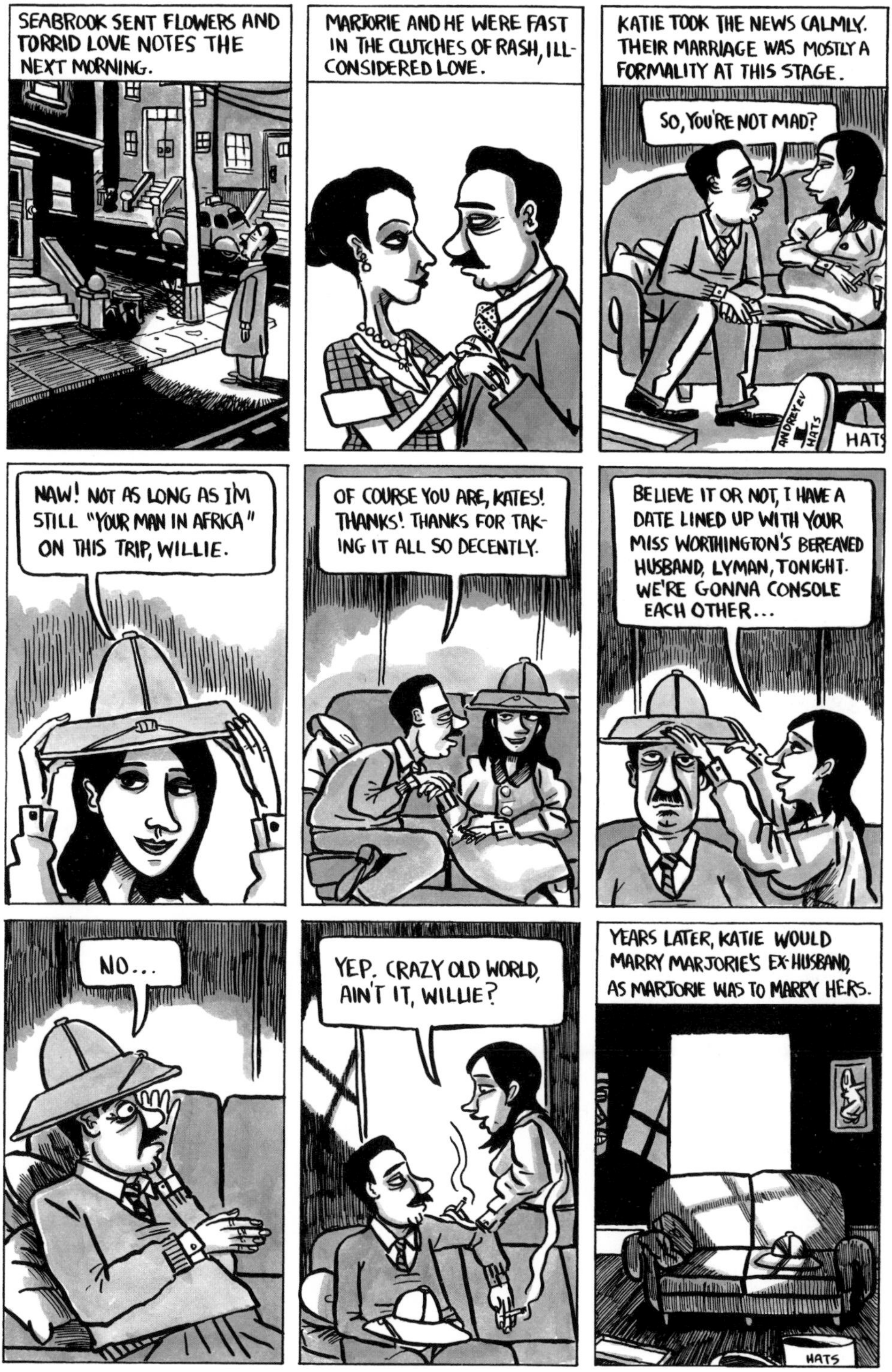
SEABROOK SENT FLOWERS AND TORRID LOVE NOTES THE NEXT MORNING.
MARJORIE AND HE WERE FAST IN THE CLUTCHES OF RASH, ILL-CONSIDERED LOVE.
KATIE TOOK THE NEWS CALMLY. THEIR MARRIAGE WAS MOSTLY A FORMALITY AT THIS STAGE.
SO, YOU'RE NOT MAD?
ANDREYEV HATS
HATS
NAW! NOT AS LONG AS I'M STILL "YOUR MAN IN AFRICA" ON THIS TRIP, WILLIE.
OF COURSE YOU ARE, KATES! THANKS! THANKS FOR TAKING IT ALL SO DECENTLY.
BELIEVE IT OR NOT, I HAVE A DATE LINED UP WITH YOUR MISS WORTHINGTON'S BEREAVED HUSBAND, LYMAN, TONIGHT. WE'RE GONNA CONSOLE EACH OTHER...
NO...
YEP. CRAZY OLD WORLD, AIN'T IT, WILLIE?
YEARS LATER, KATIE WOULD MARRY MARJORIE'S EX-HUSBAND, AS MARJORIE WAS TO MARRY HERS.
HATS

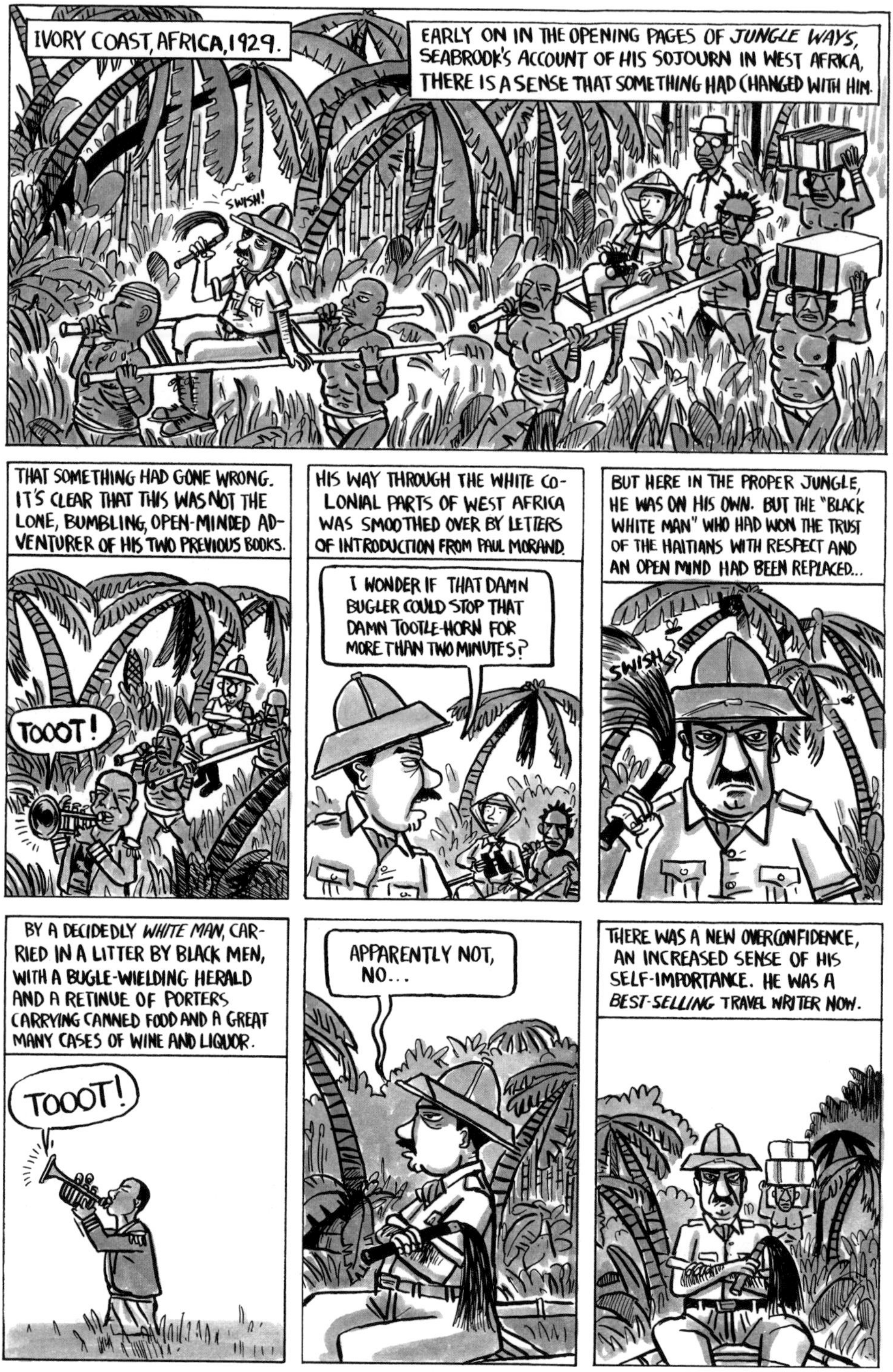
IVORY COAST, AFRICA, 1929.
EARLY ON IN THE OPENING PAGES OF JUNGLE WAYS, SEABROOK'S ACCOUNT OF HIS SOJOURN IN WEST AFRICA, THERE IS A SENSE THAT SOMETHING HAD CHANGED WITH HIM.
SWISH!
THAT SOMETHING HAD GONE WRONG. IT'S CLEAR THAT THIS WAS NOT THE LONE, BUMBLING, OPEN-MINDED ADVENTURER OF HIS TWO PREVIOUS BOOKS.
TOOOT!
HIS WAY THROUGH THE WHITE COLONIAL PARTS OF WEST AFRICA WAS SMOOTHED OVER BY LETTERS OF INTRODUCTION FROM PAUL MORAND.
I WONDER IF THAT DAMN BUGLER COULD STOP THAT DAMN TOOTLE-HORN FOR MORE THAN TWO MINUTES?
BUT HERE IN THE PROPER JUNGLE, HE WAS ON HIS OWN. BUT THE "BLACK WHITE MAN" WHO HAD WON THE TRUST OF THE HAITIANS WITH RESPECT AND AN OPEN MIND HAD BEEN REPLACED...
SWISH
BY A DECIDEDLY WHITE MAN, CARRIED IN A LITTER BY BLACK MEN, WITH A BUGLE-WIELDING HERALD AND A RETINUE OF PORTERS CARRYING CANNED FOOD AND A GREAT MANY CASES OF WINE AND LIQUOR.
TOOOT!
APPARENTLY NOT, NO...
THERE WAS A NEW OVERCONFIDENCE, AN INCREASED SENSE OF HIS SELF-IMPORTANCE. HE WAS A BEST-SELLING TRAVEL WRITER NOW.

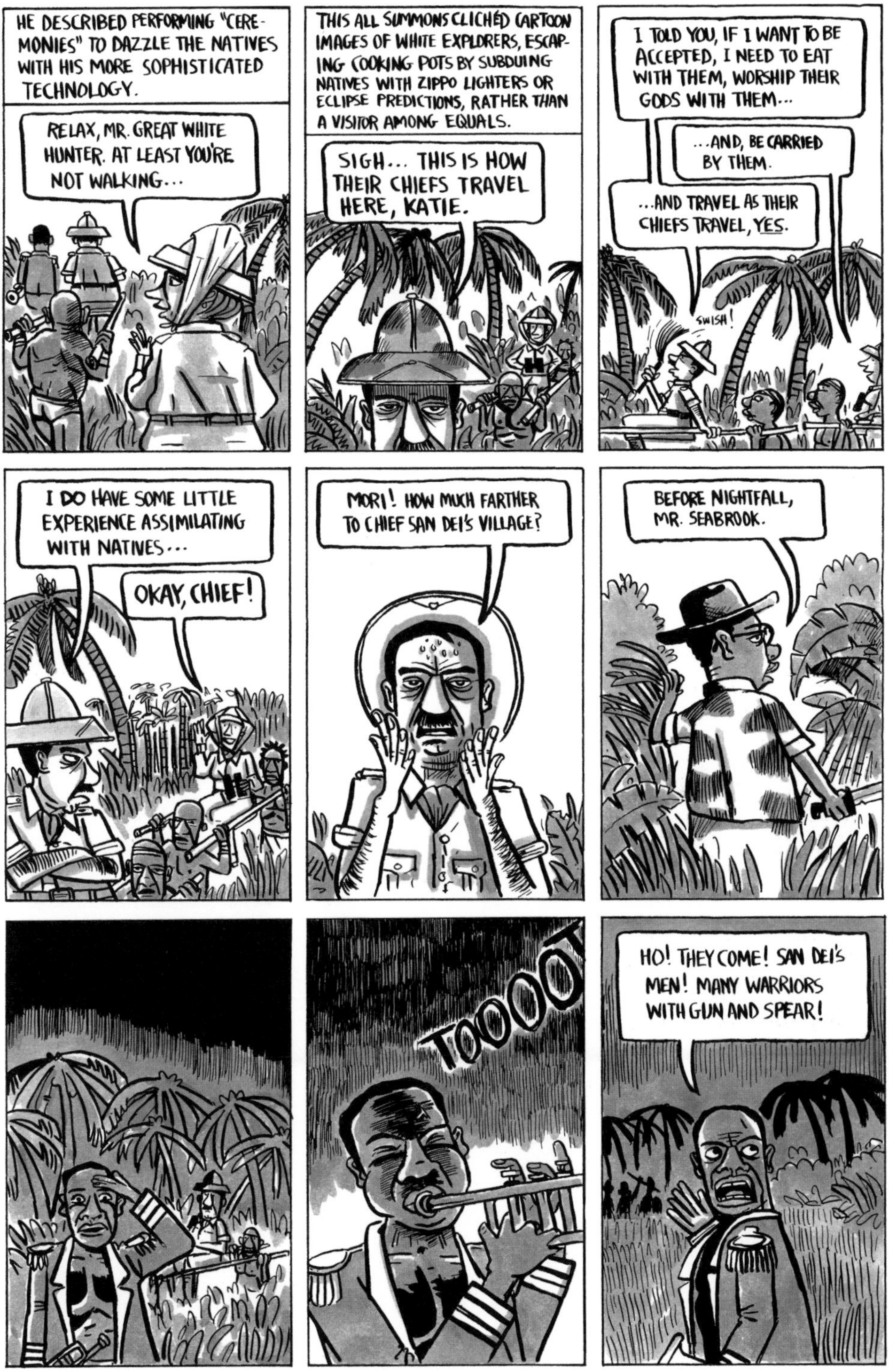
HE DESCRIBED PERFORMING "CEREMONIES" TO DAZZLE THE NATIVES WITH HIS MORE SOPHISTICATED TECHNOLOGY.
RELAX, MR. GREAT WHITE HUNTER. AT LEAST YOU'RE NOT WALKING...
THIS ALL SUMMONS CLICHÉD CARTOON IMAGES OF WHITE EXPLORERS, ESCAPING COOKING POTS BY SUBDUING NATIVES WITH ZIPPO LIGHTERS OR ECLIPSE PREDICTIONS, RATHER THAN A VISITOR AMONG EQUALS.
SIGH... THIS IS HOW THEIR CHIEFS TRAVEL HERE, KATIE.
I TOLD YOU, IF I WANT TO BE ACCEPTED, I NEED TO EAT WITH THEM, WORSHIP THEIR GODS WITH THEM...
...AND TRAVEL AS THEIR CHIEFS TRAVEL, YES.
...AND, BE CARRIED BY THEM.
SWISH!
I DO HAVE SOME LITTLE EXPERIENCE ASSIMILATING WITH NATIVES...
OKAY, CHIEF!
MORI! HOW MUCH FARTHER TO CHIEF SAN DEI'S VILLAGE?
BEFORE NIGHTFALL, MR. SEABROOK.
TOOOOOT
HO! THEY COME! SAN DEI'S MEN! MANY WARRIORS WITH GUN AND SPEAR!

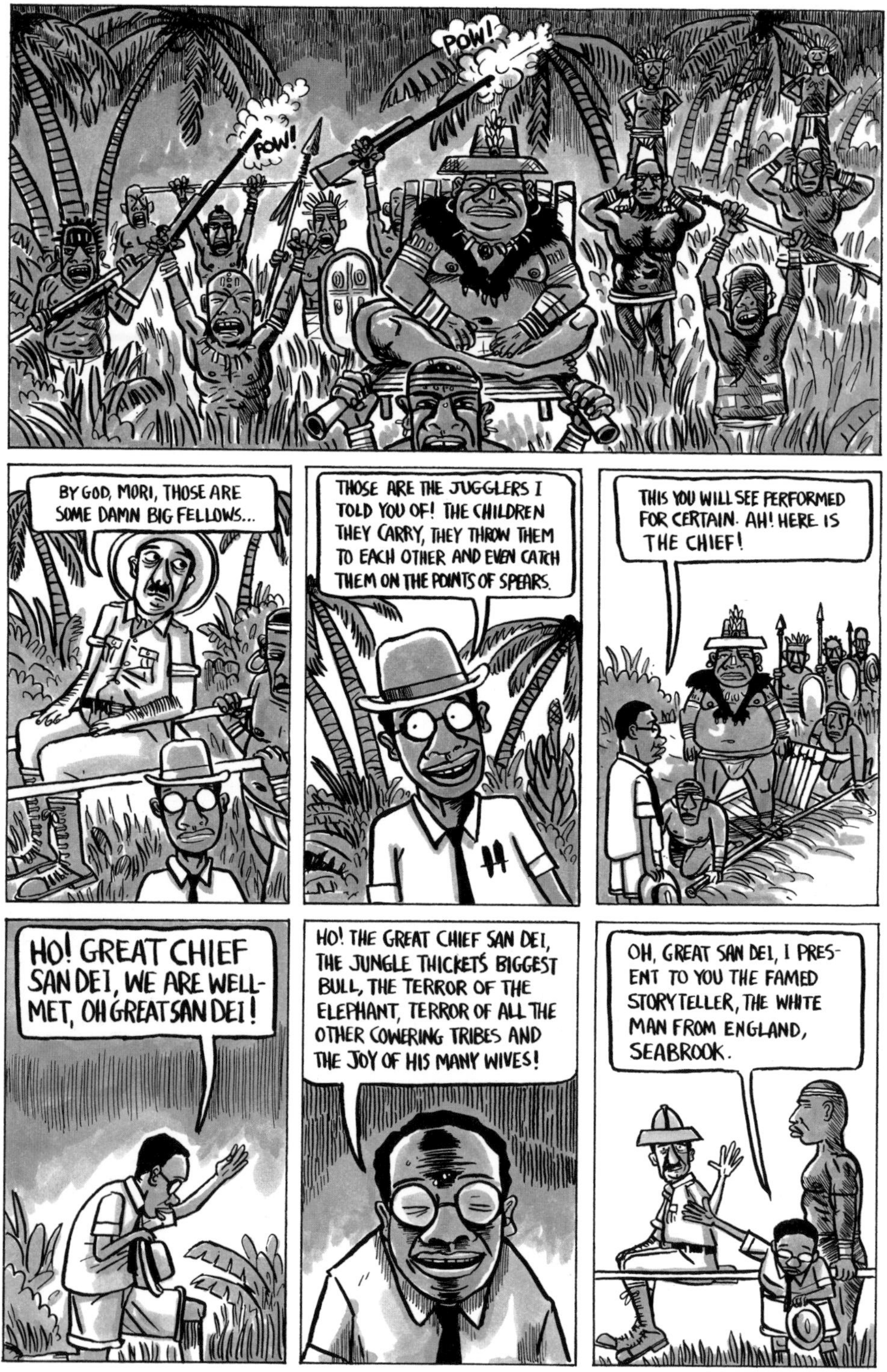
POW!
POW!
BY GOD, MORI, THOSE ARE SOME DAMN BIG FELLOWS...
THOSE ARE THE JUGGLERS I TOLD YOU OF! THE CHILDREN THEY CARRY, THEY THROW THEM TO EACH OTHER AND EVEN CATCH THEM ON THE POINTS OF SPEARS.
THIS YOU WILL SEE PERFORMED FOR CERTAIN. AH! HERE IS THE CHIEF!
HO! GREAT CHIEF SAN DEI, WE ARE WELL-MET, OH GREAT SAN DEI!
HO! THE GREAT CHIEF SAN DEI, THE JUNGLE THICKET'S BIGGEST BULL, THE TERROR OF THE ELEPHANT, TERROR OF ALL THE OTHER COWERING TRIBES AND THE JOY OF HIS MANY WIVES!
OH, GREAT SAN DEI, I PRES-ENT TO YOU THE FAMED STORYTELLER, THE WHITE MAN FROM ENGLAND, SEABROOK.

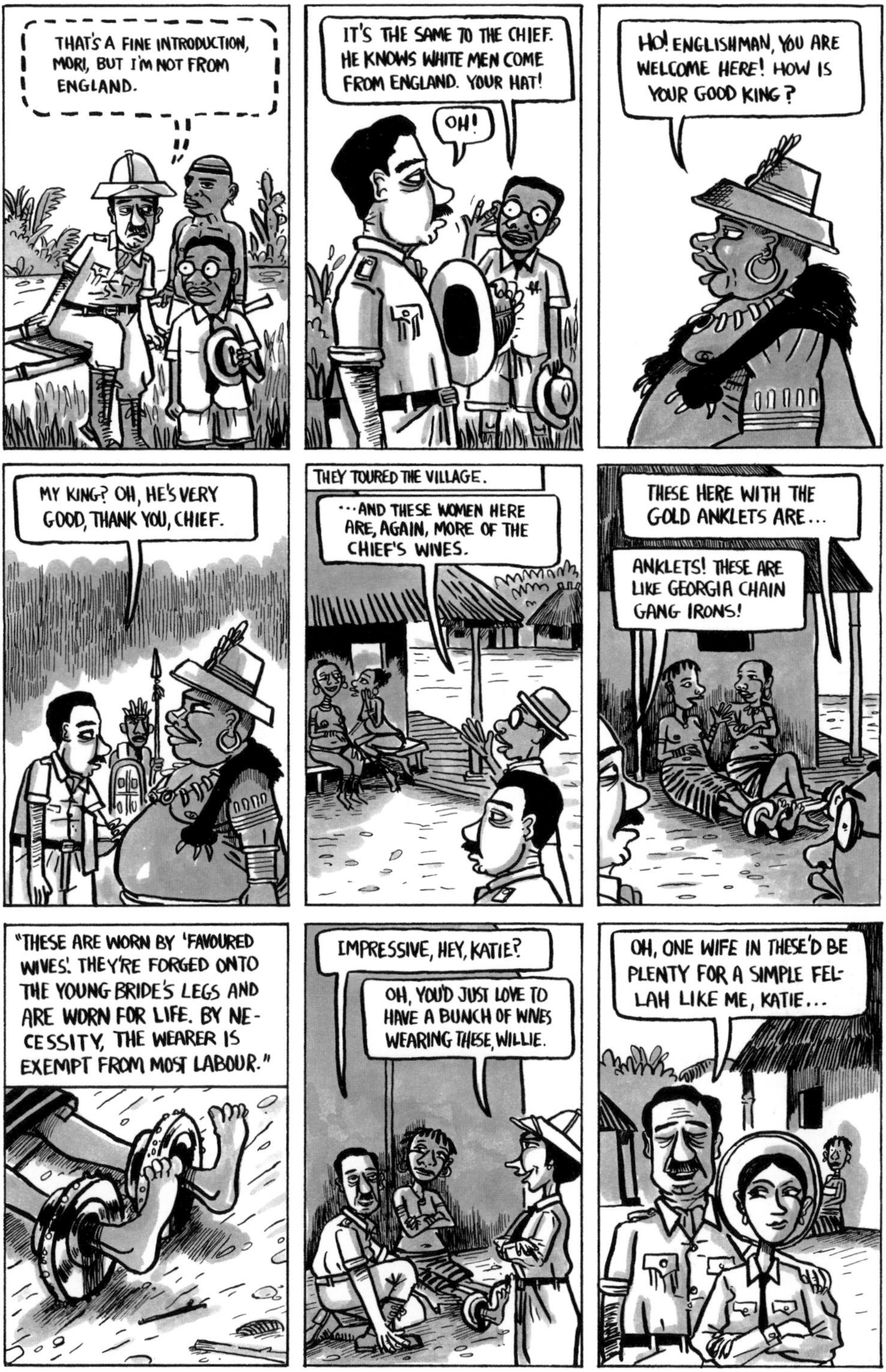
THAT'S A FINE INTRODUCTION, MORI, BUT I'M NOT FROM ENGLAND.
IT'S THE SAME TO THE CHIEF. HE KNOWS WHITE MEN COME FROM ENGLAND. YOUR HAT!
OH!
HO! ENGLISHMAN, YOU ARE WELCOME HERE! HOW IS YOUR GOOD KING?
MY KING? OH, HE'S VERY GOOD, THANK YOU, CHIEF.
THEY TOURED THE VILLAGE.
...AND THESE WOMEN HERE ARE, AGAIN, MORE OF THE CHIEF'S WIVES.
THESE HERE WITH THE GOLD ANKLETS ARE...
ANKLETS! THESE ARE LIKE GEORGIA CHAIN GANG IRONS!
"THESE ARE WORN BY 'FAVOURED WIVES'. THEY'RE FORGED ONTO THE YOUNG BRIDE'S LEGS AND ARE WORN FOR LIFE. BY NECESSITY, THE WEARER IS EXEMPT FROM MOST LABOUR."
IMPRESSIVE, HEY, KATIE?
OH, YOU'D JUST LOVE TO HAVE A BUNCH OF WIVES WEARING THESE, WILLIE.
OH, ONE WIFE IN THESE'D BE PLENTY FOR A SIMPLE FELLAH LIKE ME, KATIE...

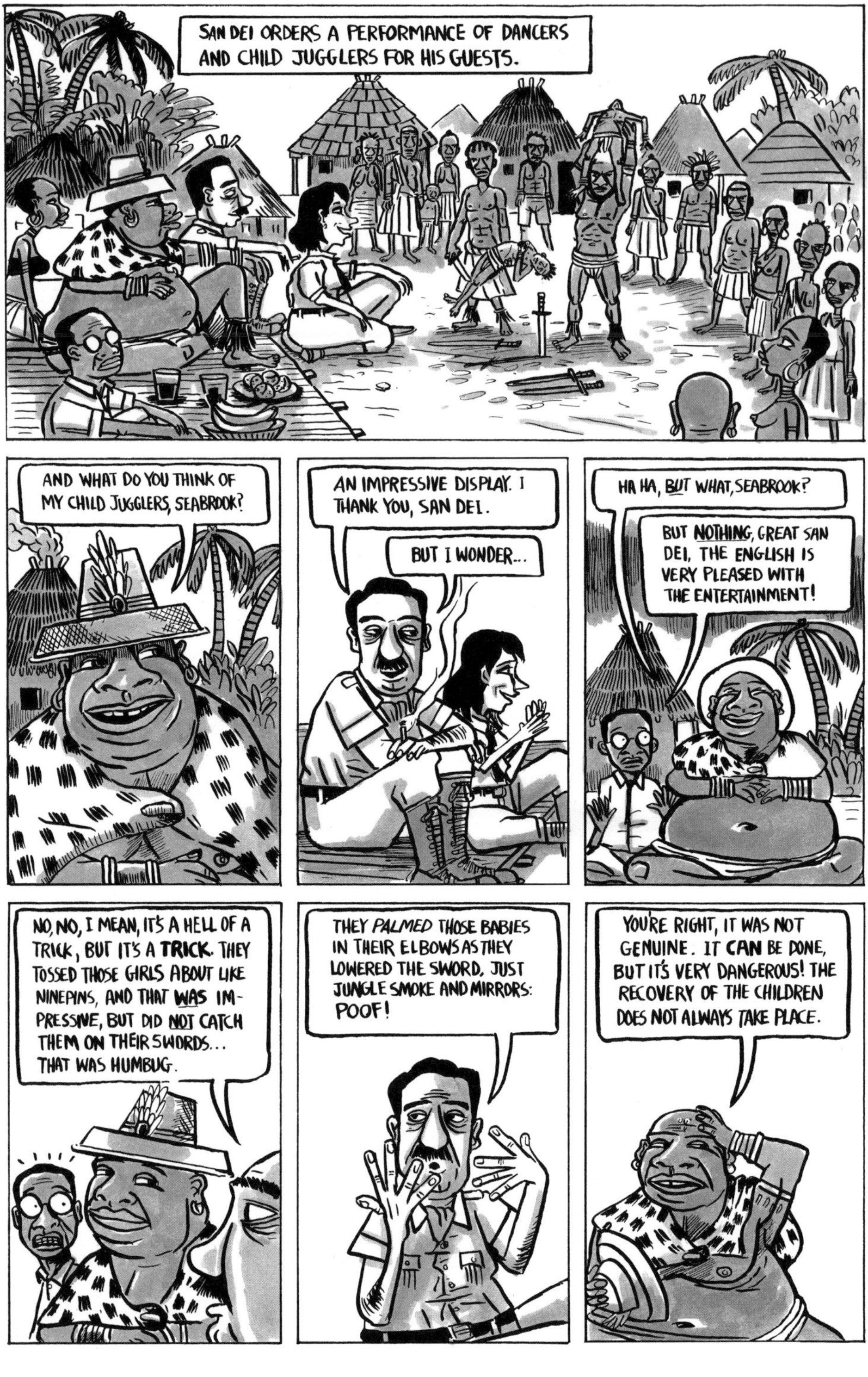
SAN DEI ORDERS A PERFORMANCE OF DANCERS AND CHILD JUGGLERS FOR HIS GUESTS.
AND WHAT DO YOU THINK OF MY CHILD JUGGLERS, SEABROOK?
AN IMPRESSIVE DISPLAY. I THANK YOU, SAN DEI.
BUT I WONDER...
HA HA, BUT WHAT, SEABROOK?
BUT NOTHING, GREAT SAN DEI, THE ENGLISH IS VERY PLEASED WITH THE ENTERTAINMENT!
NO, NO, I MEAN, IT'S A HELL OF A TRICK, BUT IT'S A TRICK. THEY TOSSED THOSE GIRLS ABOUT LIKE NINEPINS, AND THAT WAS IMPRESSIVE, BUT DID NOT CATCH THEM ON THEIR SWORDS... THAT WAS HUMBUG.
THEY PALMED THOSE BABIES IN THEIR ELBOWS AS THEY LOWERED THE SWORD, JUST JUNGLE SMOKE AND MIRRORS: POOF!
YOU'RE RIGHT, IT WAS NOT GENUINE. IT CAN BE DONE, BUT IT'S VERY DANGEROUS! THE RECOVERY OF THE CHILDREN DOES NOT ALWAYS TAKE PLACE.

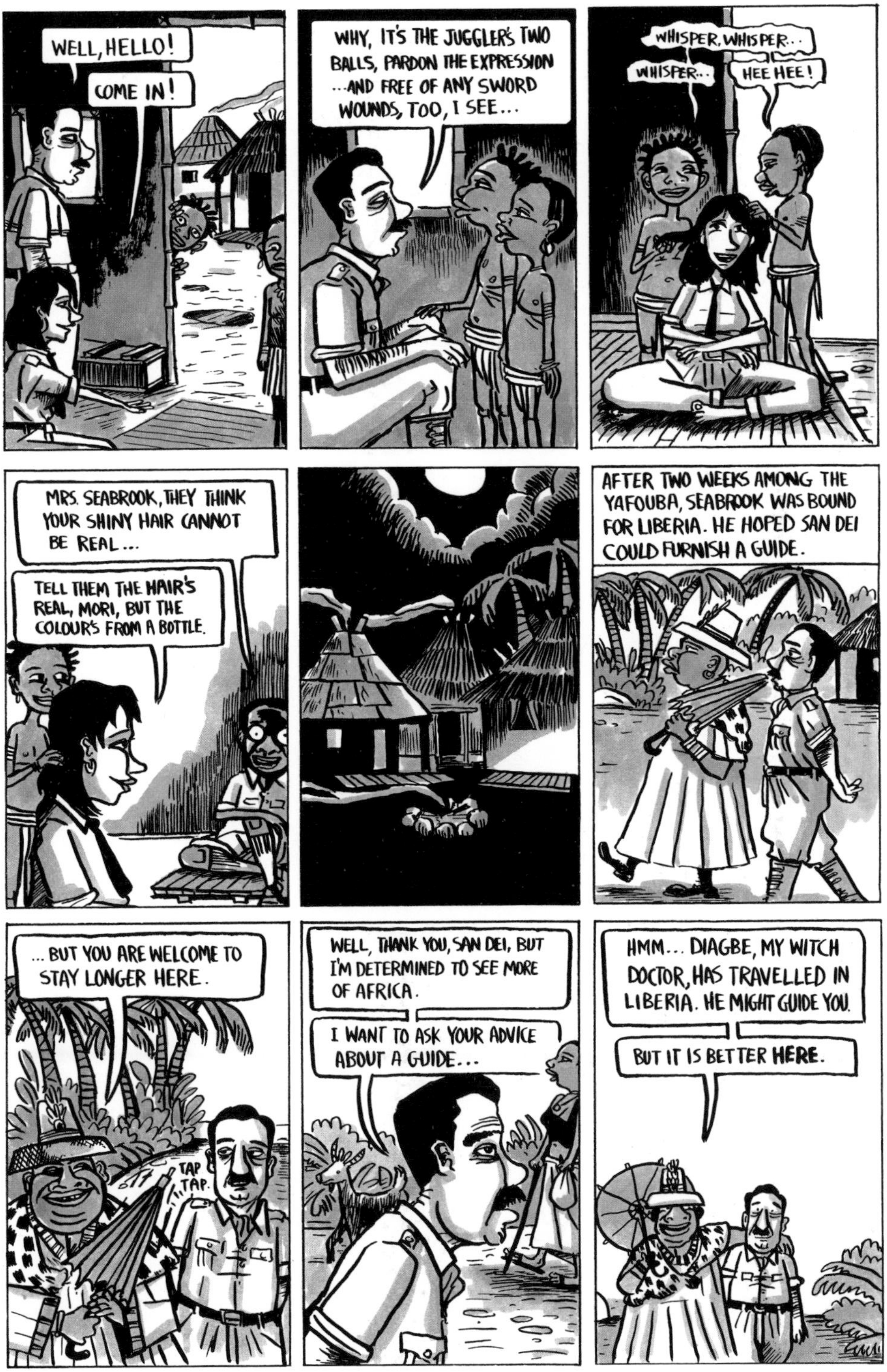
WELL, HELLO!
COME IN!
WHY, IT'S THE JUGGLER'S TWO BALLS, PARDON THE EXPRESSION ...AND FREE OF ANY SWORD WOUNDS, TOO, I SEE...
WHISPER, WHISPER...
WHISPER...
HEE HEE!
MRS. SEABROOK, THEY THINK YOUR SHINY HAIR CANNOT BE REAL...
TELL THEM THE HAIR'S REAL, MORI, BUT THE COLOUR'S FROM A BOTTLE.
AFTER TWO WEEKS AMONG THE YAFOUBA, SEABROOK WAS BOUND FOR LIBERIA. HE HOPED SAN DEI COULD FURNISH A GUIDE.
...BUT YOU ARE WELCOME TO STAY LONGER HERE.
TAP TAP.
WELL, THANK YOU, SAN DEI, BUT I'M DETERMINED TO SEE MORE OF AFRICA.
I WANT TO ASK YOUR ADVICE ABOUT A GUIDE...
HMM... DIAGBE, MY WITCH DOCTOR, HAS TRAVELLED IN LIBERIA. HE MIGHT GUIDE YOU.
BUT IT IS BETTER HERE.

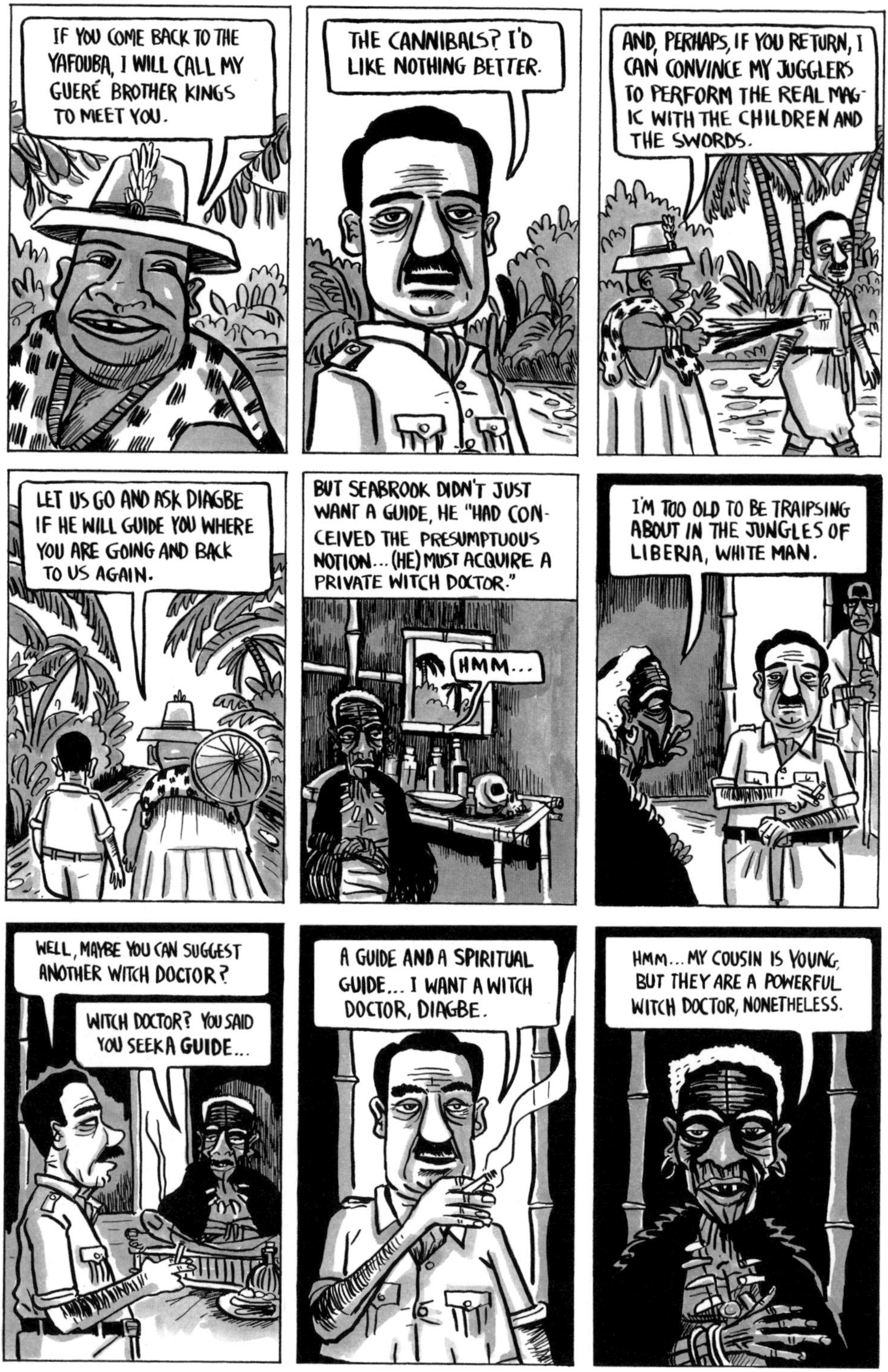
IF YOU COME BACK TO THE YAFOUBA, I WILL CALL MY GUERÉ BROTHER KINGS TO MEET YOU.
THE CANNIBALS? I'D LIKE NOTHING BETTER.
AND, PERHAPS, IF YOU RETURN, I CAN CONVINCE MY JUGGLERS TO PERFORM THE REAL MAGIC WITH THE CHILDREN AND THE SWORDS.
LET US GO AND ASK DIAGBE IF HE WILL GUIDE YOU WHERE YOU ARE GOING AND BACK TO US AGAIN.
BUT SEABROOK DIDN'T JUST WANT A GUIDE, HE "HAD CONCEIVED THE PRESUMPTUOUS NOTION... (HE) MUST ACQUIRE A PRIVATE WITCH DOCTOR."
HMM...
I'M TOO OLD TO BE TRAIPSING ABOUT IN THE JUNGLES OF LIBERIA, WHITE MAN.
WELL, MAYBE YOU CAN SUGGEST ANOTHER WITCH DOCTOR?
WITCH DOCTOR? YOU SAID YOU SEEK A GUIDE...
A GUIDE AND A SPIRITUAL GUIDE... I WANT A WITCH DOCTOR, DIAGBE.
HMM... MY COUSIN IS YOUNG, BUT THEY ARE A POWERFUL WITCH DOCTOR, NONETHELESS.

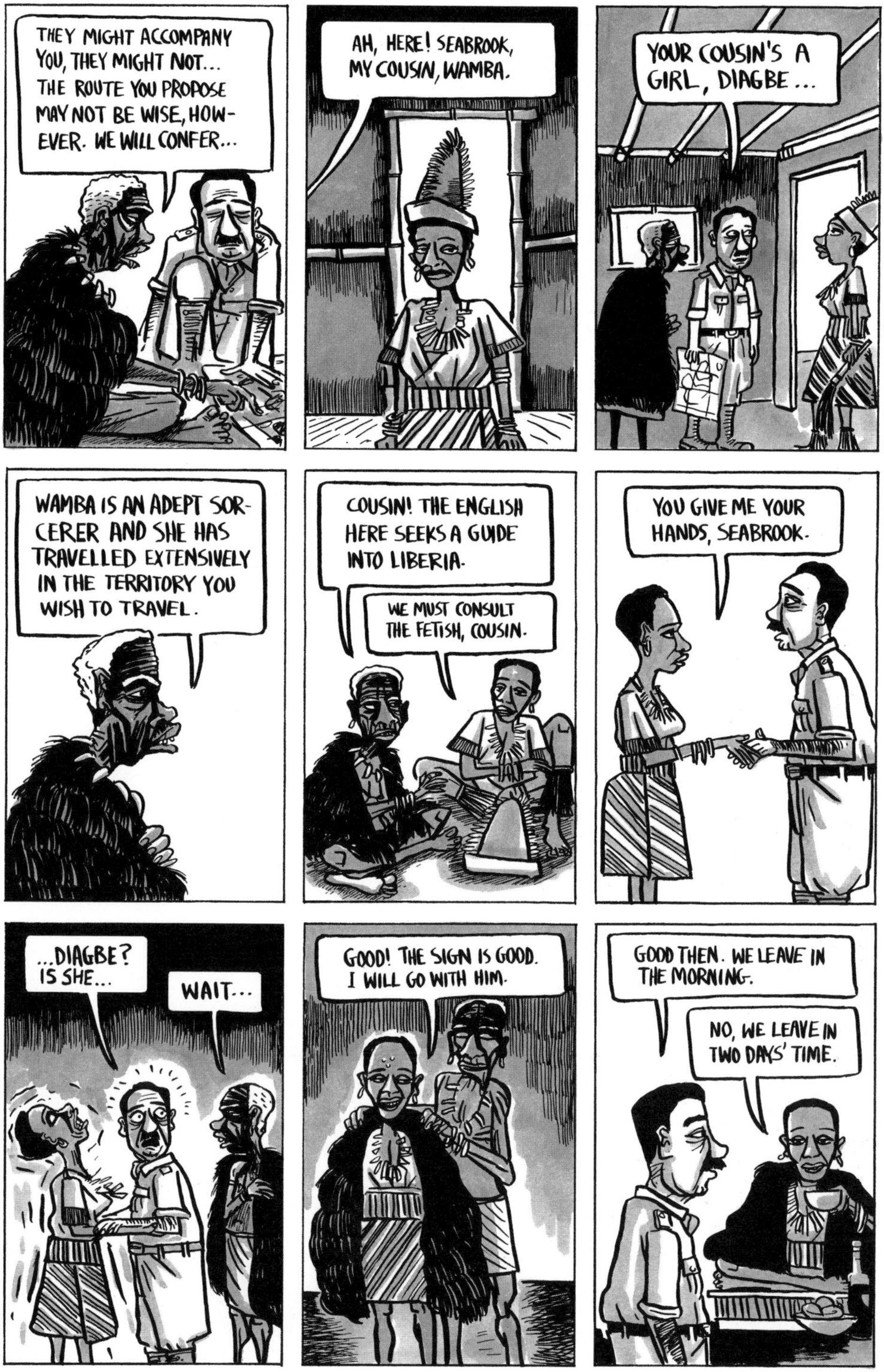
THEY MIGHT ACCOMPANY YOU, THEY MIGHT NOT... THE ROUTE YOU PROPOSE MAY NOT BE WISE, HOWEVER. WE WILL CONFER...
AH, HERE! SEABROOK, MY COUSIN, WAMBA.
YOUR COUSIN'S A GIRL, DIAGBE...
WAMBA IS AN ADEPT SORCERER AND SHE HAS TRAVELLED EXTENSIVELY IN THE TERRITORY YOU WISH TO TRAVEL.
COUSIN! THE ENGLISH HERE SEEKS A GUIDE INTO LIBERIA.
WE MUST CONSULT THE FETISH, COUSIN.
YOU GIVE ME YOUR HANDS, SEABROOK.
...DIAGBE? IS SHE...
WAIT...
GOOD! THE SIGN IS GOOD. I WILL GO WITH HIM.
GOOD THEN. WE LEAVE IN THE MORNING.
NO, WE LEAVE IN TWO DAYS' TIME.

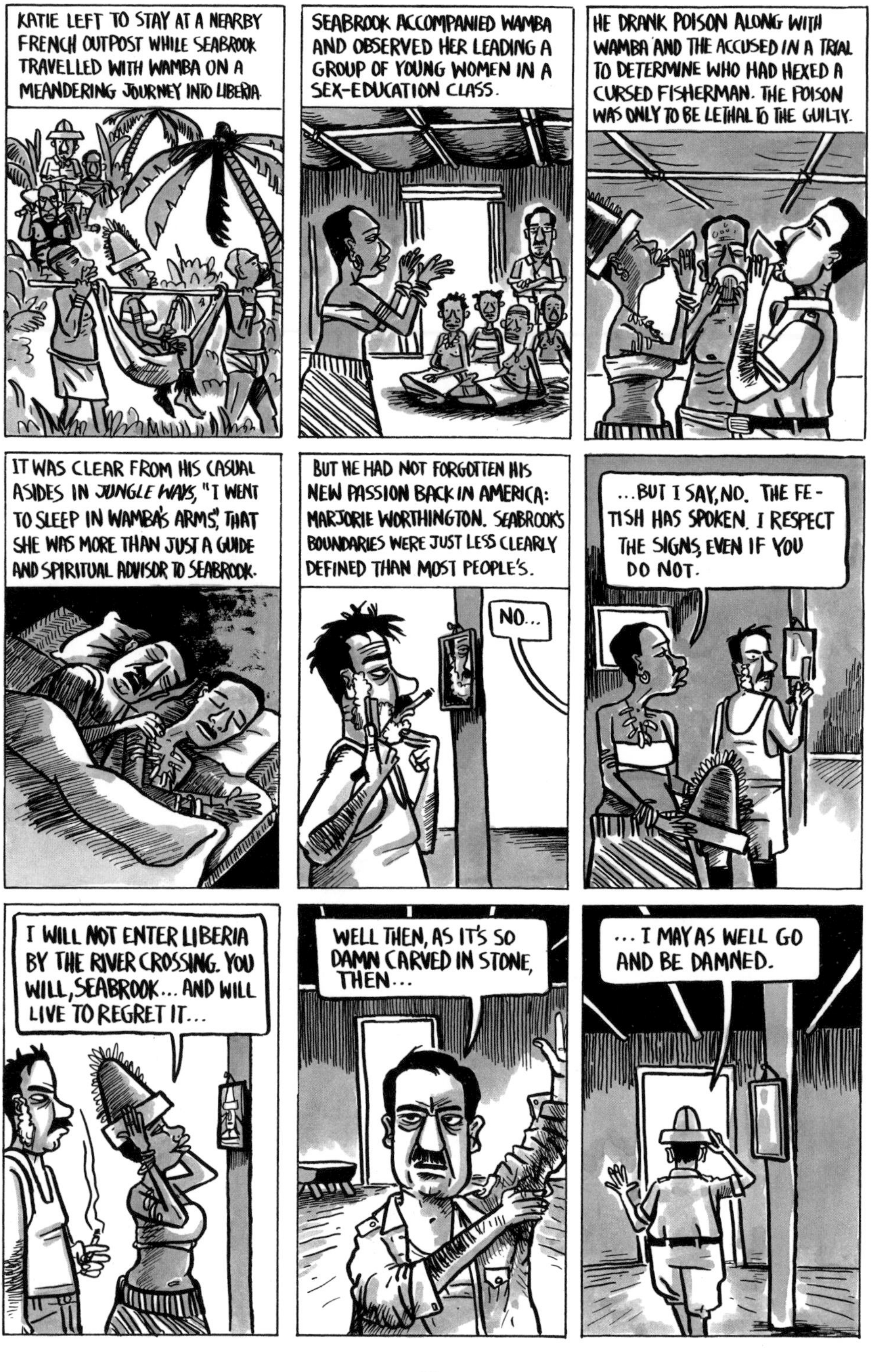
KATIE LEFT TO STAY AT A NEARBY FRENCH OUTPOST WHILE SEABROOK TRAVELLED WITH WAMBA ON A MEANDERING JOURNEY INTO LIBERIA.
SEABROOK ACCOMPANIED WAMBA AND OBSERVED HER LEADING A GROUP OF YOUNG WOMEN IN A SEX-EDUCATION CLASS.
HE DRANK POISON ALONG WITH WAMBA AND THE ACCUSED IN A TRIAL TO DETERMINE WHO HAD HEXED A CURSED FISHERMAN. THE POISON WAS ONLY TO BE LETHAL TO THE GUILTY.
IT WAS CLEAR FROM HIS CASUAL ASIDES IN *JUNGLE WAYS*, "I WENT TO SLEEP IN WAMBA'S ARMS," THAT SHE WAS MORE THAN JUST A GUIDE AND SPIRITUAL ADVISOR TO SEABROOK.
BUT HE HAD NOT FORGOTTEN HIS NEW PASSION BACK IN AMERICA: MARJORIE WORTHINGTON. SEABROOK'S BOUNDARIES WERE JUST LESS CLEARLY DEFINED THAN MOST PEOPLE'S.
NO...
...BUT I SAY, NO. THE FETISH HAS SPOKEN. I RESPECT THE SIGNS, EVEN IF YOU DO NOT.
I WILL NOT ENTER LIBERIA BY THE RIVER CROSSING. YOU WILL, SEABROOK... AND WILL LIVE TO REGRET IT...
WELL THEN, AS IT'S SO DAMN CARVED IN STONE, THEN...
... I MAY AS WELL GO AND BE DAMNED.

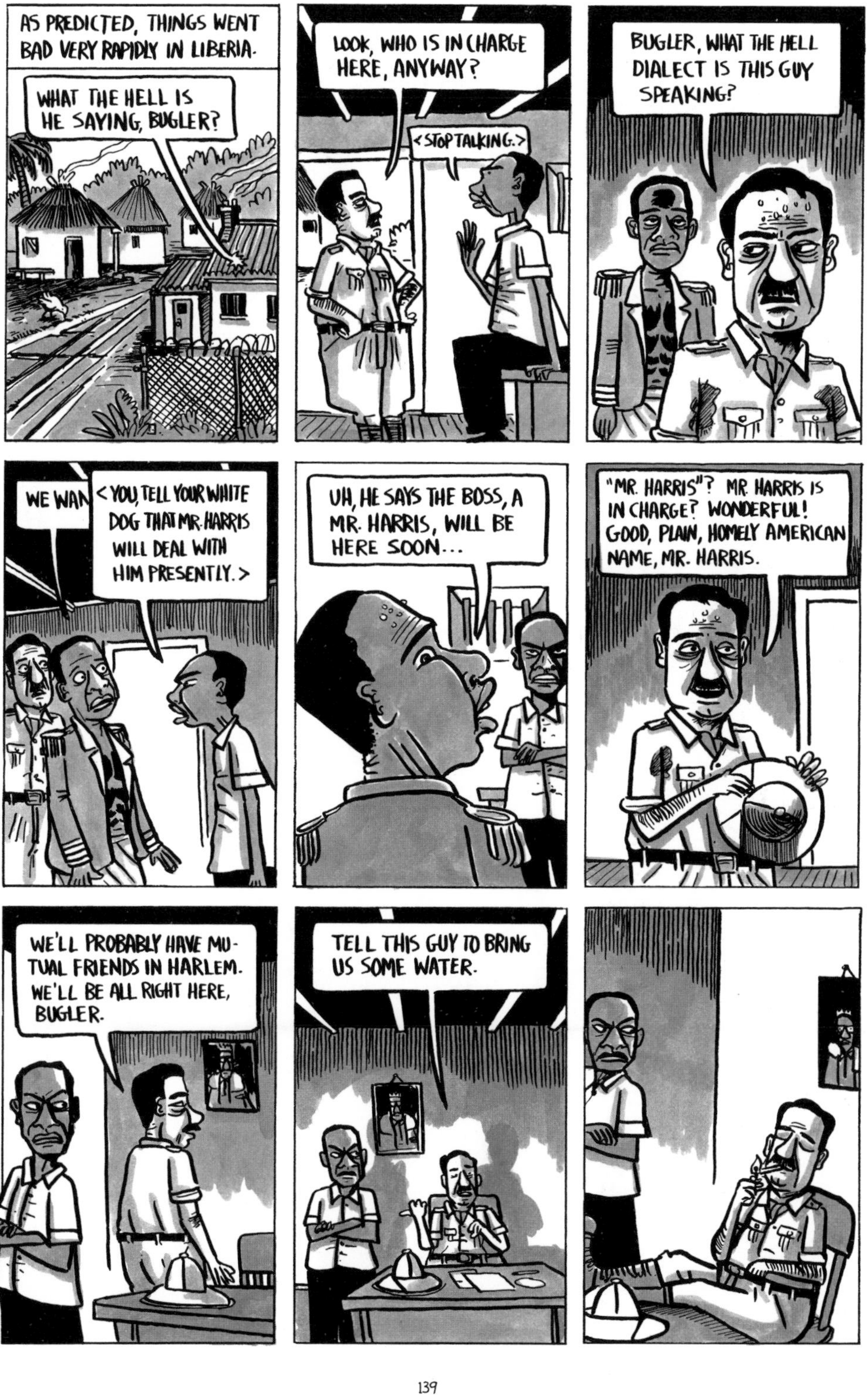
AS PREDICTED, THINGS WENT BAD VERY RAPIDLY IN LIBERIA.
WHAT THE HELL IS HE SAYING, BUGLER?
LOOK, WHO IS IN CHARGE HERE, ANYWAY?
<STOP TALKING.>
BUGLER, WHAT THE HELL DIALECT IS THIS GUY SPEAKING?
WE WAN
<YOU, TELL YOUR WHITE DOG THAT MR. HARRIS WILL DEAL WITH HIM PRESENTLY.>
UH, HE SAYS THE BOSS, A MR. HARRIS, WILL BE HERE SOON...
"MR. HARRIS"? MR. HARRIS IS IN CHARGE? WONDERFUL! GOOD, PLAIN, HOMELY AMERICAN NAME, MR. HARRIS.
WE'LL PROBABLY HAVE MU-TUAL FRIENDS IN HARLEM. WE'LL BE ALL RIGHT HERE, BUGLER.
TELL THIS GUY TO BRING US SOME WATER.

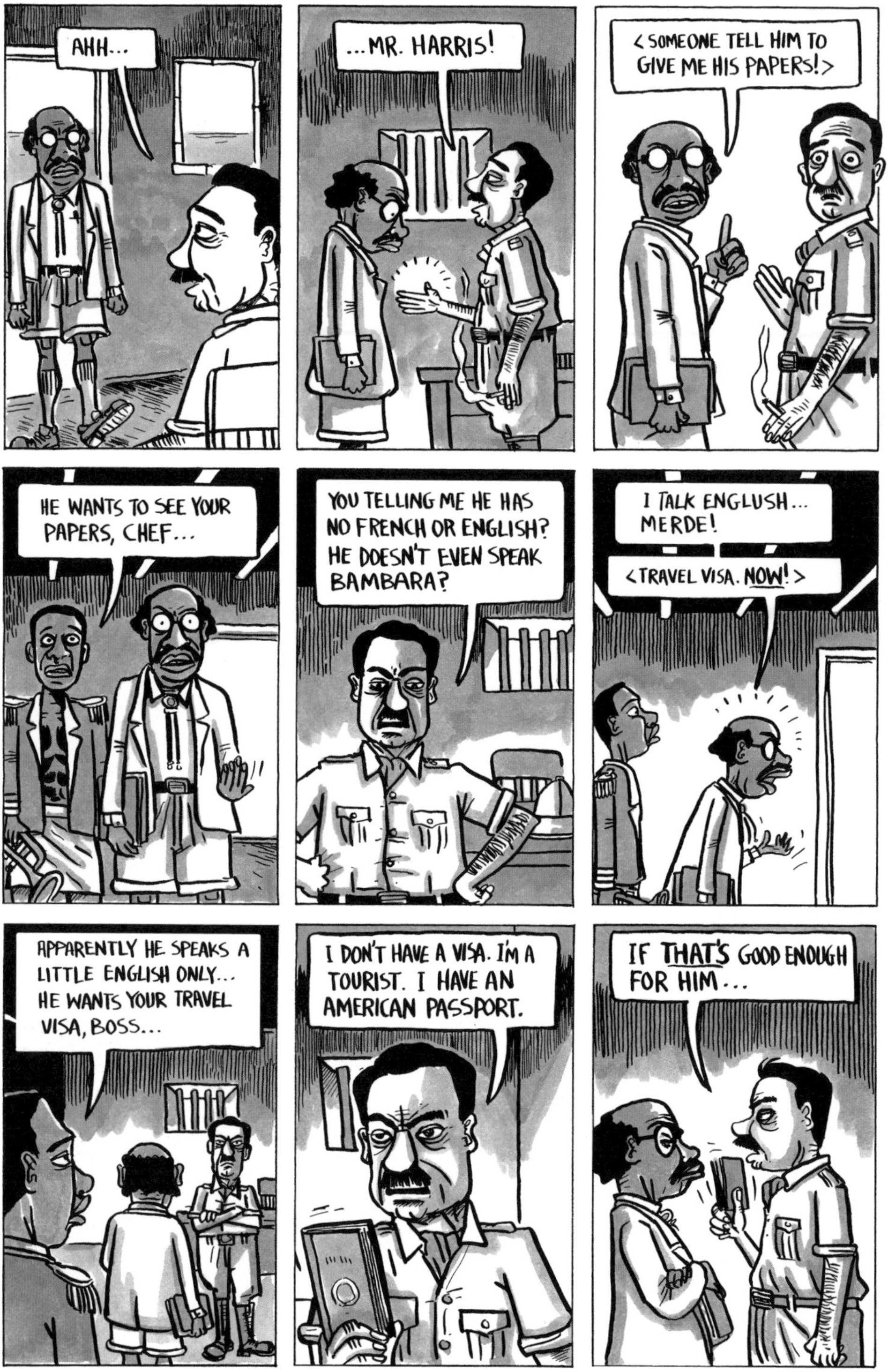
AHH...
...MR. HARRIS!
<SOMEONE TELL HIM TO GIVE ME HIS PAPERS!>
HE WANTS TO SEE YOUR PAPERS, CHEF...
YOU TELLING ME HE HAS NO FRENCH OR ENGLISH? HE DOESN'T EVEN SPEAK BAMBARA?
I TALK ENGLUSH... MERDE!
<TRAVEL VISA. NOW!>
APPARENTLY HE SPEAKS A LITTLE ENGLISH ONLY... HE WANTS YOUR TRAVEL VISA, BOSS...
I DON'T HAVE A VISA. I'M A TOURIST. I HAVE AN AMERICAN PASSPORT.
IF THAT'S GOOD ENOUGH FOR HIM...

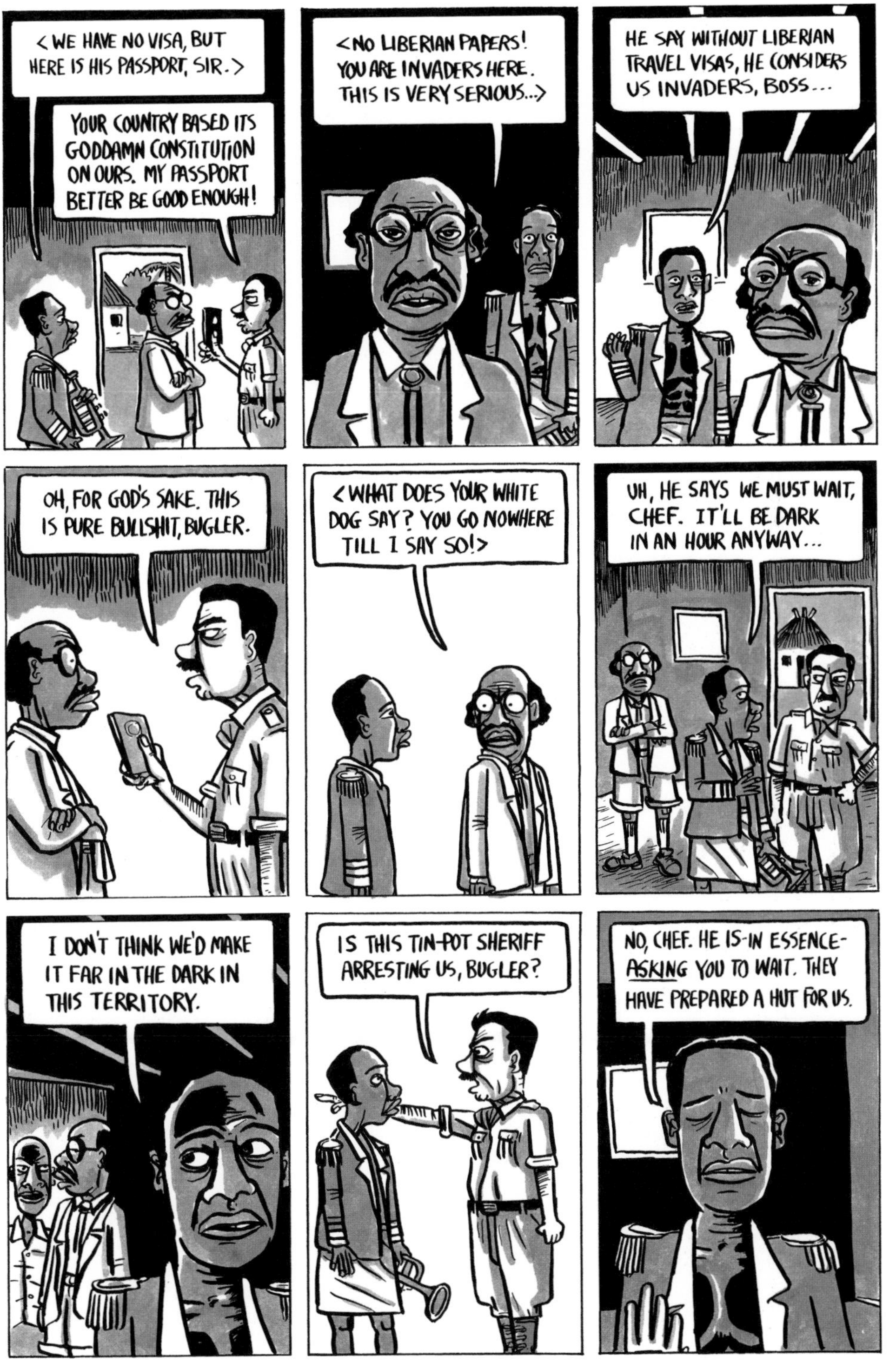
<WE HAVE NO VISA, BUT HERE IS HIS PASSPORT, SIR.>
YOUR COUNTRY BASED ITS GODDAMN CONSTITUTION ON OURS. MY PASSPORT BETTER BE GOOD ENOUGH!
<NO LIBERIAN PAPERS! YOU ARE INVADERS HERE. THIS IS VERY SERIOUS...>
HE SAY WITHOUT LIBERIAN TRAVEL VISAS, HE CONSIDERS US INVADERS, BOSS...
OH, FOR GOD'S SAKE. THIS IS PURE BULLSHIT, BUGLER.
<WHAT DOES YOUR WHITE DOG SAY? YOU GO NOWHERE TILL I SAY SO!>
UH, HE SAYS WE MUST WAIT, CHEF. IT'LL BE DARK IN AN HOUR ANYWAY...
I DON'T THINK WE'D MAKE IT FAR IN THE DARK IN THIS TERRITORY.
IS THIS TIN-POT SHERIFF ARRESTING US, BUGLER?
NO, CHEF. HE IS-IN ESSENCE-ASKING YOU TO WAIT. THEY HAVE PREPARED A HUT FOR US.

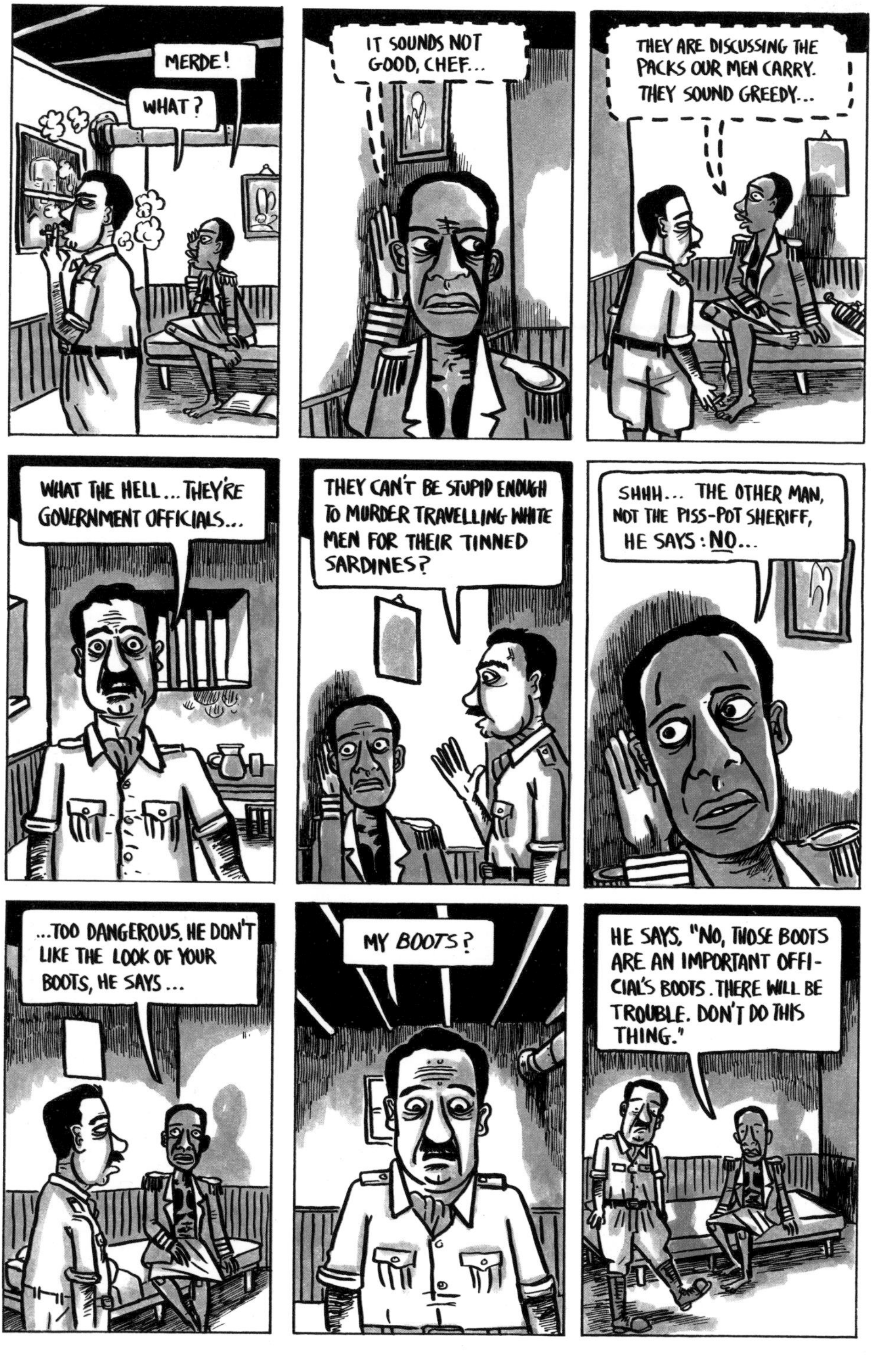
MERDE!
WHAT?
IT SOUNDS NOT GOOD, CHEF...
THEY ARE DISCUSSING THE PACKS OUR MEN CARRY. THEY SOUND GREEDY...
WHAT THE HELL... THEY'RE GOVERNMENT OFFICIALS...
THEY CAN'T BE STUPID ENOUGH TO MURDER TRAVELLING WHITE MEN FOR THEIR TINNED SARDINES?
SHHH... THE OTHER MAN, NOT THE PISS-POT SHERIFF, HE SAYS: NO...
...TOO DANGEROUS. HE DON'T LIKE THE LOOK OF YOUR BOOTS, HE SAYS...
MY *BOOTS*?
HE SAYS, "NO, THOSE BOOTS ARE AN IMPORTANT OFFICIAL'S BOOTS. THERE WILL BE TROUBLE. DON'T DO THIS THING."

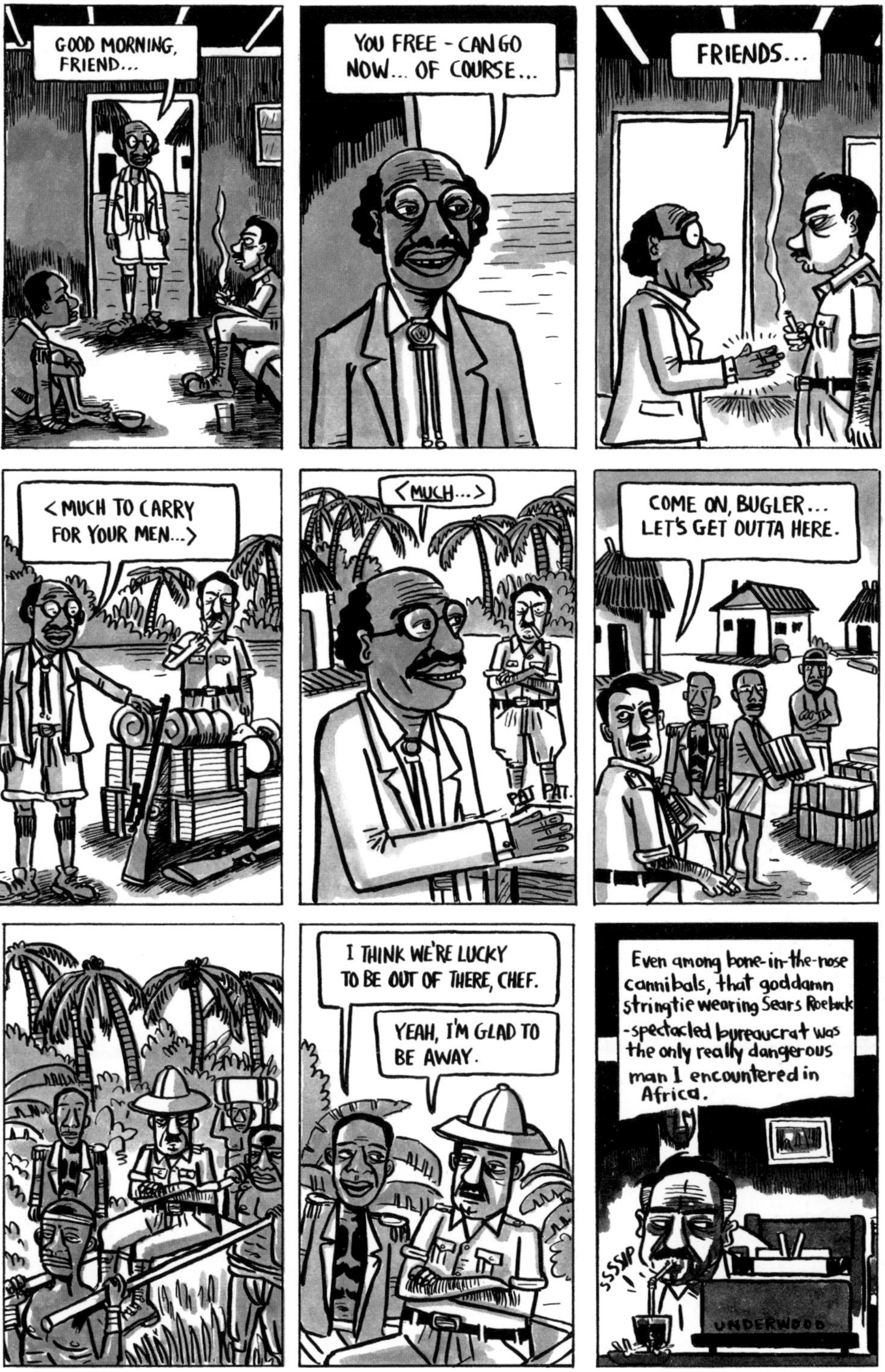
GOOD MORNING, FRIEND...
YOU FREE - CAN GO NOW... OF COURSE...
FRIENDS...
<MUCH TO CARRY FOR YOUR MEN...>
<MUCH...>
PAT PAT.
COME ON, BUGLER... LET'S GET OUTTA HERE.
I THINK WE'RE LUCKY TO BE OUT OF THERE, CHEF.
YEAH, I'M GLAD TO BE AWAY.
Even among bone-in-the-nose cannibals, that goddamn stringtie wearing Sears Roebuck -spectacled bureaucrat was the only really dangerous man I encountered in Africa.
SSSSIP
UNDERWOOD

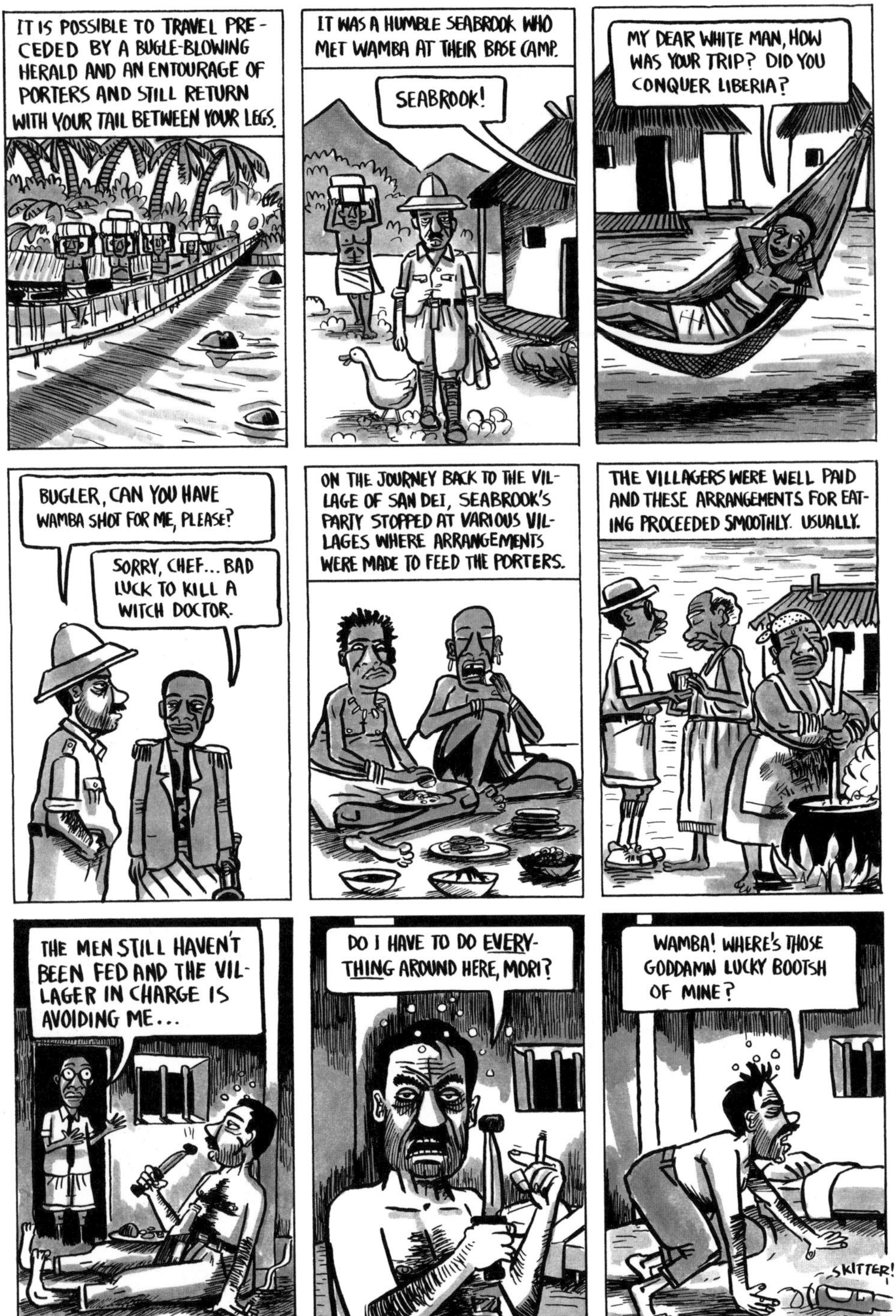

IT IS POSSIBLE TO TRAVEL PRECEDED BY A BUGLE-BLOWING HERALD AND AN ENTOURAGE OF PORTERS AND STILL RETURN WITH YOUR TAIL BETWEEN YOUR LEGS.
IT WAS A HUMBLE SEABROOK WHO MET WAMBA AT THEIR BASE CAMP.
SEABROOK!
MY DEAR WHITE MAN, HOW WAS YOUR TRIP? DID YOU CONQUER LIBERIA?
BUGLER, CAN YOU HAVE WAMBA SHOT FOR ME, PLEASE?
SORRY, CHEF... BAD LUCK TO KILL A WITCH DOCTOR.
ON THE JOURNEY BACK TO THE VILLAGE OF SAN DEI, SEABROOK'S PARTY STOPPED AT VARIOUS VILLAGES WHERE ARRANGEMENTS WERE MADE TO FEED THE PORTERS.
THE VILLAGERS WERE WELL PAID AND THESE ARRANGEMENTS FOR EATING PROCEEDED SMOOTHLY. USUALLY.
THE MEN STILL HAVEN'T BEEN FED AND THE VILLAGER IN CHARGE IS AVOIDING ME...
DO I HAVE TO DO EVERYTHING AROUND HERE, MORI?
WAMBA! WHERE'S THOSE GODDAMN LUCKY BOOTSH OF MINE?
SKITTER!

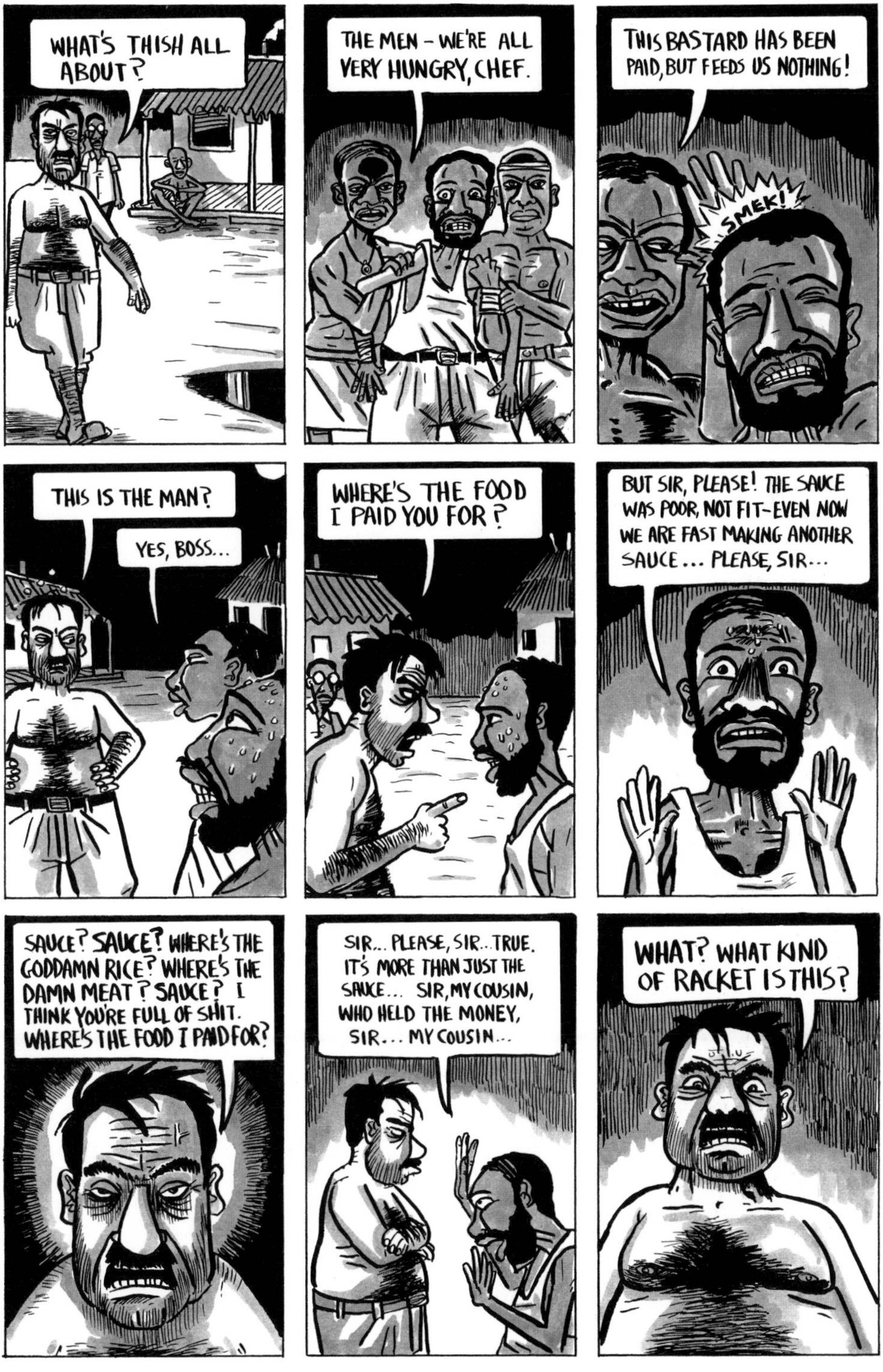
WHAT'S THISH ALL ABOUT?
THE MEN - WE'RE ALL VERY HUNGRY, CHEF.
THIS BASTARD HAS BEEN PAID, BUT FEEDS US NOTHING!
SMEK!
THIS IS THE MAN?
YES, BOSS...
WHERE'S THE FOOD I PAID YOU FOR?
BUT SIR, PLEASE! THE SAUCE WAS POOR, NOT FIT- EVEN NOW WE ARE FAST MAKING ANOTHER SAUCE... PLEASE, SIR...
SAUCE? SAUCE? WHERE'S THE GODDAMN RICE? WHERE'S THE DAMN MEAT? SAUCE? I THINK YOU'RE FULL OF SHIT. WHERE'S THE FOOD I PAID FOR?
SIR... PLEASE, SIR... TRUE. IT'S MORE THAN JUST THE SAUCE... SIR, MY COUSIN, WHO HELD THE MONEY, SIR... MY COUSIN...
WHAT? WHAT KIND OF RACKET IS THIS?

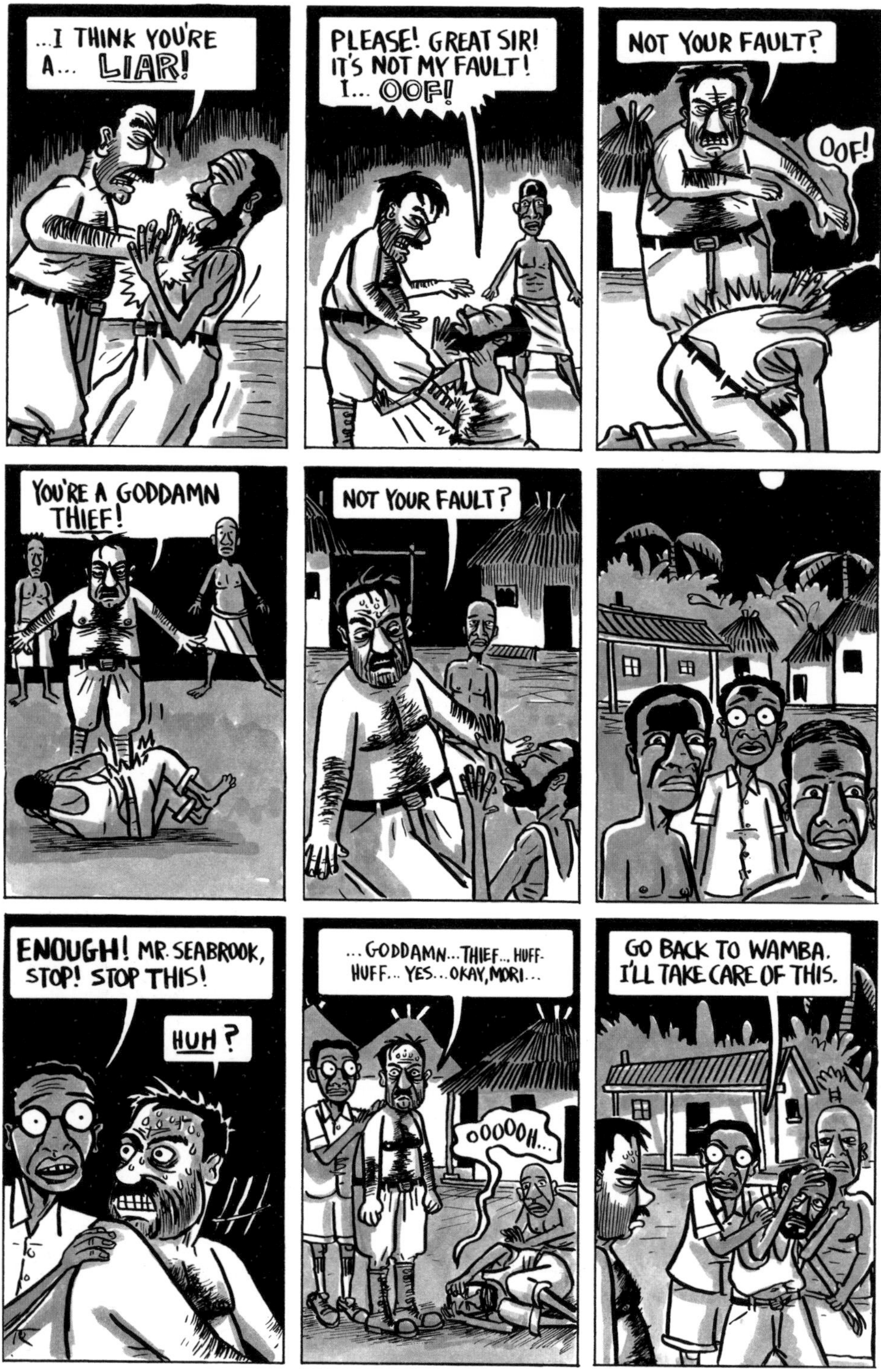

...I THINK YOU'RE A... LIAR!
PLEASE! GREAT SIR! IT'S NOT MY FAULT! I... OOF!
NOT YOUR FAULT?
OOF!
YOU'RE A GODDAMN THIEF!
NOT YOUR FAULT?
ENOUGH! MR. SEABROOK, STOP! STOP THIS!
HUH?
...GODDAMN...THIEF... HUFF-HUFF... YES...OKAY, MORI...
OOOOOH...
GO BACK TO WAMBA. I'LL TAKE CARE OF THIS.

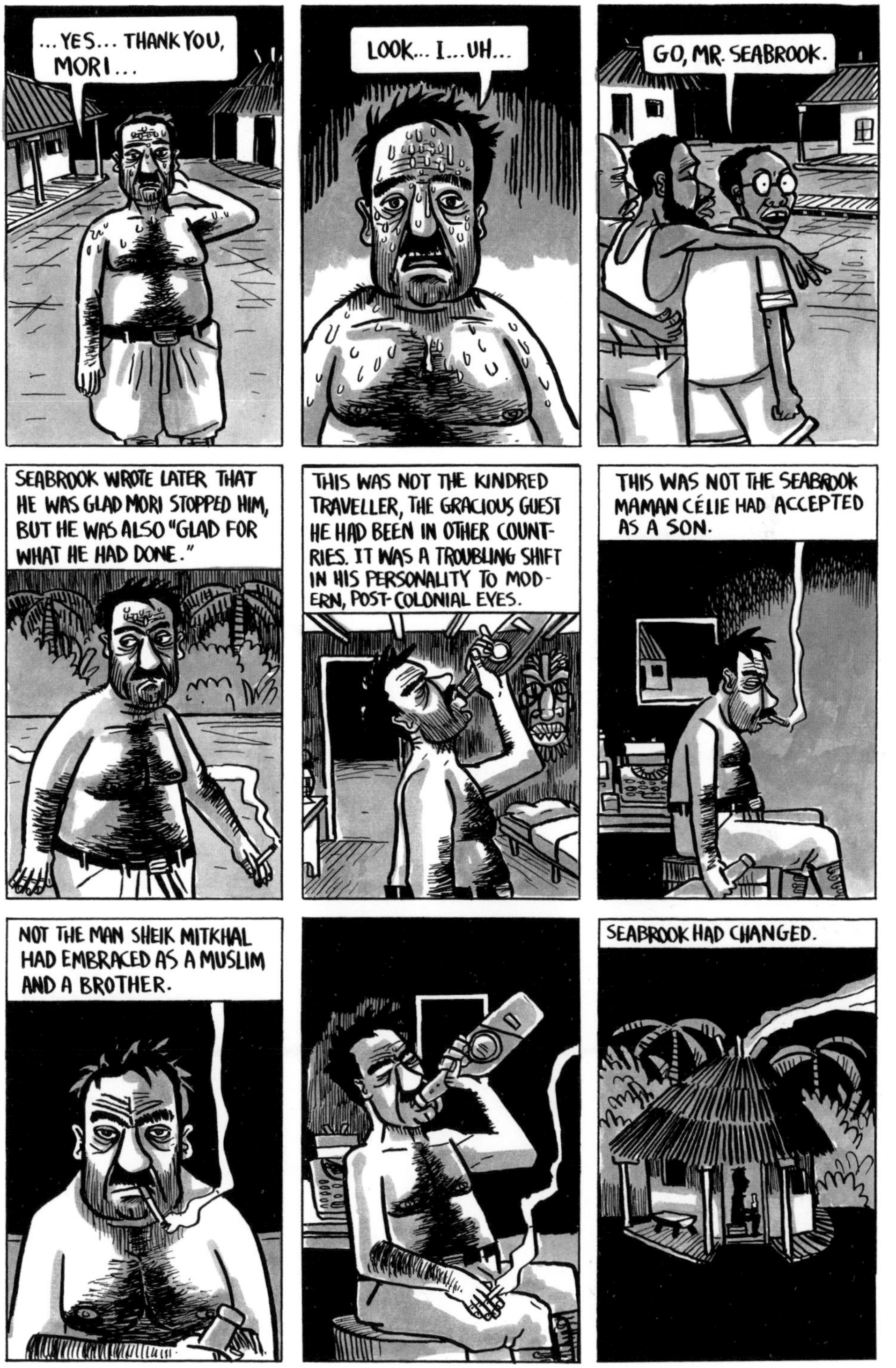
...YES... THANK YOU, MORI...
LOOK... I...UH...
GO, MR. SEABROOK.
SEABROOK WROTE LATER THAT HE WAS GLAD MORI STOPPED HIM, BUT HE WAS ALSO "GLAD FOR WHAT HE HAD DONE."
THIS WAS NOT THE KINDRED TRAVELLER, THE GRACIOUS GUEST HE HAD BEEN IN OTHER COUNTRIES. IT WAS A TROUBLING SHIFT IN HIS PERSONALITY TO MODERN, POST-COLONIAL EYES.
THIS WAS NOT THE SEABROOK MAMAN CÉLIE HAD ACCEPTED AS A SON.
NOT THE MAN SHEIK MITKHAL HAD EMBRACED AS A MUSLIM AND A BROTHER.
SEABROOK HAD CHANGED.

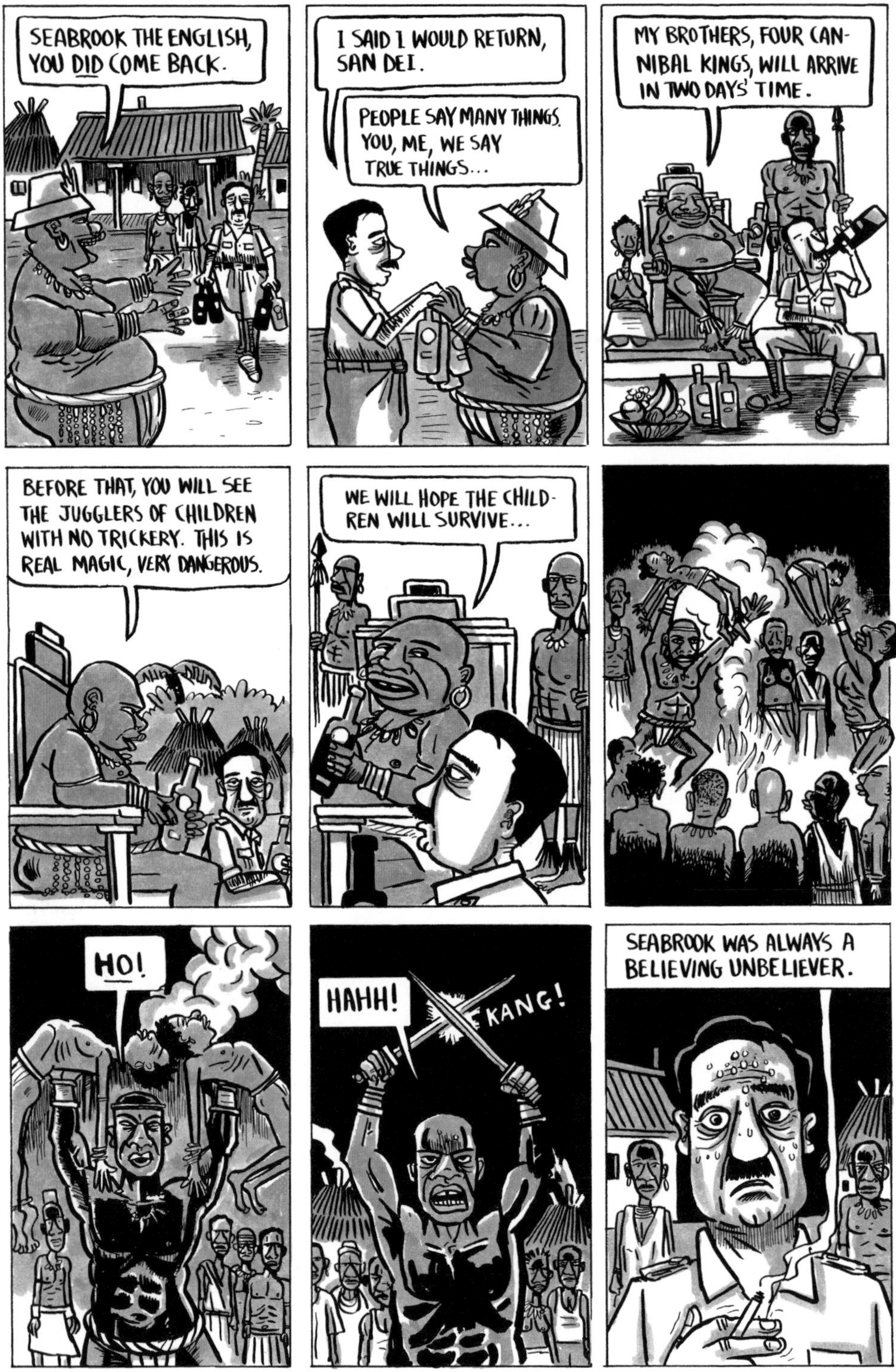
SEABROOK THE ENGLISH, YOU DID COME BACK.
I SAID I WOULD RETURN, SAN DEI.
PEOPLE SAY MANY THINGS. YOU, ME, WE SAY TRUE THINGS...
MY BROTHERS, FOUR CANNIBAL KINGS, WILL ARRIVE IN TWO DAYS' TIME.
BEFORE THAT, YOU WILL SEE THE JUGGLERS OF CHILDREN WITH NO TRICKERY. THIS IS REAL MAGIC, VERY DANGEROUS.
WE WILL HOPE THE CHILDREN WILL SURVIVE...
HO!
HAHH!
KANG!
SEABROOK WAS ALWAYS A BELIEVING UNBELIEVER.

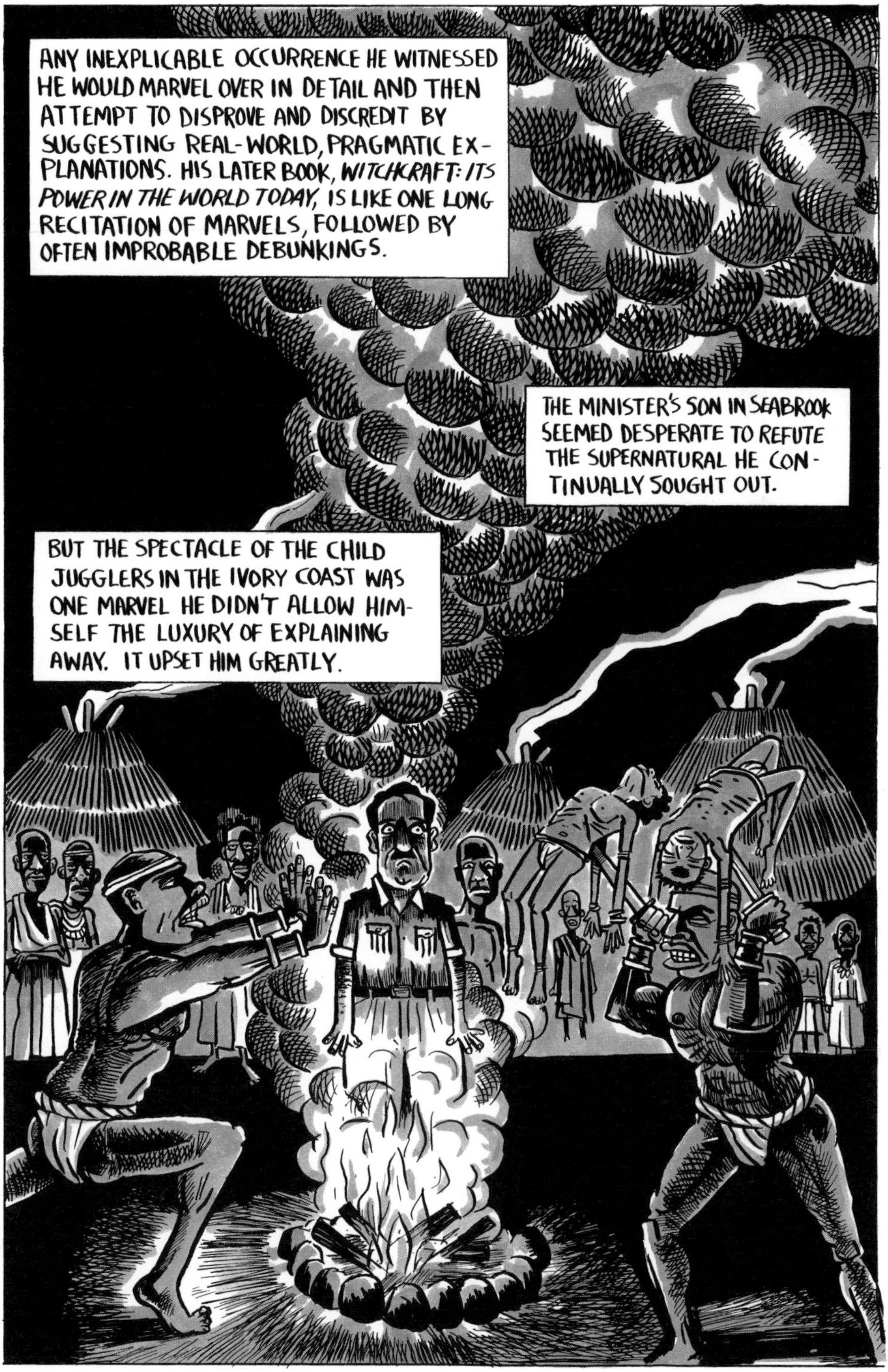
ANY INEXPLICABLE OCCURRENCE HE WITNESSED HE WOULD MARVEL OVER IN DETAIL AND THEN ATTEMPT TO DISPROVE AND DISCREDIT BY SUGGESTING REAL-WORLD, PRAGMATIC EXPLANATIONS. HIS LATER BOOK, *WITCHCRAFT: ITS POWER IN THE WORLD TODAY,* IS LIKE ONE LONG RECITATION OF MARVELS, FOLLOWED BY OFTEN IMPROBABLE DEBUNKINGS.
THE MINISTER'S SON IN SEABROOK SEEMED DESPERATE TO REFUTE THE SUPERNATURAL HE CONTINUALLY SOUGHT OUT.
BUT THE SPECTACLE OF THE CHILD JUGGLERS IN THE IVORY COAST WAS ONE MARVEL HE DIDN'T ALLOW HIMSELF THE LUXURY OF EXPLAINING AWAY. IT UPSET HIM GREATLY.

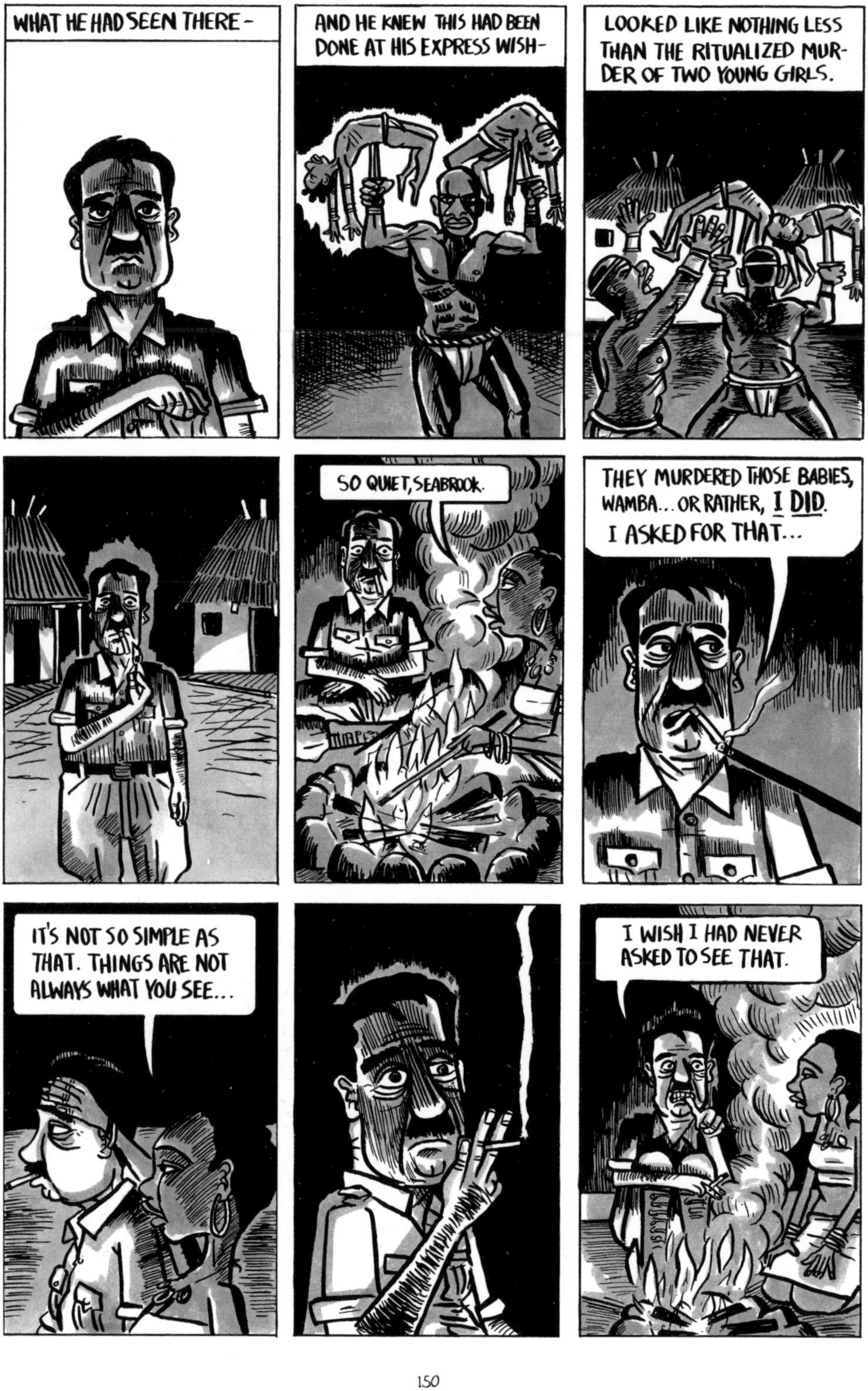
WHAT HE HAD SEEN THERE -
AND HE KNEW THIS HAD BEEN DONE AT HIS EXPRESS WISH -
LOOKED LIKE NOTHING LESS THAN THE RITUALIZED MURDER OF TWO YOUNG GIRLS.
SO QUIET, SEABROOK.
THEY MURDERED THOSE BABIES, WAMBA... OR RATHER, I DID. I ASKED FOR THAT...
IT'S NOT SO SIMPLE AS THAT. THINGS ARE NOT ALWAYS WHAT YOU SEE...
I WISH I HAD NEVER ASKED TO SEE THAT.

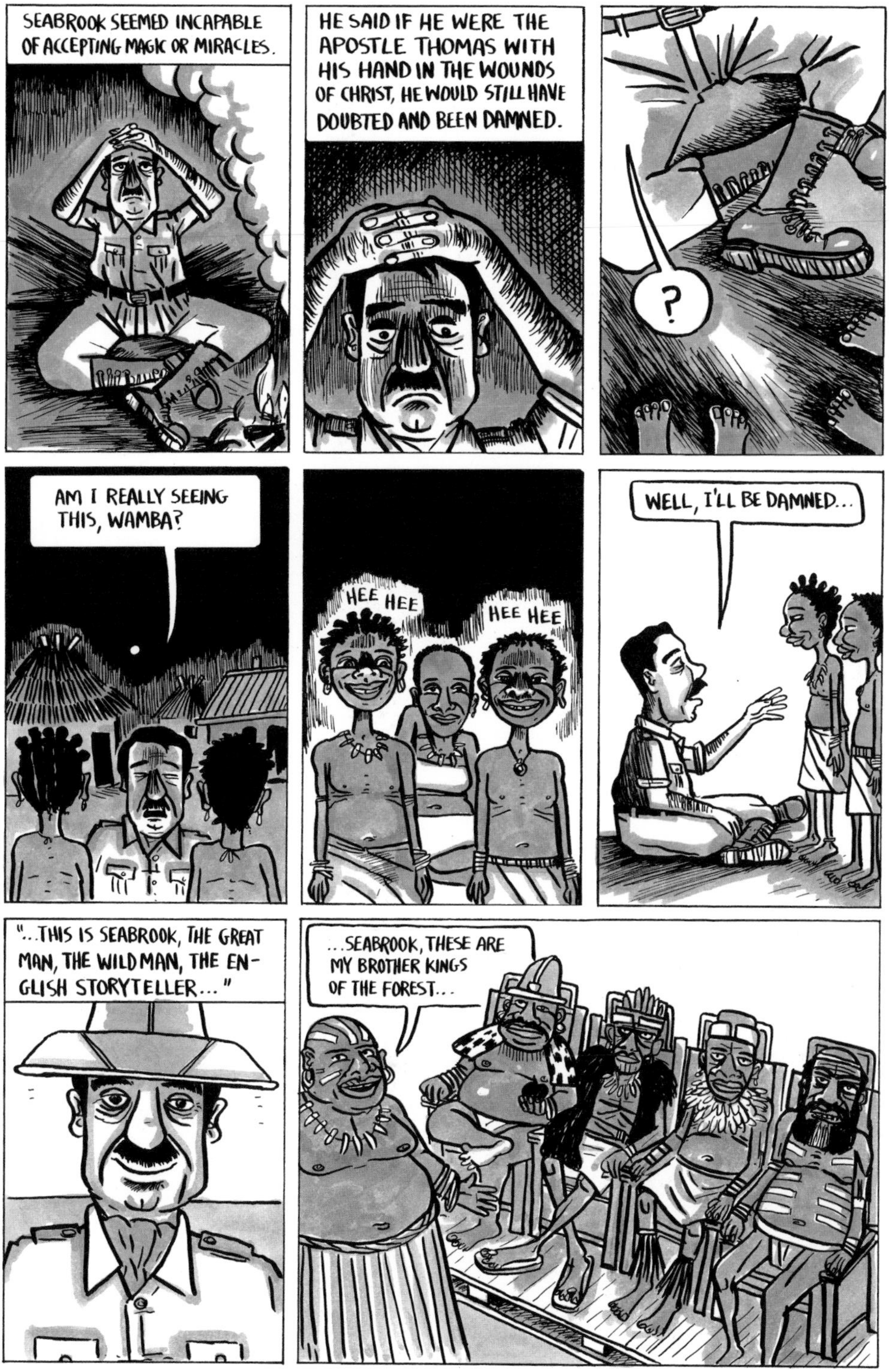
SEABROOK SEEMED INCAPABLE OF ACCEPTING MAGIC OR MIRACLES.
HE SAID IF HE WERE THE APOSTLE THOMAS WITH HIS HAND IN THE WOUNDS OF CHRIST, HE WOULD STILL HAVE DOUBTED AND BEEN DAMNED.
?
AM I REALLY SEEING THIS, WAMBA?
HEE HEE
HEE HEE
WELL, I'LL BE DAMNED...
"...THIS IS SEABROOK, THE GREAT MAN, THE WILD MAN, THE ENGLISH STORYTELLER..."
...SEABROOK, THESE ARE MY BROTHER KINGS OF THE FOREST...

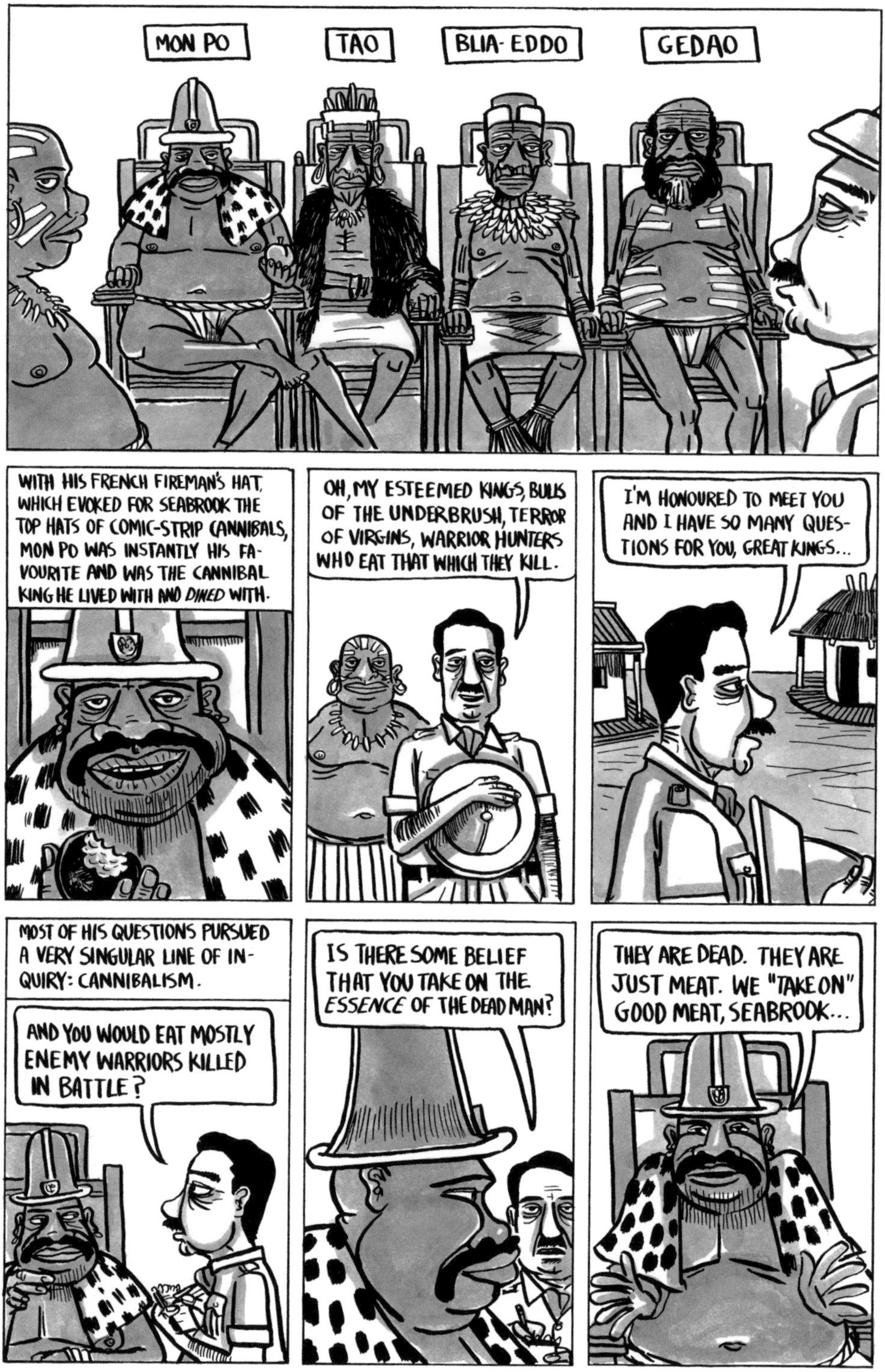
MON PO
TAO
BLIA-EDDO
GEDAO
WITH HIS FRENCH FIREMAN'S HAT, WHICH EVOKED FOR SEABROOK THE TOP HATS OF COMIC-STRIP CANNIBALS, MON PO WAS INSTANTLY HIS FAVOURITE AND WAS THE CANNIBAL KING HE LIVED WITH AND *DINED* WITH.
OH, MY ESTEEMED KINGS, BULLS OF THE UNDERBRUSH, TERROR OF VIRGINS, WARRIOR HUNTERS WHO EAT THAT WHICH THEY KILL.
I'M HONOURED TO MEET YOU AND I HAVE SO MANY QUESTIONS FOR YOU, GREAT KINGS...
MOST OF HIS QUESTIONS PURSUED A VERY SINGULAR LINE OF INQUIRY: CANNIBALISM.
AND YOU WOULD EAT MOSTLY ENEMY WARRIORS KILLED IN BATTLE?
IS THERE SOME BELIEF THAT YOU TAKE ON THE *ESSENCE* OF THE DEAD MAN?
THEY ARE DEAD. THEY ARE JUST MEAT. WE "TAKE ON" GOOD MEAT, SEABROOK...

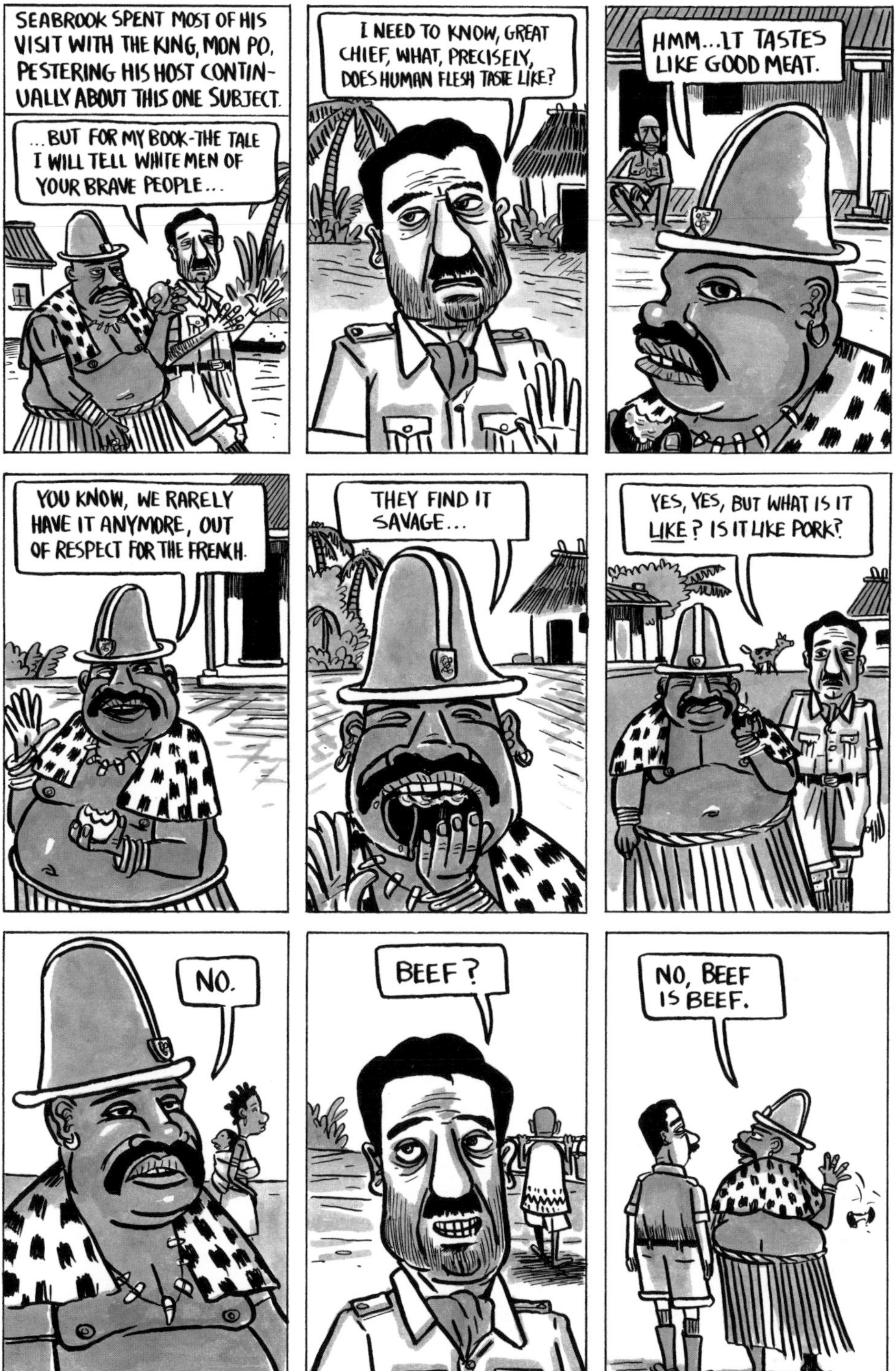
SEABROOK SPENT MOST OF HIS VISIT WITH THE KING, MON PO, PESTERING HIS HOST CONTIN-UALLY ABOUT THIS ONE SUBJECT.
...BUT FOR MY BOOK-THE TALE I WILL TELL WHITE MEN OF YOUR BRAVE PEOPLE...
I NEED TO KNOW, GREAT CHIEF, WHAT, PRECISELY, DOES HUMAN FLESH TASTE LIKE?
HMM...IT TASTES LIKE GOOD MEAT.
YOU KNOW, WE RARELY HAVE IT ANYMORE, OUT OF RESPECT FOR THE FRENCH.
THEY FIND IT SAVAGE...
YES, YES, BUT WHAT IS IT LIKE? IS IT LIKE PORK?
NO.
BEEF?
NO, BEEF IS BEEF.

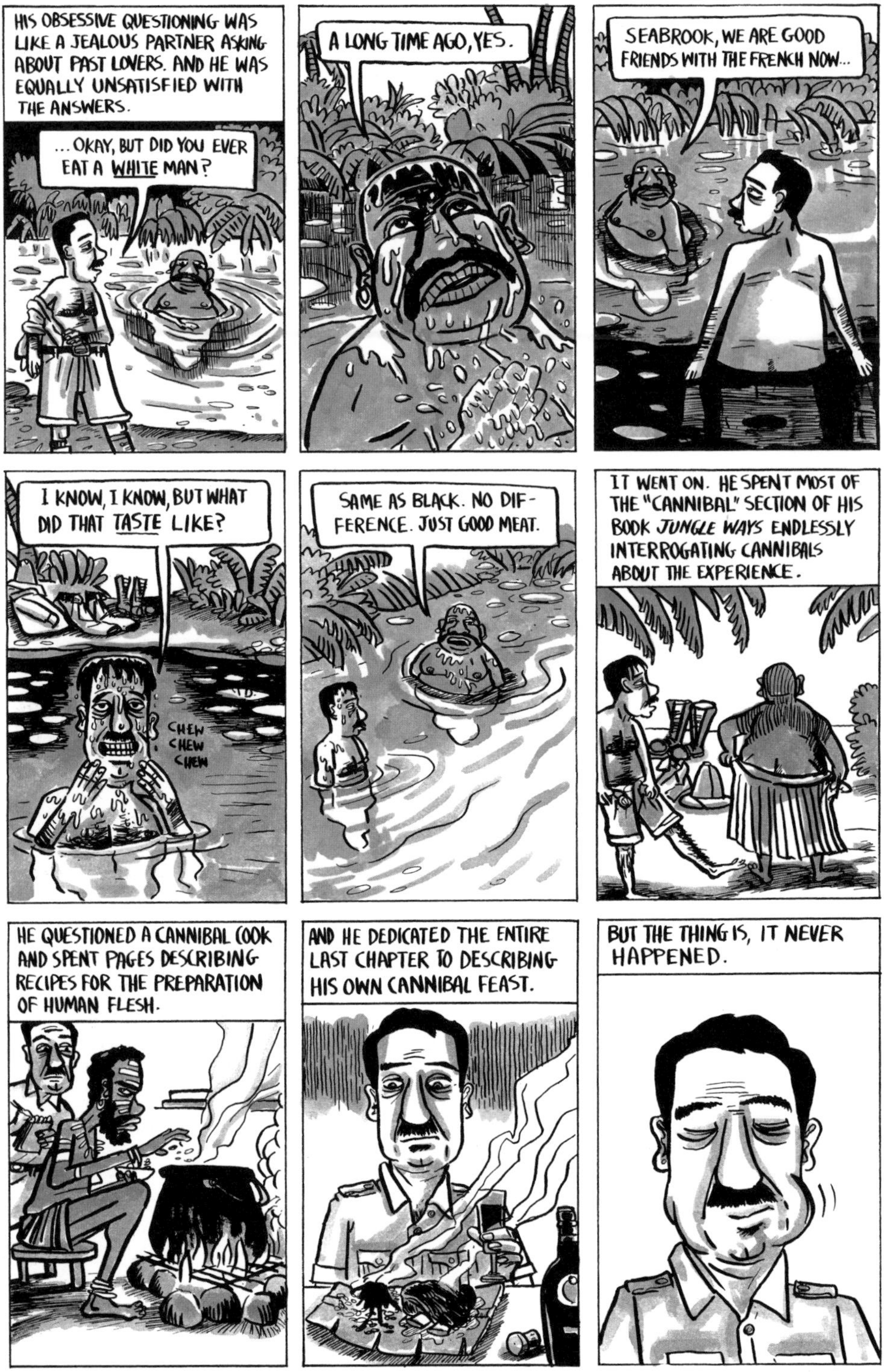
HIS OBSESSIVE QUESTIONING WAS LIKE A JEALOUS PARTNER ASKING ABOUT PAST LOVERS. AND HE WAS EQUALLY UNSATISFIED WITH THE ANSWERS.
...OKAY, BUT DID YOU EVER EAT A WHITE MAN?
A LONG TIME AGO, YES.
SEABROOK, WE ARE GOOD FRIENDS WITH THE FRENCH NOW...
I KNOW, I KNOW, BUT WHAT DID THAT TASTE LIKE?
CHEW CHEW CHEW
SAME AS BLACK. NO DIFFERENCE. JUST GOOD MEAT.
IT WENT ON. HE SPENT MOST OF THE "CANNIBAL" SECTION OF HIS BOOK JUNGLE WAYS ENDLESSLY INTERROGATING CANNIBALS ABOUT THE EXPERIENCE.
HE QUESTIONED A CANNIBAL COOK AND SPENT PAGES DESCRIBING RECIPES FOR THE PREPARATION OF HUMAN FLESH.
AND HE DEDICATED THE ENTIRE LAST CHAPTER TO DESCRIBING HIS OWN CANNIBAL FEAST.
BUT THE THING IS, IT NEVER HAPPENED.

HIS HOSTS HAD SHOWED HIM A HUMAN CORPSE, A WARRIOR KILLED IN BATTLE.

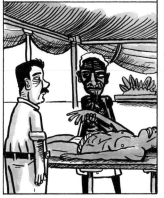

BUT IN THE END, THEY COOKED AND SERVED STEWED PIECES OF A BUTCHERED GREAT APE.

MON PO MAY HAVE WANTED TO SILENCE SEABROOK ON THE SUBJECT OF CANNIBALISM, WHILE STILL AVOIDING FRICTION WITH THE FRENCH AUTHORITIES.

YEARS LATER, SEABROOK ADMITTED THAT HE HAD REALIZED THE DECEPTION AT THE TIME.

FINGER BONES

BUT IN HIS PUBLISHED ACCOUNT, HE DESCRIBED THE COOKING AND PREPARATION OF THE DEAD MAN. HE RELATED THAT HE TOOK HIS PORTION WITH RED WINE AND A SIDE OF RICE.

"I WON'T WRITE ABOUT CANNIBALS IF I CAN'T PARTICIPATE IN THEIR FEASTS..."

REALLY?

AND WHEN IT DIDN'T HAPPEN—SEABROOK LIED.

FICTION IN A NON-FICTION BOOK IS ANATHEMA, BUT FROM HIS DAYS WRITING FOR HEARST, SEABROOK WAS USED TO "TWISTING AND DISTORTING" THE TRUTH FOR A STORY, THOUGH "OUTRIGHT LYING" WAS TABOO.

WHILE HE DIDN'T PARTICIPATE IN CANNIBALISM IN AFRICA, HE WAS CONTENT TO WRITE AS IF HE DID SO BECAUSE HE FULFILLED THE SPIRIT OF THE THING WHEN HE RETURNED TO PARIS.

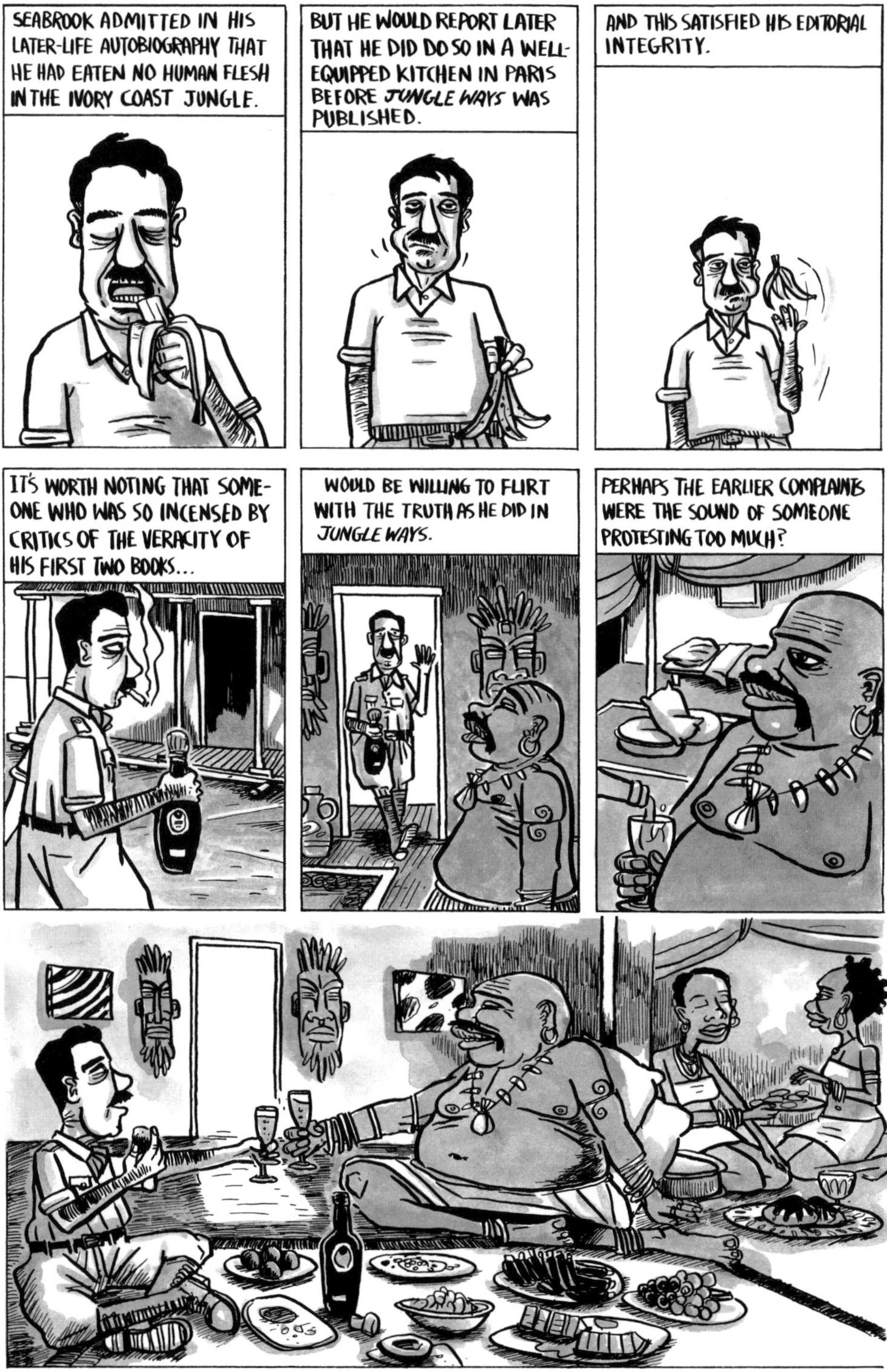
SEABROOK ADMITTED IN HIS LATER-LIFE AUTOBIOGRAPHY THAT HE HAD EATEN NO HUMAN FLESH IN THE IVORY COAST JUNGLE.
BUT HE WOULD REPORT LATER THAT HE DID DO SO IN A WELL-EQUIPPED KITCHEN IN PARIS BEFORE JUNGLE WAYS WAS PUBLISHED.
AND THIS SATISFIED HIS EDITORIAL INTEGRITY.
IT'S WORTH NOTING THAT SOME-ONE WHO WAS SO INCENSED BY CRITICS OF THE VERACITY OF HIS FIRST TWO BOOKS...
WOULD BE WILLING TO FLIRT WITH THE TRUTH AS HE DID IN JUNGLE WAYS.
PERHAPS THE EARLIER COMPLAINTS WERE THE SOUND OF SOMEONE PROTESTING TOO MUCH?

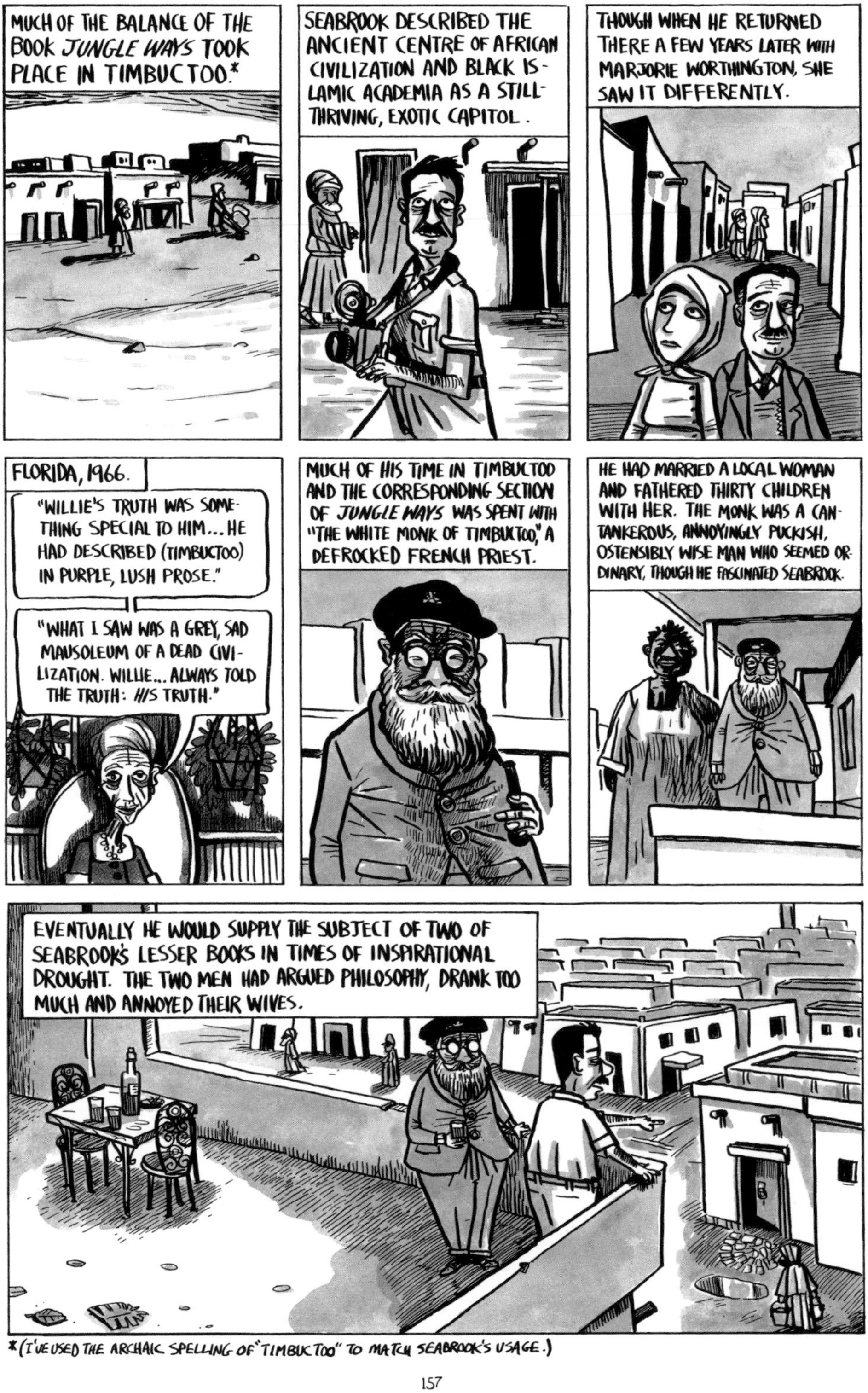

MUCH OF THE BALANCE OF THE BOOK JUNGLE WAYS TOOK PLACE IN TIMBUCTOO.*
SEABROOK DESCRIBED THE ANCIENT CENTRE OF AFRICAN CIVILIZATION AND BLACK ISLAMIC ACADEMIA AS A STILL-THRIVING, EXOTIC CAPITOL.
THOUGH WHEN HE RETURNED THERE A FEW YEARS LATER WITH MARJORIE WORTHINGTON, SHE SAW IT DIFFERENTLY.
FLORIDA, 1966.
"WILLIE'S TRUTH WAS SOMETHING SPECIAL TO HIM... HE HAD DESCRIBED (TIMBUCTOO) IN PURPLE, LUSH PROSE."
"WHAT I SAW WAS A GREY, SAD MAUSOLEUM OF A DEAD CIVILIZATION. WILLIE... ALWAYS TOLD THE TRUTH: HIS TRUTH."
MUCH OF HIS TIME IN TIMBUCTOO AND THE CORRESPONDING SECTION OF JUNGLE WAYS WAS SPENT WITH "THE WHITE MONK OF TIMBUCTOO," A DEFROCKED FRENCH PRIEST.
HE HAD MARRIED A LOCAL WOMAN AND FATHERED THIRTY CHILDREN WITH HER. THE MONK WAS A CANTANKEROUS, ANNOYINGLY PUCKISH, OSTENSIBLY WISE MAN WHO SEEMED ORDINARY, THOUGH HE FASCINATED SEABROOK.
EVENTUALLY HE WOULD SUPPLY THE SUBJECT OF TWO OF SEABROOK'S LESSER BOOKS IN TIMES OF INSPIRATIONAL DROUGHT. THE TWO MEN HAD ARGUED PHILOSOPHY, DRANK TOO MUCH AND ANNOYED THEIR WIVES.


*(I'VE USED THE ARCHAIC SPELLING OF "TIMBUCTOO" TO MATCH SEABROOK'S USAGE.)

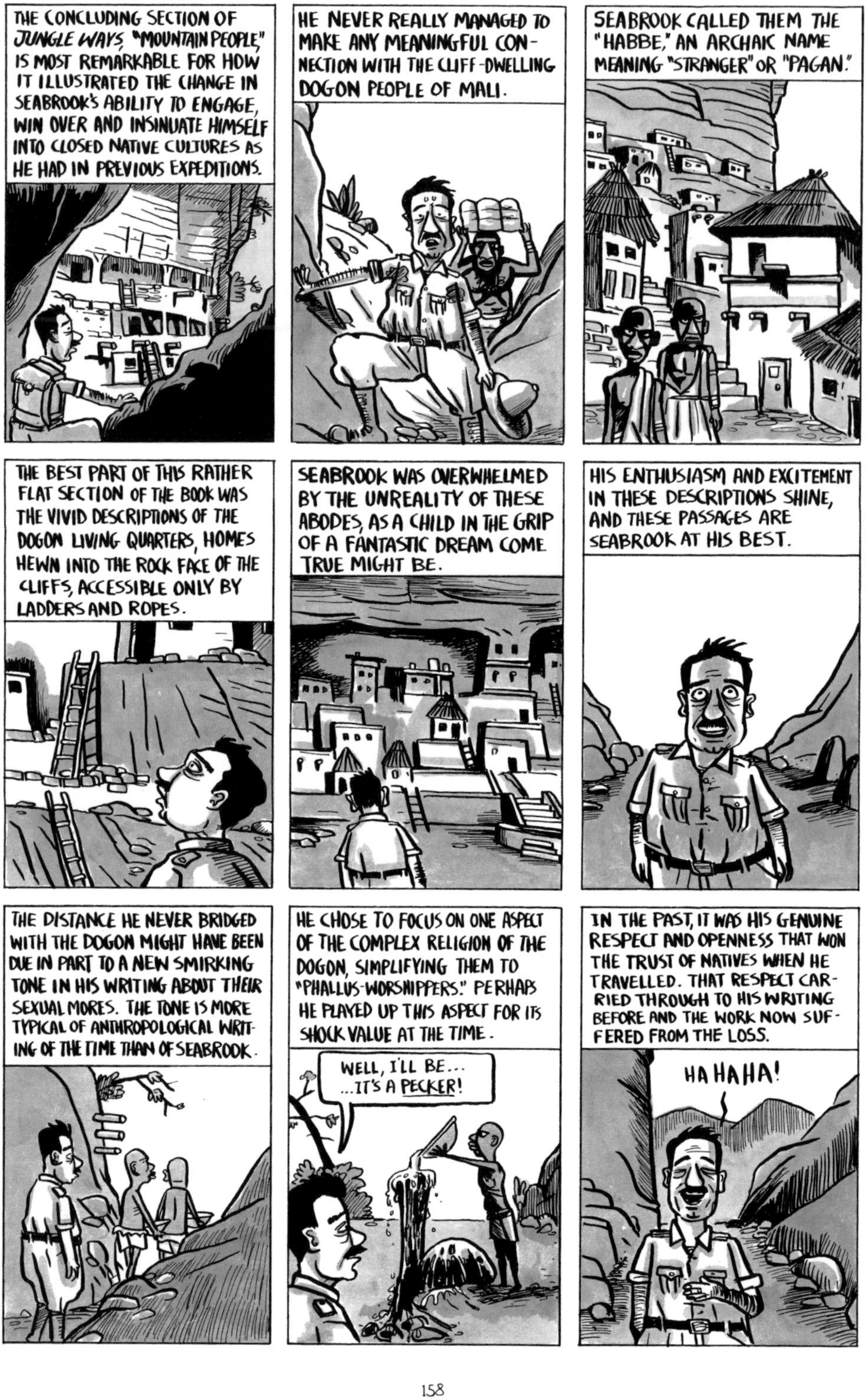
THE CONCLUDING SECTION OF JUNGLE WAYS, "MOUNTAIN PEOPLE," IS MOST REMARKABLE FOR HOW IT ILLUSTRATED THE CHANGE IN SEABROOK'S ABILITY TO ENGAGE, WIN OVER AND INSINUATE HIMSELF INTO CLOSED NATIVE CULTURES AS HE HAD IN PREVIOUS EXPEDITIONS.
HE NEVER REALLY MANAGED TO MAKE ANY MEANINGFUL CONNECTION WITH THE CLIFF-DWELLING DOGON PEOPLE OF MALI.
SEABROOK CALLED THEM THE "HABBE," AN ARCHAIC NAME MEANING "STRANGER" OR "PAGAN."
THE BEST PART OF THIS RATHER FLAT SECTION OF THE BOOK WAS THE VIVID DESCRIPTIONS OF THE DOGON LIVING QUARTERS, HOMES HEWN INTO THE ROCK FACE OF THE CLIFFS, ACCESSIBLE ONLY BY LADDERS AND ROPES.
SEABROOK WAS OVERWHELMED BY THE UNREALITY OF THESE ABODES, AS A CHILD IN THE GRIP OF A FANTASTIC DREAM COME TRUE MIGHT BE.
HIS ENTHUSIASM AND EXCITEMENT IN THESE DESCRIPTIONS SHINE, AND THESE PASSAGES ARE SEABROOK AT HIS BEST.
THE DISTANCE HE NEVER BRIDGED WITH THE DOGON MIGHT HAVE BEEN DUE IN PART TO A NEW SMIRKING TONE IN HIS WRITING ABOUT THEIR SEXUAL MORES. THE TONE IS MORE TYPICAL OF ANTHROPOLOGICAL WRITING OF THE TIME THAN OF SEABROOK.
HE CHOSE TO FOCUS ON ONE ASPECT OF THE COMPLEX RELIGION OF THE DOGON, SIMPLIFYING THEM TO "PHALLUS-WORSHIPPERS." PERHAPS HE PLAYED UP THIS ASPECT FOR ITS SHOCK VALUE AT THE TIME.
WELL, I'LL BE... ...IT'S A PECKER!
IN THE PAST, IT WAS HIS GENUINE RESPECT AND OPENNESS THAT WON THE TRUST OF NATIVES WHEN HE TRAVELLED. THAT RESPECT CARRIED THROUGH TO HIS WRITING BEFORE AND THE WORK NOW SUFFERED FROM THE LOSS.
HA HA HA!

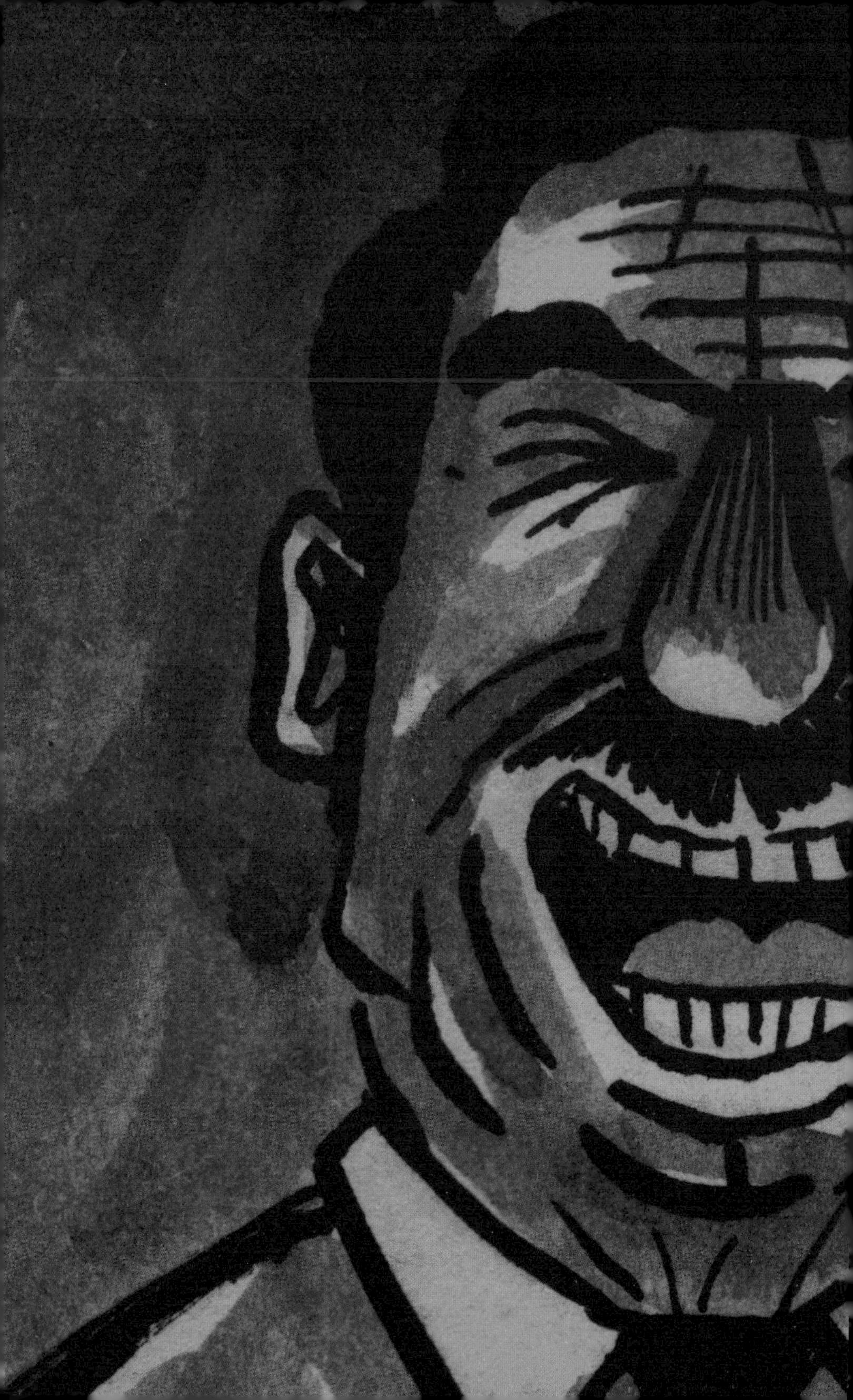

# CHAPTER FIVE
## LOST IN THE LOST GENERATION

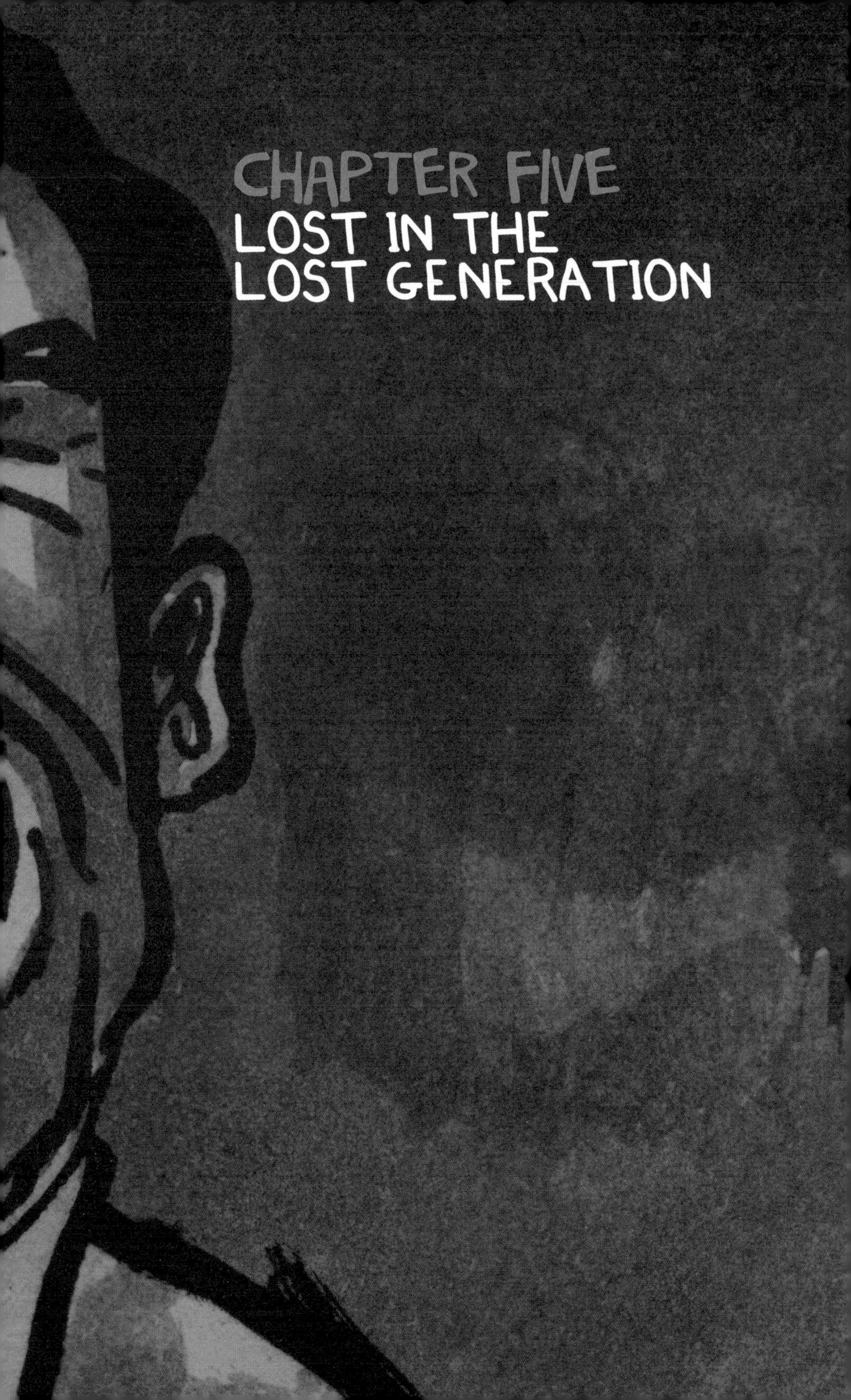

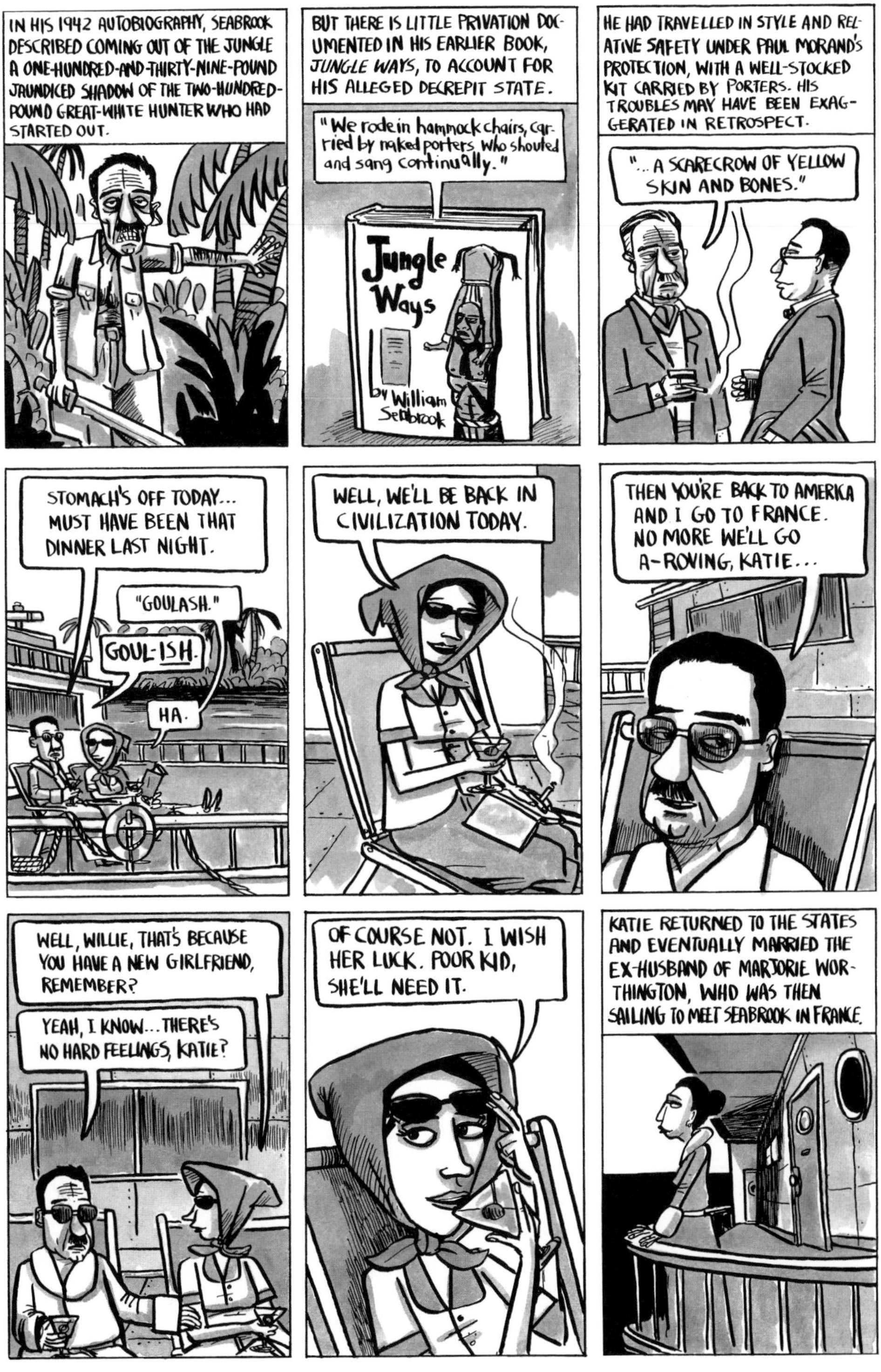
IN HIS 1942 AUTOBIOGRAPHY, SEABROOK DESCRIBED COMING OUT OF THE JUNGLE A ONE-HUNDRED-AND-THIRTY-NINE-POUND JAUNDICED SHADOW OF THE TWO-HUNDRED-POUND GREAT-WHITE HUNTER WHO HAD STARTED OUT.
BUT THERE IS LITTLE PRIVATION DOCUMENTED IN HIS EARLIER BOOK, JUNGLE WAYS, TO ACCOUNT FOR HIS ALLEGED DECREPIT STATE.
"We rode in hammock chairs, carried by naked porters who shouted and sang continually."
Jungle Ways
by William Seabrook
HE HAD TRAVELLED IN STYLE AND RELATIVE SAFETY UNDER PAUL MORAND'S PROTECTION, WITH A WELL-STOCKED KIT CARRIED BY PORTERS. HIS TROUBLES MAY HAVE BEEN EXAGGERATED IN RETROSPECT.
"... A SCARECROW OF YELLOW SKIN AND BONES."
STOMACH'S OFF TODAY... MUST HAVE BEEN THAT DINNER LAST NIGHT.
"GOULASH."
GOUL-ISH.
HA.
WELL, WE'LL BE BACK IN CIVILIZATION TODAY.
THEN YOU'RE BACK TO AMERICA AND I GO TO FRANCE. NO MORE WE'LL GO A-ROVING, KATIE...
WELL, WILLIE, THAT'S BECAUSE YOU HAVE A NEW GIRLFRIEND, REMEMBER?
YEAH, I KNOW... THERE'S NO HARD FEELINGS, KATIE?
OF COURSE NOT. I WISH HER LUCK. POOR KID, SHE'LL NEED IT.
KATIE RETURNED TO THE STATES AND EVENTUALLY MARRIED THE EX-HUSBAND OF MARJORIE WORTHINGTON, WHO WAS THEN SAILING TO MEET SEABROOK IN FRANCE.

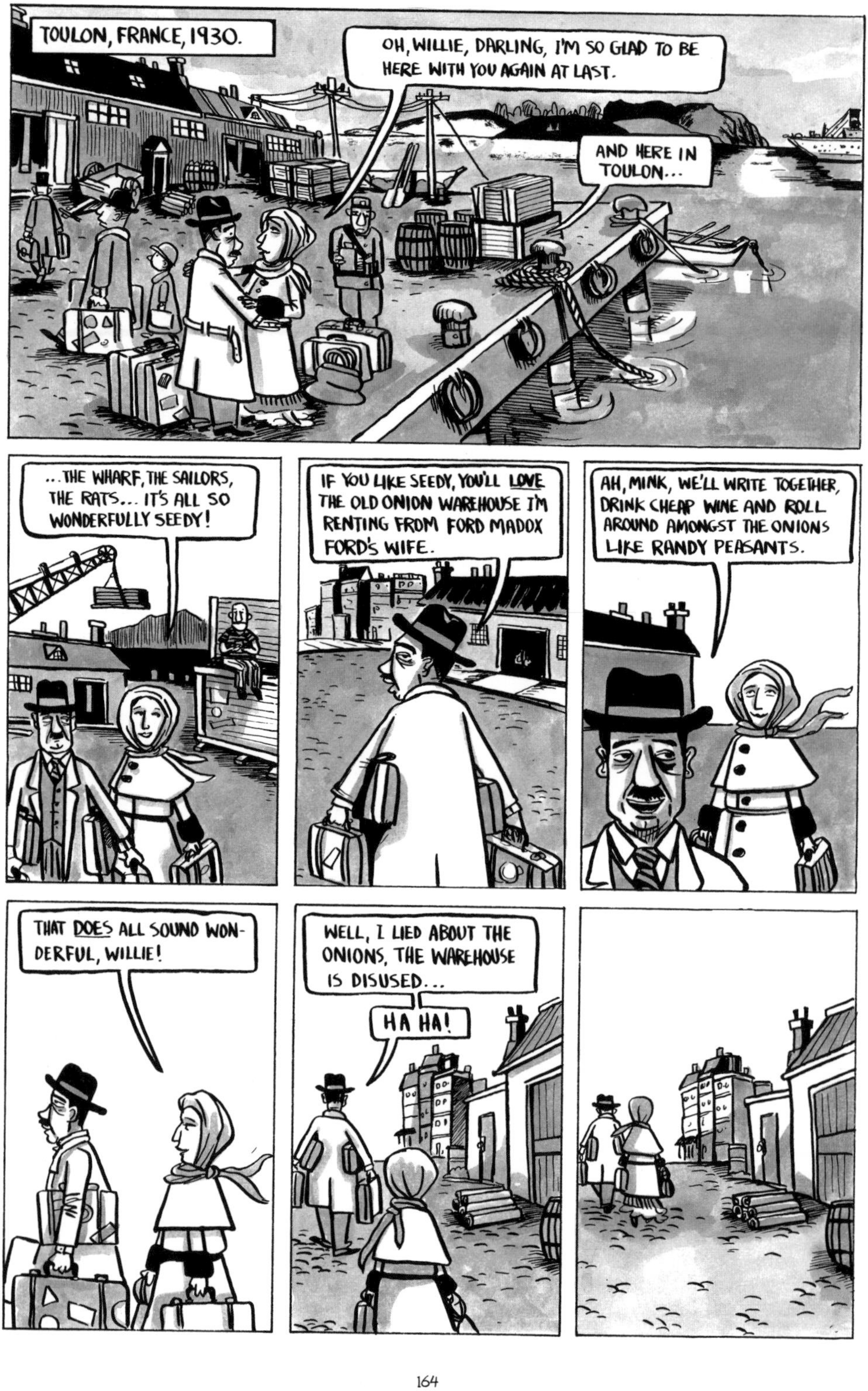
TOULON, FRANCE, 1930.
OH, WILLIE, DARLING, I'M SO GLAD TO BE HERE WITH YOU AGAIN AT LAST.
AND HERE IN TOULON...
...THE WHARF, THE SAILORS, THE RATS... IT'S ALL SO WONDERFULLY SEEDY!
IF YOU LIKE SEEDY, YOU'LL LOVE THE OLD ONION WAREHOUSE I'M RENTING FROM FORD MADOX FORD'S WIFE.
AH, MINK, WE'LL WRITE TOGETHER, DRINK CHEAP WINE AND ROLL AROUND AMONGST THE ONIONS LIKE RANDY PEASANTS.
THAT DOES ALL SOUND WON-DERFUL, WILLIE!
WELL, I LIED ABOUT THE ONIONS, THE WAREHOUSE IS DISUSED...
HA HA!

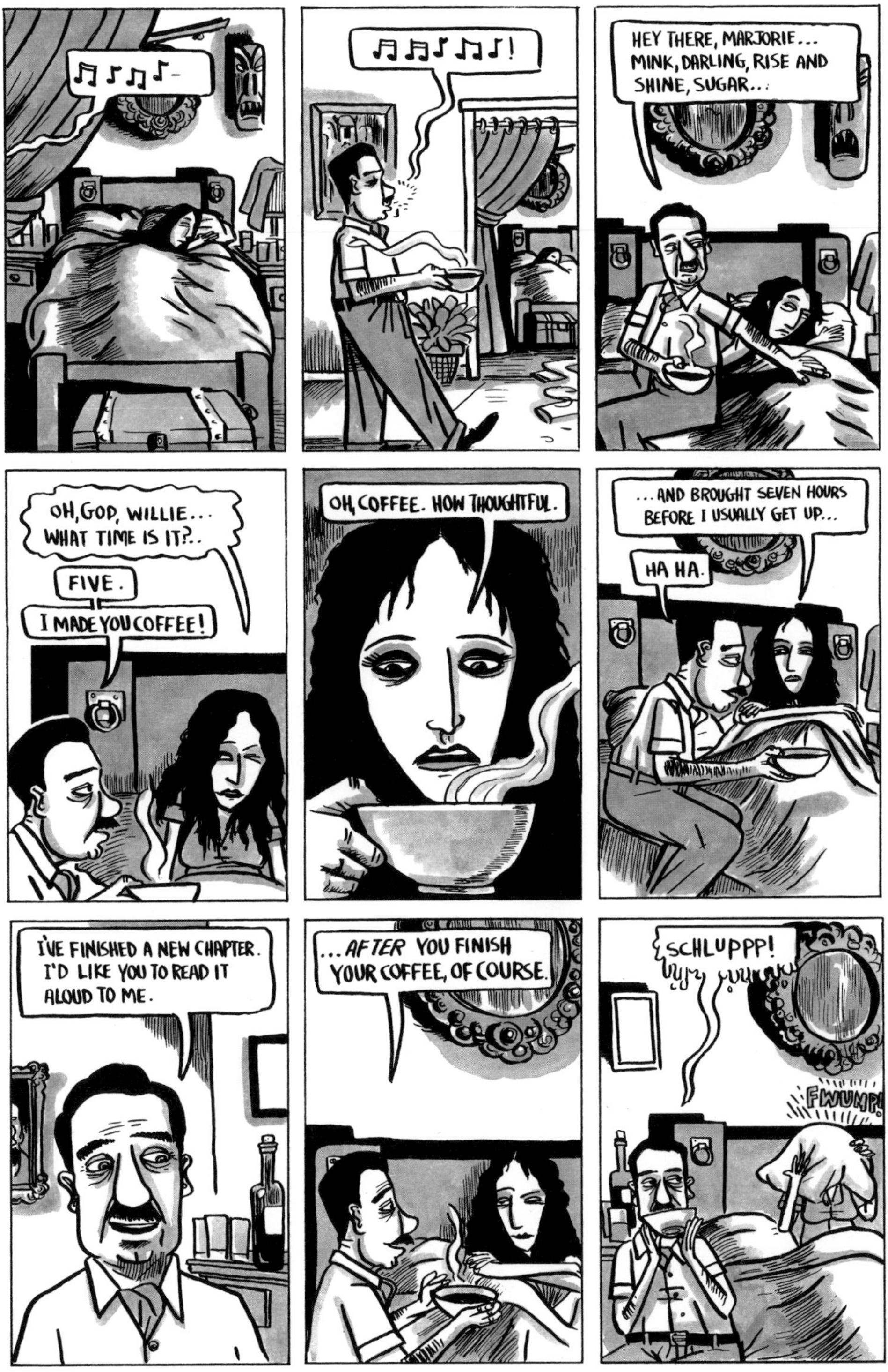
HEY THERE, MARJORIE... MINK, DARLING, RISE AND SHINE, SUGAR...
OH, GOD, WILLIE... WHAT TIME IS IT?..
FIVE.
I MADE YOU COFFEE!
OH, COFFEE. HOW THOUGHTFUL.
...AND BROUGHT SEVEN HOURS BEFORE I USUALLY GET UP...
HA HA.
I'VE FINISHED A NEW CHAPTER. I'D LIKE YOU TO READ IT ALOUD TO ME.
...AFTER YOU FINISH YOUR COFFEE, OF COURSE.
SCHLUPPP!
FWUMP!

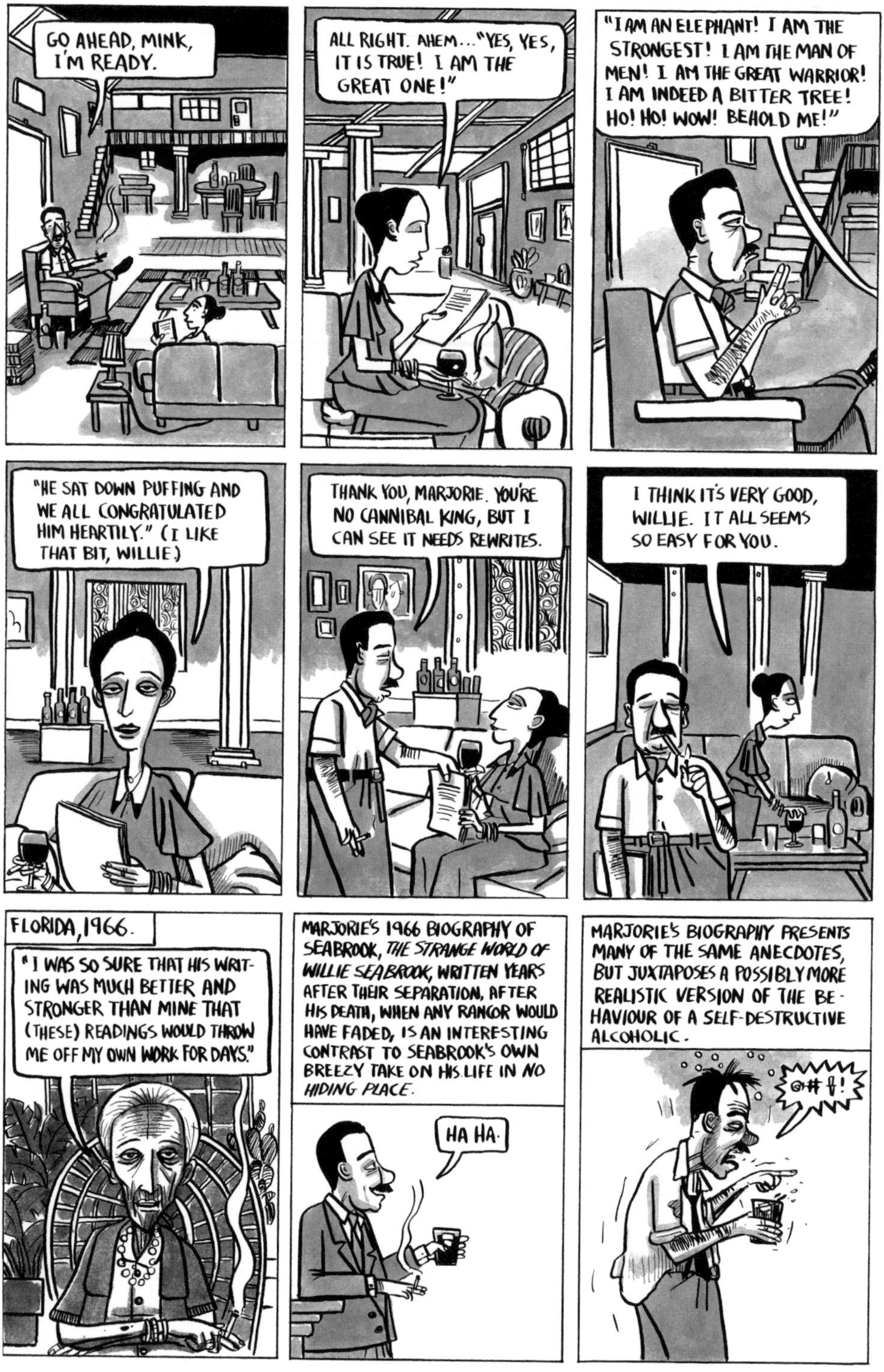
GO AHEAD, MINK, I'M READY.
ALL RIGHT. AHEM... "YES, YES, IT IS TRUE! I AM THE GREAT ONE!"
"I AM AN ELEPHANT! I AM THE STRONGEST! I AM THE MAN OF MEN! I AM THE GREAT WARRIOR! I AM INDEED A BITTER TREE! HO! HO! WOW! BEHOLD ME!"
"HE SAT DOWN PUFFING AND WE ALL CONGRATULATED HIM HEARTILY." (I LIKE THAT BIT, WILLIE.)
THANK YOU, MARJORIE. YOU'RE NO CANNIBAL KING, BUT I CAN SEE IT NEEDS REWRITES.
I THINK IT'S VERY GOOD, WILLIE. IT ALL SEEMS SO EASY FOR YOU.
FLORIDA, 1966.
"I WAS SO SURE THAT HIS WRITING WAS MUCH BETTER AND STRONGER THAN MINE THAT (THESE) READINGS WOULD THROW ME OFF MY OWN WORK FOR DAYS."
MARJORIE'S 1966 BIOGRAPHY OF SEABROOK, THE STRANGE WORLD OF WILLIE SEABROOK, WRITTEN YEARS AFTER THEIR SEPARATION, AFTER HIS DEATH, WHEN ANY RANCOR WOULD HAVE FADED, IS AN INTERESTING CONTRAST TO SEABROOK'S OWN BREEZY TAKE ON HIS LIFE IN NO HIDING PLACE.
HA HA.
MARJORIE'S BIOGRAPHY PRESENTS MANY OF THE SAME ANECDOTES, BUT JUXTAPOSES A POSSIBLY MORE REALISTIC VERSION OF THE BEHAVIOUR OF A SELF-DESTRUCTIVE ALCOHOLIC.
@#!!

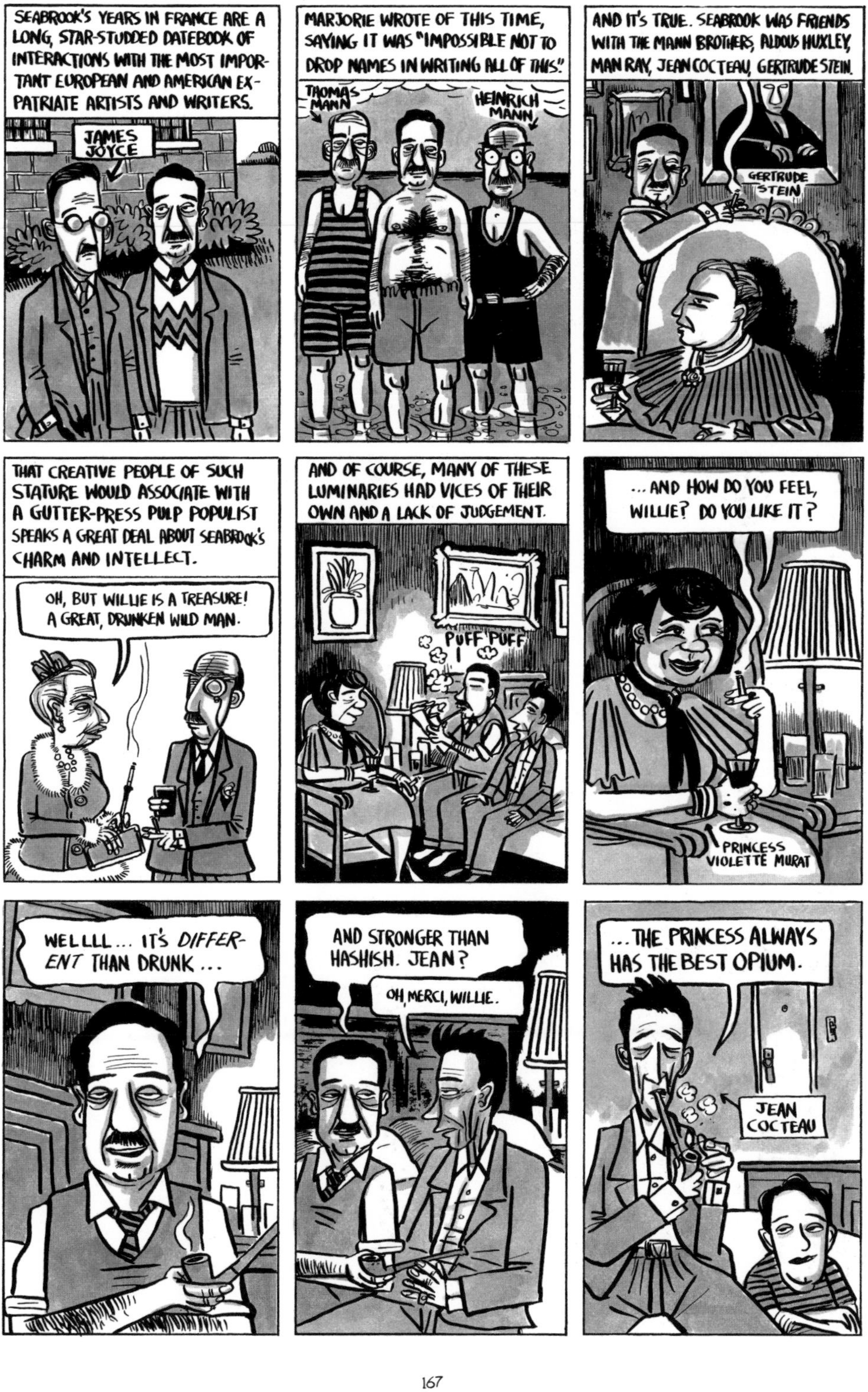
SEABROOK'S YEARS IN FRANCE ARE A LONG, STAR-STUDDED DATEBOOK OF INTERACTIONS WITH THE MOST IMPORTANT EUROPEAN AND AMERICAN EXPATRIATE ARTISTS AND WRITERS.
JAMES JOYCE
MARJORIE WROTE OF THIS TIME, SAYING IT WAS "IMPOSSIBLE NOT TO DROP NAMES IN WRITING ALL OF THIS."
THOMAS MANN
HEINRICH MANN
AND IT'S TRUE. SEABROOK WAS FRIENDS WITH THE MANN BROTHERS, ALDOUS HUXLEY, MAN RAY, JEAN COCTEAU, GERTRUDE STEIN.
GERTRUDE STEIN
THAT CREATIVE PEOPLE OF SUCH STATURE WOULD ASSOCIATE WITH A GUTTER-PRESS PULP POPULIST SPEAKS A GREAT DEAL ABOUT SEABROOK'S CHARM AND INTELLECT.
OH, BUT WILLIE IS A TREASURE! A GREAT, DRUNKEN WILD MAN.
AND OF COURSE, MANY OF THESE LUMINARIES HAD VICES OF THEIR OWN AND A LACK OF JUDGEMENT.
PUFF PUFF
... AND HOW DO YOU FEEL, WILLIE? DO YOU LIKE IT?
PRINCESS VIOLETTE MURAT
WELLLL... IT'S DIFFERENT THAN DRUNK...
AND STRONGER THAN HASHISH. JEAN?
OH, MERCI, WILLIE.
... THE PRINCESS ALWAYS HAS THE BEST OPIUM.
JEAN COCTEAU

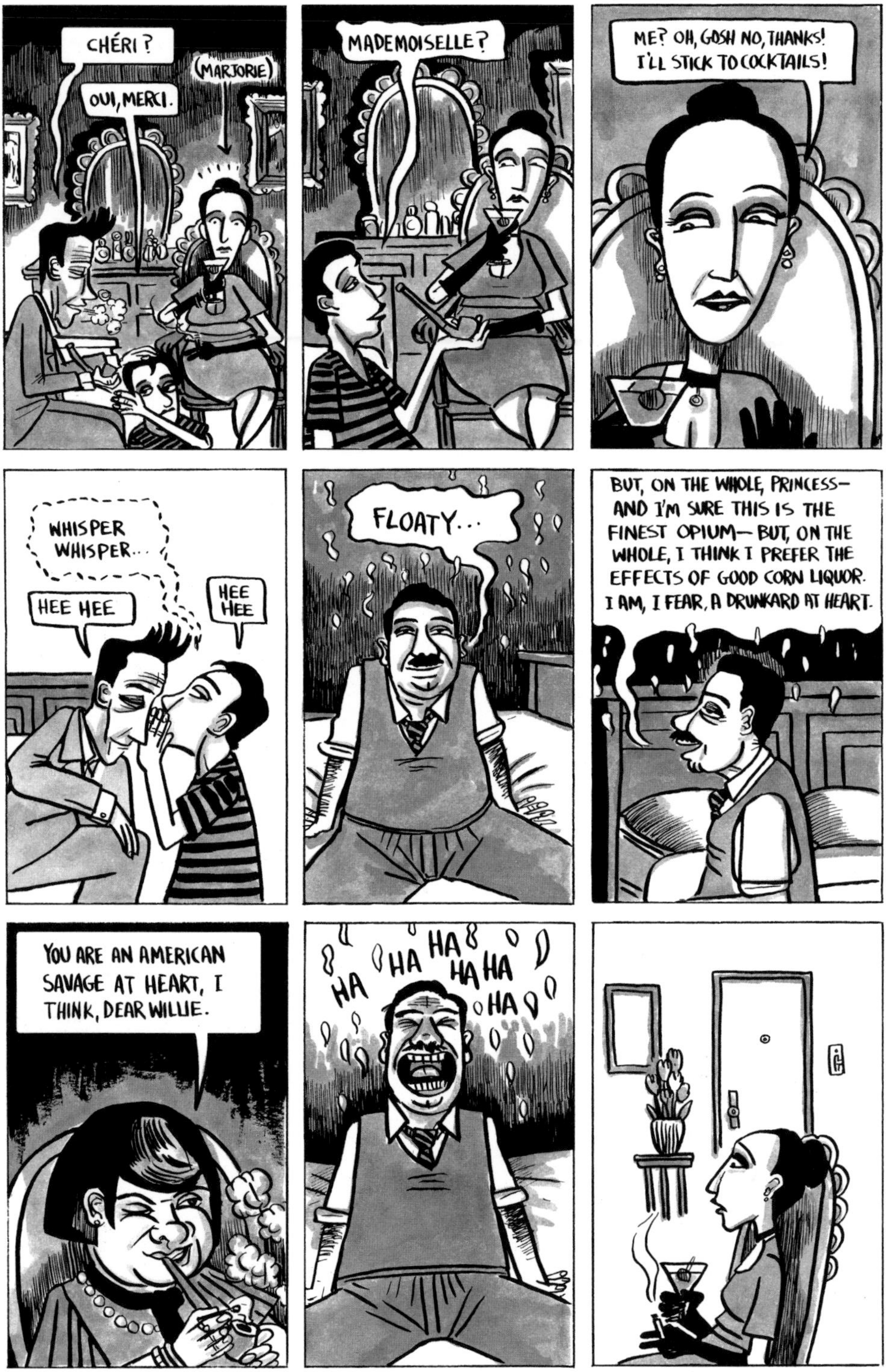
CHÉRI ?
OUI, MERCI.
(MARJORIE)
MADEMOISELLE?
ME? OH, GOSH NO, THANKS! I'LL STICK TO COCKTAILS!
WHISPER WHISPER...
HEE HEE
HEE HEE
FLOATY...
BUT, ON THE WHOLE, PRINCESS— AND I'M SURE THIS IS THE FINEST OPIUM— BUT, ON THE WHOLE, I THINK I PREFER THE EFFECTS OF GOOD CORN LIQUOR. I AM, I FEAR, A DRUNKARD AT HEART.
YOU ARE AN AMERICAN SAVAGE AT HEART, I THINK, DEAR WILLIE.
HA HA HA HA HA HA

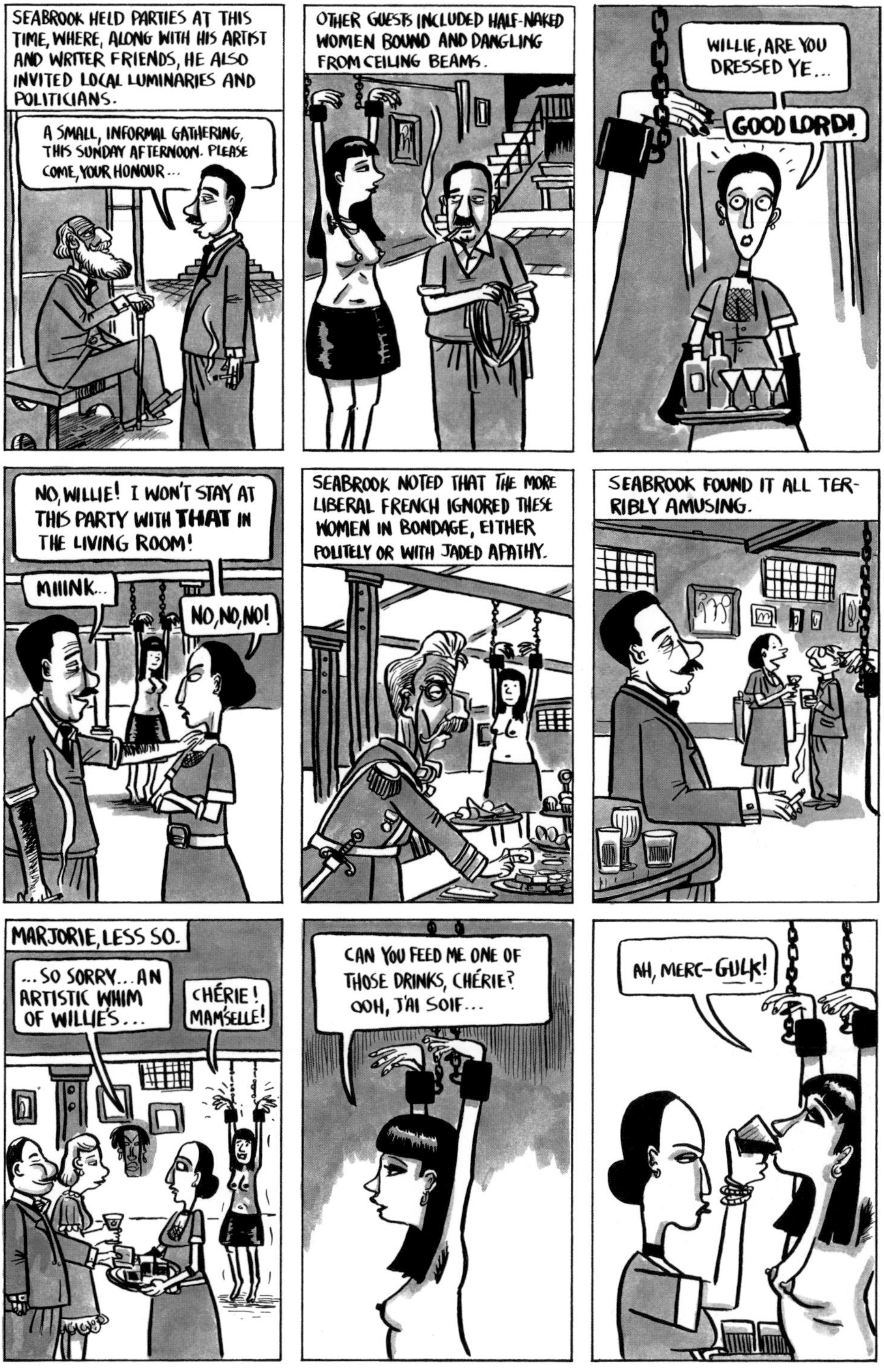
SEABROOK HELD PARTIES AT THIS TIME, WHERE, ALONG WITH HIS ARTIST AND WRITER FRIENDS, HE ALSO INVITED LOCAL LUMINARIES AND POLITICIANS.
A SMALL, INFORMAL GATHERING, THIS SUNDAY AFTERNOON. PLEASE COME, YOUR HONOUR...
OTHER GUESTS INCLUDED HALF-NAKED WOMEN BOUND AND DANGLING FROM CEILING BEAMS.
WILLIE, ARE YOU DRESSED YE...
GOOD LORD!
NO, WILLIE! I WON'T STAY AT THIS PARTY WITH THAT IN THE LIVING ROOM!
MIIINK...
NO, NO, NO!
SEABROOK NOTED THAT THE MORE LIBERAL FRENCH IGNORED THESE WOMEN IN BONDAGE, EITHER POLITELY OR WITH JADED APATHY.
SEABROOK FOUND IT ALL TERRIBLY AMUSING.
MARJORIE, LESS SO.
...SO SORRY... AN ARTISTIC WHIM OF WILLIE'S...
CHÉRIE! MAM'SELLE!
CAN YOU FEED ME ONE OF THOSE DRINKS, CHÉRIE? OOH, J'AI SOIF...
AH, MERC-GULK!

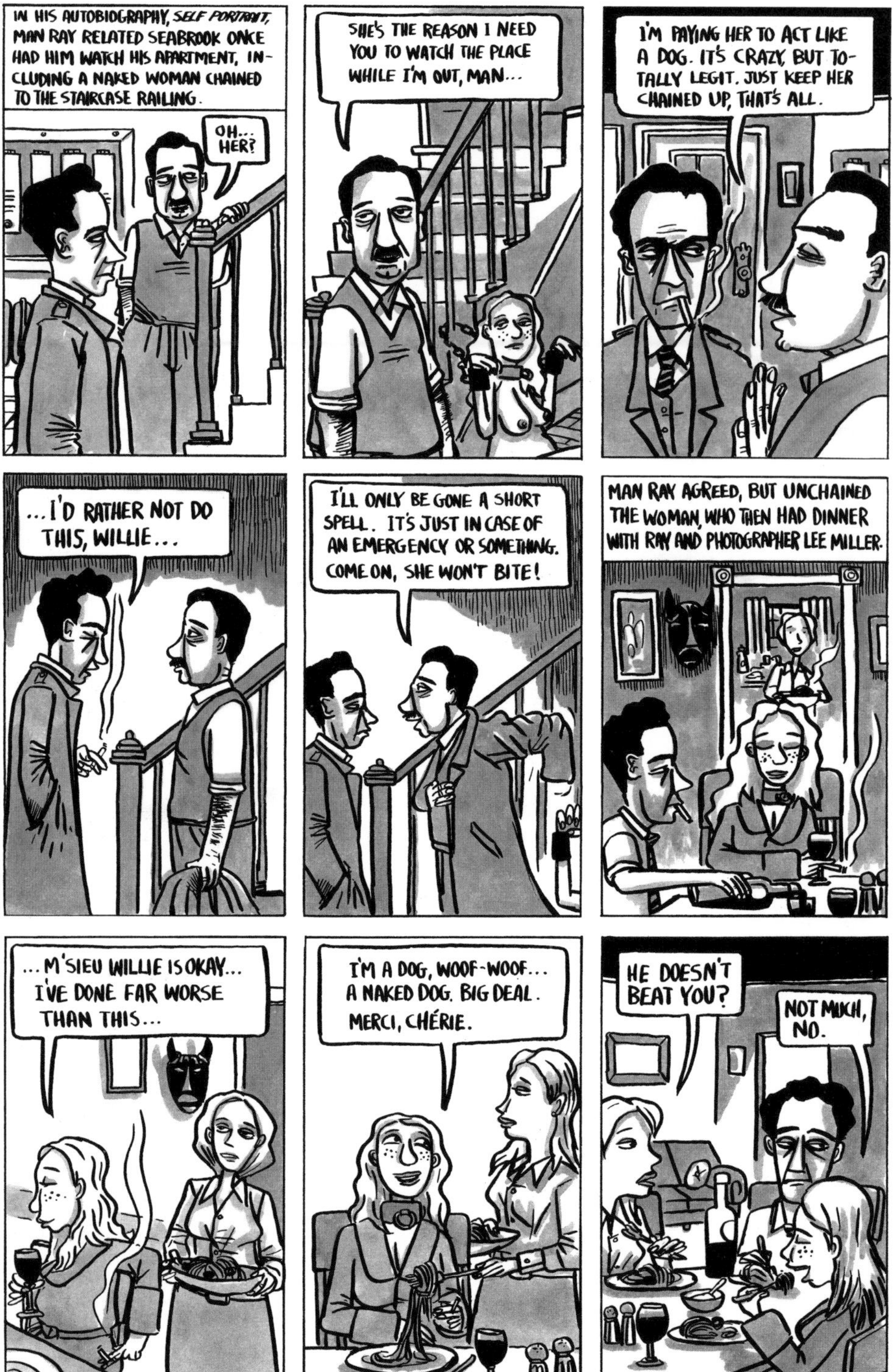
IN HIS AUTOBIOGRAPHY, SELF PORTRAIT, MAN RAY RELATED SEABROOK ONCE HAD HIM WATCH HIS APARTMENT, INCLUDING A NAKED WOMAN CHAINED TO THE STAIRCASE RAILING.
OH... HER?
SHE'S THE REASON I NEED YOU TO WATCH THE PLACE WHILE I'M OUT, MAN...
I'M PAYING HER TO ACT LIKE A DOG. IT'S CRAZY, BUT TOTALLY LEGIT. JUST KEEP HER CHAINED UP, THAT'S ALL.
...I'D RATHER NOT DO THIS, WILLIE...
I'LL ONLY BE GONE A SHORT SPELL. IT'S JUST IN CASE OF AN EMERGENCY OR SOMETHING. COME ON, SHE WON'T BITE!
MAN RAY AGREED, BUT UNCHAINED THE WOMAN, WHO THEN HAD DINNER WITH RAY AND PHOTOGRAPHER LEE MILLER.
...M'SIEU WILLIE IS OKAY... I'VE DONE FAR WORSE THAN THIS...
I'M A DOG, WOOF-WOOF... A NAKED DOG. BIG DEAL. MERCI, CHÉRIE.
HE DOESN'T BEAT YOU?
NOT MUCH, NO.

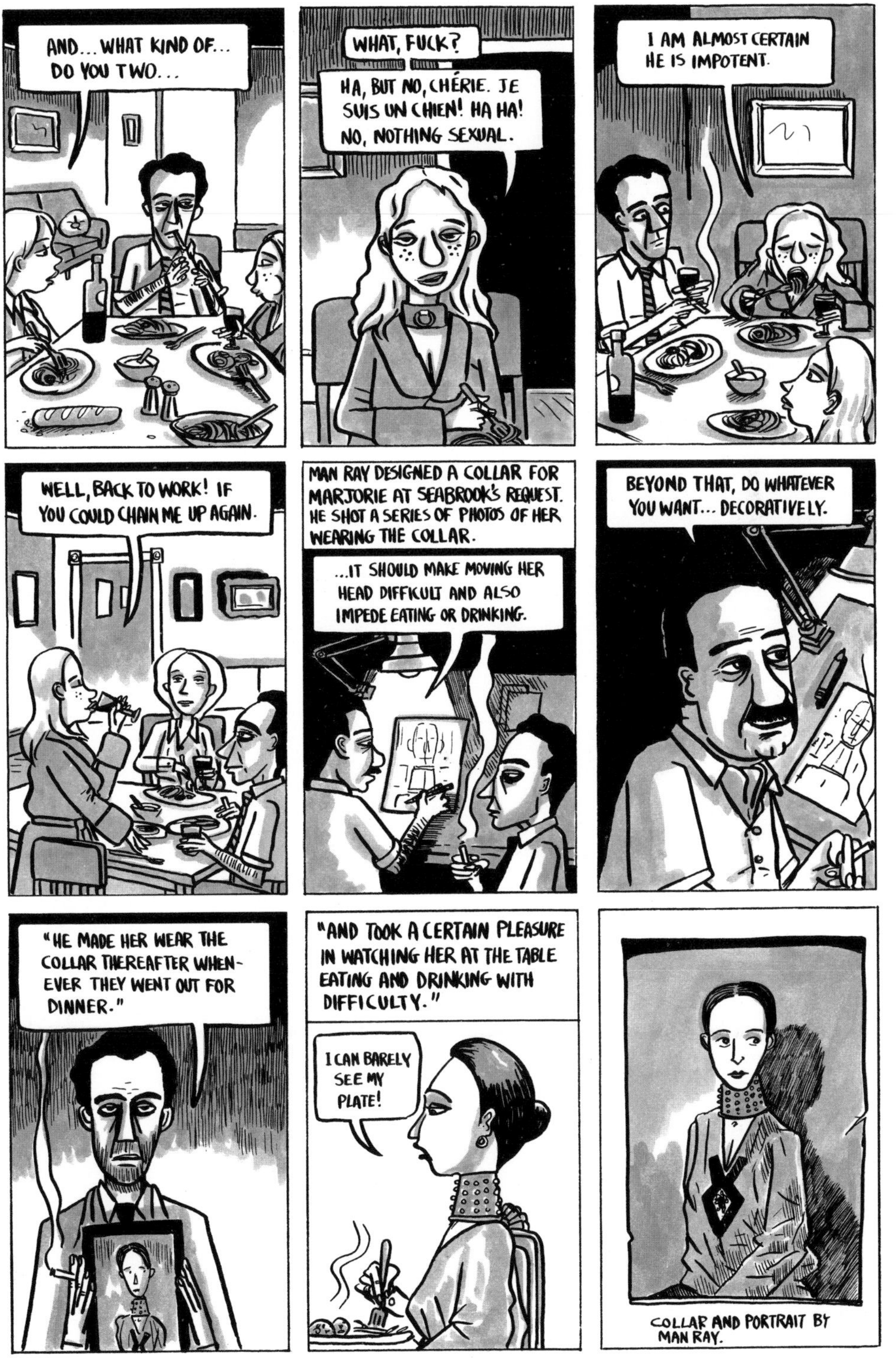
AND... WHAT KIND OF... DO YOU TWO...
WHAT, FUCK?
HA, BUT NO, CHÉRIE. JE SUIS UN CHIEN! HA HA! NO, NOTHING SEXUAL.
I AM ALMOST CERTAIN HE IS IMPOTENT.
WELL, BACK TO WORK! IF YOU COULD CHAIN ME UP AGAIN.
MAN RAY DESIGNED A COLLAR FOR MARJORIE AT SEABROOK'S REQUEST. HE SHOT A SERIES OF PHOTOS OF HER WEARING THE COLLAR.
...IT SHOULD MAKE MOVING HER HEAD DIFFICULT AND ALSO IMPEDE EATING OR DRINKING.
BEYOND THAT, DO WHATEVER YOU WANT... DECORATIVELY.
"HE MADE HER WEAR THE COLLAR THEREAFTER WHEN-EVER THEY WENT OUT FOR DINNER."
"AND TOOK A CERTAIN PLEASURE IN WATCHING HER AT THE TABLE EATING AND DRINKING WITH DIFFICULTY."
I CAN BARELY SEE MY PLATE!
COLLAR AND PORTRAIT BY MAN RAY.

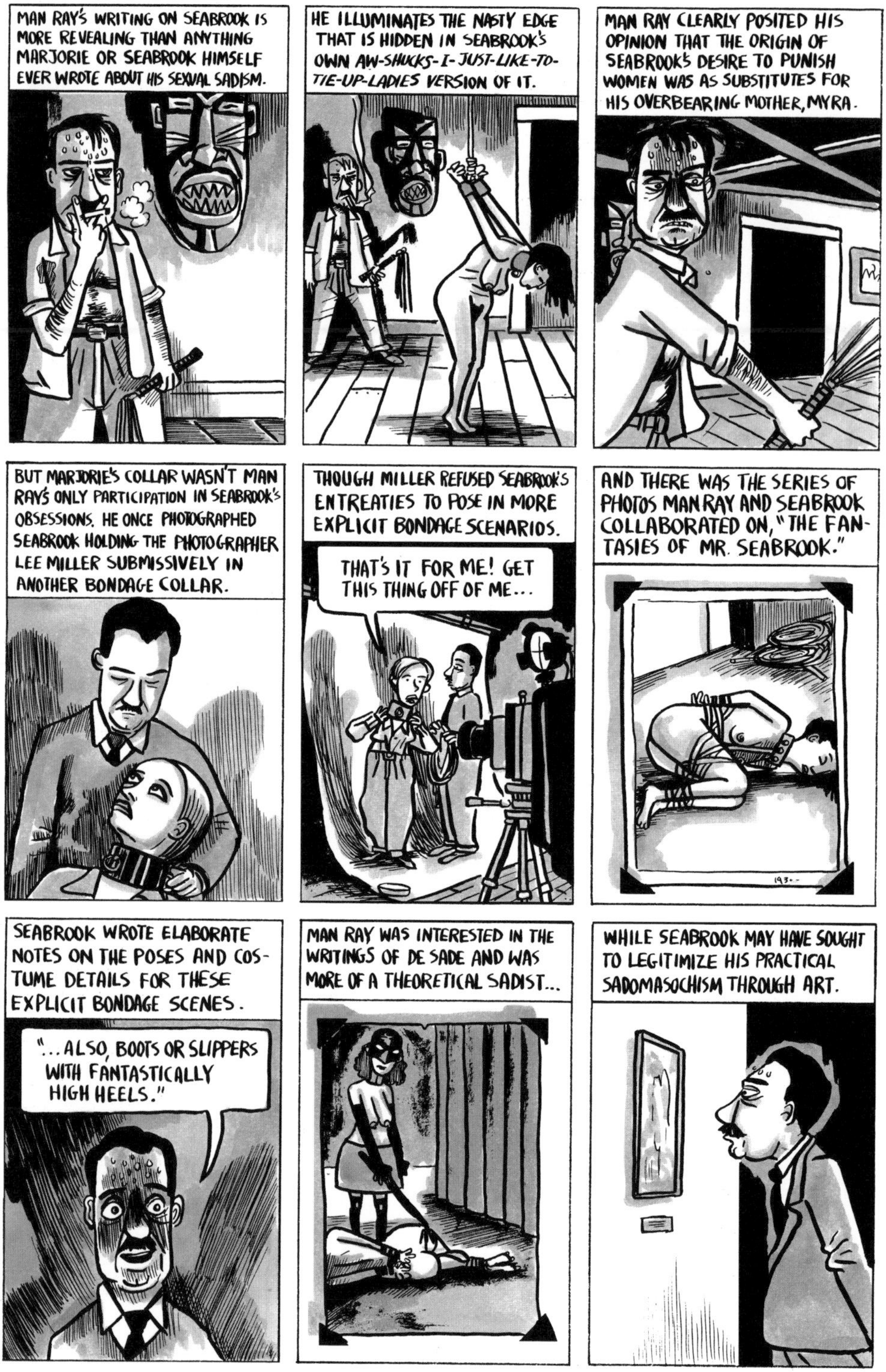
MAN RAY'S WRITING ON SEABROOK IS MORE REVEALING THAN ANYTHING MARJORIE OR SEABROOK HIMSELF EVER WROTE ABOUT HIS SEXUAL SADISM.
HE ILLUMINATES THE NASTY EDGE THAT IS HIDDEN IN SEABROOK'S OWN AW-SHUCKS-I-JUST-LIKE-TO-TIE-UP-LADIES VERSION OF IT.
MAN RAY CLEARLY POSITED HIS OPINION THAT THE ORIGIN OF SEABROOK'S DESIRE TO PUNISH WOMEN WAS AS SUBSTITUTES FOR HIS OVERBEARING MOTHER, MYRA.
BUT MARJORIE'S COLLAR WASN'T MAN RAY'S ONLY PARTICIPATION IN SEABROOK'S OBSESSIONS. HE ONCE PHOTOGRAPHED SEABROOK HOLDING THE PHOTOGRAPHER LEE MILLER SUBMISSIVELY IN ANOTHER BONDAGE COLLAR.
THOUGH MILLER REFUSED SEABROOK'S ENTREATIES TO POSE IN MORE EXPLICIT BONDAGE SCENARIOS.
THAT'S IT FOR ME! GET THIS THING OFF OF ME...
AND THERE WAS THE SERIES OF PHOTOS MAN RAY AND SEABROOK COLLABORATED ON, "THE FANTASIES OF MR. SEABROOK."
SEABROOK WROTE ELABORATE NOTES ON THE POSES AND COSTUME DETAILS FOR THESE EXPLICIT BONDAGE SCENES.
"...ALSO, BOOTS OR SLIPPERS WITH FANTASTICALLY HIGH HEELS."
MAN RAY WAS INTERESTED IN THE WRITINGS OF DE SADE AND WAS MORE OF A THEORETICAL SADIST...
WHILE SEABROOK MAY HAVE SOUGHT TO LEGITIMIZE HIS PRACTICAL SADOMASOCHISM THROUGH ART.

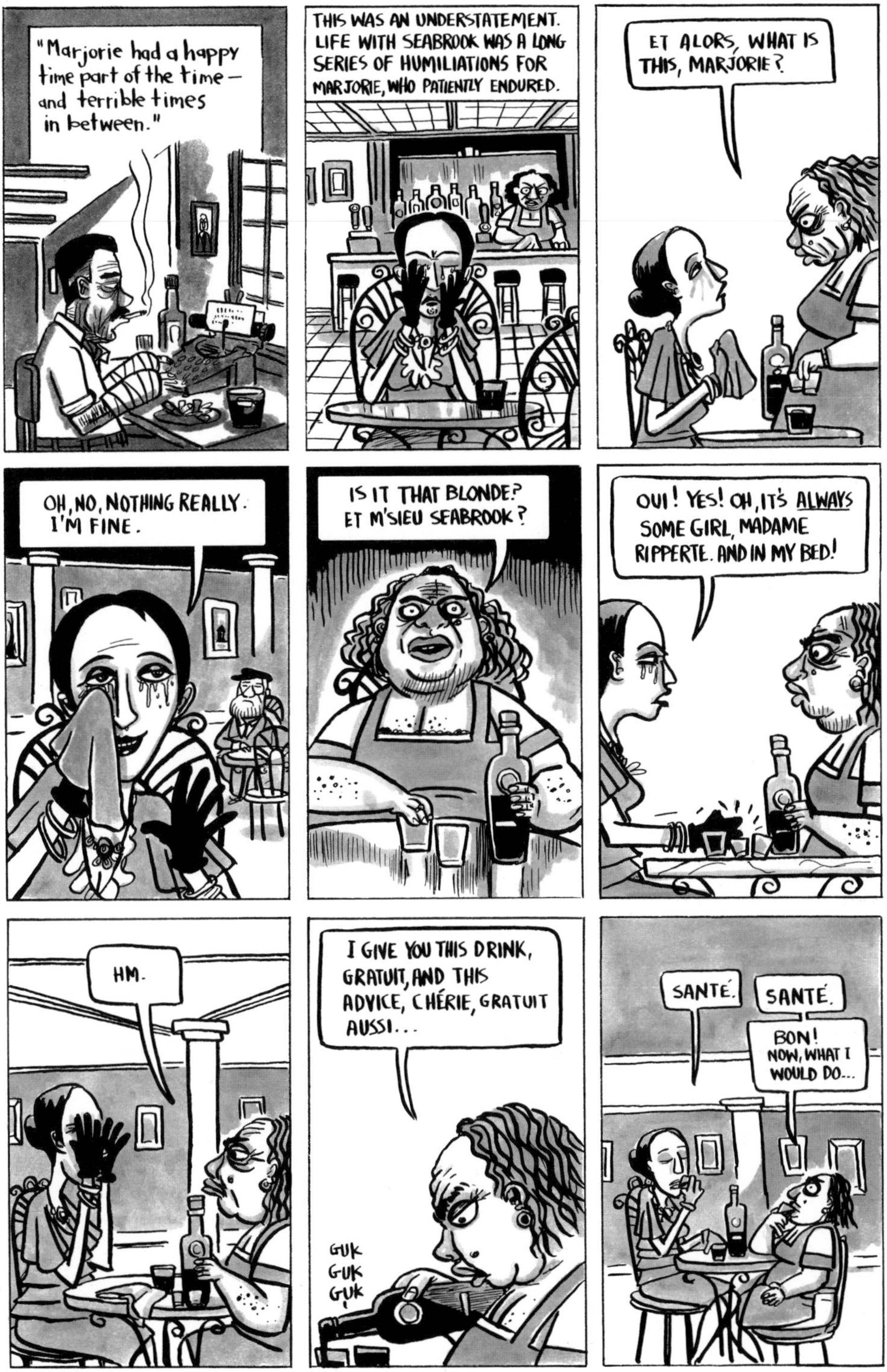
"Marjorie had a happy time part of the time — and terrible times in between."
THIS WAS AN UNDERSTATEMENT. LIFE WITH SEABROOK WAS A LONG SERIES OF HUMILIATIONS FOR MARJORIE, WHO PATIENTLY ENDURED.
ET ALORS, WHAT IS THIS, MARJORIE?
OH, NO, NOTHING REALLY. I'M FINE.
IS IT THAT BLONDE? ET M'SIEU SEABROOK?
OUI! YES! OH, IT'S ALWAYS SOME GIRL, MADAME RIPPERTE. AND IN MY BED!
HM.
I GIVE YOU THIS DRINK, GRATUIT, AND THIS ADVICE, CHÉRIE, GRATUIT AUSSI...
GUK
GUK
GUK
SANTÉ.
SANTÉ.
BON! NOW, WHAT I WOULD DO...

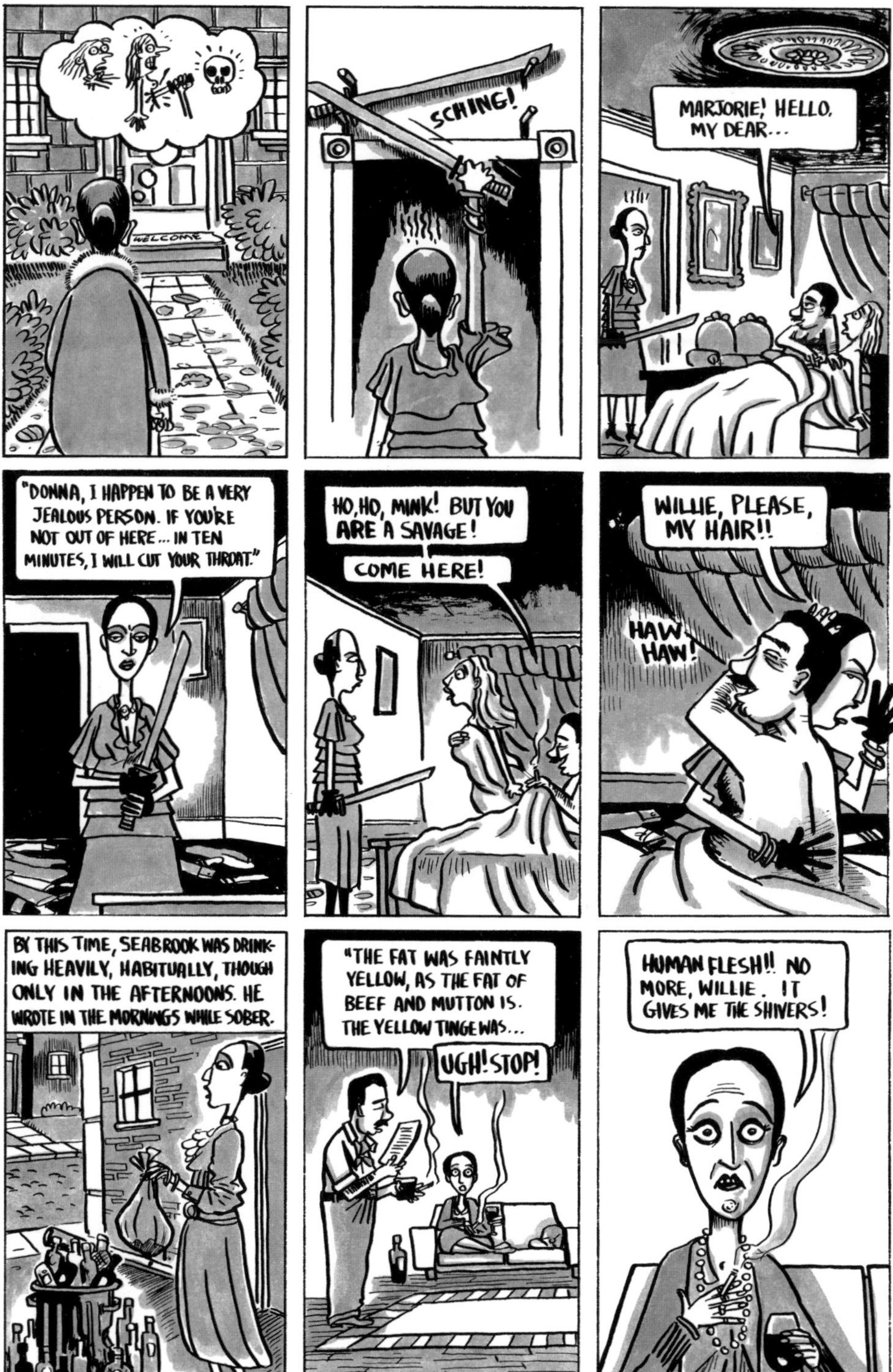
WELCOME
SCHING!
MARJORIE! HELLO, MY DEAR...
"DONNA, I HAPPEN TO BE A VERY JEALOUS PERSON. IF YOU'RE NOT OUT OF HERE... IN TEN MINUTES, I WILL CUT YOUR THROAT."
HO, HO, MINK! BUT YOU ARE A SAVAGE!
COME HERE!
WILLIE, PLEASE, MY HAIR!!
HAW HAW!
BY THIS TIME, SEABROOK WAS DRINKING HEAVILY, HABITUALLY, THOUGH ONLY IN THE AFTERNOONS. HE WROTE IN THE MORNINGS WHILE SOBER.
"THE FAT WAS FAINTLY YELLOW, AS THE FAT OF BEEF AND MUTTON IS. THE YELLOW TINGE WAS...
UGH! STOP!
HUMAN FLESH!! NO MORE, WILLIE. IT GIVES ME THE SHIVERS!

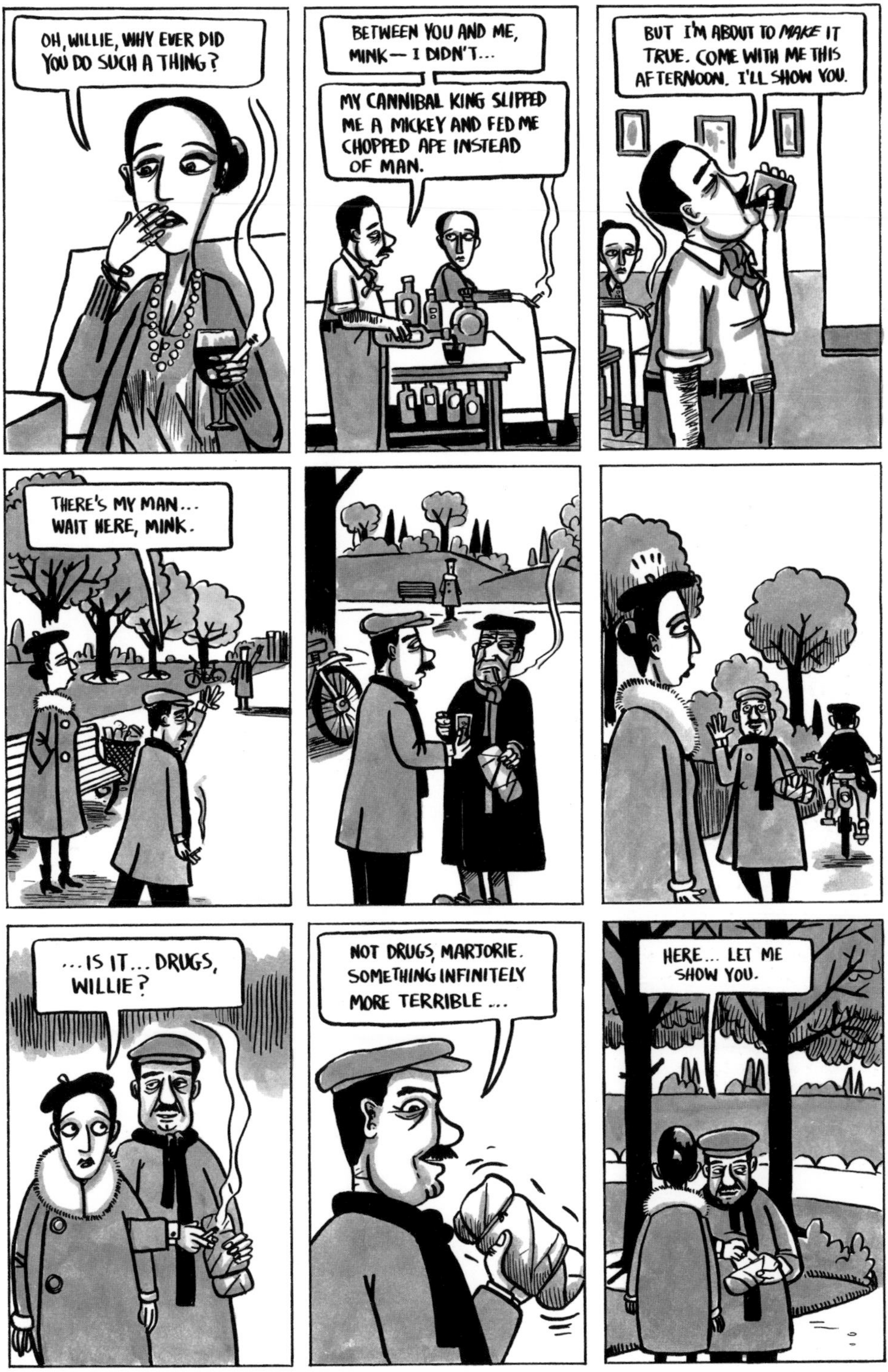
OH, WILLIE, WHY EVER DID YOU DO SUCH A THING?
BETWEEN YOU AND ME, MINK— I DIDN'T...
MY CANNIBAL KING SLIPPED ME A MICKEY AND FED ME CHOPPED APE INSTEAD OF MAN.
BUT I'M ABOUT TO *MAKE* IT TRUE. COME WITH ME THIS AFTERNOON. I'LL SHOW YOU.
THERE'S MY MAN... WAIT HERE, MINK.
...IS IT... DRUGS, WILLIE?
NOT DRUGS, MARJORIE. SOMETHING INFINITELY MORE TERRIBLE...
HERE... LET ME SHOW YOU.

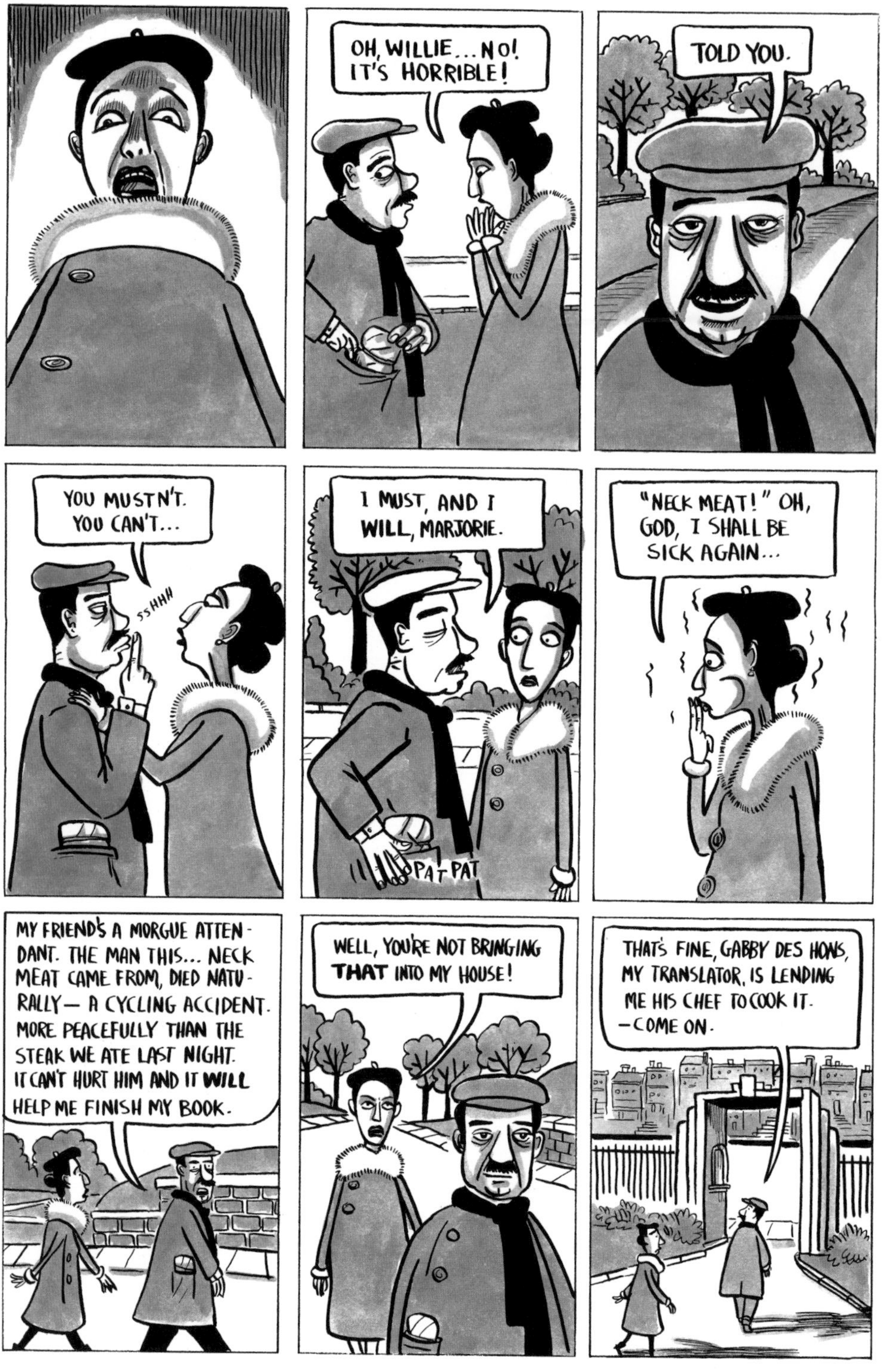
OH, WILLIE... NO! IT'S HORRIBLE!
TOLD YOU.
YOU MUSTN'T. YOU CAN'T...
SSHHH
I MUST, AND I WILL, MARJORIE.
PAT PAT
"NECK MEAT!" OH, GOD, I SHALL BE SICK AGAIN...
MY FRIEND'S A MORGUE ATTENDANT. THE MAN THIS... NECK MEAT CAME FROM, DIED NATURALLY— A CYCLING ACCIDENT. MORE PEACEFULLY THAN THE STEAK WE ATE LAST NIGHT. IT CAN'T HURT HIM AND IT WILL HELP ME FINISH MY BOOK.
WELL, YOU'RE NOT BRINGING THAT INTO MY HOUSE!
THAT'S FINE, GABBY DES HONS, MY TRANSLATOR, IS LENDING ME HIS CHEF TO COOK IT. —COME ON.

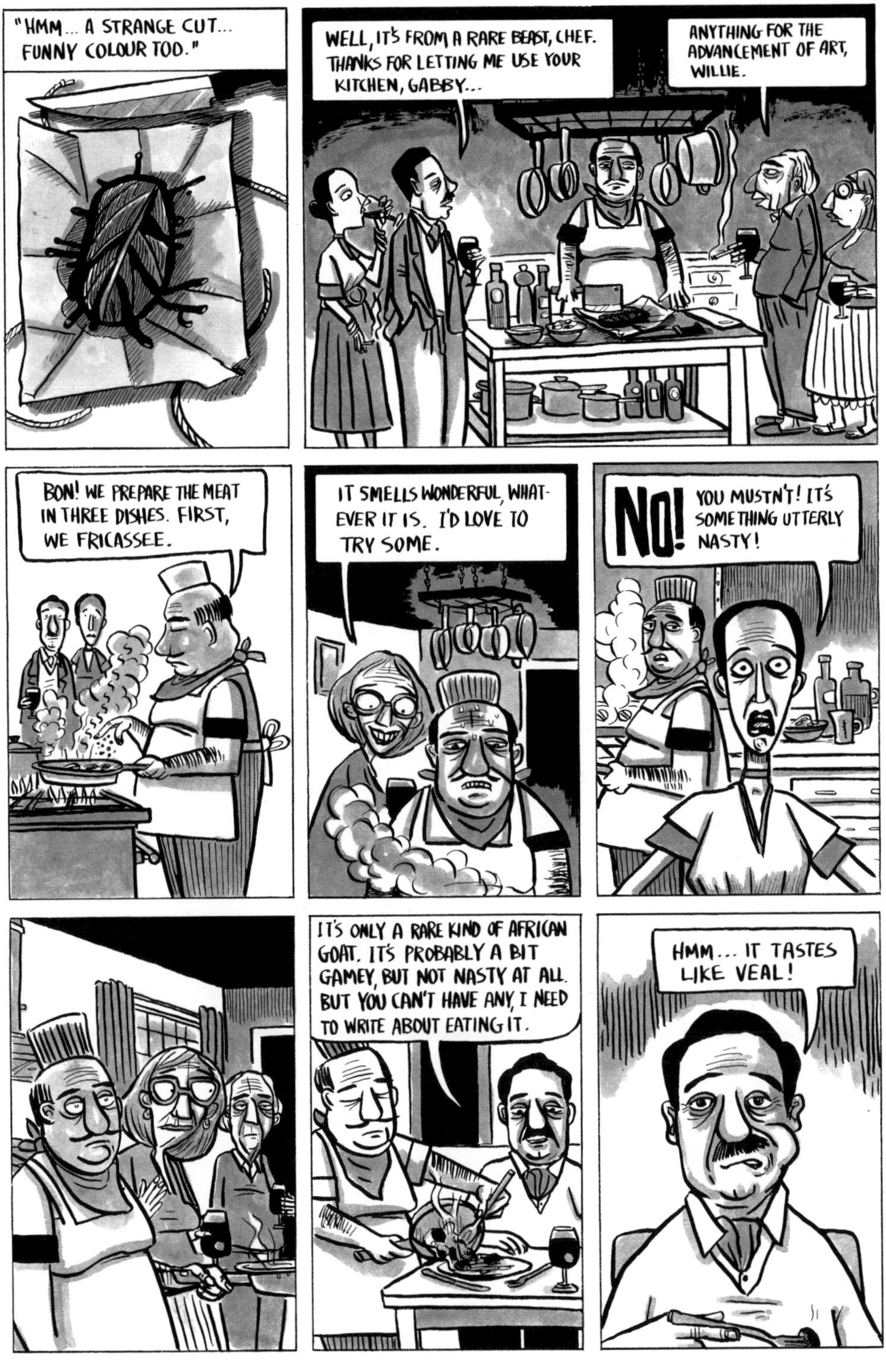
"HMM... A STRANGE CUT... FUNNY COLOUR TOO."
WELL, IT'S FROM A RARE BEAST, CHEF. THANKS FOR LETTING ME USE YOUR KITCHEN, GABBY...
ANYTHING FOR THE ADVANCEMENT OF ART, WILLIE.
BON! WE PREPARE THE MEAT IN THREE DISHES. FIRST, WE FRICASSEE.
IT SMELLS WONDERFUL, WHATEVER IT IS. I'D LOVE TO TRY SOME.
NO! YOU MUSTN'T! IT'S SOMETHING UTTERLY NASTY!
IT'S ONLY A RARE KIND OF AFRICAN GOAT. IT'S PROBABLY A BIT GAMEY, BUT NOT NASTY AT ALL. BUT YOU CAN'T HAVE ANY, I NEED TO WRITE ABOUT EATING IT.
HMM... IT TASTES LIKE VEAL!

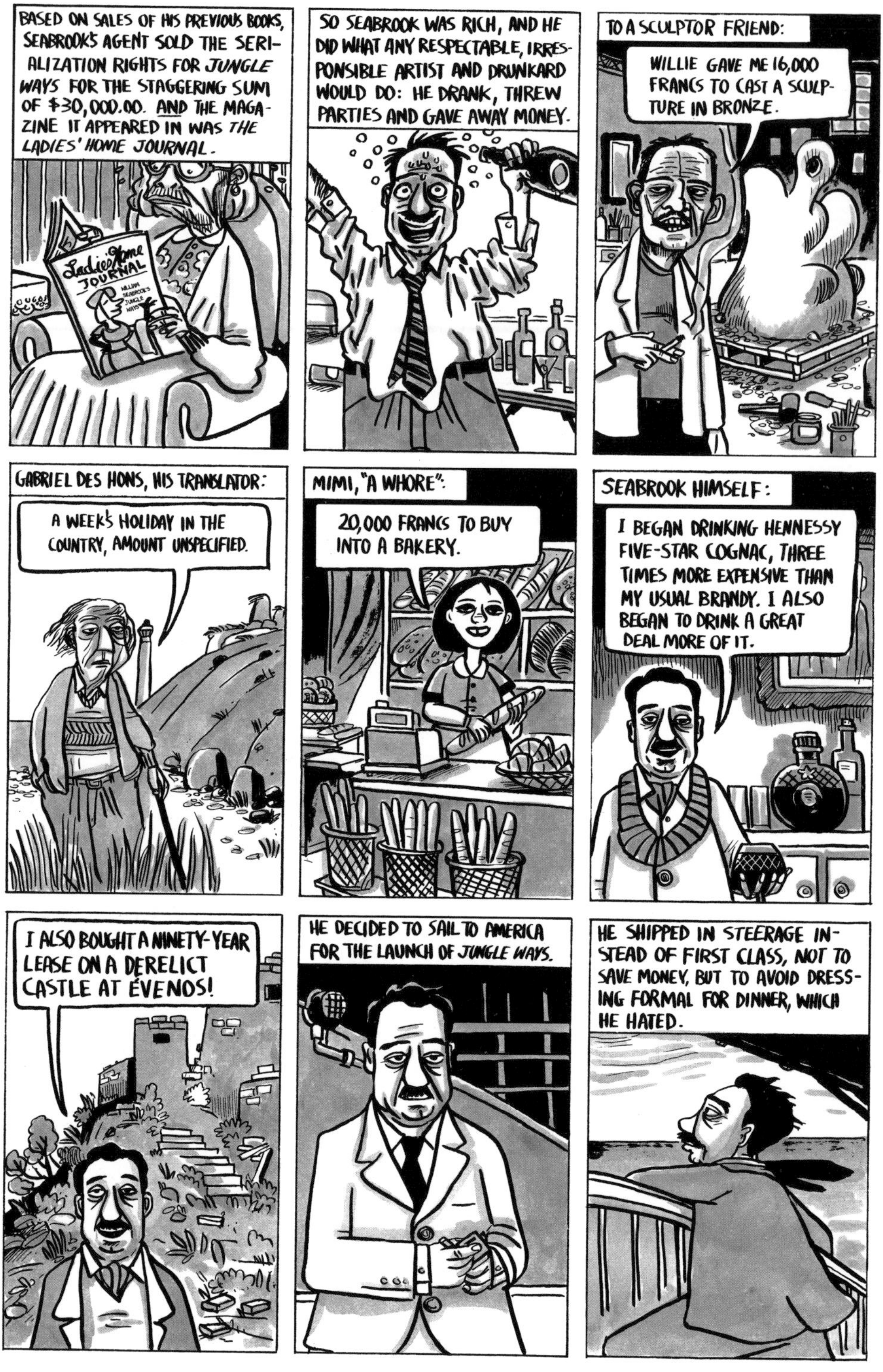
BASED ON SALES OF HIS PREVIOUS BOOKS, SEABROOK'S AGENT SOLD THE SERIALIZATION RIGHTS FOR JUNGLE WAYS FOR THE STAGGERING SUM OF $30,000.00. AND THE MAGAZINE IT APPEARED IN WAS THE LADIES' HOME JOURNAL.
Ladies' Home JOURNAL
WILLIAM SEABROOK'S JUNGLE WAYS
SO SEABROOK WAS RICH, AND HE DID WHAT ANY RESPECTABLE, IRRESPONSIBLE ARTIST AND DRUNKARD WOULD DO: HE DRANK, THREW PARTIES AND GAVE AWAY MONEY.
TO A SCULPTOR FRIEND:
WILLIE GAVE ME 16,000 FRANCS TO CAST A SCULPTURE IN BRONZE.
GABRIEL DES HONS, HIS TRANSLATOR:
A WEEK'S HOLIDAY IN THE COUNTRY, AMOUNT UNSPECIFIED.
MIMI, "A WHORE":
20,000 FRANCS TO BUY INTO A BAKERY.
SEABROOK HIMSELF:
I BEGAN DRINKING HENNESSY FIVE-STAR COGNAC, THREE TIMES MORE EXPENSIVE THAN MY USUAL BRANDY. I ALSO BEGAN TO DRINK A GREAT DEAL MORE OF IT.
I ALSO BOUGHT A NINETY-YEAR LEASE ON A DERELICT CASTLE AT ÉVENOS!
HE DECIDED TO SAIL TO AMERICA FOR THE LAUNCH OF JUNGLE WAYS.
HE SHIPPED IN STEERAGE INSTEAD OF FIRST CLASS, NOT TO SAVE MONEY, BUT TO AVOID DRESSING FORMAL FOR DINNER, WHICH HE HATED.

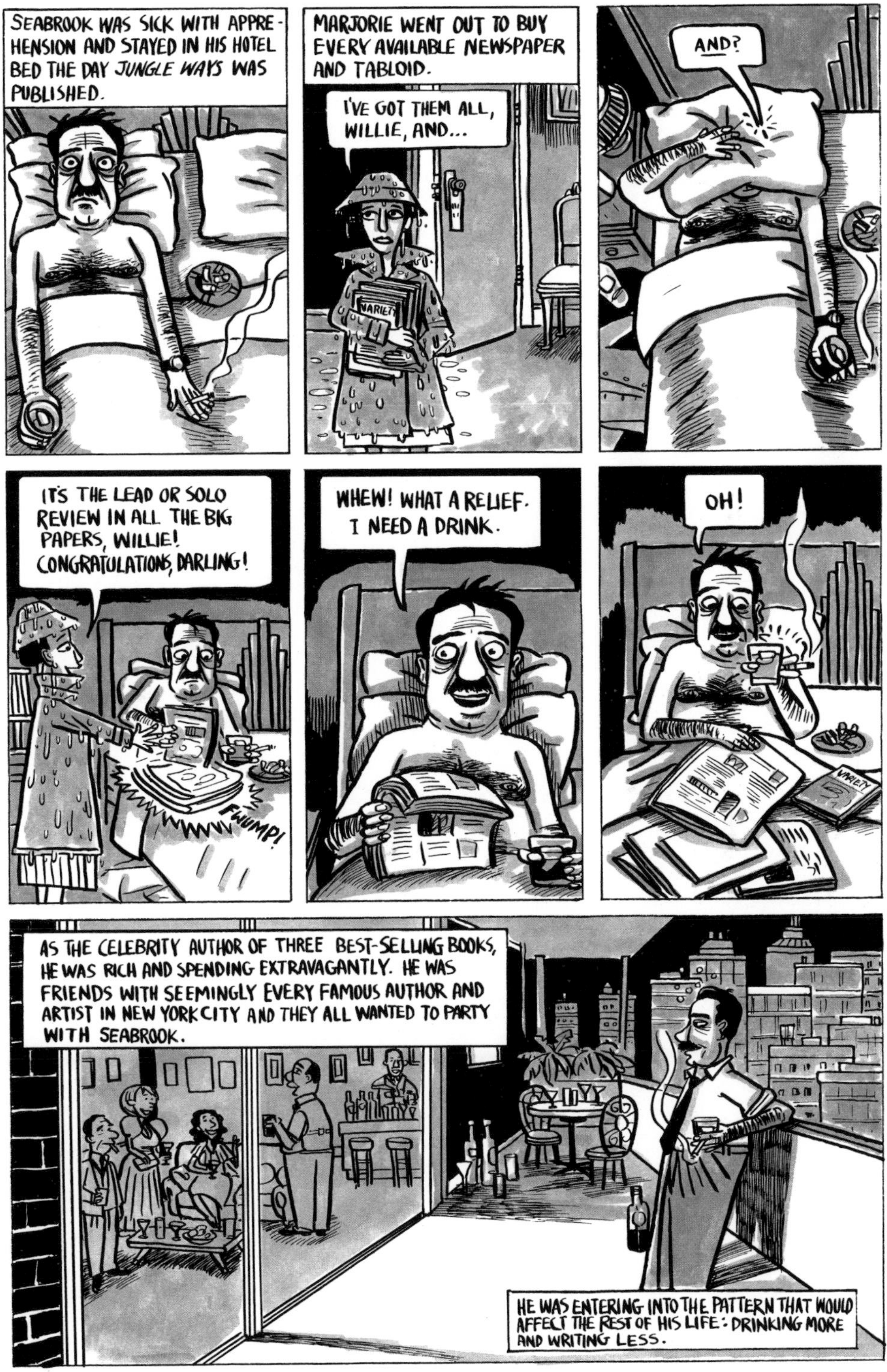
SEABROOK WAS SICK WITH APPREHENSION AND STAYED IN HIS HOTEL BED THE DAY JUNGLE WAYS WAS PUBLISHED.
MARJORIE WENT OUT TO BUY EVERY AVAILABLE NEWSPAPER AND TABLOID.
I'VE GOT THEM ALL, WILLIE, AND...
VARIETY
AND?
IT'S THE LEAD OR SOLO REVIEW IN ALL THE BIG PAPERS, WILLIE! CONGRATULATIONS, DARLING!
FWUMP!
WHEW! WHAT A RELIEF. I NEED A DRINK.
OH!
VARIETY
AS THE CELEBRITY AUTHOR OF THREE BEST-SELLING BOOKS, HE WAS RICH AND SPENDING EXTRAVAGANTLY. HE WAS FRIENDS WITH SEEMINGLY EVERY FAMOUS AUTHOR AND ARTIST IN NEW YORK CITY AND THEY ALL WANTED TO PARTY WITH SEABROOK.
HE WAS ENTERING INTO THE PATTERN THAT WOULD AFFECT THE REST OF HIS LIFE: DRINKING MORE AND WRITING LESS.

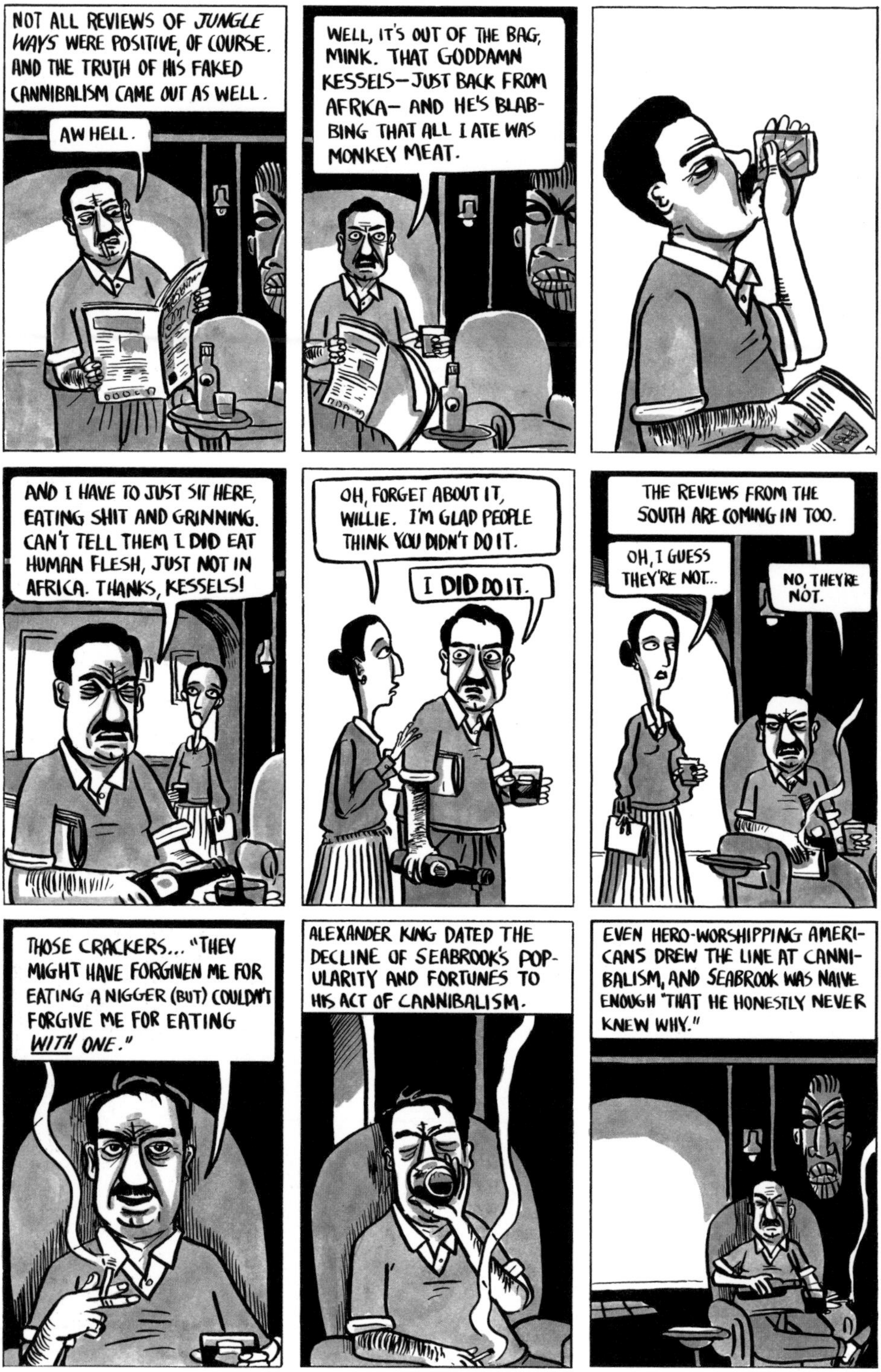
NOT ALL REVIEWS OF *JUNGLE WAYS* WERE POSITIVE, OF COURSE. AND THE TRUTH OF HIS FAKED CANNIBALISM CAME OUT AS WELL.
AW HELL.
WELL, IT'S OUT OF THE BAG, MINK. THAT GODDAMN KESSELS—JUST BACK FROM AFRKA— AND HE'S BLAB-BING THAT ALL I ATE WAS MONKEY MEAT.
AND I HAVE TO JUST SIT HERE, EATING SHIT AND GRINNING. CAN'T TELL THEM I **DID** EAT HUMAN FLESH, JUST **NOT** IN AFRICA. THANKS, KESSELS!
OH, FORGET ABOUT IT, WILLIE. I'M GLAD PEOPLE THINK YOU DIDN'T DO IT.
I **DID** DO IT.
THE REVIEWS FROM THE SOUTH ARE COMING IN TOO.
OH, I GUESS THEY'RE NOT...
NO, THEY'RE NOT.
THOSE CRACKERS... "THEY MIGHT HAVE FORGIVEN ME FOR EATING A NIGGER (BUT) COULDN'T FORGIVE ME FOR EATING *WITH ONE*."
ALEXANDER KING DATED THE DECLINE OF SEABROOK'S POPULARITY AND FORTUNES TO HIS ACT OF CANNIBALISM.
EVEN HERO-WORSHIPPING AMERICANS DREW THE LINE AT CANNIBALISM, AND SEABROOK WAS NAIVE ENOUGH "THAT HE HONESTLY NEVER KNEW WHY."

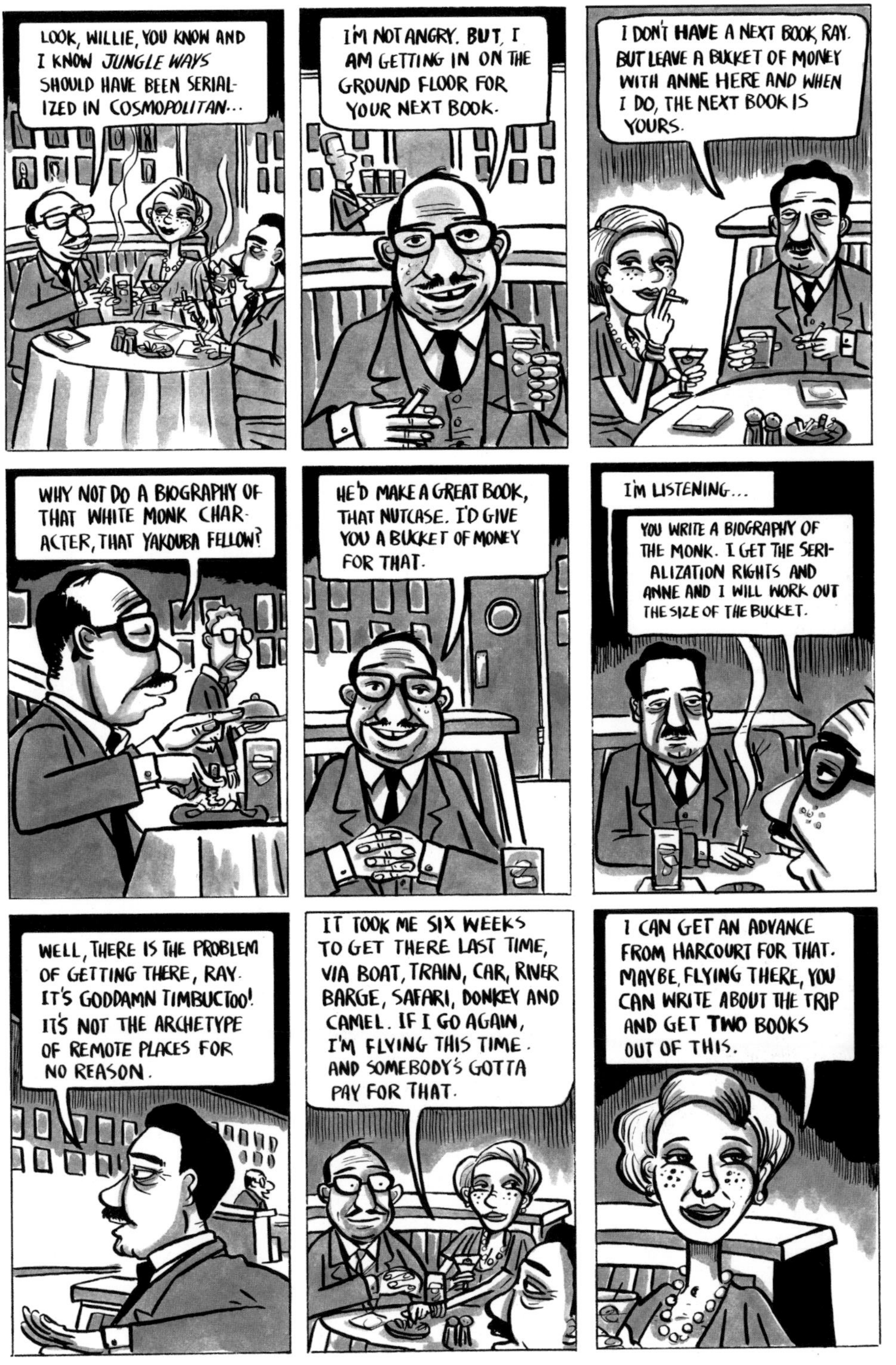
LOOK, WILLIE, YOU KNOW AND I KNOW JUNGLE WAYS SHOULD HAVE BEEN SERIALIZED IN COSMOPOLITAN...
I'M NOT ANGRY. BUT, I AM GETTING IN ON THE GROUND FLOOR FOR YOUR NEXT BOOK.
I DON'T HAVE A NEXT BOOK, RAY. BUT LEAVE A BUCKET OF MONEY WITH ANNE HERE AND WHEN I DO, THE NEXT BOOK IS YOURS.
WHY NOT DO A BIOGRAPHY OF THAT WHITE MONK CHARACTER, THAT YAKOUBA FELLOW?
HE'D MAKE A GREAT BOOK, THAT NUTCASE. I'D GIVE YOU A BUCKET OF MONEY FOR THAT.
I'M LISTENING...
YOU WRITE A BIOGRAPHY OF THE MONK. I GET THE SERIALIZATION RIGHTS AND ANNE AND I WILL WORK OUT THE SIZE OF THE BUCKET.
WELL, THERE IS THE PROBLEM OF GETTING THERE, RAY. IT'S GODDAMN TIMBUCTOO! IT'S NOT THE ARCHETYPE OF REMOTE PLACES FOR NO REASON.
IT TOOK ME SIX WEEKS TO GET THERE LAST TIME, VIA BOAT, TRAIN, CAR, RIVER BARGE, SAFARI, DONKEY AND CAMEL. IF I GO AGAIN, I'M FLYING THIS TIME. AND SOMEBODY'S GOTTA PAY FOR THAT.
I CAN GET AN ADVANCE FROM HARCOURT FOR THAT. MAYBE, FLYING THERE, YOU CAN WRITE ABOUT THE TRIP AND GET TWO BOOKS OUT OF THIS.

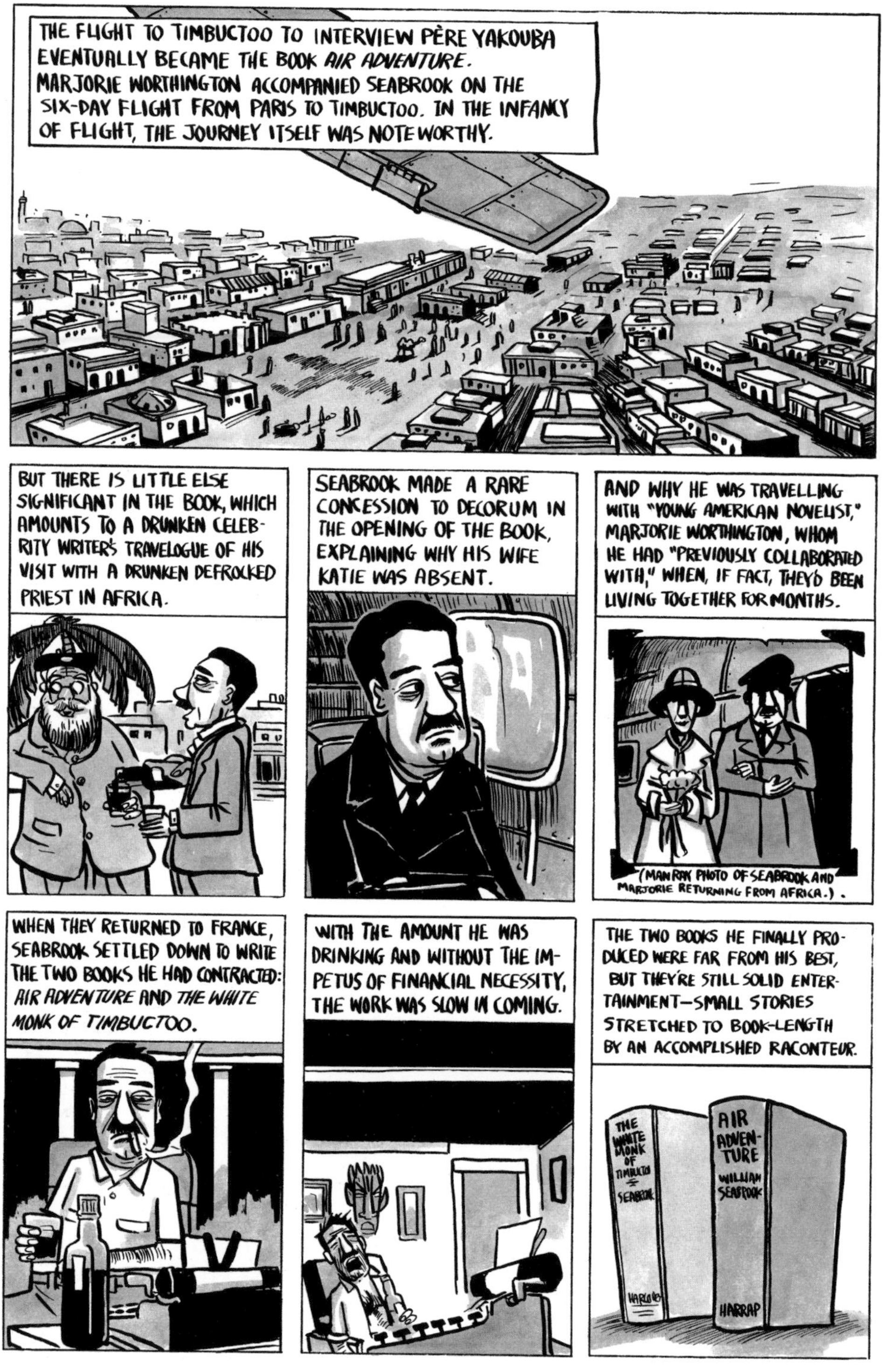
THE FLIGHT TO TIMBUCTOO TO INTERVIEW PÈRE YAKOUBA EVENTUALLY BECAME THE BOOK *AIR ADVENTURE*. MARJORIE WORTHINGTON ACCOMPANIED SEABROOK ON THE SIX-DAY FLIGHT FROM PARIS TO TIMBUCTOO. IN THE INFANCY OF FLIGHT, THE JOURNEY ITSELF WAS NOTEWORTHY.
BUT THERE IS LITTLE ELSE SIGNIFICANT IN THE BOOK, WHICH AMOUNTS TO A DRUNKEN CELEBRITY WRITER'S TRAVELOGUE OF HIS VISIT WITH A DRUNKEN DEFROCKED PRIEST IN AFRICA.
SEABROOK MADE A RARE CONCESSION TO DECORUM IN THE OPENING OF THE BOOK, EXPLAINING WHY HIS WIFE KATIE WAS ABSENT.
AND WHY HE WAS TRAVELLING WITH "YOUNG AMERICAN NOVELIST," MARJORIE WORTHINGTON, WHOM HE HAD "PREVIOUSLY COLLABORATED WITH," WHEN, IF FACT, THEY'D BEEN LIVING TOGETHER FOR MONTHS.
(MAN RAY PHOTO OF SEABROOK AND MARJORIE RETURNING FROM AFRICA.).
WHEN THEY RETURNED TO FRANCE, SEABROOK SETTLED DOWN TO WRITE THE TWO BOOKS HE HAD CONTRACTED: *AIR ADVENTURE* AND *THE WHITE MONK OF TIMBUCTOO*.
WITH THE AMOUNT HE WAS DRINKING AND WITHOUT THE IMPETUS OF FINANCIAL NECESSITY, THE WORK WAS SLOW IN COMING.
THE TWO BOOKS HE FINALLY PRODUCED WERE FAR FROM HIS BEST, BUT THEY'RE STILL SOLID ENTERTAINMENT—SMALL STORIES STRETCHED TO BOOK-LENGTH BY AN ACCOMPLISHED RACONTEUR.
AIR ADVENTURE
WILLIAM SEABROOK
HARRAP

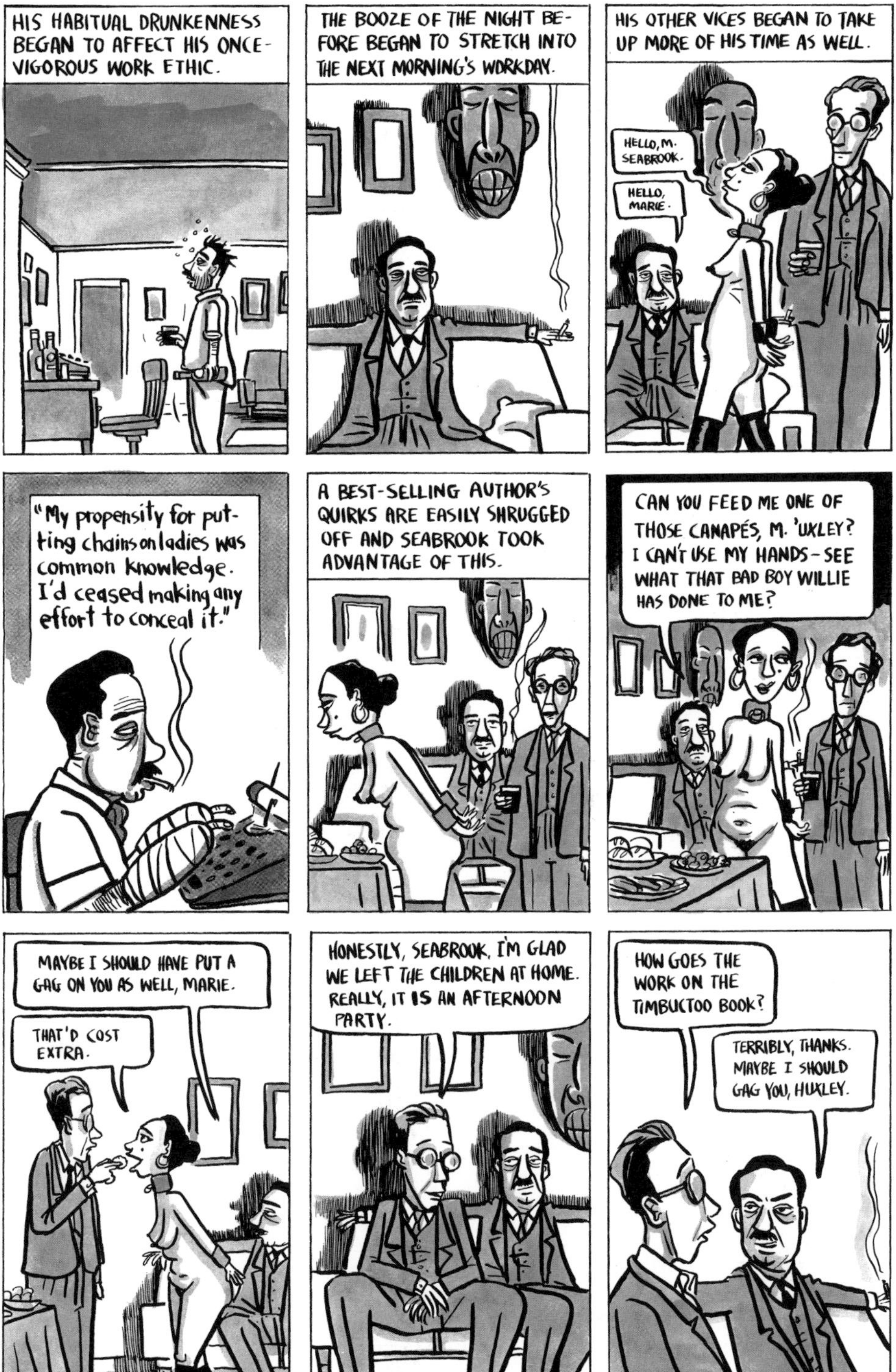
HIS HABITUAL DRUNKENNESS BEGAN TO AFFECT HIS ONCE-VIGOROUS WORK ETHIC.
THE BOOZE OF THE NIGHT BEFORE BEGAN TO STRETCH INTO THE NEXT MORNING'S WORKDAY.
HIS OTHER VICES BEGAN TO TAKE UP MORE OF HIS TIME AS WELL.
HELLO, M. SEABROOK.
HELLO, MARIE.
"My propensity for putting chains on ladies was common knowledge. I'd ceased making any effort to conceal it."
A BEST-SELLING AUTHOR'S QUIRKS ARE EASILY SHRUGGED OFF AND SEABROOK TOOK ADVANTAGE OF THIS.
CAN YOU FEED ME ONE OF THOSE CANAPÉS, M. 'UXLEY? I CAN'T USE MY HANDS - SEE WHAT THAT BAD BOY WILLIE HAS DONE TO ME?
MAYBE I SHOULD HAVE PUT A GAG ON YOU AS WELL, MARIE.
THAT'D COST EXTRA.
HONESTLY, SEABROOK, I'M GLAD WE LEFT THE CHILDREN AT HOME. REALLY, IT IS AN AFTERNOON PARTY.
HOW GOES THE WORK ON THE TIMBUCTOO BOOK?
TERRIBLY, THANKS. MAYBE I SHOULD GAG YOU, HUXLEY.

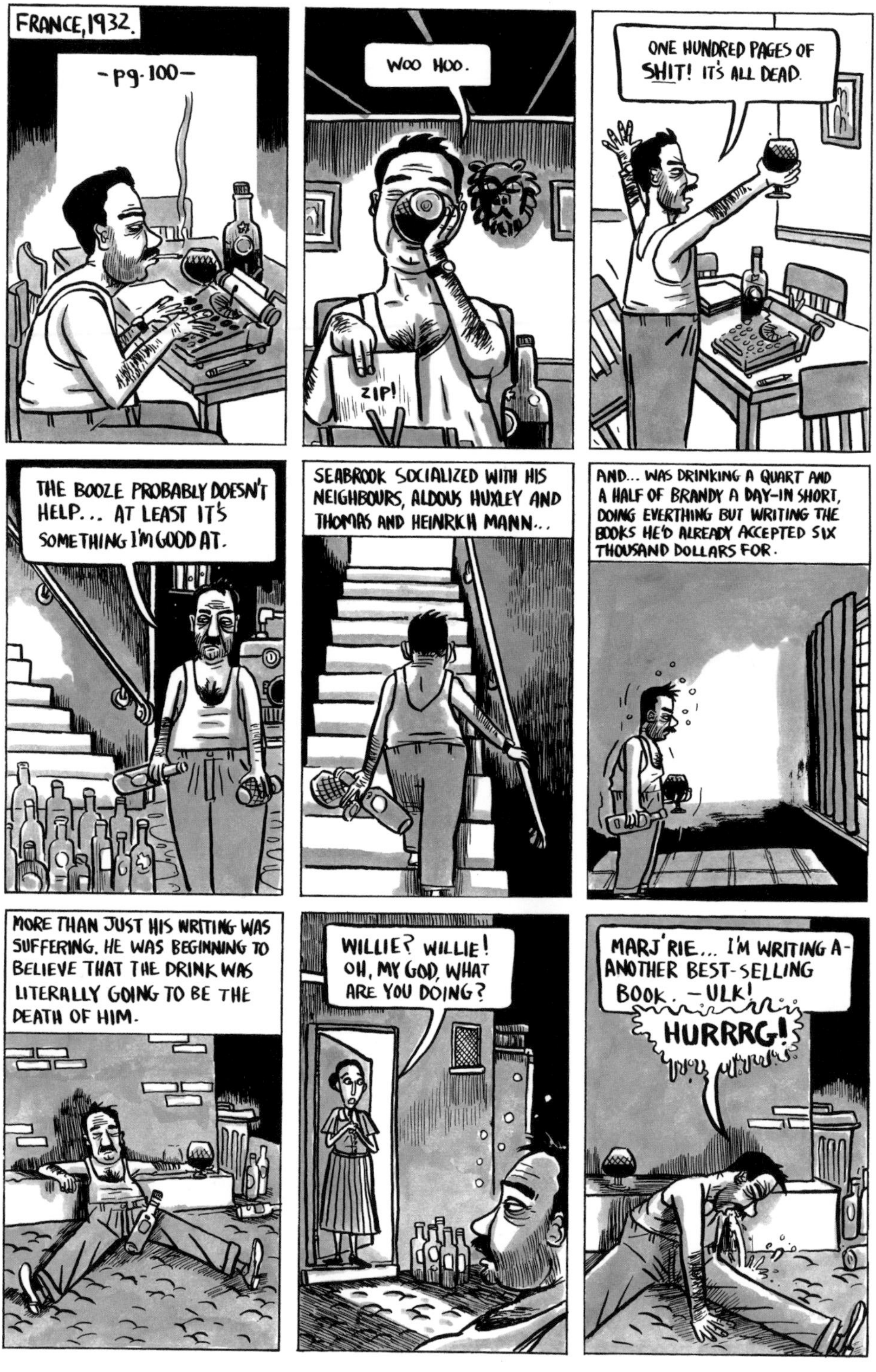
FRANCE, 1932.
-pg. 100-
WOO HOO.
ZIP!
ONE HUNDRED PAGES OF SHIT! IT'S ALL DEAD.
THE BOOZE PROBABLY DOESN'T HELP... AT LEAST IT'S SOMETHING I'M GOOD AT.
SEABROOK SOCIALIZED WITH HIS NEIGHBOURS, ALDOUS HUXLEY AND THOMAS AND HEINRICH MANN...
AND... WAS DRINKING A QUART AND A HALF OF BRANDY A DAY—IN SHORT, DOING EVERTHING BUT WRITING THE BOOKS HE'D ALREADY ACCEPTED SIX THOUSAND DOLLARS FOR.
MORE THAN JUST HIS WRITING WAS SUFFERING. HE WAS BEGINNING TO BELIEVE THAT THE DRINK WAS LITERALLY GOING TO BE THE DEATH OF HIM.
WILLIE? WILLIE! OH, MY GOD, WHAT ARE YOU DOING?
MARJ'RIE... I'M WRITING A- ANOTHER BEST-SELLING BOOK. -ULK!
HURRRG!

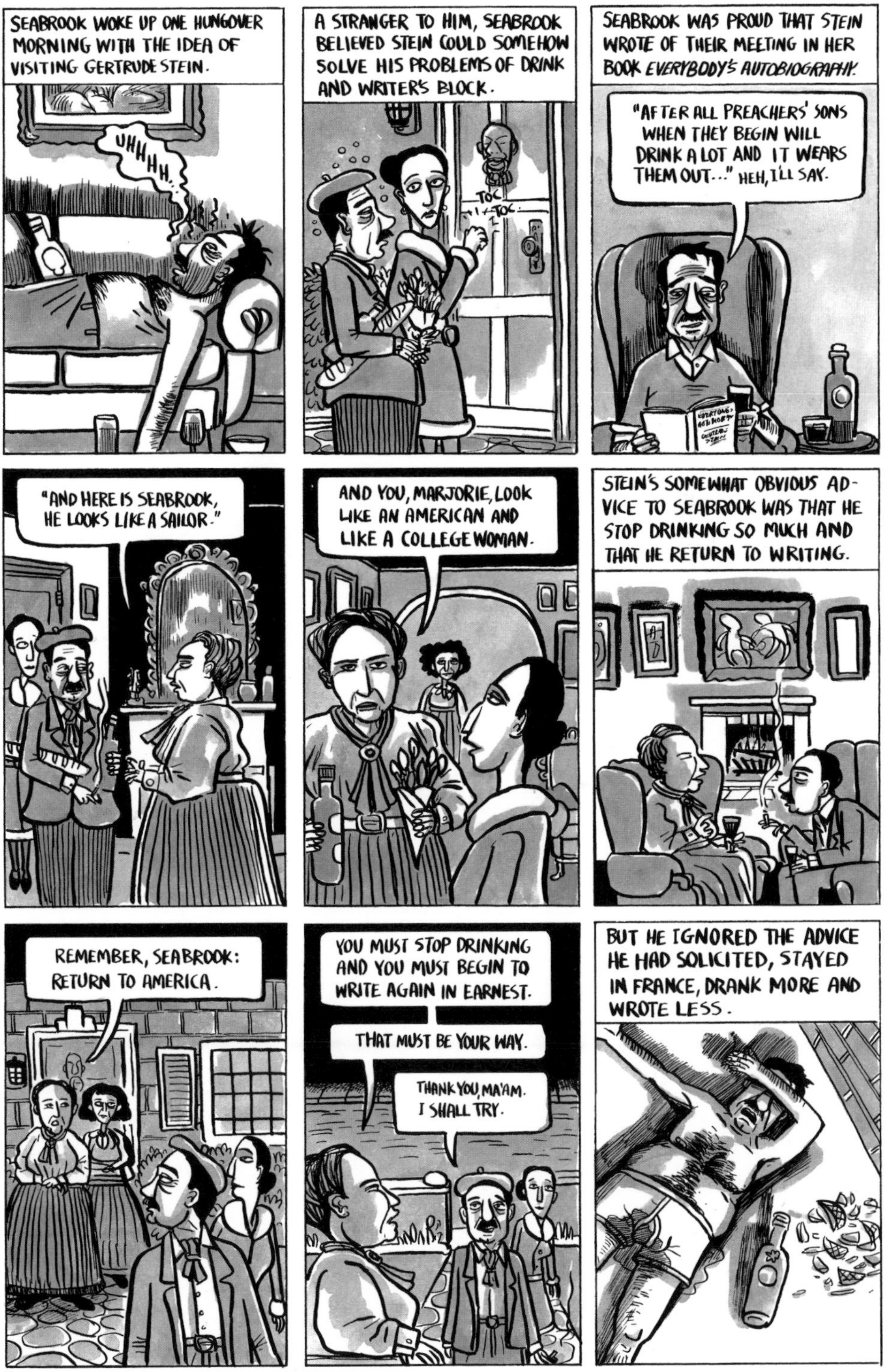
SEABROOK WOKE UP ONE HUNGOVER MORNING WITH THE IDEA OF VISITING GERTRUDE STEIN.
UHHHH.
A STRANGER TO HIM, SEABROOK BELIEVED STEIN COULD SOMEHOW SOLVE HIS PROBLEMS OF DRINK AND WRITER'S BLOCK.
TOC TOC
SEABROOK WAS PROUD THAT STEIN WROTE OF THEIR MEETING IN HER BOOK EVERYBODY'S AUTOBIOGRAPHY.
"AFTER ALL PREACHERS' SONS WHEN THEY BEGIN WILL DRINK A LOT AND IT WEARS THEM OUT..." HEH, I'LL SAY.
"AND HERE IS SEABROOK, HE LOOKS LIKE A SAILOR."
AND YOU, MARJORIE, LOOK LIKE AN AMERICAN AND LIKE A COLLEGE WOMAN.
STEIN'S SOMEWHAT OBVIOUS ADVICE TO SEABROOK WAS THAT HE STOP DRINKING SO MUCH AND THAT HE RETURN TO WRITING.
REMEMBER, SEABROOK: RETURN TO AMERICA.
YOU MUST STOP DRINKING AND YOU MUST BEGIN TO WRITE AGAIN IN EARNEST.
THAT MUST BE YOUR WAY.
THANK YOU, MA'AM. I SHALL TRY.
BUT HE IGNORED THE ADVICE HE HAD SOLICITED, STAYED IN FRANCE, DRANK MORE AND WROTE LESS.

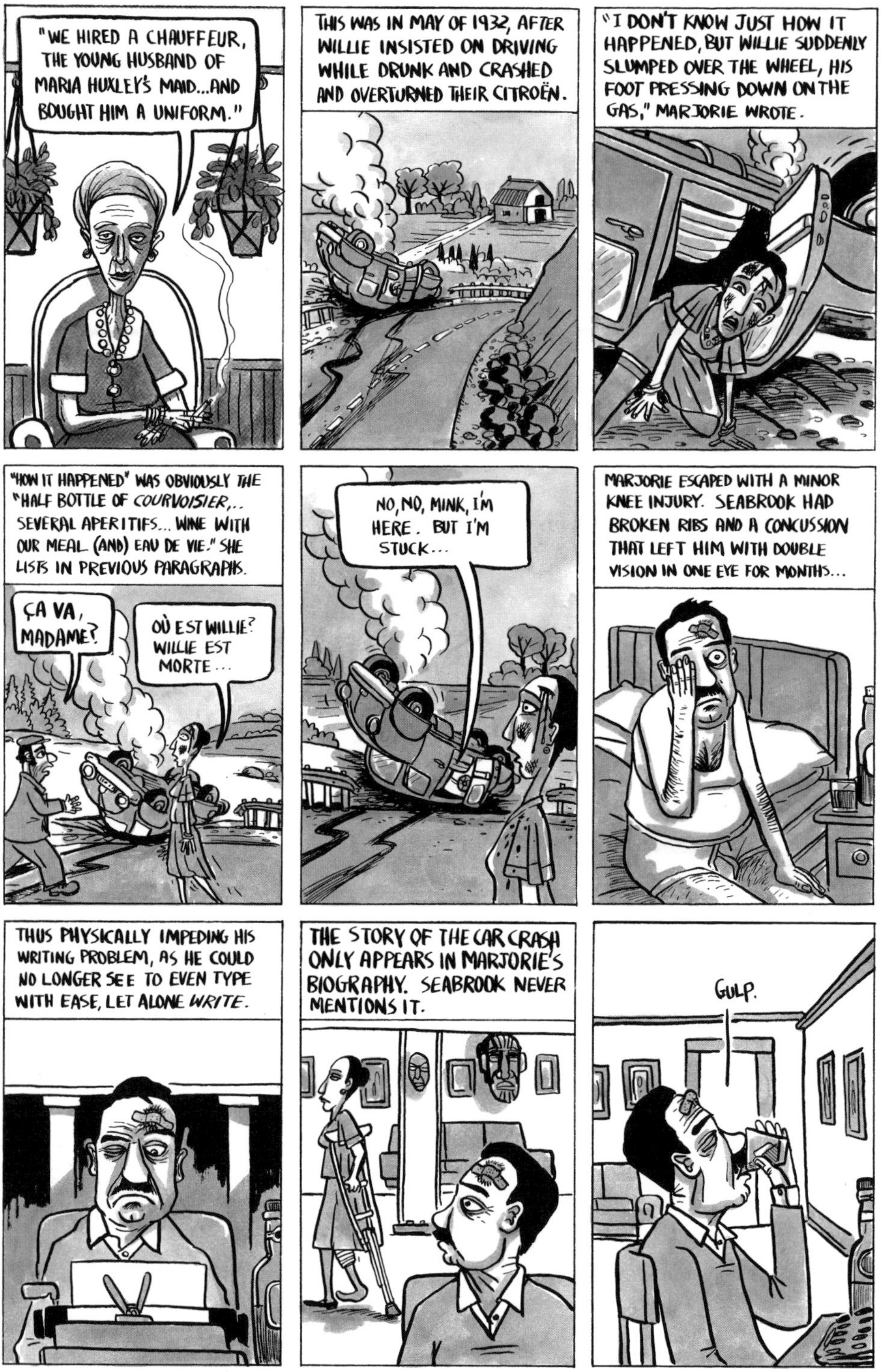
"WE HIRED A CHAUFFEUR, THE YOUNG HUSBAND OF MARIA HUXLEY'S MAID...AND BOUGHT HIM A UNIFORM."
THIS WAS IN MAY OF 1932, AFTER WILLIE INSISTED ON DRIVING WHILE DRUNK AND CRASHED AND OVERTURNED THEIR CITROËN.
"I DON'T KNOW JUST HOW IT HAPPENED, BUT WILLIE SUDDENLY SLUMPED OVER THE WHEEL, HIS FOOT PRESSING DOWN ON THE GAS," MARJORIE WROTE.
"HOW IT HAPPENED" WAS OBVIOUSLY THE "HALF BOTTLE OF COURVOISIER,.. SEVERAL APERITIFS... WINE WITH OUR MEAL (AND) EAU DE VIE." SHE LISTS IN PREVIOUS PARAGRAPHS.
ÇA VA, MADAME?
OÙ EST WILLIE? WILLIE EST MORTE...
NO, NO, MINK, I'M HERE. BUT I'M STUCK...
MARJORIE ESCAPED WITH A MINOR KNEE INJURY. SEABROOK HAD BROKEN RIBS AND A CONCUSSION THAT LEFT HIM WITH DOUBLE VISION IN ONE EYE FOR MONTHS...
THUS PHYSICALLY IMPEDING HIS WRITING PROBLEM, AS HE COULD NO LONGER SEE TO EVEN TYPE WITH EASE, LET ALONE WRITE.
THE STORY OF THE CAR CRASH ONLY APPEARS IN MARJORIE'S BIOGRAPHY. SEABROOK NEVER MENTIONS IT.
GULP.

DRUNK AND DESPERATE TO COMPLETE AT LEAST ONE OF THE BOOKS HE HAD CONTRACTED TO WRITE, SEABROOK HIRED A GHOSTWRITER TO TURN HIS NOTES INTO A COHERENT BOOK OF HIS FLIGHT TO TIMBUCTOO.

TAP TAP

EVENTUALLY, HE DECIDED TO SINK OF HIS OWN ACCORD, PAID THE WRITER OFF AND DESTROYED THE WORK, MARJORIE RECORDED.

HE THEN DRUNKENLY DICTATED THE BOOK *AIR ADVENTURE* TO MARJORIE, WHO TYPED WHILE SEABROOK DRANK TWO BOTTLES OF BRANDY DAILY.

THE BOOK WAS EVENTUALLY COMPLETED TO EVERYONE'S NEAR- OR ALMOST-SATISFACTION.

POP!

AIR ADVENTURE

BUT THERE WAS STILL THE PÈRE YAKOUBA BIOGRAPHY TO RESEARCH AND WRITE. THERE WAS NO RESPITE FROM THE PRESSURE.

SEABROOK'S DRUNKENNESS AND SELF-DESTRUCTIVE BEHAVIOUR REACHED NEW LEVELS OF INTENSITY.

WILLIE?

RUFF!

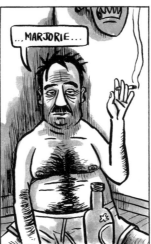

...MARJORIE...

WILLIE...

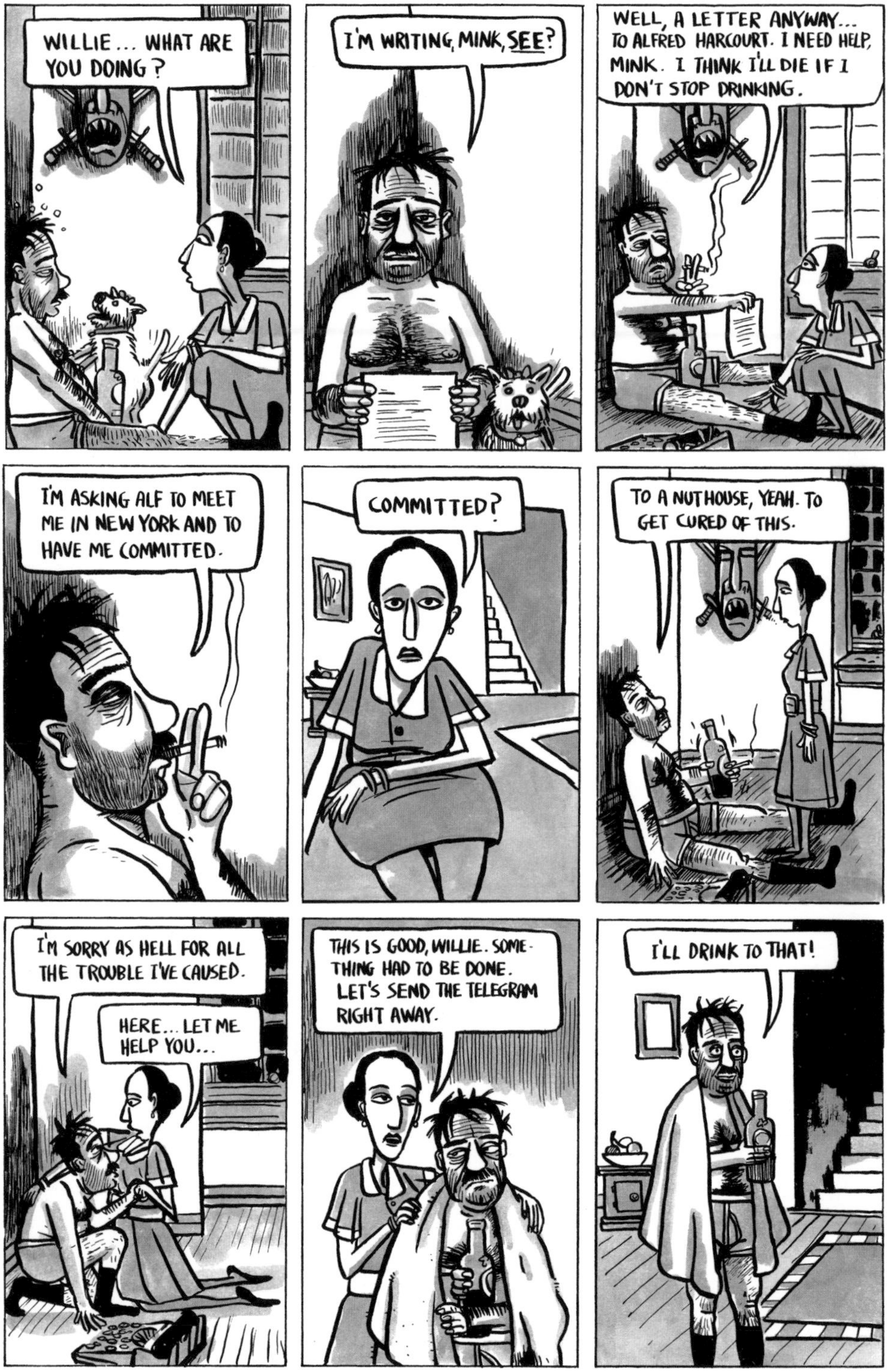
WILLIE... WHAT ARE YOU DOING?
I'M WRITING, MINK, SEE?
WELL, A LETTER ANYWAY... TO ALFRED HARCOURT. I NEED HELP, MINK. I THINK I'LL DIE IF I DON'T STOP DRINKING.
I'M ASKING ALF TO MEET ME IN NEW YORK AND TO HAVE ME COMMITTED.
COMMITTED?
TO A NUTHOUSE, YEAH. TO GET CURED OF THIS.
I'M SORRY AS HELL FOR ALL THE TROUBLE I'VE CAUSED.
HERE... LET ME HELP YOU...
THIS IS GOOD, WILLIE. SOMETHING HAD TO BE DONE. LET'S SEND THE TELEGRAM RIGHT AWAY.
I'LL DRINK TO THAT!

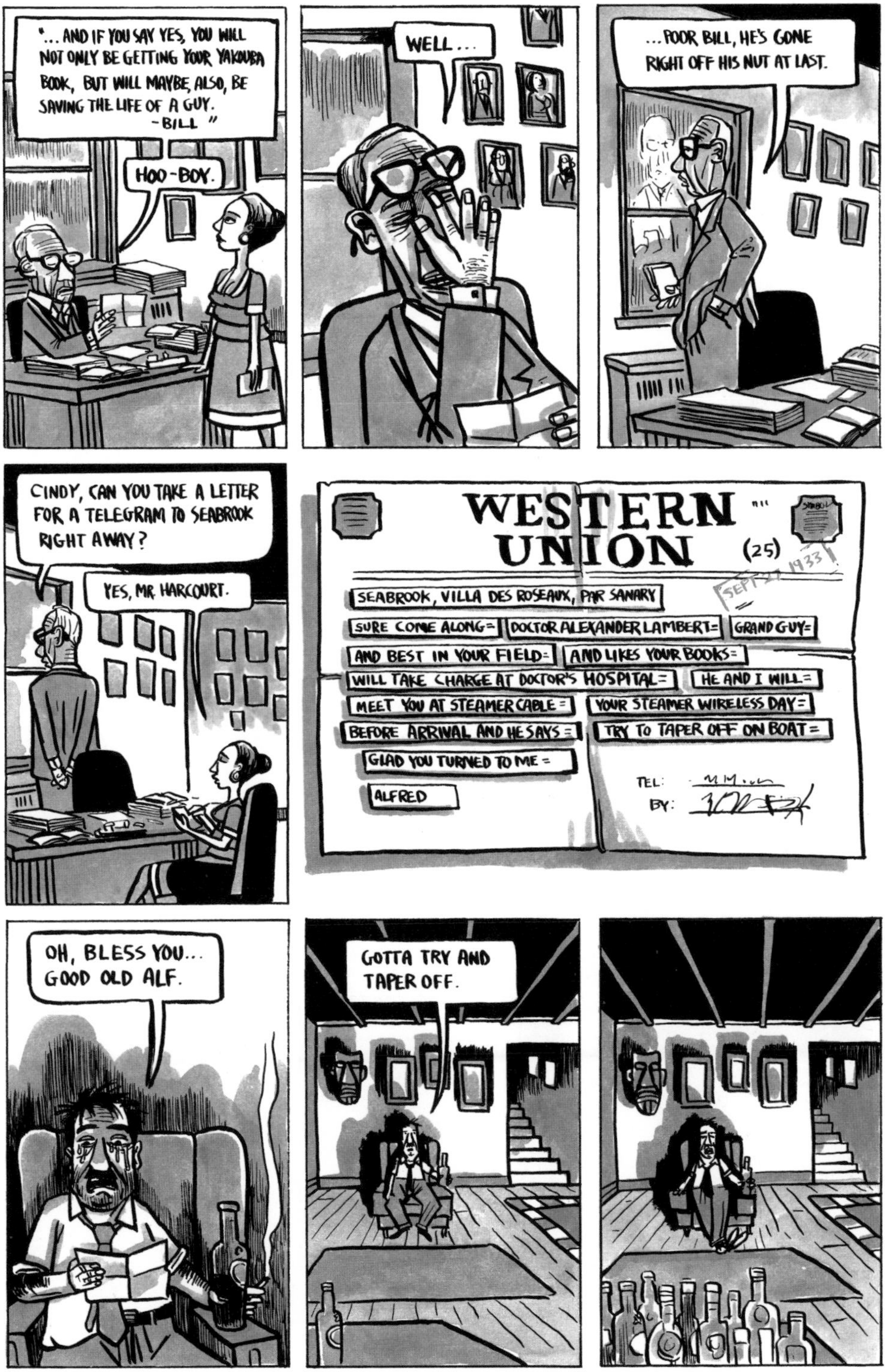
"... AND IF YOU SAY YES, YOU WILL NOT ONLY BE GETTING YOUR YAKOUBA BOOK, BUT WILL MAYBE, ALSO, BE SAVING THE LIFE OF A GUY. -BILL"
HOO-BOY.
WELL...
...POOR BILL, HE'S GONE RIGHT OFF HIS NUT AT LAST.
CINDY, CAN YOU TAKE A LETTER FOR A TELEGRAM TO SEABROOK RIGHT AWAY?
YES, MR. HARCOURT.
WESTERN UNION
(25)
SEPT 27 1933
SEABROOK, VILLA DES ROSEAUX, PAR SANARY
SURE COME ALONG= DOCTOR ALEXANDER LAMBERT= GRAND GUY=
AND BEST IN YOUR FIELD= AND LIKES YOUR BOOKS=
WILL TAKE CHARGE AT DOCTOR'S HOSPITAL= HE AND I WILL=
MEET YOU AT STEAMER CABLE= YOUR STEAMER WIRELESS DAY=
BEFORE ARRIVAL AND HE SAYS= TRY TO TAPER OFF ON BOAT=
GLAD YOU TURNED TO ME=
ALFRED
TEL:
BY:
OH, BLESS YOU... GOOD OLD ALF.
GOTTA TRY AND TAPER OFF.

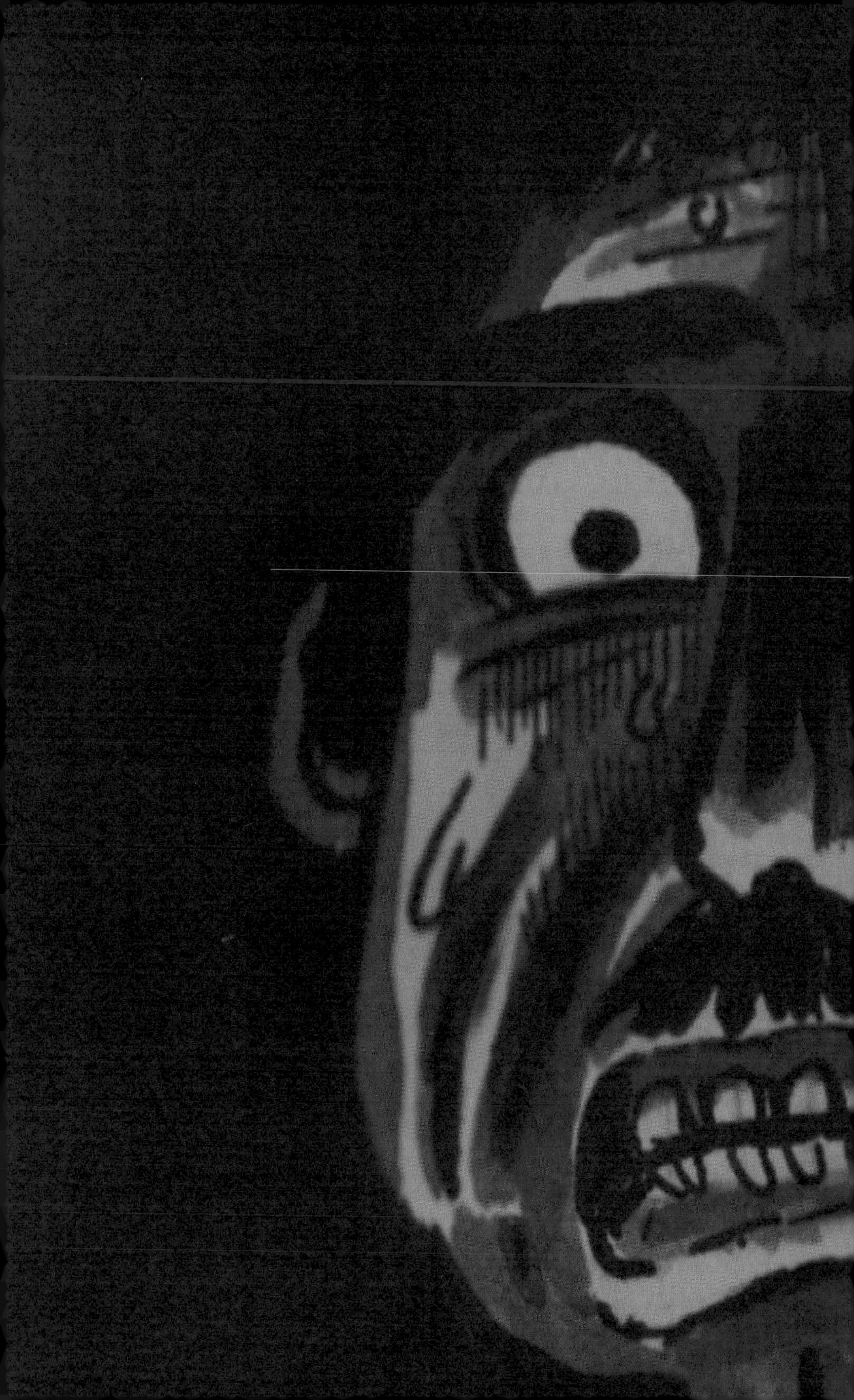

# CHAPTER SIX
# A DRUNKARD IN A MADHOUSE

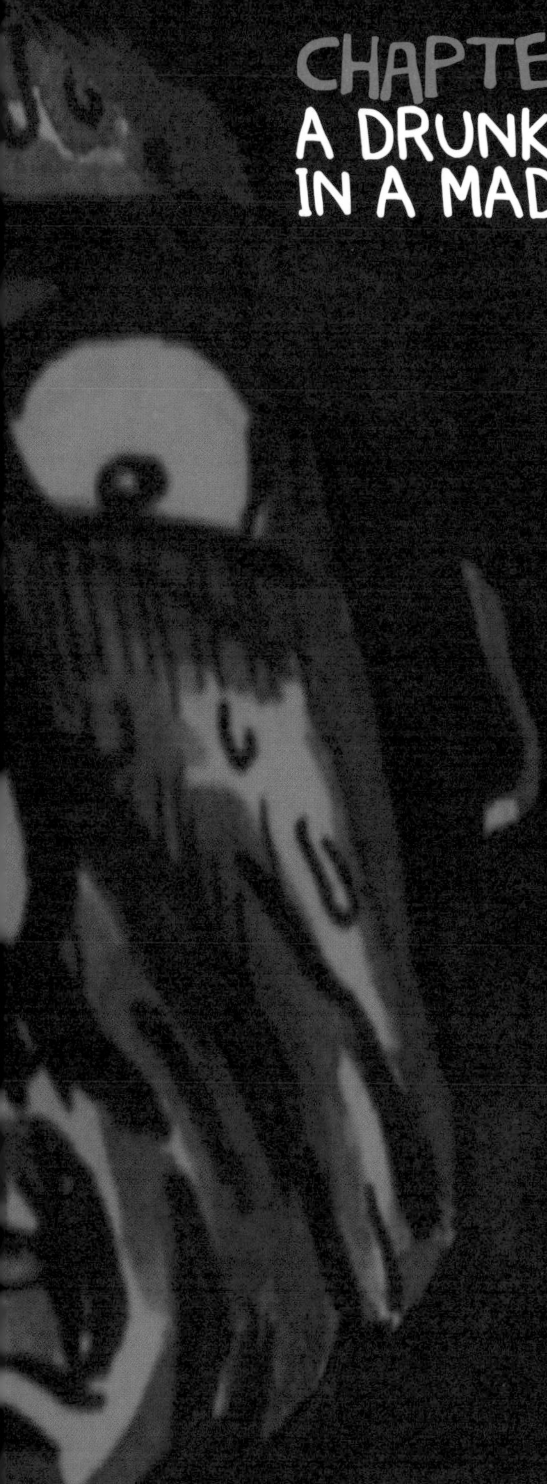

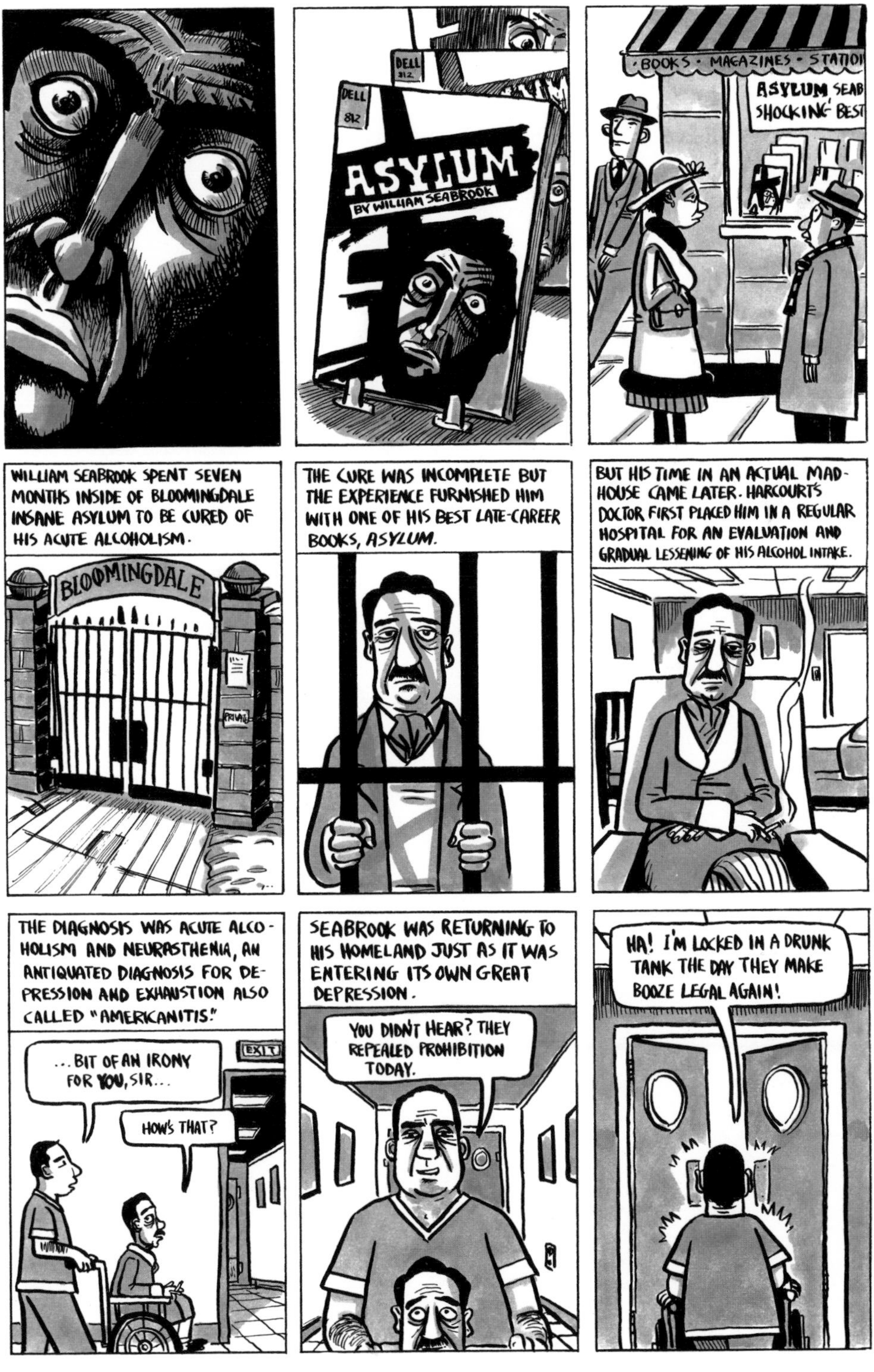
DELL 812
DELL 812
ASYLUM
BY WILLIAM SEABROOK
BOOKS · MAGAZINES · STATIO
ASYLUM SEAB
SHOCKING BEST
WILLIAM SEABROOK SPENT SEVEN MONTHS INSIDE OF BLOOMINGDALE INSANE ASYLUM TO BE CURED OF HIS ACUTE ALCOHOLISM.
BLOOMINGDALE
PRIVATE
THE CURE WAS INCOMPLETE BUT THE EXPERIENCE FURNISHED HIM WITH ONE OF HIS BEST LATE-CAREER BOOKS, ASYLUM.
BUT HIS TIME IN AN ACTUAL MAD-HOUSE CAME LATER. HARCOURT'S DOCTOR FIRST PLACED HIM IN A REGULAR HOSPITAL FOR AN EVALUATION AND GRADUAL LESSENING OF HIS ALCOHOL INTAKE.
THE DIAGNOSIS WAS ACUTE ALCO-HOLISM AND NEURASTHENIA, AN ANTIQUATED DIAGNOSIS FOR DE-PRESSION AND EXHAUSTION ALSO CALLED "AMERICANITIS."
EXIT
...BIT OF AN IRONY FOR YOU, SIR...
HOW'S THAT?
SEABROOK WAS RETURNING TO HIS HOMELAND JUST AS IT WAS ENTERING ITS OWN GREAT DEPRESSION.
YOU DIDN'T HEAR? THEY REPEALED PROHIBITION TODAY.
HA! I'M LOCKED IN A DRUNK TANK THE DAY THEY MAKE BOOZE LEGAL AGAIN!

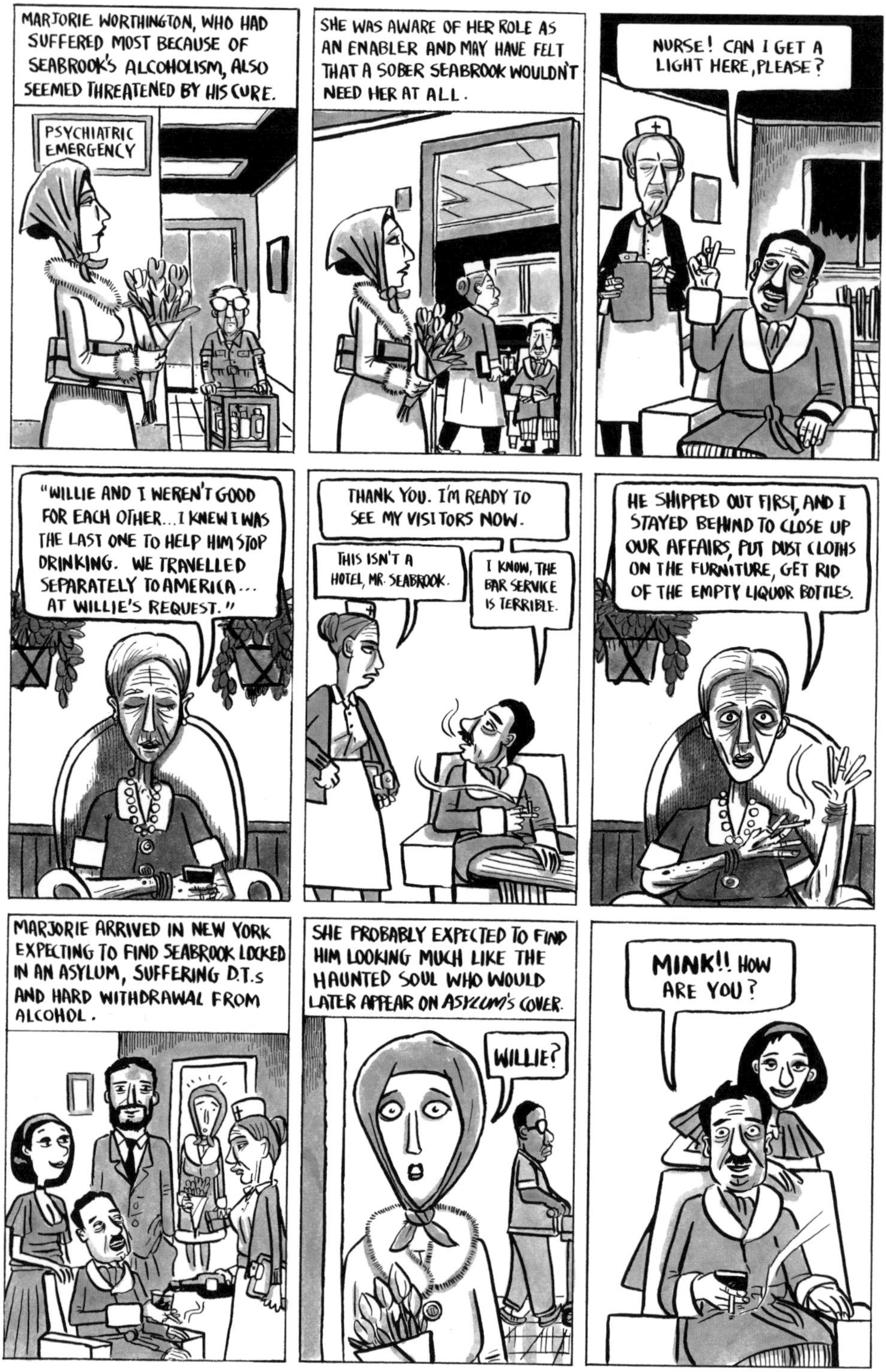
MARJORIE WORTHINGTON, WHO HAD SUFFERED MOST BECAUSE OF SEABROOK'S ALCOHOLISM, ALSO SEEMED THREATENED BY HIS CURE.
PSYCHIATRIC EMERGENCY
SHE WAS AWARE OF HER ROLE AS AN ENABLER AND MAY HAVE FELT THAT A SOBER SEABROOK WOULDN'T NEED HER AT ALL.
NURSE! CAN I GET A LIGHT HERE, PLEASE?
"WILLIE AND I WEREN'T GOOD FOR EACH OTHER... I KNEW I WAS THE LAST ONE TO HELP HIM STOP DRINKING. WE TRAVELLED SEPARATELY TO AMERICA... AT WILLIE'S REQUEST."
THANK YOU. I'M READY TO SEE MY VISITORS NOW.
THIS ISN'T A HOTEL, MR. SEABROOK.
I KNOW, THE BAR SERVICE IS TERRIBLE.
HE SHIPPED OUT FIRST, AND I STAYED BEHIND TO CLOSE UP OUR AFFAIRS, PUT DUST CLOTHS ON THE FURNITURE, GET RID OF THE EMPTY LIQUOR BOTTLES.
MARJORIE ARRIVED IN NEW YORK EXPECTING TO FIND SEABROOK LOCKED IN AN ASYLUM, SUFFERING D.T.s AND HARD WITHDRAWAL FROM ALCOHOL.
SHE PROBABLY EXPECTED TO FIND HIM LOOKING MUCH LIKE THE HAUNTED SOUL WHO WOULD LATER APPEAR ON ASYLUM'S COVER.
WILLIE?
MINK!! HOW ARE YOU?

I...

WILLIE... **WHAT** IS THAT?

HUH?

OH, THIS.

THIS IS *PRESCRIPTION* BOOZE, MINK! DON'T WORRY, THEY'VE GOT ME DOWN TO THREE OF THESE A DAY.

MARJORIE, COME, I'LL GET YOU A DRINK...

WHAT'LL YOU HAVE?

WHAT TIME DOES THE FLOOR SHOW START IN THIS CLUB, ALF?

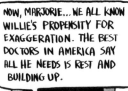

NOW, MARJORIE... WE ALL KNOW WILLIE'S PROPENSITY FOR EXAGGERATION. THE BEST DOCTORS IN AMERICA SAY ALL HE NEEDS IS REST AND BUILDING UP.

AND, YES, TO CUT DOWN ON THE BOOZE—THREE A DAY, THEN TWO AND SO ON...

HE WANTED TO BE LOCKED UP, ALF. HE **SHOULD** BE LOCKED UP... IF YOU HAD SEEN HIM IN FRANCE. HE WAS...

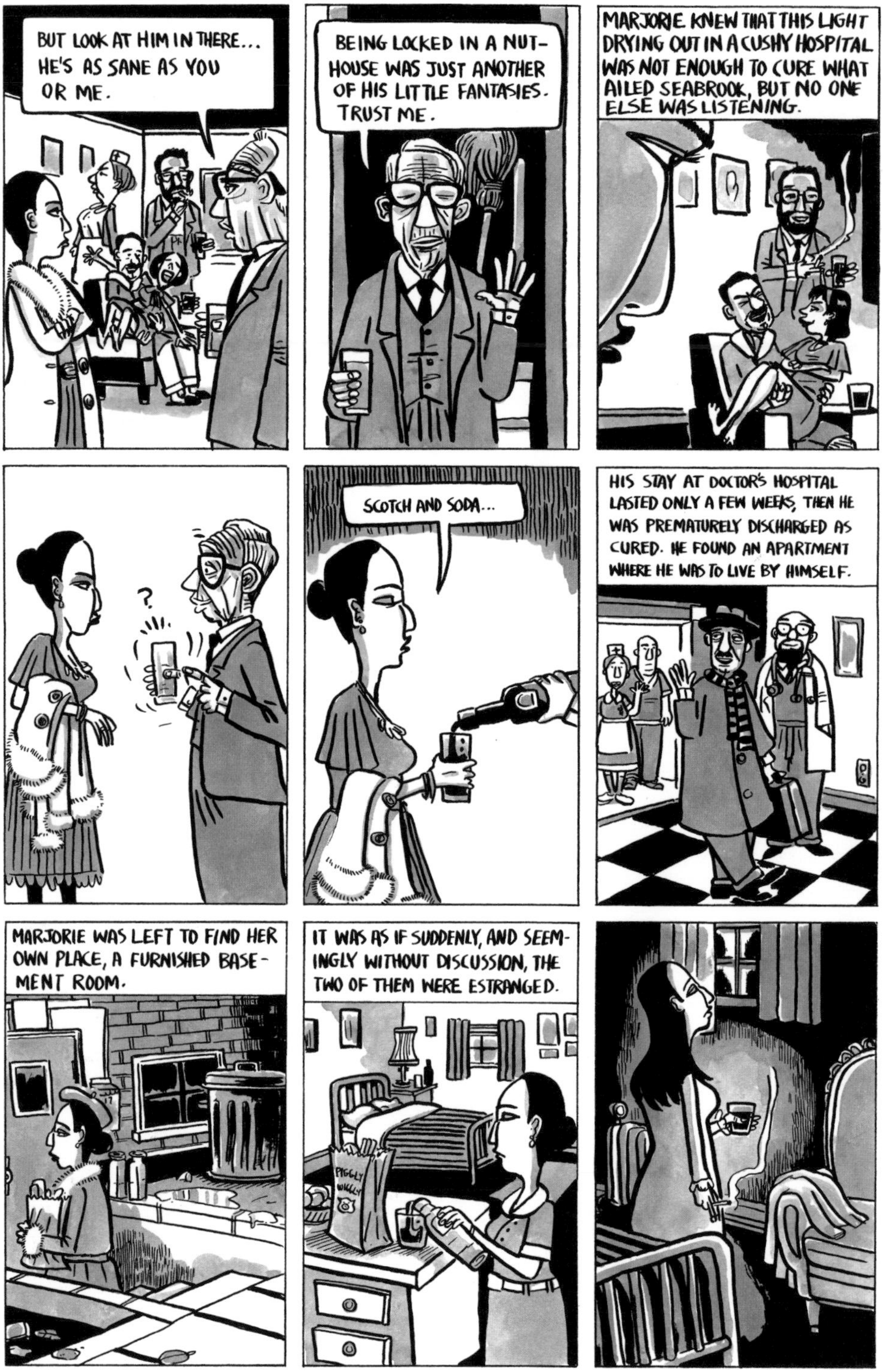
BUT LOOK AT HIM IN THERE... HE'S AS SANE AS YOU OR ME.
BEING LOCKED IN A NUT-HOUSE WAS JUST ANOTHER OF HIS LITTLE FANTASIES. TRUST ME.
MARJORIE KNEW THAT THIS LIGHT DRYING OUT IN A CUSHY HOSPITAL WAS NOT ENOUGH TO CURE WHAT AILED SEABROOK, BUT NO ONE ELSE WAS LISTENING.
?
SCOTCH AND SODA...
HIS STAY AT DOCTOR'S HOSPITAL LASTED ONLY A FEW WEEKS, THEN HE WAS PREMATURELY DISCHARGED AS CURED. HE FOUND AN APARTMENT WHERE HE WAS TO LIVE BY HIMSELF.
MARJORIE WAS LEFT TO FIND HER OWN PLACE, A FURNISHED BASE-MENT ROOM.
IT WAS AS IF SUDDENLY, AND SEEM-INGLY WITHOUT DISCUSSION, THE TWO OF THEM WERE ESTRANGED.
PIGGLY WIGGLY

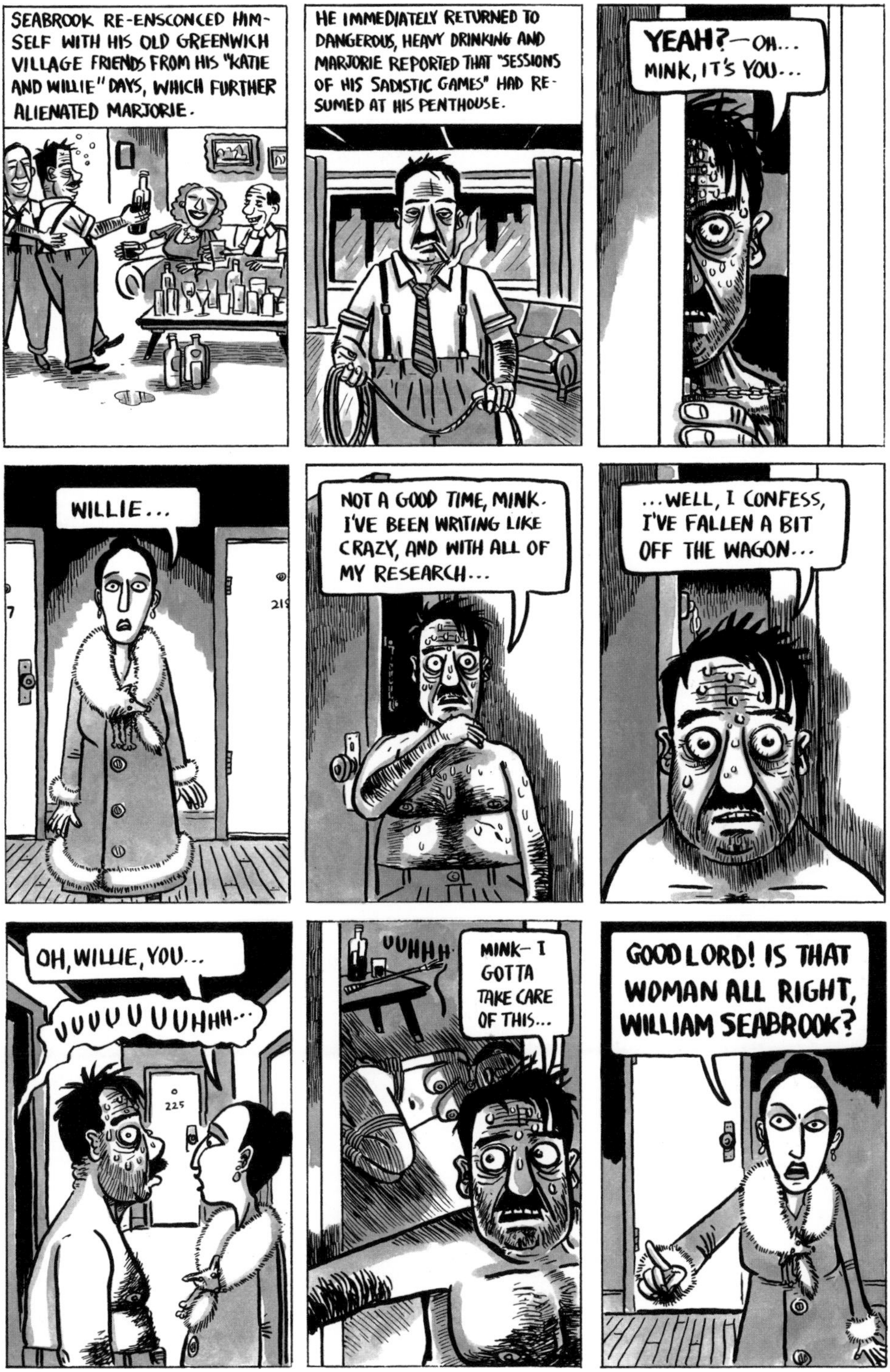
SEABROOK RE-ENSCONCED HIMSELF WITH HIS OLD GREENWICH VILLAGE FRIENDS FROM HIS "KATIE AND WILLIE" DAYS, WHICH FURTHER ALIENATED MARJORIE.
HE IMMEDIATELY RETURNED TO DANGEROUS, HEAVY DRINKING AND MARJORIE REPORTED THAT "SESSIONS OF HIS SADISTIC GAMES" HAD RESUMED AT HIS PENTHOUSE.
YEAH?—OH... MINK, IT'S YOU...
WILLIE...
NOT A GOOD TIME, MINK. I'VE BEEN WRITING LIKE CRAZY, AND WITH ALL OF MY RESEARCH...
...WELL, I CONFESS, I'VE FALLEN A BIT OFF THE WAGON...
OH, WILLIE, YOU...
UUUUUUUHHH...
UUHHH
MINK— I GOTTA TAKE CARE OF THIS...
GOOD LORD! IS THAT WOMAN ALL RIGHT, WILLIAM SEABROOK?

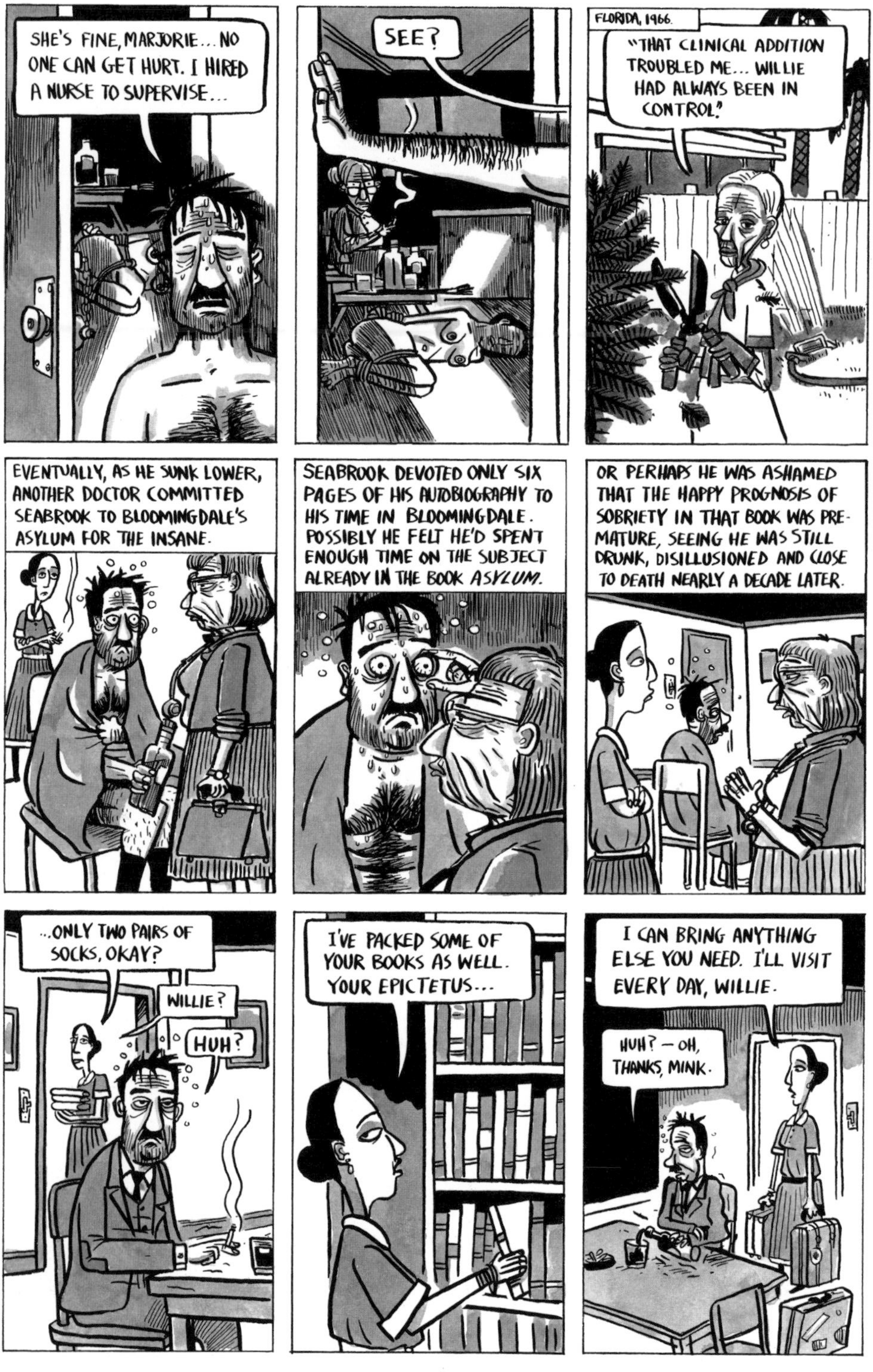
SHE'S FINE, MARJORIE... NO ONE CAN GET HURT. I HIRED A NURSE TO SUPERVISE...
SEE?
FLORIDA, 1966.
"THAT CLINICAL ADDITION TROUBLED ME... WILLIE HAD ALWAYS BEEN IN CONTROL."
EVENTUALLY, AS HE SUNK LOWER, ANOTHER DOCTOR COMMITTED SEABROOK TO BLOOMINGDALE'S ASYLUM FOR THE INSANE.
SEABROOK DEVOTED ONLY SIX PAGES OF HIS AUTOBIOGRAPHY TO HIS TIME IN BLOOMINGDALE. POSSIBLY HE FELT HE'D SPENT ENOUGH TIME ON THE SUBJECT ALREADY IN THE BOOK ASYLUM.
OR PERHAPS HE WAS ASHAMED THAT THE HAPPY PROGNOSIS OF SOBRIETY IN THAT BOOK WAS PREMATURE, SEEING HE WAS STILL DRUNK, DISILLUSIONED AND CLOSE TO DEATH NEARLY A DECADE LATER.
...ONLY TWO PAIRS OF SOCKS, OKAY?
WILLIE?
HUH?
I'VE PACKED SOME OF YOUR BOOKS AS WELL. YOUR EPICTETUS...
I CAN BRING ANYTHING ELSE YOU NEED. I'LL VISIT EVERY DAY, WILLIE.
HUH? — OH, THANKS, MINK.

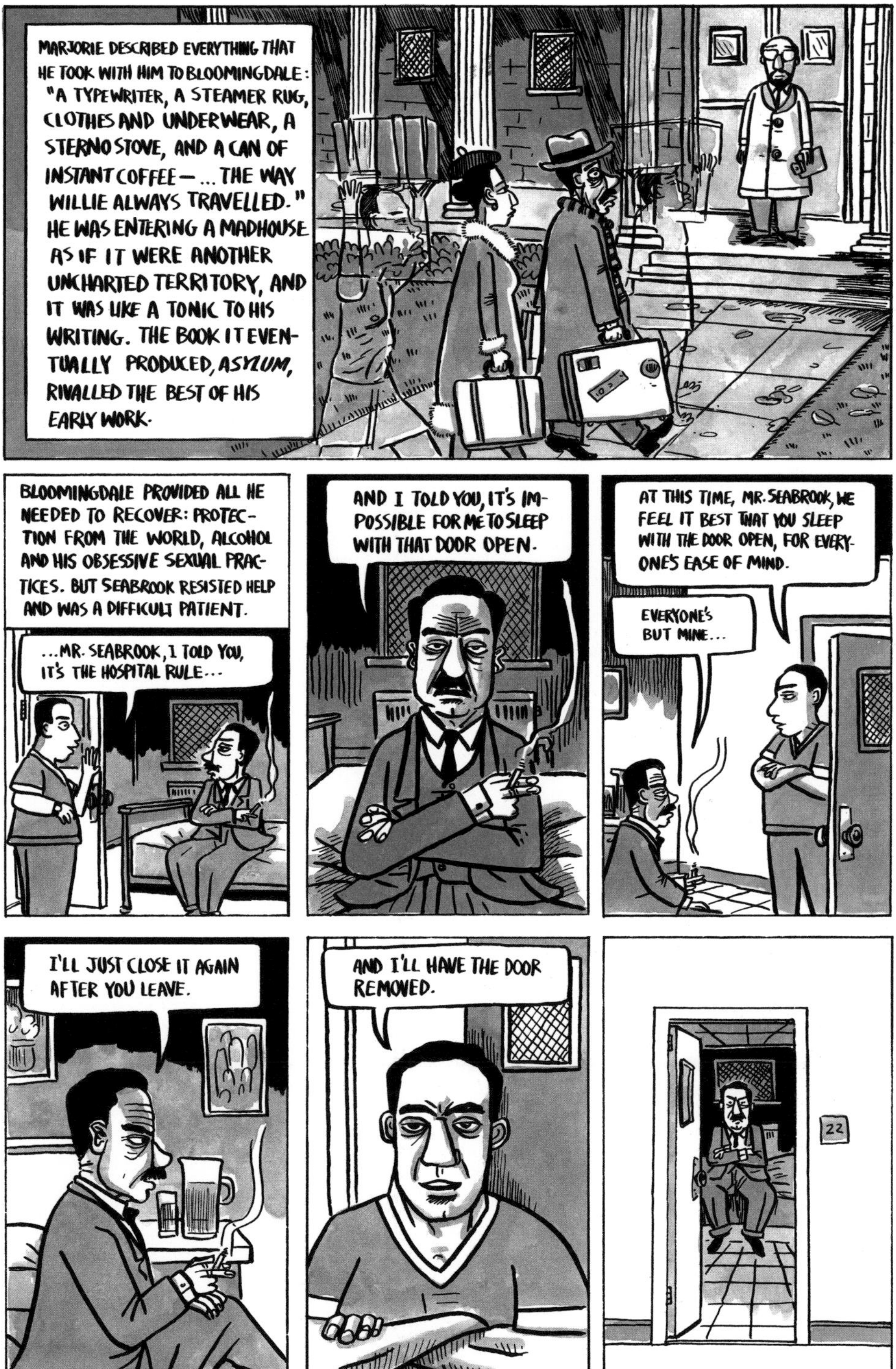
MARJORIE DESCRIBED EVERYTHING THAT HE TOOK WITH HIM TO BLOOMINGDALE: "A TYPEWRITER, A STEAMER RUG, CLOTHES AND UNDERWEAR, A STERNO STOVE, AND A CAN OF INSTANT COFFEE— ... THE WAY WILLIE ALWAYS TRAVELLED." HE WAS ENTERING A MADHOUSE AS IF IT WERE ANOTHER UNCHARTED TERRITORY, AND IT WAS LIKE A TONIC TO HIS WRITING. THE BOOK IT EVENTUALLY PRODUCED, ASYLUM, RIVALLED THE BEST OF HIS EARLY WORK.
BLOOMINGDALE PROVIDED ALL HE NEEDED TO RECOVER: PROTECTION FROM THE WORLD, ALCOHOL AND HIS OBSESSIVE SEXUAL PRACTICES. BUT SEABROOK RESISTED HELP AND WAS A DIFFICULT PATIENT.
...MR. SEABROOK, I TOLD YOU, IT'S THE HOSPITAL RULE...
AND I TOLD YOU, IT'S IMPOSSIBLE FOR ME TO SLEEP WITH THAT DOOR OPEN.
AT THIS TIME, MR. SEABROOK, WE FEEL IT BEST THAT YOU SLEEP WITH THE DOOR OPEN, FOR EVERYONE'S EASE OF MIND.
EVERYONE'S BUT MINE...
I'LL JUST CLOSE IT AGAIN AFTER YOU LEAVE.
AND I'LL HAVE THE DOOR REMOVED.
22

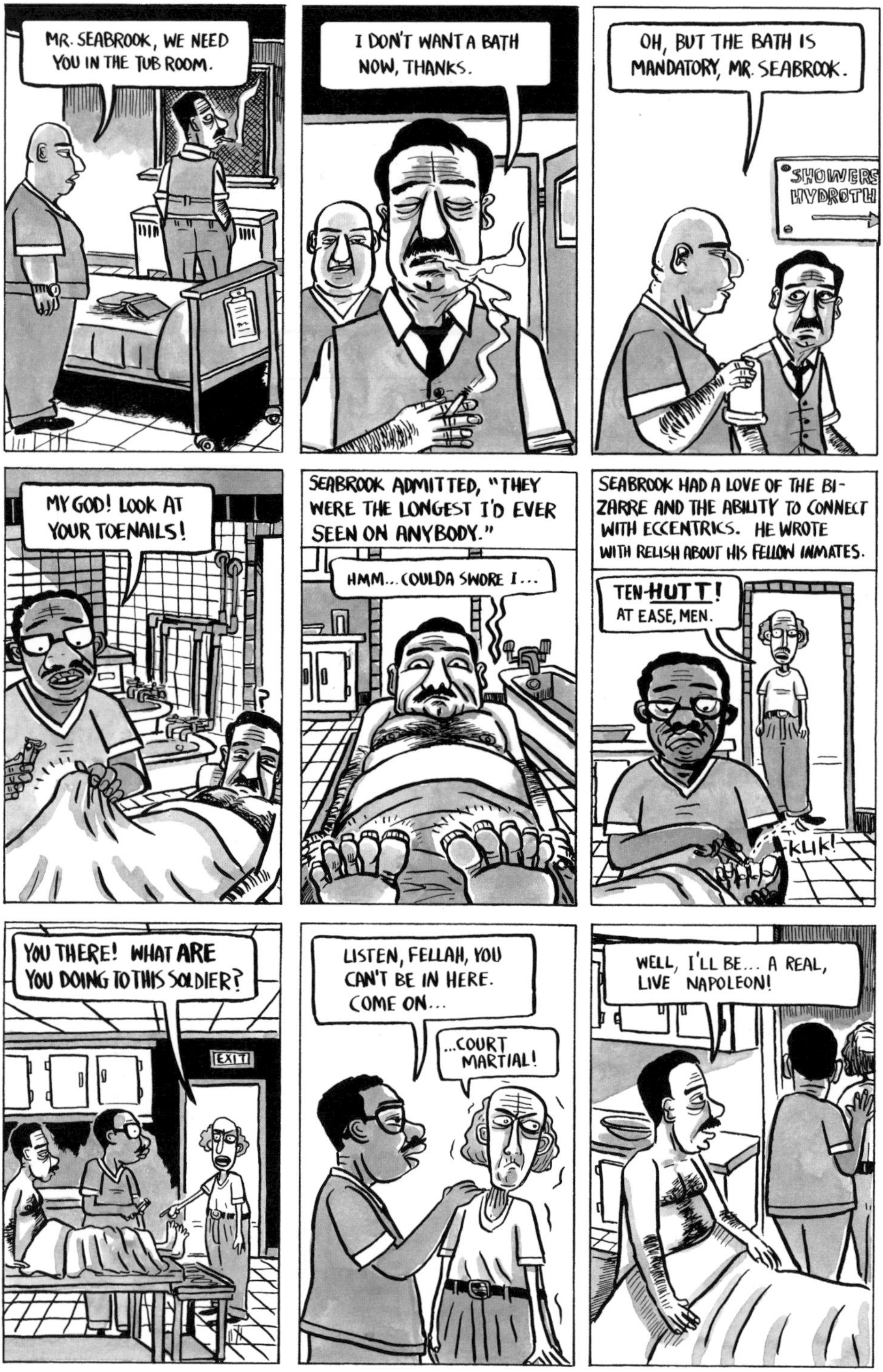
MR. SEABROOK, WE NEED YOU IN THE TUB ROOM.
I DON'T WANT A BATH NOW, THANKS.
OH, BUT THE BATH IS MANDATORY, MR. SEABROOK.
SHOWERS HYDROTH
MY GOD! LOOK AT YOUR TOENAILS!
?
SEABROOK ADMITTED, "THEY WERE THE LONGEST I'D EVER SEEN ON ANYBODY."
HMM... COULDA SWORE I...
SEABROOK HAD A LOVE OF THE BIZARRE AND THE ABILITY TO CONNECT WITH ECCENTRICS. HE WROTE WITH RELISH ABOUT HIS FELLOW INMATES.
TEN-HUTT! AT EASE, MEN.
KLIK!
YOU THERE! WHAT ARE YOU DOING TO THIS SOLDIER?
EXIT
LISTEN, FELLAH, YOU CAN'T BE IN HERE. COME ON...
...COURT MARTIAL!
WELL, I'LL BE... A REAL, LIVE NAPOLEON!

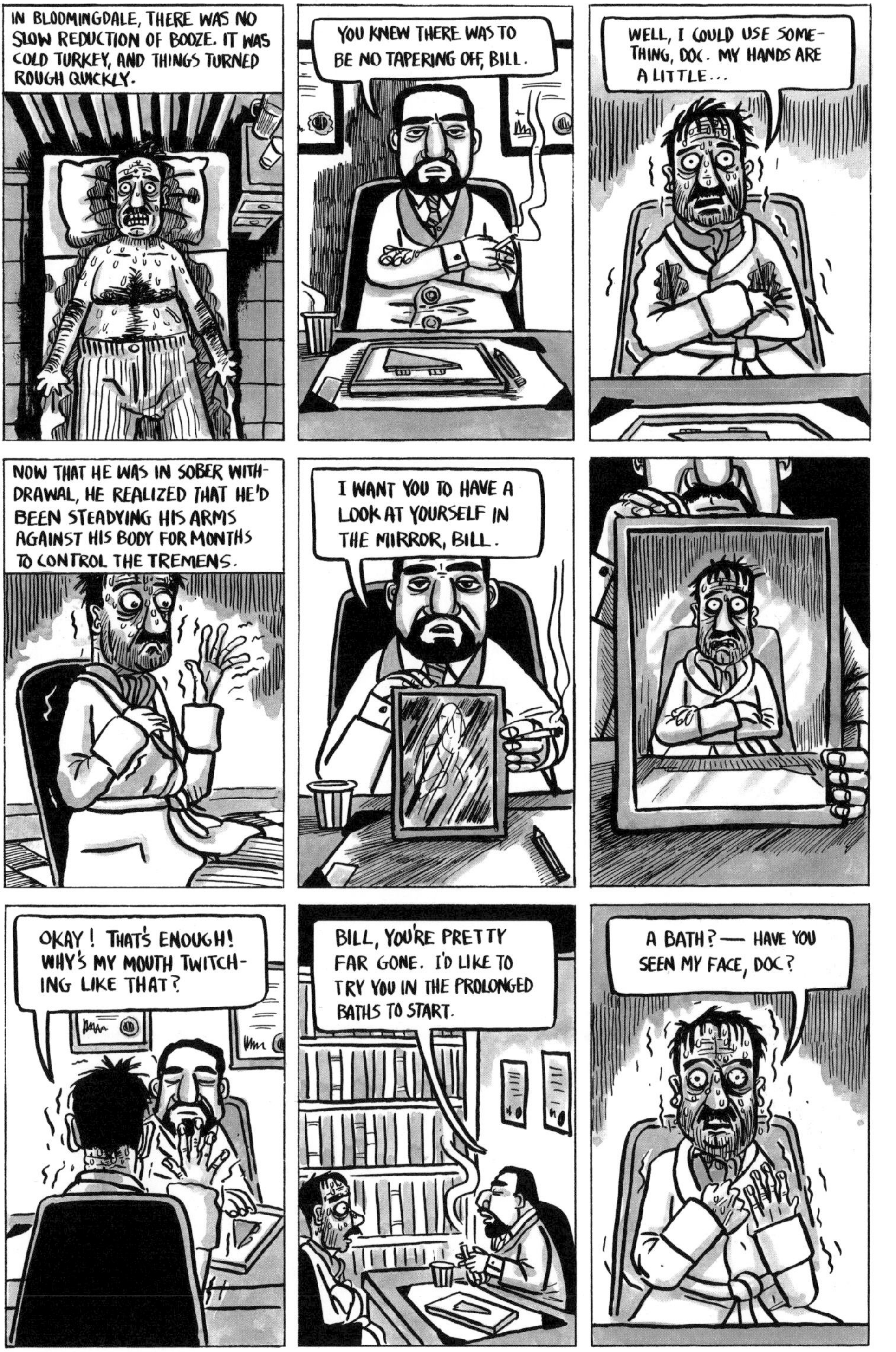
IN BLOOMINGDALE, THERE WAS NO SLOW REDUCTION OF BOOZE. IT WAS COLD TURKEY, AND THINGS TURNED ROUGH QUICKLY.
YOU KNEW THERE WAS TO BE NO TAPERING OFF, BILL.
WELL, I COULD USE SOME-THING, DOC. MY HANDS ARE A LITTLE...
NOW THAT HE WAS IN SOBER WITH-DRAWAL, HE REALIZED THAT HE'D BEEN STEADYING HIS ARMS AGAINST HIS BODY FOR MONTHS TO CONTROL THE TREMENS.
I WANT YOU TO HAVE A LOOK AT YOURSELF IN THE MIRROR, BILL.
OKAY! THAT'S ENOUGH! WHY'S MY MOUTH TWITCH-ING LIKE THAT?
BILL, YOU'RE PRETTY FAR GONE. I'D LIKE TO TRY YOU IN THE PROLONGED BATHS TO START.
A BATH? — HAVE YOU SEEN MY FACE, DOC?

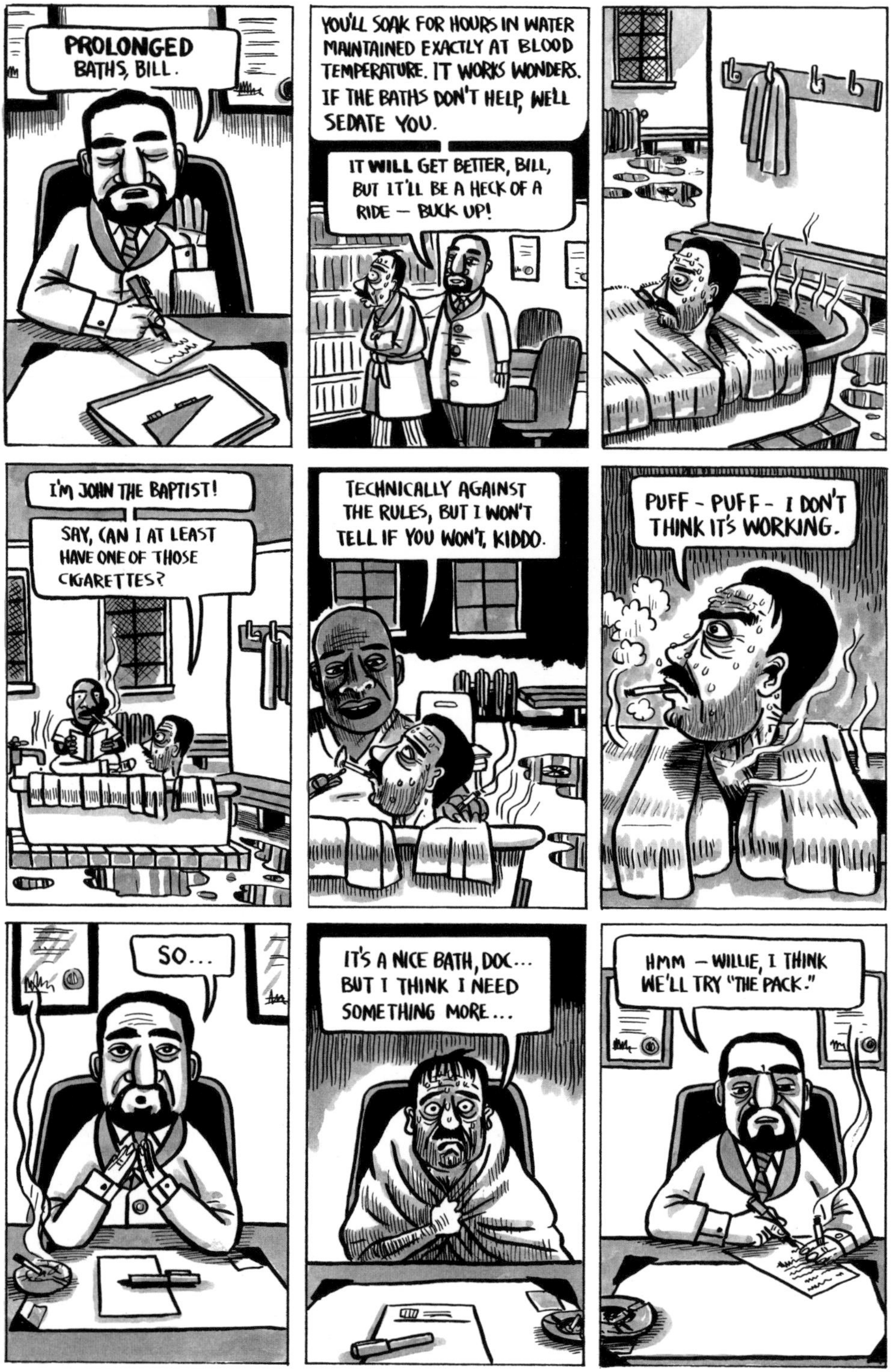
PROLONGED BATHS, BILL.
YOU'LL SOAK FOR HOURS IN WATER MAINTAINED EXACTLY AT BLOOD TEMPERATURE. IT WORKS WONDERS. IF THE BATHS DON'T HELP, WE'LL SEDATE YOU.
IT WILL GET BETTER, BILL, BUT IT'LL BE A HECK OF A RIDE — BUCK UP!
I'M JOHN THE BAPTIST!
SAY, CAN I AT LEAST HAVE ONE OF THOSE CIGARETTES?
TECHNICALLY AGAINST THE RULES, BUT I WON'T TELL IF YOU WON'T, KIDDO.
PUFF - PUFF - I DON'T THINK IT'S WORKING.
SO...
IT'S A NICE BATH, DOC... BUT I THINK I NEED SOMETHING MORE...
HMM — WILLIE, I THINK WE'LL TRY "THE PACK."

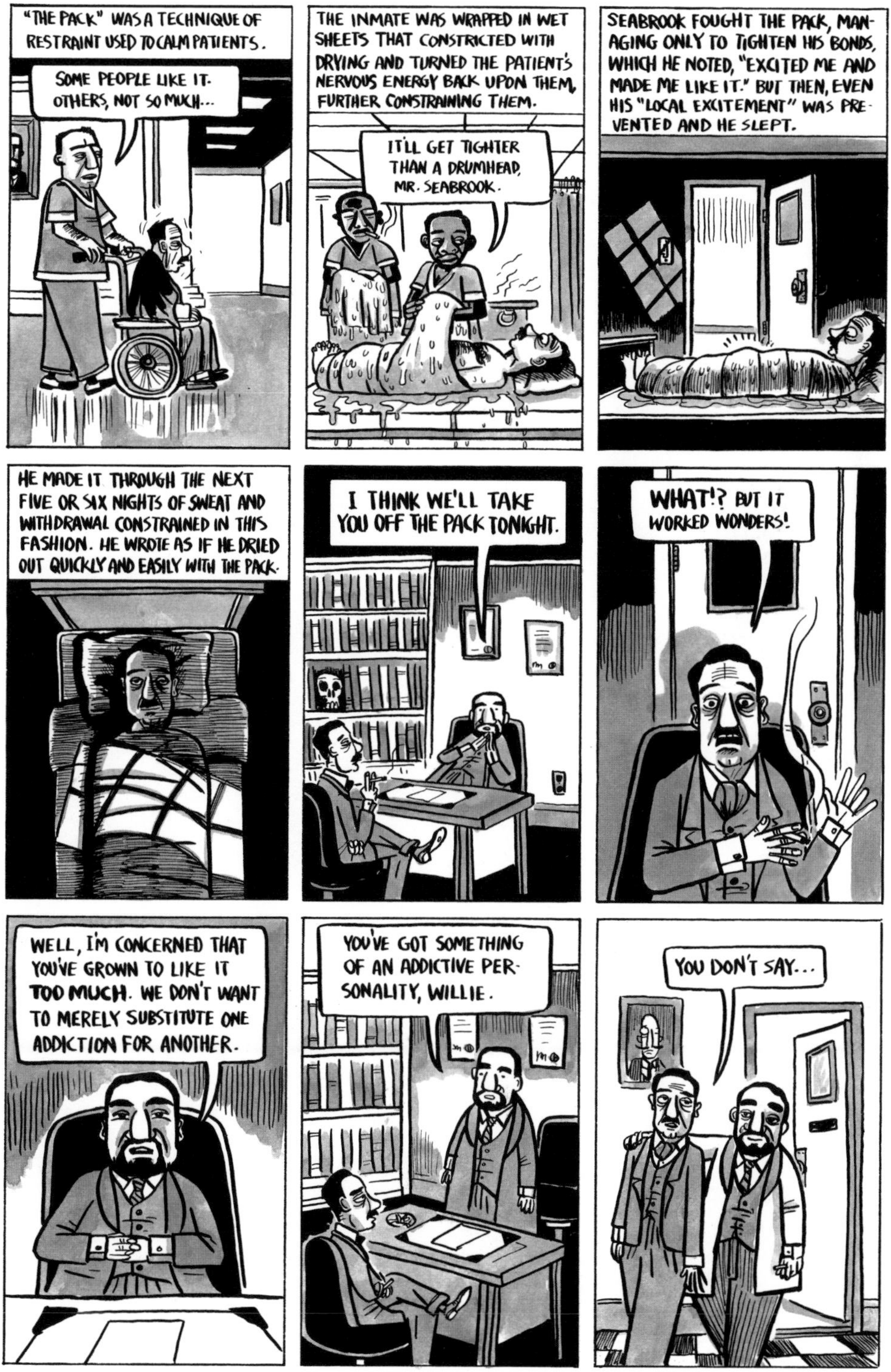
"THE PACK" WAS A TECHNIQUE OF RESTRAINT USED TO CALM PATIENTS.
SOME PEOPLE LIKE IT. OTHERS, NOT SO MUCH...
THE INMATE WAS WRAPPED IN WET SHEETS THAT CONSTRICTED WITH DRYING AND TURNED THE PATIENT'S NERVOUS ENERGY BACK UPON THEM, FURTHER CONSTRAINING THEM.
IT'LL GET TIGHTER THAN A DRUMHEAD, MR. SEABROOK.
SEABROOK FOUGHT THE PACK, MANAGING ONLY TO TIGHTEN HIS BONDS, WHICH HE NOTED, "EXCITED ME AND MADE ME LIKE IT." BUT THEN, EVEN HIS "LOCAL EXCITEMENT" WAS PREVENTED AND HE SLEPT.
HE MADE IT THROUGH THE NEXT FIVE OR SIX NIGHTS OF SWEAT AND WITHDRAWAL CONSTRAINED IN THIS FASHION. HE WROTE AS IF HE DRIED OUT QUICKLY AND EASILY WITH THE PACK.
I THINK WE'LL TAKE YOU OFF THE PACK TONIGHT.
WHAT!? BUT IT WORKED WONDERS!
WELL, I'M CONCERNED THAT YOU'VE GROWN TO LIKE IT TOO MUCH. WE DON'T WANT TO MERELY SUBSTITUTE ONE ADDICTION FOR ANOTHER.
YOU'VE GOT SOMETHING OF AN ADDICTIVE PERSONALITY, WILLIE.
YOU DON'T SAY...

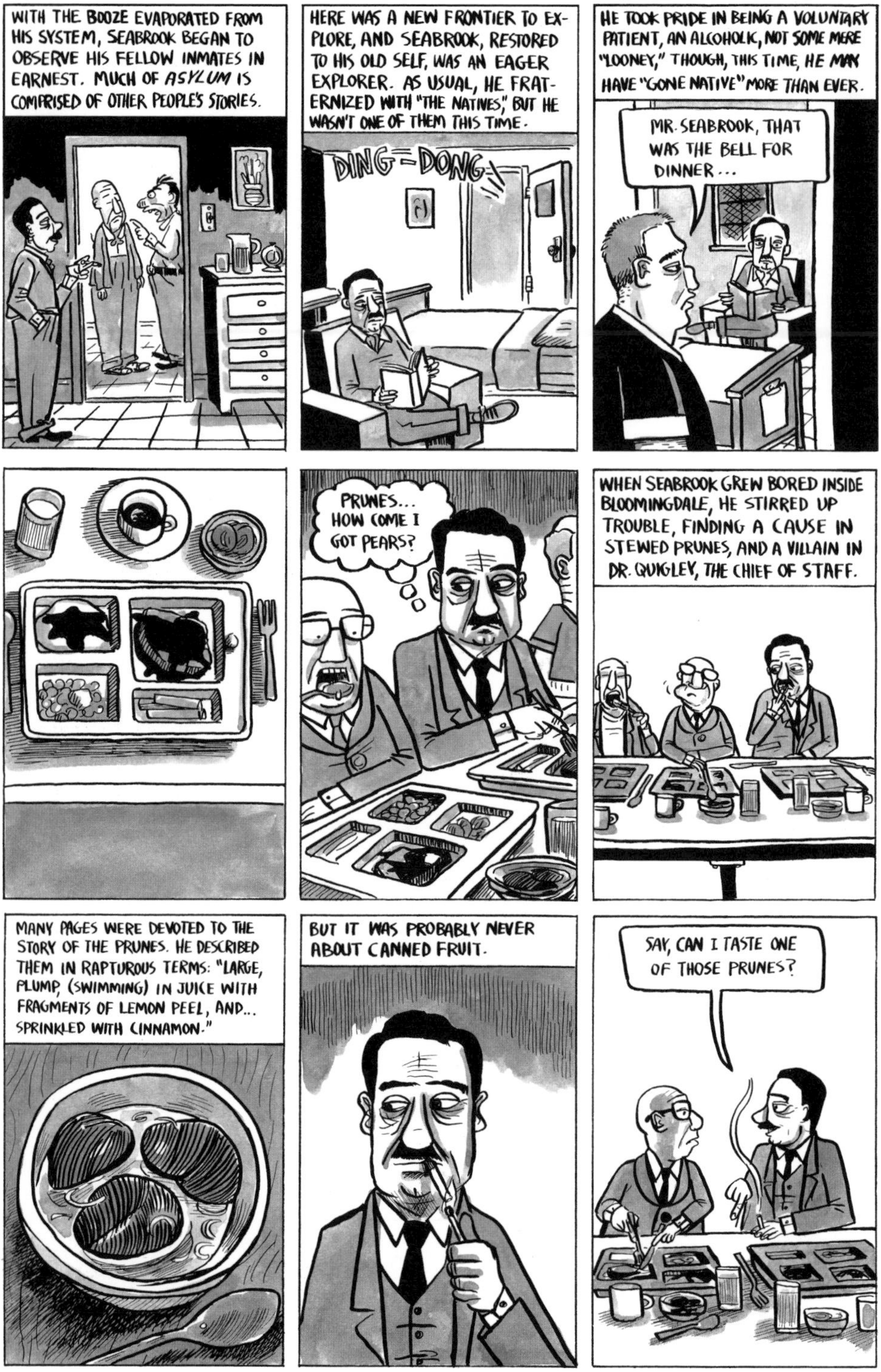
WITH THE BOOZE EVAPORATED FROM HIS SYSTEM, SEABROOK BEGAN TO OBSERVE HIS FELLOW INMATES IN EARNEST. MUCH OF ASYLUM IS COMPRISED OF OTHER PEOPLE'S STORIES.
HERE WAS A NEW FRONTIER TO EXPLORE, AND SEABROOK, RESTORED TO HIS OLD SELF, WAS AN EAGER EXPLORER. AS USUAL, HE FRATERNIZED WITH "THE NATIVES," BUT HE WASN'T ONE OF THEM THIS TIME.
DING-DONG
HE TOOK PRIDE IN BEING A VOLUNTARY PATIENT, AN ALCOHOLIC, NOT SOME MERE "LOONEY," THOUGH, THIS TIME, HE MAY HAVE "GONE NATIVE" MORE THAN EVER.
MR. SEABROOK, THAT WAS THE BELL FOR DINNER...
PRUNES... HOW COME I GOT PEARS?
WHEN SEABROOK GREW BORED INSIDE BLOOMINGDALE, HE STIRRED UP TROUBLE, FINDING A CAUSE IN STEWED PRUNES, AND A VILLAIN IN DR. QUIGLEY, THE CHIEF OF STAFF.
MANY PAGES WERE DEVOTED TO THE STORY OF THE PRUNES. HE DESCRIBED THEM IN RAPTUROUS TERMS: "LARGE, PLUMP, (SWIMMING) IN JUICE WITH FRAGMENTS OF LEMON PEEL, AND... SPRINKLED WITH CINNAMON."
BUT IT WAS PROBABLY NEVER ABOUT CANNED FRUIT.
SAY, CAN I TASTE ONE OF THOSE PRUNES?

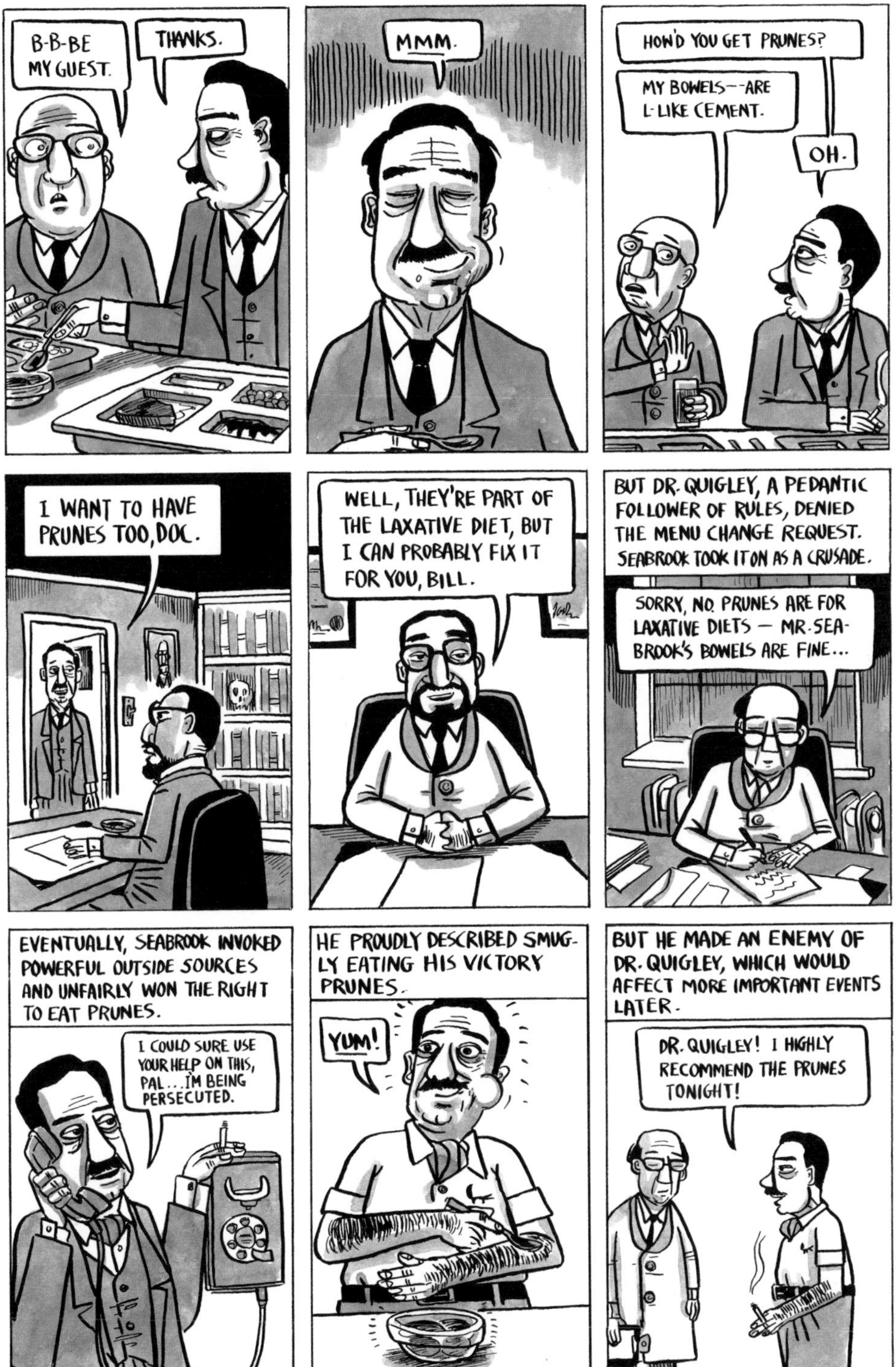
B-B-BE MY GUEST.
THANKS.
MMM.
HOW'D YOU GET PRUNES?
MY BOWELS--ARE L-LIKE CEMENT.
OH.
I WANT TO HAVE PRUNES TOO, DOC.
WELL, THEY'RE PART OF THE LAXATIVE DIET, BUT I CAN PROBABLY FIX IT FOR YOU, BILL.
BUT DR. QUIGLEY, A PEDANTIC FOLLOWER OF RULES, DENIED THE MENU CHANGE REQUEST. SEABROOK TOOK IT ON AS A CRUSADE.
SORRY, NO. PRUNES ARE FOR LAXATIVE DIETS — MR. SEABROOK'S BOWELS ARE FINE...
EVENTUALLY, SEABROOK INVOKED POWERFUL OUTSIDE SOURCES AND UNFAIRLY WON THE RIGHT TO EAT PRUNES.
I COULD SURE USE YOUR HELP ON THIS, PAL... I'M BEING PERSECUTED.
HE PROUDLY DESCRIBED SMUGLY EATING HIS VICTORY PRUNES.
YUM!
BUT HE MADE AN ENEMY OF DR. QUIGLEY, WHICH WOULD AFFECT MORE IMPORTANT EVENTS LATER.
DR. QUIGLEY! I HIGHLY RECOMMEND THE PRUNES TONIGHT!

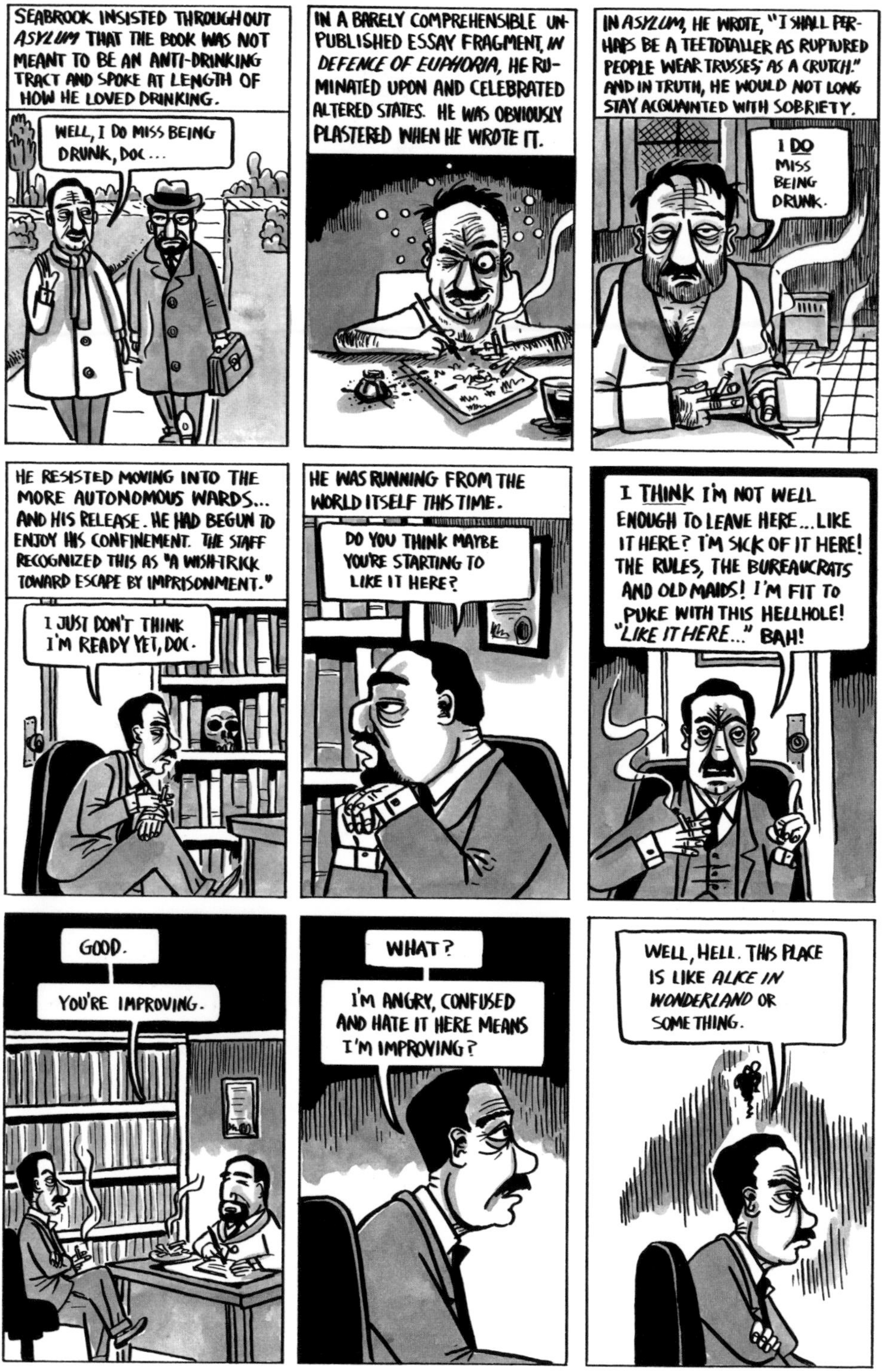
SEABROOK INSISTED THROUGHOUT ASYLUM THAT THE BOOK WAS NOT MEANT TO BE AN ANTI-DRINKING TRACT AND SPOKE AT LENGTH OF HOW HE LOVED DRINKING.
WELL, I DO MISS BEING DRUNK, DOC...
IN A BARELY COMPREHENSIBLE UNPUBLISHED ESSAY FRAGMENT, IN DEFENCE OF EUPHORIA, HE RUMINATED UPON AND CELEBRATED ALTERED STATES. HE WAS OBVIOUSLY PLASTERED WHEN HE WROTE IT.
IN ASYLUM, HE WROTE, "I SHALL PERHAPS BE A TEETOTALLER AS RUPTURED PEOPLE WEAR TRUSSES; AS A CRUTCH." AND IN TRUTH, HE WOULD NOT LONG STAY ACQUAINTED WITH SOBRIETY.
I DO MISS BEING DRUNK.
HE RESISTED MOVING INTO THE MORE AUTONOMOUS WARDS... AND HIS RELEASE. HE HAD BEGUN TO ENJOY HIS CONFINEMENT. THE STAFF RECOGNIZED THIS AS "A WISH-TRICK TOWARD ESCAPE BY IMPRISONMENT."
I JUST DON'T THINK I'M READY YET, DOC.
HE WAS RUNNING FROM THE WORLD ITSELF THIS TIME.
DO YOU THINK MAYBE YOU'RE STARTING TO LIKE IT HERE?
I THINK I'M NOT WELL ENOUGH TO LEAVE HERE... LIKE IT HERE? I'M SICK OF IT HERE! THE RULES, THE BUREAUCRATS AND OLD MAIDS! I'M FIT TO PUKE WITH THIS HELLHOLE! "LIKE IT HERE..." BAH!
GOOD.
YOU'RE IMPROVING.
WHAT?
I'M ANGRY, CONFUSED AND HATE IT HERE MEANS I'M IMPROVING?
WELL, HELL. THIS PLACE IS LIKE ALICE IN WONDERLAND OR SOMETHING.

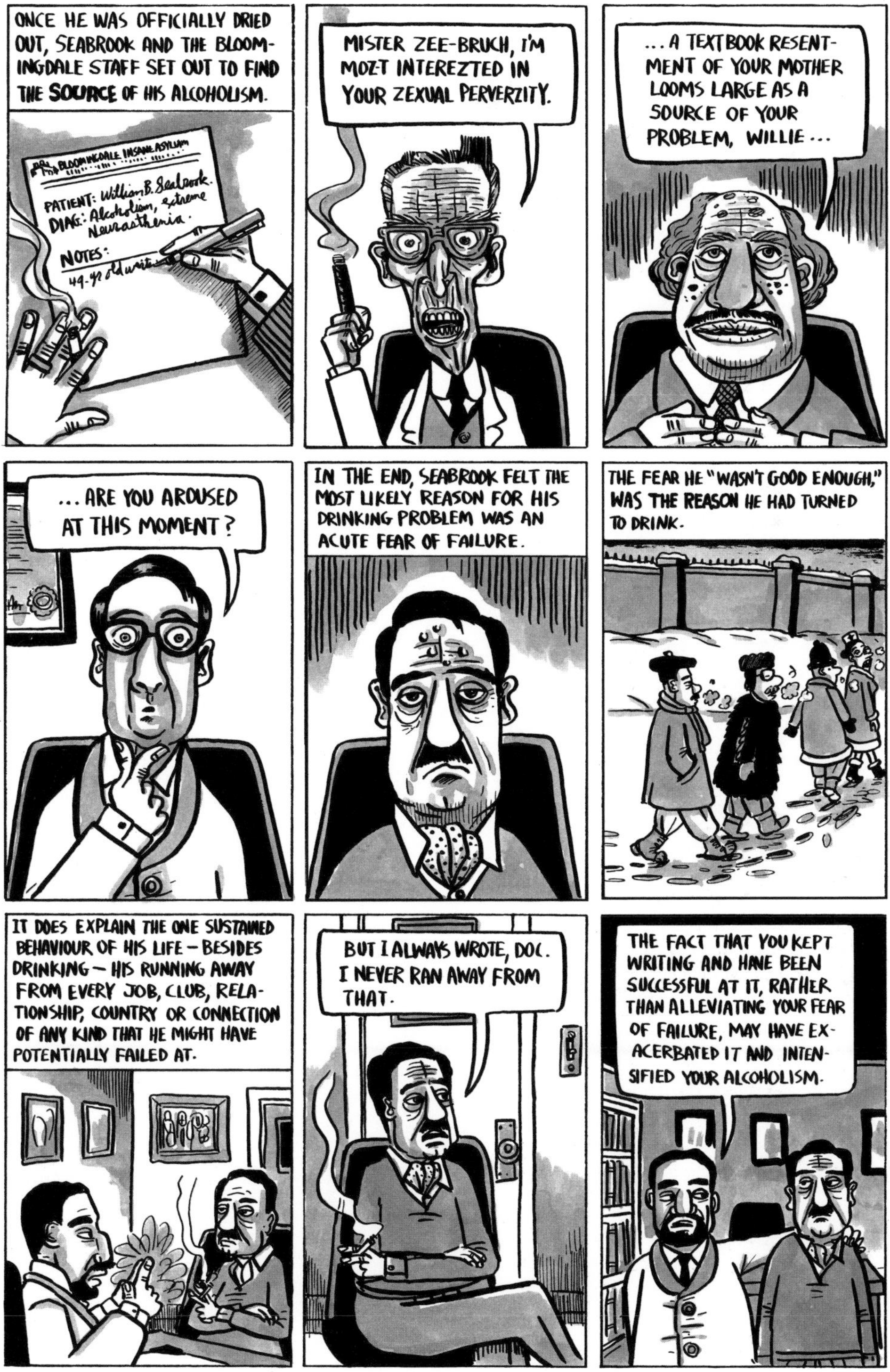
ONCE HE WAS OFFICIALLY DRIED OUT, SEABROOK AND THE BLOOMINGDALE STAFF SET OUT TO FIND THE SOURCE OF HIS ALCOHOLISM.
BLOOMINGDALE INSANE ASYLUM
PATIENT: William B. Seabrook.
DIAG: Alcoholism, extreme Neurasthenia.
NOTES:
MISTER ZEE-BRUCH, I'M MOZ-T INTEREZTED IN YOUR ZEXUAL PERVERZITY.
... A TEXTBOOK RESENTMENT OF YOUR MOTHER LOOMS LARGE AS A SOURCE OF YOUR PROBLEM, WILLIE ...
... ARE YOU AROUSED AT THIS MOMENT?
IN THE END, SEABROOK FELT THE MOST LIKELY REASON FOR HIS DRINKING PROBLEM WAS AN ACUTE FEAR OF FAILURE.
THE FEAR HE "WASN'T GOOD ENOUGH," WAS THE REASON HE HAD TURNED TO DRINK.
IT DOES EXPLAIN THE ONE SUSTAINED BEHAVIOUR OF HIS LIFE — BESIDES DRINKING — HIS RUNNING AWAY FROM EVERY JOB, CLUB, RELATIONSHIP, COUNTRY OR CONNECTION OF ANY KIND THAT HE MIGHT HAVE POTENTIALLY FAILED AT.
BUT I ALWAYS WROTE, DOC. I NEVER RAN AWAY FROM THAT.
THE FACT THAT YOU KEPT WRITING AND HAVE BEEN SUCCESSFUL AT IT, RATHER THAN ALLEVIATING YOUR FEAR OF FAILURE, MAY HAVE EXACERBATED IT AND INTENSIFIED YOUR ALCOHOLISM.

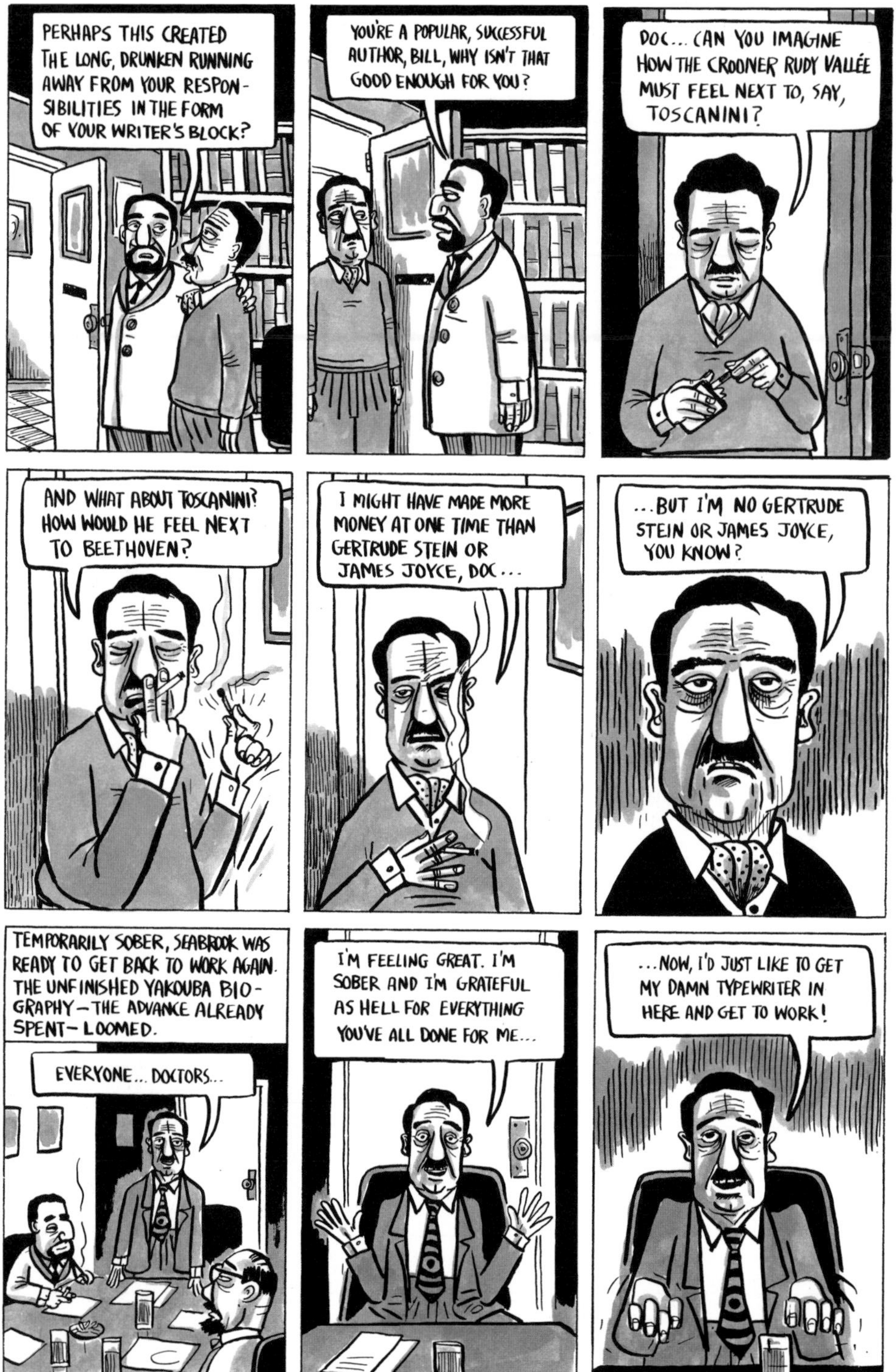
PERHAPS THIS CREATED THE LONG, DRUNKEN RUNNING AWAY FROM YOUR RESPONSIBILITIES IN THE FORM OF YOUR WRITER'S BLOCK?
YOU'RE A POPULAR, SUCCESSFUL AUTHOR, BILL, WHY ISN'T THAT GOOD ENOUGH FOR YOU?
DOC... CAN YOU IMAGINE HOW THE CROONER RUDY VALLÉE MUST FEEL NEXT TO, SAY, TOSCANINI?
AND WHAT ABOUT TOSCANINI? HOW WOULD HE FEEL NEXT TO BEETHOVEN?
I MIGHT HAVE MADE MORE MONEY AT ONE TIME THAN GERTRUDE STEIN OR JAMES JOYCE, DOC...
...BUT I'M NO GERTRUDE STEIN OR JAMES JOYCE, YOU KNOW?
TEMPORARILY SOBER, SEABROOK WAS READY TO GET BACK TO WORK AGAIN. THE UNFINISHED YAKOUBA BIOGRAPHY—THE ADVANCE ALREADY SPENT—LOOMED.
EVERYONE... DOCTORS...
I'M FEELING GREAT. I'M SOBER AND I'M GRATEFUL AS HELL FOR EVERYTHING YOU'VE ALL DONE FOR ME...
...NOW, I'D JUST LIKE TO GET MY DAMN TYPEWRITER IN HERE AND GET TO WORK!

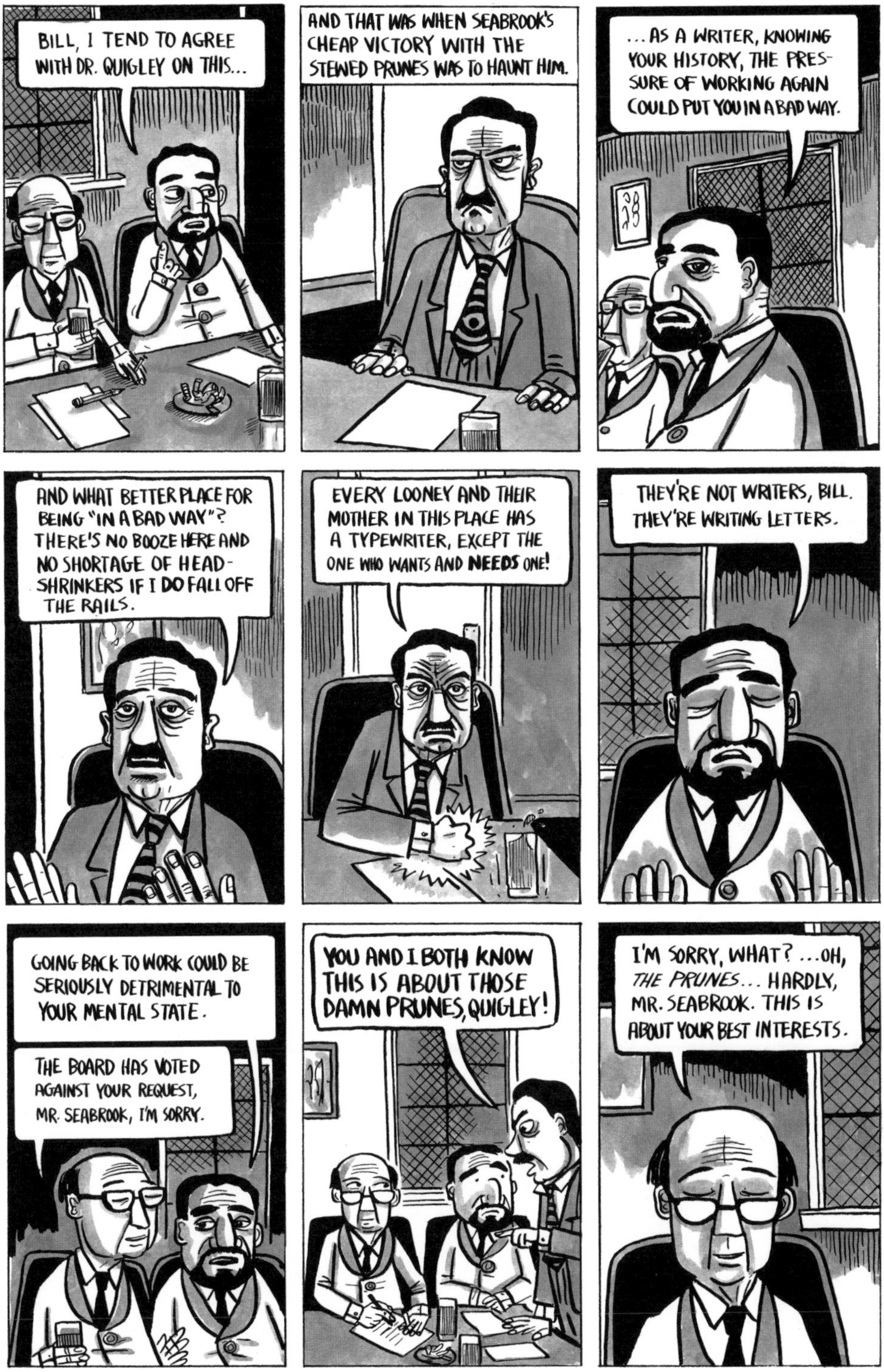
BILL, I TEND TO AGREE WITH DR. QUIGLEY ON THIS...
AND THAT WAS WHEN SEABROOK'S CHEAP VICTORY WITH THE STEWED PRUNES WAS TO HAUNT HIM.
...AS A WRITER, KNOWING YOUR HISTORY, THE PRES-SURE OF WORKING AGAIN COULD PUT YOU IN A BAD WAY.
AND WHAT BETTER PLACE FOR BEING "IN A BAD WAY"? THERE'S NO BOOZE HERE AND NO SHORTAGE OF HEAD-SHRINKERS IF I DO FALL OFF THE RAILS.
EVERY LOONEY AND THEIR MOTHER IN THIS PLACE HAS A TYPEWRITER, EXCEPT THE ONE WHO WANTS AND **NEEDS** ONE!
THEY'RE NOT WRITERS, BILL. THEY'RE WRITING LETTERS.
GOING BACK TO WORK COULD BE SERIOUSLY DETRIMENTAL TO YOUR MENTAL STATE.
THE BOARD HAS VOTED AGAINST YOUR REQUEST, MR. SEABROOK, I'M SORRY.
YOU AND I BOTH KNOW THIS IS ABOUT THOSE DAMN PRUNES, QUIGLEY!
I'M SORRY, WHAT? ...OH, *THE PRUNES*... HARDLY, MR. SEABROOK. THIS IS ABOUT YOUR BEST INTERESTS.

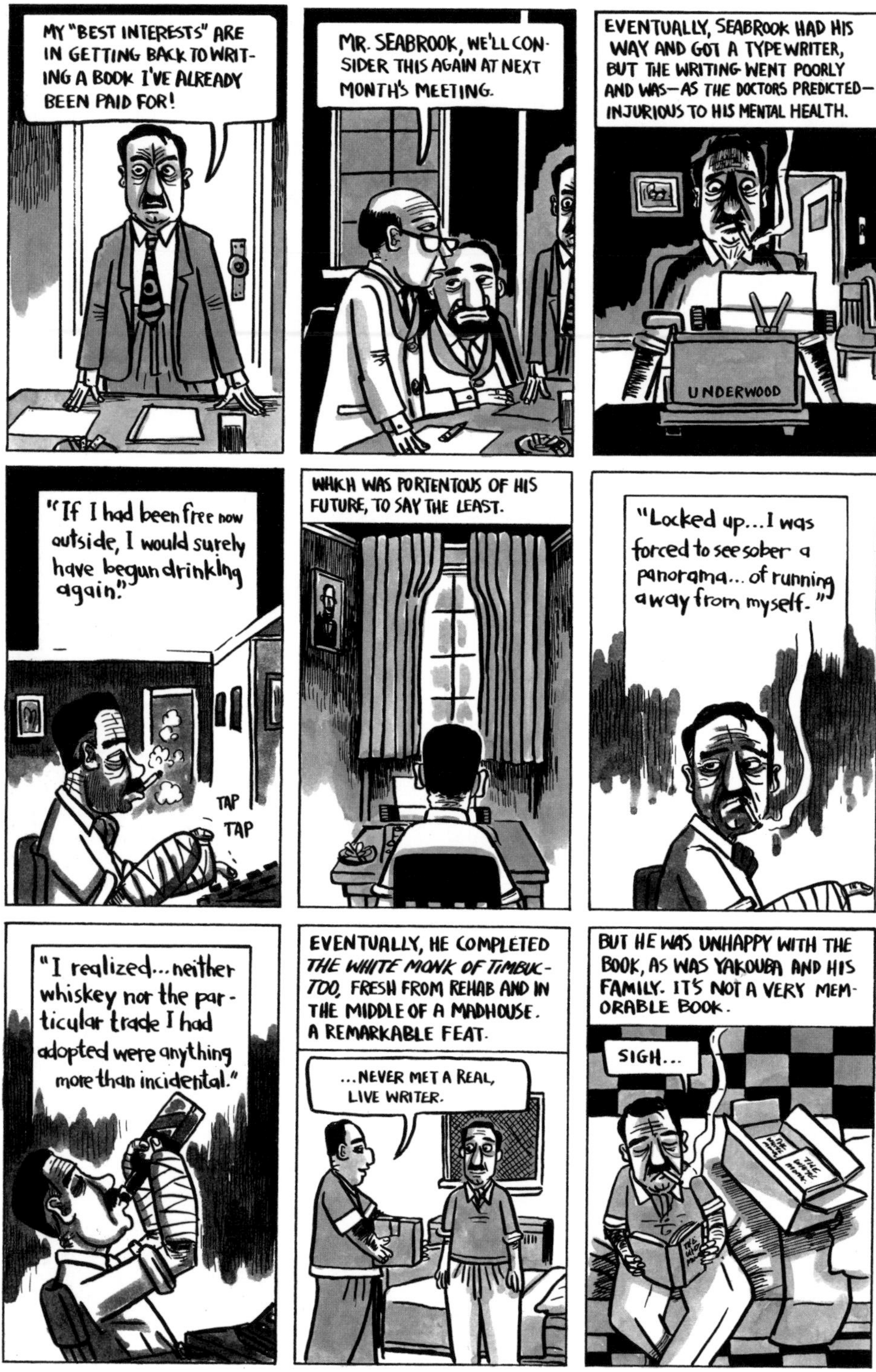
MY "BEST INTERESTS" ARE IN GETTING BACK TO WRITING A BOOK I'VE ALREADY BEEN PAID FOR!
MR. SEABROOK, WE'LL CONSIDER THIS AGAIN AT NEXT MONTH'S MEETING.
EVENTUALLY, SEABROOK HAD HIS WAY AND GOT A TYPEWRITER, BUT THE WRITING WENT POORLY AND WAS—AS THE DOCTORS PREDICTED—INJURIOUS TO HIS MENTAL HEALTH.
UNDERWOOD
"If I had been free now outside, I would surely have begun drinking again."
TAP
TAP
WHICH WAS PORTENTOUS OF HIS FUTURE, TO SAY THE LEAST.
"Locked up... I was forced to see sober a panorama... of running away from myself."
"I realized... neither whiskey nor the particular trade I had adopted were anything more than incidental."
EVENTUALLY, HE COMPLETED *THE WHITE MONK OF TIMBUCTOO*, FRESH FROM REHAB AND IN THE MIDDLE OF A MADHOUSE. A REMARKABLE FEAT.
...NEVER MET A REAL, LIVE WRITER.
BUT HE WAS UNHAPPY WITH THE BOOK, AS WAS YAKOUBA AND HIS FAMILY. IT'S NOT A VERY MEMORABLE BOOK.
SIGH...

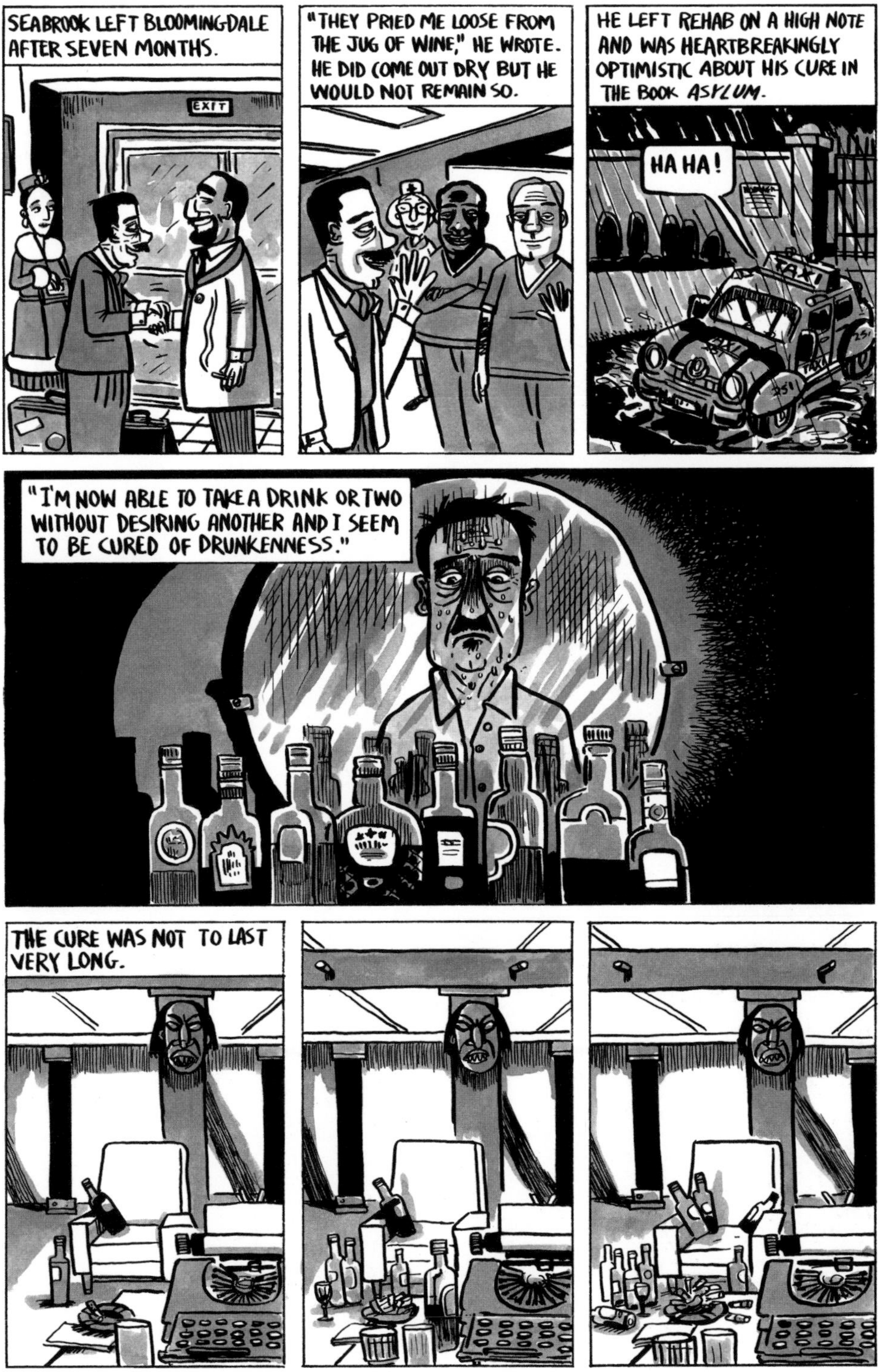
SEABROOK LEFT BLOOMINGDALE AFTER SEVEN MONTHS.
EXIT
"THEY PRIED ME LOOSE FROM THE JUG OF WINE," HE WROTE. HE DID COME OUT DRY BUT HE WOULD NOT REMAIN SO.
HE LEFT REHAB ON A HIGH NOTE AND WAS HEARTBREAKINGLY OPTIMISTIC ABOUT HIS CURE IN THE BOOK *ASYLUM*.
HA HA!
TAXI
"I'M NOW ABLE TO TAKE A DRINK OR TWO WITHOUT DESIRING ANOTHER AND I SEEM TO BE CURED OF DRUNKENNESS."
THE CURE WAS NOT TO LAST VERY LONG.

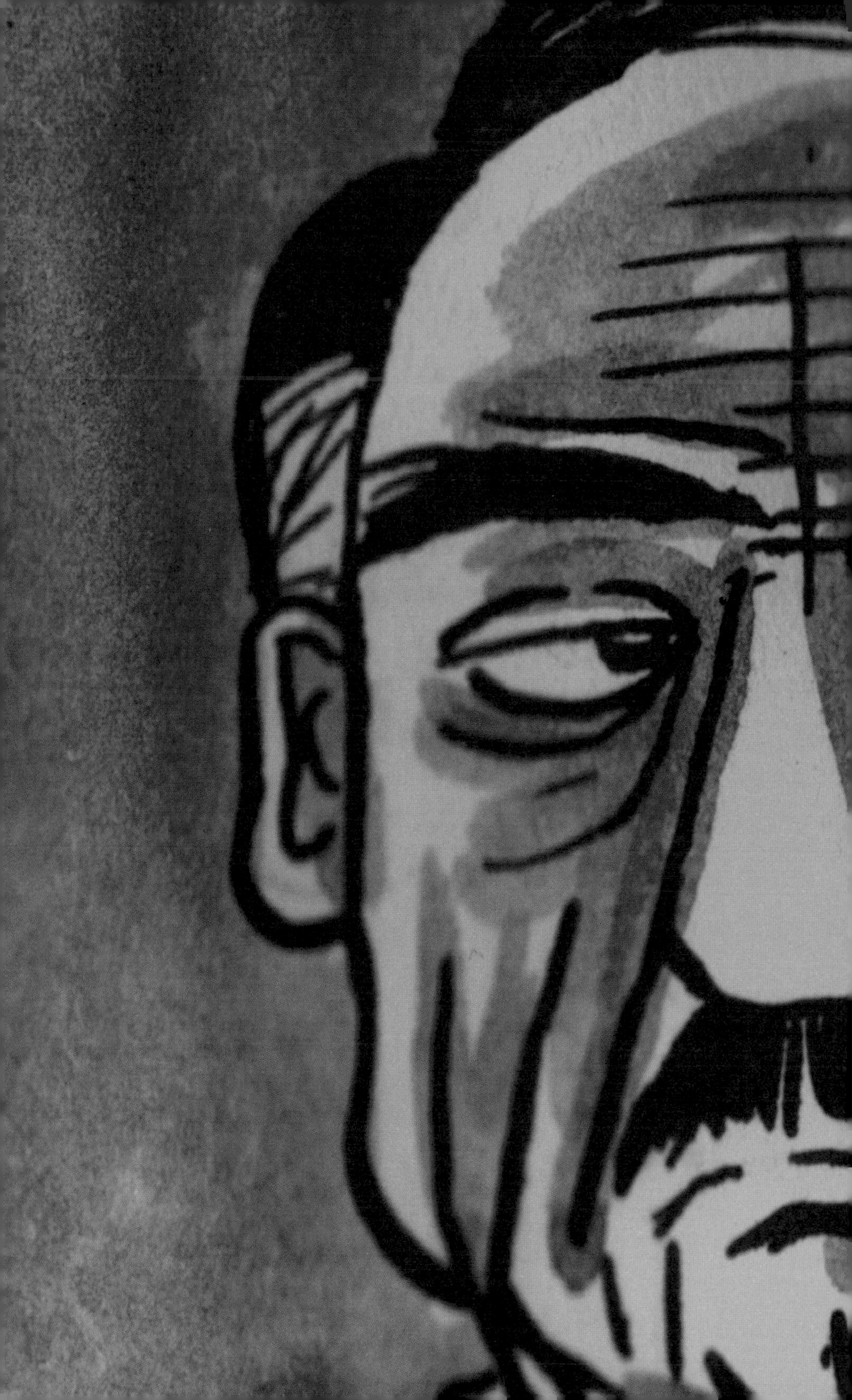

# CHAPTER SEVEN
# RHINEBECK IN CHAINS

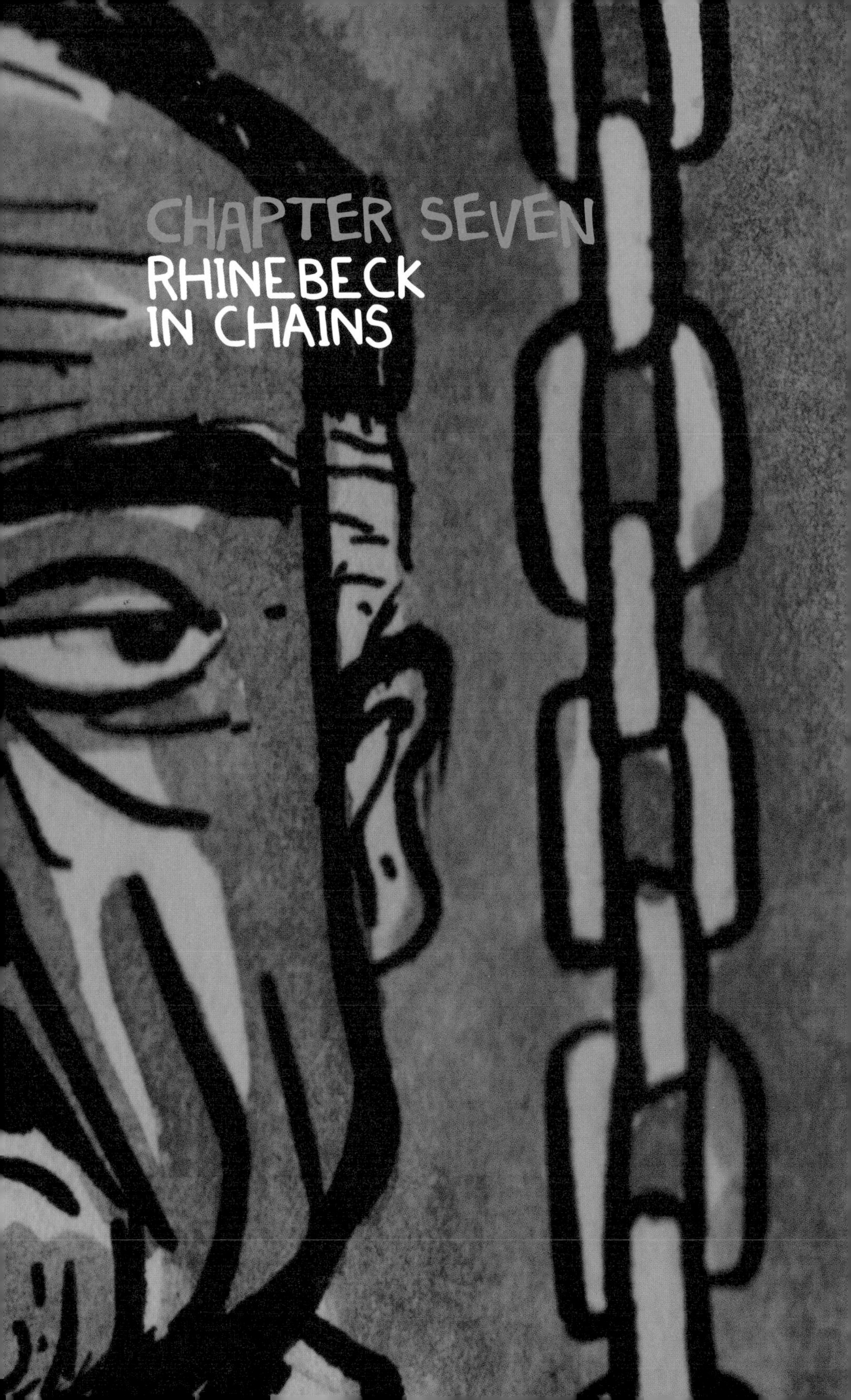

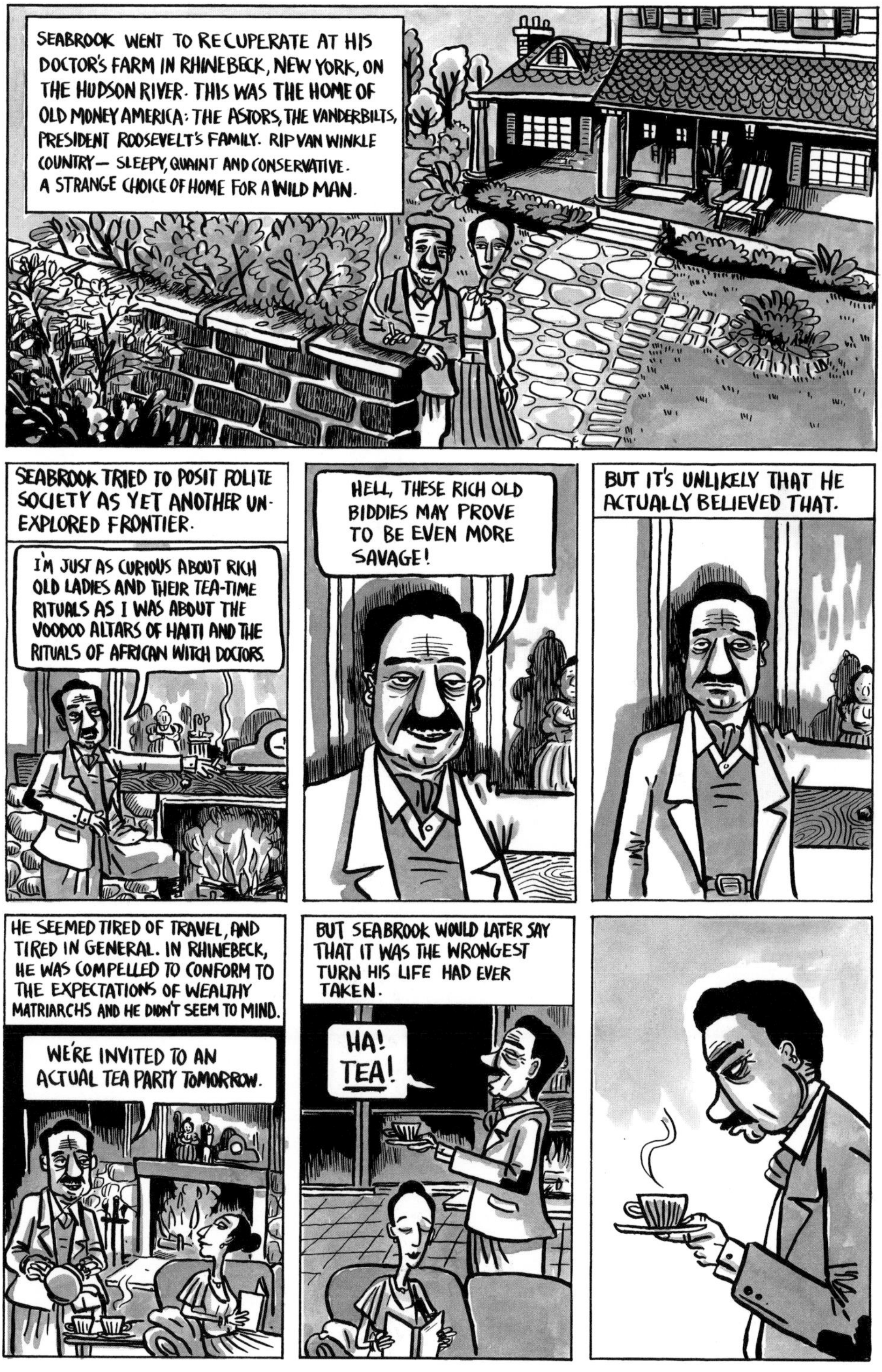
SEABROOK WENT TO RECUPERATE AT HIS DOCTOR'S FARM IN RHINEBECK, NEW YORK, ON THE HUDSON RIVER. THIS WAS THE HOME OF OLD MONEY AMERICA: THE ASTORS, THE VANDERBILTS, PRESIDENT ROOSEVELT'S FAMILY. RIP VAN WINKLE COUNTRY— SLEEPY, QUAINT AND CONSERVATIVE. A STRANGE CHOICE OF HOME FOR A WILD MAN.
SEABROOK TRIED TO POSIT POLITE SOCIETY AS YET ANOTHER UNEXPLORED FRONTIER.
I'M JUST AS CURIOUS ABOUT RICH OLD LADIES AND THEIR TEA-TIME RITUALS AS I WAS ABOUT THE VOODOO ALTARS OF HAITI AND THE RITUALS OF AFRICAN WITCH DOCTORS.
HELL, THESE RICH OLD BIDDIES MAY PROVE TO BE EVEN MORE SAVAGE!
BUT IT'S UNLIKELY THAT HE ACTUALLY BELIEVED THAT.
HE SEEMED TIRED OF TRAVEL, AND TIRED IN GENERAL. IN RHINEBECK, HE WAS COMPELLED TO CONFORM TO THE EXPECTATIONS OF WEALTHY MATRIARCHS AND HE DIDN'T SEEM TO MIND.
WE'RE INVITED TO AN ACTUAL TEA PARTY TOMORROW.
BUT SEABROOK WOULD LATER SAY THAT IT WAS THE WRONGEST TURN HIS LIFE HAD EVER TAKEN.
HA! TEA!

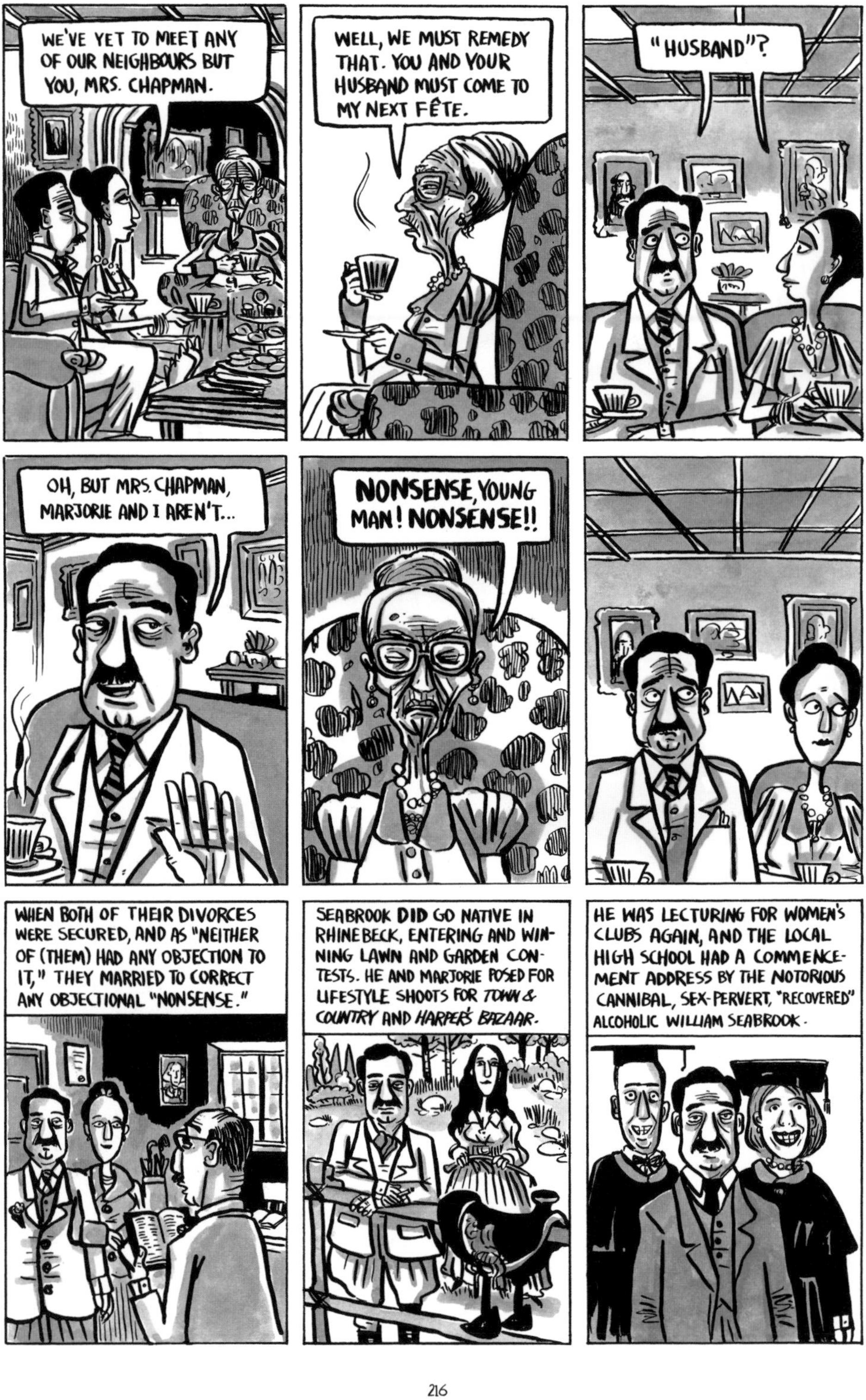
WE'VE YET TO MEET ANY OF OUR NEIGHBOURS BUT YOU, MRS. CHAPMAN.
WELL, WE MUST REMEDY THAT. YOU AND YOUR HUSBAND MUST COME TO MY NEXT FÊTE.
"HUSBAND"?
OH, BUT MRS. CHAPMAN, MARJORIE AND I AREN'T...
NONSENSE, YOUNG MAN! NONSENSE!!
WHEN BOTH OF THEIR DIVORCES WERE SECURED, AND AS "NEITHER OF (THEM) HAD ANY OBJECTION TO IT," THEY MARRIED TO CORRECT ANY OBJECTIONAL "NONSENSE."
SEABROOK DID GO NATIVE IN RHINEBECK, ENTERING AND WINNING LAWN AND GARDEN CONTESTS. HE AND MARJORIE POSED FOR LIFESTYLE SHOOTS FOR TOWN & COUNTRY AND HARPER'S BAZAAR.
HE WAS LECTURING FOR WOMEN'S CLUBS AGAIN, AND THE LOCAL HIGH SCHOOL HAD A COMMENCEMENT ADDRESS BY THE NOTORIOUS CANNIBAL, SEX-PERVERT, "RECOVERED" ALCOHOLIC WILLIAM SEABROOK.

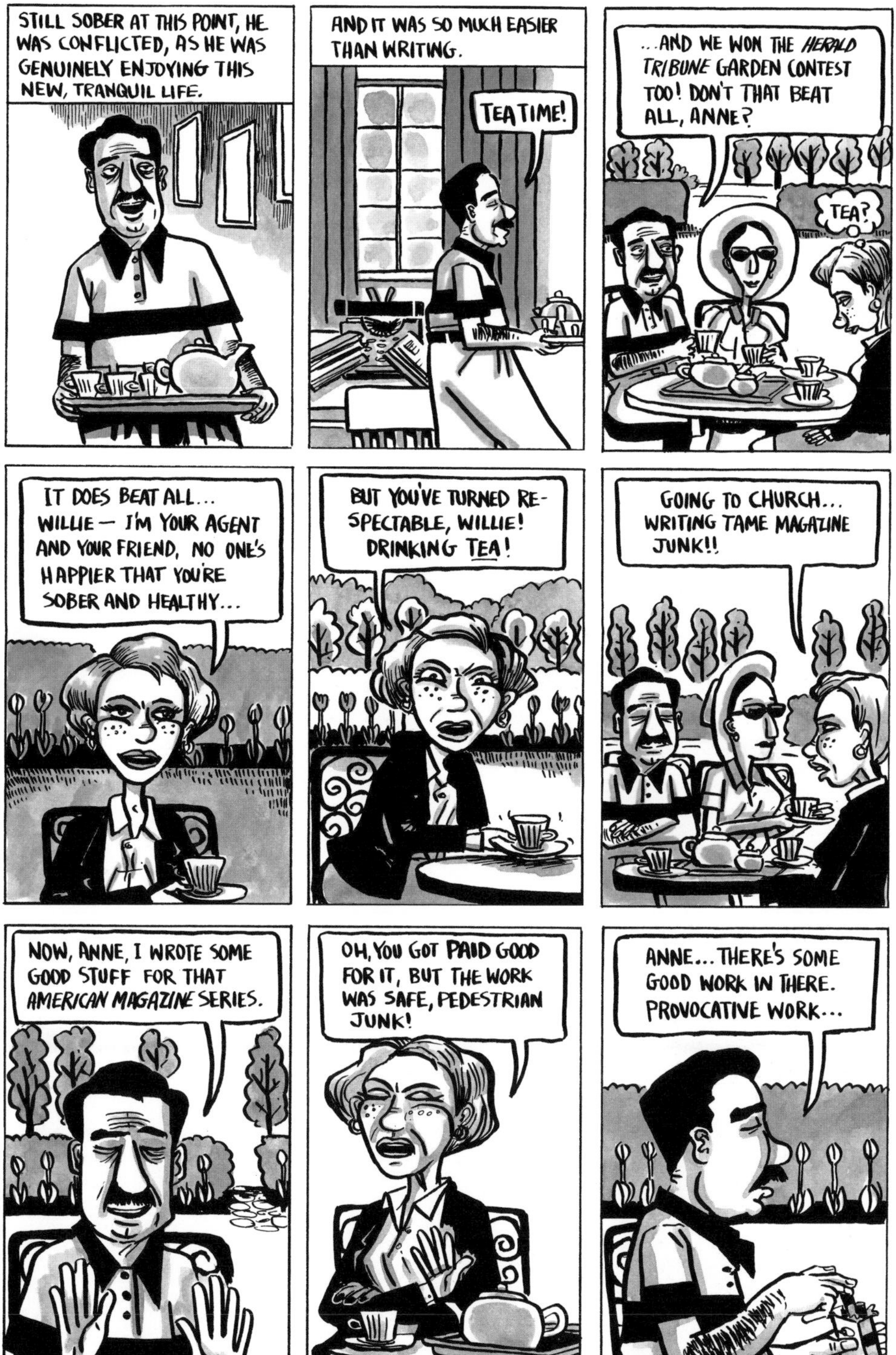
STILL SOBER AT THIS POINT, HE WAS CONFLICTED, AS HE WAS GENUINELY ENJOYING THIS NEW, TRANQUIL LIFE.
AND IT WAS SO MUCH EASIER THAN WRITING.
TEA TIME!
...AND WE WON THE HERALD TRIBUNE GARDEN CONTEST TOO! DON'T THAT BEAT ALL, ANNE?
TEA?
IT DOES BEAT ALL... WILLIE — I'M YOUR AGENT AND YOUR FRIEND, NO ONE'S HAPPIER THAT YOU'RE SOBER AND HEALTHY...
BUT YOU'VE TURNED RE-SPECTABLE, WILLIE! DRINKING TEA!
GOING TO CHURCH... WRITING TAME MAGAZINE JUNK!!
NOW, ANNE, I WROTE SOME GOOD STUFF FOR THAT AMERICAN MAGAZINE SERIES.
OH, YOU GOT PAID GOOD FOR IT, BUT THE WORK WAS SAFE, PEDESTRIAN JUNK!
ANNE... THERE'S SOME GOOD WORK IN THERE. PROVOCATIVE WORK...

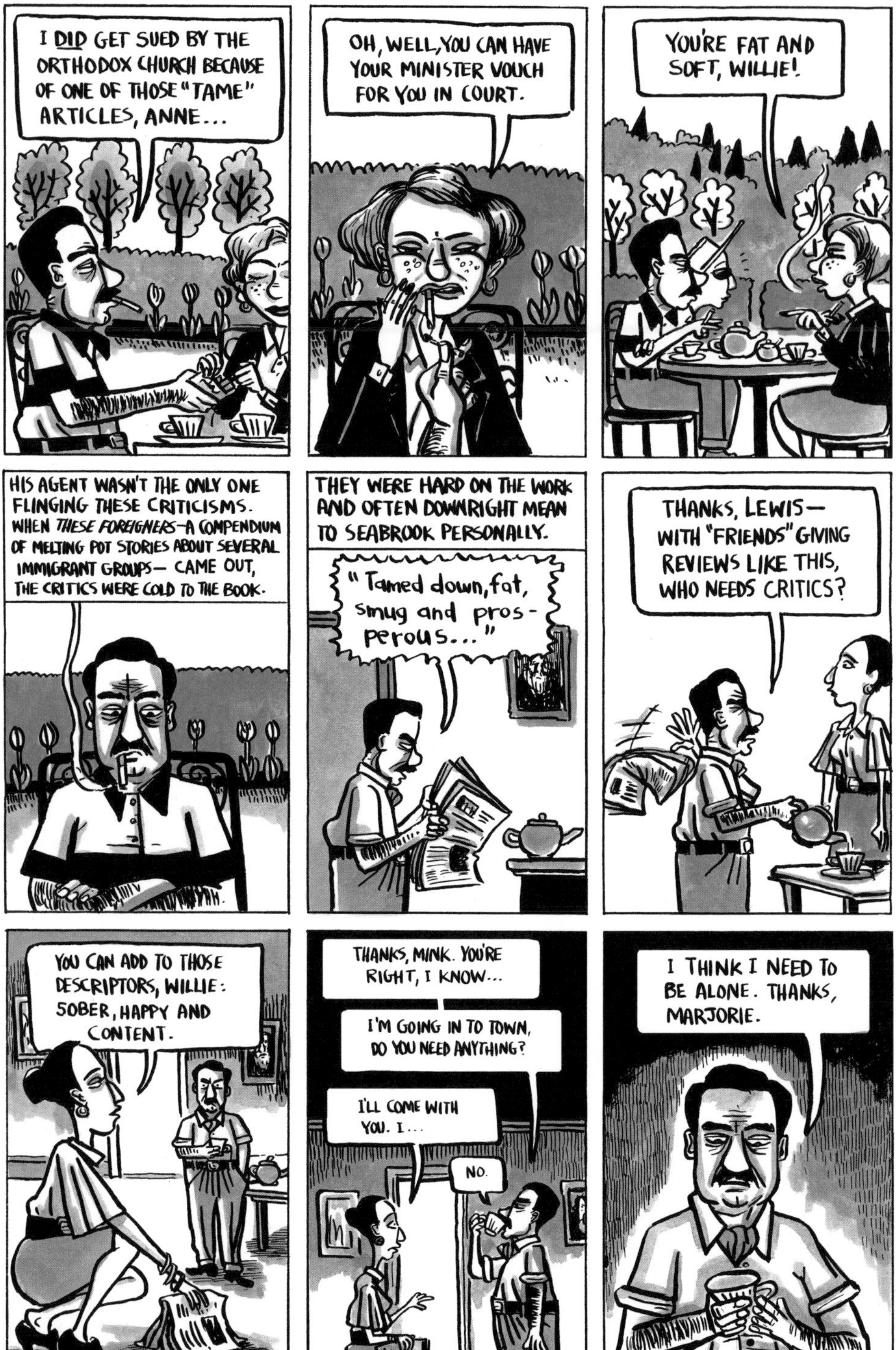
I DID GET SUED BY THE ORTHODOX CHURCH BECAUSE OF ONE OF THOSE "TAME" ARTICLES, ANNE...
OH, WELL, YOU CAN HAVE YOUR MINISTER VOUCH FOR YOU IN COURT.
YOU'RE FAT AND SOFT, WILLIE!
HIS AGENT WASN'T THE ONLY ONE FLINGING THESE CRITICISMS. WHEN *THESE FOREIGNERS*—A COMPENDIUM OF MELTING POT STORIES ABOUT SEVERAL IMMIGRANT GROUPS— CAME OUT, THE CRITICS WERE COLD TO THE BOOK.
THEY WERE HARD ON THE WORK AND OFTEN DOWNRIGHT MEAN TO SEABROOK PERSONALLY.
"Tamed down, fat, smug and pros-perous..."
THANKS, LEWIS— WITH "FRIENDS" GIVING REVIEWS LIKE THIS, WHO NEEDS CRITICS?
YOU CAN ADD TO THOSE DESCRIPTORS, WILLIE: SOBER, HAPPY AND CONTENT.
THANKS, MINK. YOU'RE RIGHT, I KNOW...
I'M GOING IN TO TOWN, DO YOU NEED ANYTHING?
I'LL COME WITH YOU. I...
NO.
I THINK I NEED TO BE ALONE. THANKS, MARJORIE.

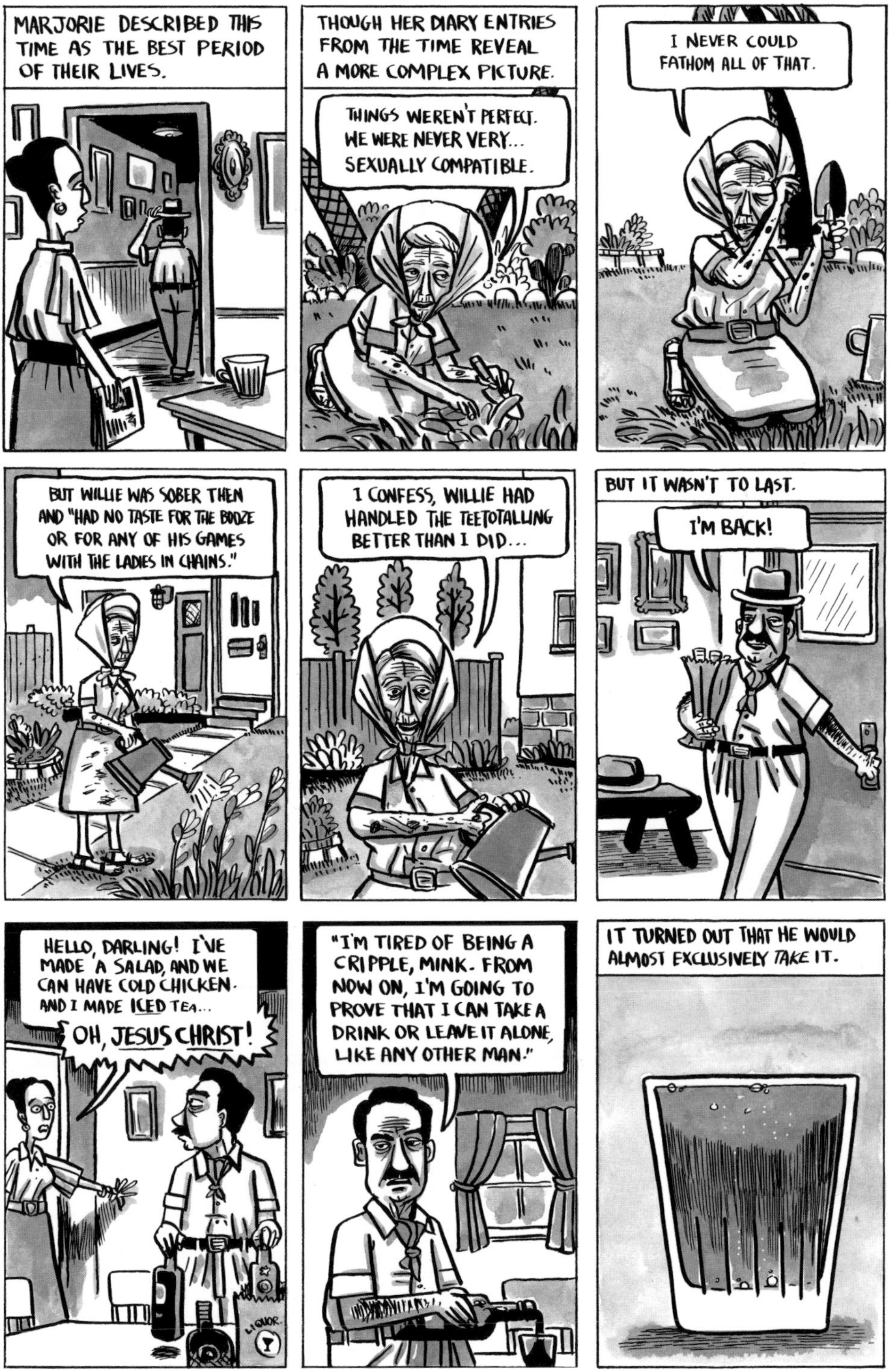
MARJORIE DESCRIBED THIS TIME AS THE BEST PERIOD OF THEIR LIVES.
THOUGH HER DIARY ENTRIES FROM THE TIME REVEAL A MORE COMPLEX PICTURE.
THINGS WEREN'T PERFECT. WE WERE NEVER VERY... SEXUALLY COMPATIBLE.
I NEVER COULD FATHOM ALL OF THAT.
BUT WILLIE WAS SOBER THEN AND "HAD NO TASTE FOR THE BOOZE OR FOR ANY OF HIS GAMES WITH THE LADIES IN CHAINS."
I CONFESS, WILLIE HAD HANDLED THE TEETOTALLING BETTER THAN I DID...
BUT IT WASN'T TO LAST.
I'M BACK!
HELLO, DARLING! I'VE MADE A SALAD, AND WE CAN HAVE COLD CHICKEN. AND I MADE ICED TEA...
OH, JESUS CHRIST!
LIQUOR
"I'M TIRED OF BEING A CRIPPLE, MINK. FROM NOW ON, I'M GOING TO PROVE THAT I CAN TAKE A DRINK OR LEAVE IT ALONE, LIKE ANY OTHER MAN."
IT TURNED OUT THAT HE WOULD ALMOST EXCLUSIVELY *TAKE* IT.

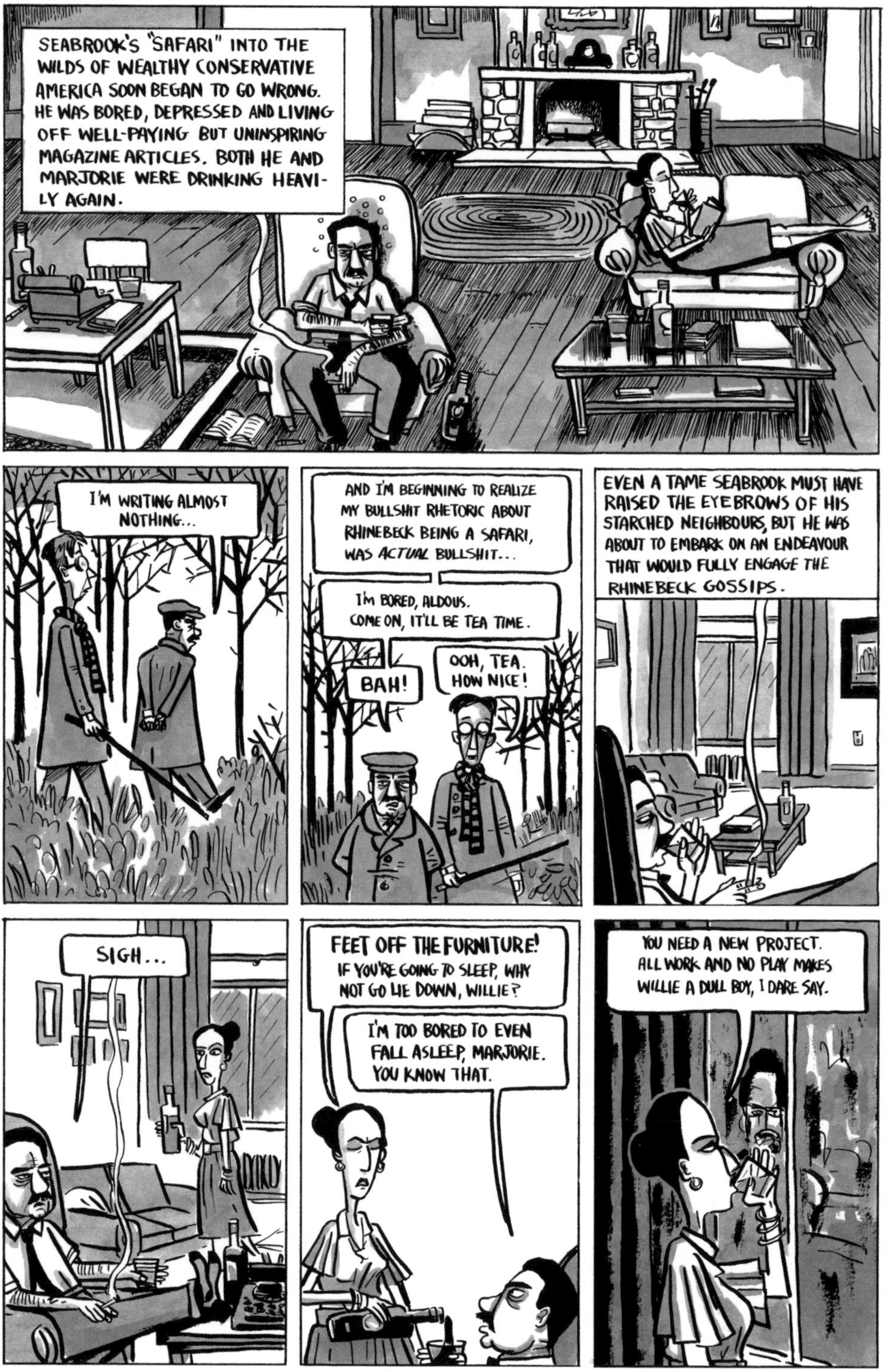
SEABROOK'S "SAFARI" INTO THE WILDS OF WEALTHY CONSERVATIVE AMERICA SOON BEGAN TO GO WRONG. HE WAS BORED, DEPRESSED AND LIVING OFF WELL-PAYING BUT UNINSPIRING MAGAZINE ARTICLES. BOTH HE AND MARJORIE WERE DRINKING HEAVILY AGAIN.
I'M WRITING ALMOST NOTHING...
AND I'M BEGINNING TO REALIZE MY BULLSHIT RHETORIC ABOUT RHINEBECK BEING A SAFARI, WAS *ACTUAL* BULLSHIT...
I'M BORED, ALDOUS. COME ON, IT'LL BE TEA TIME.
BAH!
OOH, TEA. HOW NICE!
EVEN A TAME SEABROOK MUST HAVE RAISED THE EYEBROWS OF HIS STARCHED NEIGHBOURS, BUT HE WAS ABOUT TO EMBARK ON AN ENDEAVOUR THAT WOULD FULLY ENGAGE THE RHINEBECK GOSSIPS.
SIGH...
FEET OFF THE FURNITURE! IF YOU'RE GOING TO SLEEP, WHY NOT GO LIE DOWN, WILLIE?
I'M TOO BORED TO EVEN FALL ASLEEP, MARJORIE. YOU KNOW THAT.
YOU NEED A NEW PROJECT. ALL WORK AND NO PLAY MAKES WILLIE A DULL BOY, I DARE SAY.

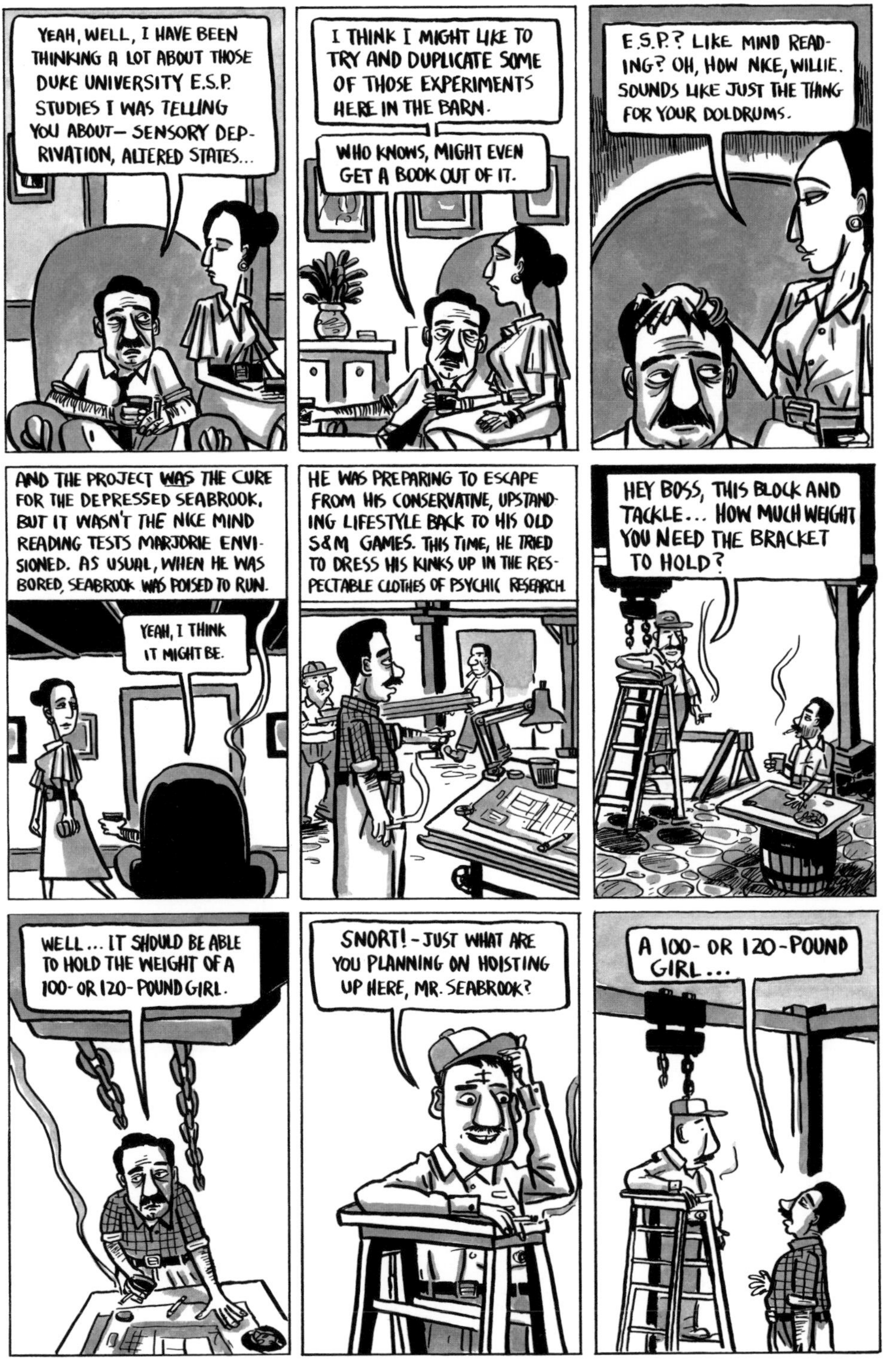
YEAH, WELL, I HAVE BEEN THINKING A LOT ABOUT THOSE DUKE UNIVERSITY E.S.P. STUDIES I WAS TELLING YOU ABOUT— SENSORY DEPRIVATION, ALTERED STATES...
I THINK I MIGHT LIKE TO TRY AND DUPLICATE SOME OF THOSE EXPERIMENTS HERE IN THE BARN.
WHO KNOWS, MIGHT EVEN GET A BOOK OUT OF IT.
E.S.P.? LIKE MIND READING? OH, HOW NICE, WILLIE. SOUNDS LIKE JUST THE THING FOR YOUR DOLDRUMS.
AND THE PROJECT WAS THE CURE FOR THE DEPRESSED SEABROOK, BUT IT WASN'T THE NICE MIND READING TESTS MARJORIE ENVISIONED. AS USUAL, WHEN HE WAS BORED, SEABROOK WAS POISED TO RUN.
YEAH, I THINK IT MIGHT BE.
HE WAS PREPARING TO ESCAPE FROM HIS CONSERVATIVE, UPSTANDING LIFESTYLE BACK TO HIS OLD S&M GAMES. THIS TIME, HE TRIED TO DRESS HIS KINKS UP IN THE RESPECTABLE CLOTHES OF PSYCHIC RESEARCH.
HEY BOSS, THIS BLOCK AND TACKLE... HOW MUCH WEIGHT YOU NEED THE BRACKET TO HOLD?
WELL... IT SHOULD BE ABLE TO HOLD THE WEIGHT OF A 100- OR 120-POUND GIRL.
SNORT! - JUST WHAT ARE YOU PLANNING ON HOISTING UP HERE, MR. SEABROOK?
A 100- OR 120-POUND GIRL...

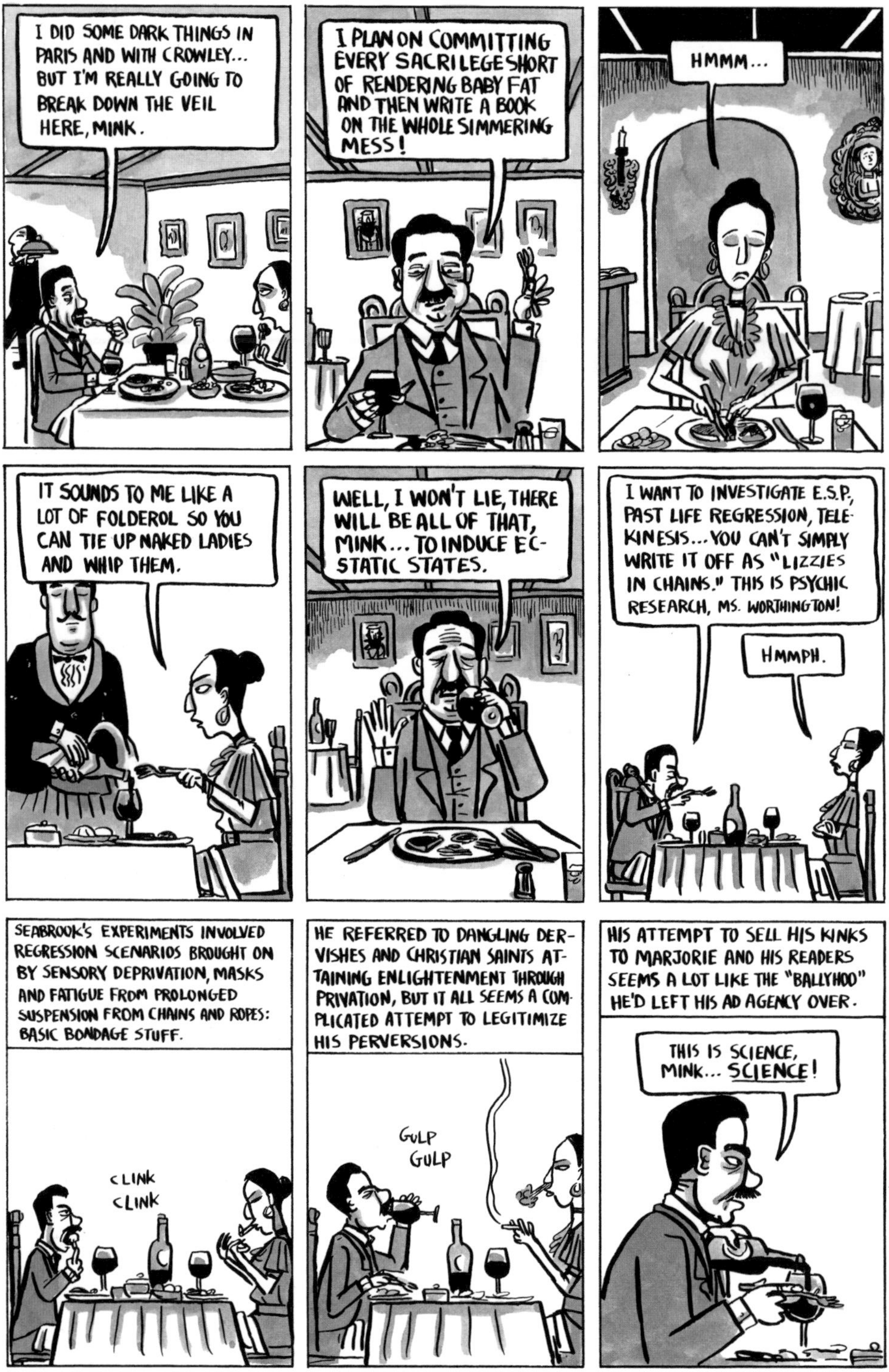
I DID SOME DARK THINGS IN PARIS AND WITH CROWLEY... BUT I'M REALLY GOING TO BREAK DOWN THE VEIL HERE, MINK.
I PLAN ON COMMITTING EVERY SACRILEGE SHORT OF RENDERING BABY FAT AND THEN WRITE A BOOK ON THE WHOLE SIMMERING MESS!
HMMM...
IT SOUNDS TO ME LIKE A LOT OF FOLDEROL SO YOU CAN TIE UP NAKED LADIES AND WHIP THEM.
WELL, I WON'T LIE, THERE WILL BE ALL OF THAT, MINK... TO INDUCE EC-STATIC STATES.
I WANT TO INVESTIGATE E.S.P., PAST LIFE REGRESSION, TELE-KINESIS... YOU CAN'T SIMPLY WRITE IT OFF AS "LIZZIES IN CHAINS." THIS IS PSYCHIC RESEARCH, MS. WORTHINGTON!
HMMPH.
SEABROOK'S EXPERIMENTS INVOLVED REGRESSION SCENARIOS BROUGHT ON BY SENSORY DEPRIVATION, MASKS AND FATIGUE FROM PROLONGED SUSPENSION FROM CHAINS AND ROPES: BASIC BONDAGE STUFF.
CLINK
CLINK
HE REFERRED TO DANGLING DER-VISHES AND CHRISTIAN SAINTS AT-TAINING ENLIGHTENMENT THROUGH PRIVATION, BUT IT ALL SEEMS A COM-PLICATED ATTEMPT TO LEGITIMIZE HIS PERVERSIONS.
GULP
GULP
HIS ATTEMPT TO SELL HIS KINKS TO MARJORIE AND HIS READERS SEEMS A LOT LIKE THE "BALLYHOO" HE'D LEFT HIS AD AGENCY OVER.
THIS IS SCIENCE, MINK... SCIENCE!

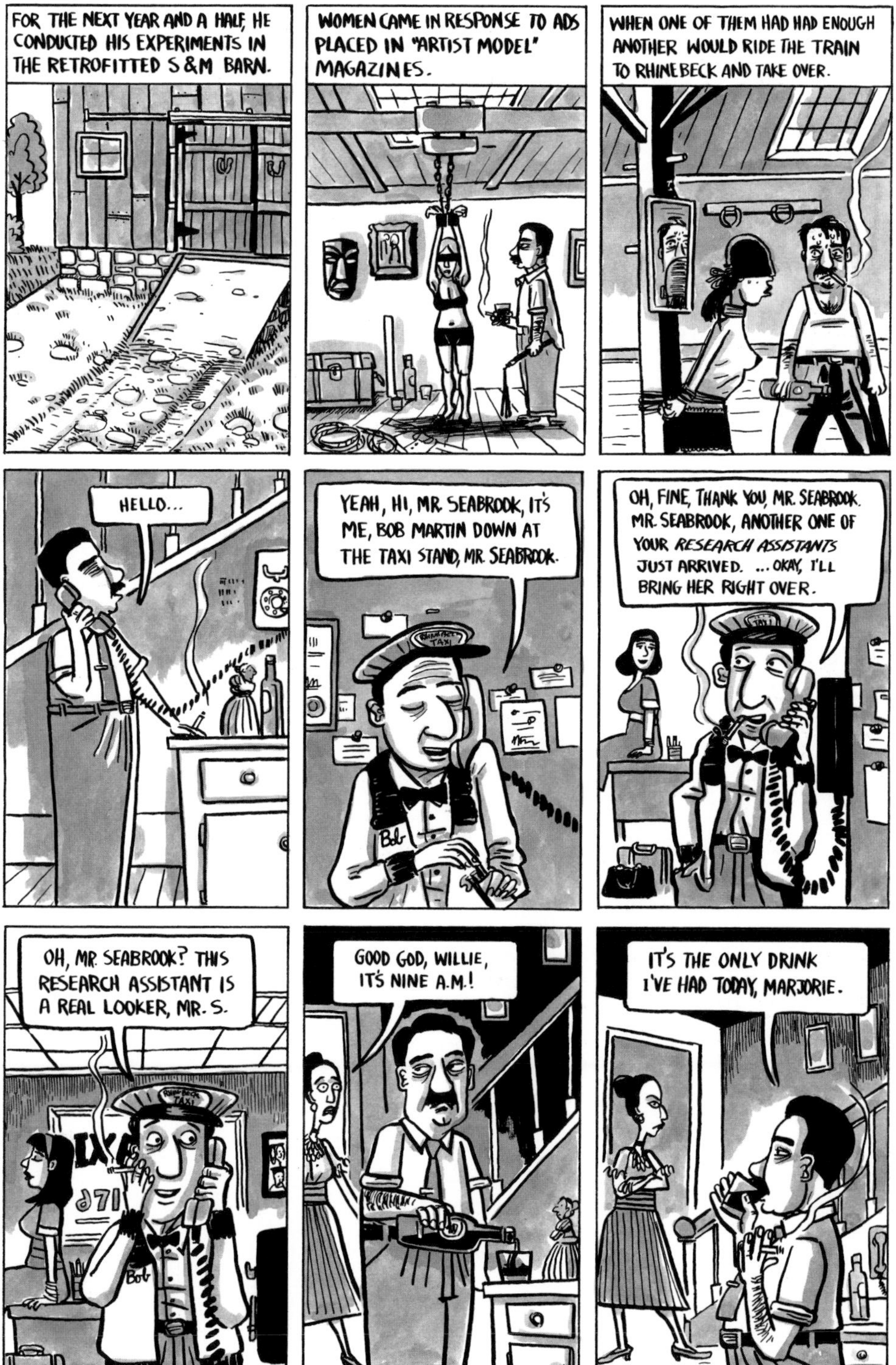
FOR THE NEXT YEAR AND A HALF, HE CONDUCTED HIS EXPERIMENTS IN THE RETROFITTED S&M BARN.
WOMEN CAME IN RESPONSE TO ADS PLACED IN "ARTIST MODEL" MAGAZINES.
WHEN ONE OF THEM HAD HAD ENOUGH ANOTHER WOULD RIDE THE TRAIN TO RHINEBECK AND TAKE OVER.
HELLO...
YEAH, HI, MR. SEABROOK, IT'S ME, BOB MARTIN DOWN AT THE TAXI STAND, MR. SEABROOK.
OH, FINE, THANK YOU, MR. SEABROOK. MR. SEABROOK, ANOTHER ONE OF YOUR *RESEARCH ASSISTANTS* JUST ARRIVED. ...OKAY, I'LL BRING HER RIGHT OVER.
OH, MR. SEABROOK? THIS RESEARCH ASSISTANT IS A REAL LOOKER, MR. S.
GOOD GOD, WILLIE, IT'S NINE A.M.!
IT'S THE ONLY DRINK I'VE HAD TODAY, MARJORIE.

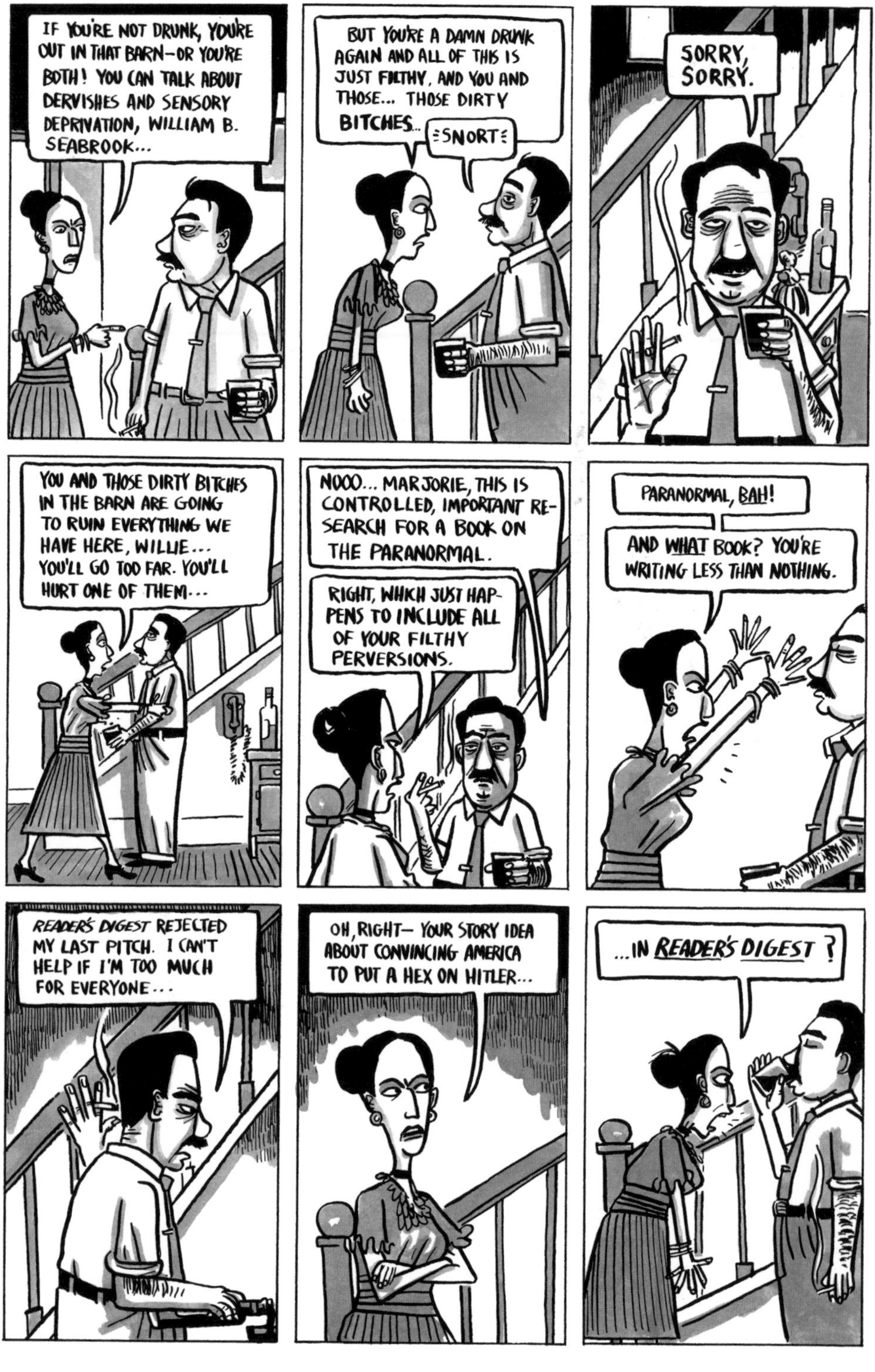
IF YOU'RE NOT DRUNK, YOU'RE OUT IN THAT BARN—OR YOU'RE BOTH! YOU CAN TALK ABOUT DERVISHES AND SENSORY DEPRIVATION, WILLIAM B. SEABROOK...
BUT YOU'RE A DAMN DRUNK AGAIN AND ALL OF THIS IS JUST FILTHY, AND YOU AND THOSE... THOSE DIRTY BITCHES...
SNORT
SORRY, SORRY.
YOU AND THOSE DIRTY BITCHES IN THE BARN ARE GOING TO RUIN EVERYTHING WE HAVE HERE, WILLIE... YOU'LL GO TOO FAR. YOU'LL HURT ONE OF THEM...
NOOO... MARJORIE, THIS IS CONTROLLED, IMPORTANT RESEARCH FOR A BOOK ON THE PARANORMAL.
RIGHT, WHICH JUST HAPPENS TO INCLUDE ALL OF YOUR FILTHY PERVERSIONS.
PARANORMAL, BAH!
AND WHAT BOOK? YOU'RE WRITING LESS THAN NOTHING.
READER'S DIGEST REJECTED MY LAST PITCH. I CAN'T HELP IF I'M TOO MUCH FOR EVERYONE...
OH, RIGHT— YOUR STORY IDEA ABOUT CONVINCING AMERICA TO PUT A HEX ON HITLER...
...IN READER'S DIGEST?

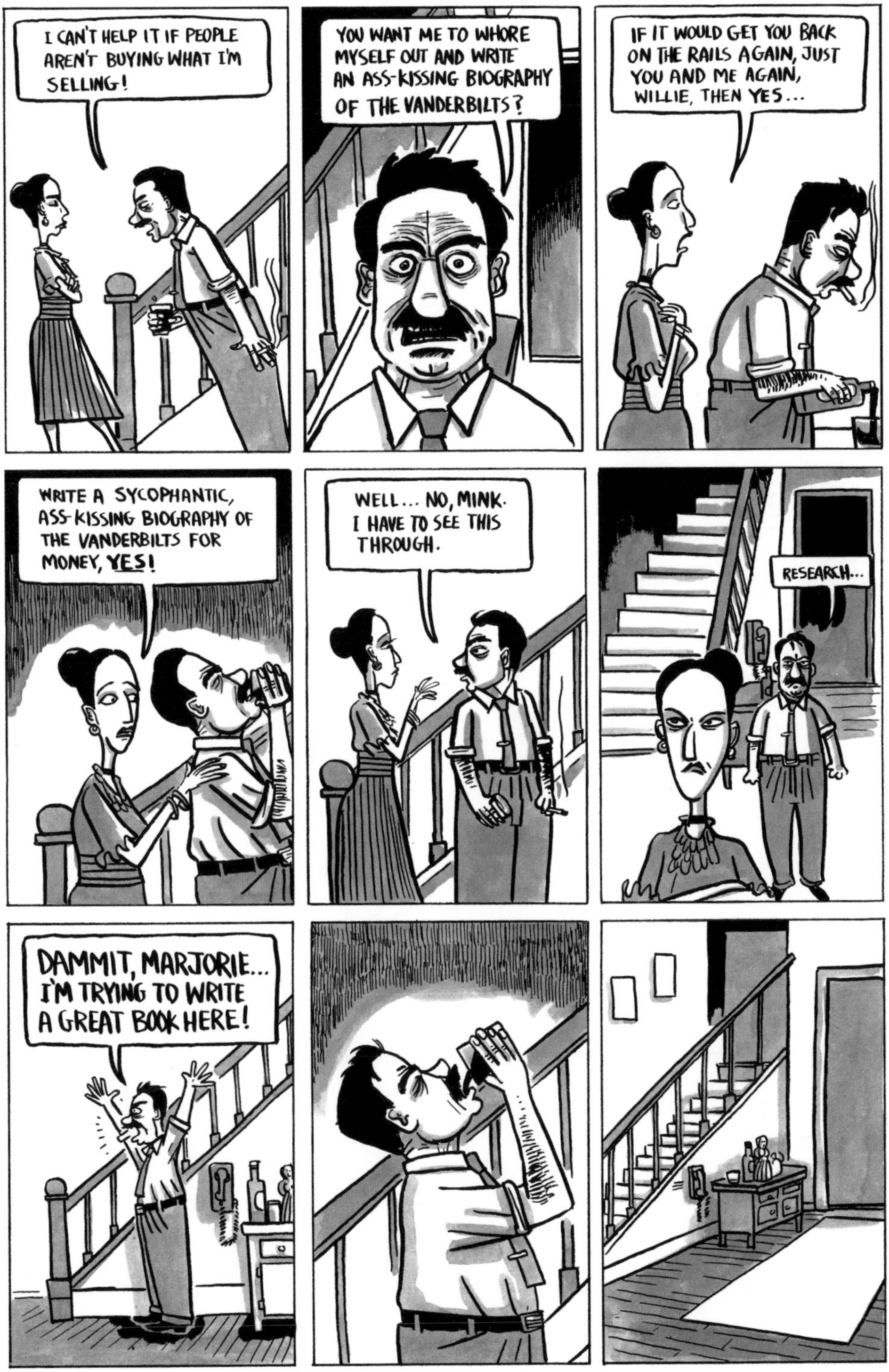
I CAN'T HELP IT IF PEOPLE AREN'T BUYING WHAT I'M SELLING!
YOU WANT ME TO WHORE MYSELF OUT AND WRITE AN ASS-KISSING BIOGRAPHY OF THE VANDERBILTS?
IF IT WOULD GET YOU BACK ON THE RAILS AGAIN, JUST YOU AND ME AGAIN, WILLIE, THEN YES...
WRITE A SYCOPHANTIC, ASS-KISSING BIOGRAPHY OF THE VANDERBILTS FOR MONEY, YES!
WELL... NO, MINK. I HAVE TO SEE THIS THROUGH.
RESEARCH...
DAMMIT, MARJORIE... I'M TRYING TO WRITE A GREAT BOOK HERE!

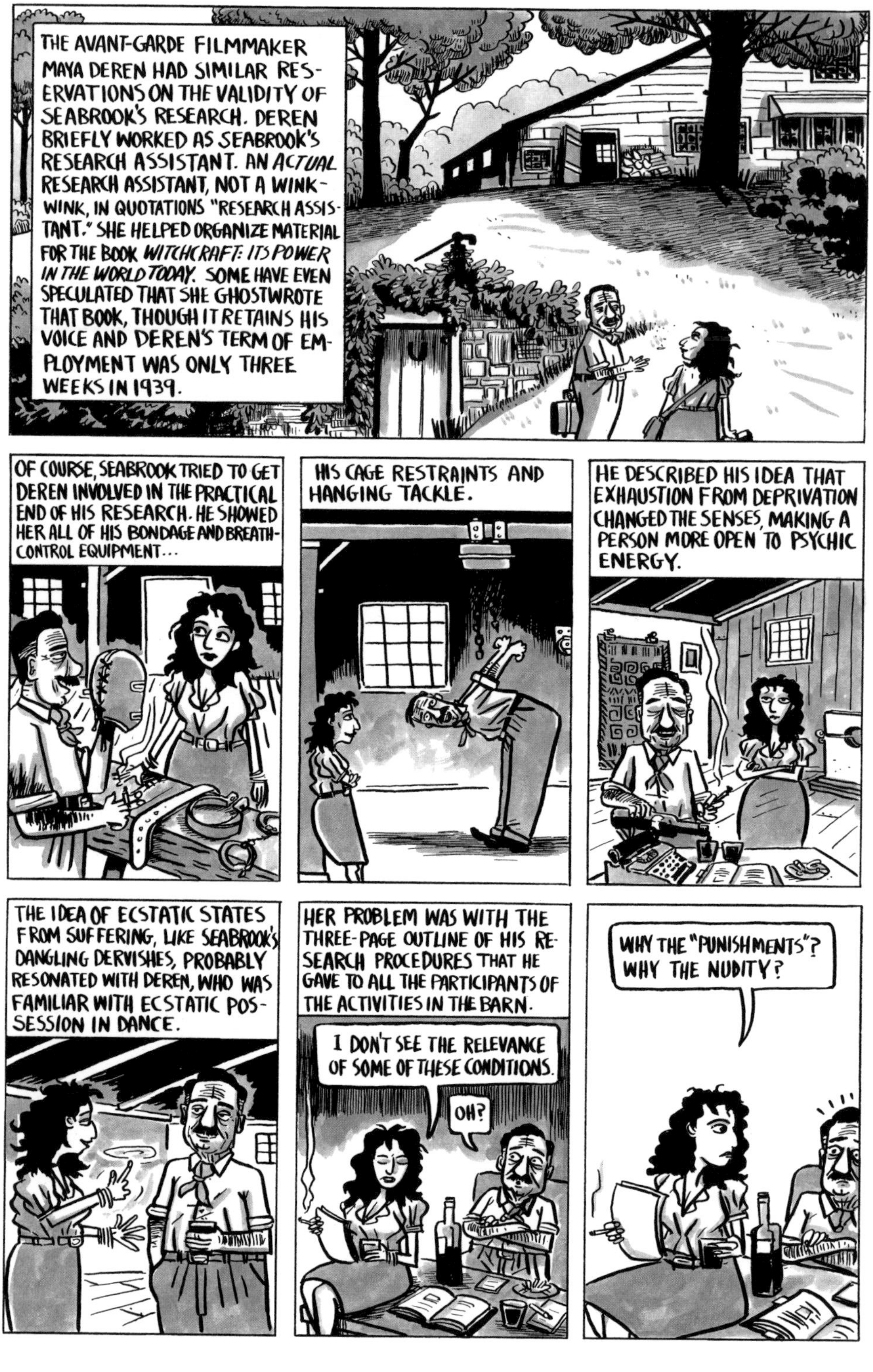
THE AVANT-GARDE FILMMAKER MAYA DEREN HAD SIMILAR RESERVATIONS ON THE VALIDITY OF SEABROOK'S RESEARCH. DEREN BRIEFLY WORKED AS SEABROOK'S RESEARCH ASSISTANT. AN *ACTUAL* RESEARCH ASSISTANT, NOT A WINK-WINK, IN QUOTATIONS "RESEARCH ASSISTANT." SHE HELPED ORGANIZE MATERIAL FOR THE BOOK *WITCHCRAFT: ITS POWER IN THE WORLD TODAY.* SOME HAVE EVEN SPECULATED THAT SHE GHOSTWROTE THAT BOOK, THOUGH IT RETAINS HIS VOICE AND DEREN'S TERM OF EMPLOYMENT WAS ONLY THREE WEEKS IN 1939.
OF COURSE, SEABROOK TRIED TO GET DEREN INVOLVED IN THE PRACTICAL END OF HIS RESEARCH. HE SHOWED HER ALL OF HIS BONDAGE AND BREATH-CONTROL EQUIPMENT...
HIS CAGE RESTRAINTS AND HANGING TACKLE.
HE DESCRIBED HIS IDEA THAT EXHAUSTION FROM DEPRIVATION CHANGED THE SENSES, MAKING A PERSON MORE OPEN TO PSYCHIC ENERGY.
THE IDEA OF ECSTATIC STATES FROM SUFFERING, LIKE SEABROOK'S DANGLING DERVISHES, PROBABLY RESONATED WITH DEREN, WHO WAS FAMILIAR WITH ECSTATIC POSSESSION IN DANCE.
HER PROBLEM WAS WITH THE THREE-PAGE OUTLINE OF HIS RESEARCH PROCEDURES THAT HE GAVE TO ALL THE PARTICIPANTS OF THE ACTIVITIES IN THE BARN.
I DON'T SEE THE RELEVANCE OF SOME OF THESE CONDITIONS.
OH?
WHY THE "PUNISHMENTS"? WHY THE NUDITY?

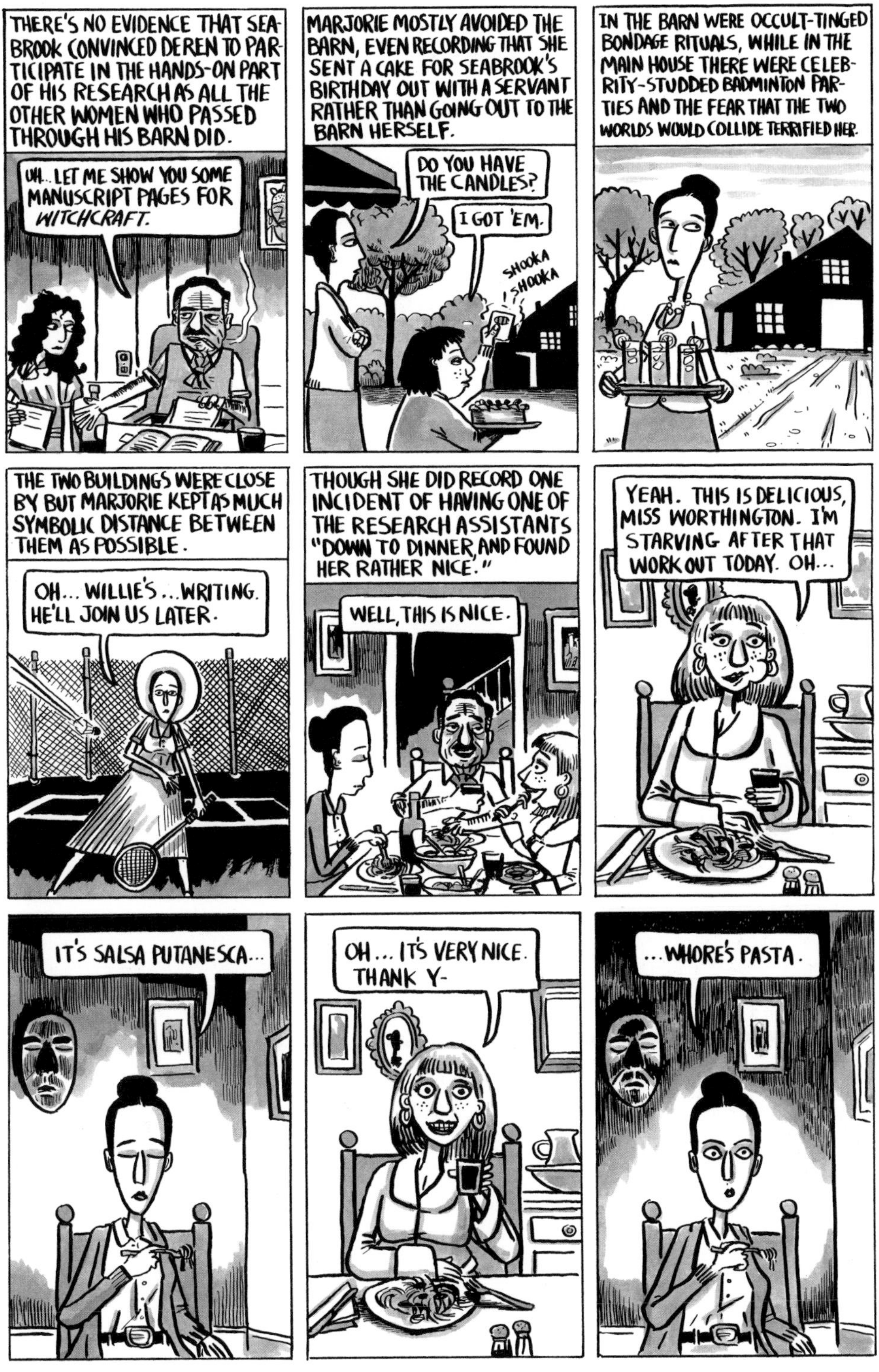
THERE'S NO EVIDENCE THAT SEABROOK CONVINCED DEREN TO PARTICIPATE IN THE HANDS-ON PART OF HIS RESEARCH AS ALL THE OTHER WOMEN WHO PASSED THROUGH HIS BARN DID.
UH... LET ME SHOW YOU SOME MANUSCRIPT PAGES FOR *WITCHCRAFT*.
MARJORIE MOSTLY AVOIDED THE BARN, EVEN RECORDING THAT SHE SENT A CAKE FOR SEABROOK'S BIRTHDAY OUT WITH A SERVANT RATHER THAN GOING OUT TO THE BARN HERSELF.
DO YOU HAVE THE CANDLES?
I GOT 'EM.
SHOOKA SHOOKA
IN THE BARN WERE OCCULT-TINGED BONDAGE RITUALS, WHILE IN THE MAIN HOUSE THERE WERE CELEBRITY-STUDDED BADMINTON PARTIES AND THE FEAR THAT THE TWO WORLDS WOULD COLLIDE TERRIFIED HER.
THE TWO BUILDINGS WERE CLOSE BY BUT MARJORIE KEPT AS MUCH SYMBOLIC DISTANCE BETWEEN THEM AS POSSIBLE.
OH... WILLIE'S... WRITING. HE'LL JOIN US LATER.
THOUGH SHE DID RECORD ONE INCIDENT OF HAVING ONE OF THE RESEARCH ASSISTANTS "DOWN TO DINNER, AND FOUND HER RATHER NICE."
WELL, THIS IS NICE.
YEAH. THIS IS DELICIOUS, MISS WORTHINGTON. I'M STARVING AFTER THAT WORK OUT TODAY. OH...
IT'S SALSA PUTANESCA...
OH... IT'S VERY NICE. THANK Y-
...WHORE'S PASTA.

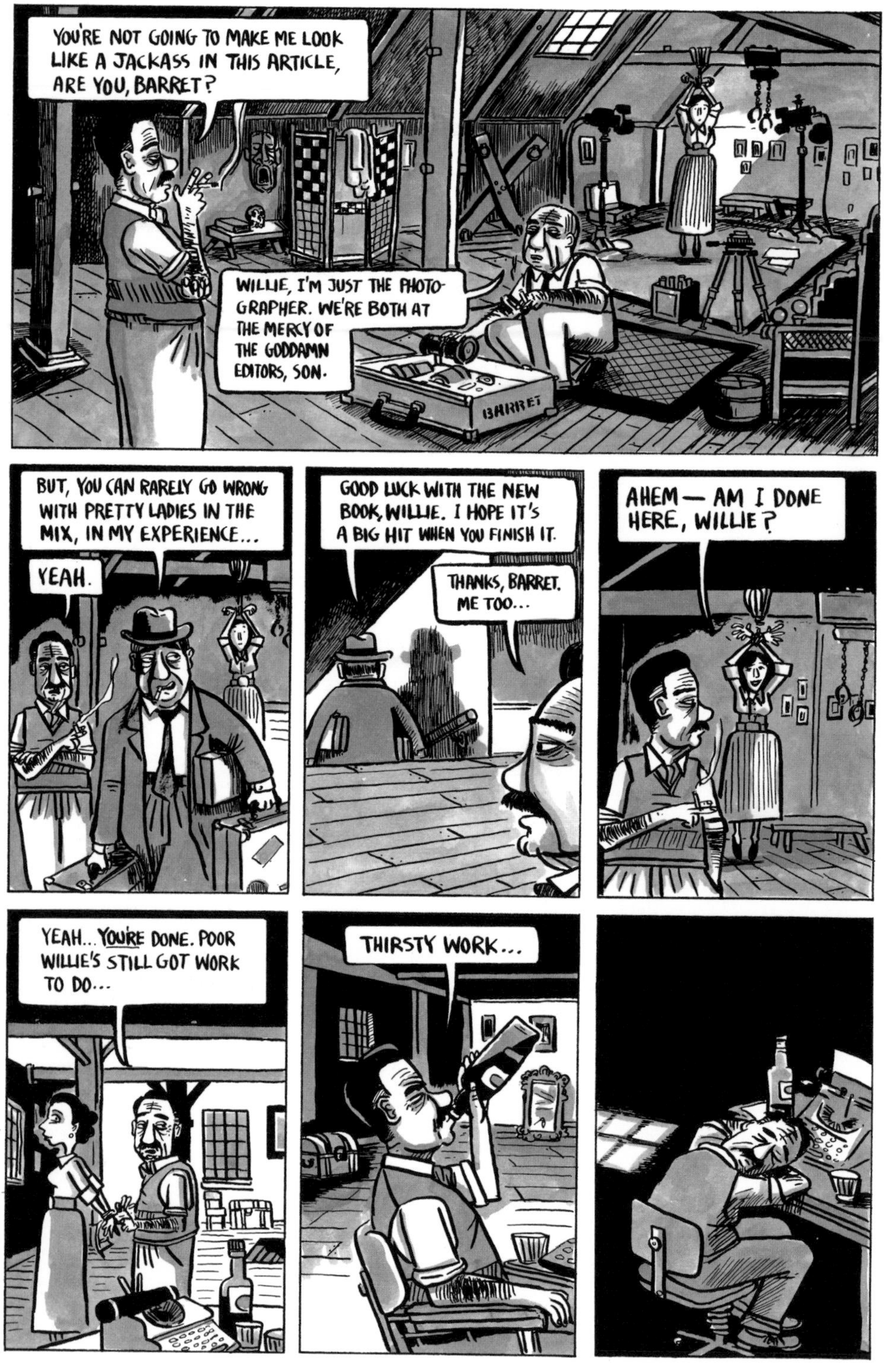
YOU'RE NOT GOING TO MAKE ME LOOK LIKE A JACKASS IN THIS ARTICLE, ARE YOU, BARRET?
WILLIE, I'M JUST THE PHOTOGRAPHER. WE'RE BOTH AT THE MERCY OF THE GODDAMN EDITORS, SON.
BARRET
BUT, YOU CAN RARELY GO WRONG WITH PRETTY LADIES IN THE MIX, IN MY EXPERIENCE...
YEAH.
GOOD LUCK WITH THE NEW BOOK, WILLIE. I HOPE IT'S A BIG HIT WHEN YOU FINISH IT.
THANKS, BARRET. ME TOO...
AHEM — AM I DONE HERE, WILLIE?
YEAH... YOU'RE DONE. POOR WILLIE'S STILL GOT WORK TO DO...
THIRSTY WORK...

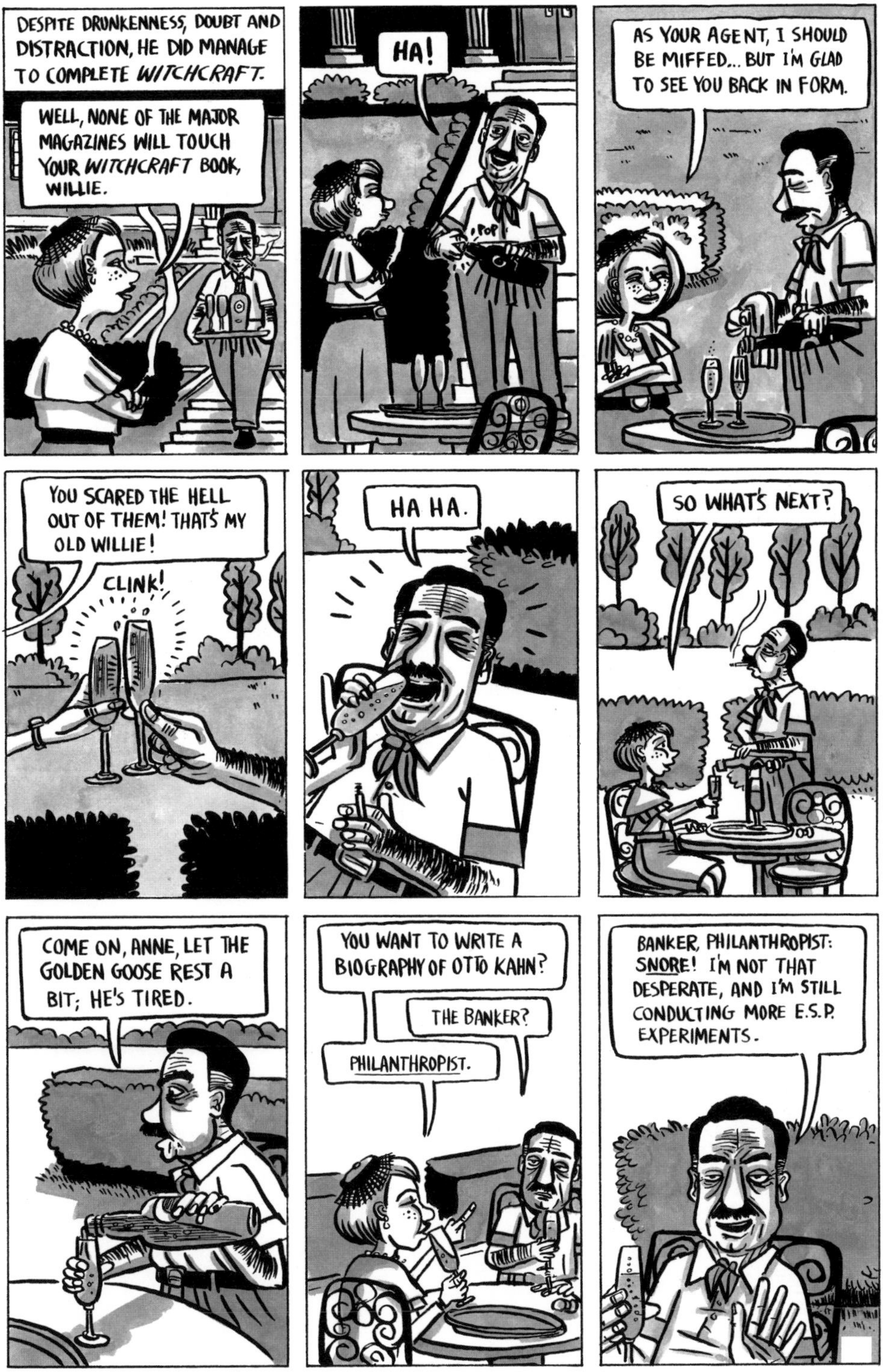
DESPITE DRUNKENNESS, DOUBT AND DISTRACTION, HE DID MANAGE TO COMPLETE WITCHCRAFT.
WELL, NONE OF THE MAJOR MAGAZINES WILL TOUCH YOUR WITCHCRAFT BOOK, WILLIE.
HA!
POP
AS YOUR AGENT, I SHOULD BE MIFFED... BUT I'M GLAD TO SEE YOU BACK IN FORM.
YOU SCARED THE HELL OUT OF THEM! THAT'S MY OLD WILLIE!
CLINK!
HA HA.
SO WHAT'S NEXT?
COME ON, ANNE, LET THE GOLDEN GOOSE REST A BIT; HE'S TIRED.
YOU WANT TO WRITE A BIOGRAPHY OF OTTO KAHN?
THE BANKER?
PHILANTHROPIST.
BANKER, PHILANTHROPIST: SNORE! I'M NOT THAT DESPERATE, AND I'M STILL CONDUCTING MORE E.S.P. EXPERIMENTS.

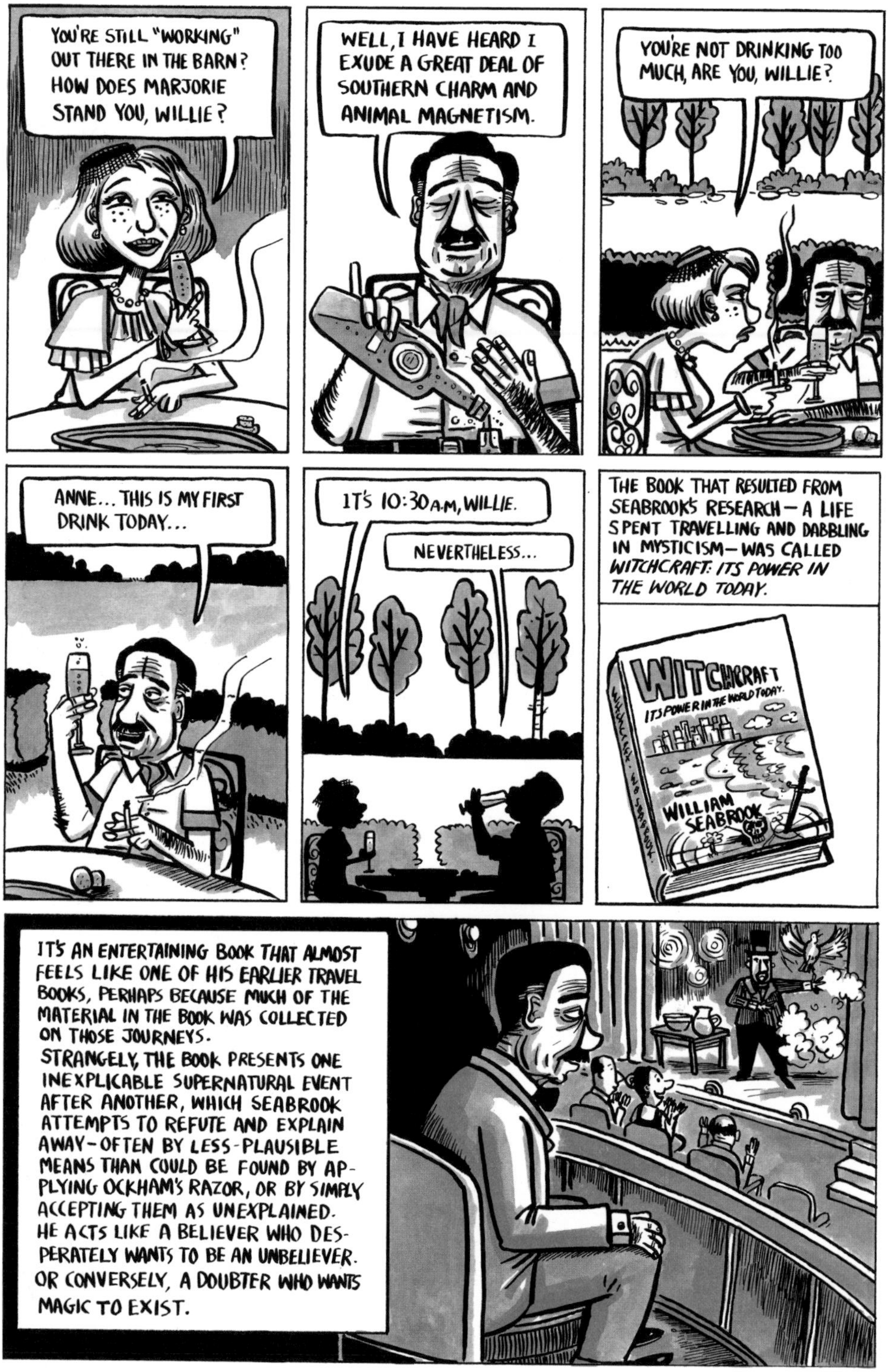
YOU'RE STILL "WORKING" OUT THERE IN THE BARN? HOW DOES MARJORIE STAND YOU, WILLIE?
WELL, I HAVE HEARD I EXUDE A GREAT DEAL OF SOUTHERN CHARM AND ANIMAL MAGNETISM.
YOU'RE NOT DRINKING TOO MUCH, ARE YOU, WILLIE?
ANNE... THIS IS MY FIRST DRINK TODAY...
IT'S 10:30 A.M, WILLIE.
NEVERTHELESS...
THE BOOK THAT RESULTED FROM SEABROOK'S RESEARCH — A LIFE SPENT TRAVELLING AND DABBLING IN MYSTICISM — WAS CALLED *WITCHCRAFT: ITS POWER IN THE WORLD TODAY.*
WITCHCRAFT
ITS POWER IN THE WORLD TODAY.
WILLIAM SEABROOK
IT'S AN ENTERTAINING BOOK THAT ALMOST FEELS LIKE ONE OF HIS EARLIER TRAVEL BOOKS, PERHAPS BECAUSE MUCH OF THE MATERIAL IN THE BOOK WAS COLLECTED ON THOSE JOURNEYS.
STRANGELY, THE BOOK PRESENTS ONE INEXPLICABLE SUPERNATURAL EVENT AFTER ANOTHER, WHICH SEABROOK ATTEMPTS TO REFUTE AND EXPLAIN AWAY — OFTEN BY LESS-PLAUSIBLE MEANS THAN COULD BE FOUND BY APPLYING OCKHAM'S RAZOR, OR BY SIMPLY ACCEPTING THEM AS UNEXPLAINED.
HE ACTS LIKE A BELIEVER WHO DESPERATELY WANTS TO BE AN UNBELIEVER.
OR CONVERSELY, A DOUBTER WHO WANTS MAGIC TO EXIST.

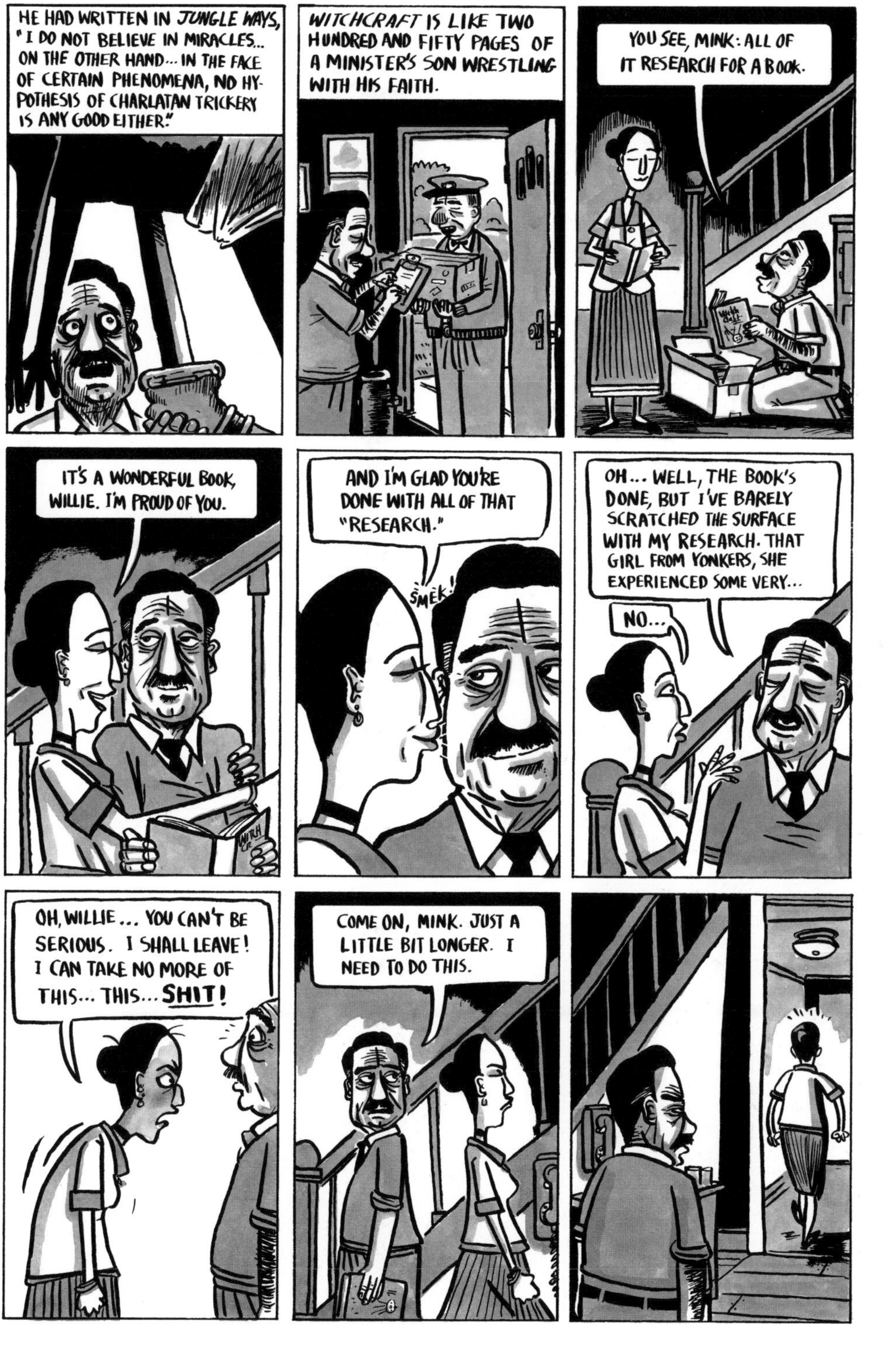
HE HAD WRITTEN IN JUNGLE WAYS, "I DO NOT BELIEVE IN MIRACLES... ON THE OTHER HAND... IN THE FACE OF CERTAIN PHENOMENA, NO HYPOTHESIS OF CHARLATAN TRICKERY IS ANY GOOD EITHER."
WITCHCRAFT IS LIKE TWO HUNDRED AND FIFTY PAGES OF A MINISTER'S SON WRESTLING WITH HIS FAITH.
YOU SEE, MINK: ALL OF IT RESEARCH FOR A BOOK.
IT'S A WONDERFUL BOOK, WILLIE. I'M PROUD OF YOU.
AND I'M GLAD YOU'RE DONE WITH ALL OF THAT "RESEARCH."
SMEK!
OH... WELL, THE BOOK'S DONE, BUT I'VE BARELY SCRATCHED THE SURFACE WITH MY RESEARCH. THAT GIRL FROM YONKERS, SHE EXPERIENCED SOME VERY...
NO...
OH, WILLIE... YOU CAN'T BE SERIOUS. I SHALL LEAVE! I CAN TAKE NO MORE OF THIS... THIS... SHIT!
COME ON, MINK. JUST A LITTLE BIT LONGER. I NEED TO DO THIS.

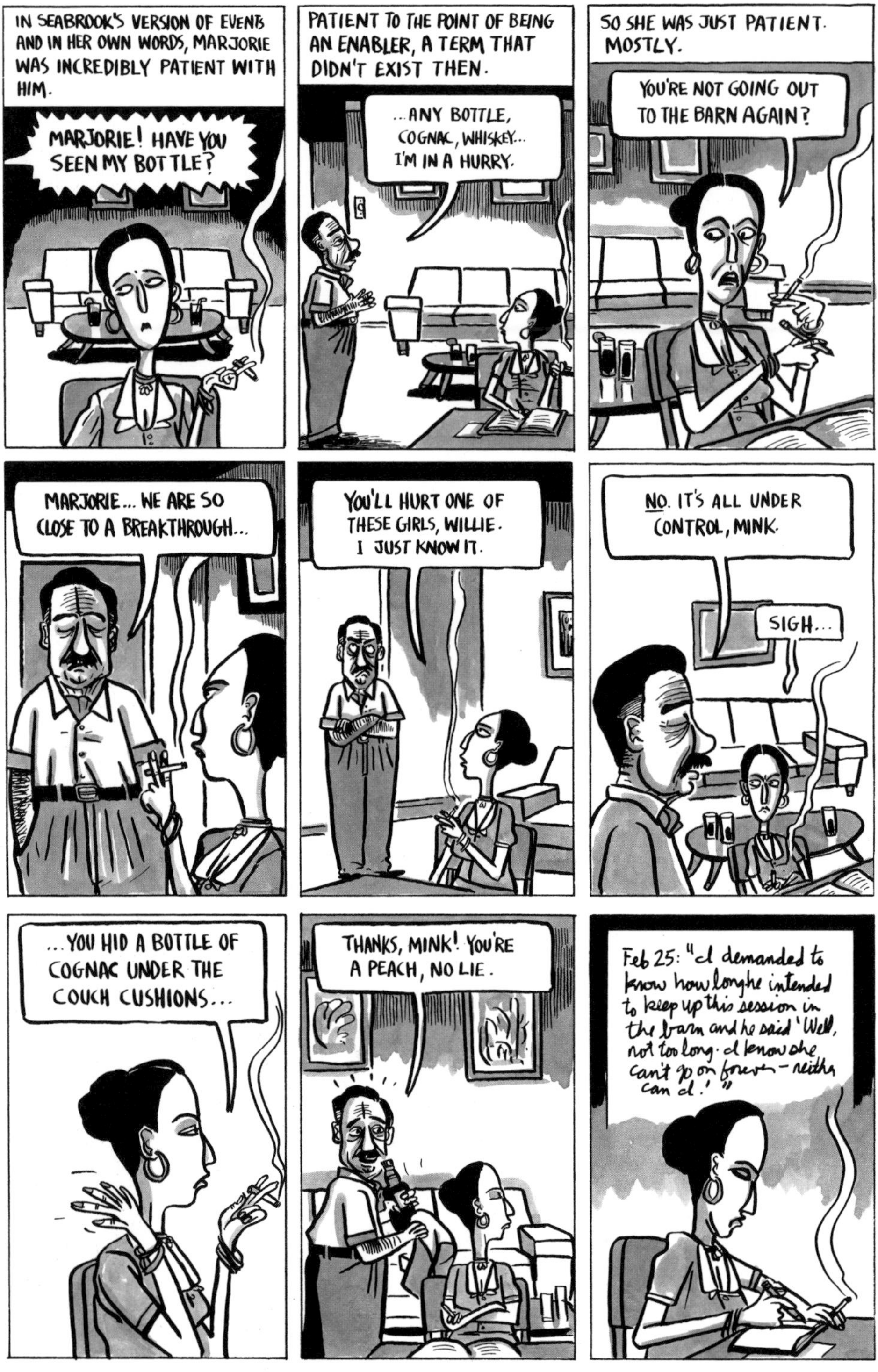
IN SEABROOK'S VERSION OF EVENTS AND IN HER OWN WORDS, MARJORIE WAS INCREDIBLY PATIENT WITH HIM.
MARJORIE! HAVE YOU SEEN MY BOTTLE?
PATIENT TO THE POINT OF BEING AN ENABLER, A TERM THAT DIDN'T EXIST THEN.
...ANY BOTTLE, COGNAC, WHISKEY... I'M IN A HURRY.
SO SHE WAS JUST PATIENT. MOSTLY.
YOU'RE NOT GOING OUT TO THE BARN AGAIN?
MARJORIE... WE ARE SO CLOSE TO A BREAKTHROUGH...
YOU'LL HURT ONE OF THESE GIRLS, WILLIE. I JUST KNOW IT.
NO. IT'S ALL UNDER CONTROL, MINK.
SIGH...
...YOU HID A BOTTLE OF COGNAC UNDER THE COUCH CUSHIONS...
THANKS, MINK! YOU'RE A PEACH, NO LIE.
Feb 25: "I demanded to know how long he intended to keep up this session in the barn and he said 'Well, not too long. I know she can't go on forever – neither can I.'"

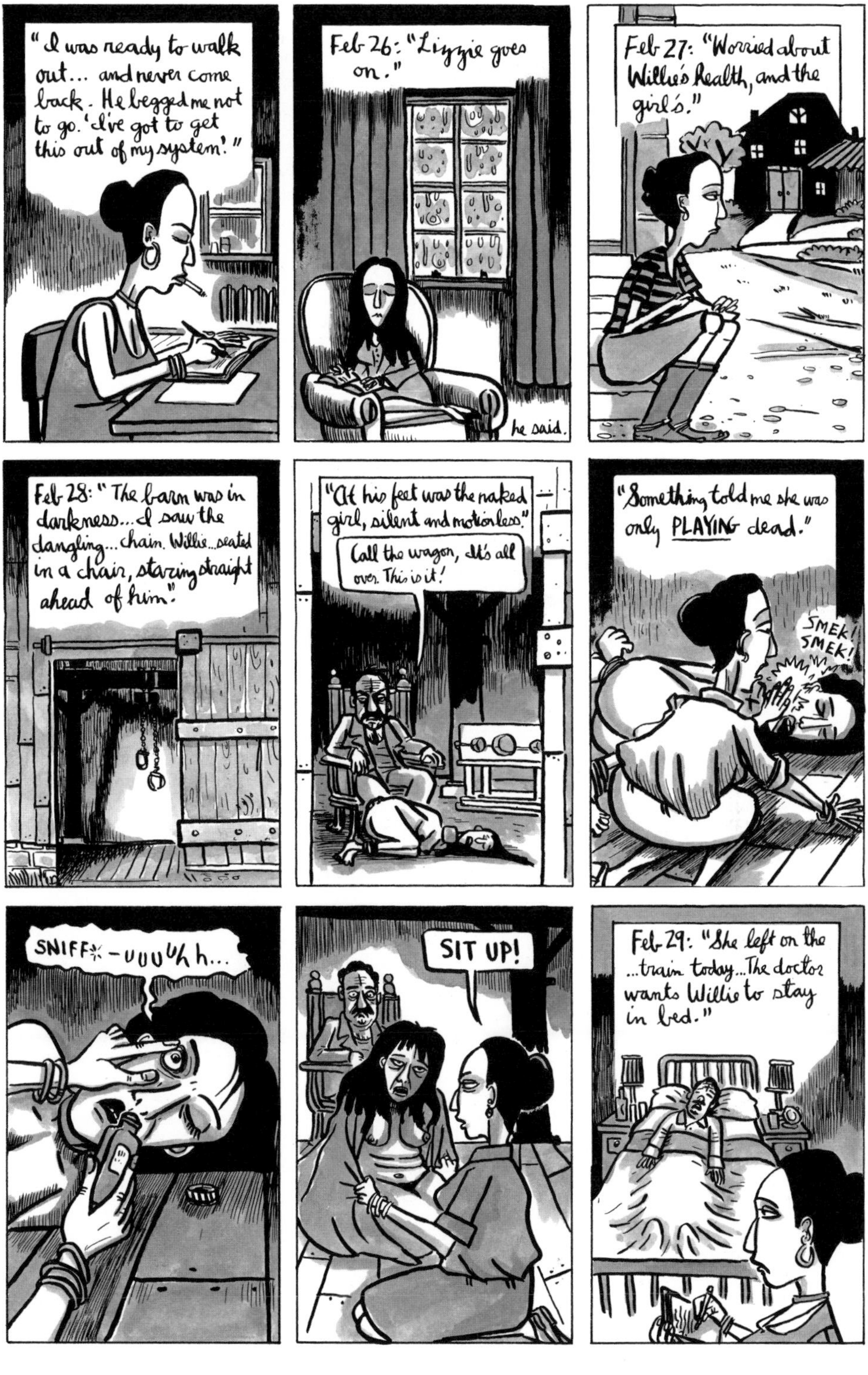
"I was ready to walk out... and never come back. He begged me not to go. 'I've got to get this out of my system!'"
Feb 26: "Lizzie goes on."
he said.
Feb 27: "Worried about Willie's health, and the girl's."
Feb 28: "The barn was in darkness... I saw the dangling... chain. Willie... seated in a chair, staring straight ahead of him."
"At his feet was the naked girl, silent and motionless."
Call the wagon, It's all over. This is it!
"Something told me she was only PLAYING dead."
SMEK! SMEK!
SNIFF -UUUUhh...
SIT UP!
Feb 29: "She left on the ...train today... The doctor wants Willie to stay in bed."

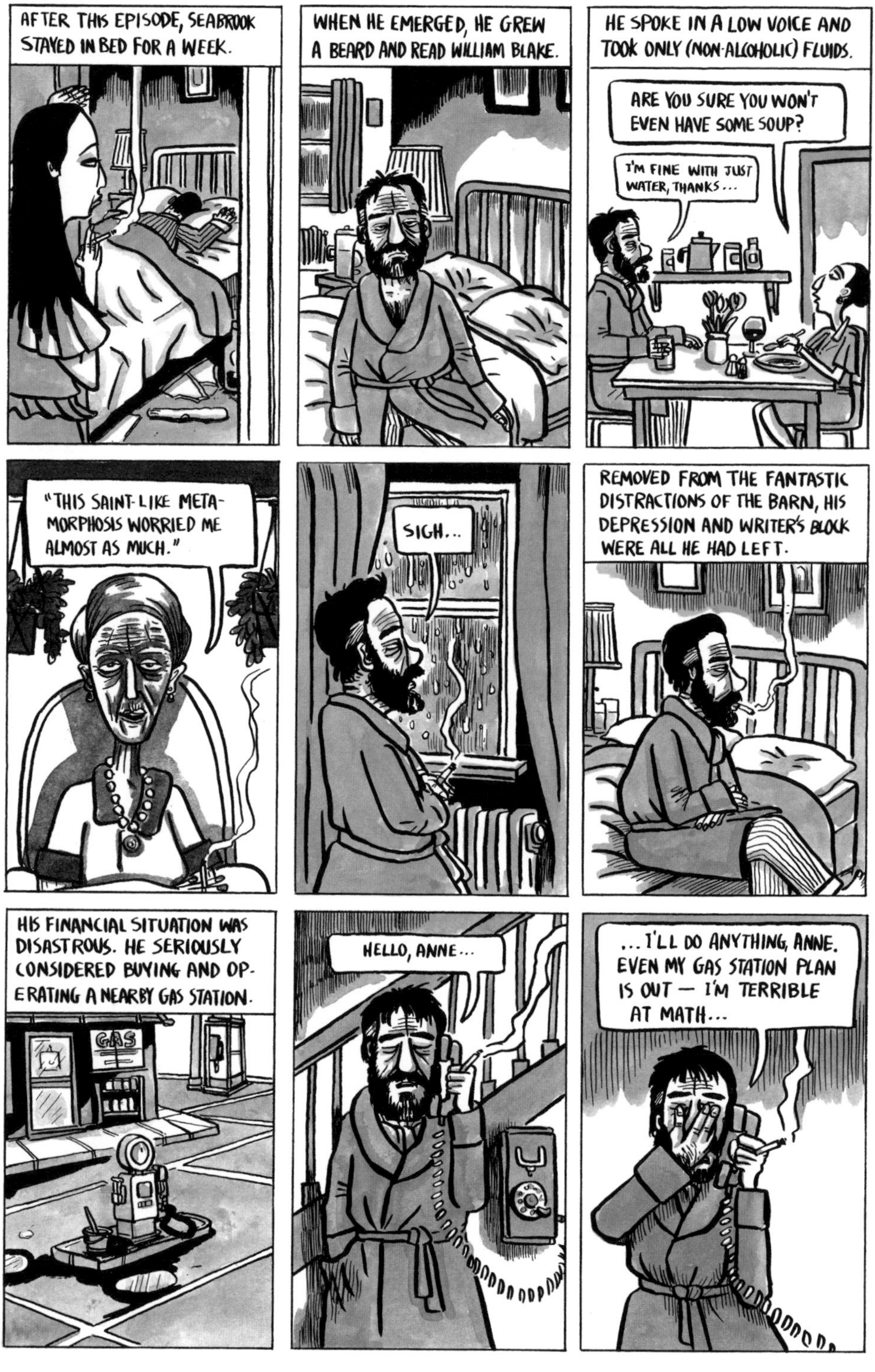
AFTER THIS EPISODE, SEABROOK STAYED IN BED FOR A WEEK.
WHEN HE EMERGED, HE GREW A BEARD AND READ WILLIAM BLAKE.
HE SPOKE IN A LOW VOICE AND TOOK ONLY (NON-ALCOHOLIC) FLUIDS.
ARE YOU SURE YOU WON'T EVEN HAVE SOME SOUP?
I'M FINE WITH JUST WATER, THANKS...
"THIS SAINT-LIKE METAMORPHOSIS WORRIED ME ALMOST AS MUCH."
SIGH...
REMOVED FROM THE FANTASTIC DISTRACTIONS OF THE BARN, HIS DEPRESSION AND WRITER'S BLOCK WERE ALL HE HAD LEFT.
HIS FINANCIAL SITUATION WAS DISASTROUS. HE SERIOUSLY CONSIDERED BUYING AND OPERATING A NEARBY GAS STATION.
GAS
HELLO, ANNE...
...I'LL DO ANYTHING, ANNE. EVEN MY GAS STATION PLAN IS OUT — I'M TERRIBLE AT MATH...

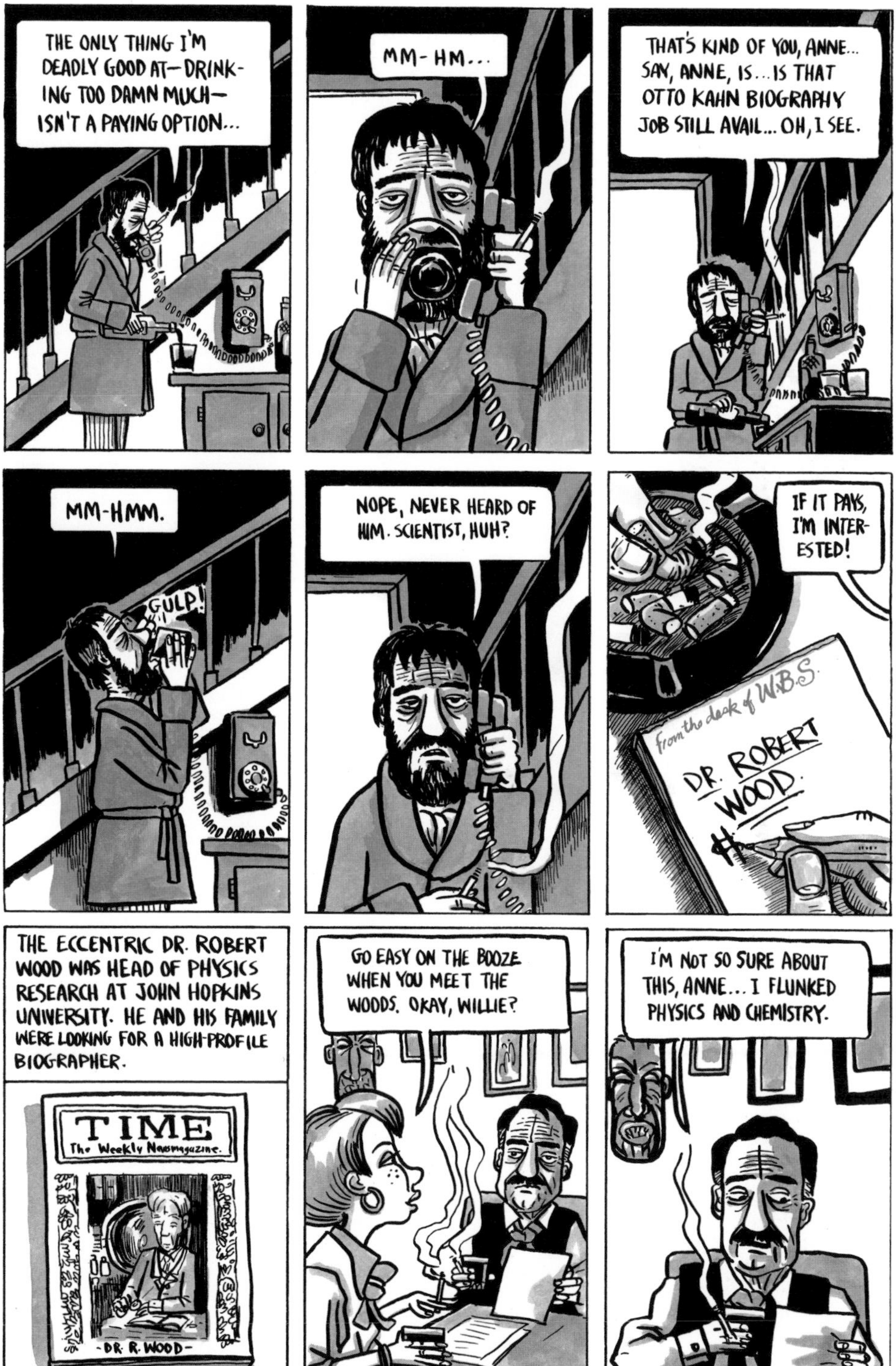
THE ONLY THING I'M DEADLY GOOD AT—DRINKING TOO DAMN MUCH—ISN'T A PAYING OPTION...
MM-HM...
THAT'S KIND OF YOU, ANNE... SAY, ANNE, IS...IS THAT OTTO KAHN BIOGRAPHY JOB STILL AVAIL... OH, I SEE.
MM-HMM.
GULP!
NOPE, NEVER HEARD OF HIM. SCIENTIST, HUH?
IF IT PAYS, I'M INTERESTED!
From the desk of W.B.S.
DR. ROBERT WOOD
THE ECCENTRIC DR. ROBERT WOOD WAS HEAD OF PHYSICS RESEARCH AT JOHN HOPKINS UNIVERSITY. HE AND HIS FAMILY WERE LOOKING FOR A HIGH-PROFILE BIOGRAPHER.
TIME
The Weekly Newsmagazine
-DR. R. WOOD-
GO EASY ON THE BOOZE WHEN YOU MEET THE WOODS. OKAY, WILLIE?
I'M NOT SO SURE ABOUT THIS, ANNE... I FLUNKED PHYSICS AND CHEMISTRY.

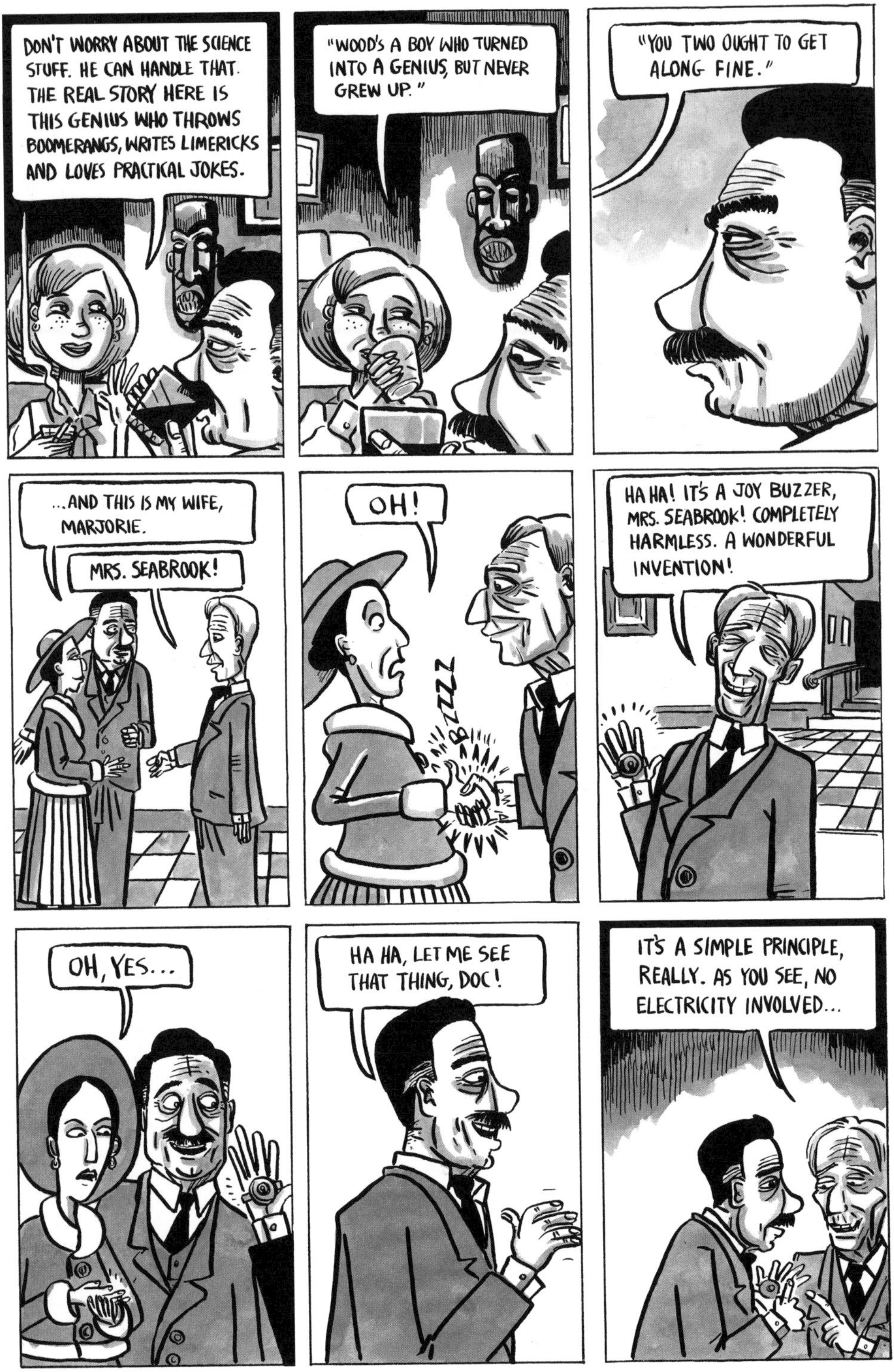
DON'T WORRY ABOUT THE SCIENCE STUFF. HE CAN HANDLE THAT. THE REAL STORY HERE IS THIS GENIUS WHO THROWS BOOMERANGS, WRITES LIMERICKS AND LOVES PRACTICAL JOKES.
"WOOD'S A BOY WHO TURNED INTO A GENIUS, BUT NEVER GREW UP."
"YOU TWO OUGHT TO GET ALONG FINE."
...AND THIS IS MY WIFE, MARJORIE.
MRS. SEABROOK!
OH!
BZZZZ
HA HA! IT'S A JOY BUZZER, MRS. SEABROOK! COMPLETELY HARMLESS. A WONDERFUL INVENTION!
OH, YES...
HA HA, LET ME SEE THAT THING, DOC!
IT'S A SIMPLE PRINCIPLE, REALLY. AS YOU SEE, NO ELECTRICITY INVOLVED...

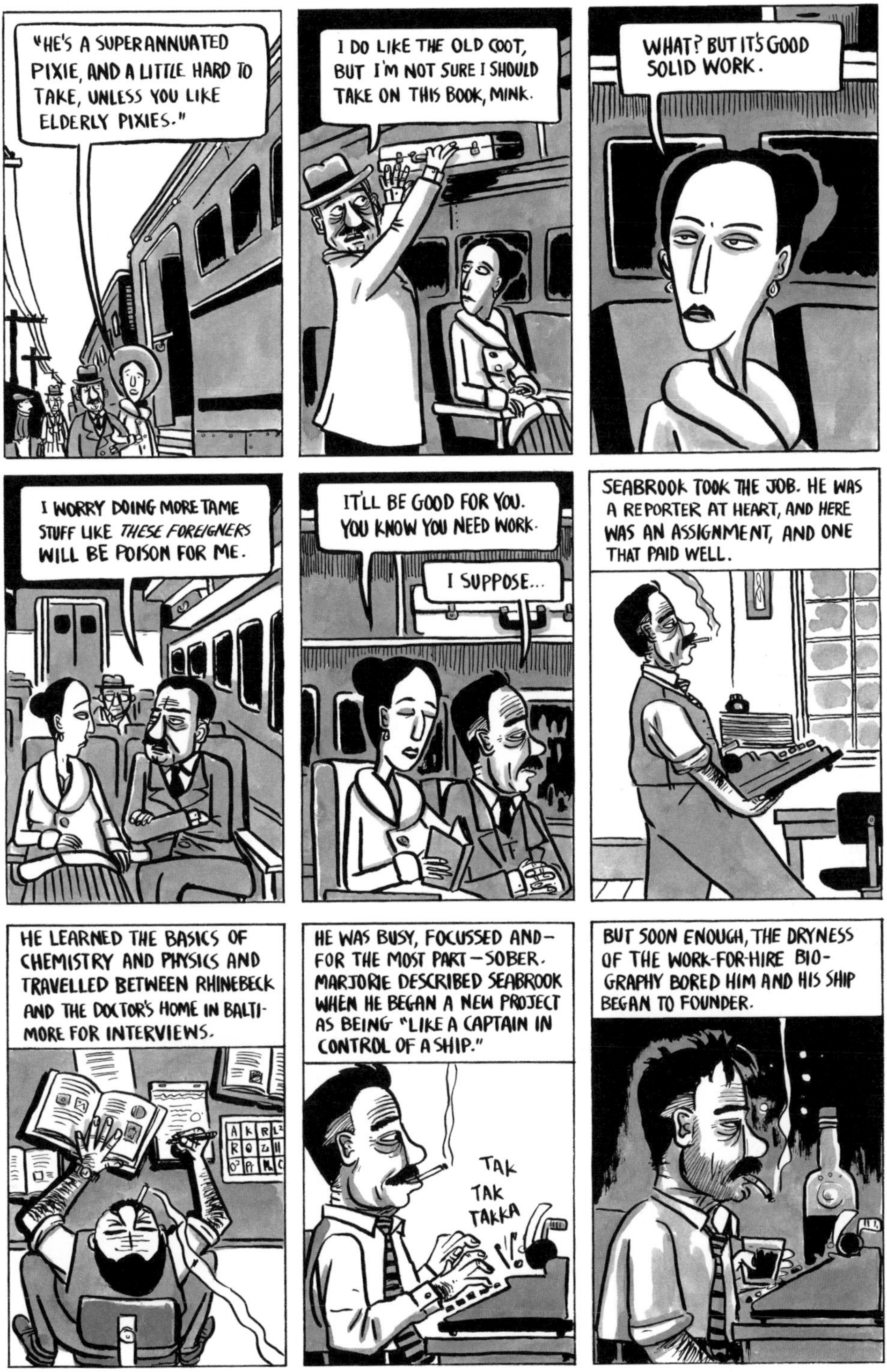
"HE'S A SUPERANNUATED PIXIE, AND A LITTLE HARD TO TAKE, UNLESS YOU LIKE ELDERLY PIXIES."
I DO LIKE THE OLD COOT, BUT I'M NOT SURE I SHOULD TAKE ON THIS BOOK, MINK.
WHAT? BUT IT'S GOOD SOLID WORK.
I WORRY DOING MORE TAME STUFF LIKE *THESE FOREIGNERS* WILL BE POISON FOR ME.
IT'LL BE GOOD FOR YOU. YOU KNOW YOU NEED WORK.
I SUPPOSE...
SEABROOK TOOK THE JOB. HE WAS A REPORTER AT HEART, AND HERE WAS AN ASSIGNMENT, AND ONE THAT PAID WELL.
HE LEARNED THE BASICS OF CHEMISTRY AND PHYSICS AND TRAVELLED BETWEEN RHINEBECK AND THE DOCTOR'S HOME IN BALTIMORE FOR INTERVIEWS.
HE WAS BUSY, FOCUSSED AND—FOR THE MOST PART—SOBER. MARJORIE DESCRIBED SEABROOK WHEN HE BEGAN A NEW PROJECT AS BEING "LIKE A CAPTAIN IN CONTROL OF A SHIP."
TAK
TAK
TAKKA
BUT SOON ENOUGH, THE DRYNESS OF THE WORK-FOR-HIRE BIOGRAPHY BORED HIM AND HIS SHIP BEGAN TO FOUNDER.

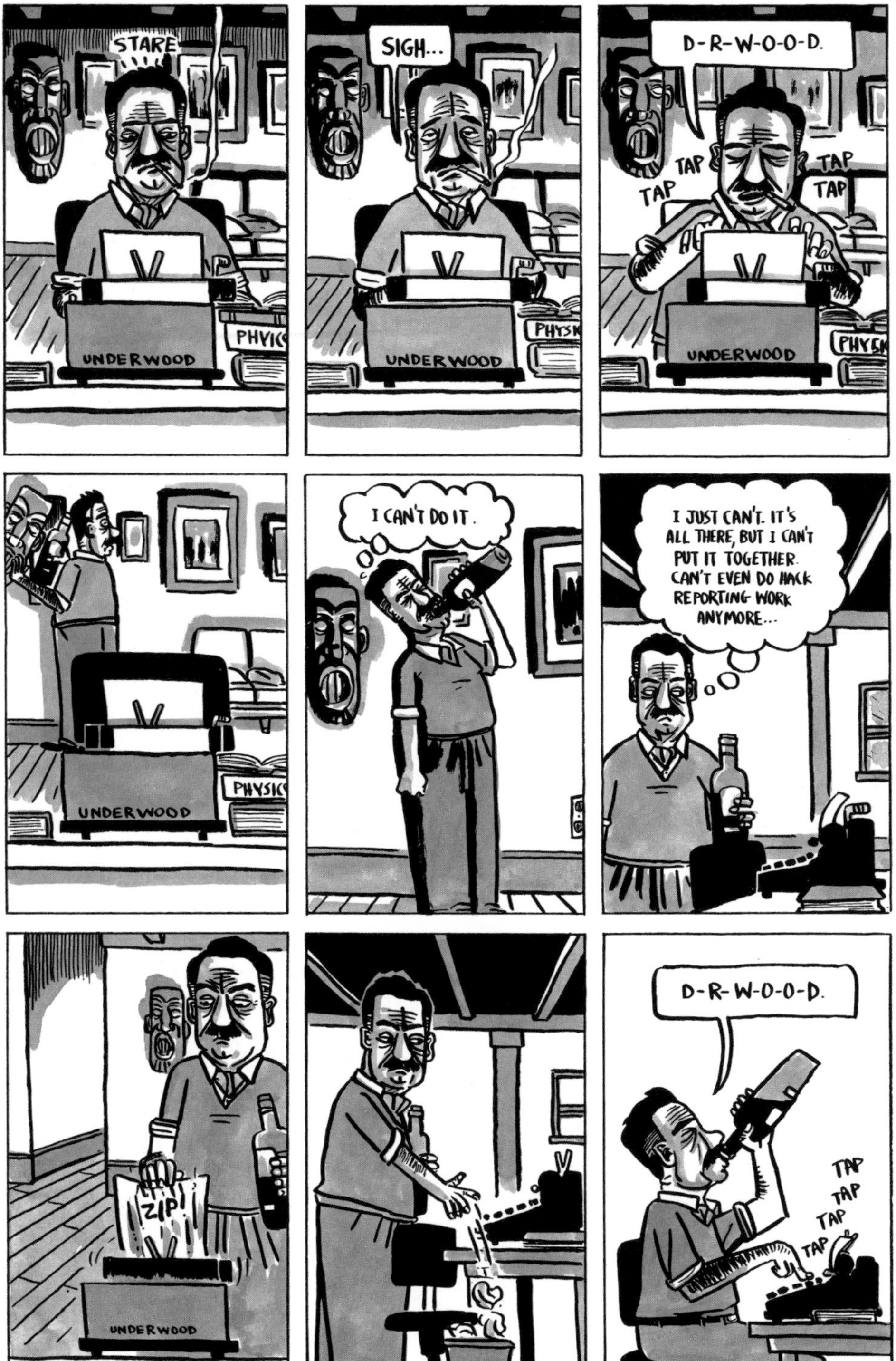
STARE
SIGH...
D-R-W-O-O-D.
TAP TAP TAP TAP
I CAN'T DO IT.
I JUST CAN'T. IT'S ALL THERE, BUT I CAN'T PUT IT TOGETHER. CAN'T EVEN DO HACK REPORTING WORK ANYMORE...
ZIP
D-R-W-O-O-D.
TAP TAP TAP TAP

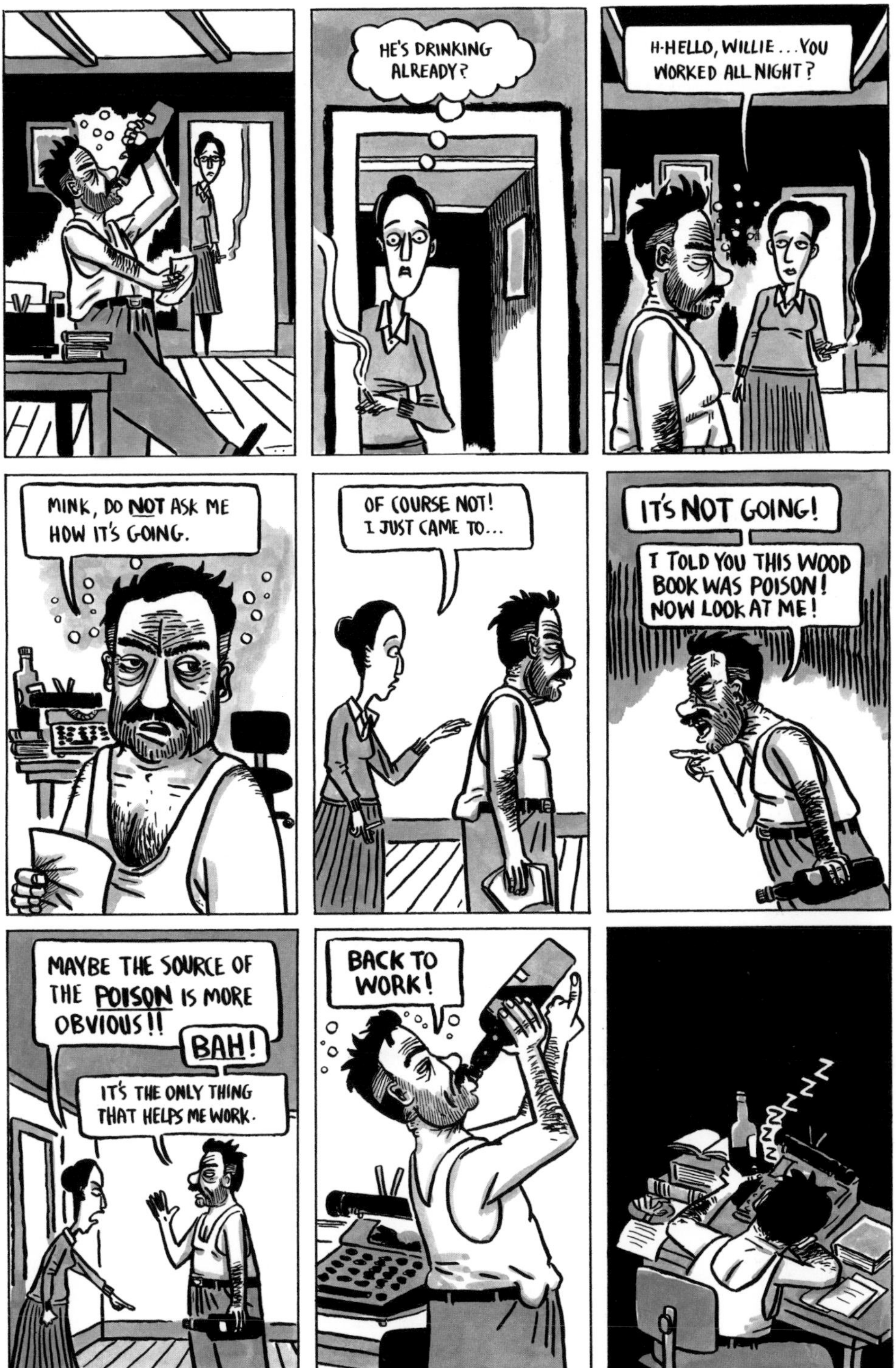
HE'S DRINKING ALREADY?
H-HELLO, WILLIE... YOU WORKED ALL NIGHT?
MINK, DO NOT ASK ME HOW IT'S GOING.
OF COURSE NOT! I JUST CAME TO...
IT'S NOT GOING!
I TOLD YOU THIS WOOD BOOK WAS POISON! NOW LOOK AT ME!
MAYBE THE SOURCE OF THE POISON IS MORE OBVIOUS!!
BAH!
IT'S THE ONLY THING THAT HELPS ME WORK.
BACK TO WORK!
ZZZZZZ

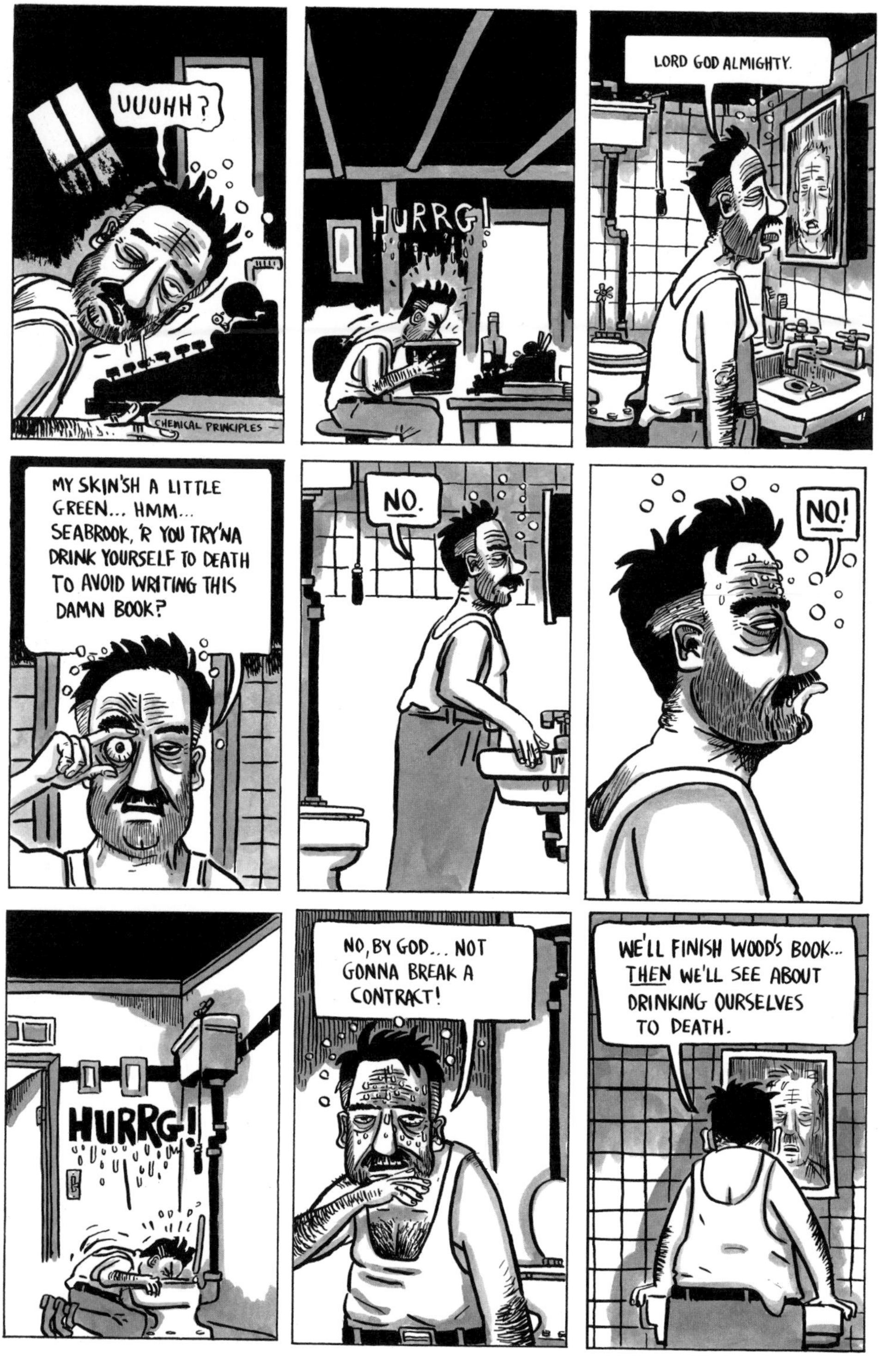
UUUHH?
CHEMICAL PRINCIPLES
HURRG!
LORD GOD ALMIGHTY.
MY SKIN'SH A LITTLE GREEN... HMM... SEABROOK, 'R YOU TRY'NA DRINK YOURSELF TO DEATH TO AVOID WRITING THIS DAMN BOOK?
NO.
NO!
HURRG!
NO, BY GOD... NOT GONNA BREAK A CONTRACT!
WE'LL FINISH WOOD'S BOOK... THEN WE'LL SEE ABOUT DRINKING OURSELVES TO DEATH.

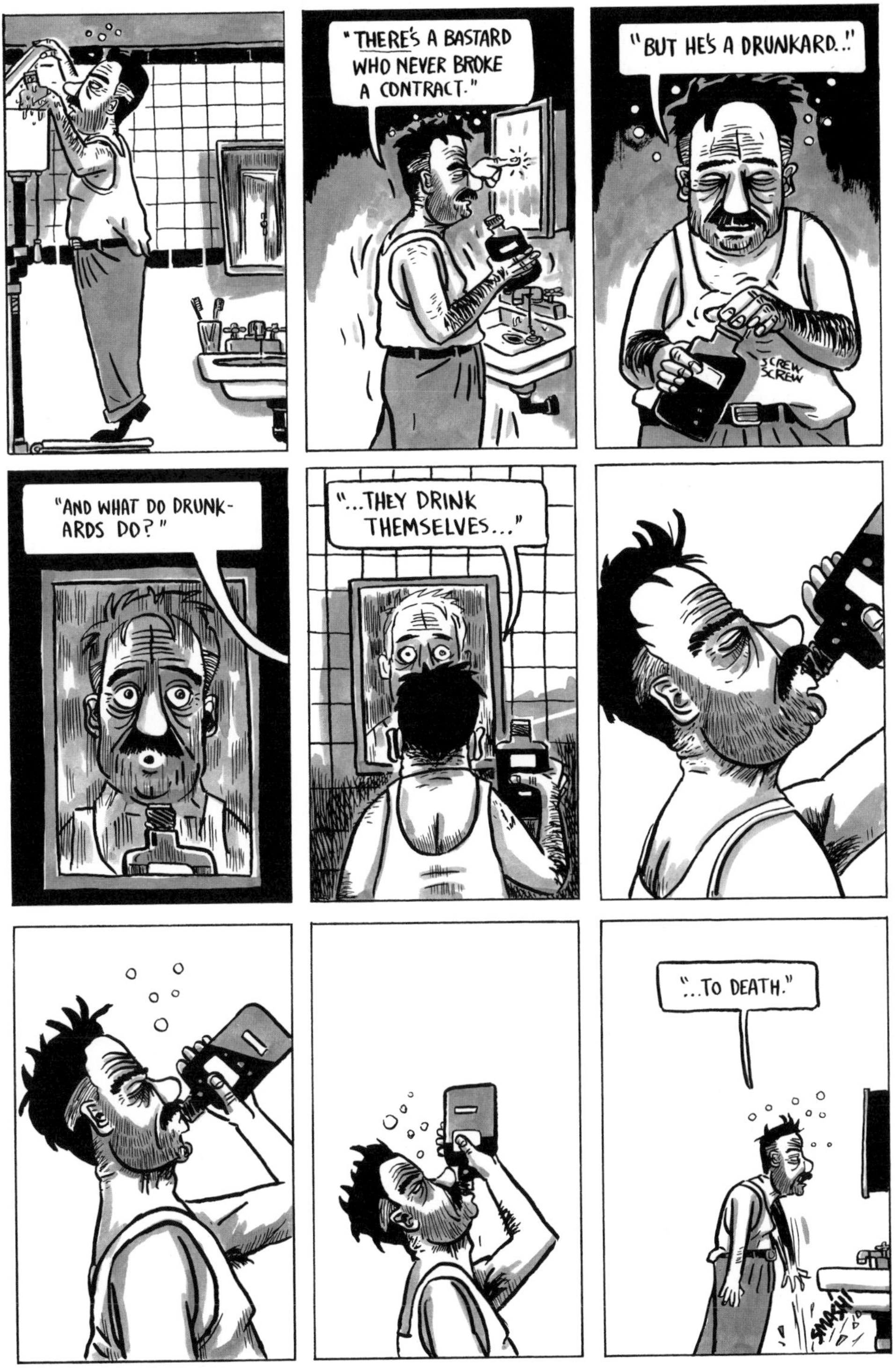
"THERE'S A BASTARD WHO NEVER BROKE A CONTRACT."
"BUT HE'S A DRUNKARD..."
SCREW SCREW
"AND WHAT DO DRUNKARDS DO?"
"...THEY DRINK THEMSELVES..."
"...TO DEATH."
SMASH!

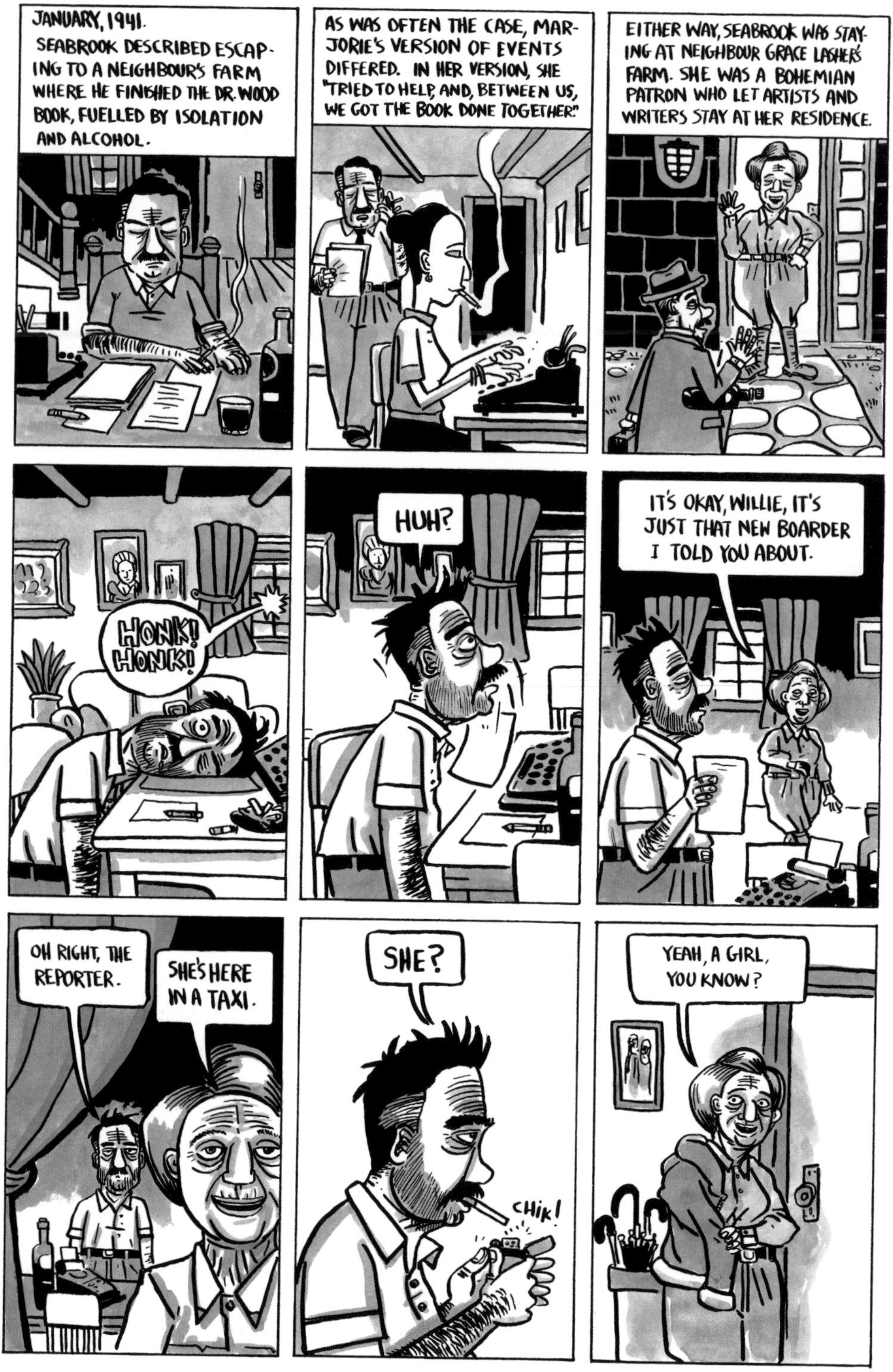
JANUARY, 1941.
SEABROOK DESCRIBED ESCAPING TO A NEIGHBOUR'S FARM WHERE HE FINISHED THE DR. WOOD BOOK, FUELLED BY ISOLATION AND ALCOHOL.
AS WAS OFTEN THE CASE, MARJORIE'S VERSION OF EVENTS DIFFERED. IN HER VERSION, SHE "TRIED TO HELP, AND, BETWEEN US, WE GOT THE BOOK DONE TOGETHER."
EITHER WAY, SEABROOK WAS STAYING AT NEIGHBOUR GRACE LASHER'S FARM. SHE WAS A BOHEMIAN PATRON WHO LET ARTISTS AND WRITERS STAY AT HER RESIDENCE.
HONK! HONK!
HUH?
IT'S OKAY, WILLIE, IT'S JUST THAT NEW BOARDER I TOLD YOU ABOUT.
OH RIGHT, THE REPORTER.
SHE'S HERE IN A TAXI.
SHE?
CHIK!
YEAH, A GIRL, YOU KNOW?

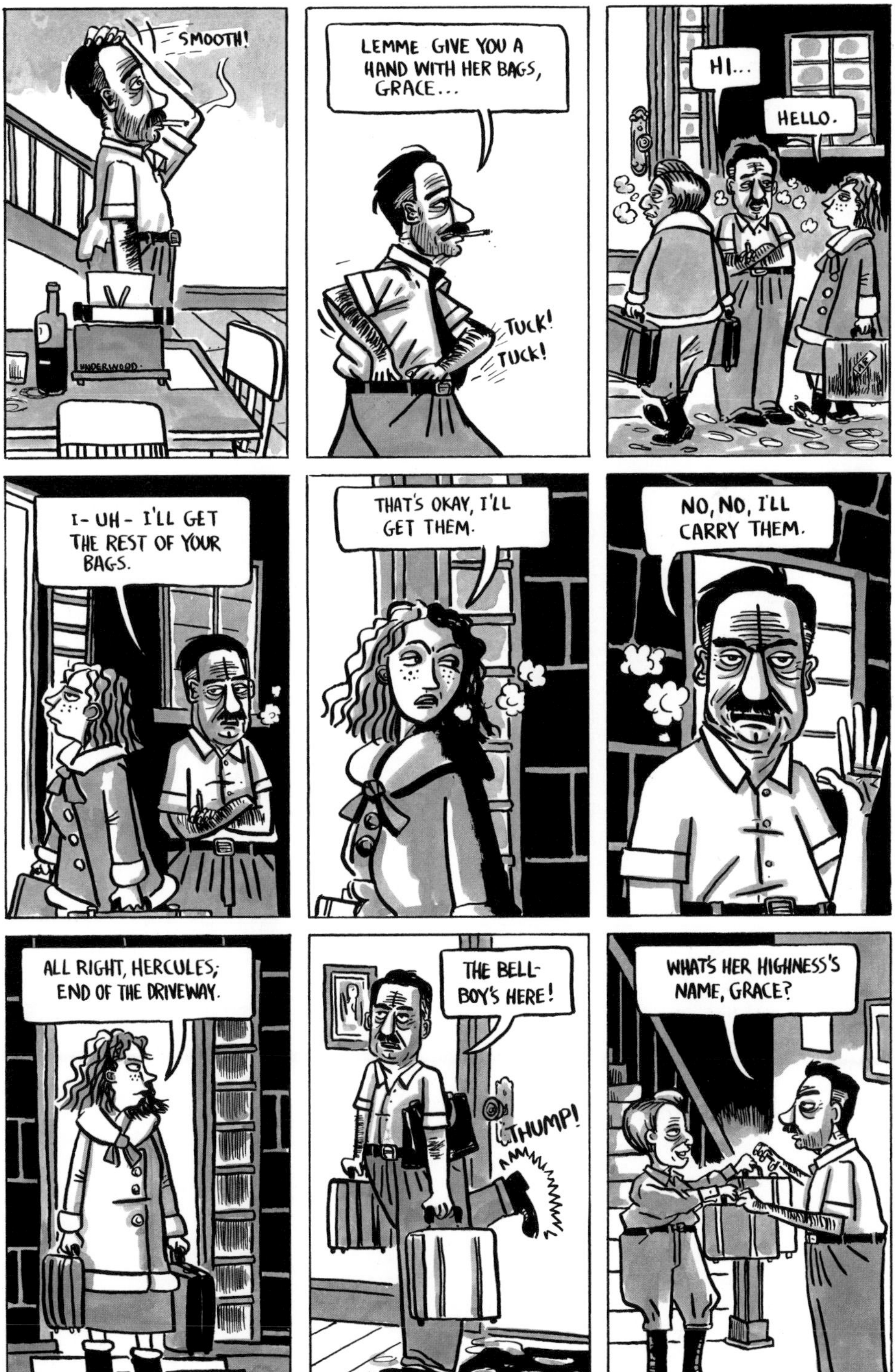
SMOOTH!
LEMME GIVE YOU A HAND WITH HER BAGS, GRACE...
TUCK!
TUCK!
HI...
HELLO.
I- UH- I'LL GET THE REST OF YOUR BAGS.
THAT'S OKAY, I'LL GET THEM.
NO, NO, I'LL CARRY THEM.
ALL RIGHT, HERCULES; END OF THE DRIVEWAY.
THE BELL-BOY'S HERE!
THUMP!
WHAT'S HER HIGHNESS'S NAME, GRACE?

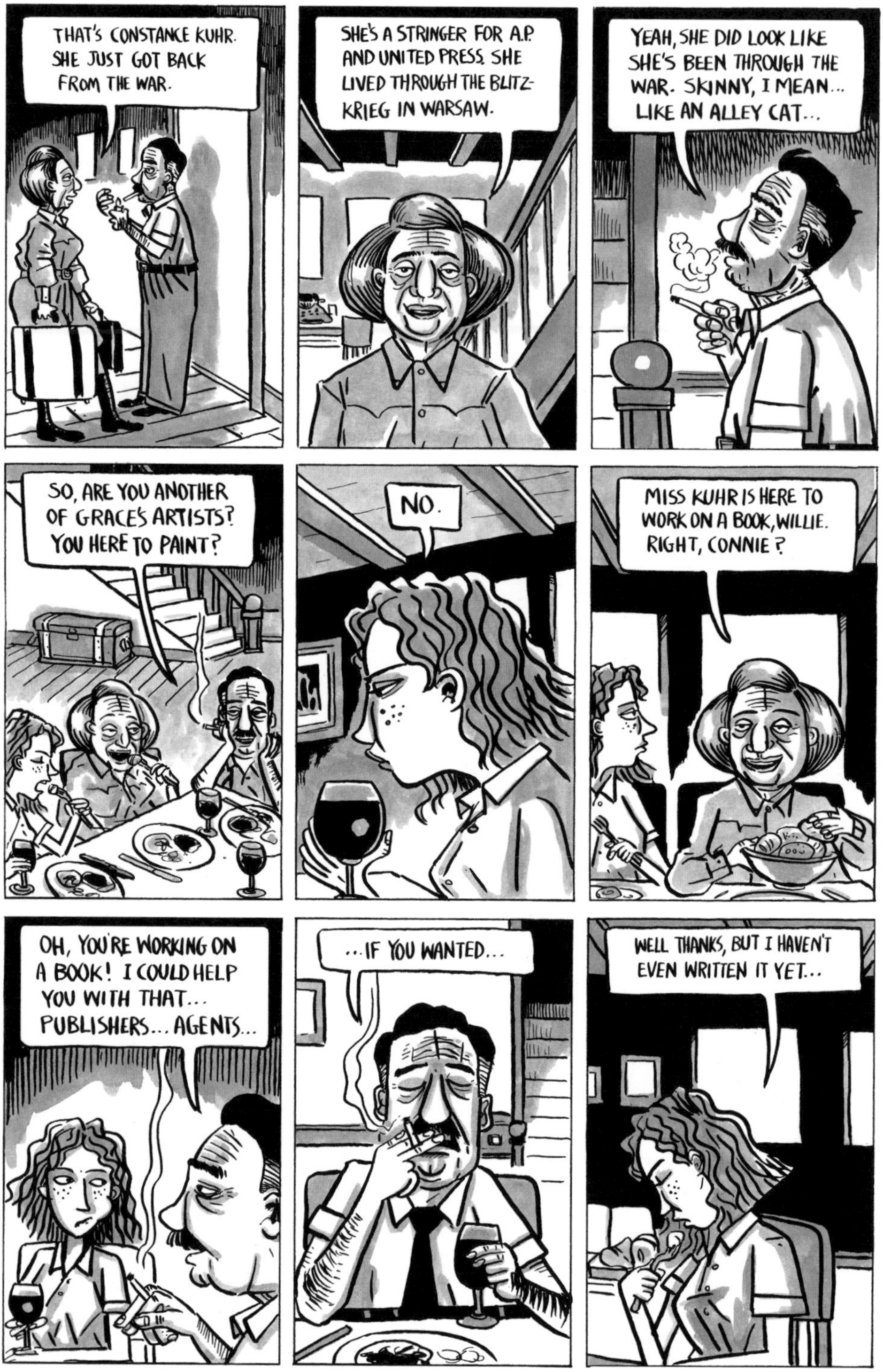
THAT'S CONSTANCE KUHR. SHE JUST GOT BACK FROM THE WAR.
SHE'S A STRINGER FOR A.P. AND UNITED PRESS. SHE LIVED THROUGH THE BLITZ-KRIEG IN WARSAW.
YEAH, SHE DID LOOK LIKE SHE'S BEEN THROUGH THE WAR. SKINNY, I MEAN... LIKE AN ALLEY CAT...
SO, ARE YOU ANOTHER OF GRACE'S ARTISTS? YOU HERE TO PAINT?
NO.
MISS KUHR IS HERE TO WORK ON A BOOK, WILLIE. RIGHT, CONNIE?
OH, YOU'RE WORKING ON A BOOK! I COULD HELP YOU WITH THAT... PUBLISHERS... AGENTS...
...IF YOU WANTED...
WELL THANKS, BUT I HAVEN'T EVEN WRITTEN IT YET...

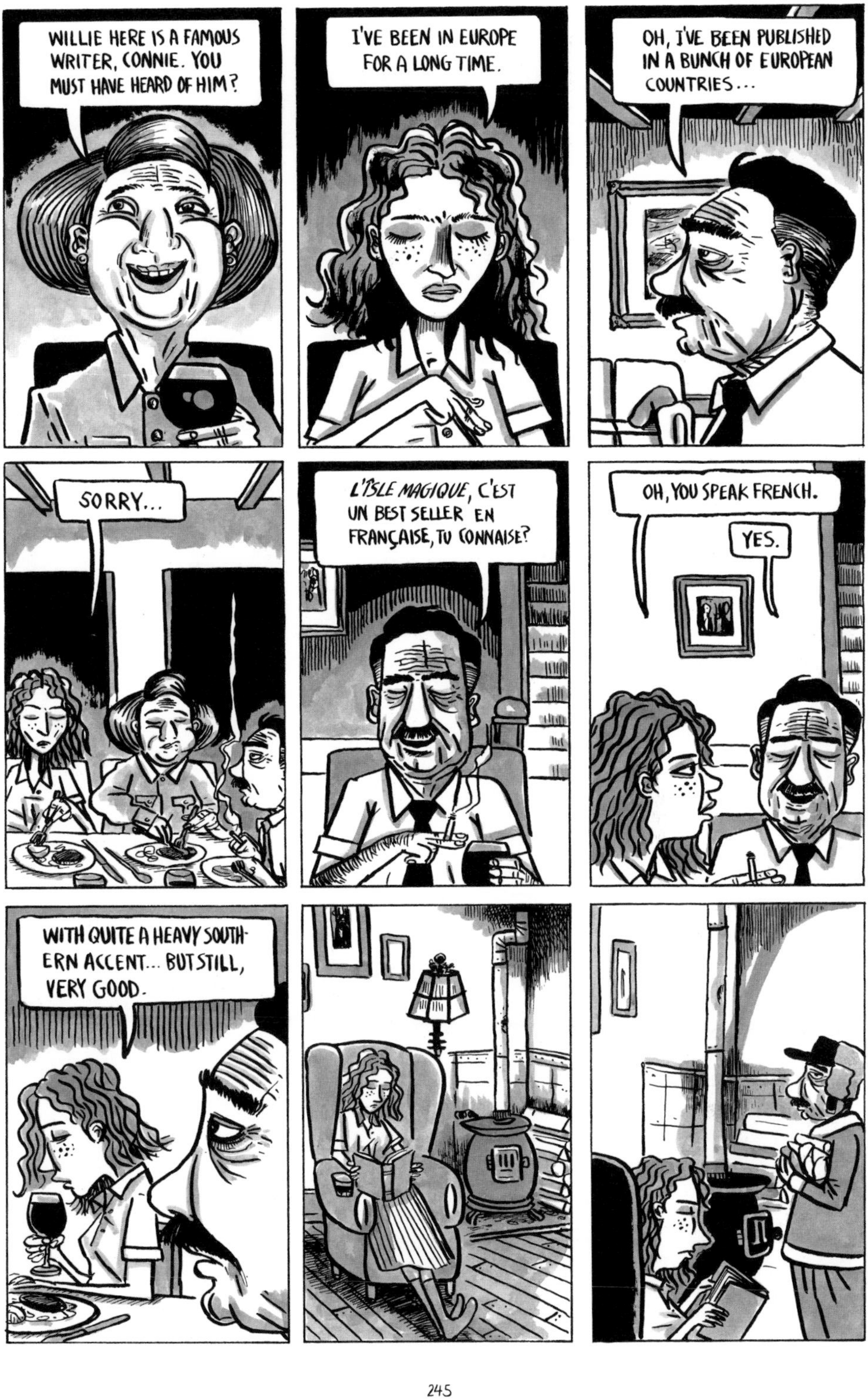
WILLIE HERE IS A FAMOUS WRITER, CONNIE. YOU MUST HAVE HEARD OF HIM?
I'VE BEEN IN EUROPE FOR A LONG TIME.
OH, I'VE BEEN PUBLISHED IN A BUNCH OF EUROPEAN COUNTRIES...
SORRY...
L'ISLE MAGIQUE, C'EST UN BEST SELLER EN FRANÇAISE, TU CONNAISE?
OH, YOU SPEAK FRENCH.
YES.
WITH QUITE A HEAVY SOUTHERN ACCENT... BUT STILL, VERY GOOD.

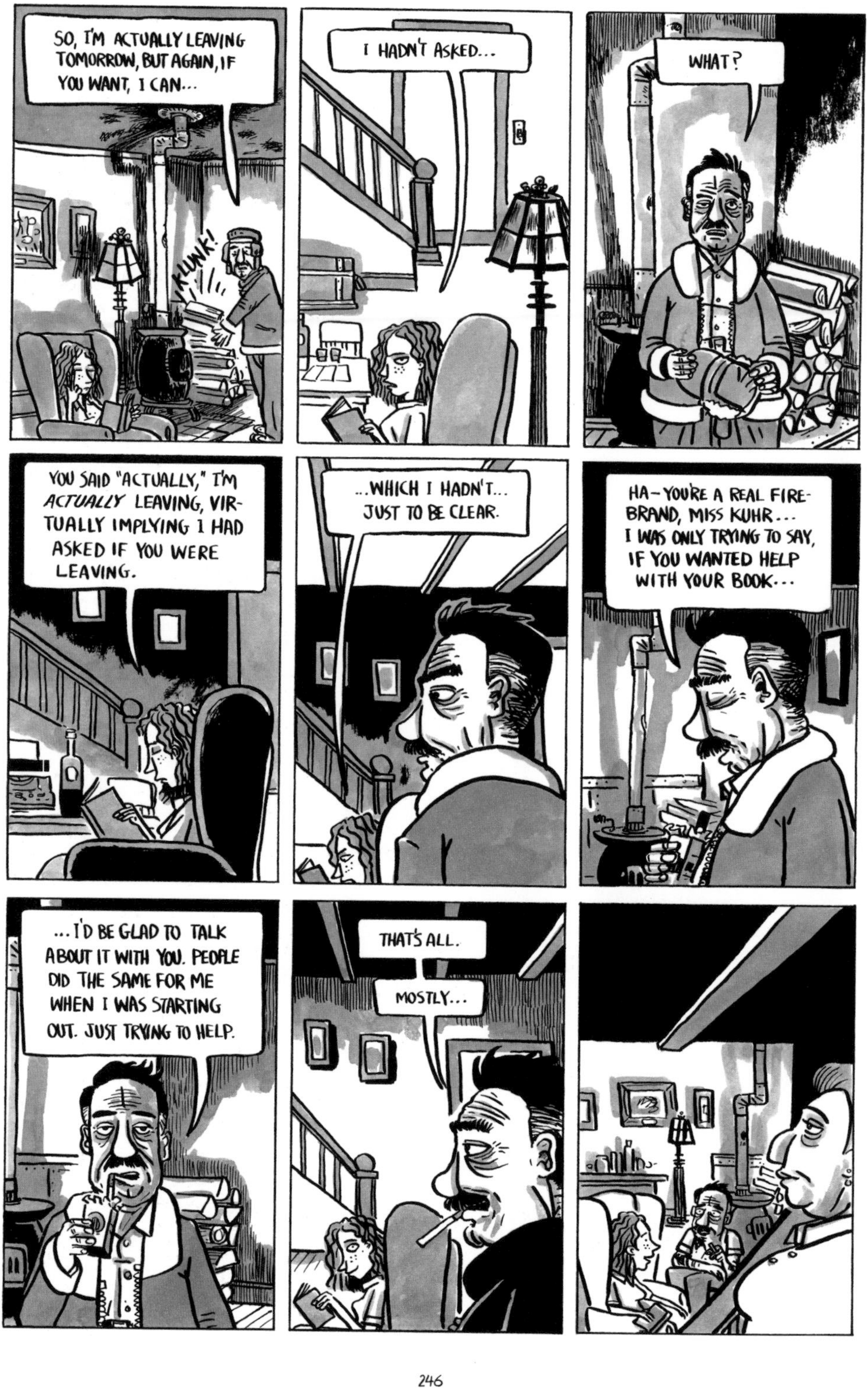
SO, I'M ACTUALLY LEAVING TOMORROW, BUT AGAIN, IF YOU WANT, I CAN...
KLUNK!
I HADN'T ASKED...
WHAT?
YOU SAID "ACTUALLY," I'M *ACTUALLY* LEAVING, VIRTUALLY IMPLYING I HAD ASKED IF YOU WERE LEAVING.
...WHICH I HADN'T... JUST TO BE CLEAR.
HA-- YOU'RE A REAL FIREBRAND, MISS KUHR... I WAS ONLY TRYING TO SAY, IF YOU WANTED HELP WITH YOUR BOOK...
...I'D BE GLAD TO TALK ABOUT IT WITH YOU. PEOPLE DID THE SAME FOR ME WHEN I WAS STARTING OUT. JUST TRYING TO HELP.
THAT'S ALL.
MOSTLY...

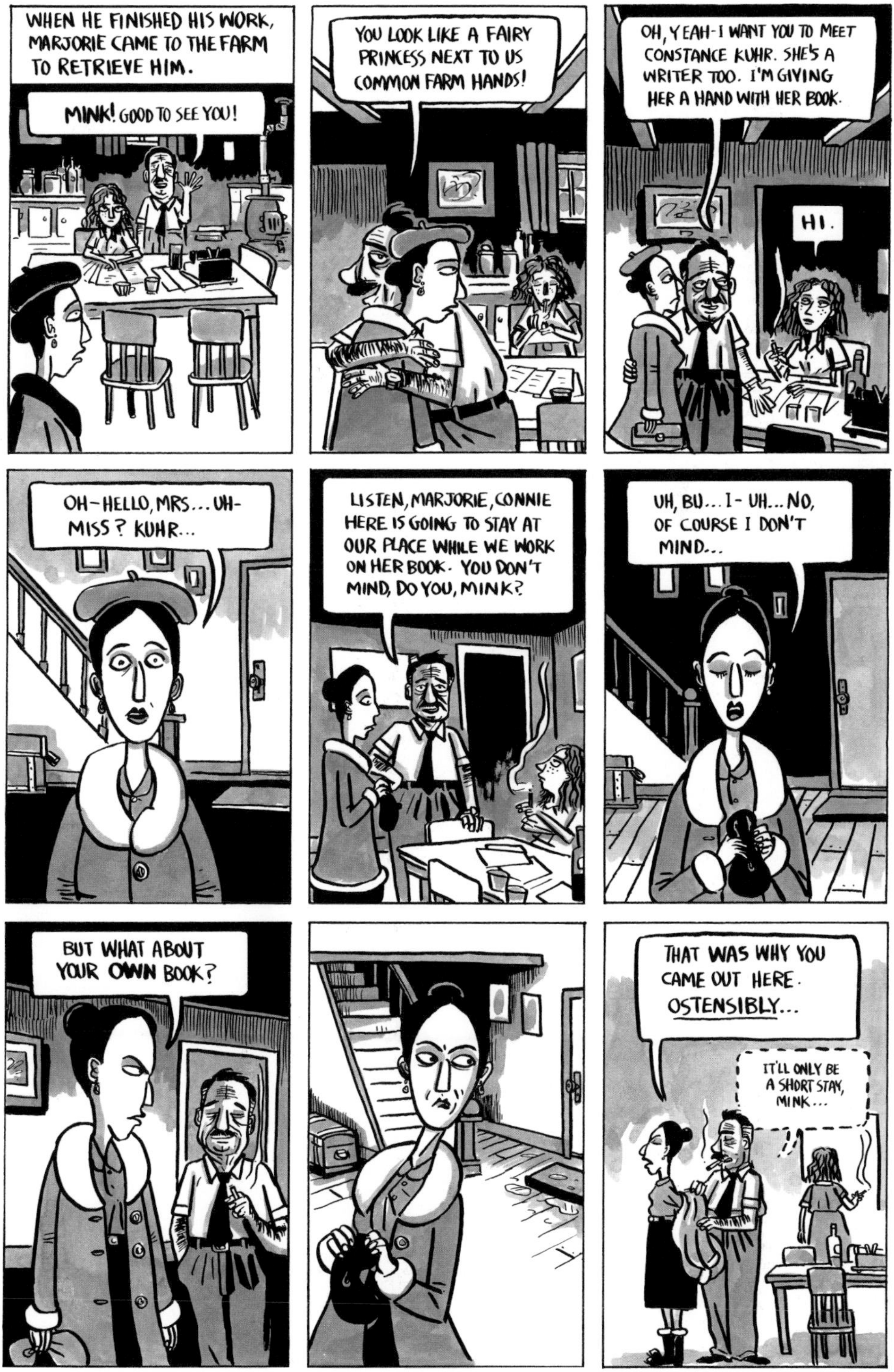
WHEN HE FINISHED HIS WORK, MARJORIE CAME TO THE FARM TO RETRIEVE HIM.
MINK! GOOD TO SEE YOU!
YOU LOOK LIKE A FAIRY PRINCESS NEXT TO US COMMON FARM HANDS!
OH, YEAH- I WANT YOU TO MEET CONSTANCE KUHR. SHE'S A WRITER TOO. I'M GIVING HER A HAND WITH HER BOOK.
HI.
OH- HELLO, MRS... UH- MISS? KUHR...
LISTEN, MARJORIE, CONNIE HERE IS GOING TO STAY AT OUR PLACE WHILE WE WORK ON HER BOOK. YOU DON'T MIND, DO YOU, MINK?
UH, BU... I- UH... NO, OF COURSE I DON'T MIND...
BUT WHAT ABOUT YOUR OWN BOOK?
THAT WAS WHY YOU CAME OUT HERE. OSTENSIBLY...
IT'LL ONLY BE A SHORT STAY, MINK...

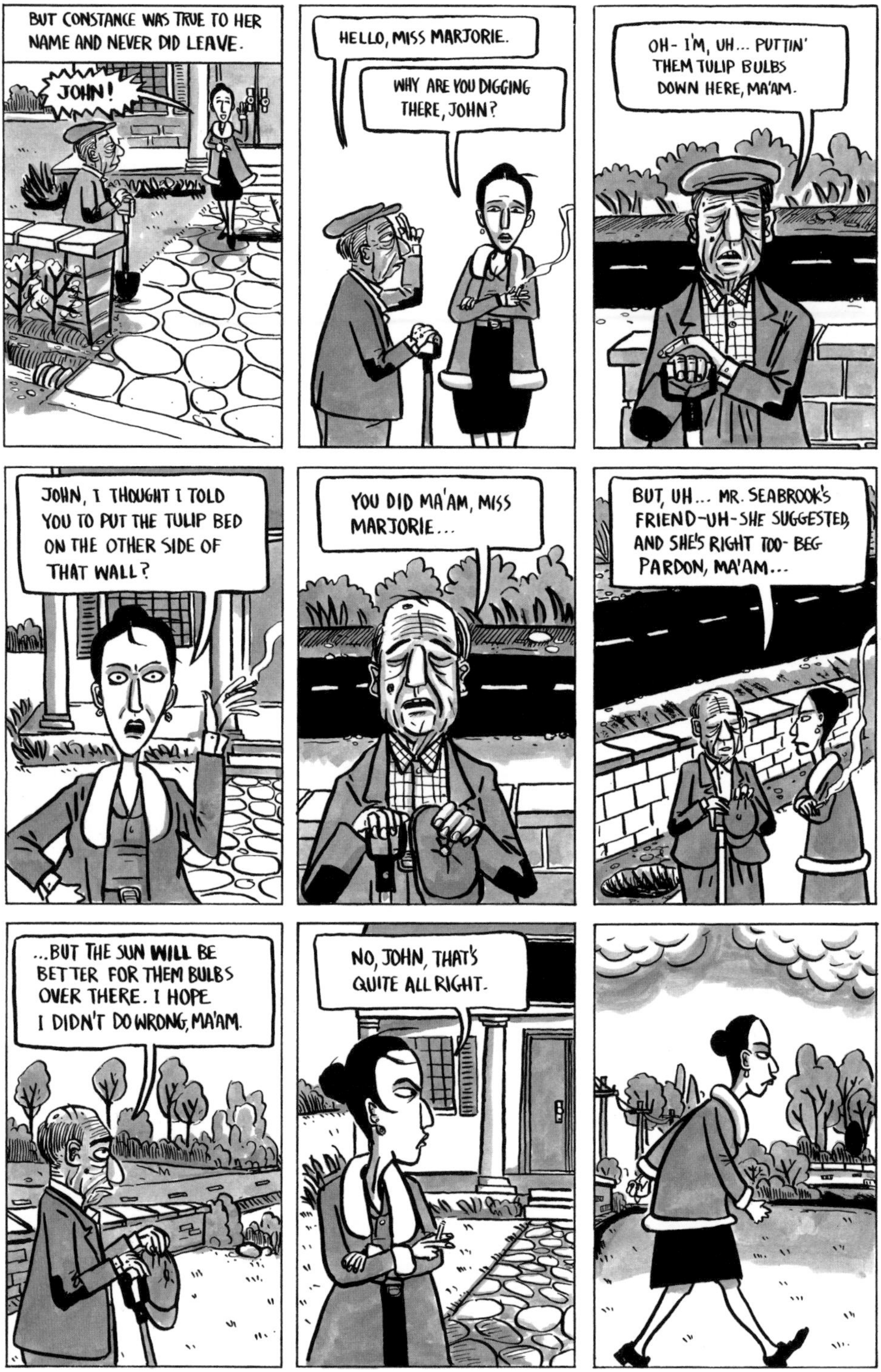
BUT CONSTANCE WAS TRUE TO HER NAME AND NEVER DID LEAVE.
JOHN!
HELLO, MISS MARJORIE.
WHY ARE YOU DIGGING THERE, JOHN?
OH- I'M, UH... PUTTIN' THEM TULIP BULBS DOWN HERE, MA'AM.
JOHN, I THOUGHT I TOLD YOU TO PUT THE TULIP BED ON THE OTHER SIDE OF THAT WALL?
YOU DID MA'AM, MISS MARJORIE...
BUT, UH... MR. SEABROOK'S FRIEND-UH-SHE SUGGESTED, AND SHE'S RIGHT TOO- BEG PARDON, MA'AM...
...BUT THE SUN WILL BE BETTER FOR THEM BULBS OVER THERE. I HOPE I DIDN'T DO WRONG, MA'AM.
NO, JOHN, THAT'S QUITE ALL RIGHT.

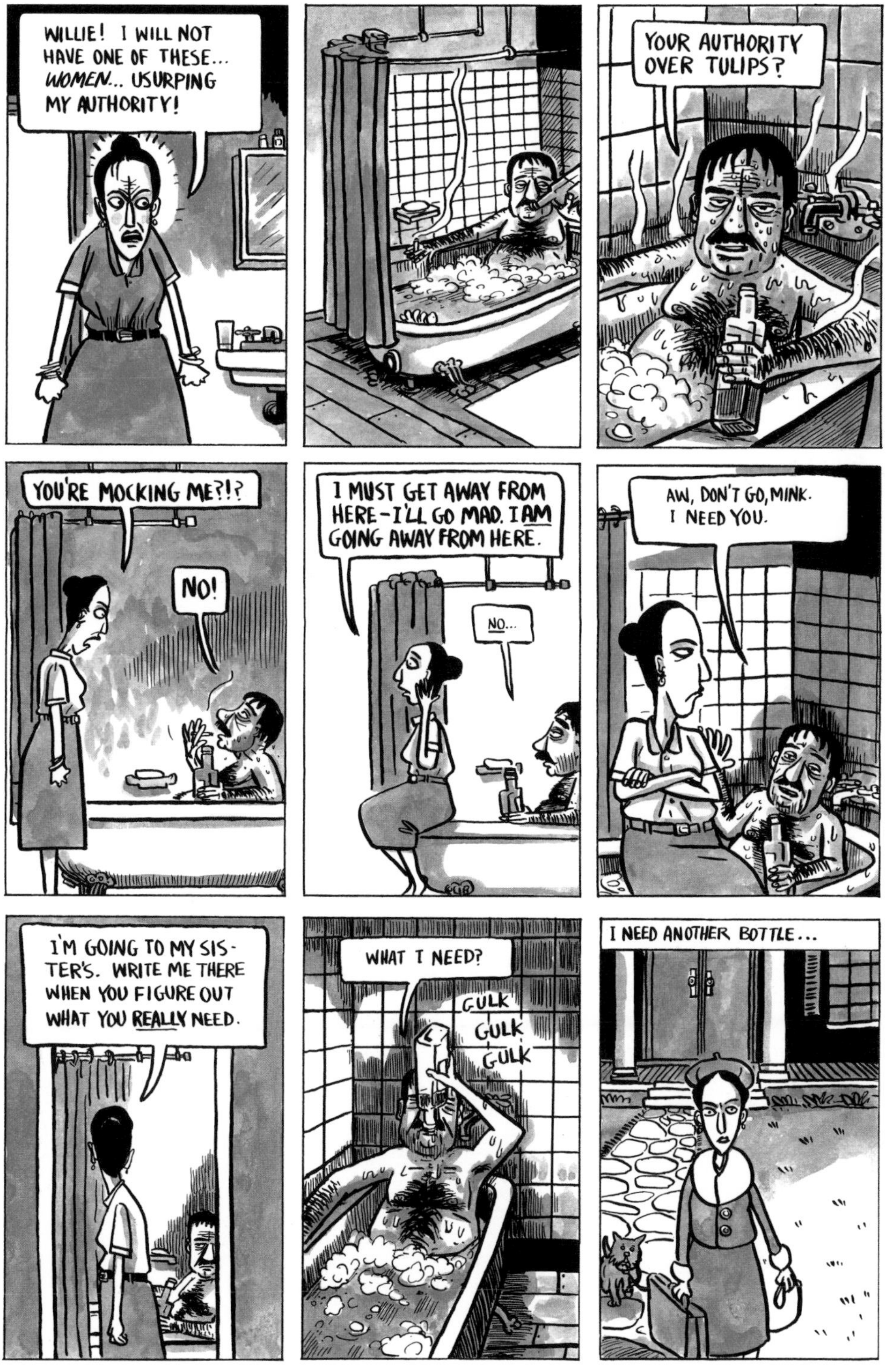

WILLIE! I WILL NOT HAVE ONE OF THESE... *WOMEN*... USURPING MY AUTHORITY!
YOUR AUTHORITY OVER TULIPS?
YOU'RE MOCKING ME?!?
NO!
I MUST GET AWAY FROM HERE—I'LL GO MAD. I AM GOING AWAY FROM HERE.
NO...
AW, DON'T GO, MINK. I NEED YOU.
I'M GOING TO MY SISTER'S. WRITE ME THERE WHEN YOU FIGURE OUT WHAT YOU REALLY NEED.
WHAT I NEED?
GULK
GULK
GULK
I NEED ANOTHER BOTTLE...

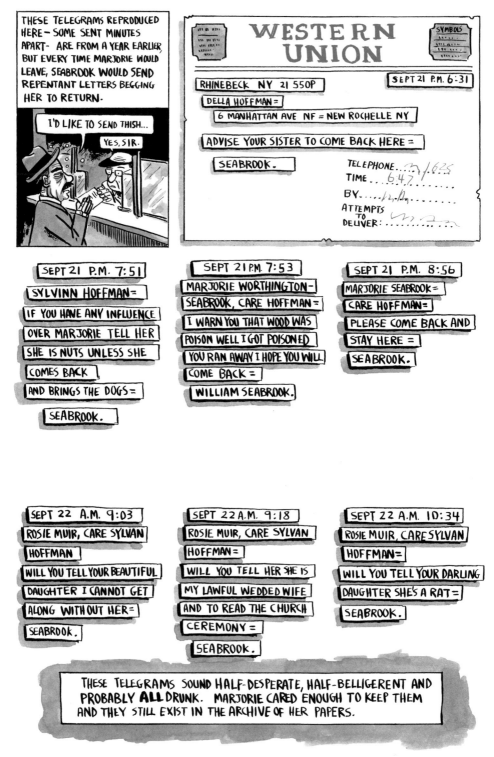

THESE TELEGRAMS REPRODUCED HERE— SOME SENT MINUTES APART— ARE FROM A YEAR EARLIER, BUT EVERY TIME MARJORIE WOULD LEAVE, SEABROOK WOULD SEND REPENTANT LETTERS BEGGING HER TO RETURN.

I'D LIKE TO SEND THISH...

YES, SIR.

WESTERN UNION

SYMBOLS

RHINEBECK NY 21 550P

SEPT 21 P.M. 6:31

DELLA HOFFMAN =

6 MANHATTAN AVE NF = NEW ROCHELLE NY

ADVISE YOUR SISTER TO COME BACK HERE =

SEABROOK.

TELEPHONE....37/625
TIME.... 647
BY.....Mdg
ATTEMPTS TO DELIVER: Mrs

SEPT 21 P.M. 7:51

SYLVINN HOFFMAN =

IF YOU HAVE ANY INFLUENCE OVER MARJORIE TELL HER SHE IS NUTS UNLESS SHE COMES BACK AND BRINGS THE DOGS =

SEABROOK.

SEPT 21 P.M. 7:53

MARJORIE WORTHINGTON- SEABROOK, CARE HOFFMAN =

I WARN YOU THAT WOOD WAS POISON WELL I GOT POISONED YOU RAN AWAY I HOPE YOU WILL COME BACK =

WILLIAM SEABROOK.

SEPT 21 P.M. 8:56

MARJORIE SEABROOK =

CARE HOFFMAN =

PLEASE COME BACK AND STAY HERE =

SEABROOK.

SEPT 22 A.M. 9:03

ROSIE MUIR, CARE SYLVAN HOFFMAN

WILL YOU TELL YOUR BEAUTIFUL DAUGHTER I CANNOT GET ALONG WITHOUT HER =

SEABROOK.

SEPT 22 A.M. 9:18

ROSIE MUIR, CARE SYLVAN HOFFMAN =

WILL YOU TELL HER SHE IS MY LAWFUL WEDDED WIFE AND TO READ THE CHURCH CEREMONY =

SEABROOK.

SEPT 22 A.M. 10:34

ROSIE MUIR, CARE SYLVAN HOFFMAN =

WILL YOU TELL YOUR DARLING DAUGHTER SHE'S A RAT =

SEABROOK.

THESE TELEGRAMS SOUND HALF-DESPERATE, HALF-BELLIGERENT AND PROBABLY **ALL** DRUNK. MARJORIE CARED ENOUGH TO KEEP THEM AND THEY STILL EXIST IN THE ARCHIVE OF HER PAPERS.

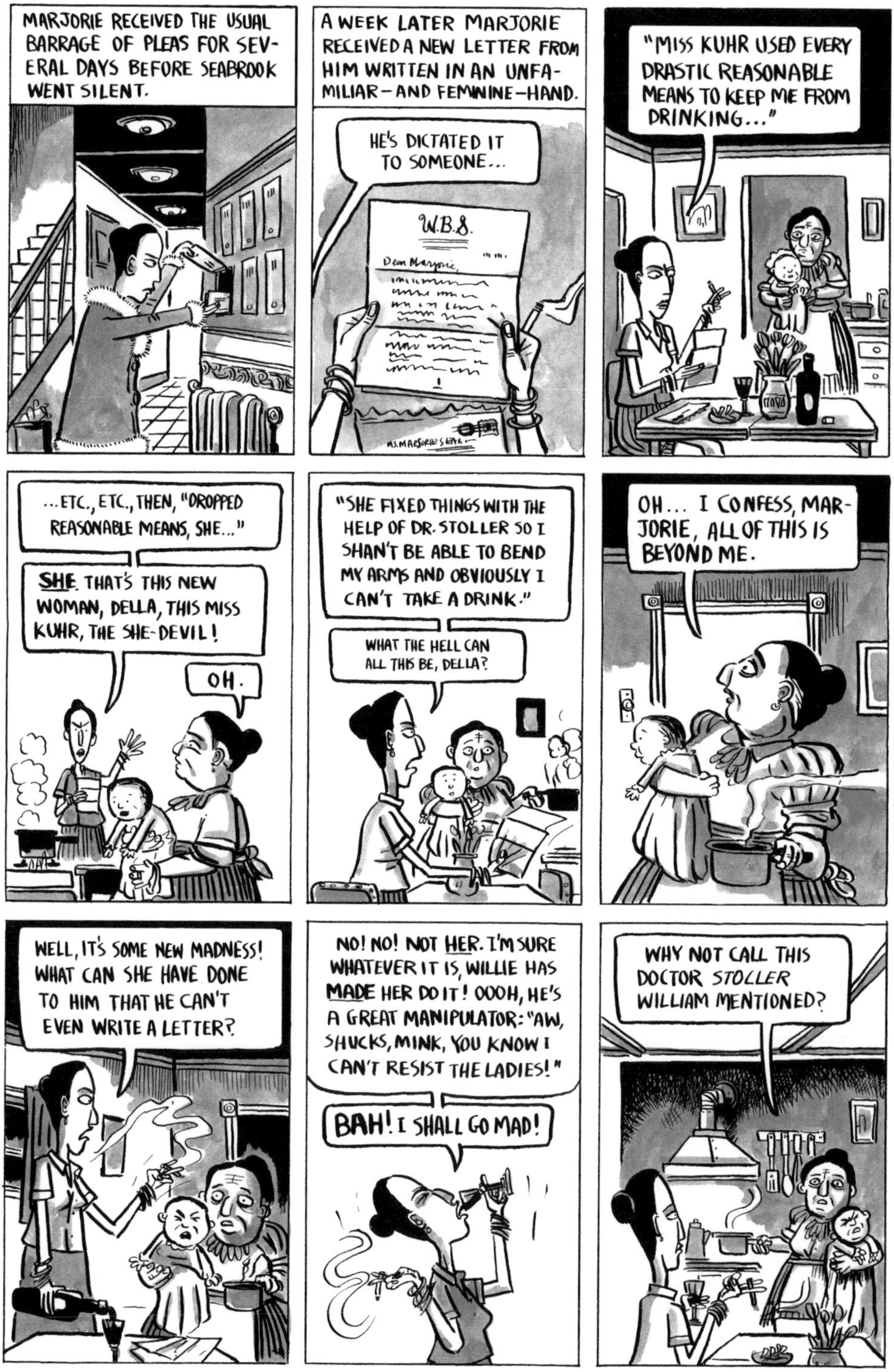
MARJORIE RECEIVED THE USUAL BARRAGE OF PLEAS FOR SEVERAL DAYS BEFORE SEABROOK WENT SILENT.
A WEEK LATER MARJORIE RECEIVED A NEW LETTER FROM HIM WRITTEN IN AN UNFAMILIAR—AND FEMININE—HAND.
HE'S DICTATED IT TO SOMEONE...
W.B.S.
Dear Marjorie,
"MISS KUHR USED EVERY DRASTIC REASONABLE MEANS TO KEEP ME FROM DRINKING..."
...ETC., ETC., THEN, "DROPPED REASONABLE MEANS, SHE..."
SHE. THAT'S THIS NEW WOMAN, DELLA, THIS MISS KUHR, THE SHE-DEVIL!
OH.
"SHE FIXED THINGS WITH THE HELP OF DR. STOLLER SO I SHAN'T BE ABLE TO BEND MY ARMS AND OBVIOUSLY I CAN'T TAKE A DRINK."
WHAT THE HELL CAN ALL THIS BE, DELLA?
OH... I CONFESS, MARJORIE, ALL OF THIS IS BEYOND ME.
WELL, IT'S SOME NEW MADNESS! WHAT CAN SHE HAVE DONE TO HIM THAT HE CAN'T EVEN WRITE A LETTER?
NO! NO! NOT HER. I'M SURE WHATEVER IT IS, WILLIE HAS MADE HER DO IT! OOOH, HE'S A GREAT MANIPULATOR: "AW, SHUCKS, MINK, YOU KNOW I CAN'T RESIST THE LADIES!"
BAH! I SHALL GO MAD!
WHY NOT CALL THIS DOCTOR STOLLER WILLIAM MENTIONED?

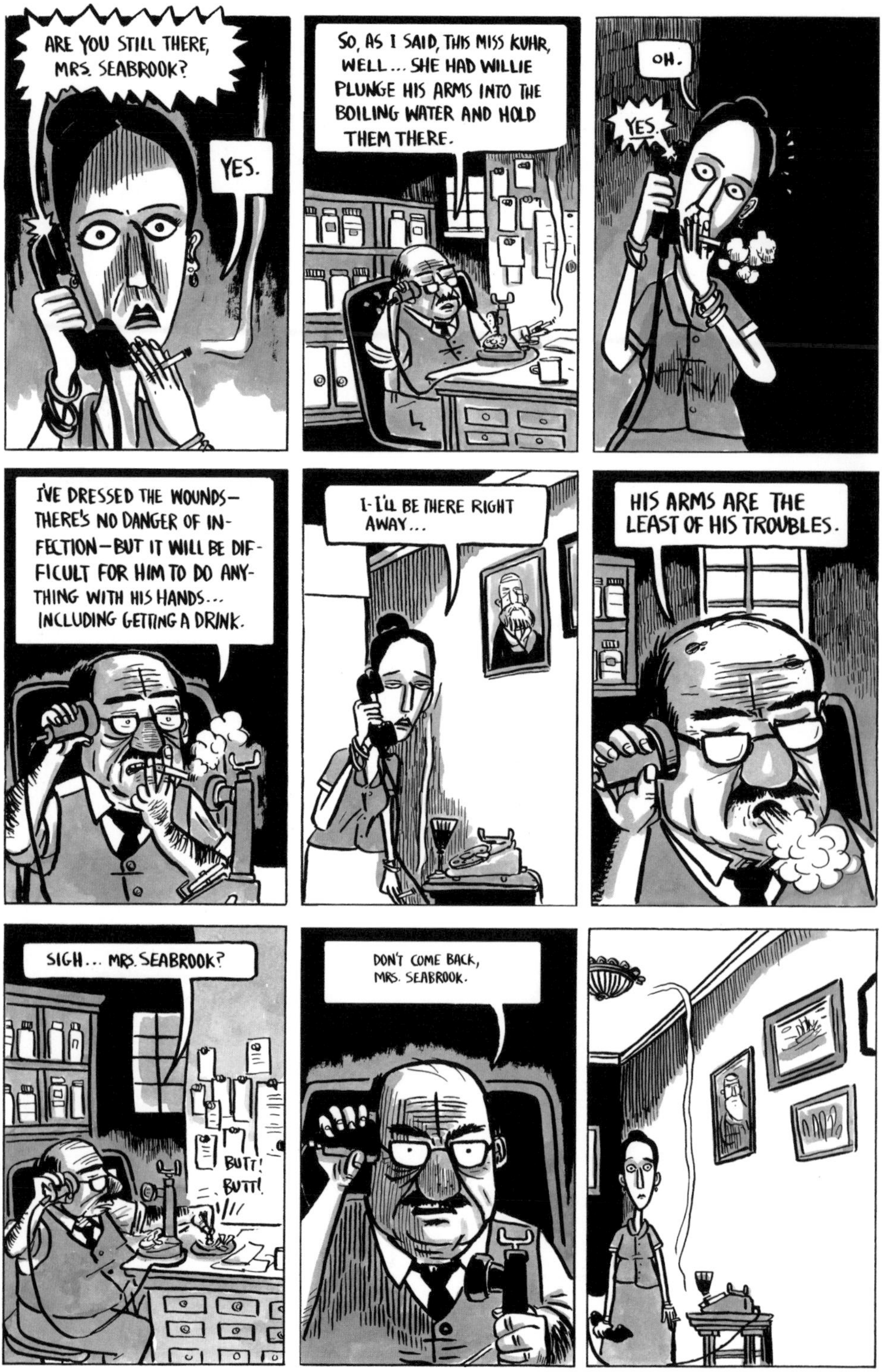
ARE YOU STILL THERE, MRS. SEABROOK?
YES.
SO, AS I SAID, THIS MISS KUHR, WELL... SHE HAD WILLIE PLUNGE HIS ARMS INTO THE BOILING WATER AND HOLD THEM THERE.
OH.
YES.
I'VE DRESSED THE WOUNDS— THERE'S NO DANGER OF INFECTION—BUT IT WILL BE DIFFICULT FOR HIM TO DO ANYTHING WITH HIS HANDS... INCLUDING GETTING A DRINK.
I-I'LL BE THERE RIGHT AWAY...
HIS ARMS ARE THE LEAST OF HIS TROUBLES.
SIGH... MRS. SEABROOK?
BUTT! BUTT!
DON'T COME BACK, MRS. SEABROOK.

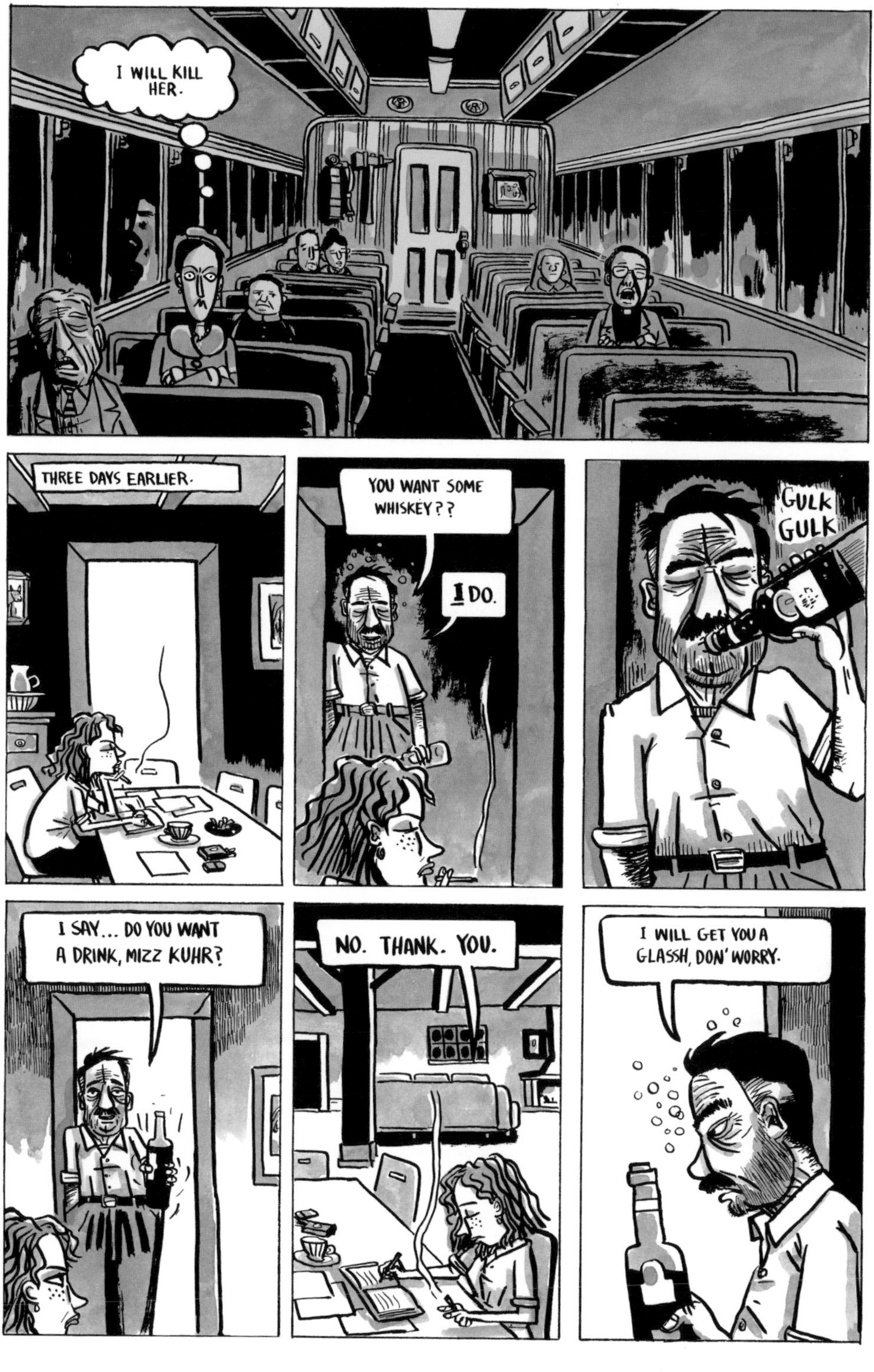
I WILL KILL HER.
THREE DAYS EARLIER.
YOU WANT SOME WHISKEY??
I DO.
GULK GULK
I SAY... DO YOU WANT A DRINK, MIZZ KUHR?
NO. THANK. YOU.
I WILL GET YOU A GLASSH, DON' WORRY.

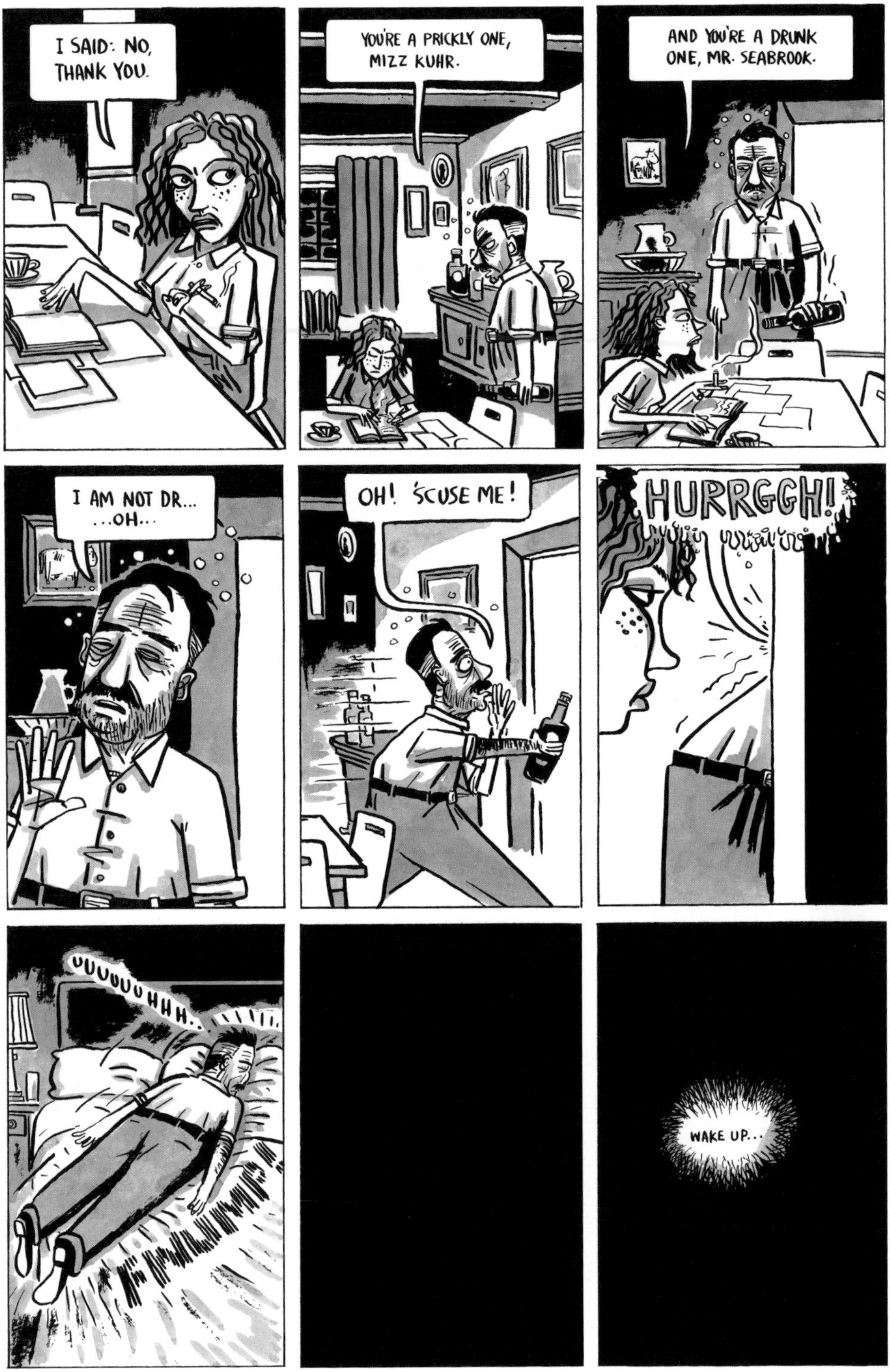
I SAID: NO, THANK YOU.
YOU'RE A PRICKLY ONE, MIZZ KUHR.
AND YOU'RE A DRUNK ONE, MR. SEABROOK.
I AM NOT DR... ...OH...
OH! 'SCUSE ME!
HURRGGH!
UUUUUUHHH...
WAKE UP...

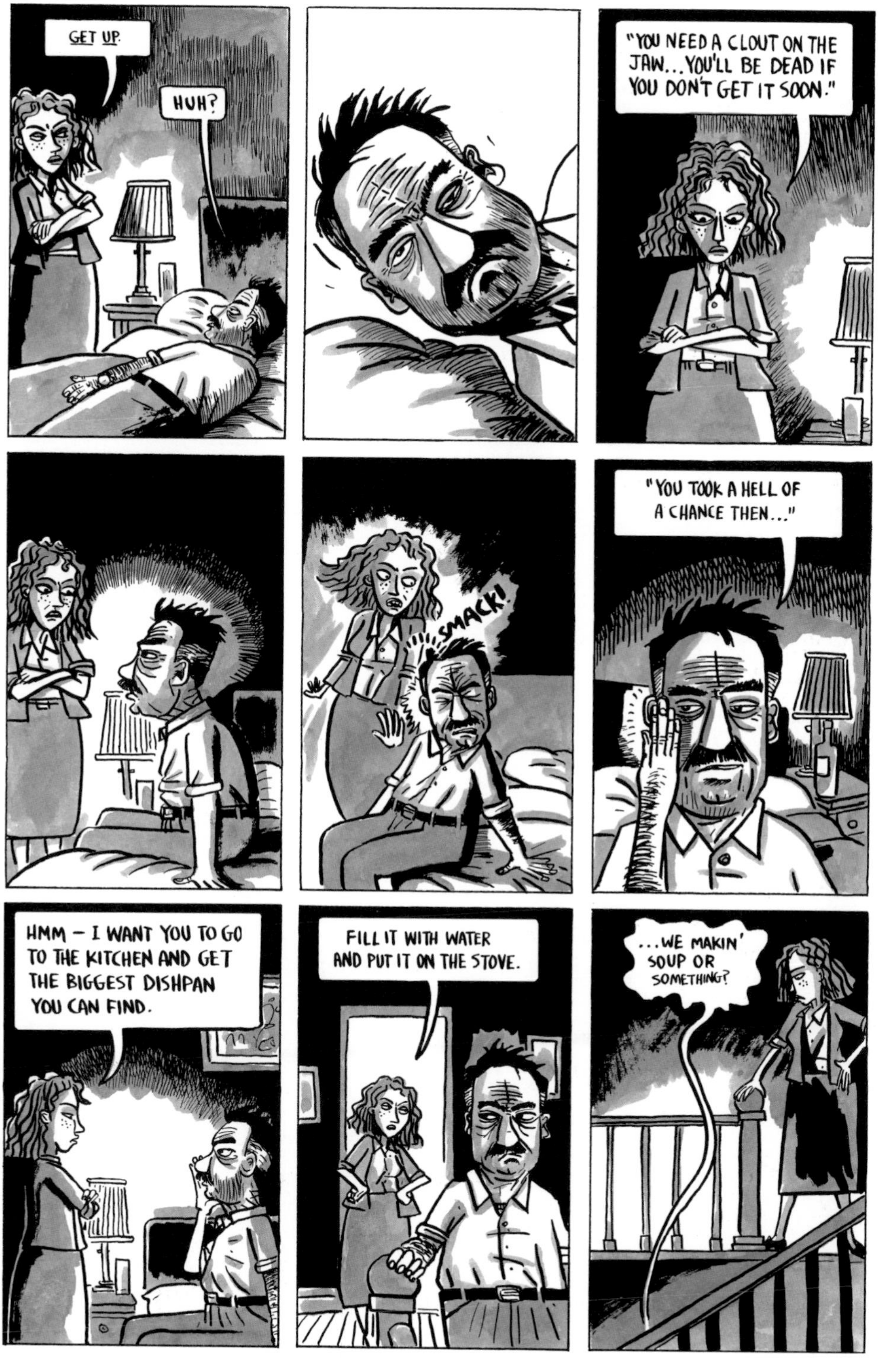
GET UP.
HUH?
"YOU NEED A CLOUT ON THE JAW... YOU'LL BE DEAD IF YOU DON'T GET IT SOON."
SMACK!
"YOU TOOK A HELL OF A CHANCE THEN..."
HMM – I WANT YOU TO GO TO THE KITCHEN AND GET THE BIGGEST DISHPAN YOU CAN FIND.
FILL IT WITH WATER AND PUT IT ON THE STOVE.
...WE MAKIN' SOUP OR SOMETHING?

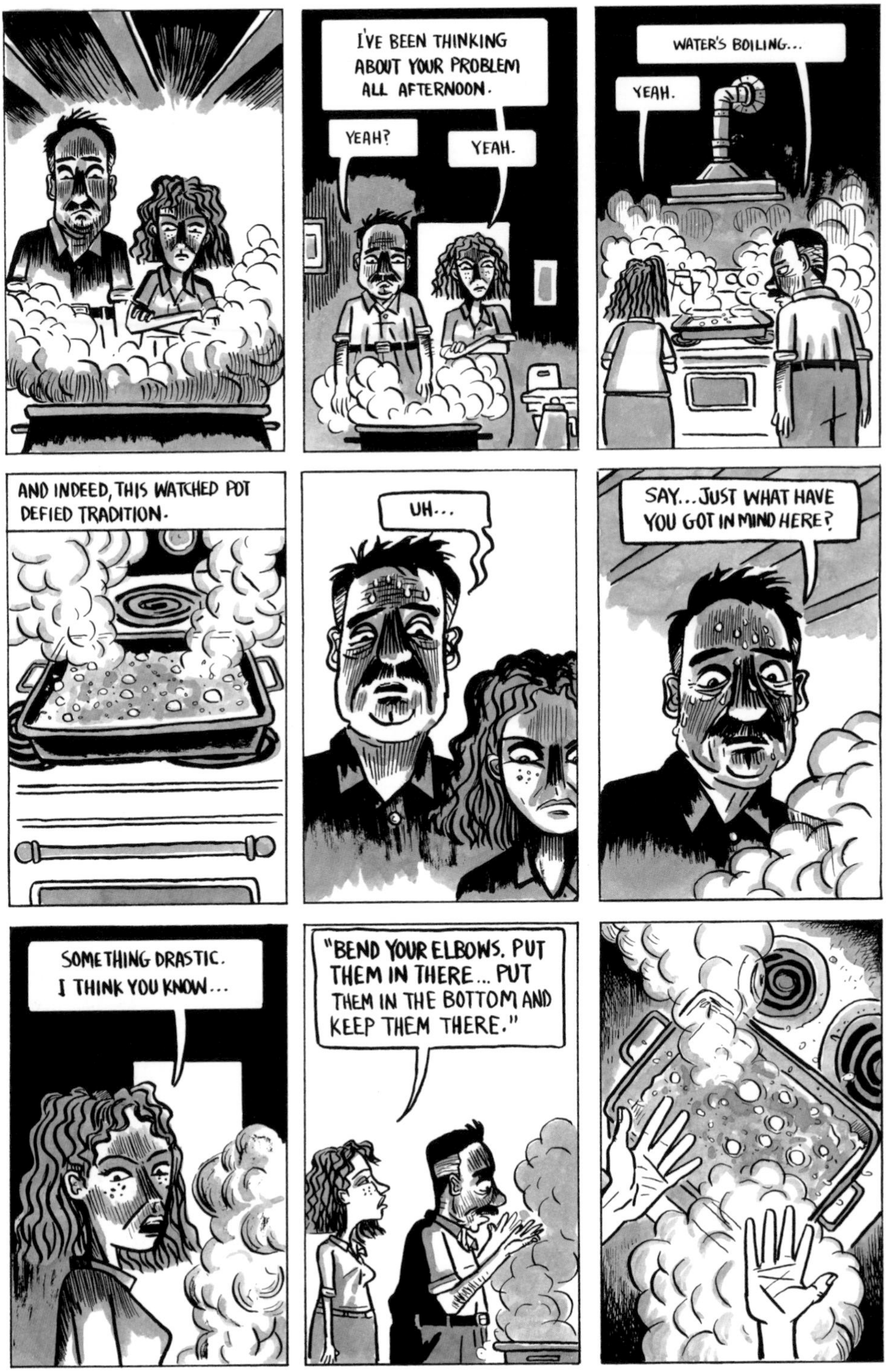
I'VE BEEN THINKING ABOUT YOUR PROBLEM ALL AFTERNOON.
YEAH?
YEAH.
WATER'S BOILING...
YEAH.
AND INDEED, THIS WATCHED POT DEFIED TRADITION.
UH...
SAY... JUST WHAT HAVE YOU GOT IN MIND HERE?
SOMETHING DRASTIC. I THINK YOU KNOW...
"BEND YOUR ELBOWS. PUT THEM IN THERE... PUT THEM IN THE BOTTOM AND KEEP THEM THERE."

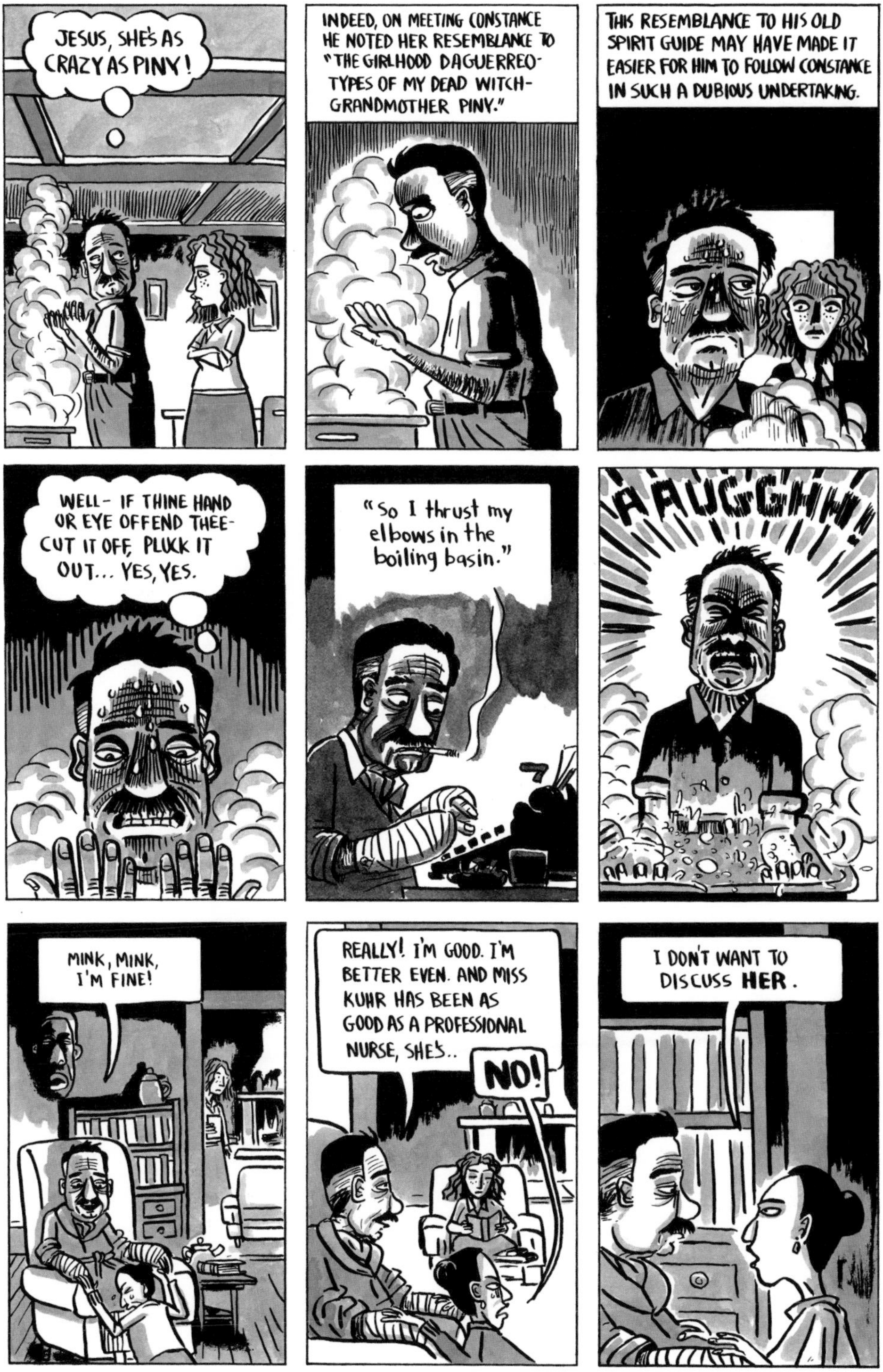
JESUS, SHE'S AS CRAZY AS PINY!
INDEED, ON MEETING CONSTANCE HE NOTED HER RESEMBLANCE TO "THE GIRLHOOD DAGUERREOTYPES OF MY DEAD WITCH-GRANDMOTHER PINY."
THIS RESEMBLANCE TO HIS OLD SPIRIT GUIDE MAY HAVE MADE IT EASIER FOR HIM TO FOLLOW CONSTANCE IN SUCH A DUBIOUS UNDERTAKING.
WELL- IF THINE HAND OR EYE OFFEND THEE- CUT IT OFF, PLUCK IT OUT... YES, YES.
"So I thrust my elbows in the boiling basin."
AAUGGHH!
MINK, MINK, I'M FINE!
REALLY! I'M GOOD. I'M BETTER EVEN. AND MISS KUHR HAS BEEN AS GOOD AS A PROFESSIONAL NURSE, SHE'S..
NO!
I DON'T WANT TO DISCUSS HER.

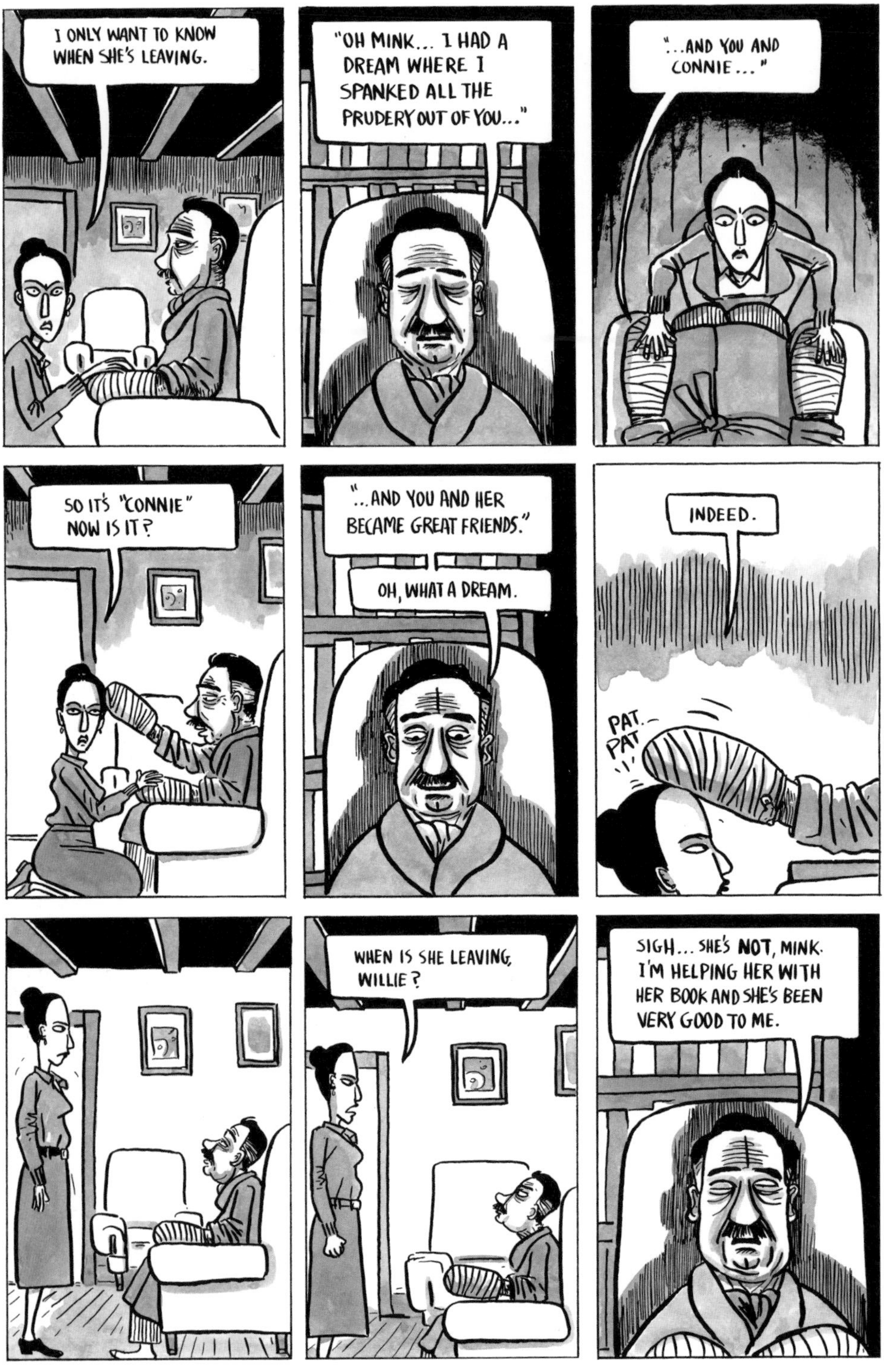
I ONLY WANT TO KNOW WHEN SHE'S LEAVING.
"OH MINK... I HAD A DREAM WHERE I SPANKED ALL THE PRUDERY OUT OF YOU..."
"...AND YOU AND CONNIE..."
SO IT'S "CONNIE" NOW IS IT?
"...AND YOU AND HER BECAME GREAT FRIENDS."
OH, WHAT A DREAM.
INDEED.
PAT. PAT
WHEN IS SHE LEAVING, WILLIE?
SIGH... SHE'S NOT, MINK. I'M HELPING HER WITH HER BOOK AND SHE'S BEEN VERY GOOD TO ME.

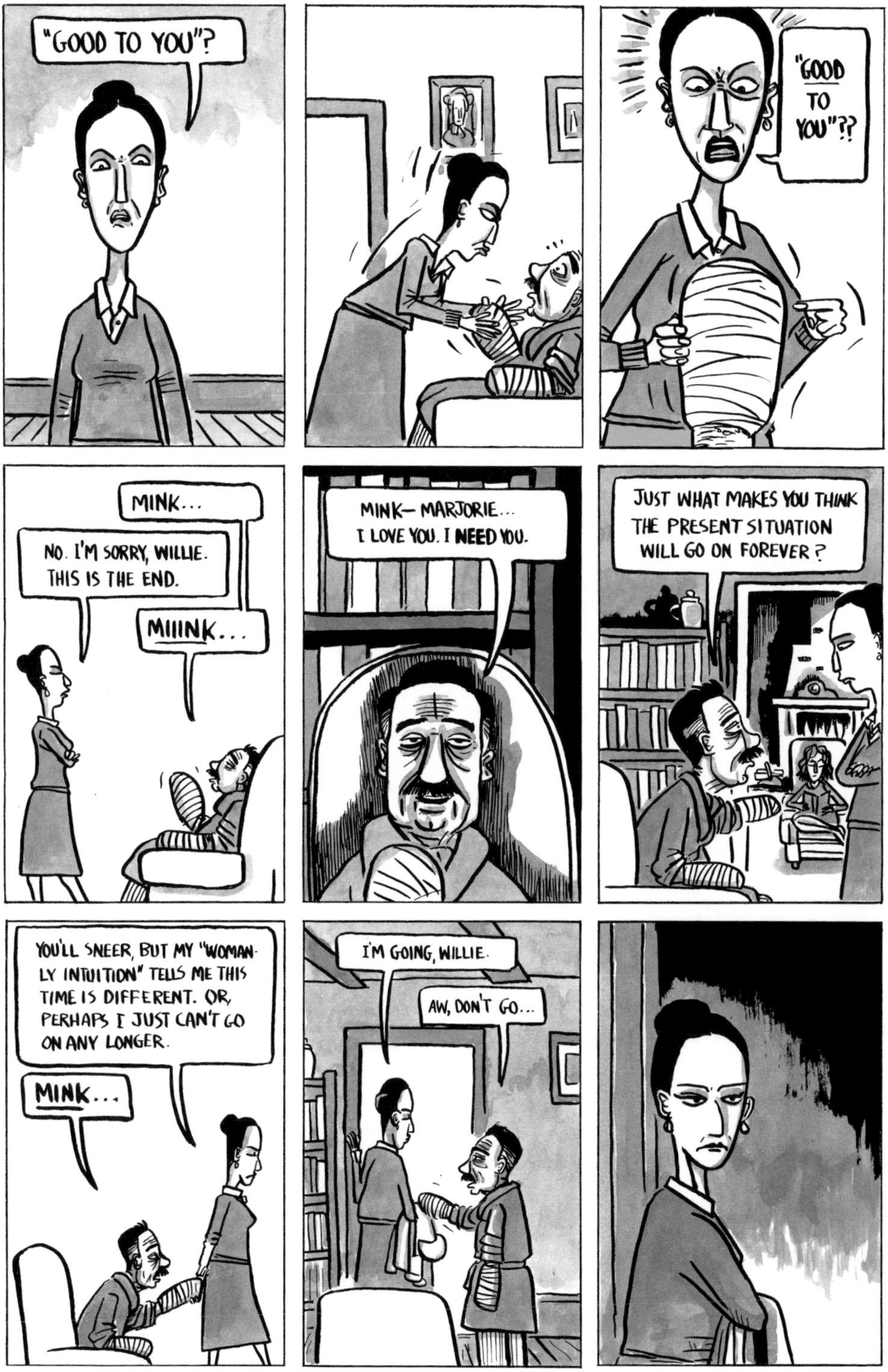
"GOOD TO YOU"?
"GOOD TO YOU"??
MINK...
NO. I'M SORRY, WILLIE. THIS IS THE END.
MIIINK...
MINK— MARJORIE... I LOVE YOU. I NEED YOU.
JUST WHAT MAKES YOU THINK THE PRESENT SITUATION WILL GO ON FOREVER?
YOU'LL SNEER, BUT MY "WOMANLY INTUITION" TELLS ME THIS TIME IS DIFFERENT. OR, PERHAPS I JUST CAN'T GO ON ANY LONGER.
MINK...
I'M GOING, WILLIE.
AW, DON'T GO...

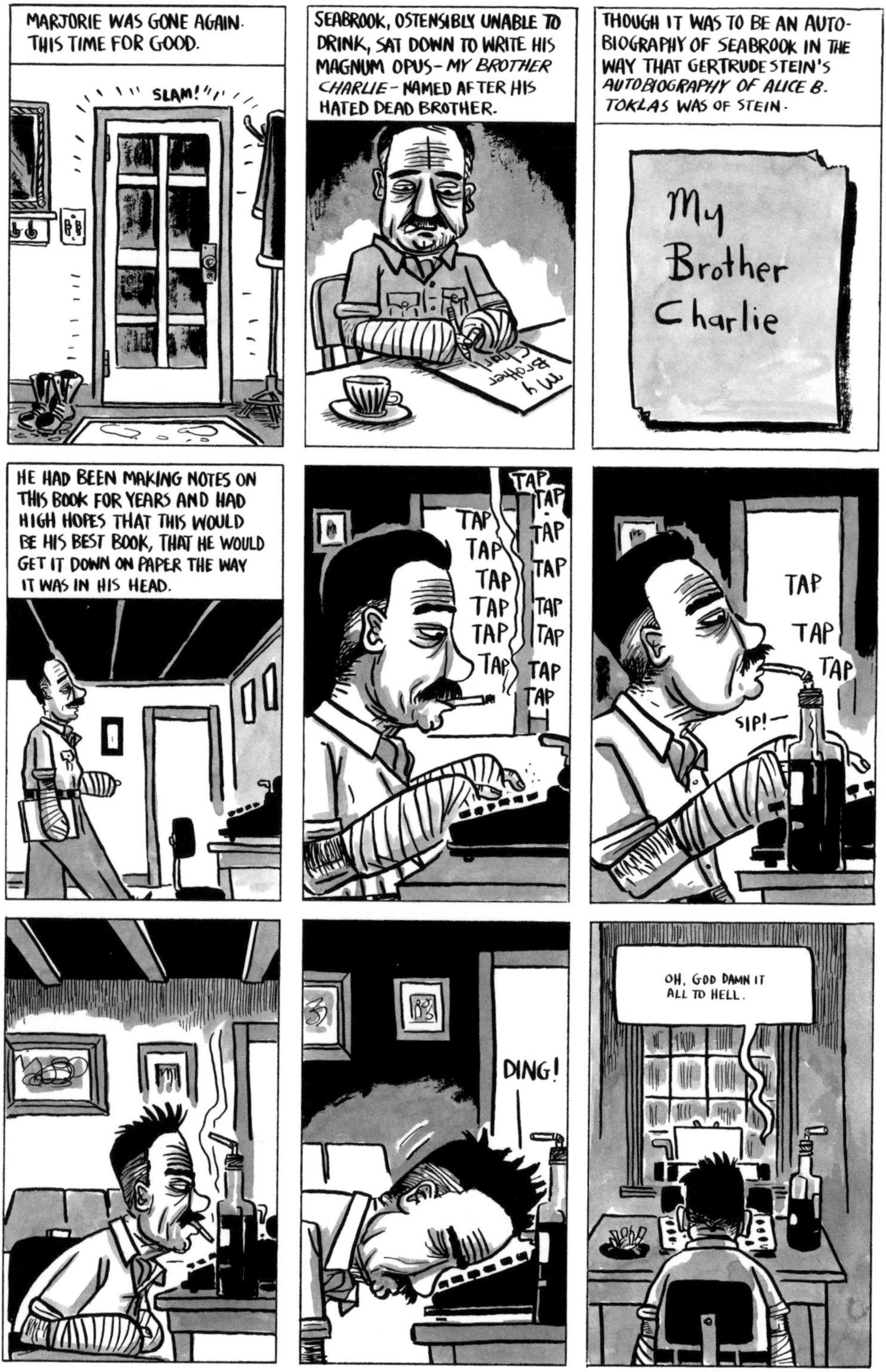
MARJORIE WAS GONE AGAIN. THIS TIME FOR GOOD.
SLAM!
SEABROOK, OSTENSIBLY UNABLE TO DRINK, SAT DOWN TO WRITE HIS MAGNUM OPUS– *MY BROTHER CHARLIE*– NAMED AFTER HIS HATED DEAD BROTHER.
My Brother Charlie
THOUGH IT WAS TO BE AN AUTOBIOGRAPHY OF SEABROOK IN THE WAY THAT GERTRUDE STEIN'S *AUTOBIOGRAPHY OF ALICE B. TOKLAS* WAS OF STEIN.
My Brother Charlie
HE HAD BEEN MAKING NOTES ON THIS BOOK FOR YEARS AND HAD HIGH HOPES THAT THIS WOULD BE HIS BEST BOOK, THAT HE WOULD GET IT DOWN ON PAPER THE WAY IT WAS IN HIS HEAD.
TAP TAP TAP TAP TAP TAP TAP TAP TAP TAP TAP TAP TAP TAP
TAP TAP TAP
SIP!–
DING!
OH, GOD DAMN IT ALL TO HELL.

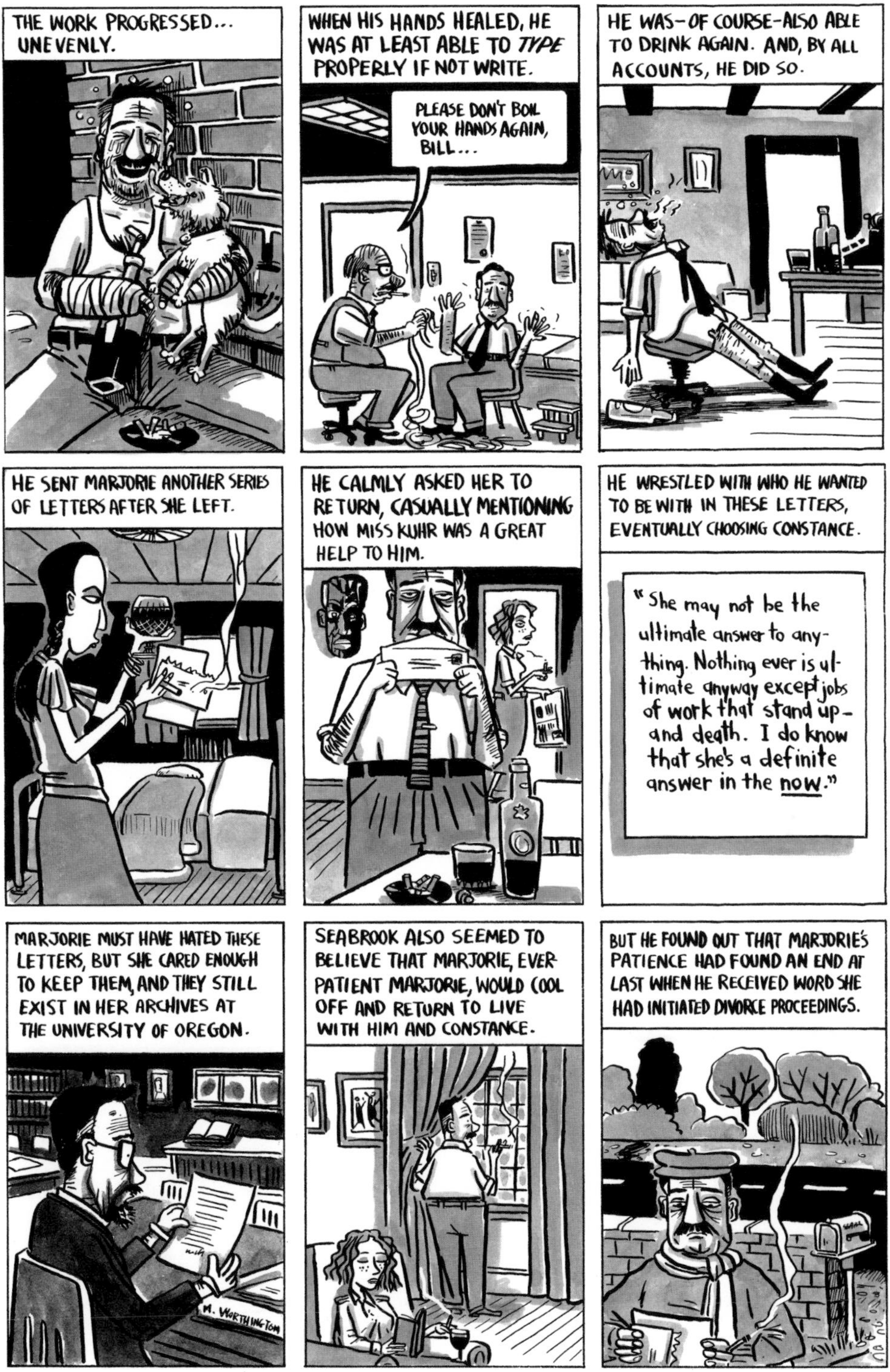
THE WORK PROGRESSED... UNEVENLY.
WHEN HIS HANDS HEALED, HE WAS AT LEAST ABLE TO *TYPE* PROPERLY IF NOT WRITE.
PLEASE DON'T BOIL YOUR HANDS AGAIN, BILL...
HE WAS—OF COURSE—ALSO ABLE TO DRINK AGAIN. AND, BY ALL ACCOUNTS, HE DID SO.
HE SENT MARJORIE ANOTHER SERIES OF LETTERS AFTER SHE LEFT.
HE CALMLY ASKED HER TO RETURN, CASUALLY MENTIONING HOW MISS KUHR WAS A GREAT HELP TO HIM.
HE WRESTLED WITH WHO HE WANTED TO BE WITH IN THESE LETTERS, EVENTUALLY CHOOSING CONSTANCE.
"She may not be the ultimate answer to anything. Nothing ever is ultimate anyway except jobs of work that stand up—and death. I do know that she's a definite answer in the now."
MARJORIE MUST HAVE HATED THESE LETTERS, BUT SHE CARED ENOUGH TO KEEP THEM, AND THEY STILL EXIST IN HER ARCHIVES AT THE UNIVERSITY OF OREGON.
M. WORTHINGTON
SEABROOK ALSO SEEMED TO BELIEVE THAT MARJORIE, EVER-PATIENT MARJORIE, WOULD COOL OFF AND RETURN TO LIVE WITH HIM AND CONSTANCE.
BUT HE FOUND OUT THAT MARJORIE'S PATIENCE HAD FOUND AN END AT LAST WHEN HE RECEIVED WORD SHE HAD INITIATED DIVORCE PROCEEDINGS.

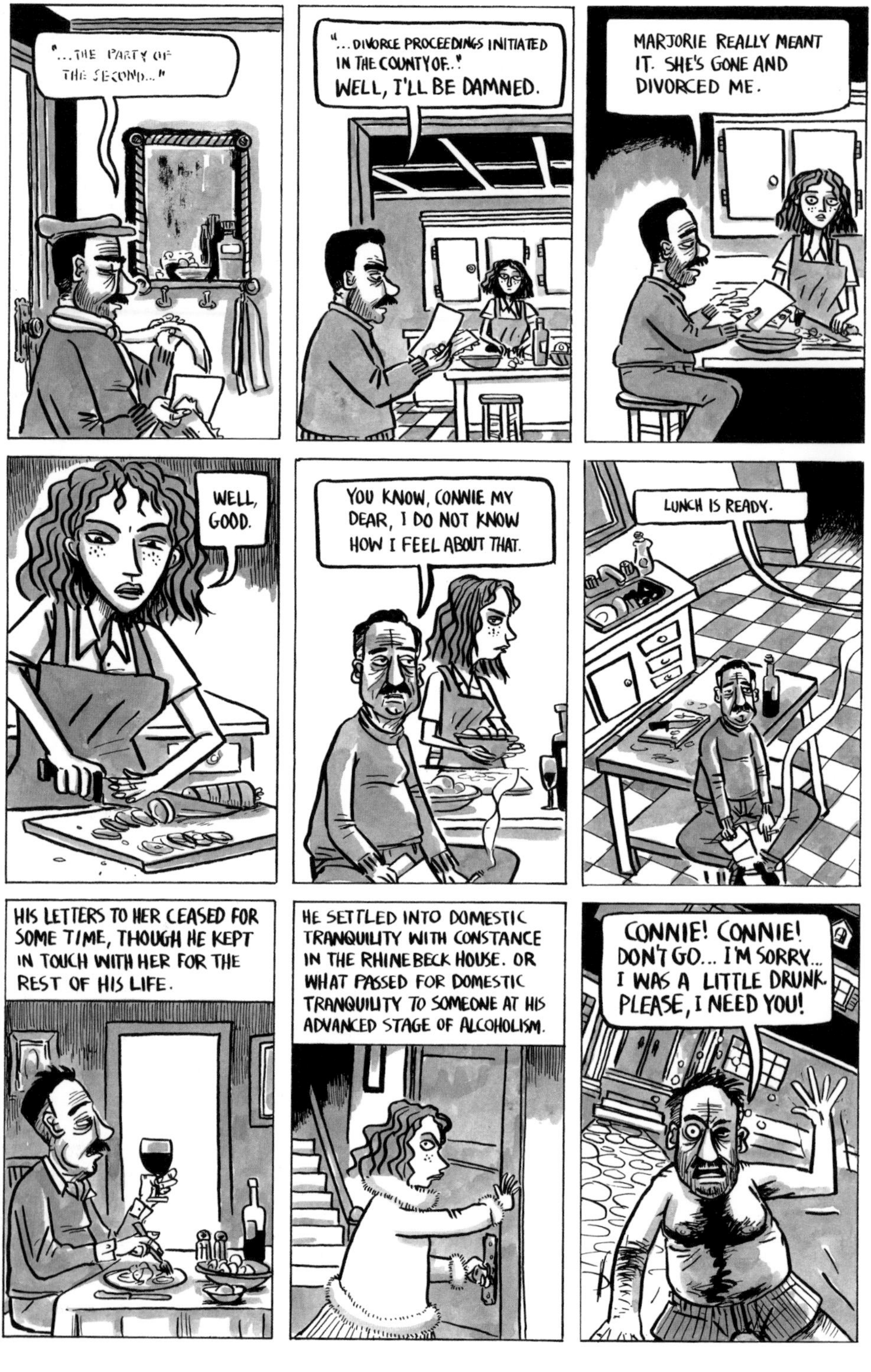
"...THE PARTY OF THE SECOND..."
"...DIVORCE PROCEEDINGS INITIATED IN THE COUNTY OF.." WELL, I'LL BE DAMNED.
MARJORIE REALLY MEANT IT. SHE'S GONE AND DIVORCED ME.
WELL, GOOD.
YOU KNOW, CONNIE MY DEAR, I DO NOT KNOW HOW I FEEL ABOUT THAT.
LUNCH IS READY.
HIS LETTERS TO HER CEASED FOR SOME TIME, THOUGH HE KEPT IN TOUCH WITH HER FOR THE REST OF HIS LIFE.
HE SETTLED INTO DOMESTIC TRANQUILITY WITH CONSTANCE IN THE RHINEBECK HOUSE. OR WHAT PASSED FOR DOMESTIC TRANQUILITY TO SOMEONE AT HIS ADVANCED STAGE OF ALCOHOLISM.
CONNIE! CONNIE! DON'T GO... I'M SORRY... I WAS A LITTLE DRUNK. PLEASE, I NEED YOU!

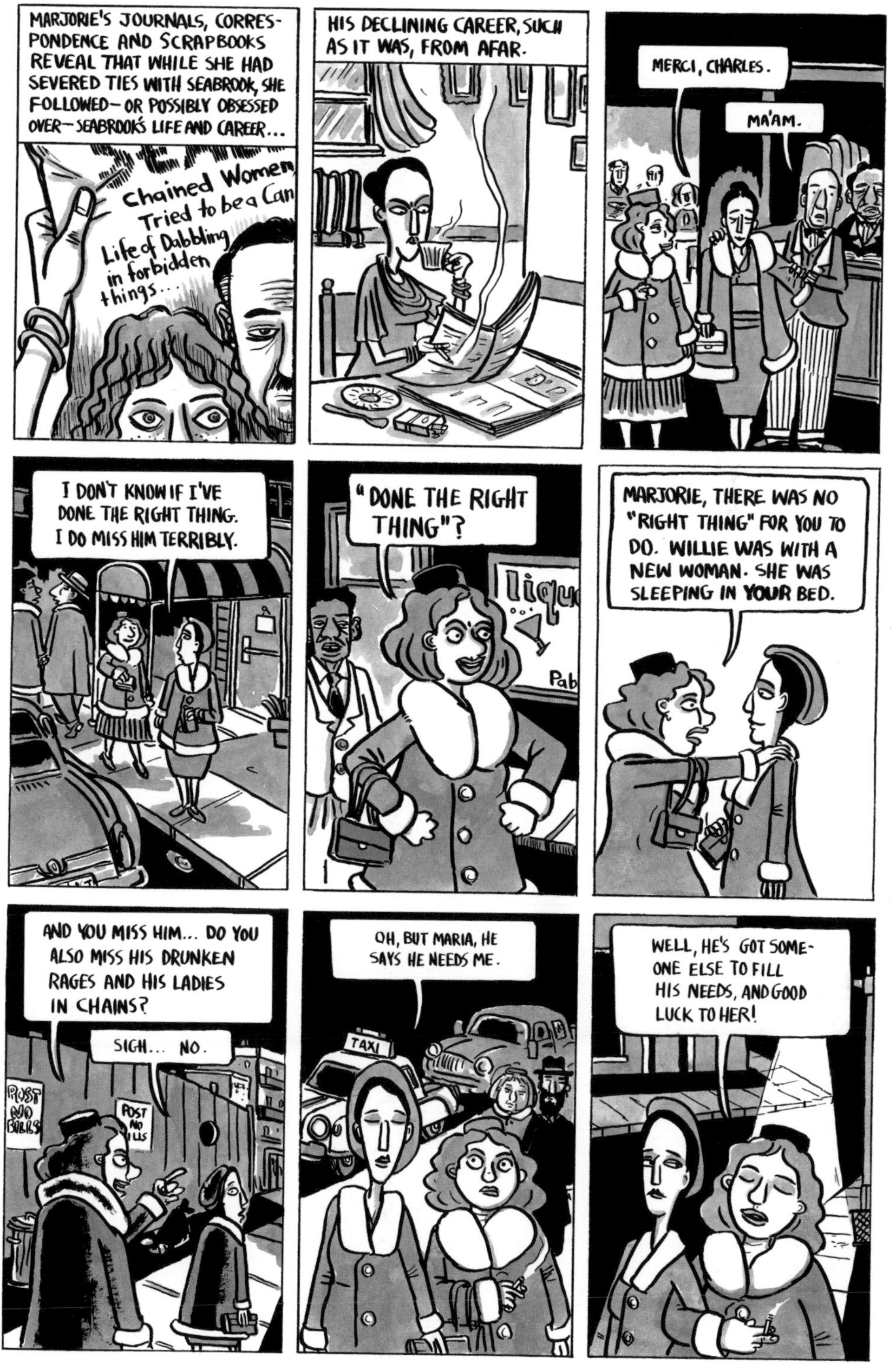
MARJORIE'S JOURNALS, CORRESPONDENCE AND SCRAPBOOKS REVEAL THAT WHILE SHE HAD SEVERED TIES WITH SEABROOK, SHE FOLLOWED— OR POSSIBLY OBSESSED OVER— SEABROOK'S LIFE AND CAREER...
Chained Women
Tried to be a Can
Life of Dabbling in forbidden things...
HIS DECLINING CAREER, SUCH AS IT WAS, FROM AFAR.
MERCI, CHARLES.
MA'AM.
I DON'T KNOW IF I'VE DONE THE RIGHT THING. I DO MISS HIM TERRIBLY.
"DONE THE RIGHT THING"?
MARJORIE, THERE WAS NO "RIGHT THING" FOR YOU TO DO. WILLIE WAS WITH A NEW WOMAN. SHE WAS SLEEPING IN YOUR BED.
AND YOU MISS HIM... DO YOU ALSO MISS HIS DRUNKEN RAGES AND HIS LADIES IN CHAINS?
SIGH... NO.
POST NO BILLS
OH, BUT MARIA, HE SAYS HE NEEDS ME.
TAXI
WELL, HE'S GOT SOMEONE ELSE TO FILL HIS NEEDS, AND GOOD LUCK TO HER!

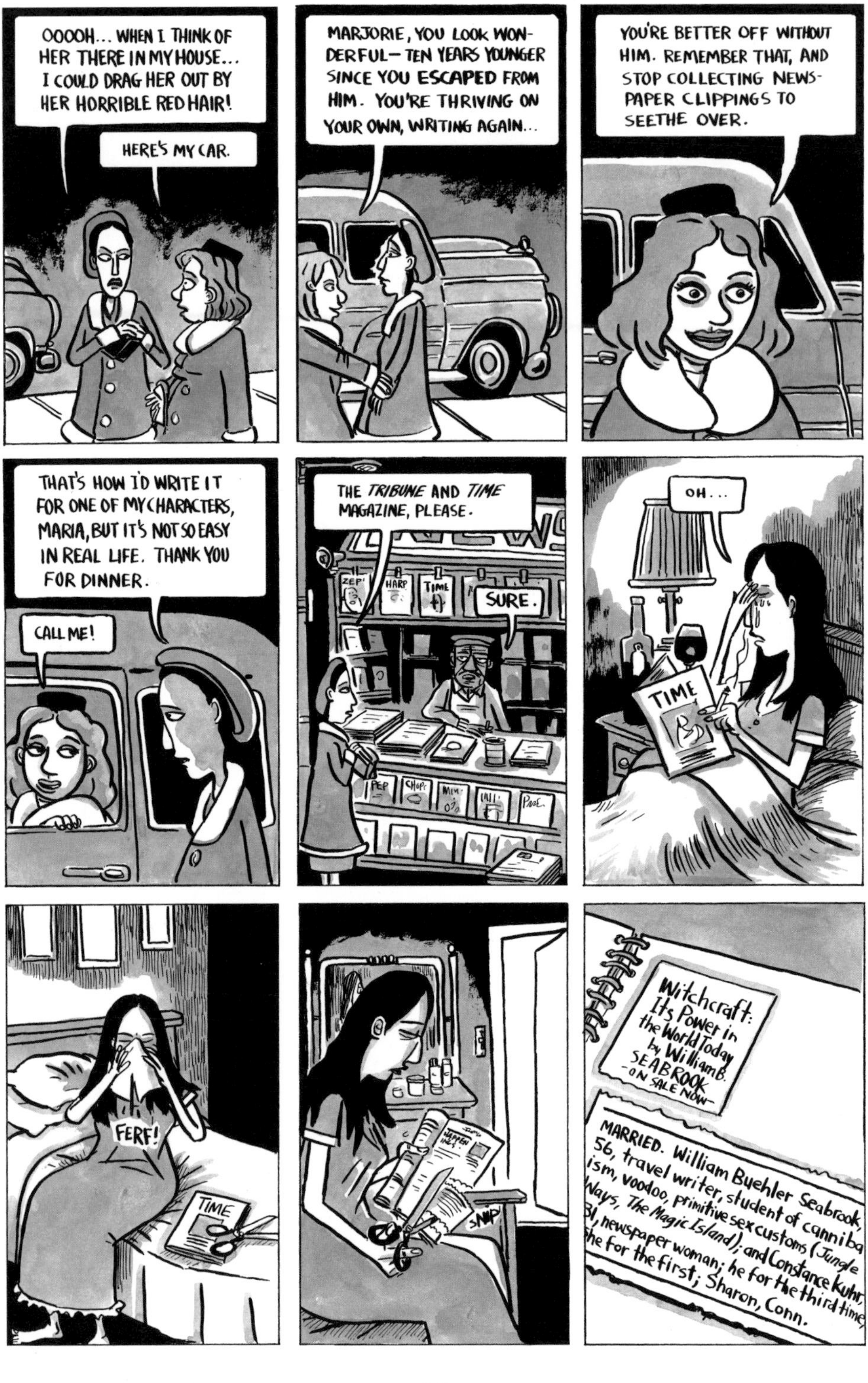
OOOOH... WHEN I THINK OF HER THERE IN MY HOUSE... I COULD DRAG HER OUT BY HER HORRIBLE RED HAIR!
HERE'S MY CAR.
MARJORIE, YOU LOOK WONDERFUL— TEN YEARS YOUNGER SINCE YOU ESCAPED FROM HIM. YOU'RE THRIVING ON YOUR OWN, WRITING AGAIN...
YOU'RE BETTER OFF WITHOUT HIM. REMEMBER THAT, AND STOP COLLECTING NEWSPAPER CLIPPINGS TO SEETHE OVER.
THAT'S HOW I'D WRITE IT FOR ONE OF MY CHARACTERS, MARIA, BUT IT'S NOT SO EASY IN REAL LIFE. THANK YOU FOR DINNER.
CALL ME!
THE *TRIBUNE* AND *TIME* MAGAZINE, PLEASE.
SURE.
OH...
TIME
FERF!
TIME
SNIP
Witchcraft: Its Power in the World Today by William B. SEABROOK -ON SALE NOW-
MARRIED. William Buehler Seabrook, 56, travel writer, student of canniba
ism, voodoo, primitive sex customs (*Jungle Ways*, *The Magic Island*); and Constance Kuhr,
31, newspaper woman; he for the third time,
she for the first; Sharon, Conn.

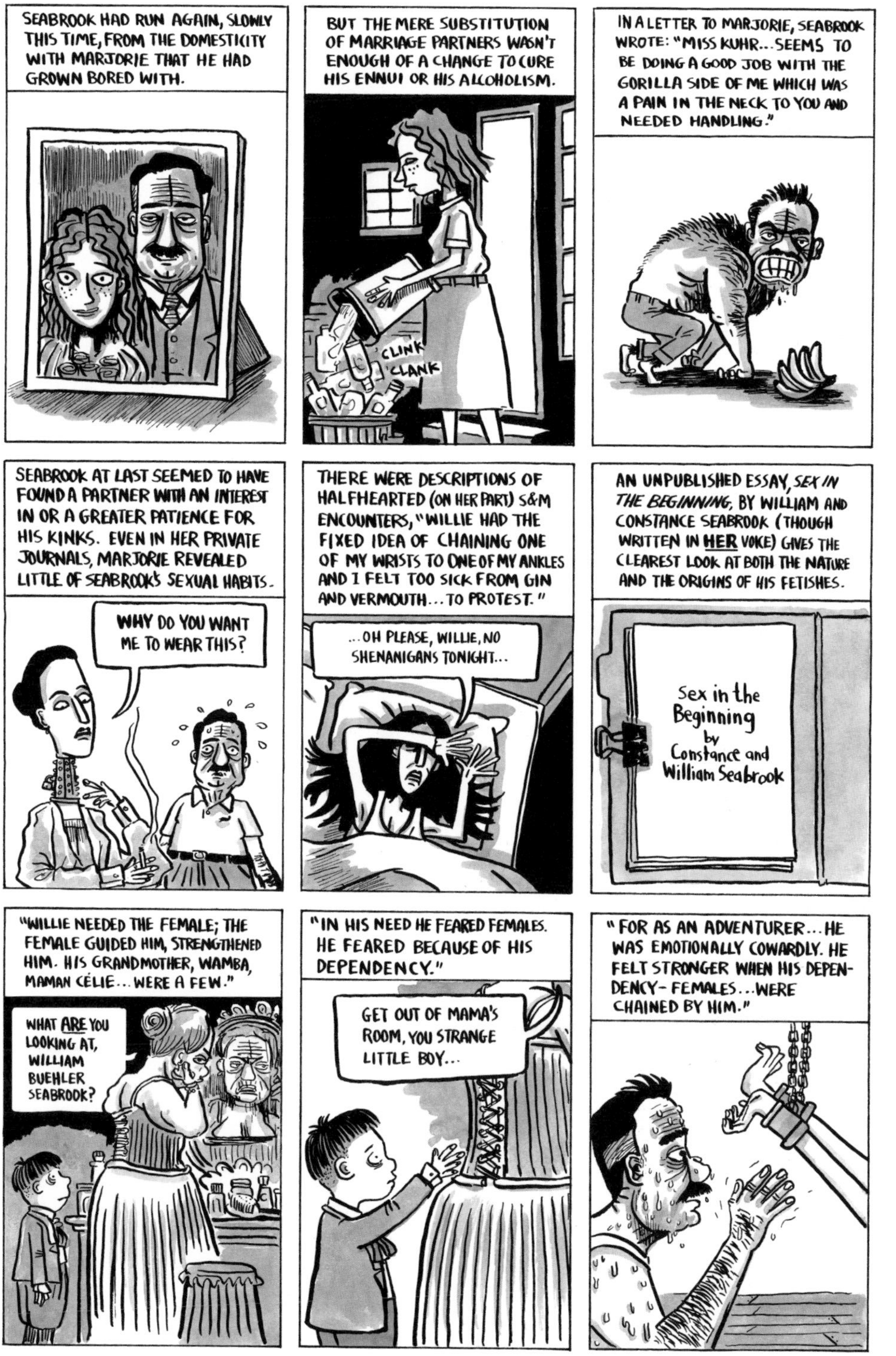
SEABROOK HAD RUN AGAIN, SLOWLY THIS TIME, FROM THE DOMESTICITY WITH MARJORIE THAT HE HAD GROWN BORED WITH.
BUT THE MERE SUBSTITUTION OF MARRIAGE PARTNERS WASN'T ENOUGH OF A CHANGE TO CURE HIS ENNUI OR HIS ALCOHOLISM.
CLINK
CLANK
IN A LETTER TO MARJORIE, SEABROOK WROTE: "MISS KUHR... SEEMS TO BE DOING A GOOD JOB WITH THE GORILLA SIDE OF ME WHICH WAS A PAIN IN THE NECK TO YOU AND NEEDED HANDLING."
SEABROOK AT LAST SEEMED TO HAVE FOUND A PARTNER WITH AN INTEREST IN OR A GREATER PATIENCE FOR HIS KINKS. EVEN IN HER PRIVATE JOURNALS, MARJORIE REVEALED LITTLE OF SEABROOK'S SEXUAL HABITS.
WHY DO YOU WANT ME TO WEAR THIS?
THERE WERE DESCRIPTIONS OF HALFHEARTED (ON HER PART) S&M ENCOUNTERS, "WILLIE HAD THE FIXED IDEA OF CHAINING ONE OF MY WRISTS TO ONE OF MY ANKLES AND I FELT TOO SICK FROM GIN AND VERMOUTH... TO PROTEST."
...OH PLEASE, WILLIE, NO SHENANIGANS TONIGHT...
AN UNPUBLISHED ESSAY, *SEX IN THE BEGINNING*, BY WILLIAM AND CONSTANCE SEABROOK (THOUGH WRITTEN IN **HER** VOICE) GIVES THE CLEAREST LOOK AT BOTH THE NATURE AND THE ORIGINS OF HIS FETISHES.
Sex in the Beginning by Constance and William Seabrook
"WILLIE NEEDED THE FEMALE; THE FEMALE GUIDED HIM, STRENGTHENED HIM. HIS GRANDMOTHER, WAMBA, MAMAN CÉLIE... WERE A FEW."
WHAT ARE YOU LOOKING AT, WILLIAM BUEHLER SEABROOK?
"IN HIS NEED HE FEARED FEMALES. HE FEARED BECAUSE OF HIS DEPENDENCY."
GET OUT OF MAMA'S ROOM, YOU STRANGE LITTLE BOY...
"FOR AS AN ADVENTURER... HE WAS EMOTIONALLY COWARDLY. HE FELT STRONGER WHEN HIS DEPENDENCY- FEMALES... WERE CHAINED BY HIM."

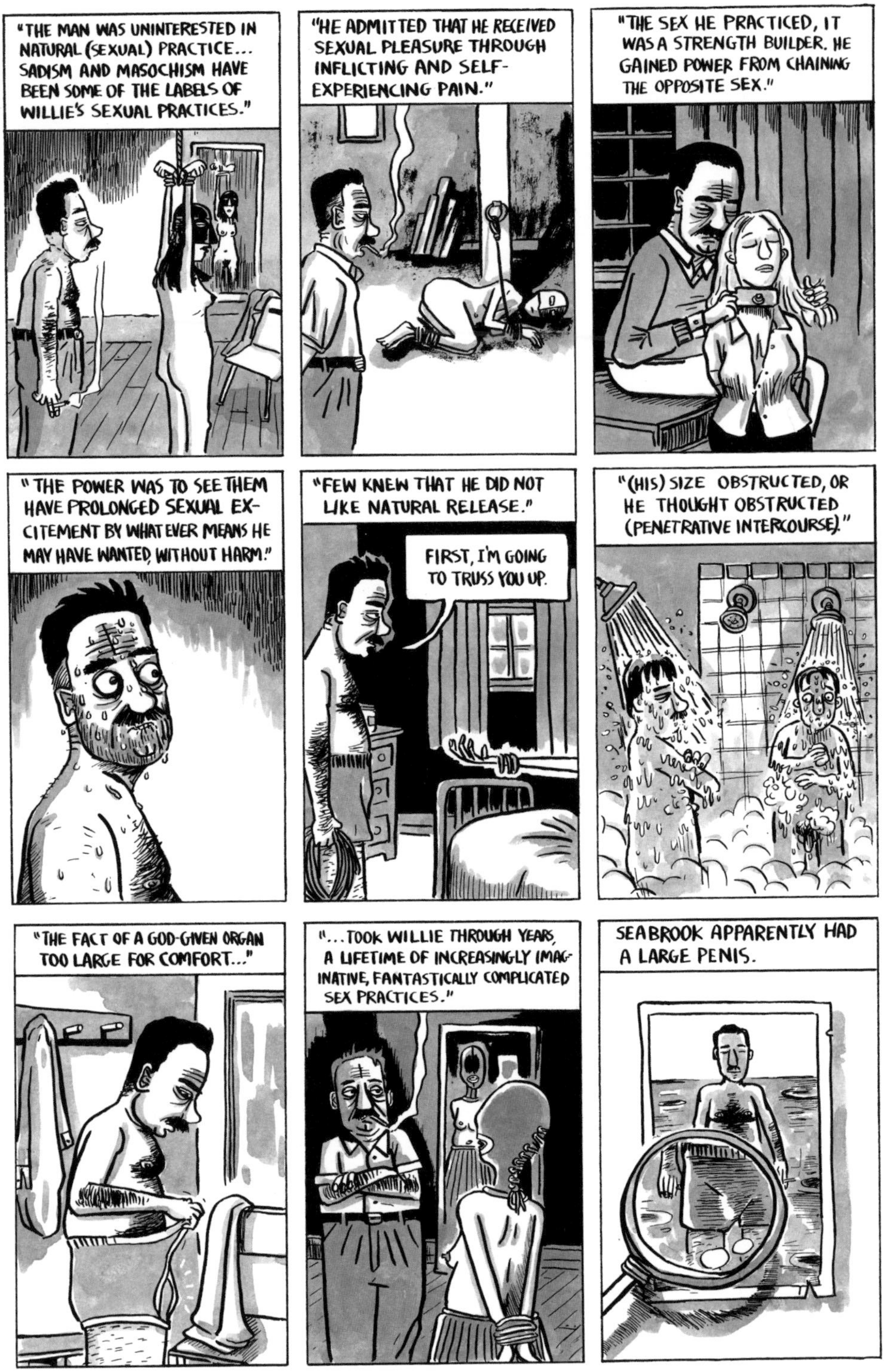
"THE MAN WAS UNINTERESTED IN NATURAL (SEXUAL) PRACTICE... SADISM AND MASOCHISM HAVE BEEN SOME OF THE LABELS OF WILLIE'S SEXUAL PRACTICES."
"HE ADMITTED THAT HE RECEIVED SEXUAL PLEASURE THROUGH INFLICTING AND SELF-EXPERIENCING PAIN."
"THE SEX HE PRACTICED, IT WAS A STRENGTH BUILDER. HE GAINED POWER FROM CHAINING THE OPPOSITE SEX."
"THE POWER WAS TO SEE THEM HAVE PROLONGED SEXUAL EXCITEMENT BY WHAT EVER MEANS HE MAY HAVE WANTED, WITHOUT HARM."
"FEW KNEW THAT HE DID NOT LIKE NATURAL RELEASE."
FIRST, I'M GOING TO TRUSS YOU UP.
"(HIS) SIZE OBSTRUCTED, OR HE THOUGHT OBSTRUCTED (PENETRATIVE INTERCOURSE)."
"THE FACT OF A GOD-GIVEN ORGAN TOO LARGE FOR COMFORT..."
"...TOOK WILLIE THROUGH YEARS, A LIFETIME OF INCREASINGLY IMAGINATIVE, FANTASTICALLY COMPLICATED SEX PRACTICES."
SEABROOK APPARENTLY HAD A LARGE PENIS.

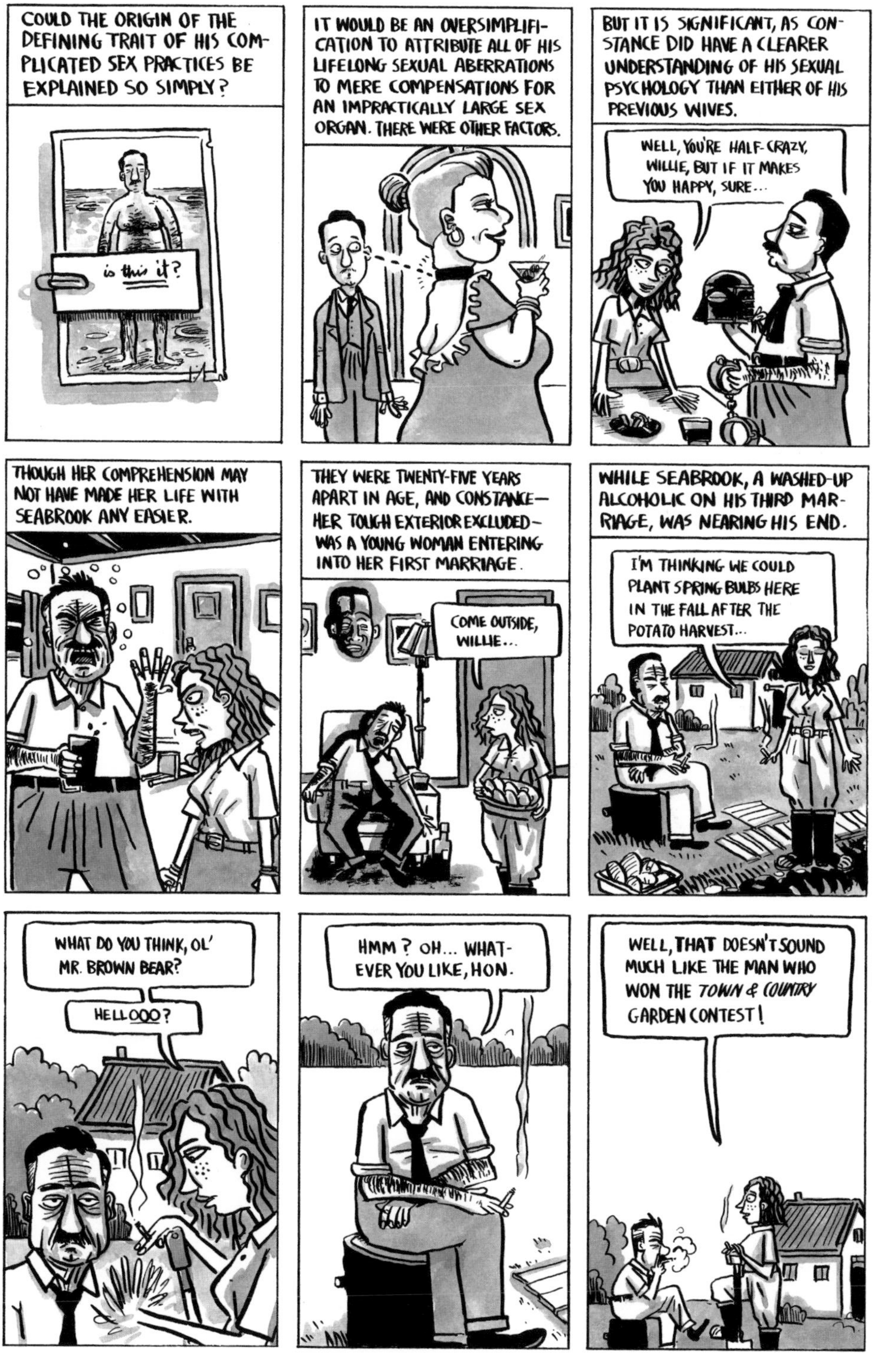
COULD THE ORIGIN OF THE DEFINING TRAIT OF HIS COMPLICATED SEX PRACTICES BE EXPLAINED SO SIMPLY?
is this it?
IT WOULD BE AN OVERSIMPLIFICATION TO ATTRIBUTE ALL OF HIS LIFELONG SEXUAL ABERRATIONS TO MERE COMPENSATIONS FOR AN IMPRACTICALLY LARGE SEX ORGAN. THERE WERE OTHER FACTORS.
BUT IT IS SIGNIFICANT, AS CONSTANCE DID HAVE A CLEARER UNDERSTANDING OF HIS SEXUAL PSYCHOLOGY THAN EITHER OF HIS PREVIOUS WIVES.
WELL, YOU'RE HALF-CRAZY, WILLIE, BUT IF IT MAKES YOU HAPPY, SURE...
THOUGH HER COMPREHENSION MAY NOT HAVE MADE HER LIFE WITH SEABROOK ANY EASIER.
THEY WERE TWENTY-FIVE YEARS APART IN AGE, AND CONSTANCE—HER TOUGH EXTERIOR EXCLUDED—WAS A YOUNG WOMAN ENTERING INTO HER FIRST MARRIAGE.
COME OUTSIDE, WILLIE...
WHILE SEABROOK, A WASHED-UP ALCOHOLIC ON HIS THIRD MARRIAGE, WAS NEARING HIS END.
I'M THINKING WE COULD PLANT SPRING BULBS HERE IN THE FALL AFTER THE POTATO HARVEST...
WHAT DO YOU THINK, OL' MR. BROWN BEAR?
HELLOOO?
HMM? OH... WHATEVER YOU LIKE, HON.
WELL, THAT DOESN'T SOUND MUCH LIKE THE MAN WHO WON THE TOWN & COUNTRY GARDEN CONTEST!

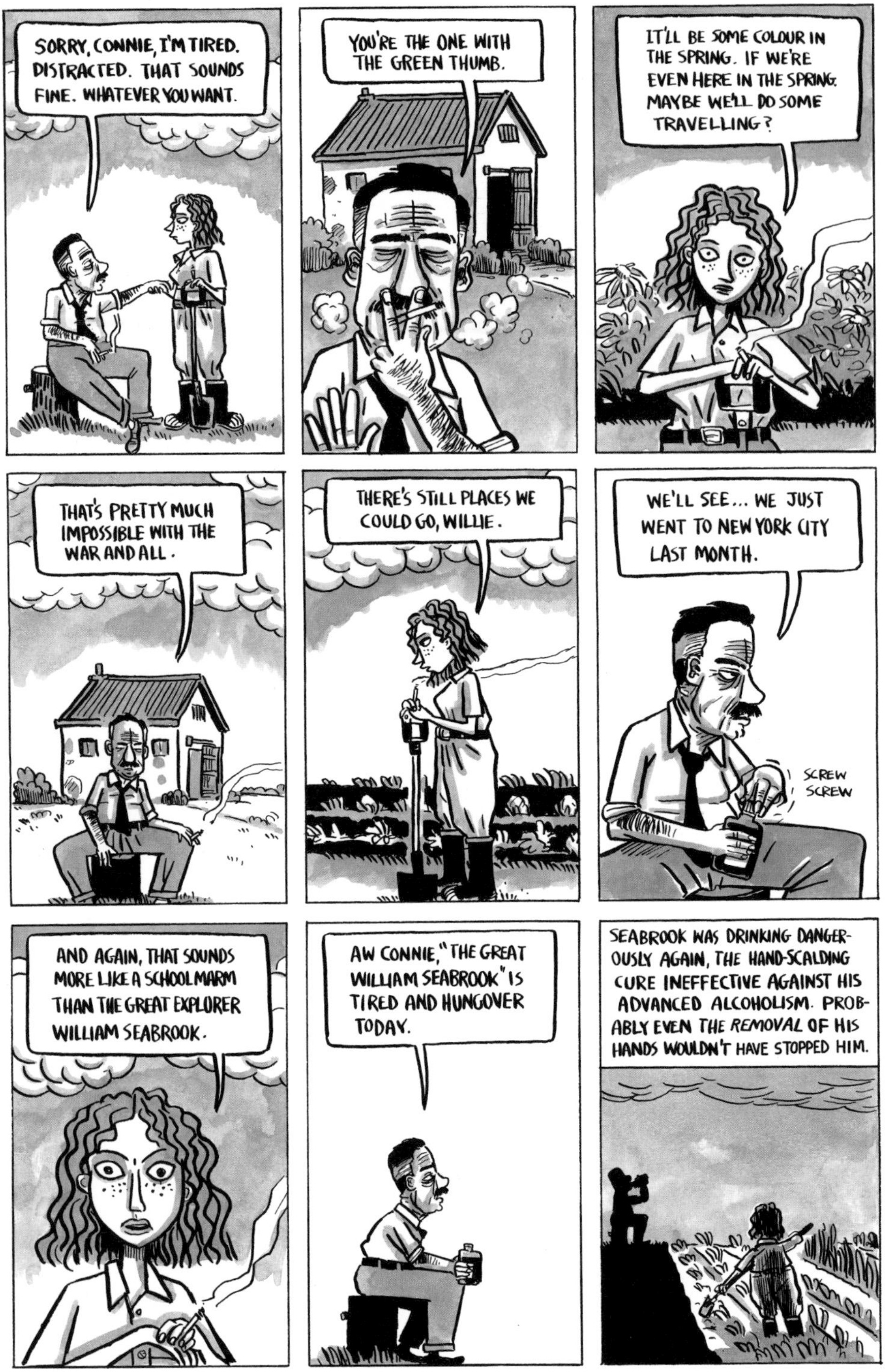
SORRY, CONNIE, I'M TIRED. DISTRACTED. THAT SOUNDS FINE. WHATEVER YOU WANT.
YOU'RE THE ONE WITH THE GREEN THUMB.
IT'LL BE SOME COLOUR IN THE SPRING. IF WE'RE EVEN HERE IN THE SPRING. MAYBE WE'LL DO SOME TRAVELLING?
THAT'S PRETTY MUCH IMPOSSIBLE WITH THE WAR AND ALL.
THERE'S STILL PLACES WE COULD GO, WILLIE.
WE'LL SEE... WE JUST WENT TO NEW YORK CITY LAST MONTH.
SCREW SCREW
AND AGAIN, THAT SOUNDS MORE LIKE A SCHOOLMARM THAN THE GREAT EXPLORER WILLIAM SEABROOK.
AW CONNIE, "THE GREAT WILLIAM SEABROOK" IS TIRED AND HUNGOVER TODAY.
SEABROOK WAS DRINKING DANGEROUSLY AGAIN, THE HAND-SCALDING CURE INEFFECTIVE AGAINST HIS ADVANCED ALCOHOLISM. PROBABLY EVEN THE *REMOVAL* OF HIS HANDS WOULDN'T HAVE STOPPED HIM.

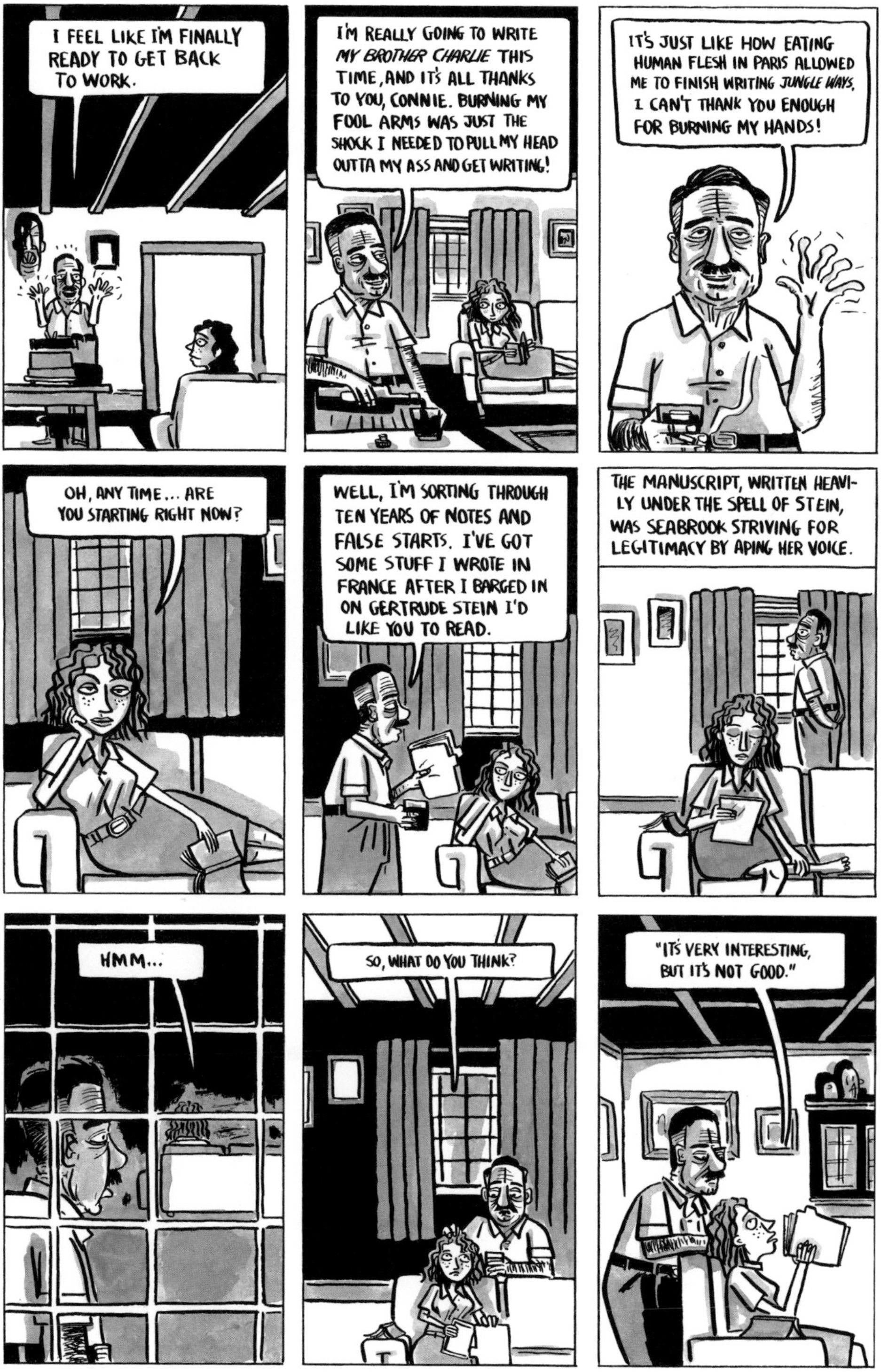
I FEEL LIKE I'M FINALLY READY TO GET BACK TO WORK.
I'M REALLY GOING TO WRITE *MY BROTHER CHARLIE* THIS TIME, AND IT'S ALL THANKS TO YOU, CONNIE. BURNING MY FOOL ARMS WAS JUST THE SHOCK I NEEDED TO PULL MY HEAD OUTTA MY ASS AND GET WRITING!
IT'S JUST LIKE HOW EATING HUMAN FLESH IN PARIS ALLOWED ME TO FINISH WRITING *JUNGLE WAYS*, I CAN'T THANK YOU ENOUGH FOR BURNING MY HANDS!
OH, ANY TIME... ARE YOU STARTING RIGHT NOW?
WELL, I'M SORTING THROUGH TEN YEARS OF NOTES AND FALSE STARTS. I'VE GOT SOME STUFF I WROTE IN FRANCE AFTER I BARGED IN ON GERTRUDE STEIN I'D LIKE YOU TO READ.
THE MANUSCRIPT, WRITTEN HEAVILY UNDER THE SPELL OF STEIN, WAS SEABROOK STRIVING FOR LEGITIMACY BY APING HER VOICE.
HMM...
SO, WHAT DO YOU THINK?
"IT'S VERY INTERESTING, BUT IT'S NOT GOOD."

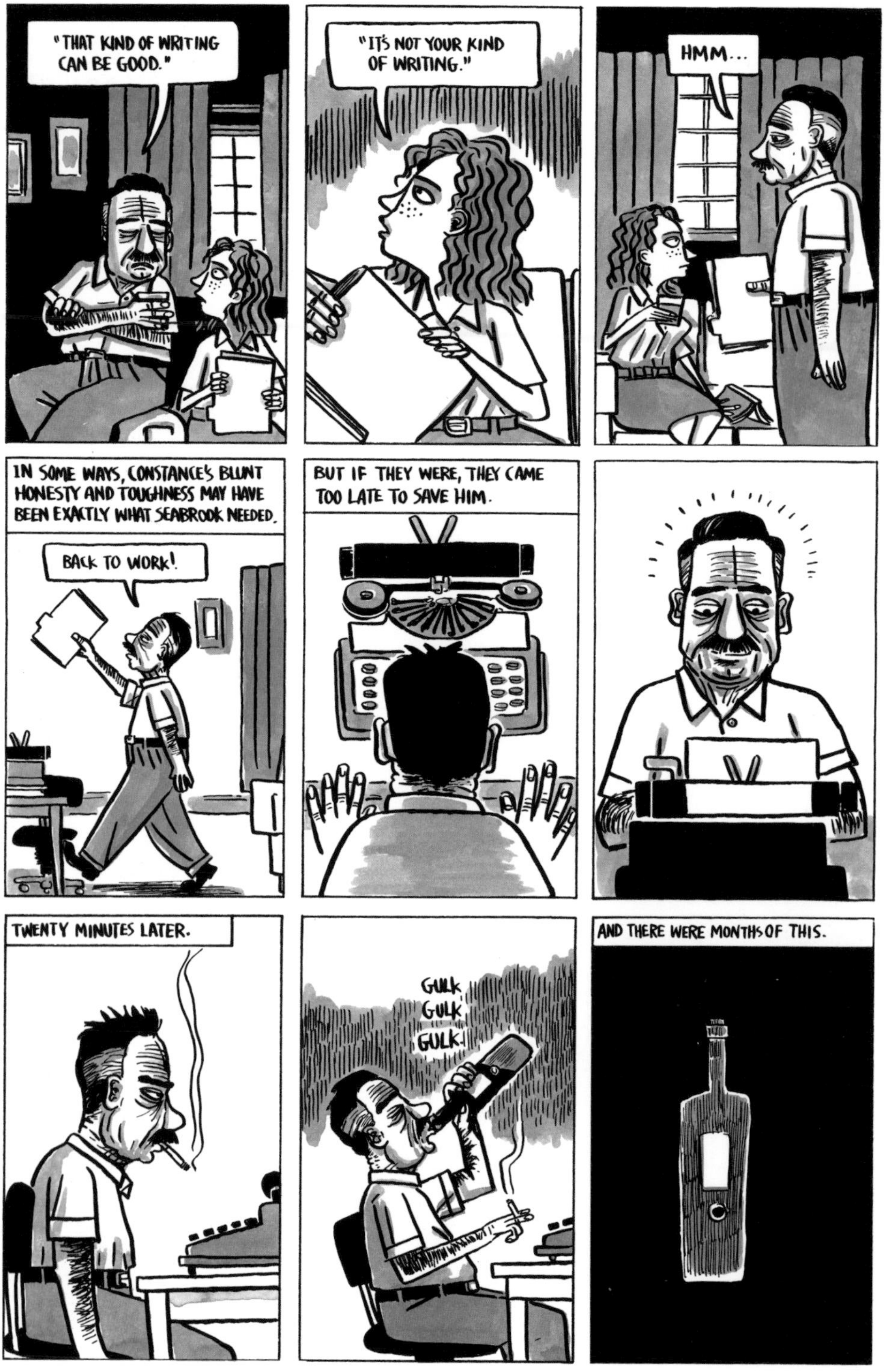
"THAT KIND OF WRITING CAN BE GOOD."
"IT'S NOT YOUR KIND OF WRITING."
HMM...
IN SOME WAYS, CONSTANCE'S BLUNT HONESTY AND TOUGHNESS MAY HAVE BEEN EXACTLY WHAT SEABROOK NEEDED.
BACK TO WORK!
BUT IF THEY WERE, THEY CAME TOO LATE TO SAVE HIM.
TWENTY MINUTES LATER.
GULK
GULK
GULK
AND THERE WERE MONTHS OF THIS.

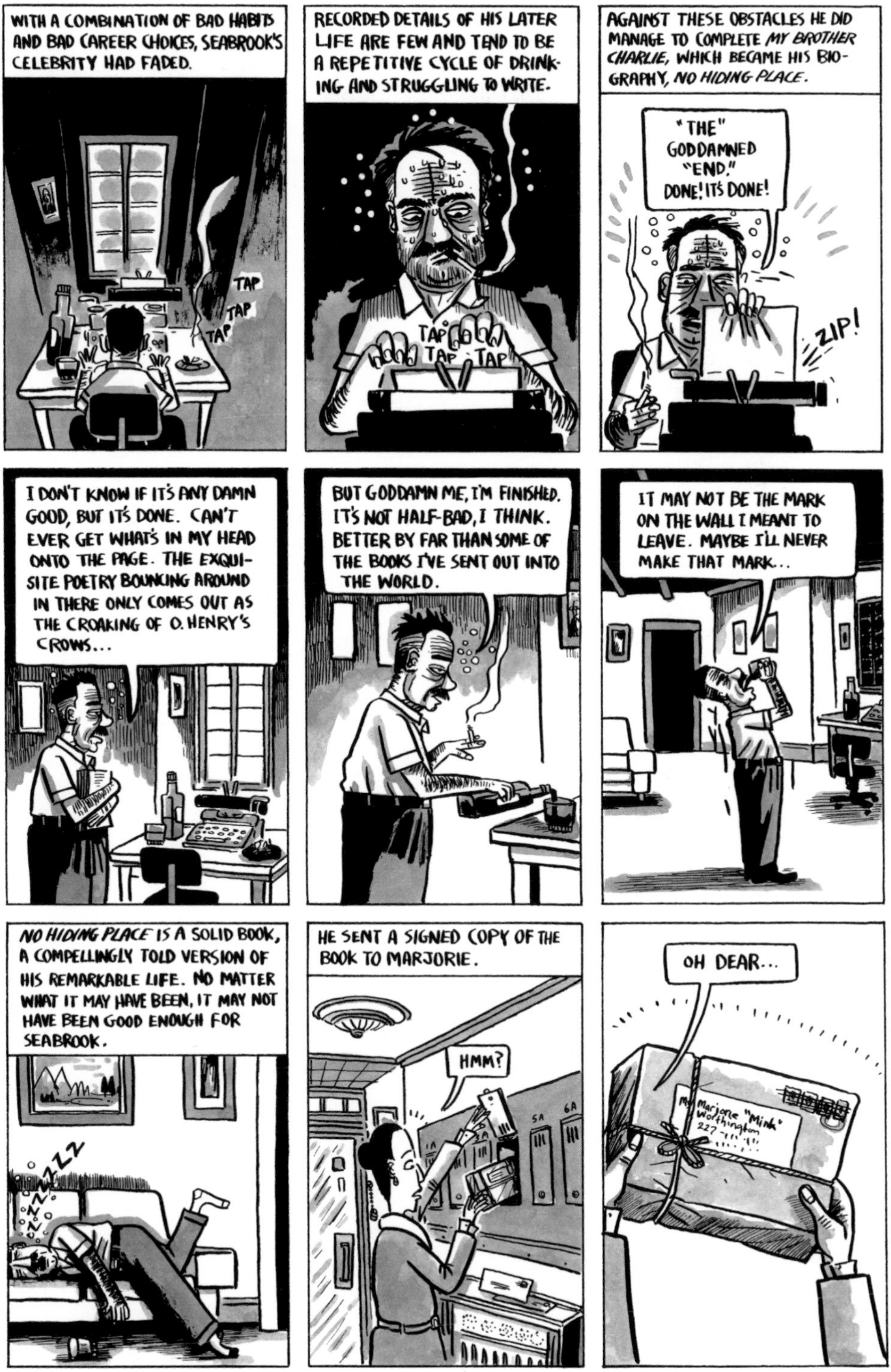
WITH A COMBINATION OF BAD HABITS AND BAD CAREER CHOICES, SEABROOK'S CELEBRITY HAD FADED.
TAP TAP TAP
RECORDED DETAILS OF HIS LATER LIFE ARE FEW AND TEND TO BE A REPETITIVE CYCLE OF DRINKING AND STRUGGLING TO WRITE.
TAP TAP TAP
AGAINST THESE OBSTACLES HE DID MANAGE TO COMPLETE *MY BROTHER CHARLIE*, WHICH BECAME HIS BIOGRAPHY, *NO HIDING PLACE*.
"THE" GODDAMNED "END." DONE! IT'S DONE!
ZIP!
I DON'T KNOW IF IT'S ANY DAMN GOOD, BUT IT'S DONE. CAN'T EVER GET WHAT'S IN MY HEAD ONTO THE PAGE. THE EXQUISITE POETRY BOUNCING AROUND IN THERE ONLY COMES OUT AS THE CROAKING OF O. HENRY'S CROWS...
BUT GODDAMN ME, I'M FINISHED. IT'S NOT HALF-BAD, I THINK. BETTER BY FAR THAN SOME OF THE BOOKS I'VE SENT OUT INTO THE WORLD.
IT MAY NOT BE THE MARK ON THE WALL I MEANT TO LEAVE. MAYBE I'LL NEVER MAKE THAT MARK...
*NO HIDING PLACE* IS A SOLID BOOK, A COMPELLINGLY TOLD VERSION OF HIS REMARKABLE LIFE. NO MATTER WHAT IT MAY HAVE BEEN, IT MAY NOT HAVE BEEN GOOD ENOUGH FOR SEABROOK.
ZZZ
HE SENT A SIGNED COPY OF THE BOOK TO MARJORIE.
HMM?
5A
6A
OH DEAR...
Marjorie "Mink" Worthington

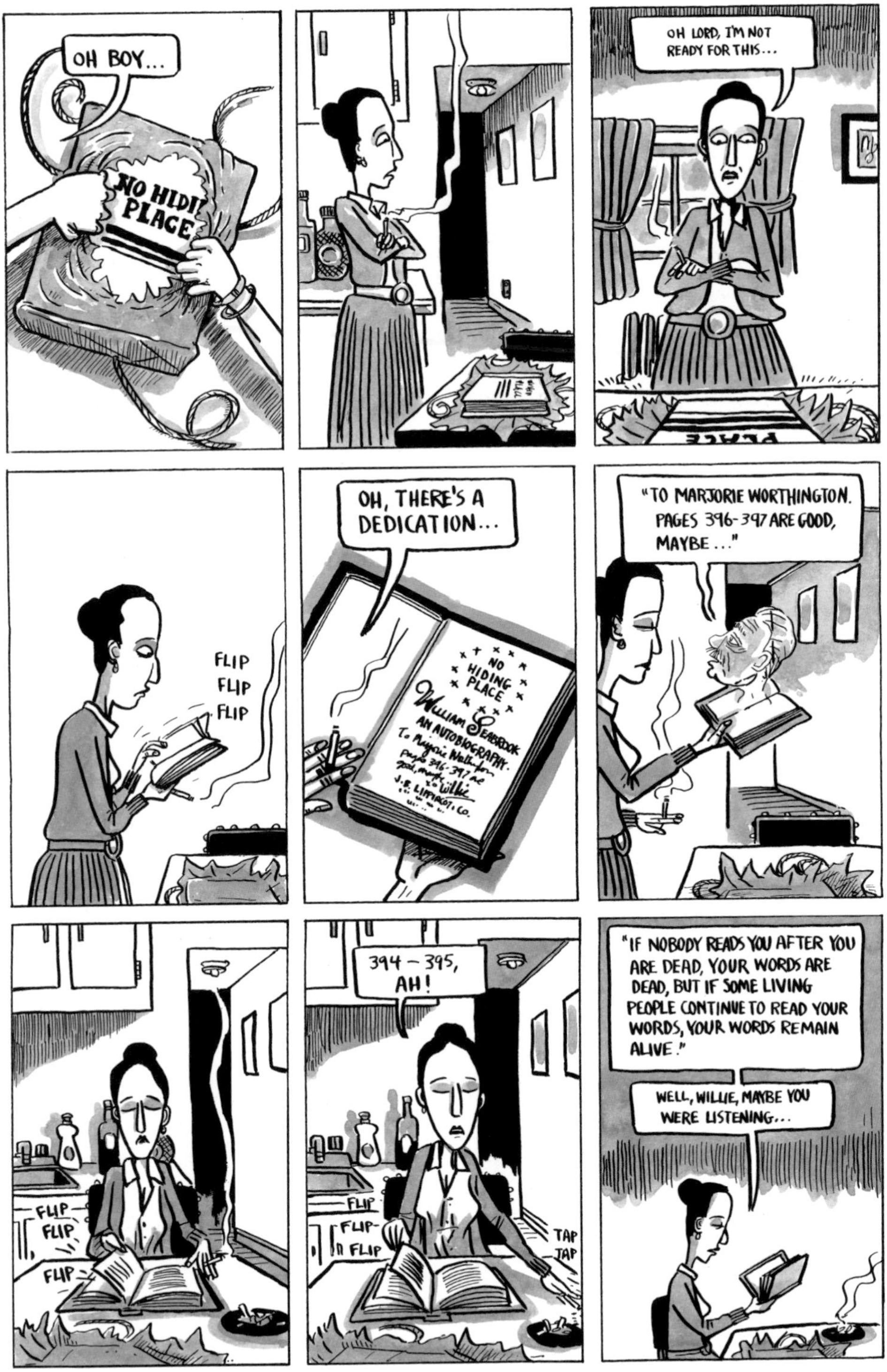
OH BOY...
NO HIDI
PLACE
OH LORD, I'M NOT READY FOR THIS...
FLIP
FLIP
FLIP
OH, THERE'S A DEDICATION...
NO HIDING PLACE
WILLIAM SEABROOK
AN AUTOBIOGRAPHY.
"TO MARJORIE WORTHINGTON. PAGES 396-397 ARE GOOD, MAYBE..."
FLIP
FLIP
FLIP
394 — 395, AH!
FLIP
FLIP
FLIP
TAP
TAP
"IF NOBODY READS YOU AFTER YOU ARE DEAD, YOUR WORDS ARE DEAD, BUT IF SOME LIVING PEOPLE CONTINUE TO READ YOUR WORDS, YOUR WORDS REMAIN ALIVE."
WELL, WILLIE, MAYBE YOU WERE LISTENING...

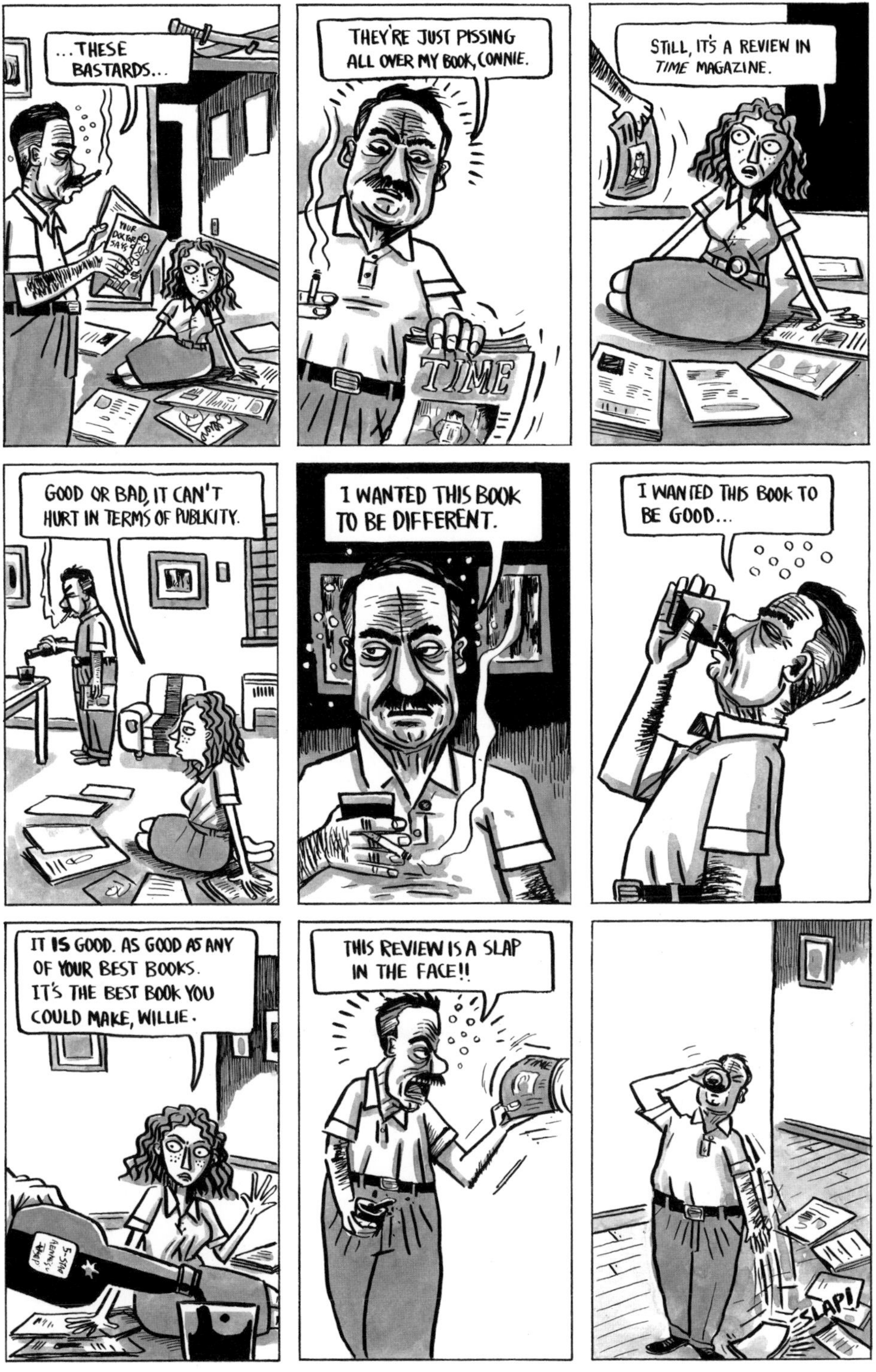
...THESE BASTARDS...
THEY'RE JUST PISSING ALL OVER MY BOOK, CONNIE.
STILL, IT'S A REVIEW IN *TIME* MAGAZINE.
TIME
GOOD OR BAD, IT CAN'T HURT IN TERMS OF PUBLICITY.
I WANTED THIS BOOK TO BE DIFFERENT.
I WANTED THIS BOOK TO BE GOOD...
IT **IS** GOOD. AS GOOD AS ANY OF YOUR BEST BOOKS. IT'S THE BEST BOOK YOU COULD MAKE, WILLIE.
THIS REVIEW IS A SLAP IN THE FACE!!
SLAP!

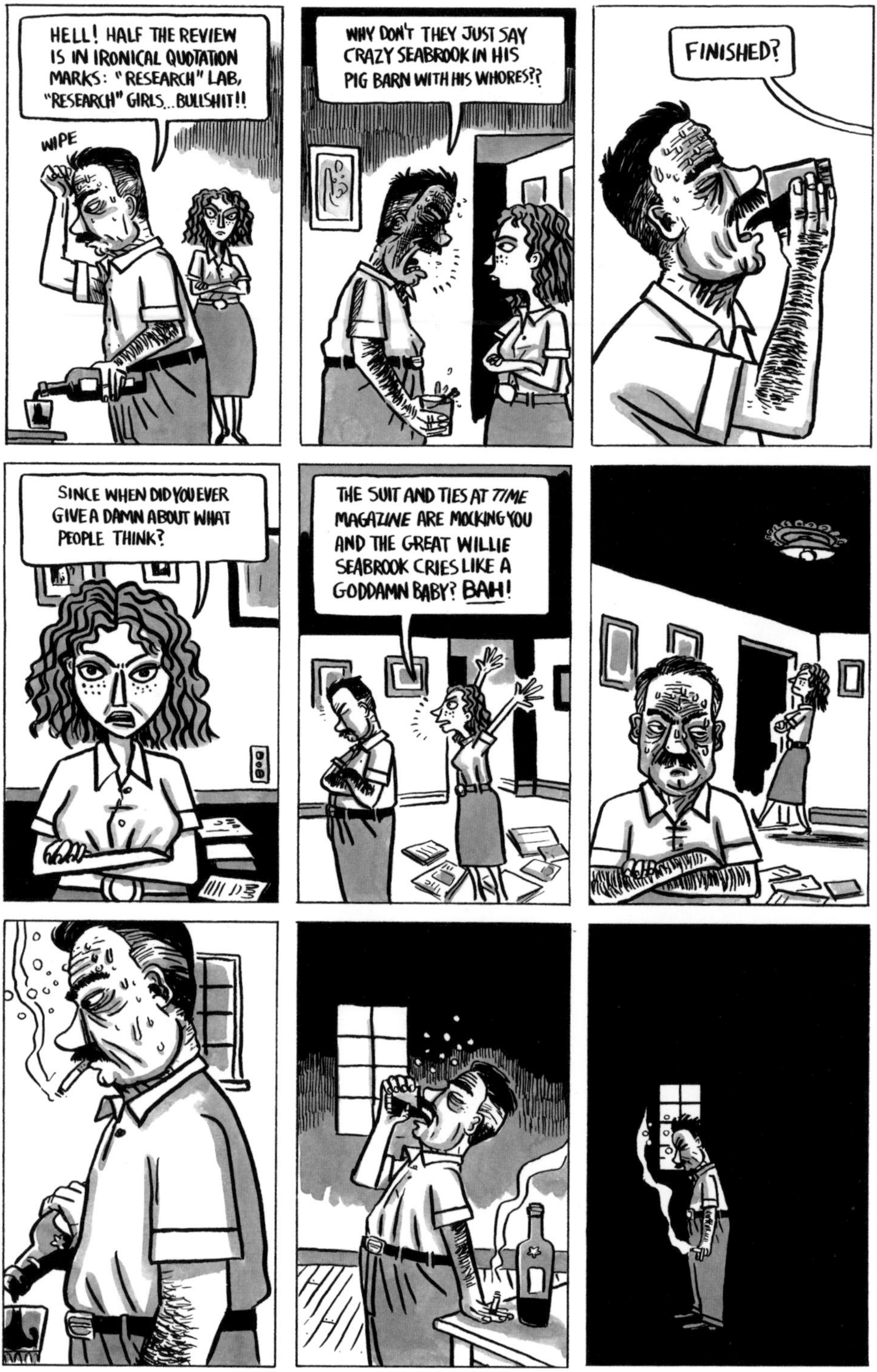
HELL! HALF THE REVIEW IS IN IRONICAL QUOTATION MARKS: "RESEARCH" LAB, "RESEARCH" GIRLS... BULLSHIT!!
WIPE
WHY DON'T THEY JUST SAY CRAZY SEABROOK IN HIS PIG BARN WITH HIS WHORES??
FINISHED?
SINCE WHEN DID YOU EVER GIVE A DAMN ABOUT WHAT PEOPLE THINK?
THE SUIT AND TIES AT *TIME MAGAZINE* ARE MOCKING YOU AND THE GREAT WILLIE SEABROOK CRIES LIKE A GODDAMN BABY? BAH!

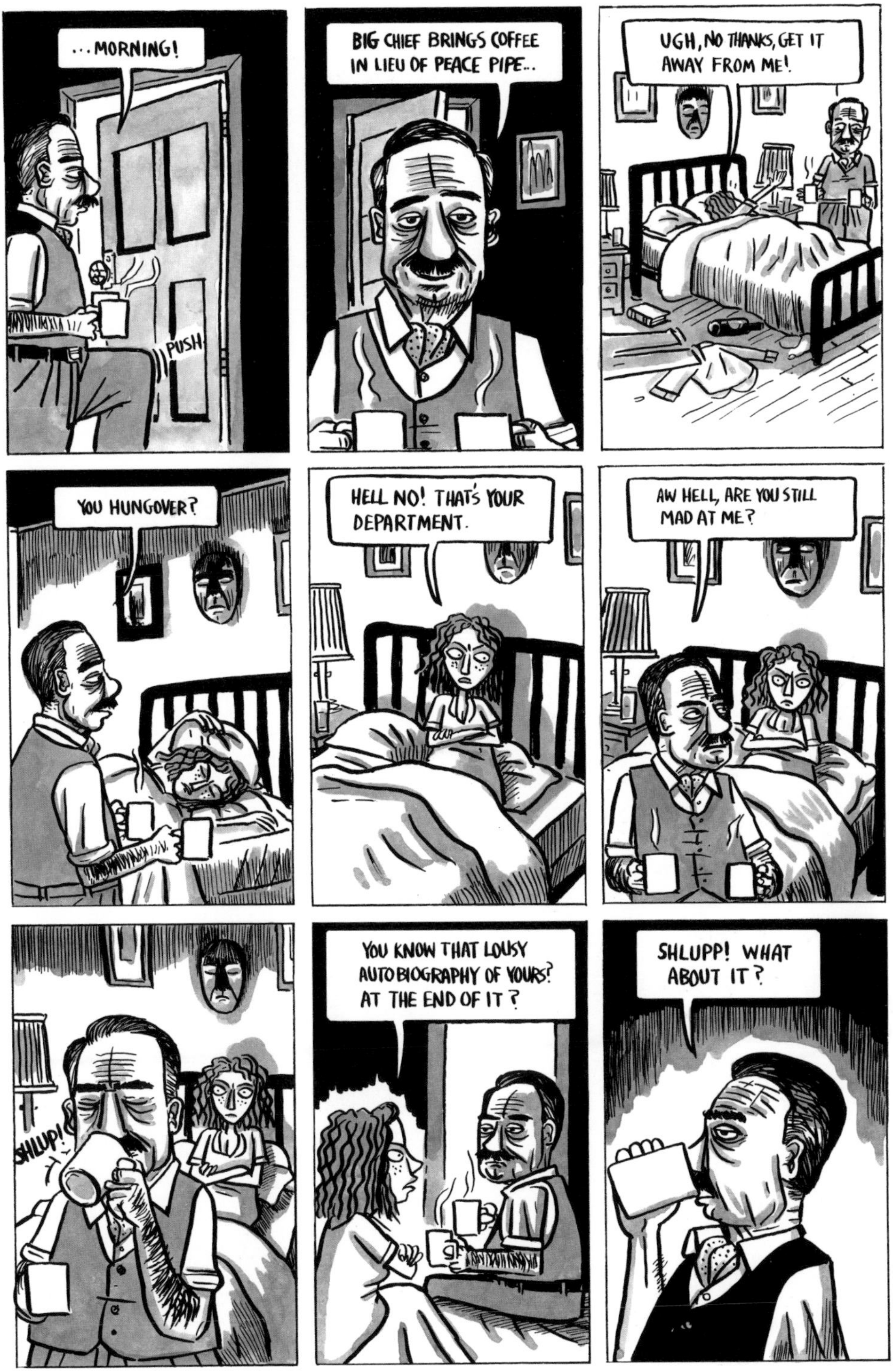
...MORNING!
PUSH
BIG CHIEF BRINGS COFFEE IN LIEU OF PEACE PIPE...
UGH, NO THANKS, GET IT AWAY FROM ME!
YOU HUNGOVER?
HELL NO! THAT'S YOUR DEPARTMENT.
AW HELL, ARE YOU STILL MAD AT ME?
SHLUP!
YOU KNOW THAT LOUSY AUTOBIOGRAPHY OF YOURS? AT THE END OF IT?
SHLUPP! WHAT ABOUT IT?

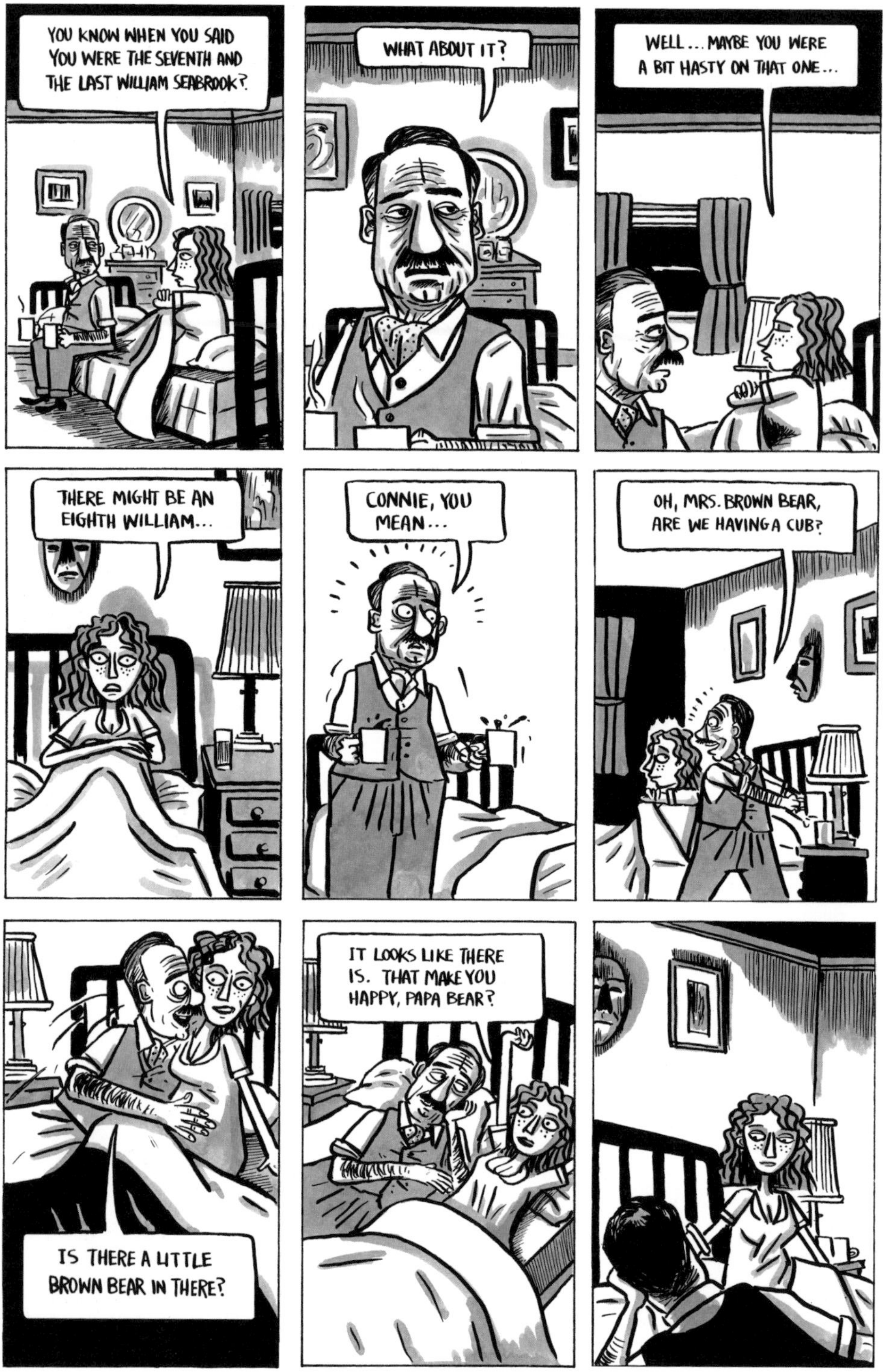

YOU KNOW WHEN YOU SAID YOU WERE THE SEVENTH AND THE LAST WILLIAM SEABROOK?
WHAT ABOUT IT?
WELL... MAYBE YOU WERE A BIT HASTY ON THAT ONE...
THERE MIGHT BE AN EIGHTH WILLIAM...
CONNIE, YOU MEAN...
OH, MRS. BROWN BEAR, ARE WE HAVING A CUB?
IS THERE A LITTLE BROWN BEAR IN THERE?
IT LOOKS LIKE THERE IS. THAT MAKE YOU HAPPY, PAPA BEAR?

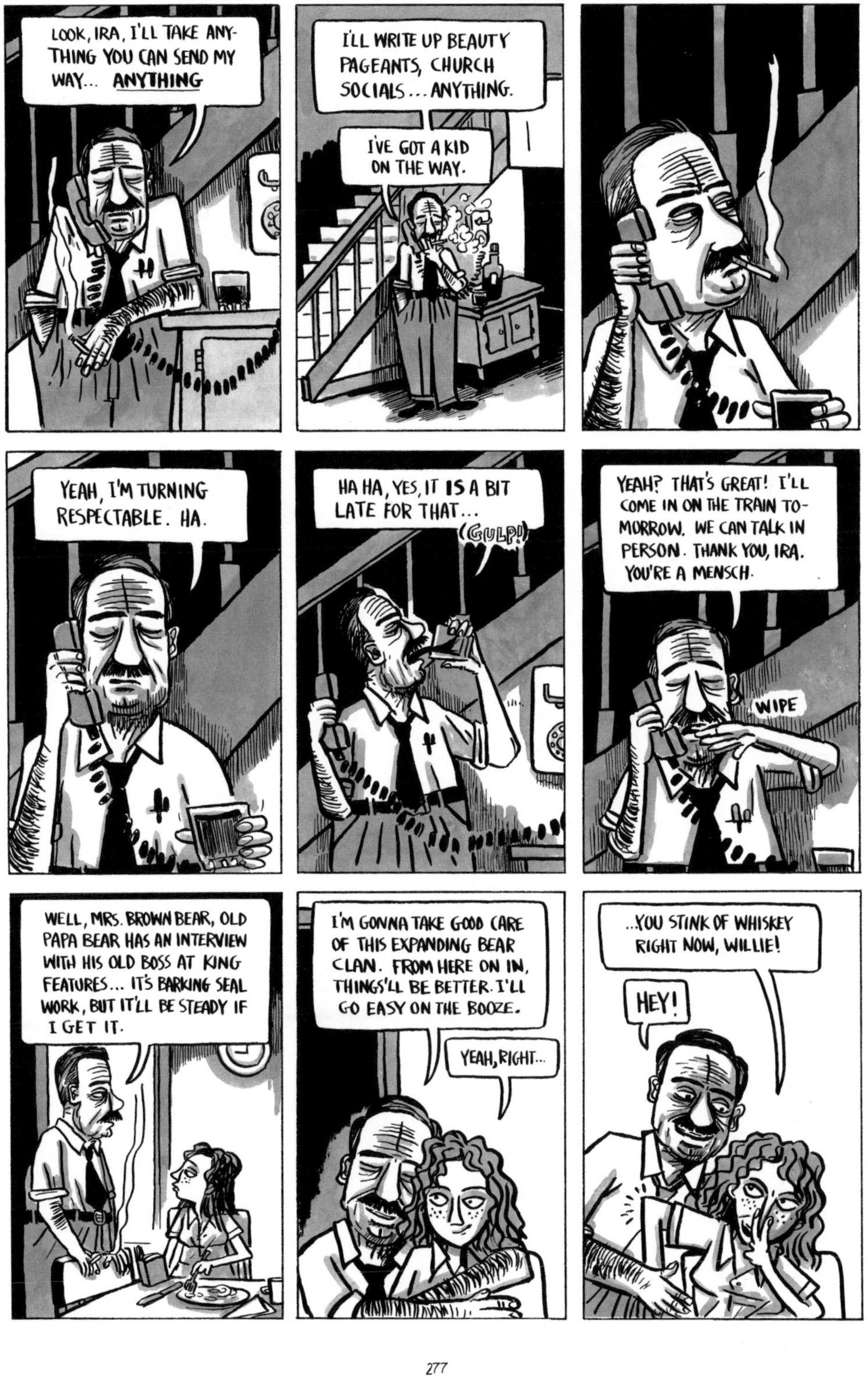
LOOK, IRA, I'LL TAKE ANYTHING YOU CAN SEND MY WAY... ANYTHING
I'LL WRITE UP BEAUTY PAGEANTS, CHURCH SOCIALS... ANYTHING.
I'VE GOT A KID ON THE WAY.
YEAH, I'M TURNING RESPECTABLE. HA.
HA HA, YES, IT IS A BIT LATE FOR THAT...
(GULP!)
YEAH? THAT'S GREAT! I'LL COME IN ON THE TRAIN TOMORROW. WE CAN TALK IN PERSON. THANK YOU, IRA. YOU'RE A MENSCH.
WIPE
WELL, MRS. BROWN BEAR, OLD PAPA BEAR HAS AN INTERVIEW WITH HIS OLD BOSS AT KING FEATURES... IT'S BARKING SEAL WORK, BUT IT'LL BE STEADY IF I GET IT.
I'M GONNA TAKE GOOD CARE OF THIS EXPANDING BEAR CLAN. FROM HERE ON IN, THINGS'LL BE BETTER. I'LL GO EASY ON THE BOOZE.
YEAH, RIGHT...
...YOU STINK OF WHISKEY RIGHT NOW, WILLIE!
HEY!

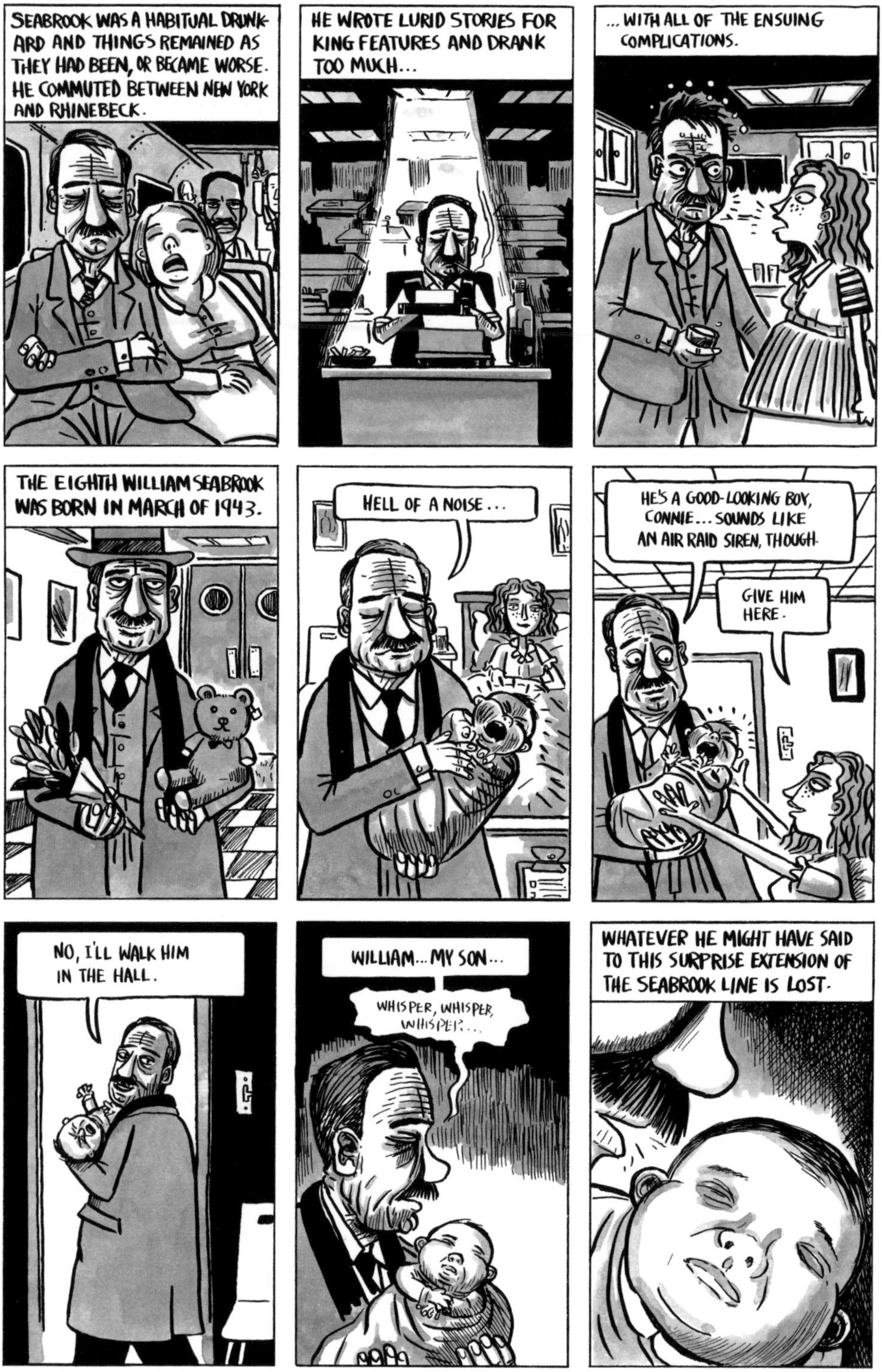
SEABROOK WAS A HABITUAL DRUNKARD AND THINGS REMAINED AS THEY HAD BEEN, OR BECAME WORSE. HE COMMUTED BETWEEN NEW YORK AND RHINEBECK.
HE WROTE LURID STORIES FOR KING FEATURES AND DRANK TOO MUCH...
...WITH ALL OF THE ENSUING COMPLICATIONS.
THE EIGHTH WILLIAM SEABROOK WAS BORN IN MARCH OF 1943.
HELL OF A NOISE...
HE'S A GOOD-LOOKING BOY, CONNIE... SOUNDS LIKE AN AIR RAID SIREN, THOUGH.
GIVE HIM HERE.
NO, I'LL WALK HIM IN THE HALL.
WILLIAM... MY SON...
WHISPER, WHISPER, WHISPER...
WHATEVER HE MIGHT HAVE SAID TO THIS SURPRISE EXTENSION OF THE SEABROOK LINE IS LOST.

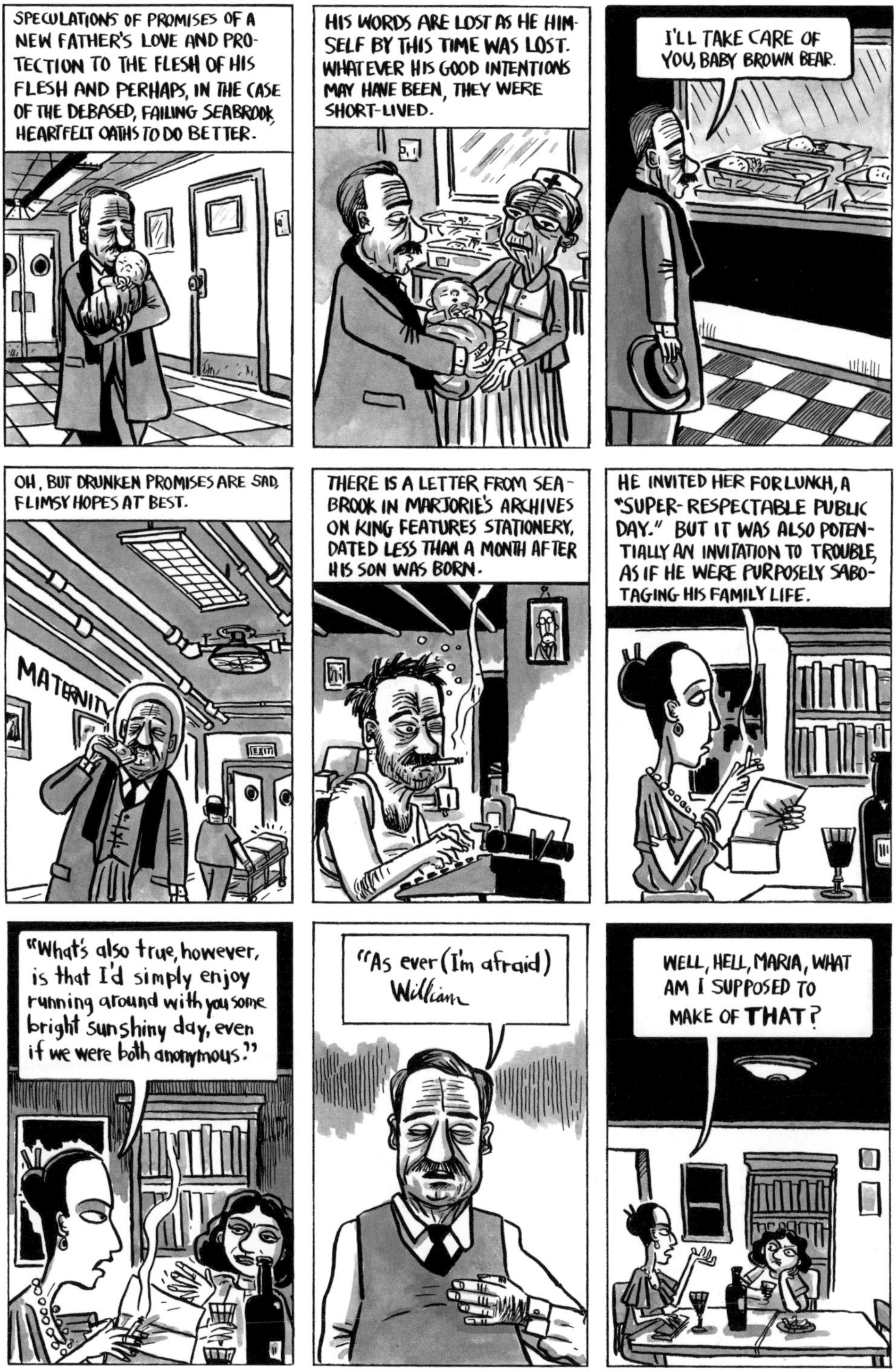
SPECULATIONS OF PROMISES OF A NEW FATHER'S LOVE AND PROTECTION TO THE FLESH OF HIS FLESH AND PERHAPS, IN THE CASE OF THE DEBASED, FAILING SEABROOK, HEARTFELT OATHS TO DO BETTER.
HIS WORDS ARE LOST AS HE HIMSELF BY THIS TIME WAS LOST. WHATEVER HIS GOOD INTENTIONS MAY HAVE BEEN, THEY WERE SHORT-LIVED.
I'LL TAKE CARE OF YOU, BABY BROWN BEAR.
OH, BUT DRUNKEN PROMISES ARE SAD, FLIMSY HOPES AT BEST.
MATERNITY
EXIT
THERE IS A LETTER FROM SEABROOK IN MARJORIE'S ARCHIVES ON KING FEATURES STATIONERY, DATED LESS THAN A MONTH AFTER HIS SON WAS BORN.
HE INVITED HER FOR LUNCH, A "SUPER-RESPECTABLE PUBLIC DAY." BUT IT WAS ALSO POTENTIALLY AN INVITATION TO TROUBLE, AS IF HE WERE PURPOSELY SABOTAGING HIS FAMILY LIFE.
"What's also true, however, is that I'd simply enjoy running around with you some bright sunshiny day, even if we were both anonymous."
"As ever (I'm afraid) William
WELL, HELL, MARIA, WHAT AM I SUPPOSED TO MAKE OF THAT?

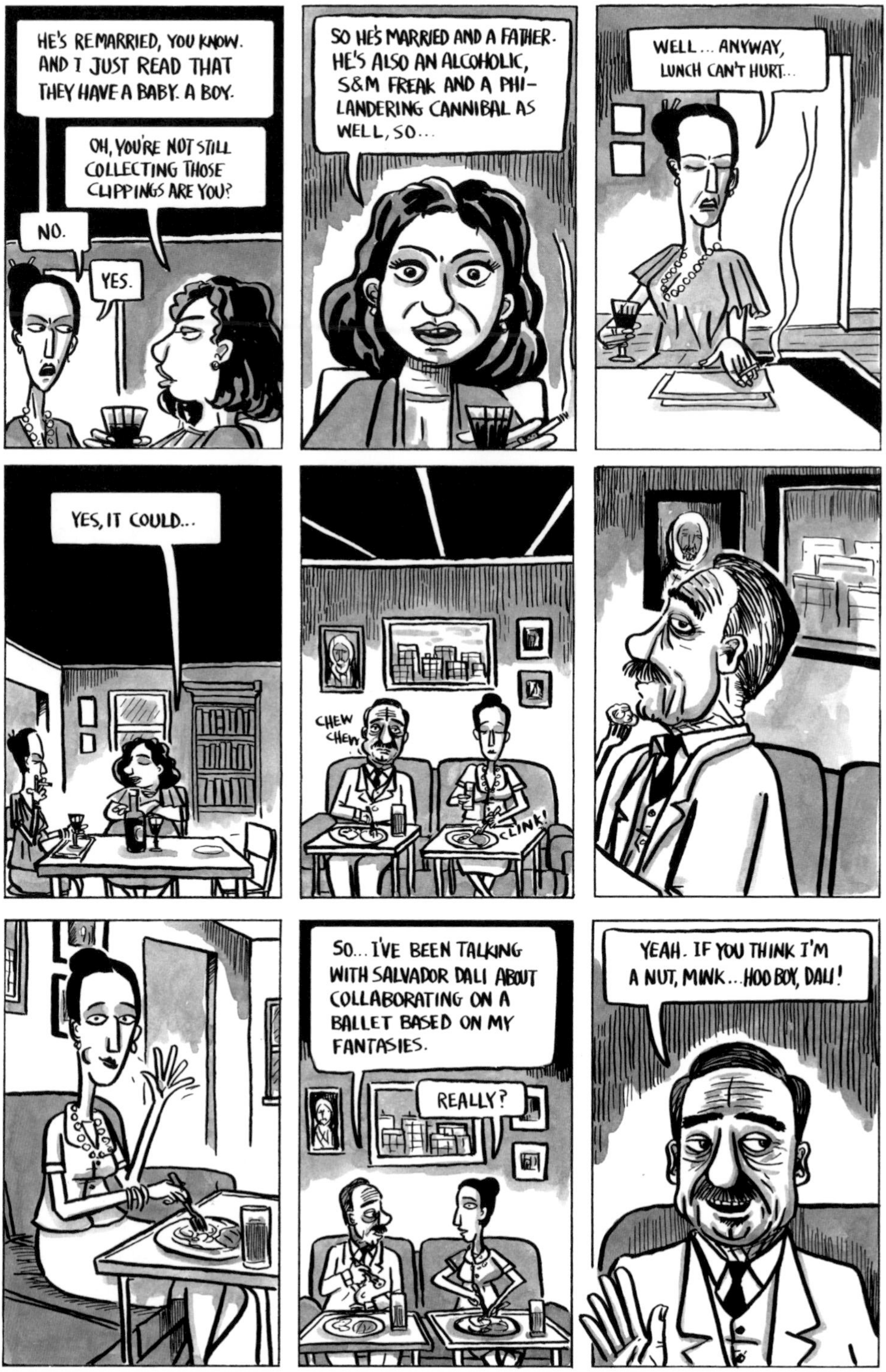
HE'S REMARRIED, YOU KNOW. AND I JUST READ THAT THEY HAVE A BABY. A BOY.
OH, YOU'RE NOT STILL COLLECTING THOSE CLIPPINGS ARE YOU?
NO.
YES.
SO HE'S MARRIED AND A FATHER. HE'S ALSO AN ALCOHOLIC, S&M FREAK AND A PHILANDERING CANNIBAL AS WELL, SO...
WELL... ANYWAY, LUNCH CAN'T HURT...
YES, IT COULD...
CHEW CHEW
CLINK!
SO... I'VE BEEN TALKING WITH SALVADOR DALI ABOUT COLLABORATING ON A BALLET BASED ON MY FANTASIES.
REALLY?
YEAH. IF YOU THINK I'M A NUT, MINK... HOO BOY, DALI!

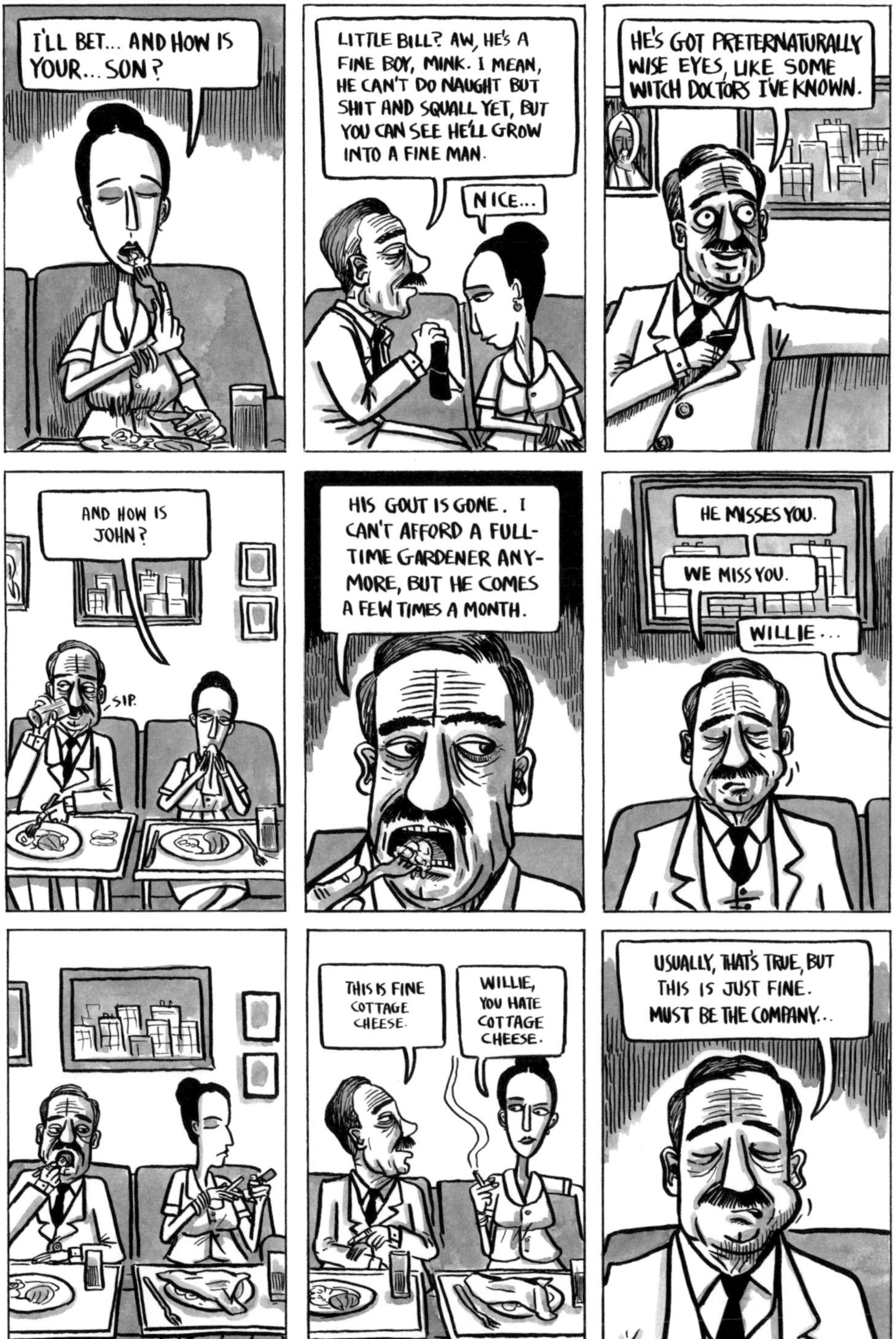
I'LL BET... AND HOW IS YOUR... SON?
LITTLE BILL? AW, HE'S A FINE BOY, MINK. I MEAN, HE CAN'T DO NAUGHT BUT SHIT AND SQUALL YET, BUT YOU CAN SEE HE'LL GROW INTO A FINE MAN.
NICE...
HE'S GOT PRETERNATURALLY WISE EYES, LIKE SOME WITCH DOCTORS I'VE KNOWN.
AND HOW IS JOHN?
SIP.
HIS GOUT IS GONE. I CAN'T AFFORD A FULL-TIME GARDENER ANYMORE, BUT HE COMES A FEW TIMES A MONTH.
HE MISSES YOU.
WE MISS YOU.
WILLIE...
THIS IS FINE COTTAGE CHEESE.
WILLIE, YOU HATE COTTAGE CHEESE.
USUALLY, THAT'S TRUE, BUT THIS IS JUST FINE. MUST BE THE COMPANY...

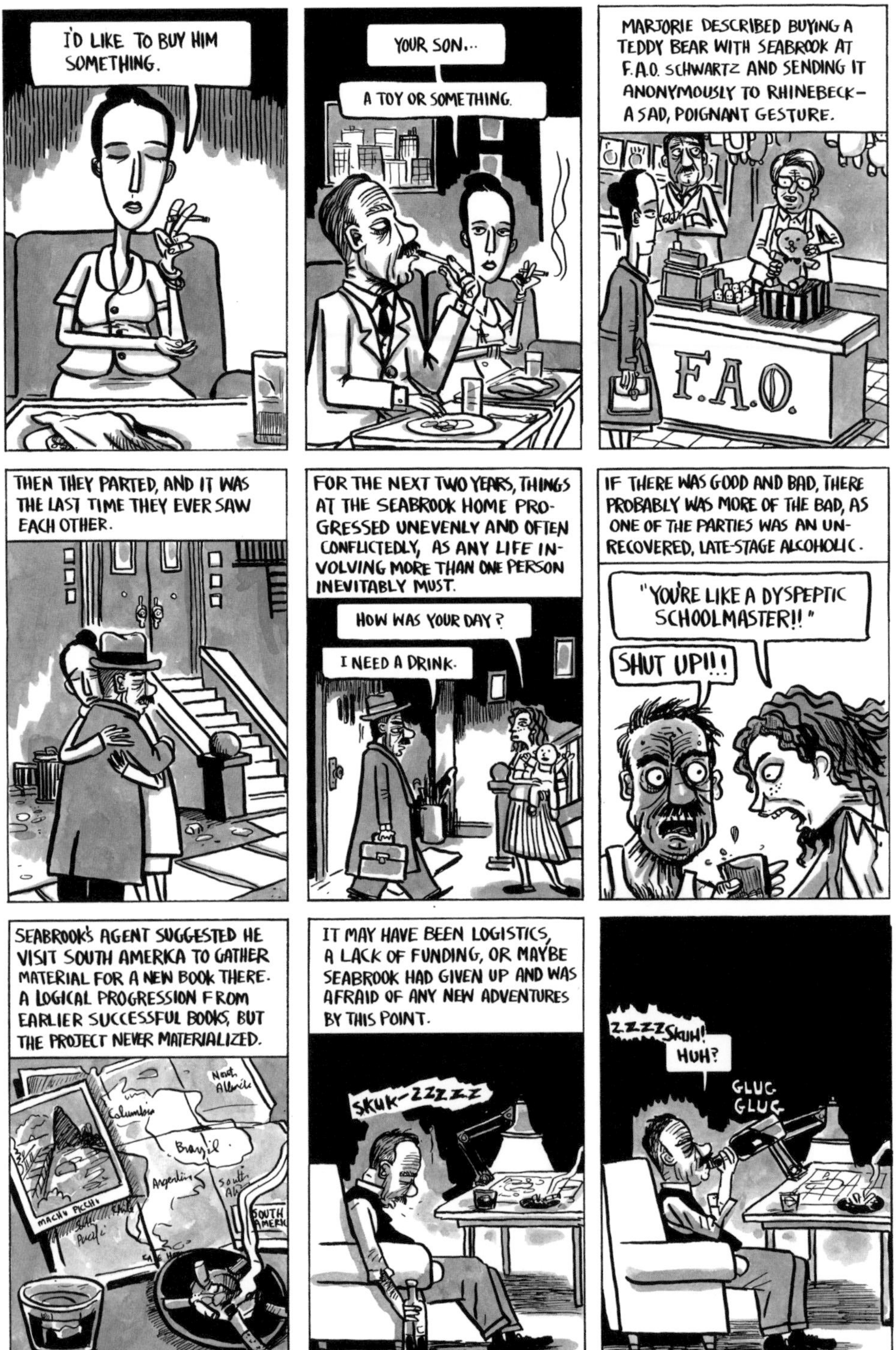
I'D LIKE TO BUY HIM SOMETHING.
YOUR SON...
A TOY OR SOMETHING.
MARJORIE DESCRIBED BUYING A TEDDY BEAR WITH SEABROOK AT F.A.O. SCHWARTZ AND SENDING IT ANONYMOUSLY TO RHINEBECK- A SAD, POIGNANT GESTURE.
F.A.O.
THEN THEY PARTED, AND IT WAS THE LAST TIME THEY EVER SAW EACH OTHER.
FOR THE NEXT TWO YEARS, THINGS AT THE SEABROOK HOME PROGRESSED UNEVENLY AND OFTEN CONFLICTEDLY, AS ANY LIFE INVOLVING MORE THAN ONE PERSON INEVITABLY MUST.
HOW WAS YOUR DAY?
I NEED A DRINK.
IF THERE WAS GOOD AND BAD, THERE PROBABLY WAS MORE OF THE BAD, AS ONE OF THE PARTIES WAS AN UNRECOVERED, LATE-STAGE ALCOHOLIC.
"YOU'RE LIKE A DYSPEPTIC SCHOOLMASTER!!"
SHUT UP!!!
SEABROOK'S AGENT SUGGESTED HE VISIT SOUTH AMERICA TO GATHER MATERIAL FOR A NEW BOOK THERE. A LOGICAL PROGRESSION FROM EARLIER SUCCESSFUL BOOKS, BUT THE PROJECT NEVER MATERIALIZED.
IT MAY HAVE BEEN LOGISTICS, A LACK OF FUNDING, OR MAYBE SEABROOK HAD GIVEN UP AND WAS AFRAID OF ANY NEW ADVENTURES BY THIS POINT.
SKUK-ZZZZZ
ZZZZSKUH!
HUH?
GLUG GLUG

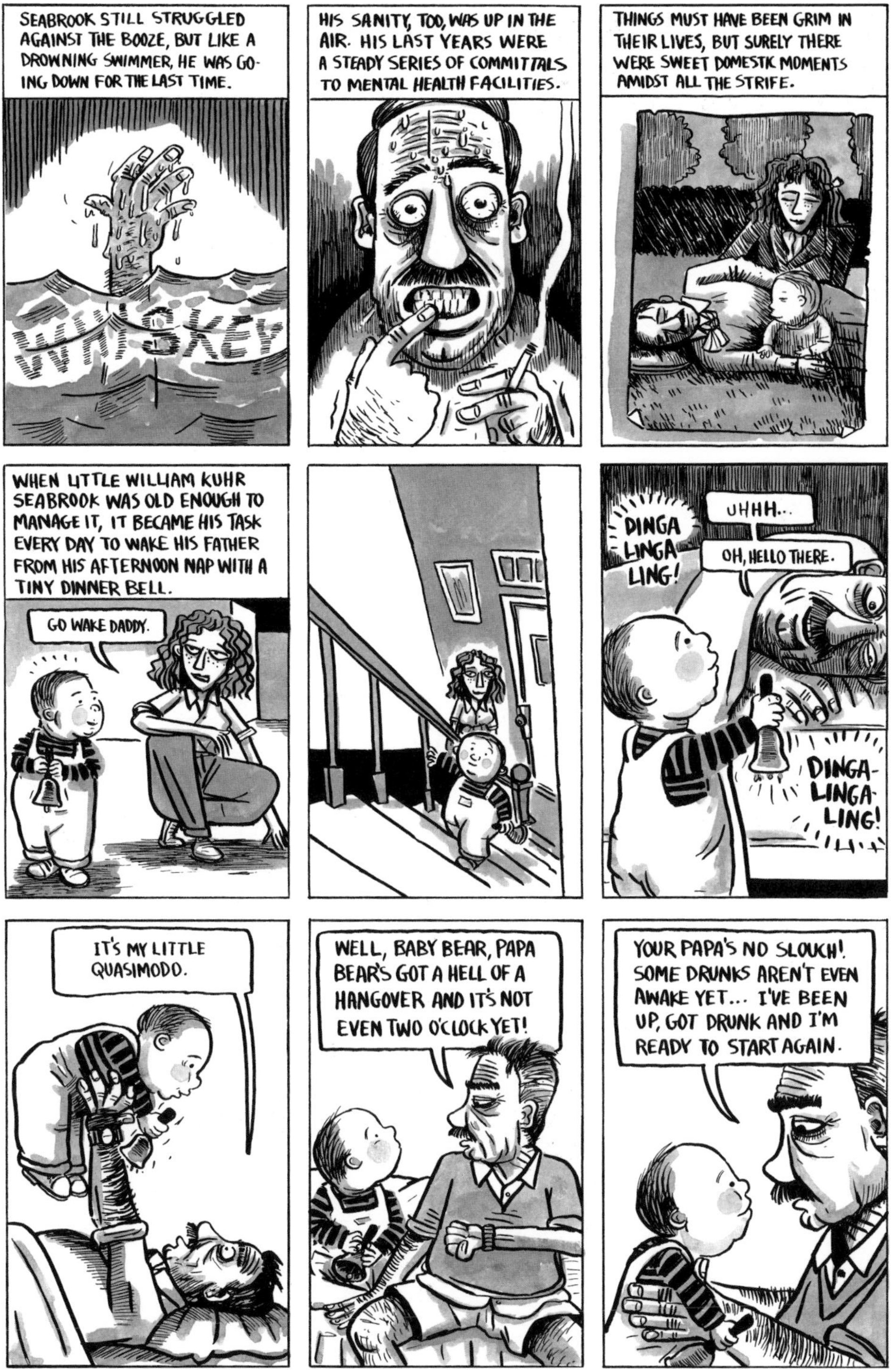
SEABROOK STILL STRUGGLED AGAINST THE BOOZE, BUT LIKE A DROWNING SWIMMER, HE WAS GOING DOWN FOR THE LAST TIME.
WHISKEY
HIS SANITY, TOO, WAS UP IN THE AIR. HIS LAST YEARS WERE A STEADY SERIES OF COMMITTALS TO MENTAL HEALTH FACILITIES.
THINGS MUST HAVE BEEN GRIM IN THEIR LIVES, BUT SURELY THERE WERE SWEET DOMESTIC MOMENTS AMIDST ALL THE STRIFE.
WHEN LITTLE WILLIAM KUHR SEABROOK WAS OLD ENOUGH TO MANAGE IT, IT BECAME HIS TASK EVERY DAY TO WAKE HIS FATHER FROM HIS AFTERNOON NAP WITH A TINY DINNER BELL.
GO WAKE DADDY.
DINGA LINGA LING!
UHHH...
OH, HELLO THERE.
DINGA-LINGA-LING!
IT'S MY LITTLE QUASIMODO.
WELL, BABY BEAR, PAPA BEAR'S GOT A HELL OF A HANGOVER AND IT'S NOT EVEN TWO O'CLOCK YET!
YOUR PAPA'S NO SLOUCH! SOME DRUNKS AREN'T EVEN AWAKE YET... I'VE BEEN UP, GOT DRUNK AND I'M READY TO START AGAIN.

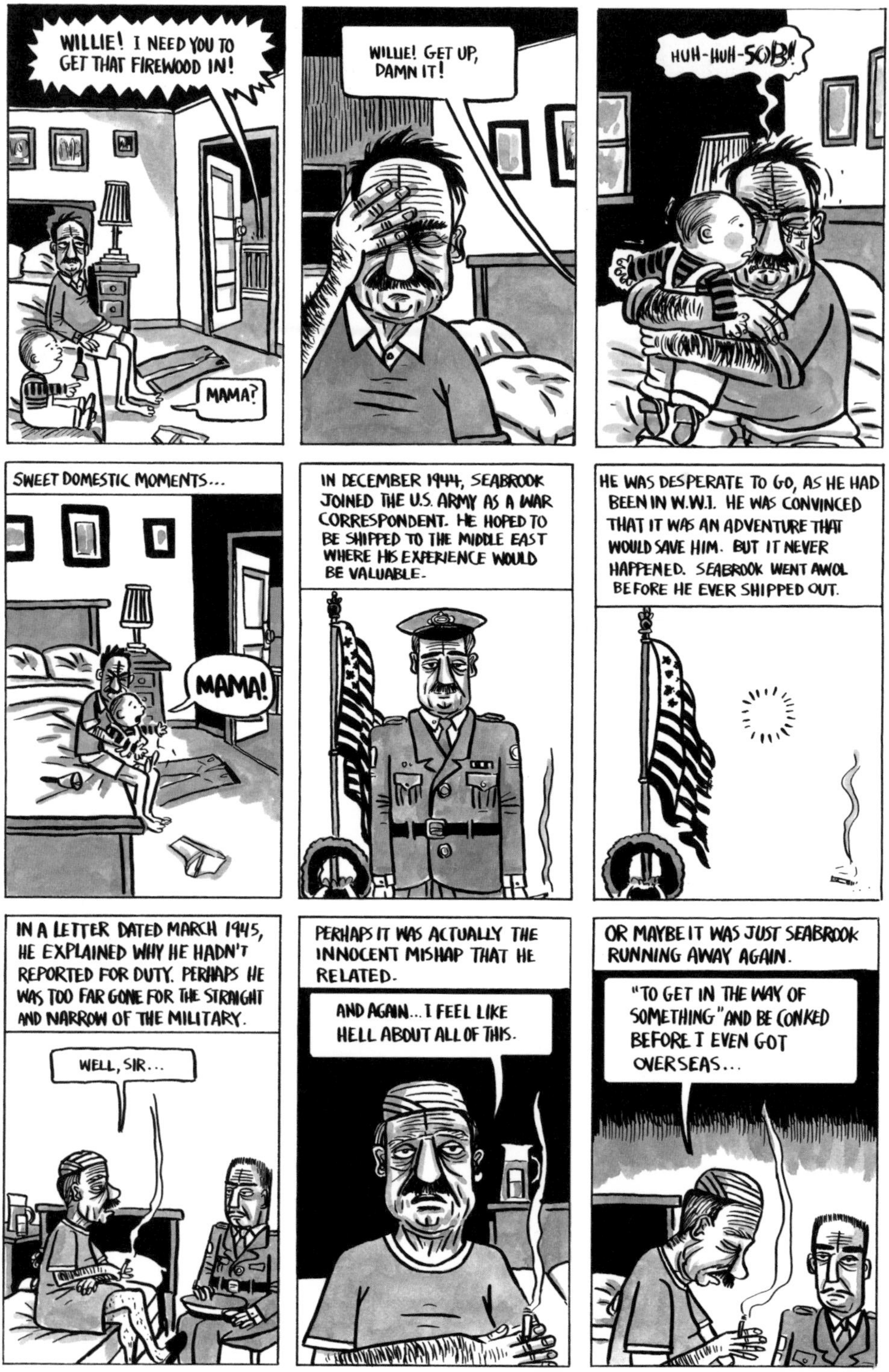
WILLIE! I NEED YOU TO GET THAT FIREWOOD IN!
MAMA?
WILLIE! GET UP, DAMN IT!
HUH-HUH-SOB!
SWEET DOMESTIC MOMENTS...
MAMA!
IN DECEMBER 1944, SEABROOK JOINED THE U.S. ARMY AS A WAR CORRESPONDENT. HE HOPED TO BE SHIPPED TO THE MIDDLE EAST WHERE HIS EXPERIENCE WOULD BE VALUABLE.
HE WAS DESPERATE TO GO, AS HE HAD BEEN IN W.W.I. HE WAS CONVINCED THAT IT WAS AN ADVENTURE THAT WOULD SAVE HIM. BUT IT NEVER HAPPENED. SEABROOK WENT AWOL BEFORE HE EVER SHIPPED OUT.
IN A LETTER DATED MARCH 1945, HE EXPLAINED WHY HE HADN'T REPORTED FOR DUTY. PERHAPS HE WAS TOO FAR GONE FOR THE STRAIGHT AND NARROW OF THE MILITARY.
WELL, SIR...
PERHAPS IT WAS ACTUALLY THE INNOCENT MISHAP THAT HE RELATED.
AND AGAIN... I FEEL LIKE HELL ABOUT ALL OF THIS.
OR MAYBE IT WAS JUST SEABROOK RUNNING AWAY AGAIN.
"TO GET IN THE WAY OF SOMETHING" AND BE CONKED BEFORE I EVEN GOT OVERSEAS...

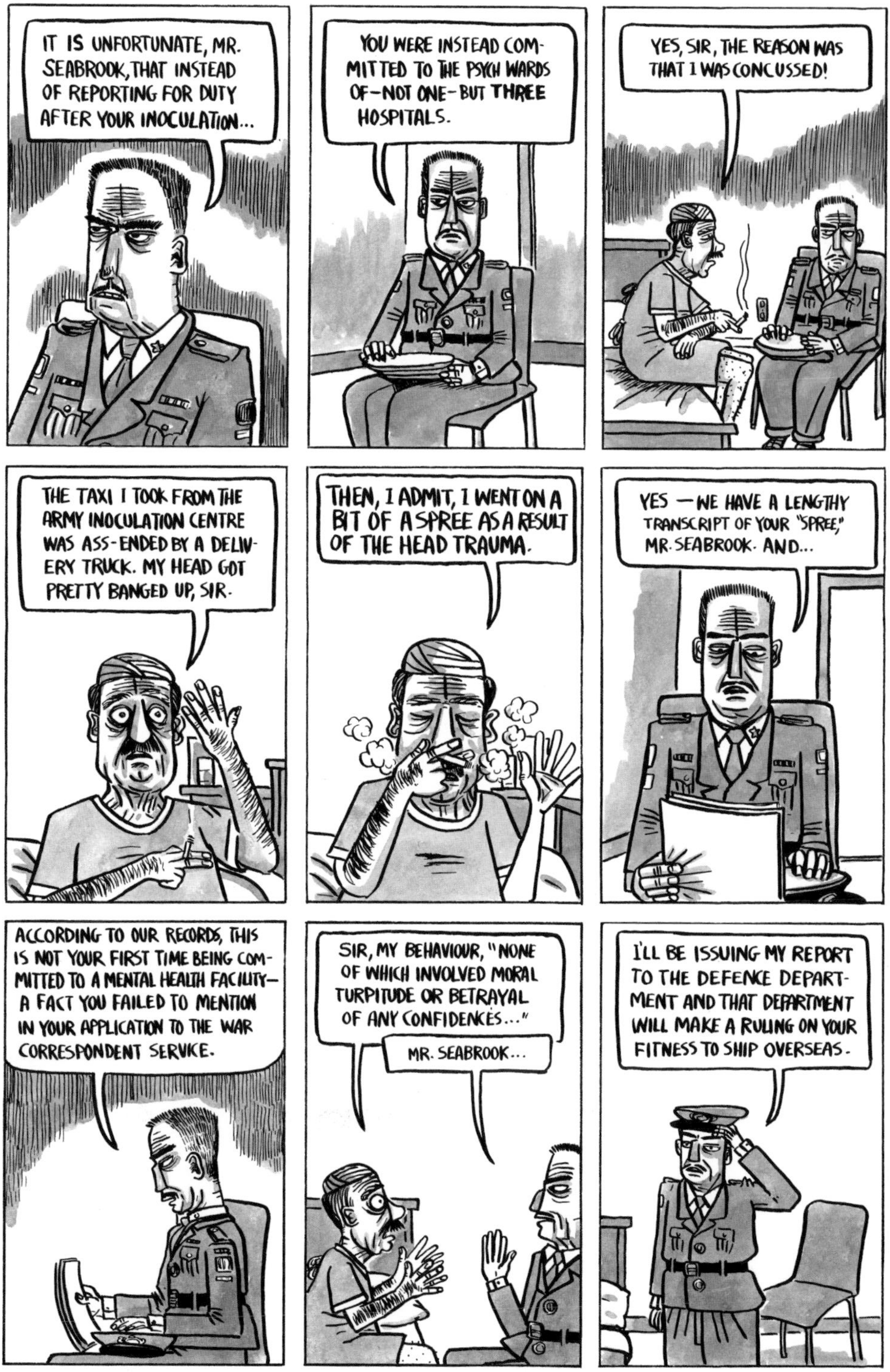
IT IS UNFORTUNATE, MR. SEABROOK, THAT INSTEAD OF REPORTING FOR DUTY AFTER YOUR INOCULATION...
YOU WERE INSTEAD COMMITTED TO THE PSYCH WARDS OF—NOT ONE—BUT THREE HOSPITALS.
YES, SIR, THE REASON WAS THAT I WAS CONCUSSED!
THE TAXI I TOOK FROM THE ARMY INOCULATION CENTRE WAS ASS-ENDED BY A DELIVERY TRUCK. MY HEAD GOT PRETTY BANGED UP, SIR.
THEN, I ADMIT, I WENT ON A BIT OF A SPREE AS A RESULT OF THE HEAD TRAUMA.
YES —WE HAVE A LENGTHY TRANSCRIPT OF YOUR "SPREE," MR. SEABROOK. AND...
ACCORDING TO OUR RECORDS, THIS IS NOT YOUR FIRST TIME BEING COMMITTED TO A MENTAL HEALTH FACILITY—A FACT YOU FAILED TO MENTION IN YOUR APPLICATION TO THE WAR CORRESPONDENT SERVICE.
SIR, MY BEHAVIOUR, "NONE OF WHICH INVOLVED MORAL TURPITUDE OR BETRAYAL OF ANY CONFIDENCES..."
MR. SEABROOK...
I'LL BE ISSUING MY REPORT TO THE DEFENCE DEPARTMENT AND THAT DEPARTMENT WILL MAKE A RULING ON YOUR FITNESS TO SHIP OVERSEAS.

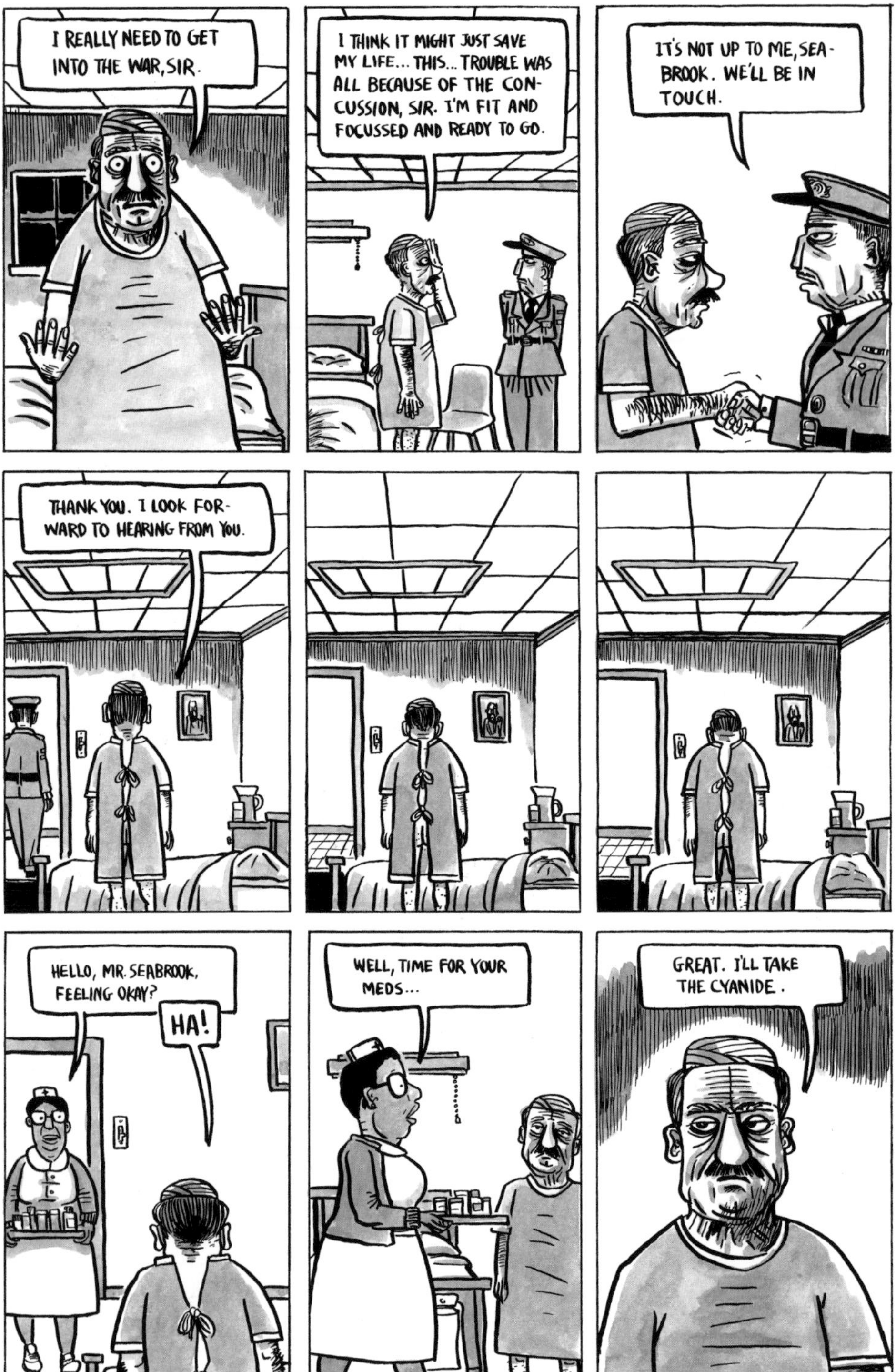
I REALLY NEED TO GET INTO THE WAR, SIR.
I THINK IT MIGHT JUST SAVE MY LIFE... THIS... TROUBLE WAS ALL BECAUSE OF THE CONCUSSION, SIR. I'M FIT AND FOCUSSED AND READY TO GO.
IT'S NOT UP TO ME, SEABROOK. WE'LL BE IN TOUCH.
THANK YOU. I LOOK FORWARD TO HEARING FROM YOU.
HELLO, MR. SEABROOK, FEELING OKAY?
HA!
WELL, TIME FOR YOUR MEDS...
GREAT. I'LL TAKE THE CYANIDE.

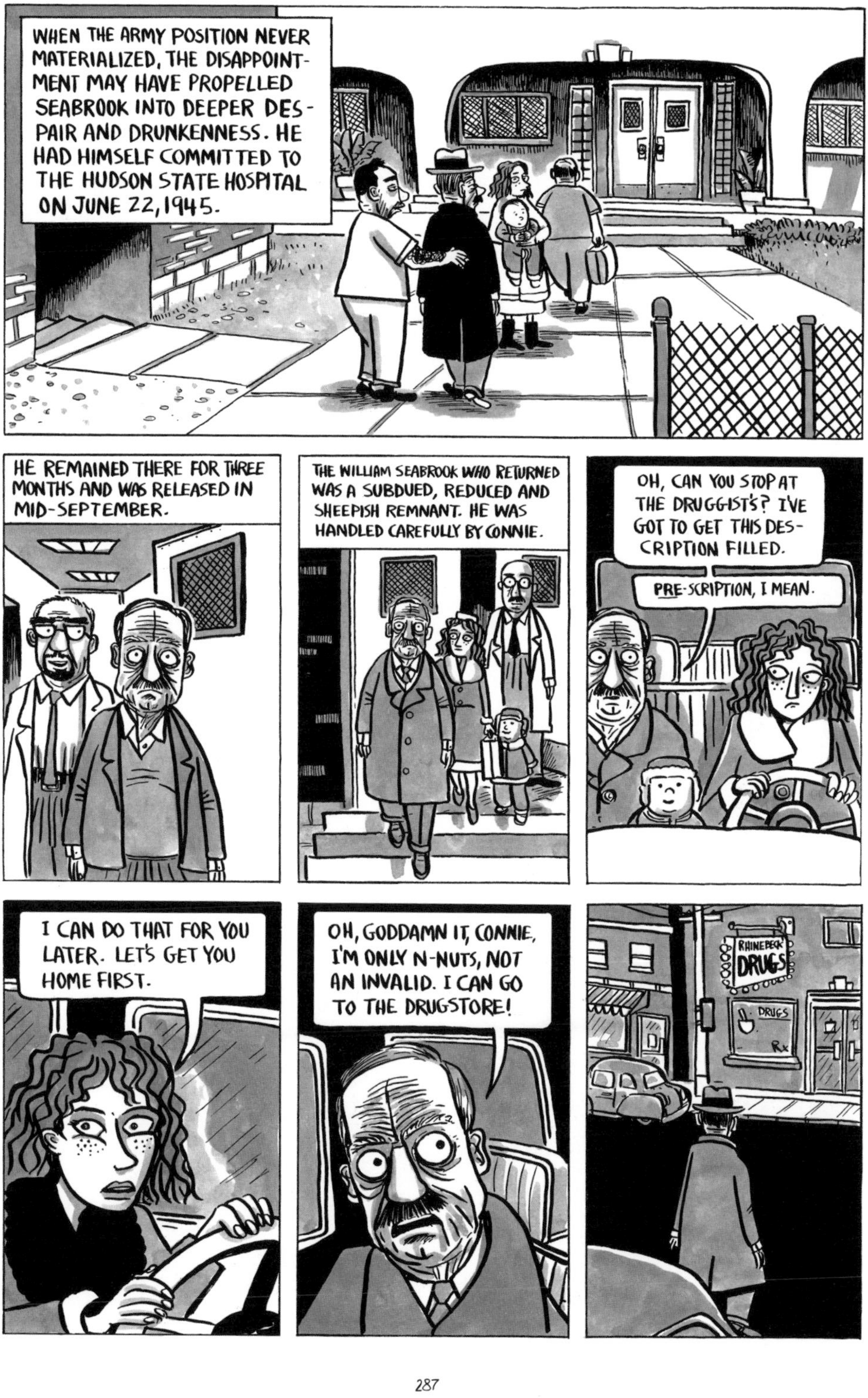
WHEN THE ARMY POSITION NEVER MATERIALIZED, THE DISAPPOINTMENT MAY HAVE PROPELLED SEABROOK INTO DEEPER DESPAIR AND DRUNKENNESS. HE HAD HIMSELF COMMITTED TO THE HUDSON STATE HOSPITAL ON JUNE 22, 1945.
HE REMAINED THERE FOR THREE MONTHS AND WAS RELEASED IN MID-SEPTEMBER.
THE WILLIAM SEABROOK WHO RETURNED WAS A SUBDUED, REDUCED AND SHEEPISH REMNANT. HE WAS HANDLED CAREFULLY BY CONNIE.
OH, CAN YOU STOP AT THE DRUGGIST'S? I'VE GOT TO GET THIS DESCRIPTION FILLED.
PRE-SCRIPTION, I MEAN.
I CAN DO THAT FOR YOU LATER. LET'S GET YOU HOME FIRST.
OH, GODDAMN IT, CONNIE, I'M ONLY N-NUTS, NOT AN INVALID. I CAN GO TO THE DRUGSTORE!
RHINEBECK DRUGS
DRUGS
Rx

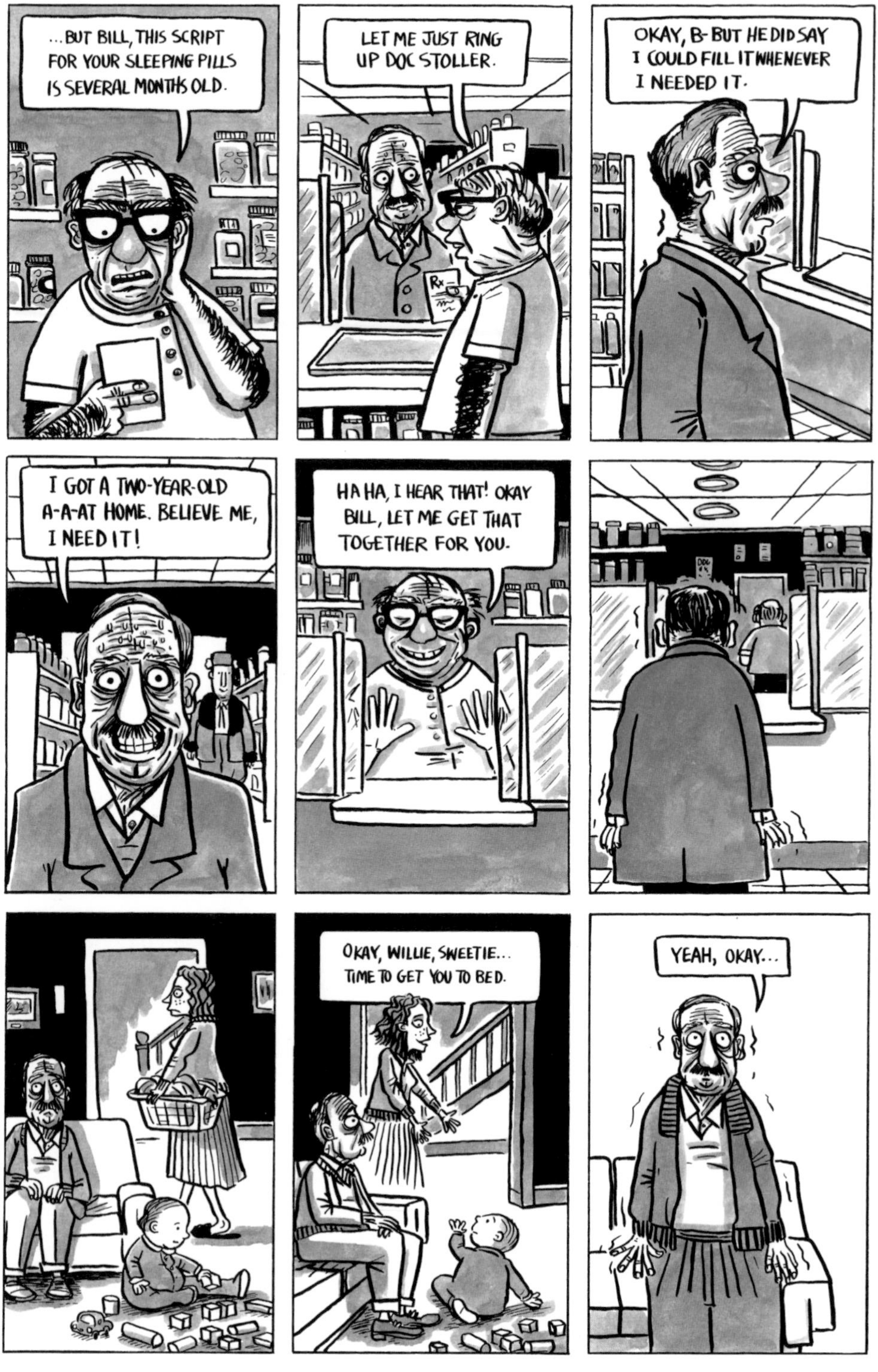
...BUT BILL, THIS SCRIPT FOR YOUR SLEEPING PILLS IS SEVERAL MONTHS OLD.
LET ME JUST RING UP DOC STOLLER.
OKAY, B-BUT HE DID SAY I COULD FILL IT WHENEVER I NEEDED IT.
I GOT A TWO-YEAR-OLD A-A-AT HOME. BELIEVE ME, I NEED IT!
HA HA, I HEAR THAT! OKAY BILL, LET ME GET THAT TOGETHER FOR YOU.
OKAY, WILLIE, SWEETIE... TIME TO GET YOU TO BED.
YEAH, OKAY...

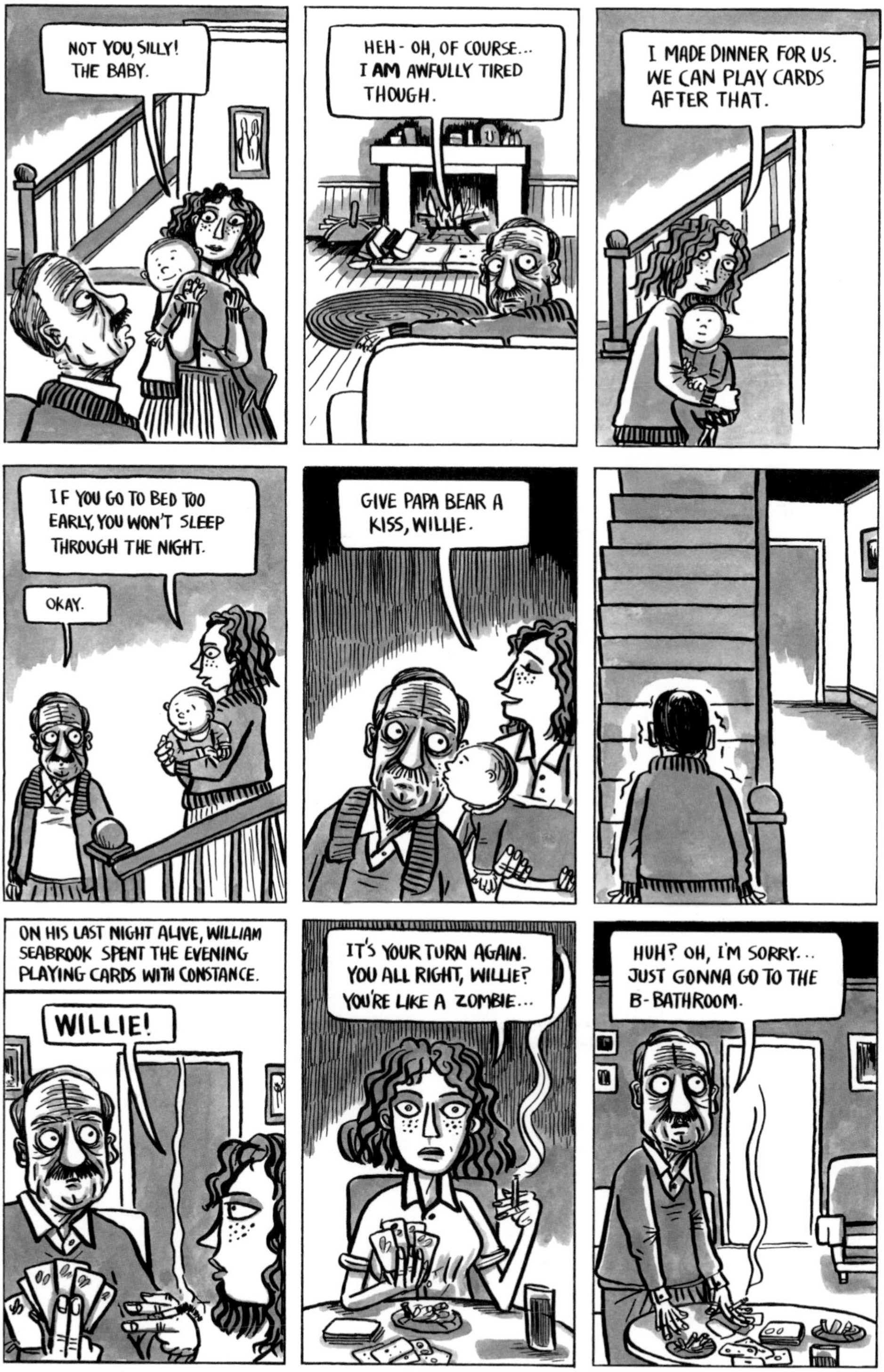
NOT YOU, SILLY! THE BABY.
HEH - OH, OF COURSE... I AM AWFULLY TIRED THOUGH.
I MADE DINNER FOR US. WE CAN PLAY CARDS AFTER THAT.
IF YOU GO TO BED TOO EARLY, YOU WON'T SLEEP THROUGH THE NIGHT.
OKAY.
GIVE PAPA BEAR A KISS, WILLIE.
ON HIS LAST NIGHT ALIVE, WILLIAM SEABROOK SPENT THE EVENING PLAYING CARDS WITH CONSTANCE.
WILLIE!
IT'S YOUR TURN AGAIN. YOU ALL RIGHT, WILLIE? YOU'RE LIKE A ZOMBIE...
HUH? OH, I'M SORRY... JUST GONNA GO TO THE B-BATHROOM.

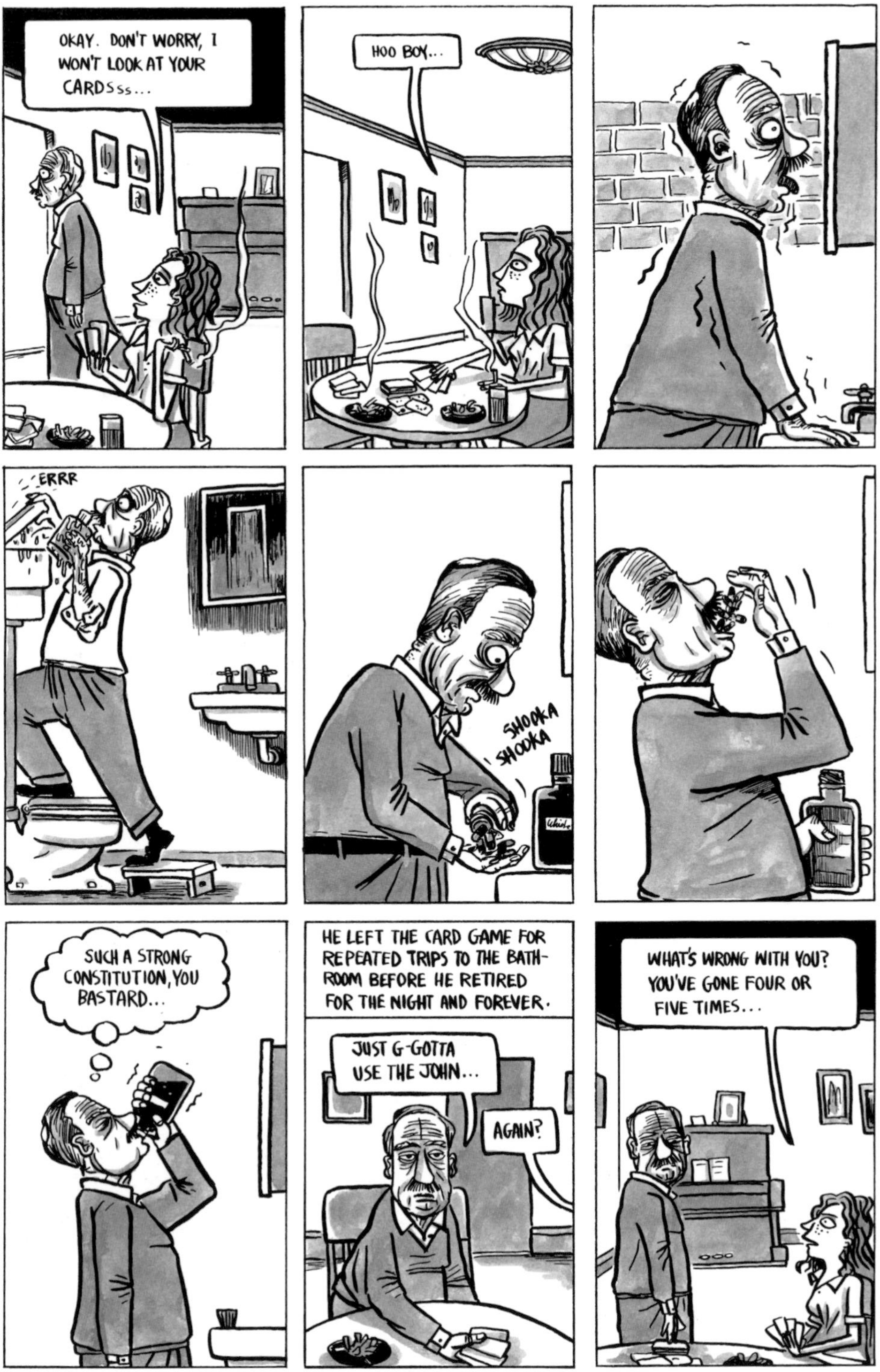
OKAY. DON'T WORRY, I WON'T LOOK AT YOUR CARDSsss...
HOO BOY...
ERRR
SHOOKA SHOOKA
SUCH A STRONG CONSTITUTION, YOU BASTARD...
HE LEFT THE CARD GAME FOR REPEATED TRIPS TO THE BATHROOM BEFORE HE RETIRED FOR THE NIGHT AND FOREVER.
JUST G-GOTTA USE THE JOHN...
AGAIN?
WHAT'S WRONG WITH YOU? YOU'VE GONE FOUR OR FIVE TIMES...

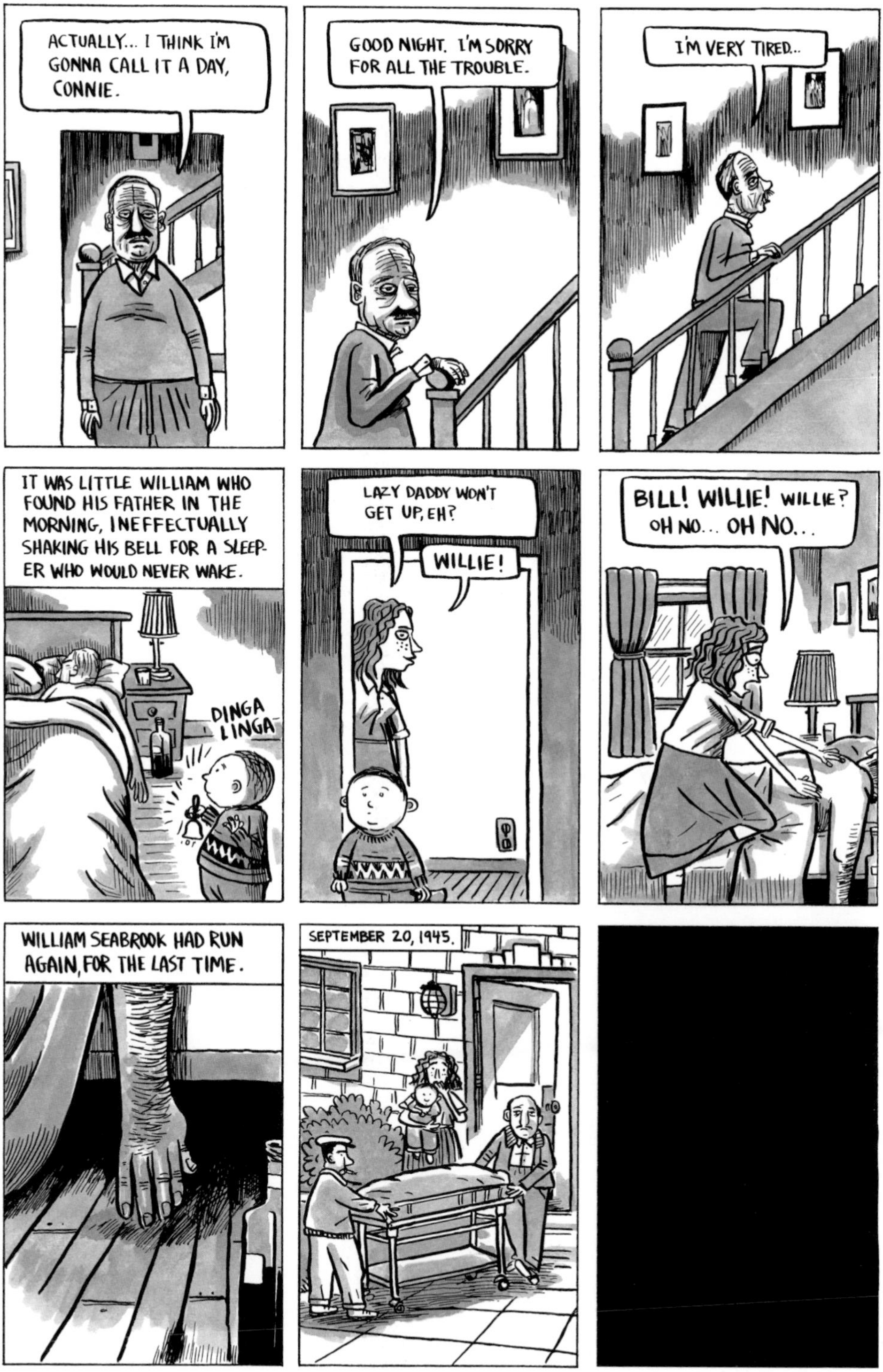
ACTUALLY... I THINK I'M GONNA CALL IT A DAY, CONNIE.
GOOD NIGHT. I'M SORRY FOR ALL THE TROUBLE.
I'M VERY TIRED...
IT WAS LITTLE WILLIAM WHO FOUND HIS FATHER IN THE MORNING, INEFFECTUALLY SHAKING HIS BELL FOR A SLEEPER WHO WOULD NEVER WAKE.
DINGA LINGA
LAZY DADDY WON'T GET UP, EH?
WILLIE!
BILL! WILLIE! WILLIE?
OH NO... OH NO...
WILLIAM SEABROOK HAD RUN AGAIN, FOR THE LAST TIME.
SEPTEMBER 20, 1945.

THE FOLLOWING IS NOT MEANT TO IMPLY "HEAVEN," BUT MERELY A POSSIBLE CONSTRUCT OF THE DYING SEABROOK'S MIND.

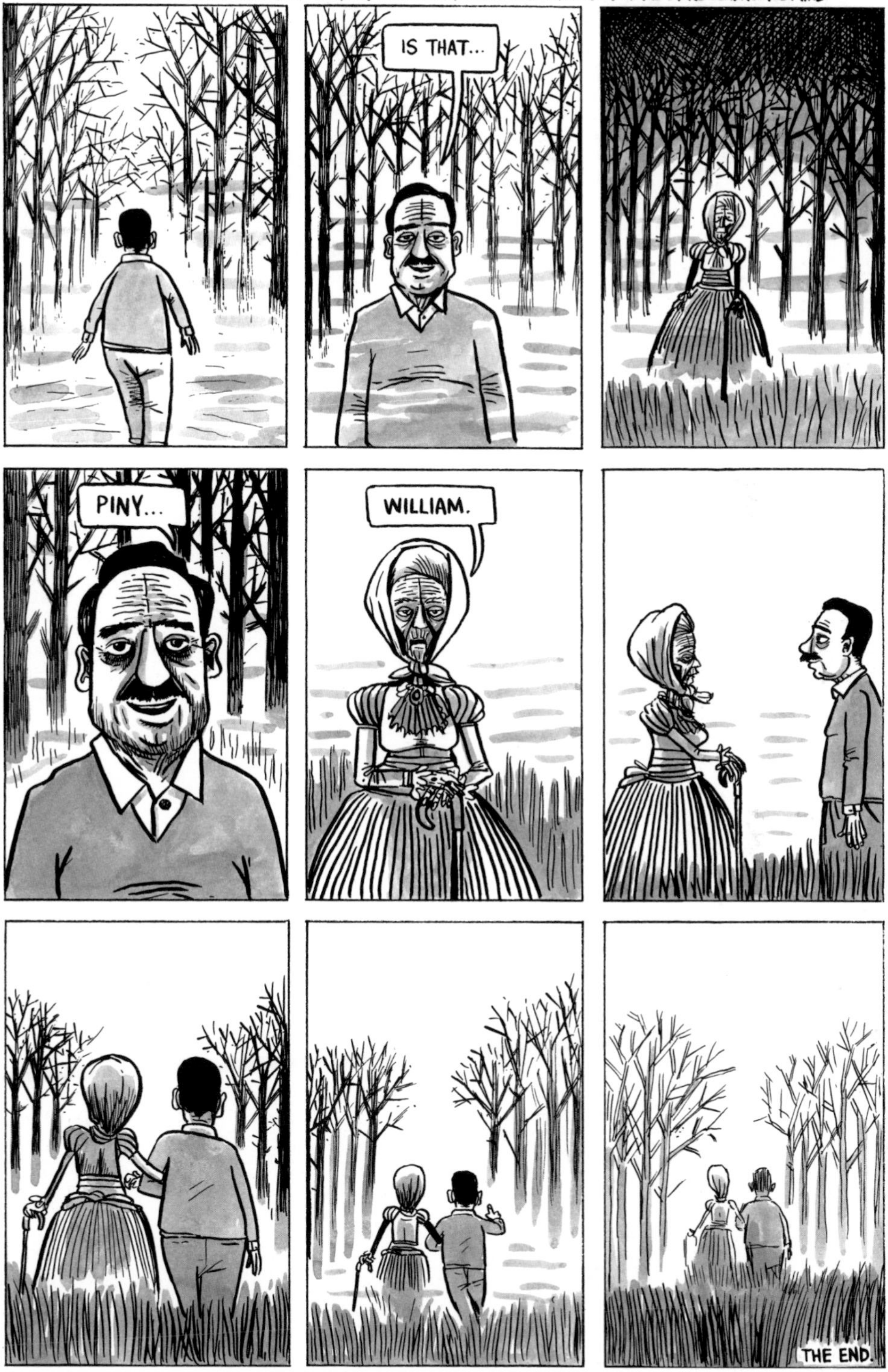
IS THAT...
PINY...
WILLIAM.
THE END.

# EPILOGUE

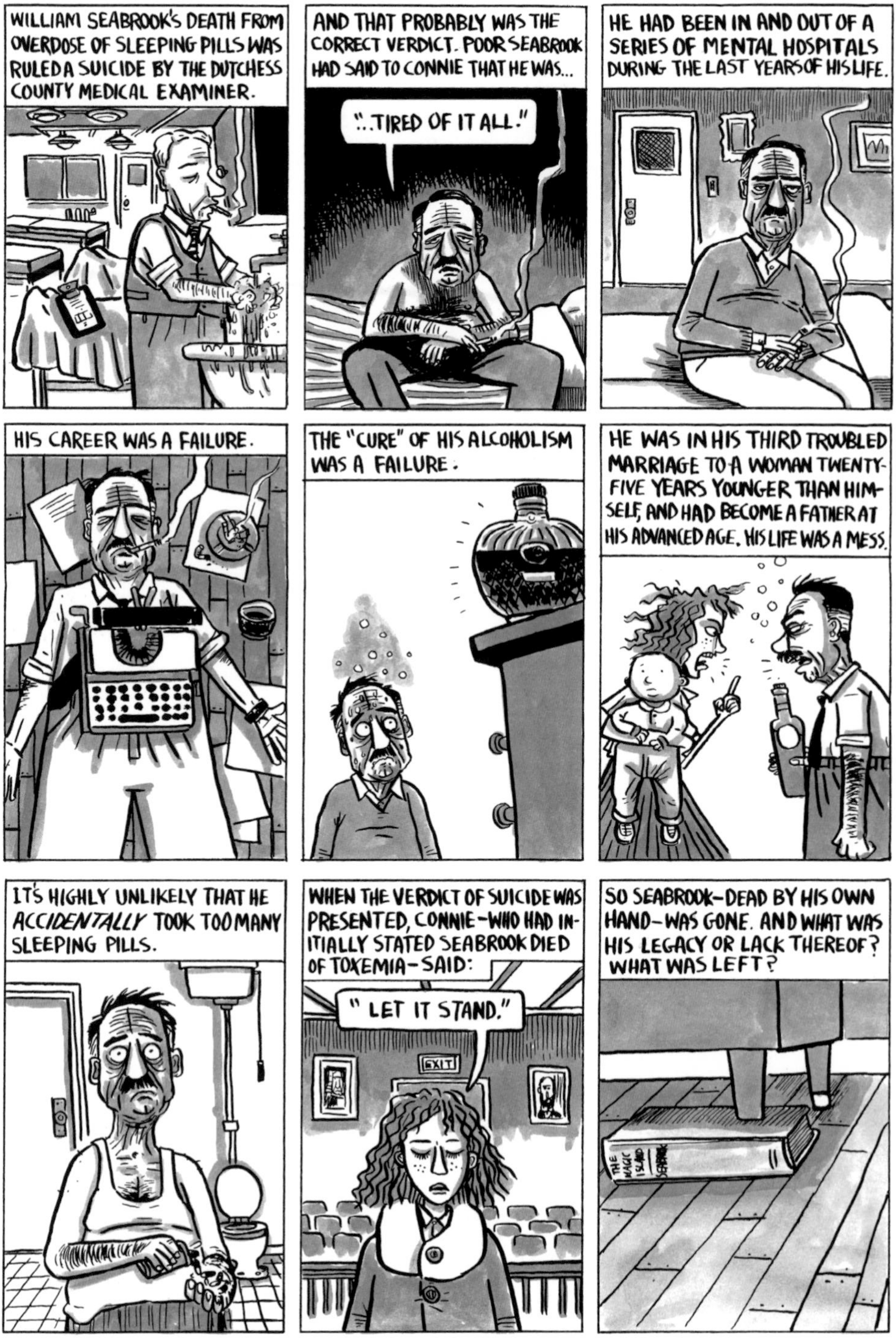

WILLIAM SEABROOK'S DEATH FROM OVERDOSE OF SLEEPING PILLS WAS RULED A SUICIDE BY THE DUTCHESS COUNTY MEDICAL EXAMINER.
AND THAT PROBABLY WAS THE CORRECT VERDICT. POOR SEABROOK HAD SAID TO CONNIE THAT HE WAS...
"...TIRED OF IT ALL."
HE HAD BEEN IN AND OUT OF A SERIES OF MENTAL HOSPITALS DURING THE LAST YEARS OF HIS LIFE.
HIS CAREER WAS A FAILURE.
THE "CURE" OF HIS ALCOHOLISM WAS A FAILURE.
HE WAS IN HIS THIRD TROUBLED MARRIAGE TO A WOMAN TWENTY-FIVE YEARS YOUNGER THAN HIMSELF, AND HAD BECOME A FATHER AT HIS ADVANCED AGE. HIS LIFE WAS A MESS.
IT'S HIGHLY UNLIKELY THAT HE *ACCIDENTALLY* TOOK TOO MANY SLEEPING PILLS.
WHEN THE VERDICT OF SUICIDE WAS PRESENTED, CONNIE—WHO HAD INITIALLY STATED SEABROOK DIED OF TOXEMIA—SAID:
" LET IT STAND."
EXIT
SO SEABROOK—DEAD BY HIS OWN HAND—WAS GONE. AND WHAT WAS HIS LEGACY OR LACK THEREOF? WHAT WAS LEFT?
THE MAGIC ISLAND

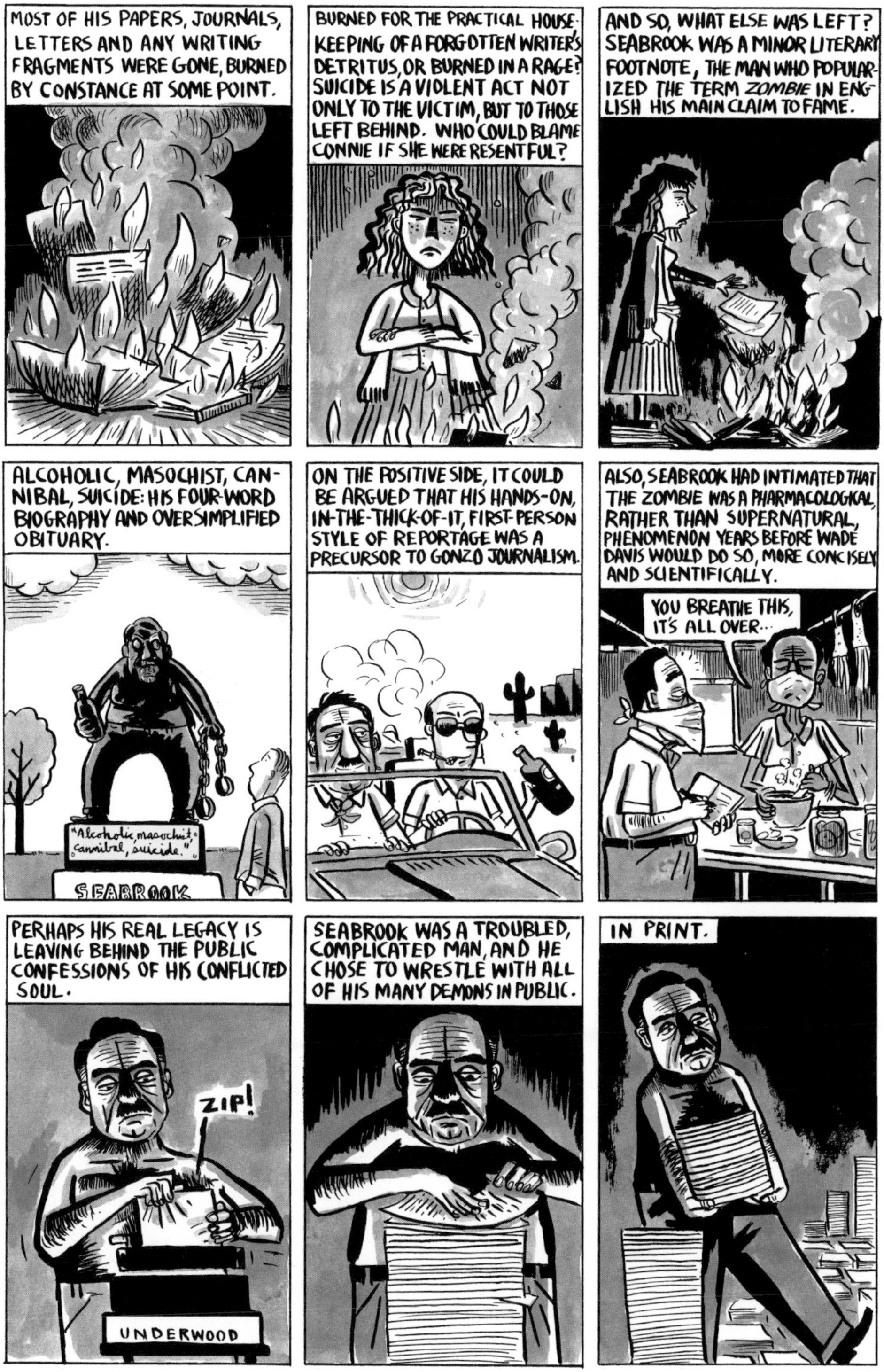
MOST OF HIS PAPERS, JOURNALS, LETTERS AND ANY WRITING FRAGMENTS WERE GONE, BURNED BY CONSTANCE AT SOME POINT.
BURNED FOR THE PRACTICAL HOUSE-KEEPING OF A FORGOTTEN WRITER'S DETRITUS, OR BURNED IN A RAGE? SUICIDE IS A VIOLENT ACT NOT ONLY TO THE VICTIM, BUT TO THOSE LEFT BEHIND. WHO COULD BLAME CONNIE IF SHE WERE RESENTFUL?
AND SO, WHAT ELSE WAS LEFT? SEABROOK WAS A MINOR LITERARY FOOTNOTE, THE MAN WHO POPULARIZED THE TERM ZOMBIE IN ENGLISH HIS MAIN CLAIM TO FAME.
ALCOHOLIC, MASOCHIST, CANNIBAL, SUICIDE: HIS FOUR-WORD BIOGRAPHY AND OVERSIMPLIFIED OBITUARY.
"Alcoholic, masochist, cannibal, suicide."
SEABROOK
ON THE POSITIVE SIDE, IT COULD BE ARGUED THAT HIS HANDS-ON, IN-THE-THICK-OF-IT, FIRST-PERSON STYLE OF REPORTAGE WAS A PRECURSOR TO GONZO JOURNALISM.
ALSO, SEABROOK HAD INTIMATED THAT THE ZOMBIE WAS A PHARMACOLOGICAL, RATHER THAN SUPERNATURAL, PHENOMENON YEARS BEFORE WADE DAVIS WOULD DO SO, MORE CONCISELY AND SCIENTIFICALLY.
YOU BREATHE THIS, IT'S ALL OVER...
PERHAPS HIS REAL LEGACY IS LEAVING BEHIND THE PUBLIC CONFESSIONS OF HIS CONFLICTED SOUL.
ZIP!
UNDERWOOD
SEABROOK WAS A TROUBLED, COMPLICATED MAN, AND HE CHOSE TO WRESTLE WITH ALL OF HIS MANY DEMONS IN PUBLIC.
IN PRINT.

HE WROTE AS IF HE WERE PHYSICALLY INCAPABLE OF DISHONESTY, THOUGH THERE WAS THAT TIME HE LIED ABOUT HIS CANNIBALISM IN A NON-FICTION BOOK.

HE WROTE WITHOUT SHAME ABOUT HIS BONDAGE PRACTICES, THOUGH HE SEEMED COMPELLED TO LEGITIMIZE THEM IN THE GUISE OF PSYCHIC RESEARCH.

HE WAS PROGRESSIVE, OPEN TO OTHER CULTURES AND LARGELY RESPECTFUL TO OTHER RACES, THOUGH HE WAS PROUD OF BEATING AN AFRICAN MAN HE THOUGHT HAD CHEATED HIM.

HE WAS A COMPLICATED, TROUBLED MAN WHO LEFT BEHIND AN UNEVEN, MINOR LITERARY LEGACY.

HE HAD GONE FROM BEING ONE OF THE BEST-SELLING, HIGHEST-PAID WRITERS OF HIS DAY, A FRIEND AND CONTEMPORARY OF GREAT WRITERS, TO BEING LARGELY FORGOTTEN.

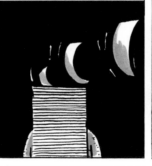

ALL OF HIS BOOKS WERE OUT OF PRINT. THERE WERE ONLY A FEW ONLINE RESOURCES THAT SHARED INFORMATION AMONG HIS FEW AVID ENTHUSIASTS.

BUT RECENTLY, SEABROOK HAS BEGUN TO BE REDISCOVERED FROM THE FEW CLUES LEFT TO SEEKERS. HIS BOOKS ARE COMING BACK IN PRINT. ARTICLES ARE BEING WRITTEN, BIOGRAPHIES AND FILMS ARE BEING CONSIDERED.

THIS NEW AUDIENCE FOR SEABROOK'S FRANK, HONEST WRITING MAY BE SURPRISED AT ITS QUALITY—THAT HE IS A BETTER WRITER THAN ONE WOULD EXPECT FOR A GUTTER PRESS JOURNALIST.

MAYBE SEABROOK'S HOPE WILL BE FULFILLED:

"IF NOBODY READS YOU AFTER YOU ARE DEAD, YOUR WORDS ARE DEAD, BUT IF SOME LIVING PEOPLE CONTINUE TO READ YOUR WORDS, YOUR WORDS REMAIN ALIVE..."

# NOTES

PAGE 1– THIS PROLOGUE IS PURE SPECULATION ON WHAT A NIGHT NEAR THE END OF SEABROOK'S LIFE MIGHT HAVE BEEN LIKE, BASED ON WHAT WE KNOW: THAT HE HAD BEEN ACCEPTED INTO THE WAR CORRESPONDENT CORPS OF THE U.S. ARMY. MARJORIE WROTE THAT HE WORE HIS UNIFORM WHEN THEY MET IN N.Y.C., THAT, BESIDES THEIR HOUSE IN RHINEBECK, HE KEPT AN APARTMENT IN GREENWICH VILLAGE AT THE TIME AND THAT HE WAS DRINKING HEAVILY AND WAS FEELING HIS AGE AND THE FAILURE OF HIS CAREER.

PAGE 15, PANEL 7– THE PULLMAN AD. SEABROOK WAS A BIG ENOUGH LITERARY STAR THAT HE DID CELEBRITY ENDORSEMENTS.

PAGE 16– HIS MOTHER. SEABROOK HAD AN INCREDIBLY COMPLICATED RELATIONSHIP WITH HIS MOTHER. SHE LOOMS LARGE IN HIS LIFE. MAN RAY SUGGESTED SHE WAS THE REASON SEABROOK USED BONDAGE TO PUNISH WOMEN: AS SURROGATES FOR HIS MOTHER. I MAY HAVE PORTRAYED HER TOO HARSHLY IN THIS BOOK, SO KEEP IN MIND MY ONLY SOURCE ON HER BEHAVIOUR IS SEABROOK.

PAGE 20, PANEL 2– "PINY'S CAUL." YOU ALL KNOW ABOUT CAULS, RIGHT? IF NOT, A CAUL IS A PIECE OF MEMBRANE THAT CAN COVER A NEWBORN INFANT'S FACE. IT IS EASILY REMOVED, AND A CHILD BORN WITH A CAUL HAS – SINCE MEDIEVAL TIMES – BEEN THOUGHT TO BE LUCKY OR TO POSSESS SUPERNATURAL ABILITIES. IN THE VICTORIAN ERA, CAULS WERE LISTED FOR SALE IN WANT ADS AND WERE BOUGHT BY SAILORS AS PROTECTION AGAINST DROWNING. DICKENS'S DAVID COPPERFIELD WAS BORN WITH A CAUL.

PAGE 23 – SEABROOK DESCRIBED THE BIRDS IN HIS VISION AS BEAUTIFUL AND BRIGHTPLUMAGED, YET I DREW THEM BASICALLY AS LARGE CHICKENS. SEABROOK WAS PRONE TO EXAGGERATION AND I SPECULATED THAT MAYBE HIS CHILDHOOD VISIONS WERE LESS FANCIFUL THAN HE DESCRIBED LATER IN LIFE.

PAGE 42– KATIE SEABROOK SEEMED TO HAVE BEEN EXTREMELY EASY GOING. SHE AND SEABROOK HAD THE LEAST TROUBLED RELATIONSHIP OF ALL HIS MARRIAGES. SHE WROTE A CHILDREN'S BOOK CALLED GAO OF THE IVORY COAST.

PAGE 59– DEBORAH LURIS. I HAD HOPED TO FIND SOME REFERENCE TO HER REAL NAME IN MARJORIE'S ARCHIVES. MAYBE A PROPER RESEARCHER WOULD HAVE DISCOVERED HER IDENTITY. IT DOESN'T MATTER ULTIMATELY. THE MAIN THING ABOUT HER IMPORTANCE IN SEABROOK'S LIFE IS AS THE FIRST WILLING COLLABORATOR IN HIS BONDAGE FANTASIES. SHE WORKED FOR TONY SARG, THE GREAT PUPPETEER, ANIMATOR AND CARTOONIST. SARG DESIGNED THE HELIUM-FILLED FLOATS IN THE FIRST MACY'S THANKSGIVING PARADE.

PAGE 63, PANEL 8– THEODORE DREISER WAS SEABROOK'S LITERARY HERO, SO IT WAS SAD THAT WHEN THEY MET, DREISER TREATED HIM TERRIBLY, "HE WAS A BITTER AND UNHAPPY STRONG MAN, ALREADY FAMOUS BUT STILL STRUGGLING ECONOMICALLY, WHO TOOK IT OUT ON NOBODIES AND WEAKLINGS." AFTERWARD, HE STILL ACKNOWLEDGED DREISER'S GENIUS, BUT HE WOULD "LOITER OR CROSS THE STREET TO AVOID (MEETING HIM)."

PAGE 69, PANEL 1 — AGAIN, SEABROOK IS A TEXTBOOK UNRELIABLE NARRATOR. HE BLITHELY MENTIONS CUTTING REGULAR CHEQUES FOR HIS PARENTS LIKE A BIG SHOT, BUT THEN THERE'S THE LETTER FROM HIS SISTER, FRANCES, BEGGING THAT HE'LL HELP THEIR FINANCIALLY DESPERATE PARENTS.

PAGE 78, PANEL 7 — MITKHAL PASHA EL FAYIZ, LEADER OF THE BENI SAKHR BEDOUIN WHO LIVED OUTSIDE OF JORDAN. HE WAS ONE OF THE ARAB DELEGATION WHO NEGOTIATED WITH THE ZIONIST ORGANIZATION IN PALESTINE IN 1933 AND LATER GAVE UP THE NOMADIC LIFE IN EXCHANGE FOR FINANCIAL AID FROM THE RULING BRITISH COLONIAL GOVERNMENT THAT OCCUPIED JORDAN.

PAGE 82, PANEL 2 — MORE DIFFERING ACCOUNTS OF EVENTS. THERE ARE MANY INSTANCES WHERE SEABROOK WROTE ABOUT AN EVENT IN ONE OF HIS EARLIER BOOKS, THEN DESCRIBES THE SAME EVENT DIFFERENTLY IN THE MUCH LATER AUTOBIOGRAPHY, NO HIDING PLACE. THEN, THERE ARE MARJORIE'S VERSIONS OF EVENTS, WHICH ARE, AGAIN, OFTEN QUITE DIFFERENT THAN HIS. AS MARJORIE SAID: "WILLIE... ALWAYS TOLD THE TRUTH. HIS TRUTH."

PAGE 98, PANEL 4 — SEABROOK SPEAKING "PIDGIN" FRENCH IS SPECULATION BY ME. I COULD FIND NO REFERENCE TO HIS LANGUAGE SKILLS. I SUSPECT, LIKE MANY NORTH AMERICANS SPEAKING ANOTHER LANGUAGE, THEY WERE PROBABLY LIMITED, AT LEAST IN TERMS OF ACCENT. (I HAVE A RECORDING OF A RADIO SHOW OF SEABROOK SPEAKING WITH A PRONOUNCED SOUTHERN ACCENT.) I MAY BE TOTALLY OFF BASE ON THIS, BUT I USED IT AS A CHANCE TO TURN AROUND THE USUAL CLICHÉ OF THE PERSON OF COLOUR SPEAKING MANGLED ENGLISH BY HAVING SEABROOK BOTCHING THE FRENCH. AS I COULDN'T CONFIRM IT, I ONLY INTRODUCE THE NOTION BRIEFLY, THEN DROP IT, AS IF HE WERE LEARNING THE LANGUAGE AND IMPROVING.

PAGE 102 — ZOMBIES ARE HIS CLAIM TO FAME. THERE'S THE BÉLA LUGOSI FILM, *WHITE ZOMBIE*, THE FACT THAT HE'S CREDITED BY SOME AS INTRODUCING THE WORD *ZOMBIE* TO ENGLISH AUDIENCES, AND THAT HE PROPOSED THAT THE ZOMBIE WAS A CHEMICAL AND NOT A SUPERNATURAL EVENT, LONG BEFORE ZORA NEALE HURSTON DID IN *TELL MY HORSE* OR ETHNOBOTANIST WADE DAVIS DID MOST SUCCINCTLY IN *THE SERPENT AND THE RAINBOW*.

PAGE 152 — MON PO THE CANNIBAL KING. I DREW HIM WRONG! BUT IT WAS TOO LATE/ I WAS TOO LAZY TO CORRECT IT. REREADING *JUNGLE WAYS*, I SAW SEABROOK DESCRIBED HIM AS "A MUSCULAR LITTLE MAN." NOT THE HEAVY MAN I DREW. OF COURSE, HIS CARRIAGE IS NOT CRUCIAL TO THE STORY, BUT I DO APOLOGIZE TO MON PO.

PAGE 157 — MARJORIE MUIR WORTHINGTON (1900–1976) PUBLISHED ELEVEN BOOKS IN HER LIFETIME, THE LAST BEING *THE STRANGE WORLD OF WILLIE SEABROOK*. MARJORIE WAS AN INCREDIBLE RESOURCE TO ME IN PROVIDING ALTERNATE VIEWS OF SEABROOK'S STORIES. *THE STRANGE WORLD...* IS A GOOD, ENGAGING BIOGRAPHY. SHE REALLY LOVED THE GUY; YOU COULD STILL FEEL IT IN THE PAGES WHEN SHE WROTE THE BOOK IN 1966, TWENTY-ONE YEARS AFTER HE DIED. I'M ALSO INDEBTED TO THE UNIVERSITY OF OREGON FOR ALLOWING ME INTO THEIR ARCHIVES OF MARJORIE'S PAPERS, WHICH WERE A TREASURE TROVE, INCLUDING LETTERS FROM ALDOUS HUXLEY AND MAN RAY! (FOR A BRIEF MOMENT, AS I WENT THROUGH BOXES WITH THE LITTLE WHITE GLOVES ON—FEELING LIKE A CHARACTER IN A.S. BYATT'S *POSSESSION*— I "DISCOVERED" A NEW, UNPUBLISHED SEABROOK MANUSCRIPT, *AFRICA!* IT TURNED OUT TO BE JUST AN EARLIER DRAFT OF *JUNGLE WAYS*.) MARJORIE'S DIARIES CONFIRMED

IN REALITY, STORIES I KNEW SO WELL, THEY SEEMED LIKE MYTHOLOGY. SHE WAS MORE REALISTIC THAN SEABROOK WAS ABOUT THE EFFECTS OF HIS ALCOHOLISM, WHICH HE TENDED TO PASS OFF IN A LIGHTHEARTED FASHION WITH HIMSELF MAINLY THE VICTIM. MARJORIE ENDURED A LOT, AND WITH HER ARCHIVES AND THE BIO OF SEABROOK, SHE PLAYED A LARGE PART IN KEEPING HIS LEGACY ALIVE. I'M INCREDIBLY BEHOLDEN TO HER.

PAGE 169, PANEL 2 — I WORRIED ABOUT DRAWING ALL THIS BONDAGE STUFF, AND PASCAL GIRARD GAVE ME THE ADVICE TO BE VERY EXPLICIT, BUT NOT TO MAKE IT SEXY, WHICH IS WHAT I TRIED TO DO.

PAGE 172 — IN HIS AUTOBIO, *SELF-PORTRAIT*, MAN RAY HAD MORE INSIGHT (RIGHT OR WRONG) ABOUT SEABROOK'S SEXUALITY THAN ANYONE. THEIR PHOTO COLLABORATIONS, *THE FANTASIES OF MR. SEABROOK*, ARE WIDELY AVAILABLE TO BE SEEN ONLINE.

PAGE 224 — THE HEX ON HITLER. I LOVE THAT HE TRIED TO SELL THIS IDEA TO *READER'S DIGEST*. SEABROOK ACTUALLY DID THIS HEX, AND *LIFE* MAGAZINE PUBLISHED A PHOTO ESSAY OF IT, WHICH IS AVAILABLE ONLINE. IN 2011, A KANSAS THEATRE PRODUCED A PLAY OF THIS EVENT.

PAGE 251, PANEL 2 — I SAW THESE LETTERS IN MARJORIE'S ARCHIVES, INCLUDING ONE THAT SEABROOK WROTE HIMSELF IN GIANT, CHILD-LIKE, MISSHAPEN LETTERS, FORMED WITH A PENCIL CLUTCHED BETWEEN BURNT, BANDAGED HANDS.

PAGE 264 — MARJORIE'S SCRAPBOOK OF SEABROOK'S LIFE IS IN HER ARCHIVE. IT IS EXTENSIVE AND HAS ARTICLES ABOUT HIM UP TO AND AFTER HIS DEATH. I DON'T THINK SHE EVER GOT OVER HIM, AND WRITING THE BIOGRAPHY WAS PROBABLY THERAPEUTIC FOR HER.

PAGE 267 — SEABROOK'S ABNORMALLY LARGE SEX ORGAN! IT COULD EXPLAIN SOME, BUT NOT ALL, OF HIS SEX PRACTICES. I HAVE NEVER SEEN THIS FACT PUBLISHED ANYWHERE ELSE IN ANYTHING I'VE READ ABOUT SEABROOK.

PAGE 284, PANEL 7— I'VE SEEN SEABROOK'S LETTER TO THE WAR DEPARTMENT AND MAYBE HE DID HAVE A REACTION TO HIS INOCULATIONS AND A BUMP ON THE HEAD IN A CAR CRASH THAT PUT HIM OFF THE RAILS, OR MAYBE IT WAS JUST ANOTHER SPREE. WHO KNOWS. HE WAS DESPERATE TO CHARM HIS WAY BACK INTO THE ARMY'S GOOD GRACES. I THINK THE WAR CORRESPONDENT JOB WOULD HAVE GIVEN HIM A PURPOSE, MADE HIM FEEL YOUNGER, AND THAT GOING INTO A WAR ZONE MIGHT, IRONICALLY, HAVE EXTENDED HIS LIFE.

THERE WASN'T ROOM FOR EVERYTHING IN THIS BOOK, BUT I WANT TO MENTION THIS INTERESTING BIT THAT MARJORIE ALSO EDITED OUT OF HER BOOK— OF A VISIT TO SCULPTOR ALEXANDER CALDER'S STUDIO IN PARIS. THEY WATCHED HIM PERFORM A TINY CIRCUS, WITH HIS KINETIC SCULPTURES AND TOYS. THAT'S ALL, IT WASN'T IMPORTANT, I JUST LOVE CALDER AND WOULD HAVE LOVED TO INCLUDE THIS. THERE'S A 1955 PATHÉ VIDEO OF THIS PERFORMANCE BY CALDER YOU CAN SEE ONLINE.

I GUESS THAT'S IT. I'M SURE I'VE FORGOTTEN THINGS. IT DOESN'T MATTER, NO ONE HAS READ THIS FAR IN THE NOTES EXCEPT CHESTER, ANYWAY. HI, CHESTER!

THANK YOU...

WILLIAM SEABROOK, MARJORIE WORTHINGTON, THE UNIVERSITY OF OREGON SPECIAL COLLECTIONS, PETER HAINING, THE SEABROOK LIVEJOURNAL GROUP, TAIEN, SAM, MEAGHAN, LIZ, DREW FORD, ANDY BROWN, DAVE LAPP, PASCAL GIRARD, SETH, CHRIS, TOM, PEGGY, TRACY, JULIA, ALL THE D+Q PEOPLE, HOWARD CHACKOWICZ, BILLY MAVREAS, TODD STEWART, MURRAY LIGHTBURN, ANNIE KOYAMA, MOM, DAD, CONAN TOBIAS, THE CANADA COUNCIL FOR THE ARTS, THE ONTARIO ARTS COUNCIL.

SPECIAL THANKS TO INCREDIBLE COPY EDITS BY LUCIE, ALICE AND GILLIAN. TRACY HURREN, THANKS FOR OVERSEEING ALL OF THIS. YOUR SUGGESTIONS MADE THIS A BETTER BOOK.

THANK YOU ALL. ♥

## BIBLIOGRAPHY

THE WORKS OF WILLIAM SEABROOK:
DIARY OF SECTION VIII, (1917)
ADVENTURES IN ARABIA, (1927)
THE MAGIC ISLAND, (1929)
JUNGLE WAYS, (1930)
AIR ADVENTURE, (1933)
THE WHITE MONK OF TIMBUCTOO, (1934)
ASYLUM, (1935)
THESE FOREIGNERS: AMERICANS ALL, (1938)
WITCHCRAFT: ITS POWER IN THE WORLD TODAY, (1940)
DOCTOR WOOD: MODERN WIZARD OF THE LABORATORY, (1941)
NO HIDING PLACE: AN AUTOBIOGRAPHY, (1942)

MARJORIE WORTHINGTON, THE STRANGE WORLD OF
WILLIE SEABROOK, (1966)

MAN RAY, SELF-PORTRAIT

ALEXANDER KING, MINE ENEMY GROWS OLDER

GERTRUDE STEIN, EVERYBODY'S AUTOBIOGRAPHY

NEIL BALDWIN, MAN RAY, AMERICAN ARTIST

ZORA NEALE HURSTON, TELL MY HORSE

GARY DON RHODES, WHITE ZOMBIE: ANATOMY OF
A HORROR FILM

ROBERT NORTH, THE GRIMOIRE OF MARIA
DE NAGLOWSKA

MARJORIE WORTHINGTON'S ARCHIVE AT THE
UNIVERSITY OF OREGON.

This is not a proper bibliography, but I'm not a proper
academic, so sue me. (Please, don't sue me.)

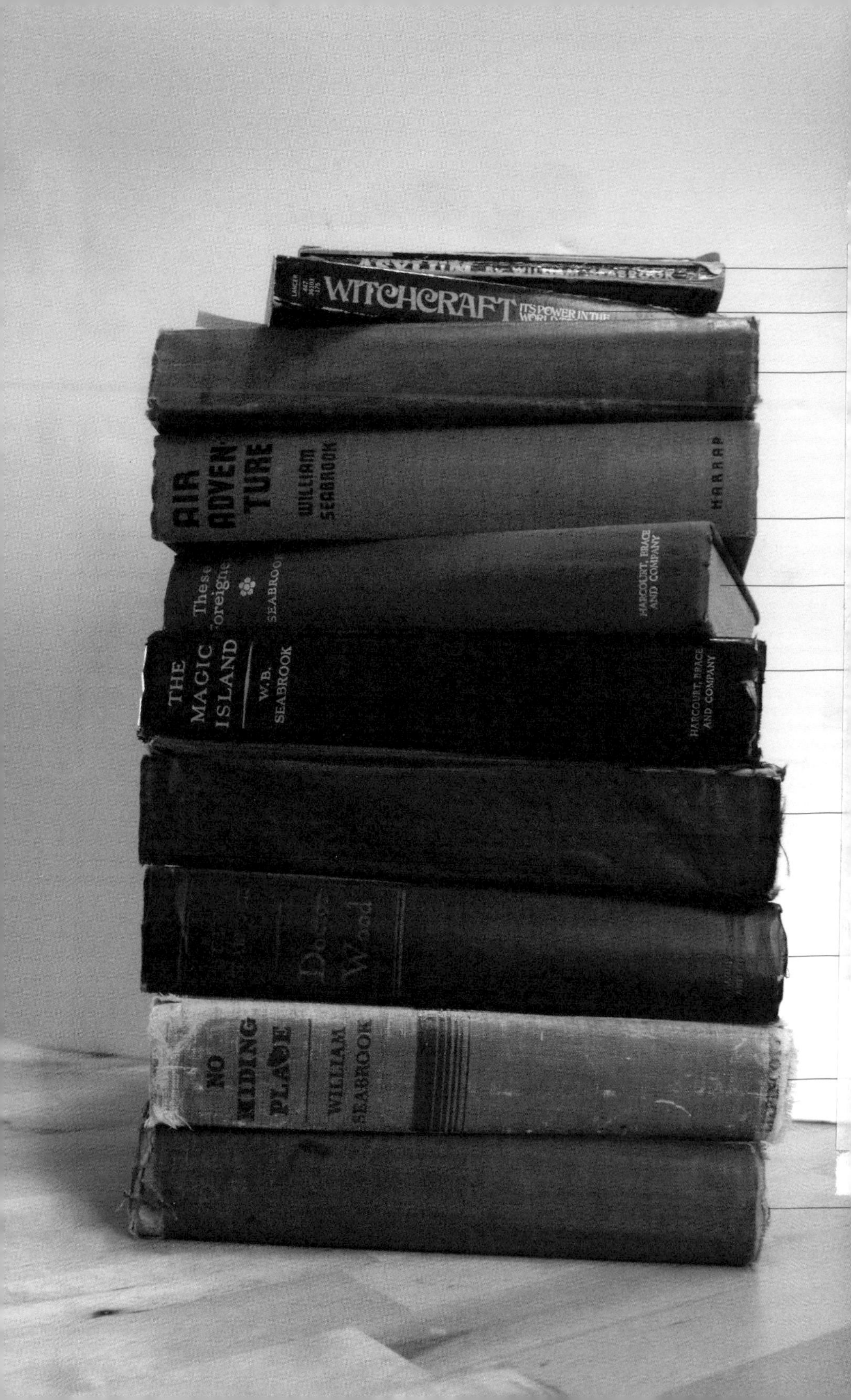
WITCHCRAFT
ITS POWER IN THE
AIR ADVEN-TURE
WILLIAM SEABROOK
HARRAP
These
SEABROOK
HARCOURT, BRACE AND COMPANY
THE MAGIC ISLAND
W. B. SEABROOK
HARCOURT, BRACE AND COMPANY
Doctor Wood
NO HIDING PLACE
WILLIAM SEABROOK

BECAUSE LITERALLY NO ONE ASKED FOR IT:
## WILLIAM SEABROOK'S BOOKS (AS RATED BY ME)

(2) ASYLUM - 1935 - ONE OF HIS BEST, DESPITE A LAGGING MIDDLE SECTION.
BACK IN PRINT (WITH COVER AND INTRO BY ME!) FROM DOVER.

(6) WITCHCRAFT: ITS POWER IN THE WORLD TODAY - 1940
- A SOLID BOOK, IF ONE THAT READS LIKE A BUNCH OF
MAGAZINE ARTICLES STRUNG TOGETHER.

(9) THE WHITE MONK OF TIMBUCTOO - 1934 - I DIDN'T LIKE THE
SUBJECT OF THIS BIO - HE GRATED ON ME. BUT IT'S
NOT A GREAT BOOK ANYWAY.

(8) AIR ADVENTURES - 1933 - THIS WOULD PROBABLY HAVE BEEN OF MORE
INTEREST AT PUBLICATION, IN THE INFANCY OF FLIGHT.

(7) THESE FOREIGNERS - 1938 - SOLID CELEBRATION OF IMMIGRATION.
SEABROOK'S LOVE OF PEOPLE AND HIS SKILL AS A
REPORTER MADE THIS BOOK GOOD.

(3) MAGIC ISLAND - 1929 - GREAT TRAVELOGUE, CULTURAL HISTORY
AND ANTHROPOLOGICAL STUDY OF HAITI.
ALSO IN REPRINT FROM DOVER WITH FOREWORD AND
AFTERWORD BY GEORGE ROMERO AND WADE DAVIS!
(ALSO COVER AND COMICS INTRO BY ME.)

(4) ADVENTURES IN ARABIA - 1927 - GREAT INSIDER VIEW OF BEDOUIN
LIFE IN THE 1920S. LARGELY RESPECTFUL
OF ARAB CULTURE!

(10) DR. WOOD - 1941 - SMELLS LIKE WORK FOR HIRE. NOT HIS BEST.

(1) NO HIDING PLACE - 1942 - A FITTING FINAL BOOK. A SOLID BIOGRAPHY.

(5) JUNGLE WAYS - 1930 - HIS LAST GREAT TRAVEL BOOK. MARRED BY
HIS CHANGED ATTITUDE TO THE NATIVE PEOPLE OF THE
COUNTRY HE'S VISITING. HE'S LESS A KINDRED SPIRIT IN AFRICA
THAN A "GREAT WHITE HUNTER."

THESE ARE JUST MY HUMBLE OPINIONS.

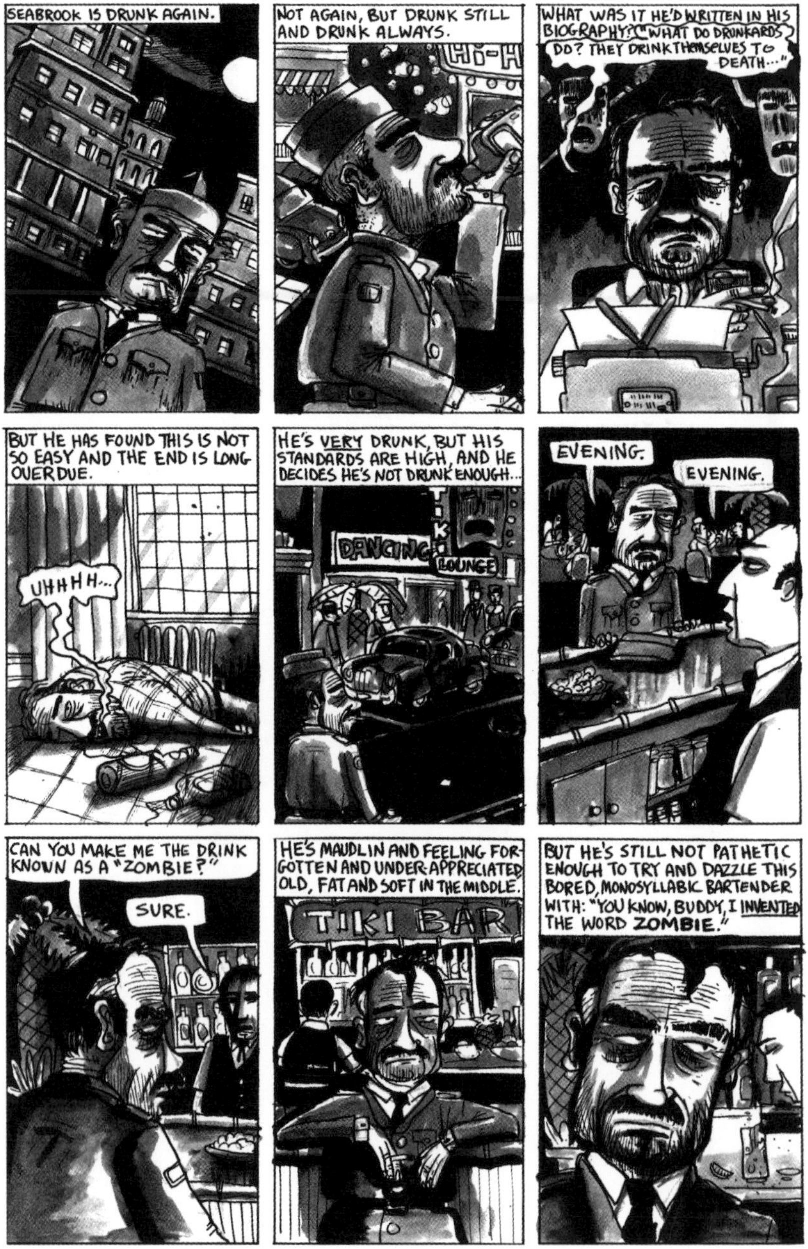
SEABROOK IS DRUNK AGAIN.
NOT AGAIN, BUT DRUNK STILL AND DRUNK ALWAYS.
WHAT WAS IT HE'D WRITTEN IN HIS BIOGRAPHY? "WHAT DO DRUNKARDS DO? THEY DRINK THEMSELVES TO DEATH..."
BUT HE HAS FOUND THIS IS NOT SO EASY AND THE END IS LONG OVERDUE.
UHHHH...
HE'S VERY DRUNK, BUT HIS STANDARDS ARE HIGH, AND HE DECIDES HE'S NOT DRUNK ENOUGH...
DANCING
LOUNGE
EVENING.
EVENING.
CAN YOU MAKE ME THE DRINK KNOWN AS A "ZOMBIE?"
SURE.
HE'S MAUDLIN AND FEELING FORGOTTEN AND UNDER-APPRECIATED, OLD, FAT AND SOFT IN THE MIDDLE.
TIKI BAR
BUT HE'S STILL NOT PATHETIC ENOUGH TO TRY AND DAZZLE THIS BORED, MONOSYLLABIC BARTENDER WITH: "YOU KNOW, BUDDY, I INVENTED THE WORD ZOMBIE."

THIS WAS AN EARLY TEST PAGE. I DIDN'T HAVE A HANDLE ON HIM YET (I'M NOT SURE I HAVE A HANDLE ON HIM NOW, FIVE YEARS LATER). I DO LIKE THIS LOOSER WORK. LOOSEN UP!

## THE "*ASYLUM*" COCKTAIL

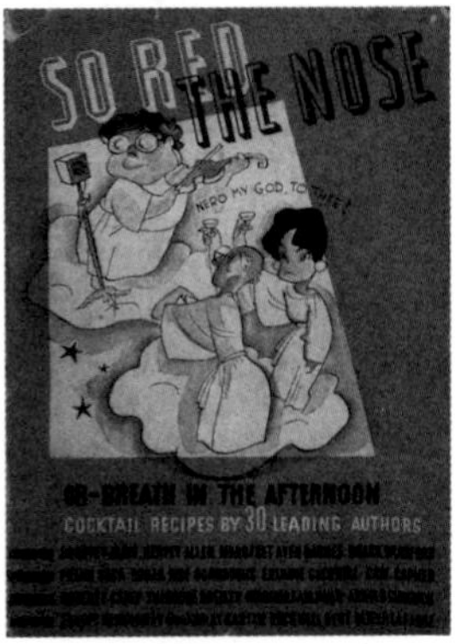
SO RED THE NOSE
NERO MY GOD, TO THEE!
OR—BREATH IN THE AFTERNOON
COCKTAIL RECIPES BY 30 LEADING AUTHORS

THE CELEBRITY OF WILLIAM SEABROOK AT THE HEIGHT OF HIS CAREER ALWAYS ASTOUNDS ME. ESPECIALLY WHEN CONTRASTED WITH HIS OBSCURITY IN HIS LATER LIFE AND ALMOST TOTAL NEGLECT AFTER HIS DEATH.

SEABROOK APPEARED IN *SO RED THE NOSE*, A 1935 BOOK OF COCKTAIL RECIPES BY "30 LEADING AUTHORS," IN THE COMPANY OF HEMINGWAY, DREISER AND EDGAR RICE BURROUGHS OF *TARZAN* FAME.

HE WAS STILL MAKING LIGHT OF HIS ALCOHOLISM AND CONFIDENT IN HIS CURE. THIS WAS THE SAME YEAR HIS BOOK *ASYLUM* WAS PUBLISHED AND HE CALLED HIS DRINK CREATION "WILLIAM SEABROOK'S *ASYLUM* COCKTAIL." I KNOW I'M A HUMOURLESS TEETOTALLER AND SEABROOK WOULD HAVE DESPISED ME FOR IT, BUT HIM MAKING LIGHT OF HIS ALCOHOLISM THAT WRECKED HIM MAKES ME TERRIBLY SAD.

ANYWAY... HERE'S THAT RECIPE:

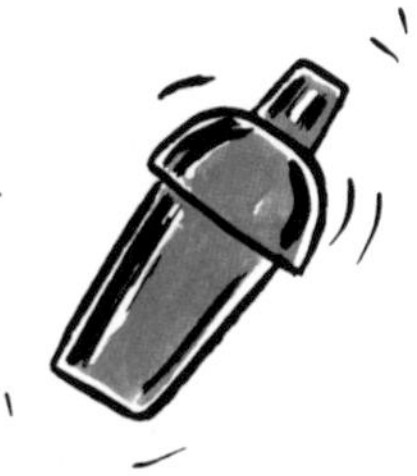

### WILLIAM SEABROOK'S *ASYLUM* COCKTAIL

1 PART GIN

1 PART PERNOD

DASH OF GRENADINE

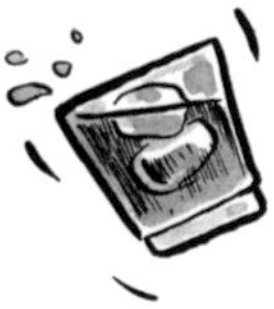

POUR OVER LARGE LUMPS OF ICE
DO NOT SHAKE

IT WILL "MAKE YOU PLENTY CRAZY." - WILLIAM SEABROOK

Seabrook in a striped shirt. Date unknown.